American Dreaming,
Global Realities

D1466098

American Dreaming, Global Realities

Rethinking U.S.
Immigration History

EDITED BY
Donna R. Gabaccia
and Vicki L. Ruiz

UNIVERSITY OF ILLINOIS PRESS
URBANA AND CHICAGO

Library of Congress
Cataloging-in-Publication Data
American dreaming, global realities : rethinking U.S.
immigration history / edited by Donna R. Gabaccia and
Vicki L. Ruiz.
p. cm. — (Statue of Liberty–Ellis Island Centennial
series)
Includes bibliographical references and index.
ISBN-13: 978-0-252-03064-2 (cloth : alk. paper)
ISBN-10: 0-252-03064-8 (cloth : alk. paper)
ISBN-13: 978-0-252-07305-2 (pbk. : alk. paper)
ISBN-10: 0-252-07305-3 (pbk. : alk. paper) 1. Immigrants—
United States—History. 2. United States—Emigration
and immigration—History. I. Gabaccia, Donna R., 1949–
II. Ruiz, Vicki. III. Series.
JV6450.A585   2006
304.8'73—dc22   2005028935

Contents

Acknowledgments

Assembling a reader is always an act of faith. Although an anthology can indirectly influence future research by luring potential undergraduate scholars into the field, its main purpose is to educate undergraduates who will not in all likelihood become historians, but rather teachers, business people, attorneys, nurses, doctors, public servants, and parents. We remain indebted to our students, from whom we have learned so much. Indeed, our students kept us motivated during the work process, which proved longer, more arduous, and more costly than either of us anticipated at the outset.

We wish to thank the four anonymous readers of this collection. Their careful attention to our introduction and selections confirmed our initial sense that we were "onto something," and that we had identified important pieces missing in the current literature available to educators and students of immigration history. More important, they pushed us toward greater conceptual clarity.

Several individuals and institutions assisted our work with financial and collegial aid. Donna Gabaccia thanks her colleagues at the University of North Carolina at Charlotte, the University of Minnesota, and the University of Pittsburgh (especially her student assistants, Reg Gingell, Mike Silliman, and Kenyon Zimmer). At the Immigration History Research Center, Judy Rosenblatt provided invaluable and timely help with editing. Last minute assistance from Jeffrey Pilcher allowed us to finish in a timely fashion. Financial assistance came from the Andrew K. Mellon endowment in the School of Arts and Sciences at the University of Pittsburgh and the Rudolph J. Vecoli Chair in Immigration History Research at the University of Minnesota.

Vicki L. Ruiz thanks her colleagues in history and Chicano/Latino studies at the University of California, Irvine, as well as Stella Ginez, the business manager of Chicano/Latino studies, and John Chao, an undergraduate assistant in the history department. In addition, Vicki acknowledges the following UCI doctoral students who challenge and support one another and their advisor—Beth Anderson, Margie Brown-Coronel, Julie Cohen, Ryan Kray, Kara O'Keefe, Soledad Vidal, and Bart Wisialowski. Margie Brown-Coronel deserves special mention for preparation of the index along with the expert advice and assistance of Sharon Block, associate professor of history, and David

Newman, research scientist in the department of computer science at UCI. She is also grateful to UCI's Center for Research on Latinos in a Global Society for additional research support. Financial assistance for permissions derived from Vicki's research account in UCI's School of Social Sciences.

We appreciate the understanding, professionalism, and dogged determination of our editor, Joan Catapano. We are also grateful to Ms. Catapano's assistants, Marla Osterbur and Christina Walter, for their efficiency and hard work. Ms. Walter, especially, took great care with this collection and we appreciate her extra efforts.

As anyone who has attempted it knows, collaboration can become a difficult experience. Ours was not. Donna thanks Vicki for her patience, persistence, good humor, and never-flagging levels of enthusiasm and attention to detail as well as her introduction to several great West Coast restaurants. Vicki thanks Donna for her intellectual insights, perseverance, patience, amazing energy, and, most of all, her *corazón*.

Intellectual work does not take place in an emotional vacuum. To acknowledge our personal support networks is perhaps a small token of our gratitude, but it is nevertheless heartfelt. Donna thanks the usual suspects—Jeanne, Jeffrey, Leslie, Marilyn, Tamino, and Thomas. Vicki acknowledges her family—Victor, Miguel, and Dan.

American Dreaming, Global Realities

Introduction

DONNA R. GABACCIA AND VICKI L. RUIZ

> No matter how bleak and constrained the situation, some form of improvisation and coping takes place. No matter what happens, people go on telling stories about it and bequeath them to the future. No matter how static and despairing the present looks, the past reminds us that change can occur. . . . The past is an unending source of interest and can even be a source for hope.
>
> —Natalie Zemon Davis

The stories told by our students are often the most instructive. Carmen, an undergraduate at the University of Texas, El Paso, who came to the United States as a young girl, revealed in a personal essay that "the daily struggles for survival of the immigrant are known only to the immigrant. Books can expose details and experiences but never thoughts and intensity of feelings. Endurance and its reasons are hard to convey."[1] Working daily with students such as Carmen replenishes our commitment to a scholarly field in which immigration exists in the present, not just the past, and in which emotion and lived experience have not been erased. As we push the conceptual and methodological boundaries of immigration history, we also write a more inclusive history of immigrants—in their homelands and in the United States, at home, at school, and at work, as men and women, whether rich or poor, and regardless of age and geography.

As immigration changes, so does its history. Writing at a time when the United States was tightening restrictions on immigration, historians first described immigration as comparable to the "frontier" in its formative influence on national American life. Taking their cue from Frederick Jackson Turner's famed "frontier thesis," these scholars envisioned immigration as central to nation building and democracy; but just as Turner noted the closing of the western frontier in 1893, immigration historians during the 1920s also considered the mass migrations of peoples to the United States to be a fading memory. Taking a different view, a few scholars approached immigration as a form of social and cultural connection between the old and new worlds. Somewhat later, other historians borrowed a theory of assimilation from the Chicago School of Sociology and charted immigrants' transformation from alienated European newcomers to assimilated members of American life. These narratives told of a linear "march of progress" that emphasized generational mobility and the creation of white, middle-class American identities among European immigrants.

Immigration history became an established field of scholarly inquiry only after the United States reformed its restrictive immigration policy in 1965 to eliminate racial discrimination at the border and to allow for rising levels of immigration. For the next two decades, social historians of European, Asian, and Latin American immigration turned their attention to studying working-class communities and the lives of immigrant women. As part of a general ethnic revival that was a direct product of the U.S. civil rights movement, historians began to question whether ethnicity had, in fact, died or had merely been transformed. Infused with cultural nationalism and a quest for social justice, scholars of color looked to reclaim histories long buried or hidden from public view. However, too often their social history monographs tended to focus only on one group or one coast and few conversations developed across subfields. For example, historians of Mexican immigration would more likely identify themselves (and still do) as Chicana/o historians or U.S. Western historians rather than as immigration scholars. In one of the earliest conversations between the coeditors, in 1986, they engaged in a spirited (but in hindsight fruitless) discussion about which U.S. city had the most diversity—New York City or Los Angeles. The state of the field in the 1970s and 1980s revolved around two binaries—East Coast/West Coast or European/non-European.

However, immigration history continued to evolve (as did our own conversations about the field). Scholars now frequently focus on the effect of globalization on immigration and immigrants' place in U.S. society. They explore the intricate overlapping of race, class, and gender on ethnic identity and on American citizenship. And they join social scientists and scholars in ethnic and women's studies in their efforts to understand the lives of immigrants in the twentieth century, groups that cut across class and nation-states with a decided emphasis on migration from Asia and Latin America and on issues related to political and economic colonialism. Immigration history no longer focuses so exclusively on life within the boundaries of the United States, but treats migration as a form of connection between locality, nation, and the wider world.

American Dreaming, Global Realities represents some of the best of this new research on immigration. The twenty-two articles respond to contemporary political debates about the future of the United States. Who, among the millions of people always on the move, are considered immigrants? How have the ties of newcomers to their homelands changed over the centuries? Does maintenance of such transnational bonds mean that today's immigrants will follow paths different from the earlier groups of largely European immigrants and from each other? How do race, class, gender, and region shape the mutual adjustments of natives and newcomers? What is the definition of an "American"? *American Dreaming, Global Realities* does not provide easy answers to these questions. Instead, it encourages students to think about how the study of immigration history can help them confront with greater critical awareness issues inherent in a multicultural "Nation of Immigrants."

Rethinking Immigration History

All scholarly fields change with time. In the past decade, scholars in immigration history have raised questions about many concepts fundamental to an analysis of migration and immigrant life. And they have continued their predecessors' critical engagement with theories of assimilation based on the Chicago School of Sociology's understanding of how European immigrants joined the American mainstream. By defining "immigrants" as foreigners who settle in the United States to become citizens, and by contrasting "immigrants" to "Americans," we are forced to consider the possibility that we exaggerate differences between natives and newcomers. Both groups have long been "on the move." Essays by Martha Hodes, Shirley Yee, and John Hart remind us that long-distance migrations and cultural negotiations were common experiences for women (and men) born in the United States, some of whom ultimately left the country—to marry, to escape slavery, or to work in Mexico. Considering these immigration experiences outside the United States, such as the Euro-American settlements John Hart explores in Mexico, destabilizes any linear narrative of assimilation and integration. Furthermore, a chapter by Thomas Andrews tells the story of English-speaking, U.S. citizen teachers who migrated to a rural Oglala Lakota reservation in their efforts to inculcate American values and cultural practices in American Indian children, thus mirroring activities in urban settlements that worked with foreign-born children, such as Jane Addams's famed Hull House in Chicago or the Methodist-sponsored Rose Gregory Houchen settlement in El Paso. Coeditor Vicki L. Ruiz posits the notion of cultural coalescence as an interpretative lens through which to understand how predominantly Catholic Mexican mothers availed themselves of Houchen's medical services and early childhood educational programs while discarding or ignoring missionary messages of Protestant conversion. The Lebanese described by Akram Fouad Khater, moreover, force us to reconsider whether immigration always equals settlement or a path to citizenship: these sojourners never intended to remain in the United States and most left after only a few years. The significant impact of their migrations was on the homeland, not on the receiving society.

Recent scholarship has also forced us to question and to be simultaneously more precise and more flexible in our definitions of both "immigrants" and "Americans." Such questions have strengthened immigration historians' long-standing ambivalence toward the concept of assimilation as developed within sociology in the 1920s and 1930s. Although sociologists once described all immigrants as marching generationally in logical, measured fashion along a straight path from "foreignness" to full assimilation as middle-class citizens, present-day historians continue to focus on the complexity— perhaps even the "messiness"—of human identity, experience, and relationships. Long-distance migrations have guaranteed that the very meaning of the "mainstream" differs across the many regions of the United States. Race, class, gender, generation, and social location, including colonial/historical contexts, further complicate the newcomers' accommodations to and search for a place within U.S. society. As many chapters in this book reveal, an immigrant does not simply "become American": she becomes an American woman or a Mexican American or "black." And for some immigrants—like Filipina adolescents—adopting typical American teenage behavior is not necessarily a desirable goal.

The essays in *American Dreaming, Global Realities* are presented chronologically, beginning with studies of the early decades of the nineteenth century and ending with analyses of today's world. They can be read in chronological order or by theme. We consciously selected chapters that could engage in multiple conversations and address overlapping issues. Here we present four thematic markers or buoys to guide readers through this collection and through the general sea of immigration history. These four buoys include transnationalism, community building, making home, and citizenship.

Transnationalism

Historians' skepticism about assimilation as the end product of all immigration has been heightened recently by the discovery of the strength and persistence of ties between international migrants and the countries of their origin. Today these bonds are sometimes called "transnational" (connecting life in two countries) or "translocal" (connecting life in a village or region of one country and a particular city or town in another). All the transnational and translocal analyses in *American Dreaming, Global Realities* explore connections between a site in the United States and in at least one other nation, although Donna Gabaccia's study on Italians emphasizes that the United States is not always the only, or even the more important, "node" in transnational networks of migration, exchange, and family or community solidarity.

Collectively, essays by Martha Hodes, Erika Lee, Donna Gabaccia, Akram Fouad Khater, Gunther Peck, and Nancy Foner establish that immigrants have long maintained ties to their homelands, often over extended periods of time, and often involving considerable back-and-forth movement across international boundaries. Work and family complicate in different ways transnational modalities and communities. Erika Lee, Evelyn Nakano Glenn, and Gunther Peck illuminate the ways in which immigrants accommodate to life in the United States through the workplace, whereas Khater, Gabaccia, Vicki Ruiz, and Yen Le Espiritu focus on families and on their routines, dreams, and choices. Politics, too, can be transnational. Nancy Raquel Mirabal's chapter examines Cuban immigration before the exodus following the Cuban Revolution of 1959. Through the prism of José Martí's "nuestra America," Mirabal historicizes the Cuban presence in the United States since the late nineteenth century and within contemporary transnational networks. Moreover, transnational and translocal ties shape the contours of immigrant lives in the United States. Even so, as Nancy Foner suggests in her concluding essay to *American Dreaming, Global Realities,* there can be little doubt that new technologies of communication and transportation enable recent arrivals to maintain transnational bonds with greater ease than in the past. Air travel and video, satellite, and digital communication should encourage us to wonder how immigrants' transnational ties will alter our understanding of assimilation and of the United States as a nation of immigrants into the future. As sociologist Yen Le Espiritu has so astutely observed, "migration is not necessarily—or at least not always—an act of leaving."[2] Instead, immigrants can remain enmeshed in family, kin, and community life stretching across borders and oceans.

Building Community

In exploring the creation of communities—whether rooted in place, culture, or interests—social historians rely on the building blocks of race, class, and gender. As an example, Martha Hodes offers an intimate portrait of a Yankee textile worker who marries a successful mixed-race African sea captain from Grand Cayman, teasing out comparative racializations and the possibilities of movement and transnational circuits. Decentering the United States as the only destination underscores a wider view. Shirley Yee delineates the role of African American women, many formerly enslaved, who forged new communities and identities in Canada. Moreover, physical location shapes (and perhaps even determines) immigrant expectations and everyday life. Linda Pickle's chapter lends insight into the rhythms and challenges of a rural setting, chronicling the array of adjustments, at even the most mundane level, faced by nineteenth-century immigrants in isolated hinterlands of the Midwest. We should also keep in mind the gendered dimensions of women's and men's community experiences and community representations. Karen Leong and Erika Lee interrogate meanings of manhood among the Chinese, including the perspectives of both the immigrants themselves and of U.S. policy makers and politicians. In deciphering daily lives and aspirations, Erika Lee is especially mindful of the power of the state in shaping the contours of entry and of the communities immigrants can create once in the United States.

Drawing on feminist historiography that seeks to integrate women's public and private lives, Judy Wu introduces us to Dr. Margaret Chung. Chung, the first Chinese American woman to become a doctor, lived in San Francisco's Chinatown community, a close-knit world rife with gossip and innuendo, including gossip about Chung's sexuality. The "porch culture" of gossip that existed in native-born small towns apparently had its equivalent even in urban immigrant communities, where women's (and men's) networks and conversations could support or undermine individual reputations.[3]

Yet we also want to remind readers that the very term "community building" should be approached with a certain caution lest we are lulled into comforting tropes of harmonious ethnic neighborhoods filled with nationalist pride and solidarity. Gunther Peck's research clearly documents that southern European immigrants were not above exploiting one another on the job site; similarly, Matt García interrogates the gender-coded tensions that erupted between Mexican Americans and Mexican nationals with the arrival of *braceros* (contract laborers) into southern California during World War II. Communities were not peaceful or unified; like families, they could be united by quarrels and enmity as well as by solidarity and mutual support.

Making Home

For immigrants, images of "home" conjure up a myriad of meanings — from a birthplace far away to the *casita* down the street. Women and men engage in making home both literally and figuratively. Homeland can be imagined in the minds of second-generation youth who have never stepped foot in the land of their parents or as an actual place of intimate familiarity. Yen Le Espiritu offers the most incisive definition of "home making," which she describes as "the processes by which diverse subjects imagine and make themselves at home in various geographic locations."[4] As Donna Gabaccia points out in her article on Italian family economies, home making is neither linear nor temporal but can reflect elements of both permanence and transiency within the same communities; individuals and families can and do make decisions about shifting the location of their home base while remaining engaged in transnational practices. Focusing on the lives of immigrants after World War II, Mary Patrice Erdmans brings out generational cleavages between Polish Americans and their recent immigrant cousins, each group bearing radically different visions of home (Poland), and shows how these intergenerational tensions played themselves out on a daily basis. Complicating notions of citizenship, making home also merges public and private spaces. Joyce Antler's essay provides a sweeping survey of political activism among Jewish women during the twentieth century, couching struggles for social justice within a Jewish American domestic sensibility.

Home making is also integrally related to the context of colonialism, past and present. Filipinos, Puerto Ricans, and Mexicans have all felt the weight of U.S. political and economic dominance despite their differing physical locations. U.S. corporate influence in Mexico did not begin with the North American Free Trade Agreement (NAFTA) or with the globalization policies of the past twenty years; rather, this unequal symbiotic relationship emerged more than a century ago, first with the Treaty of Guadalupe Hidalgo in 1848 and then a few decades later with the entrance of extensive U.S. investment in Mexico. Puerto Ricans and Filipinos still feel the legacies of imperialism wrought by the U.S. war with Spain, especially given Puerto Rico's ambiguous commonwealth status and economic dependency. As Espiritu's essay on Filipina youth culture suggests, colonial legacies extend across families, generations, and transnational communities.

Citizenship

At its most basic, citizenship is a timeless legal and juridical concept, a sense and obligation of civic culture and enfranchisement. Central to U.S. citizenship is the exercise of rights guaranteed under the U.S. Constitution and the promises of the Declaration of Independence. As Jon Gjerde's chapter suggests, even those European immigrants of the early nineteenth century who enthusiastically embraced citizenship and liberty as a signifier of national belonging often discovered the pains of cultural transformation inherent in each form of Americanization. Furthermore, citizenship was not open to all immigrants, but only to whites. And not all citizens, even when native-born, have enjoyed full civil rights. The essays by Nakano Glenn, Foley, Wu, and Foner (among others) demonstrate how gender, race, class, and sexuality create boundaries around or different routes to the privileges of citizenship. In her study of Hawaii, Evelyn Nakano Glenn brings out the constant interplay of race, gender, labor, and local practice, emphasizing how, on a day-to-day basis, people have maintained as well as resisted such boundaries.

Significantly, however, the promises of citizenship also provided the grounds for an excluded group to mobilize for civil rights and social justice. Neil Foley discusses the long-term consequences for intergenerational relations of both native- and foreign-born Mexicans' access to citizenship, which was based on their juridical (although not always phenotypic) "whiteness." Luis León, moreover, suggests that joining the American nation is more than a matter of citizenship and color; becoming American is often a form of religious accommodation. American religion typically emphasizes more voluntaristic, individualist, enthusiastic, and evangelical expression of faith than many immigrants experienced at home.

Although the full effect on U.S. immigration policies and practices in the wake of September 11th remains to be seen, contemporary concerns about civil liberties and citizenship resonate among natives and newcomers alike, sparking new debates about American identity and American power. At the dawn of the twenty-first century, trans-nationalism, community building, making home, and citizenship recur as salient constructs for individuals, groups, and nation-states. In addressing what it means to be an immigrant in the United States and, conversely, what it means when Americans emigrate to other places, we seek to juxtapose images of "the lady with the light" (as articulated by one Cambodian refugee) with past and present geopolitical realities.[5] This volume emphasizes the centrality of immigration in American history from the period of the early republic to the present. This centrality is not just a question of new groups arriving and climbing the ladder of social mobility (a model anthropologist Aihwa Ong critiques as "ethnic succession"),[6] but also of historicizing migration as part of the process that defines who we are as Americans.

Rethinking U.S. immigration history requires students to consider a plurality of specific historical, economic, regional, familial, and cultural contexts. Such a history reveals resistance and accommodation, persistent older traditions and Americanization, and the creation of new cultural forms that blend old and new. With *American Dreaming, Global Realities,* we seek to explore the ways in which immigrant lives and those of their children are shaped by transnational bonds, globalization, family ties, and personal choice as well as the ways in which the immigrants engender a sense of belonging and a sense of themselves as "Americans."

Notes

The epigraph for this chapter is from Natalie Zemon Davis, "A Life of Learning," Charles Homer Haskins Lecture for 1997, ACLS Occasional Paper, no. 39 (1997), 23.

1. "Carmen's Story" (personal files of Vicki L. Ruiz).

2. Yen Le Espiritu, *Home Bound: Filipino American Lives Across Cultures, Communities, and Countries* (Berkeley: University of California Press, 2003), 85.

3. Jacquelyn Dowd Hall et al., *Like a Family: The Making of a Southern Cotton Mill World* (Chapel Hill: University of North Carolina Press, 1987).

4. Espiritu, *Home Bound*, 2.

5. Aihwa Ong, *Buddha Is Hiding: Refugees, Citizenship, the New America* (Berkeley: University of California Press, 2003), 69.

6. Ibid., 3–4.

The Burden of Their Song

Immigrant Encounters with the Republic

JON GJERDE

When Bishop Mathias Loras called upon a dying Irish immigrant on the Iowa frontier in the early 1840s, the feeble man's poignant plea to the priest was simple: "Like my ancestors in Ireland, I should like to repose in the holy ground under the shadow of the cross. The sanctified earth would be no longer to me a strange land and I should less regret the tombs of my country." Heeding the dying man's requests, Loras and the small Irish colony inaugurated a new sacralization of space by erecting a twelve-foot-high oak cross, which, according to the bishop, successfully served "to protect the land cultivated by our Christians and to stretch forth its arms to the savages who inhabit the neighboring forests."[1] Loras's work is emblematic of the prominent role played by Roman Catholic missionaries who early on made a cultural imprint on the Middle West. Working initially with Native Americans, Roman Catholic priests turned their attention to European settlers when waves of migrants entered the West. They soon became active in encouraging and directing migration and settlement.[2]

The story of these early missionaries parallels in some ways and cross-cuts in others the narratives of the American-born leaders who were simultaneously moving westward. As emigration from Europe swelled in the mid-nineteenth century, western Catholics, not unlike their Protestant adversaries, perceived the temporal and spiritual promise of the West. "I do wish," wrote Father Francis Pierz in 1855, "that the choicest pieces of land in this delightful Territory [of Minnesota] would become the property of thrifty Catholics who would make an earthly paradise of this Minnesota which Heaven has so richly blessed, and who would bear out the opinion that Germans prove to be the best farmers and the best Christians in America."[3] Loras arrived at similar conclusions. "No section of the country offered finer soil or climate," he wrote following his extensive travels throughout eastern Iowa, "or provided more favorable opportunities for an industrious agricultural population."[4]

One even discerns in the writings of the Catholic clergy a sense of providence regarding the West and America comparable to that expressed in the American-born. In 1844, Father Samuel Mazzuchelli thanked the Lord, "who is rich in mercy," for providing an effective means of spreading the "Truth" of Catholicism throughout the United States. Through the War of Independence, "the designs of Divine Wisdom" had freed the country from the domination of England, which in turn had precipitated the "emigration of many Catholic families from Europe," who could now live as Catholics in a more abundant environment.[5] The signs of providence were wondrous, even miraculous. "On the feast of the Epiphany," wrote Pierz in 1855, "there was seen here in Minnesota . . . a remarkable apparition of the holy cross in the sky. As the full moon arose at eight o'clock in the evening the holy cross appeared in yellowish hue and most heavenly brilliance upon the rising moon. . . . The cross was surrounded by a bright nimbus of the rarest and loveliest of colors. The whole phenomenon," he concluded, "was entrancingly beautiful and bright." Pierz divined the significance of the spectacle by noting that "the holy cross, seeming to rest on Minnesota's soil and to expand far and wide with the rising moon," was a clear symbol that the Minnesota Territory would soon be populated by Christians, undoubtedly Catholic and probably German.[6]

Besides providing better material conditions, this providential West also enabled isolated settlement, which Catholic leaders saw as a solution to the increasingly hostile nativism in the East. Loras, writing in an eastern Catholic paper, encouraged migration to the West for this very reason. "Many Catholics will certainly be induced to emigrate toward the western regions of Iowa," he predicted. "I persevere in the conviction that they can hardly do anything better [and] I speak chiefly of those who now live in that New England where Catholicity is so shamefully persecuted."[7] Other missionary bishops and priests flooded eastern newspapers, in particular Catholic journals such as the *Catholic Observer* and the *Boston Pilot,* with accounts of the advantages of western residence.[8] At the same time, they successfully appealed to Europe for funds that would enable a safer and larger Catholic emigration.[9]

Whereas both the foreign- and American-born could agree that the West held material and spiritual promise, then, immigrants saw that promise as based in part on the opportunity to seclude themselves in isolated settlements sheltered both from direct nativist hostility and from "American" tutelage—precisely what the nativists feared most.[10] The fact that American nativists feared the specter of growing rural European settlements is dripping with irony. It was nativist hostility in the East, Catholic leaders observed, that served in part to encourage Catholic migration westward to the region that many of the native-born considered the key to the destiny of the American Republic. Moreover, it was the vast tracts of rich land uninhabited by American citizens—a central component of exceptionalist beliefs about the West—that enabled Europeans to seclude themselves and maintain their beliefs.

Yet American nativists largely misinterpreted the meaning of the European migration and misunderstood the challenges immigrant leaders faced. European immigrants, like their American-born counterparts, not only perceived the great promise of the West but also tended to accept, if somewhat uncritically, many of the tropes and myths of the American nation. Many applauded a spirit of "freedom" that seemingly had not existed at home. To be sure, the region was desirable in part because it fostered the potential for self-contained societies. Yet even here, it was the "freedom" to form isolated communities and maintain cultural patterns that was one of the reasons for celebrating life in the United States. Whereas Americans tended to view immigration to the West as a validation of others' faith in their Republic, Europeans viewed the promise of the Republic as an explanation for their immigration.

These predispositions ought not discount the challenges that a massive immigration posed to the immigrant community, its leadership, and the nation as a whole. The nation faced the unavoidable fact that the vast majority of immigrants had indeed previously lived as subjects. The United States thus was forced to grapple with the immigrants' transformation into citizens. The nation had to contend with questions concerning how to educate people who were previously tied to fundamentally different political systems in American government. Immigrants had to address issues involving how they could be schooled in the American system so that they could realize the promise immigration offered. In short, they had to "learn republicanism."

The process of learning republicanism was advanced and simplified, I argue in this chapter, by access to a citizenship that did not demand that immigrants forsake their cultural pasts. Indeed, a political environment that permitted immigrants to maintain their religious beliefs and converse in their home language worked to augment loyalties to the nation. Newspapers and printed tracts instructed non-English speakers in the precepts, responsibilities, and rights inherent in the Republic. Seen from this perspective, allegiances to ethnic subgroup and nation were mutually supportive. An ethnic pluralism sustained the American polity.

This self-reinforcing relationship between nation and ethnic subgroup was more problematic, however, when it involved religious organizations, with which most immigrants identified and which were typically institutional centers in the rural immigrant community. Immigrant spiritual leaders repeatedly affirmed their loyalty to American institutions and to the American republican system. They frequently celebrated the freedom to practice their religion in the United States and the fact that the American free church was an institution that fostered their Christian beliefs. Yet they were also forced to ponder the apparent inconsistencies between republican citizenship and spiritual guidance. They often expressed concerns that their flocks were learning the precepts of liberal democracy all too well, as immigrants left the faith or proposed electoral solutions to spiritual problems that could not be solved by majority rule. In sum, whereas they were comforted by freedoms of religion, many religious leaders feared the consequences when putatively "free" patterns of behavior and belief spread seemingly out of control and interfered with church, home, and community.

The "Complementary Identity" and
Learning American Republicanism

> One of the Swede's flaxen-headed boys wanted to know if the king of
> Minnesota was a good man, and on being told that the king was dead and the
> country was ruled by a gentleman hired for the purpose called the governor,
> the little boy replied that he was sorry to hear of the king's death, and he
> hoped that he had a fitting monument.
>
> —*Stillwater (Minnesota) Gazette,* 18 May 1881

> These [Irish immigrants] became more American than the Americans
> and knew how to appreciate the blessing of civic freedom far better than
> the natives, who had always enjoyed such blessing. They looked up to the
> Fathers of the Republic as to *the saints.*
>
> —John Talbot Smith, *History of the Catholic Church in New York* (1905;
>   emphasis added)

Americans in the mid-nineteenth century celebrated the many ways in which their Republic improved upon the tired systems of the old European states. As they invented an American nationality that allegedly reflected these advancements, they stressed the conviction that their nation was structured according to abstract notions of freedom, equality, and self-government. This was necessary, Hans Kohn argued, because Americans of British descent could be distinct from their British past only insofar as they evinced a commitment to the ideological constructs—such as "freedom" and "self-rule"—that were a basis of their rebellion.[11] Alexis de Tocqueville observed that "the sovereignty of the people is . . . the last link in a chain of opinions which binds around the whole Anglo-American world." For Americans, "though in practice a republican government often behaves badly," he averred, "the theory is always good, and in the end the people's actions always conform to it."[12] If nations are formed as "imagined communities," then, the United States as a nation was visualized by its citizenry in the early nineteenth century in ideological terms: the American past, according to Herbert Croly, was "informed by an idea."[13]

This intellectual framework simultaneously placed a great responsibility on the citizenry and enabled relatively simple access to citizenship for those defined as "white."[14] For them, as Carl Friedrich wrote some years ago, "to be an American is an ideal," compared to being a Frenchman, which was "a fact."[15] An immigrant to the United States could become a citizen merely by consenting to the political ideology that defined its citizenry. Significantly, although they were required to renounce loyalties to foreign governments, immigrants and their descendants were not forced to forsake the cultural baggage with which they had arrived.[16]

Many American nativists, as we have observed, believed these circumstances posed acute problems with regard to immigrants arriving from the benighted European lands. They doubted that immigrants could learn the lessons of freedom. "*Subjects,*" wrote Thomas R. Whitney, "cannot become good *citizens* in a moment. Men must be *educated* to freedom."[17] Traits such as "independence of character," he commented, "were rarely found in one trained to submission." Told that "he inhabits a land of liberty and equality," the immigrant "gets a confused notion that a great change has taken place in his condition. . . . He has heard something about 'liberty' before, without knowing what was meant, but the word 'equality,' is not found in his lexicon, and he can't make out how it is that he is 'as good as other people.'" Engraved on his mind "by the hand of a stern artist" were "thoughts and fancies adapted to his former state—lessons . . . of low, slavish, abject submission," which "are difficult to rub out."[18] Immigrants, in short, were untrained in the responsibilities of citizenship. In learning the intricacies of republican citizenship, they needed to comprehend the dangers of the abuse of freedoms on the one hand and of servile dependence on the other. American nativists questioned whether the European mind could avoid either extreme, especially considering the indoctrination immigrants carried with them. Catholic immigrants were human beings, Samuel F. B. Morse admitted, but "oppression has blotted out their reason and conscience and thought." As a result, "their liberty, is licentiousness, their freedom, strife and debauchery."[19]

These complaints had some merit. Europeans often failed to comprehend the basics of American republicanism when they arrived in the United States. It is true that some had been instructed prior to their emigration by guidebooks that described life in the United States, including its government, and introduced them to concepts of an American exceptionalism. "The United States," explained Ole Rynning in his guidebook published for Norwegian immigrants in 1838, "has no king. Nonetheless, there is always a man who has almost a king's authority. . . . Here there are laws, government, and authorities as in Norway. But *everything*," he concluded, "is intended to maintain people's *natural freedom and equality*."[20]

Yet even when immigrants had this guidance, the learning process often took some time. Ole Munch Ræder wrote in the 1840s that Norwegian immigrants had "not reached beyond the first rudiments of a republican education." Not only were many ignorant of political party differences, but a few settlers still called the government price on land "the king's price," an example of the persistence of the use of European terms as frames of reference.[21] C. L. Clausen, editor of the Norwegian paper *Emigranten,* detected similar conditions in 1852 when he expressed his amazement "at the lack of interest of our people in the West regarding political matters." Referring to the approaching presidential election, Clausen feared that "if some farm work is to be done on election day, [Norwegians] will fail to go to the polls even though the work could easily be postponed. It is a sad situation," he concluded, for "it indicates that the Norwegian-American has no conception of what it means to be an American citizen." Yet he betrayed a hope that the immigrants would "acquire this training in citizenship," and he urged his countrymen to "try to create a little political instinct in ourselves!"[22] Circumstances were similar, suggested the *Dubuque National Demokrat* some years later, among German immigrant farmers. Shortly after their arrival, German immigrants presumed that the "government goes on without them." Only after some time did they realize that as citizens, they were "part of the system."[23]

Like nativist critics, moreover, some Europeans were also distressed by diminished social controls that resulted from abuses and misunderstandings about the meaning of concepts such as liberty. One Irishman, writing home in 1826, denounced the Irish as "the worst conditioned people in this Country." "On their first landing," he argued, "they are extremely mean and servile." Yet "after meeting a short time with their Countrymen and hearing that all men are here free and equal in respect to their rights," he observed, "they think that freedom consists in being at liberty to do as they please and they become intolerably insolent."[24] Father Joseph Cretin commented on a comparable spiritual degeneration following a confrontation with his parishioners. "I did not believe the Irish character susceptible to this kind of malice against their own pastors," he complained. After all, "they are so docile in Ireland under the absolute and often arbitrary empire of their high clergy."[25] Freedom and liberty obviously could be abused.

They could also be misunderstood. Europeans often affiliated with political organizations because of vaguely understood appeals. German immigrants became Democrats in the 1840s, wrote one German, simply because "'Democracy' stood for 'Freiheit.'"[26] The Democratic Daily Wisconsin Banner solicited German votes in 1850 by suggesting a similar, if more intricate, interpretation. "'Democracy,'" the editor wrote, "is a glorious word. There are few other words, in any language, which can be compared to it. To the poor man it is peculiarly precious since he is aware that he owes to it his escape from the serfdom in which his oppressors held him, and can now look up into heaven and thank his God that he has ceased to be a serf."[27] Vaguely articulated terms rather than political platforms often had greater appeal to the unschooled immigrant.

As they were introduced to the rhetoric and institutions of American exceptionalism, immigrants showed an inclination to celebrate the American political and social system. As we have seen, mid-nineteenth-century European immigrants commonly praised the economic possibilities that defined the nation and especially the West. They were also predisposed to esteem the "natural freedom and equality" of the nation's political institutions. These identifications were powerful forces in encouraging recent arrivals to develop loyalties to the United States and to learn about its institutions. Certainly for some the initial contact with the democratic culture in the United States was unnerving. Democracy so pervaded all "national habits" in the United States, Michel Chevalier remarked, that "it besets and startles at every step the foreigner who, before landing in the country, had no suspicion to what a degree every nerve and fibre had been steeped in aristocracy by a European education."[28] Yet those immigrants who had been touched by the flames of republicanism in Europe or influenced by the pronouncements of American liberty and opportunity often eagerly embraced the rhetoric of American republicanism. "In America," trumpeted Nordlyset, "liberty advances as proudly and deliberately as its gigantic rivers. [In Europe,] absolute despots or kings are everywhere in power. . . . Just let them sit on their thrones, wearing their robes of sable, and oppressing mankind! Here in America at any rate, there is neither king nor tyrant."[29] "Liberty in Norway was merely a dead letter on the statute book," agreed the editor of Folkets Røst in an 1858 editorial. "How greatly different [it is] in this country [where] we can . . . in common with the native-born Americans settle the political questions of the country." Here, in short, was "unmistakable evidence that in this country, freedom and equality exist in reality."[30]

Johan R. Reiersen, who journeyed throughout the United States in 1843, agreed. The fact that the American government was unhampered by monarchical and aristocratic interests, he argued, promoted a "spirit of progress, improvements in all directions, and a feeling for popular liberty and of the rights of the great masses exceeding that of any land in Europe." As a result, the republican government would not fail, in large part because "the masses" would never be "reduced—through the power of individuals or of capital— to the same slavish dependence that supports the thrones of Europe. Personal freedom is something the people suck in with their mother's milk," he concluded. "It seems to have become as essential to every citizen of the United States as the air he breathes."[31] The letters of members of a Norwegian correspondence society likewise stressed the spirit of freedom in the United States, which, they maintained, contained "the secret of general equality."[32] A German immigrant, writing to his kin in Europe at about the same time, compared his former home to his new one. In Germany, "alas, common sense and free speech lie in shackles," he wrote. If his relatives wished "to obtain a clear notion of *genuine* public life, freedom of the people and sense of being a nation," he contended, they should emigrate. "I have never regretted that I came here, and never! never! again shall I bow my head under the yoke of despotism and folly."[33] Other immigrants writing in different languages used nearly identical imagery: one Norwegian wrote that his people enjoyed tasting "the satisfaction of being liberated from the effect of all yoke and despotism."[34] Decades later, American "freedom" remained a trope for Germans explaining their forebears' migration to the United States. "Discontent prevailed in all classes of German society," wrote R. Puchner. "There was a longing for free political and free religious ideas; the old institutions seemed rotten and sick unto death; there was . . . only the ocean in between them [and] the new land of promise, the mighty republican Empire of America."[35]

These examples do not prove, of course, that all immigrants were satisfied with their decision to emigrate. Immigrants often returned home unhappy with life in the United States. Others remained in America but were despondent over their prospects. Nor did all immigrants find the degree of freedom they had anticipated. "It sounds ridiculous to hear a man speak of freedom," wrote a German worker in 1886, "when he is still enslaved by a *Corporation* as he was not in Germany."[36]

This evidence does indicate, however, that immigrants' steady rhetoric about salutary encounters with American conditions tended to mute their criticism of the new land. Immigrants' predisposition to glorify the possibilities of American citizenship, oftentimes uncritically, likely worked to hasten their integration into American society. The writings of Russian populist Grigorij Machtet during a journey in Kansas in 1874 described how immigrants were changed and their criticism of the American nation was softened by their encounters with American life. To be sure, the "raw material" of immigrant peoples had to be "processed and mastered by America."[37] Clearly, "many dark aspects, many blemishes," marred the United States. But the "mass of immigrants, uncertainly seeking a different way of life," tended to observe their new home through rose-colored glasses. Thus, although many Americans viewed Europeans with "a mixture of scorn, offensive pity, and sympathy," wrote Machtet, they could anticipate a transformation of immigrants because of their predisposition not to criticize American society. "Out of this stalwart but downtrodden, fearful, and hesitant German," he concluded, "must be created a citizen who is both competent and free; out of this ever drunk, ever swearing, ever fighting, fanatical Irishman must be created not only a harmless person but also a competent and free citizen." Despite such worrisome character defects, within five years in the United States the immigrant was indeed "reborn": "it is as though he has become a different person, as though he has 'been born into God's world.'" Importantly, Machtet believed that a person's inclination to embrace the American system of government not only remade the person but also powerfully muted criticisms of the United States. As long as immigrant discourse presupposed the salutary influences of American freedoms, expressions that emphasized American "blemishes" would be tempered. And celebrations of American life would continue.[38]

The absorption of national myths, however, did not mean that cultural pasts were discarded. On the contrary, immigrants seized on common national, linguistic, and religious traditions as cornerstones for fashioning their ethnic collectivities. These ethnic groups created boundaries, oftentimes reconfiguring common pasts, that were instrumental to ethnic leaders in a pluralist society.[39] Ethnic institutions, based on common intellectual, geographical, or linguistic pasts originating in Europe, were created in the United States to support interest-group associations in the polity and society. This process of "ethnicization" also did not nullify the development of loyalties to the United States. Rather than competing, the dual loyalties to nation and subgroup, invented under the auspices of an American creed, could be complementary.[40]

The ideological underpinnings of citizenship that privileged "freedom" and "self-rule" in fact enabled immigrants to nurture simultaneously their bonds to nation and to ethnic subgroup. Tropes of "freedom" and "liberty," perhaps because their meanings were so pliant, proved to be malleable concepts that fostered an appreciation among immigrants of the responsibilities and rights of American citizenship. Yet the very concept of freedom could also nurture the maintenance of Old World ties. One sense of "freedom," after all, implied the liberty to maintain patterns of life that varied from those of native-born Americans. Immigrants became citizens of the United States and theoretically performed the obligations of citizens, but basic rights inherent in their citizenship status allowed them to retain ethnic and religious allegiances they carried from Europe. Ironically, then, immigrants and their children could simultaneously—in a complementary, self-reinforcing fashion—maintain allegiances to the United States and to their former identities outside its borders.

In this way, faithfulness to an ethnic subgroup within a "complementary identity" theoretically fostered a magnified loyalty to the United States. Ethnic allegiances encouraged affinities with nation.[41] As Samuel P. Huntington has argued, "Defining and maintaining an ethnic identity was an essential building block in the process of creating an American national identity."[42] The ideologically based national identity, on the other hand, enabled people to reformulate former beliefs and fostered the formation of ethnic groups in the United States. In its stable form, then, the complementary identity represented more than the opportunity to develop a dual identity to nation and ethnic subgroup: it was a self-reinforcing concept that powerfully promoted an allegiance to American institutions at the same time that it fostered a maintenance of ethnic forms. Pluralism was embedded within national loyalty.

Evidence from memoirs and newspapers indicates that mid-nineteenth-century immigrants almost intuitively understood this complementarity. "Americanization" typically had a very different meaning for the myriad ethnic communities in the United States than it did for American-born nativists.[43] The editor of *Den Swenske Republikanen,* for example, argued in 1857 that his paper indeed intended to "Americanize" its readers, which to him meant that it sought "to acquaint them with the republican institutions of America and make those institutions respected and loved."[44] Immigrants thus did not necessarily have to become "Americans" to be "Americanized." Nativists notwithstanding, other European observers argued that the American system *was* inclusive, pointing out that Europeans who pledged allegiance to their "American" refuge did not lose their old national culture. "The American character," wrote Ole Munch Ræder in the mid-1840s, "is not yet so fixed and established that it excludes all others. The Americans," he concluded, referring here to the native-born, "are satisfied with demanding a few general traits of political rather than of really national significance." Repeating a contention made decades earlier by J. Hector St. John de Crèvecoeur, Ræder argued that "under such lenient influences, the aliens are elevated and improved, rather than changed."[45] Immigrants, in short, could be loyal citizens of the United States and members of ethnic groups simultaneously. Many different immigrants found it simple to translate Carl Schurz's advice to his male German counterparts: "I love Germany as my mother. America as my bride."[46]

Ethnic Americans throughout the nineteenth century ingenuously conflated these multiple loyalties. Public celebrations of national holidays, for example, consolidated images of both the European past and the American present. Irish immigrants in Dubuque merged an 1883 Fourth of July celebration with advocacy of the Irish National Land League and of independence for Ireland.[47] Swiss Americans saw no incongruity in incorporating the history of Switzerland into their Fourth of July observance in 1876. Their centennial parade float contained representations of Helvetia and Columbia surrounded by images of the Swiss cantons with their coats-of-arms.[48] Members of a rural German community six years later celebrated American life by reading the Declaration of Independence and listening to a speaker discuss the role of Germans in the Revolutionary War, "a chapter in American history," reported a German-language newspaper, "too little known."[49] "The jewels of Isabella the Catholic," Bishop John Hughes reportedly observed, "would be an appropriate ornament for the sword of Washington."[50] Some years later, Cardinal James Gibbons, upon watching the American and papal flags carried side by side in a parade, observed, "I always wish to see those two flags lovingly entwined, for no one can be faithful to God without being faithful to his country."[51] And Roman Catholic newspaper mastheads juxtaposed portraits of George Washington and Pope Pius X, a clear illustration of the importance and compatibility of allegiance to both church and state.[52]

The private correspondence of immigrants, like their public displays, also illustrates the fusion of new and old loyalties. A German Catholic tenant farmer in 1886, for instance, noted that a farmer in Europe had to perform grinding labor every day of the week. "If we asked permission [of the landlord] to go to Church on Sunday, then the man abused us . . . every time and said: 'You won't always need to be running after the priest if you find yourselves in the alms house.' And so," he concluded, "I am going to America [where] on Sundays as many as wish to may go to church. My children shall not imitate my slavery."[53] American freedoms provided the opportunity to practice Catholic beliefs.[54]

This complementarity would endure well into the nineteenth century. A remarkable correspondence between historian Kate Everest and spokesmen for German communities in late-nineteenth-century Wisconsin time and again demonstrated that old and new loyalties were self-reinforcing, that indeed they strengthened both allegiances. Ernest Mayerhoff, writing from Juneau County, stressed that his neighbors "want to become good American citizens, make use of the english language and try to master it for themselves and for their children, but they wish to retain also the German language and the Lutheran faith." In this way, he noted, his people enriched the United States just as their new country bettered them. "They accommodate to the english manners and customs," he continued, "when they think it is for the good, but retain their German customs, when they think the english are bad ones." As a result, Mayerhoff concluded, "they have improved in America in every direction and have learned not to be servants of mankind, but servants of God; and to become true citizens and to take care of the welfare of the country."[55]

Other respondents were more defensive about their place in the United States, but they continued to stress the value of dual loyalties. When asked if the German inhabitants intermarried with "Americans," a resident of Sheboygan County, Wisconsin, wrote that "there are not English Americans here to intermarry with." As he continued writing, he revealed his impatience. "This question," he claimed, "seems to take for granted, that only English or Irish blood makes an American." His neighbors, he continued, desired to maintain their customs and beliefs, including their mother tongue, and it "would be a sad loss to them and the state if they didn't." "If to get rid of all these things . . . good [though] they may be, means *to become Americanized,*" he surmised, "why I suppose they are still rude German barbarians." On the other hand, "they and especially their children are learning the English language, the History & Constitution of the U.S., they read the newspapers, quite a number of English ones; they are intelligent voters, peaceable and industrious citizens, many of them English teachers in the public schools. . . . If you call that Americanizing," he concluded, "why then they desire it."[56] Joh. Kilian, writing in German about his Dodge County, Wisconsin, neighbors, contended that "they are all good American citizens [who] hold true and firm to their old Lutheran beliefs and virtuous customs."[57] Kilian evinced no impression that his statement, which succinctly and simply fused American identity with the maintenance of European customs, was incongruous.

Participants in the complementary identity often found it simple to proceed one step further and stress that they were better Americans than the native-born who questioned the extent of their loyalty. "I am as good an American as the most blue-blooded Yankee can be," emphasized a German Catholic priest in defense of an association of priests to which he belonged. The association was "American above all" since it could only have been formed "in the atmosphere of our glorious American constitution, which guarantees liberty to all—liberty of thought . . . liberty of association, [and] liberty of religious worship." Indeed, he concluded, it was those who attempted to "infringe this liberty" to maintain Catholic organizations who were "truly un-American."[58]

Expressions reflecting a complementary identity with nation and subgroup were thus

American in conception and origin. Immigrants and their leaders invented and continually modified both a sense of allegiance to an imagined community composed of Americans and a reified notion of a common preimmigration past.[59] These identities, when developed in tandem, modulated in relation to one another. Ethnic leaders therefore compared conditions in the United States with those in Europe and, using a biblical allusion, stressed that immigrants "had shaken the dust [of Europe] from their feet and have reached the shores of this continent to lead a dignified life once again."[60] Or they spoke of their old country as a "land of tyranny."[61] Yet their reverence for their new country and their "patriotism" were often based on their freedom to be ethnically and religiously distinct. The cornerstone of the edifice of a Catholic church in rural Iowa contained an inscription that is an apt example of a mature dual identity. The inscription, composed in Latin, was a reminder that "while our sacred religion has been viciously persecuted at home for ten years, we may enjoy in this rich and beautiful country a perfect peace and the most wonderful religious liberty." Yet it also asked descendants of the German immigrants "to remain Catholics and down-to-earth and upright Germans." It solicited "God's abiding blessing," which it trusted the church would receive since the large, tall-steepled church "will show the blasé and utterly materialistic Yankee what Catholic faith and German spirit of sacrifice can achieve."[62] Several decades earlier, a German-language newspaper reported that a Democratic Party rally manifested a "fire of patriotism" that "stirred the Americans up."[63] Patriotism, it was clear, was not dependent on being "American," nor was a European national identity dependent on remaining loyal to Old World governments.

Thus, as a layered array of allegiances that linked particular local identities to a national membership, a complementary identity could strengthen allegiances to both a national and an ethnic identification.[64] As such, it could be simultaneously acculturative while it facilitated the construction of a pluralist society. Kerby A. Miller argues, for example, that the Irish American leadership successfully used a reified Irish nationalism and a sanitized Americanism to gain "social and cultural hegemony" over its "lower classes" while it simultaneously sought acceptance from and access to the larger native institutions. A syncretic ethnic culture that joined Catholicity, Democracy, trade unionism, and loyalty to the cause of Ireland enabled the Irish leadership to assert that Irish immigrants were simultaneously "good Irish Americans" and "good Americans."[65]

While pluralist structures could evolve from a complementary identity, some contemporaries emphasized the assimilative properties associated with a complementary identity. As Machtet had noted, the tendency to glorify the United States, in part because of its freedoms, also prompted those dissatisfied with their experiences to mute their discontent. Yet there was more: the complementary identity provided immigrant communities with a certain amount of latitude, a sort of safety zone in which they could maintain their ethnic allegiance as they moved first to American citizenship and then to "American" behavior. As a prominent Roman Catholic leader pointed out, "Anything which makes immigrants more satisfied," which could include maintaining old beliefs, "also makes them better citizens."[66] Thus the tension inherent in the complementary identity could ultimately hasten the metamorphosis of immigrants from loyal and patriotic citizens to loyal "Americans." It permitted immigrants to identify with their ethnic past in the context of their adopted nation, and thus it granted them the leeway to celebrate both. In this sense, a dynamic occasioned by the complementary identity worked as many Americans hoped it would: it ultimately was acculturative.

Some immigrants confidently predicted this progression. C. L. Clausen, editor of *Emigranten,* wrote in English "to our American friends" in the premier issue of his paper in 1852. "We came here as strangers and friendless," he wrote, "ignorant of your institutions, your language and your customs." Nonetheless, "you extended to us the rights of citizenship and equal participation in your privileges." In response to this "friendly welcome," through the pages of the new paper, Clausen pledged to "hurry the process of Americanization of our immigrated countrymen" so that they could be "one people with the Americans" and "contribute their part to the final development of the character of this Great Nation."[67] Five years later, "Typo," also writing in English in *Emigranten,* argued that the Norwegian immigrants had experienced "progress." "When we first landed on the shores of this continent," he noted, "we knew no more of the English language than 'yes' and 'no.'" After a few years, most of the immigrants could conduct business with the American-born, and some worked in the "legislative halls of this country." "This," he concluded, "is decidedly Progress." Regarding the Norwegian-language press, "Typo" contended that its "duty" was to "assimilate the heterogeneous elements of society, and consolidate a great nation with a government of the people."[68]

Church leaders—including Roman Catholics—occasionally echoed the views of the secular press. Liberal Catholic Bishop Clement Smyth, for example, argued that the loyalty of Catholics during the Civil War had resulted in "the advancement of the interests of [the Catholic] church in this country." Whereas the church had once been looked upon "with suspicion and was considered even as hostile to republican institutions," Smyth argued, it now attracted "the attention of thinking Protestants" and "excited their admiration of its governing principles."[69] Such a hope undergirded the attitudes of the liberal "Americanizers" within the Catholic Church in the late nineteenth century. Cardinal James Gibbons in 1891 urged his flock to "glory in the title of American citizen. We owe our allegiance to one country, and that country is America. We must be in harmony with our political institutions" because the United States "is the land of our destiny." Since "patriotism is a sentiment commended by almighty God Himself," he concluded, "loyalty to God's Church and to our country" should be "our religious and political faith."[70]

The firmly held belief that contemporary conditions enabled one to be simultaneously a better American and a better Catholic or Norwegian or Irishman, however, was not without its risks for ethnic leaders. As immigrant society enjoyed and celebrated the American freedoms to be ethnic, a complementary identity tended to nudge such discussions into a bourgeois and liberal discourse that muted debates about class and culture.[71] In the political sphere, Amy Bridges argues, immigrants and their children were encouraged, in an arena of competing identifications under the rubric of American citizenship, to develop loyalties to new institutions, such as the political party, that challenged or reformulated former ethnic allegiances. Changing institutional affiliations threatened ethnic leaders as they regulated immigrant discourse. They represented both the potential to empower immigrants politically and socially, as in the case of urban American labor, and the potential to channel and constrain that power within such American institutions as the political party.[72] Editors of non-English-language papers for their part attempted to instruct their readership about life in the United States, but they obviously hoped that readers would continue to consult media written for a non-English-reading audience. And although Gibbons hoped to merge a "religious and political faith," he certainly did not contemplate that his followers would privilege citizenship over belief.

The structures of belonging in families and ethnic communities, moreover, did not always correspond to those of American citizenship. Whereas the relationship between the liberal state and its citizenry was perceived by many to be the sum of the individual contracts, it was complicated by connections within families and within ethnic communities that could rival the rights and duties of citizenship. Perhaps some saw families as miniature republics, as Michel Chevalier contended in 1839.[73] But for many, families were not small building blocks of the state so much as institutional structures that competed with and in some cases theoretically superseded it. The complementary identity becomes complicated in this context when societies were conceived, as they tended to be among European immigrants, as more organic and less contractual, more corporate and less individually based.[74]

These quandaries were particularly salient for European religious groups. To be sure, religious leaders were predisposed to celebrate American life and the inherent freedoms of the Republic. They frequently noted that America gave them the freedom to worship on Sunday. Although the state enabled the practice of religious belief, however, religious belief itself was not subject to allegiance to the state and therefore was not connected to citizenship. Societal structures based on particular religious ideas, moreover, did not necessarily conform to liberal, republican notions that were the basis for citizenship in an evolving American polity. The next section of this chapter argues that religious leaders treasured the conditions that permitted freedom of belief. Yet they were challenged when asked to revere a liberal society that permitted them, among other things, religious freedom but also imperiled communal beliefs and practices because of the society's penchant for stressing individual rights and freedoms. Ultimately, they found that they somehow had to nurture a reverence for "freedom" without discarding moral postures that might be at risk to the logical outcome of American liberty.

The Immigrants' Critique of American Society

> The Americans are fond of the word liberty; it is indeed the burden of their song, their glory and their pride. In some respects this is praiseworthy—an essential ingredient in national honour and national greatness; but in my opinion it is carried too far when it enters the sanctuary. . . . And yet religion is only one, the gospel is only one; and consequently no two conflicting creeds can be both right.
>
> —Rebecca Burlend, *A True Picture of Emigration* (1848)

Beneath a veneer of consensus among immigrants that celebrated the Republic lay profoundly different interpretations of the possibilities of American citizenship and the meaning of its concepts of liberty and freedom. European critics remained mindful of the importance of a state and society that enabled them the freedom to practice diverse customs. Yet they also feared that the very freedom to maintain their faith could also propagate license among their peers that would erode the central beliefs that knit them together. "Freedom" was a malleable concept, and its practice could begin an insidious process whose intrusion into every arena of life would be difficult to impede, especially since it was accepted and celebrated in the abstract. Thus the Norwegian newspaper *Emigranten* could lecture its immigrant readership on the differences between "freedom under law and order" and "licence."[75] Many European leaders therefore concurred with their American adversaries: liberty could lead to a self-indulgence deleterious to society at large.

Yet immigrant leaders who sought to transplant their cultural systems from Europe encountered even more pressing challenges. The many European immigrant traditions—with their Roman Catholic, Reformed, Calvinist, and Lutheran components—that were resituated in the Middle West resembled what Ernst Troeltsch termed church-types—inclusive institutions into which, as in a family or community, one was born.[76] Stressing hierarchical structures, these churches were likely to be influenced by contemporary movements that emphasized a corporatism and organicism. Those influenced by these ideas saw individual freedoms and volunteerism in a liberal republic as potential threats to corporatist societal structures. It is true that some immigrant sects and communities of belief that had embraced a nineteenth-century pietist sensibility found it more practical to merge religious beliefs with American society. They often skirmished with the more corporate wings within their church organizations over these very issues. Influential segments within the Roman Catholic community argued that even their church hierarchy should be adapted to the American Republic.[77] They believed that their faith—a conversation across continents and over centuries—had adjusted to secular political societies in the past and would continue to do so in the future.

A significant segment of European American cultural leaders, however, remained leery of the legacy of the Enlightenment upon which republican experiments were based. They encountered the internal contradictions of their churches nested in a society whose religious structures were based on voluntary membership and sectarianism. At the very least, many of them worried that the increasingly liberal tone in nineteenth-century American society would create a society of excess, materialism, and individualism.[78] Ironically, they valued the freedom that permitted people to reestablish communities of belief in America, but they feared the logical outcome when those within such communities also claimed their individual freedoms. What if an individualism that grew out of liberalism was valued in society and polity but was inadvisable in family life, community structures, or religious belief? And why were some freedoms acceptable whereas others were to be rejected? Religious leaders were well aware in the early nineteenth century of what Walter Lippmann would later term the "acids of modernity."[79] In this sense, they were concerned that their people might lose track of what they themselves considered the real purpose of existence on this earth. Like Rebecca Burlend, many European immigrants and their leaders were troubled when love of American political culture superseded or came into conflict with more meaningful beliefs.

Thus one of the great differences between the Yankee mind and the foreign mind concerned the relationship between church and state. Americans seemed to envision "sacred Republicanism" as marching across the continent hand in hand with "secular Republicanism."[80] Tocqueville argued that "in America it is religion which leads to enlightenment and the observance of divine laws which leads men to liberty." He contended that "freedom sees religion as the companion of its struggles and triumphs, the cradle of its infancy, and the divine source of its rights. Religion is considered as the guardian of mores, and mores are regarded as the guarantee of the laws and pledge for the maintenance of freedom itself." "Despotism may govern without faith," he wrote, "but liberty cannot."[81]

Many European religious leaders, in contrast, saw their faith as not so much a vehicle for the social control necessary to a republic as a set of beliefs central to their existence independent of the state. They perceived tensions between religion and the state and were forced, as a result, to tread the fine line between celebrating freedoms to practice diverse faiths and countenancing excessive liberties that jeopardized their own beliefs. To that end, they often criticized the increased prerogatives of the individual at the expense of institutions such as the church and family that mediated between individuals and the state. European leaders foresaw a society spinning out of control as individuals were cut adrift from their moorings. A Norwegian Lutheran pastor thus could express his admiration for the American Republic at the same time that he confessed a fear of "men who embraced a false humanism and were intoxicated with the modern rage for 'natural and inalienable human rights,' who considered outward, temporal freedom *absolutely* necessary to human beings."[82]

These leaders, from very early on, tended to express concerns that their adopted society was characterized by political immoderation, economic excess, and inordinate individualism. They worried, first, that the American polity would incline its citizens toward political intemperance. The "democratic institutions are no doubt very beneficial," admitted Ræder in 1847. Yet even in constitutional monarchies, such as in Norway, "there is a constant clamor for more and more rights and a continual striving toward democratic government." Republics such as the United States, he continued, "soon [had] a tendency to run to still greater extremes." Political rights, which "awaken the intellect" and "cause us to look around," lead "in many cases . . . to practical results," Ræder concluded. But they also "lead us into meditations, sensible or foolish according to our understanding and temperament."[83]

Fears about political immoderation were coupled with concerns that economic excess would stem from a proclivity toward materialism that pervaded American life. Whereas admirers of the American Republic connected the freedoms of the political environment to the genius of economic growth, immigrants occasionally expressed concerns about the long-term results of economic development. They feared that economic freedom—the "Yankee spirit," as one called it—had led to an overemphasis on material prosperity at the expense of more purposeful secular concerns. "Here is neither art, poetry, nor science," wrote a Norwegian clergyman simply. "Here are dollars and steam—that is all."[84] Dollars and steam, moreover, did not necessarily create a better society, especially when its citizens acted out of avarice. It was clear, the editor of *Emigranten* argued in 1857, that the immigrant should not be like the American, "who conducts his 'business' not for the benefit of his fellow man or society, but selfishly to 'make money' with the most complete unscrupulousness."[85] As a result, wrote a Norwegian clergyman to his relatives in Europe, "there is truly so little honesty and authority that one shudders." "I really do not know how long I can endure living under these beautiful republican conditions," he concluded sarcastically, "where the American God 'Money' holds the scepter of righteousness and where law and order are held in lowest esteem."[86]

A land where money implied right was a place that would challenge spiritual leaders for decades. Reverend Anton H. Walburg, a German Roman Catholic, maintained in the late nineteenth century that the materialism inherent in American culture would prove detrimental to his flock and his church. Enticements to "assimilate" would "lead our simple, straight-forward, honest Germans and Irish into this whirlpool of American life, this element wedded to this world, bent upon riches, upon political distinction, where their consciences will be stifled, their better sentiments trampled under foot."[87] Norwegian immigrants, according to one of their clergymen, likewise should not allow "themselves to become so engrossed in their worldly occupations that they were carried away by a materialism murderous to all spiritual interest, with every earnest thought destroyed by the thirst for gold and the coveting of earthly happiness."[88]

At the root of these political and material excesses, for many European leaders, was an individualism that had dangerous implications for both the spiritual and secular spheres. Such concerns were especially urgent for Roman Catholic immigrant leaders, who maintained religious beliefs that emphasized a natural order that relied on a web of institutions, above the individual and antecedent to the state, to order society. To be sure, American Catholic leaders had been influenced by a Catholic Enlightenment in the late eighteenth century, but by the mid-nineteenth century, many feared a "spirit" of Protestantism based on a freedom of religion that made private spiritual interpretations commonplace.[89] Many Roman Catholics were concerned that the sum of competing individual beliefs had created a sort of marketplace of creeds. According to Father Samuel Mazzuchelli, a pioneer priest in Wisconsin, "Protestantism has degenerated into a purely negative doctrine founded on *individual caprice and understanding,* influenced by every human passion and frailty." As a result, "in America, where the spirit of personal independence is carried to the extreme," individual understanding and sectarian competition became a mean-spirited popularity contest. "Sectarians," Mazzuchelli argued, "are even more disposed to deny what others believe, in order to give free rein to the suggestions of pride, malice, self-interest, passions, fanaticism, and *individual delusions.*" Truth was thus the ultimate loser as "the authority and teachings of all the ages are laid low before the defective and fallacious reasoning of every sectarian with the proud exclamation, 'I am free!'"[90] Freedom and majority rule, in short, which were proudly proclaimed in the political sphere, failed when they entered the sanctuary. Yet in the United States, "the political principle that the majority ought to rule," Mazzuchelli insisted, also regulated religious matters in every Protestant denomination. The maxim "I am free" thus extended beyond politics and became "the source of innumerable intellectual vagaries" enabling "the public preaching of the most extreme religious doctrines."[91] When political freedoms diffused into the spiritual world, the concept of freedom became incongruous.

Religious freedom not only created spiritual individualism but fostered a relativity of issues that, to Mazzuchelli and others, were absolute. The great number of sects in America, according to Father Wilhelm P. Bigot, existed because "the authorities have free access to the Holy Bible, but no one to explain it." As a result, religion in the United States "is like arriving at Babel, with a Babylonish confusion." Such "confusion" was due to a lack of authority and a paucity of leadership, which contradicted the true composition of the church.[92] "In North America," Bigot concluded, "every religious and irreligious have their own opinion of their representative, from superstition we are not free, from disbelief not far.... From year to year it is getting more variegated and more insane."[93]

Mazzuchelli also deprecated the spiritual repercussions of a Protestant relativism. Not only could all ministers interpret the faith, but also "all persons are imbued with a spirit of misunderstood religious independence, which leads them to consider themselves sole and absolute masters and competent judges of the truths to be believed and the morality to be practiced." It thus followed that "in America the opinion of the one who teaches is considered no more worthy of belief than that of his pupil; the interpretation of the hearer is considered of equal authority with that of the minister; and the meanings of Holy Scripture are such and so many that it is absolutely impossible to find any uniformity in them."[94] The sacred world thus had come to resemble the secular world. The fact that individuals belonged to a certain sect did not mean that they held a steadfast conviction in its teachings but rather that in a spiritual marketplace they preferred one preacher to another. The church, its leaders hoped, would "soften the manners of society" and "curb the spirit of pride which denies respect to superior authority, or tends to a belief that we were created to be independent of each other,—ideas unfortunately too common in the early stages of democracy."[95] Yet here again individuals could choose their own authority and foster their own pride. And the possibilities of religion were endless. "Any religious novelty whatsoever," Mazzuchelli judged, "when supported and promulgated by biblical fanaticism, by the secret financial or political interests of any shrewd hypocrites, will make proselytes." Americans, Mazzuchelli stressed, "like a flock without a shepherd, go here and there to listen to anyone who can offer them beautiful words." Perhaps such words were beautiful, but they were not necessarily "true."[96]

Protestant Europeans were also not at ease with what one Lutheran clergyman called "these blooming vagaries about freedom [*disse velsignede Frihedsgriller*]."[97] Although Protestant sects shared an animosity toward the Church of Rome, they often feared the consequences of freedoms of religion as well. European Protestant religious traditions, particularly the more liturgical branches of the Lutheran and Reformed Churches, also struggled with the many manifestations of what one Lutheran called a "churchly confusion ... in this land harrowed by so many erring sects" that followed directly from religious freedom.[98] First, Protestant leaders grappled with a religious freedom that bred disarray among sects and congregations. The wife of a Norwegian Lutheran pastor believed that two congregations under the leadership of her husband "were insane." "They want to build churches," she wrote, "but they are to be open to any odd tramp who wants to come and preach to them, and of these there are a large number in this country.... This is a free country, they say, and everyone can do as he pleases."[99] Second, an infatuation with democracy within the church could taint religious truth. Some argued that if majority rule functioned in government, it should also be practiced in the church. Even Europeans enamored of the Republic and the separation of church and state expressed amazement that, as one put it, congregations were "given a formal right to act contrary to God's Word if [they] can merely summon a two-thirds majority for a decision."[100]

Despite these deeply held fears, it is remarkable that these same church leaders nonetheless remained optimistic about the future of their faiths in the United States. That optimism was based on yet another instance of complementary identity, a syncretism that applauded both American freedom and religious truth. The structures of religious freedom, argued immigrant clergymen, actually would strengthen the faith and result in a victory of religious belief. The perspective of Norwegian Lutheran pastor Herman Amberg Preus, therefore, who worried about "the modern rage for 'natural and inalienable human rights,'" treasured the separation of church and state. The church, he observed, was protected, if not supported, by the state. And precisely because that support was lacking, the state could not dictate church policy. Thus in America the church body was not sustained by "ordinances of human devising . . . or privileges under civil law, but only [by] God's Word." In the United States, a pure church could be maintained only if "every activity can be directed according to God's Word" and its leadership could "work for the salvation of souls" and act as "servants of the Word without being hemmed in by the prejudices, constraints, and burdens of the state church."[101]

Even a Catholic leader such as Mazzuchelli was hopeful that truth would emerge victorious despite, or perhaps because of, the tendencies of excess. "The press and free preaching," he argued, "carry religious innovations to extremes as soon as they are born." Yet Catholic writers "whose pens are never idle" could attack that fanaticism. Using superior logic and armed with spiritual truth, they could check "the innate tendency to non-Catholic principles." As the church combated error, it was certain that "the followers of error must eventually submit and profess the truth or else, rejecting every religious system whatsoever, abandon themselves to unbelief which is, in its effects, little different from paganism." Precisely because of the freedoms of religion and the press and political equality, Mazzuchelli argued, Catholics would be able to maintain their beliefs and eventually exert some influence in the governing of the nation. Thus he was able to praise the opportunity to preserve differing religious convictions and simultaneously maintain his absolutist faith in the validity of the church. Ironically, his optimism about the future of Roman Catholicism was based on an acknowledgment of American immoderation: the excesses of freedom of belief would ultimately create a path toward belief in absolute Catholic principles.[102] Whereas Preus perceived a church free from the dictates of the state, Mazzuchelli envisioned an untrammeled discourse that would lead to a stronger church.

As powerful and compelling as these formulations based on the complementary identity may have seemed to immigrant leaders, they often created intellectual quandaries. For one thing, they suffered from an underlying paradox that Peter Berger and others call "cognitive contamination."[103] By attempting to control the modernizing forces that swirled around nineteenth-century American life, the leadership was attempting to guide them. In striving to regulate these forces, they were accepting ideas—the possibilities of choice, the use of manipulation—that were "modern" in and of themselves. By making compromises, they were implicitly accepting terms with which they disagreed.

In a more immediate sense, their solutions begged the questions underlying spiritual confrontation. Perhaps American providence would result in a Catholic or Lutheran "victory." Perhaps one religion would "win" because it would naturally occur to the citizenry that it was better. But how should the leadership of one faith, or one ethnic predilection, confront "defeat" if its adversary won the war for the hearts and minds of the West? How would such leaders be able to accept the idea of majority rule when the majority might not necessarily be right? And how were they to stem the tide of freedoms in the family and community if they were celebrated in the region and the polity? These questions would endure among the immigrant families embedded in the rural communities that dotted the nineteenth-century Middle West.

Notes

1. Cited in "Rt. Rev. Mathias Loras, D.D., First Bishop of Dubuque," *Annals of Iowa* 3 (1899): 591.

2. For a good overview of Catholic colonization, see Sister Mary Gilbert Kelly, *Catholic Immigrant Colonization Projects in the United States, 1815–1860* (New York: United States Catholic Historical Society, 1939).

3. Rev. Francis X. Pierz, *Die Indianer in Nord-America, ihre Lebenweise, Sitten, Gebräusche, u.s.w.* (St. Louis: Franz Saler, 1855), appendix, translated in *Acta et Dicta* 7 (1935): 121–30.

4. Mathias Loras memoirs, cited in Sister Mary Cleo Tritz, "St. Donatus: A Settlement of Luxemburgers in Northeastern Iowa" (M.A. thesis, Catholic University of America, 1954), 14–15.

5. Samuel Mazzuchelli, *The Memoirs of Father Samuel Mazzuchelli, O.P.* (1844; Chicago: Priory Press, 1967), 300. Here is a good example of the variations in the invented meanings of historical events. The American-born often posed the American Revolution as a successful overthrow of the papists of England.

6. Pierz, *Die Indianer in Nord-America,* 121–30. Germans would lead the settlement, according to Pierz, since they were the first Europeans in the vicinity and had beheld the apparition of the cross.

7. *Freeman's Journal and Catholic Register* (New York), 2 September 1854, cited in Kelly, *Catholic Immigrant Colonization Projects,* 155.

8. See, for example, "Letters and Documents," *Iowa Catholic Historical Review* 6 (1933): 40–42. See also M. M. Hoffmann, *The Church Founders of the Northwest* (Milwaukee: Bruce Publishing, 1937), and Kelly, *Catholic Immigrant Colonization Projects.*

9. The Propagation of the Faith Society of Lyons, the Leopoldine Society of Vienna, and the Ludwig Missions-Verein of Munich sent millions of francs and thousands of florins to the Catholic hierarchy in the West. See, for example, A. J. Rezek, "The Leopoldine Society (Leopoldinen Stiftung)," *Acta et Dicta* 3 (1914): 305–20, and M. M. Hoffmann, "Europe's Pennies and Iowa's Missions," *Iowa Catholic Historical Review* 5 (1932): 39–48.

10. Catholic leaders were often explicit about their attempts to sequester their flocks from contact with incorrect beliefs. Pierz, for example, challenged potential migrants to Catholic settlements to "prove yourselves good Catholics [by not bringing] with you any free-thinkers, red republicans, atheists, or agitators" (Pierz: *Die Indianer in Nord-America,* 121–30).

11. Hans Kohn, *American Nationalism: An Interpretative Essay* (New York: Macmillan, 1957). See also Yehoshua Arieli, *Individualism and Nationalism in American Ideology* (Cambridge: Harvard Uni-

versity Press, 1964); Paul Nagle, *This Sacred Trust: American Nationality, 1798–1898* (New York: Oxford University Press, 1971); and Samuel P. Huntington, *American Politics: The Promise of Disharmony* (Cambridge: Harvard University Press, 1981).

12. Alexis de Tocqueville, *Democracy in America,* ed. J. P. Mayer, trans. George Lawrence (New York: Anchor Books, 1969), 396–97.

13. Benedict Anderson, *Imagined Communities: Reflections on the Origins and Spread of Nationalism,* rev. ed. (London: Verso, 1991); Herbert David Croly, *Promise of American Life* (Cambridge: Harvard University Press, 1965), 3. On nationalism, see also Ernest Gellner, *Nations and Nationalism* (Ithaca: Cornell University Press, 1983), and Eric J. Hobsbawm, *Nations and Nationalism since 1870: Programme, Myth, Reality,* 2d ed. (New York: Cambridge University Press, 1992).

14. It must be underscored that these paragraphs speak of the overwhelming majority of immigrants to the West who were of European background and therefore defined as "white." The naturalization acts of the United States from 1790 until the aftermath of the Civil War defined access to citizenship according to "whiteness." The relatively simple passage to citizenship was restricted to "white" immigrants, whose encounters with the American nation, it goes without saying, contrasted starkly with those who were defined as "nonwhite." On citizenship, see James H. Kettner, *The Development of American Citizenship, 1608–1870* (Chapel Hill: University of North Carolina Press, 1978). On the construction of whiteness, see David R. Roediger, *Wages of Whiteness: Race and the Making of the American Working Class* (New York: Verso, 1991).

15. Carl J. Friedrich et al., *Problems of the American Public Service* (New York: McGraw Hill, 1935), 12, cited in Huntington, *American Politics,* 30.

16. See Philip Gleason, "American Identity and Americanization," in *Harvard Encyclopedia of American Ethnic Groups,* ed. Stephan Thernstrom (Cambridge: Harvard University Press, 1980), 31–34; Kathleen Neils Conzen et al., "The Invention of Ethnicity: A Perspective from the U.S.A.," *Journal of American Ethnic History* 12 (1992): 6–9; and John Higham, "Integrating America: The Problem of Assimilation in the Nineteenth Century," *Journal of American Ethnic History* 1 (1981): 7–16.

17. Thomas R. Whitney, *A Defence of the American Policy* (New York: DeWitt & Davenport, 1856), 29 (emphasis in original).

18. Ibid., 129–30.

19. Samuel F. B. Morse, *Foreign Conspiracy against the Liberties of the United States* (New York: Leavitt, Lord, 1835), 167–71.

20. Ole Rynning, *Ole Rynning's True Account of America,* ed. and trans. Theodore C. Blegen (Minneapolis: Norwegian-American Historical Association, 1926), 22–23 (emphasis added).

21. Ole Munch Ræder, *America in the Forties: The Letters of Ole Munch Ræder,* ed. and trans. Gunnar J. Malmin (Minneapolis: Norwegian-American Historical Association, 1929), 22.

22. *Emigranten,* 17 September 1852, cited in Harold M. Tolo, "The Political Position of *Emigranten* in the Election of 1852," *Norwegian-American Studies and Records* 8 (1934): 105–6.

23. *Dubuque National Demokrat,* 1 February 1859, 1, trans. J. K. Downing, CDH.

24. G. Unthank letter, 16 February 1826, MHS.

25. Mary Kevin Gallagher, ed., *Seed/Harvest* (Dubuque: Archdiocese of Dubuque Press, 1987), 13.

26. Karl Mathie, Marathon, Marathon County, 1893, Kate Levi field notes, Kate Levi papers, SHSW.

27. Cited in Joseph Schafer, "The Yankee and the Teuton in Wisconsin: V. Social Harmonies and Discords," *Wisconsin Magazine of History* 7 (1923): 158–59. Ræder observed a similar misidentification of Democrat with democracy among German, Irish, and Norwegian immigrants. On the other hand, "Englishmen, who have a constitutional education and have learned to think for themselves, or, as the Locofocos would say, have been corrupted by the aristocracy which infests Great Britain, willingly take sides with the Whigs" (Ræder, *America in the Forties,* 22–23).

28. Michel Chevalier, *Society, Manners, and Politics in the United States: Being a Series of Letters on North America* (Boston: Weeks, Jordan, 1839), 187.

29. *Nordlyset,* cited in Ræder, *America in the Forties,* 180.

30. *Folkets Røst,* 24 July 1858, 2.

31. Johan Reinert Reiersen, *Pathfinder for Norwegian Emigrants by Johan Reinert Reiersen,* ed. and trans. Frank G. Nelson (Northfield, Minn.: Norwegian-American Historical Association, 1981), 176, 182–83.

32. Lars Fletre, "The Vossing Correspondence Society of 1848 and the Report of Adam Löven-skjold," *Norwegian-American Studies* 28 (1979): 267.

33. August Blümner to his relatives, 3 April 1838, in *News from the Land of Freedom: German Immigrants Write Home,* ed. Walter D. Kamphoefner, Wolfgang Helbich, and Ulrike Sommer (Ithaca: Cornell University Press, 1991), 103 (emphasis in original). See also letters in ibid., 164–65, 307, 393, 427, 478, 481–82, 494, 585, 602.

34. Fletre, "Vossing Correspondence Society," 267.

35. R. Puchner to Kate Everest, New Holstein, Calumet County, 1890, Kate Levi Papers, State Historical Society of Wisconsin Archives, Madison, Wisconsin (hereafter SHSW).

36. Ludwig Dilger to parents and brothers and sisters, 5 November 1886, cited in Kamphoefner, Helbich, and Sommer, *News from the Land of Freedom,* 494 (emphasis in original). Despite his disparagement of American freedom, it is noteworthy that later in his letter Dilger wrote that "the worker will soon realize what his freedom is all about," as evidenced by the recent electoral victories among socialists.

37. Grigorij Machtet, "The Prairie and the Pioneers," *The Week,* nos. 47 and 48 (November 1874), in *America through Russian Eyes, 1874–1926,* ed. and trans. Olga Peters Hasty and Susanne Fusso (New Haven: Yale University Press, 1988), 21–22. Machtet was a member of the "American circle" of Russian populists, who attempted to form settlements in the United States in the 1870s.

38. Ibid. On the importance of myths of mobility and the influence of electoral politics in muting criticism of U.S. society, see, for example, Ira Katznelson, *City Trenches: Urban Politics and the Patterning of Class in the United States* (Chicago: University of Chicago Press, 1981); Stephan Thernstrom, *Poverty and Progress: Social Mobility in a Nineteenth Century City* (Cambridge: Harvard University Press, 1964); and Alan Dawley, *Class and Community: The Industrial Revolution and Lynn* (Cambridge: Harvard University Press, 1976).

39. Jonathan D. Sarna notes that larger collectivities were configured out of previously divisive groups in "From Immigrants to Ethnics: Toward a New Theory of 'Ethnicization,'" *Ethnicity* 5 (1978): 370–78. On "boundaries," see Fredrik Barth, *Ethnic Groups and Boundaries: The Social Organization of Cultural Difference* (Boston: Little, Brown, 1969), 9–38. See also William L. Yancey et al., "Emergent Ethnicity: A Review and Reformulation," *American Sociological Review* 41 (1976): 391–403, and Nathan Glazer and Daniel P. Moynihan, *Beyond the Melting Pot: The Negroes, Puerto Ricans, Jews, Italians, and Irish of New York City* (Cambridge: Massachusetts Institute of Technology Press, 1963).

40. The subgroup within the complementary identity, as I shall outline it, could be based on class and status identification. It is very important to keep in mind, however, that divisions at mid-century tended to be based on racial, religious, and ethnic concerns. See Conzen et al., "The Invention of Ethnicity," 8.

41. On the concept of a "complementary identity," see Peter A. Munch, "In Search of Identity: Ethnic Awareness and Ethnic Attitudes among Scandinavian Immigrants, 1840–1860," in *Scandinavians in America: Literary Life,* ed. J. R. Christianson (Decorah, Iowa: Symra Literary Society, 1985), 1–24. See also David M. Potter, "The Historian's Use of Nationalism and Vice Versa," in *History and American Society* (New York: Oxford University Press, 1973), 74–75, and Morton Grodzins, *The Loyal and the Disloyal: Social Boundaries of Patriotism and Treason* (Chicago: University of Chicago Press, 1956).

42. Huntington, *American Politics,* 27.

43. Indeed, immigrants saw "Americans" as those with Anglo-Saxon backgrounds. "Americanization," from this perspective, was impossible.

44. *Den Swenske Republikanen,* 21 August 1857, cited in Munch, "In Search of Identity," 7.

45. Ræder, *America in the Forties,* 19.

46. Cited in Joseph Schröder, *Verhandlungen der vierten allgemeinen Versammlung der Katholiken*

deutscher Zunge der Vereinigten Staaten von Nord-Amerika in Pittsburgh, Pa., Am 22, 23, 24 und 25 September, 1890 (Pittsburgh, 1890), 69–70, cited in Colman J. Barry, *The Catholic Church and German Americans* (Washington, D.C.: Catholic University of America Press, 1953), 124. Father Goller extended the metaphor when he noted that immigrants "may still treasure in their hearts the sweet memories of childhood; for only the renegade can forget the mother that bore him." But "far more dearer to them than the memories of childhood is the strong and beautiful bride, Columbia, who taught them to walk erect on God's earth in the proud consciousness of manhood" (ibid., 173).

47. See, for example, *Die Iowa,* 12 July 1883, 8.

48. *Dubuque National Demokrat,* 16 March 1876, 3, trans. J. K. Downing, Center for Dubuque History Archives, Lovas College, Dubuque, Iowa (hereafter CDH).

49. *Die Iowa,* 13 July 1882, 5.

50. Whitney, *Defence of the American Policy,* 71. This quotation was intended to indict Hughes for substituting "the mitre for our liberty cap" and blending "the crozier with the stars and stripes." Yet it also clearly indicates the attempts to fuse the symbols of America with those of Catholicism in order to augment loyalties to both.

51. Cited in Dorothy Dohen, *Nationalism and American Catholicism* (New York: Sheed and Ward, 1967), 114.

52. See Sister Mary De Paul Faber, "*The Luxemberger Gazette:* A Catholic German Language Paper of the Middle West, 1872–1918" (M.A. thesis, Catholic University of America, 1948), 31.

53. Letter reproduced in *St. Raphaels Blatt* 1 (January 1886): 7, cited in Barry, *The Catholic Church and German Americans,* 7.

54. German Catholic immigrants during the *Kulturkampf* were especially sensitive to American religious freedom. A German immigrant, wrote a countryman who sustained his Catholic faith along with his uncritical acceptance of an American creed, becomes "as good an American citizen as those of any other nationality. He has as much love for free American institutions; there is certainly no danger that the German Catholics will prefer the hegemony of Prussia and of Bismarckism to the greatest and freest republic in the world, with its flag of stars and stripes and its glorious constitution" (Father Farber and Reverend Innocent Wapelhorst, *The Future of Foreign Born Catholics; and Fear and Hopes for the Catholic Church and Schools in the United States* [St. Louis, 1884], 12–14, cited in Barry, *The Catholic Church and German Americans,* 53–54).

55. Ernest Mayerhoff to Kate Everest, Wanewoc, Juneau County, 1893, Kate Levi Papers, SHSW.

56. Unnamed correspondent to Kate Everest, Centerville Township, Sheboygan County, 1892, Kate Levi Papers, SHSW. Other, more concise respondents made similar points. A correspondent from Jefferson County wrote that nearly all residents of his community were "proud to be *German*-Americans" (unnamed correspondent to Kate Everest, Jefferson, Jefferson County, 1892, Kate Levi Papers, SHSW).

57. Joh. Kilian to Kate Everest, Theresa, Dodge County, 1892, Kate Levi Papers, SHSW.

58. Fr. Farber, *Church Progress,* 13 June 1891, cited in Barry, *The Catholic Church and German Americans,* 147. The contention that "Americans" were "un-American," or somehow less American than their immigrant counterparts, was raised in the context of public celebrations as well as private beliefs. Protestant ministers, reported a German Catholic paper, refused to participate in Decoration Day ceremonies in 1880 because the holiday fell on a Sunday. "Curious people, these puritans!" the editor concluded (*Die Iowa,* 10 June 1880, 8). Following President Garfield's assassination, the Catholic Benevolent Association float in yet another parade contained thirty-eight girls representing the states of the Union. "It shows that Protestants and Unbelievers," argued a German Catholic, "do not have a corner on patriotism" (*Die Iowa,* 29 August 1881, 8).

59. Traditions invented in the United States by ethnic groups were often the reformulations of conventions developed in specific European homelands. As Kathleen Conzen points out, for example, nationalist rituals enacted in the German states were a basis of German American institutions and ritual traditions that affirmed dual loyalties in the United States. Dorothy Dohen argues that Irish nationalism in the United States was powerfully informed by Irish nationalism in

Ireland. See Kathleen Neils Conzen, "Ethnicity as Festive Culture: Nineteenth-Century German America on Parade," in *The Invention of Ethnicity,* ed. Werner Sollors (New York: Oxford University Press, 1989), 44–76, and Dohen, *Nationalism and American Catholicism,* 59–63.

60. *Die Iowa,* 7 July 1881, 8. The scriptural allusion illustrates immigrants' belief that true faith could be cultivated in the United States away from meddling European states. But it also suggests the division between true believers and those outside the faith. See Matthew 10:14, Mark 6:7–13, and Luke 9:1–6.

61. *Die Iowa,* 30 May 1878, 8. These expressions of distaste for Germany were made amid the anti-Catholic *Kulturkampf.*

62. "X," *Die Iowa,* 4 May 1882, 5.

63. *Dubuque National Demokrat,* 5 July 1858, 3, trans. J. K. Downing, CDH.

64. Since varying sets of people were theoretically bound together depending on which level of identity was expressed, the boundaries that separated them differed according to the level of identity. It therefore seems problematic to conceptualize ethnic relationships, as Barth does, in terms of one set of boundaries that separated reified groups. Since multiple boundaries built on different levels existed, shared cultural constructions could conceivably divide and unite people simultaneously. See Barth, *Ethnic Groups and Boundaries.*

65. Kerby A. Miller, *Emigrants and Exiles: Ireland and the Irish Exodus to North America* (New York: Oxford University Press, 1985). See Kerby A. Miller, "Class, Culture, and Immigrant Group Identity in the United States: The Case of Irish-American Ethnicity," in *Immigration Reconsidered: History, Sociology, and Politics,* ed. Virginia Yans-McLaughlin (New York: Oxford University Press, 1990), for an abbreviated statement of the argument. See also Katznelson, *City Trenches.*

66. John Lancaster Spaulding, *St. Raphaels Blatt* 6 (1891): 63, cited in Barry, *The Catholic Church and German Americans,* 167.

67. *Emigranten,* 23 January 1852, cited in Tolo, "Political Position of *Emigranten,*" 95–96.

68. *Emigranten,* 20 April 1857, 3. The editor of *Emigranten* was now less sanguine about the benefits of acculturation. Writing in English, he agreed that "our countrymen . . . benefitted by the intercourse with American-born fellow-citizens" and that they "generally appropriate for themselves as quickly as possible the *desirable* qualities and customs of the Americans." But, he concluded, "it cannot however be wondered at if some of the nobler traits in the Norwegian Character is somewhat injured by the materialism inseparable from the life and pursuits in a country like this" (emphasis in original).

69. "Clement Smyth, Second Bishop of Iowa," *Iowa Catholic Historical Review* 9 (1936): 17.

70. James Cardinal Gibbons, *A Retrospect of Fifty Years,* 2 vols. (New York, 1916), 2:148–55, cited in Barry, *The Catholic Church and German Americans,* 163.

71. Bruce Levine hints at this problem in *The Migration of Ideology and the Contested Meaning of Freedom: German Americans in the Mid-Nineteenth Century* (Washington, D.C.: German Historical Institute, 1992).

72. See Amy Bridges, "Becoming American: The Working Classes in the United States before the Civil War," in *Working-Class Formation: Nineteenth-Century Patterns in Western Europe and the United States,* ed. Ira Katznelson and Aristide R. Zolberg (Princeton: Princeton University Press, 1986), 157–96.

73. Chevalier, *Society, Manners, and Politics,* 369.

74. Often these competing structures are not adequately addressed by scholars. Samuel Huntington, for example, argues correctly that the "American" ties within ethnic communities were "political and ideological" whereas the ethnic ties were "organic." Yet he is less willing to consider the consequences of a conflict between organic ideals nurtured in ethnic communities and political conceptions of individual freedom. Werner Sollors likewise has portrayed the contention between consent and descent as a fundamental means of understanding the possibilities of surpassing ethnicity. Yet the conflict between consent and descent, which is metaphorically a tension between two axes, is complicated if the cultures of descent relied on communal control that obviated pure individual consent. See Huntington, *American Politics,* 27, and Werner

Sollors, *Beyond Ethnicity: Consent and Descent in American Culture* (New York: Oxford University Press, 1986).

75. See "Tidsaanden: Vi boe i et frit land," *Emigranten*, 18 August 1855, and P. L. Mosstu, "Frihedens sande væsen og betydning," *Emigranten*, 2 May 1856, both cited in Peter A. Munch, "Authority and Freedom: Controversy in Norwegian-American Congregations," *Norwegian-American Studies* 28 (1979): 28.

76. Ernst Troeltsch, *Religion in History*, trans. and ed. James Luther Adams and Walter F. Bense (Minneapolis: Fortress Press, 1991), 210–34, 324–26.

77. See, for example, Patrick W. Carey, *People, Priests, and Prelates: Ecclesiastical Democracy and the Tensions of Trusteeism* (Notre Dame: University of Notre Dame Press, 1987).

78. These ideas emanated from a broad array of church leaders. Groups within Scandinavian and German Lutheranism, Dutch Calvinism, and Irish and German Catholicism evinced a suspicion of the rationalism and liberalism that were hallmarks of the Enlightenment. As the nineteenth century unfolded, European church leaders in the United States voiced increasingly powerful reactions. Among the vast literature, see George M. Stephenson, *The Religious Aspects of Swedish Immigration: A Study of Immigrant Churches* (Minneapolis: University of Minnesota Press, 1932), 1–48; E. Clifford Nelson and Eugene L. Fevold, *The Lutheran Church among Norwegian Americans: A History of the Evangelical Lutheran Church*, 2 vols. (Minneapolis: Augsburg Publishing House, 1960), 1:3–45; Heinrich H. Maurer, "The Problems of a National Church before 1860," *American Journal of Sociology* 30 (1925): 534–50, and "The Problems of Group-Consensus: Founding the Missouri Synod," *American Journal of Sociology* 30 (1925): 665–82; Miller, *Emigrants and Exiles*, 492–568; Philip Gleason, *The Conservative Reformers: German-American Catholics and the Social Order* (Notre Dame: University of Notre Dame Press, 1968); and James D. Bratt, *Dutch Calvinism in Modern America: A History of a Conservative Subculture* (Grand Rapids: William B. Eerdmans, 1984), 3–13.

79. Walter Lippmann, *A Preface to Morals* (New York: Macmillan, 1929), 8.

80. Ephraim Adams expressed this image in *The Iowa Band* (Boston: Congregational Publishing Society, 1870), 11. See Chapter 1. European immigrants, of course, were not the only Americans who feared the excesses of individualism. George M. Fredrickson cites examples of American-born conservatives such as Horace Bushnell and Orestes Brownson who dreaded the ideas of the so-called anti-institutionalists. Yet he also dismisses the extent of the influence of "the church-centered, organic view of society, with its stress on tradition and authority," as "clearly out of tune with the dominant trends of American thought" (George M. Fredrickson, *The Inner Civil War: Northern Intellectuals and the Crisis of the Union* [New York: Harper and Row, 1965], 28). One wonders if he would have arrived at the same conclusion if he had been mindful that some one-quarter of adults in the northern United States in 1860 were foreign-born. See ibid., chap. 2.

81. Tocqueville, *Democracy in America*, 1:45, 47. Orestes Brownson, on the contrary noted the tension between American Protestantism and American "civility." See, for example, Orestes Brownson, "Missions of America," *Brownson's Quarterly Review* 1 (1856): 409–44.

82. Herman Amberg Preus, *Syv Foredrag over de kirkelige Forholde blandt de Norske i Amerika* (Christiania, Norway: Jac. Dybwad, 1867), translated in *Vivacious Daughter: Seven Lectures on the Religious Situation among Norwegians in America by Herman Amberg Preus*, ed. and trans. Todd W. Nichol (Northfield, Minn.: Norwegian-American Historical Association, 1990), 166 (emphasis in original).

83. Ræder, *America in the Forties*, 69. Ræder also tried to convince Americans, without much success, that "a monarchical form of government can be combined with any liberty." After all, he wrote, a limited monarchy "must yield to the wishes of the majority" and "protect the minority against oppression so that everyone may enjoy a certain amount of liberty or, at any rate, freedom from arbitrariness on the part of anyone" (ibid., 84).

84. Jacob A. Ottesen to friends, 20 November 1852, in *Den Norske Tilskuer* (The Norwegian spectator), cited in Theodore Blegen, *Land of Their Choice: The Immigrants Write Home* (Minneapolis: University of Minnesota Press, 1955), 287.

85. *Emigranten*, 27 May 1857, cited in Munch, "In Search of Identity," 8. See also *Democraten*, 21,

28 September 1850; *Den Swenska Republikanen,* 31 July 1857; and *Hemlandet,* 4 April 1859, for similar appraisals. Some years later, Dr. Guy Hinsdale argued that the extraordinarily high rates of insanity among Scandinavians were due to "the restlessness and competition which characterize the social and industrial life in America," which "surpassed their limited strength" (*Swenska Amerikanska Posten,* 9 August 1892, 1).

86. O. F. Duus to Dear Ones at Home, 3 February 1856, in *Frontier Parsonage: The Letters of Olaus Fredrik Duus, Norwegian Pastor in Wisconsin, 1855–1858,* ed. Theodore C. Blegen (Northfield, Minn.: Norwegian-American Historical Association, 1947), 17. Duus's letters unconsciously underscore the challenges the leadership faced, for as he inveighs against materialism, he meticulously reports his speculative gains in land purchases. Blegen observes that "he seems to discern the will of God, and not a crass materialism," in his transactions (ibid., vi).

87. Anton H. Walburg, *The Question of Nationality in Its Relations to the Catholic Church in the United States* (Cincinnati, 1889), 44–45.

88. Preus, *Syv Foredrag,* in Nichol, *Vivacious Daughter,* 106.

89. See Jay P. Dolan, *The American Catholic Experience: A History from Colonial Times to the Present* (Garden City, N.Y.: Doubleday, 1985), for an overview of the Catholic Enlightenment and questions of authority raised by church leaders in the nineteenth century. See also Carey, *People, Priests, and Prelates,* for an optimistic portrayal of the Catholic Church's facility to balance "republicanism" and Catholic belief.

90. Mazzuchelli, *Memoirs,* 283–84 (emphasis added).

91. Ibid., 284.

92. Wilhelm P. Bigot, "Report to Germany about My First Work," in *Annalen der St. Michaelsgemeinde in Loramie [Berlin], Shelby County, Ohio, in der Erzdiözese Cincinnati von 1838 bis 1903* (Sidney, Ohio: Shelby County Anzeiger, 1907), 75, translated in *Annals of St. Michael's Parish in Loramie [Berlin], Shelby County, Ohio in the Archdiocese of Cincinnati from 1838 to 1903,* 65. After all, Bigot stressed, "not in vain did the Lord pray to his heavenly Father: 'I pray that all who believe in me, be one, and entirely one.' We Catholics know, acknowledge, and respect such a teacher, in the follower for whom the Lord prayed."

93. Ibid., 64.

94. Mazzuchelli, *Memoirs,* 284.

95. Cited in "Grand Scheme for Planting Irish Catholic Colonies in the Western States," *Home Missionary* 15 (1842): 154.

96. Mazzuchelli, *Memoirs,* 284, 290.

97. E. Clifford Nelson, ed., *A Pioneer Churchman: J. W. C. Dietrichson in Wisconsin, 1844–1850* (New York: Twayne Publishers, 1973), 143.

98. J. W. C. Dietrichson, in Munch, "Authority and Freedom," 15.

99. Caja Munch to her parents, 31 May–1 June 1857, in *The Strange American Way: Letters of Caja Munch from Wiota, Wisconsin, 1855–1859, with "An American Adventure" by Johan Storm Munch,* ed. and trans. Helene Munch and Peter A. Munch (Carbondale: Southern Illinois University Press, 1970), 97.

100. Preus, *Syv Foredrag,* in Nichol, *Vivacious Daughter,* 150. In this context, Preus was criticizing the Swedish Augustana Synod. Some church bodies, such as the Norwegian Synod, made distinctions between spiritual and temporal authority rooted in the Augsburg Confession so that the former was held solely by the clergy.

101. Ibid., 53, 178. See also J. St. Munch to Andreas Munch, 16 November 1857, in Munch and Munch, *Strange American Way,* 111. C. F. W. Walther, a leader of the German Missouri Synod, concurred with Preus and Munch. Reminding us again of a complementary identity, he wrote that "we live here in a State in which the church enjoys a freedom unsurpassed since its origin, and at present to be found scarcely anywhere else in the world. Our rulers, instead of allowing attacks to be made upon the rights of the church, exert all their power for the protection of these rights. We have here full liberty to regulate everything according to God's word." It was different in Germany, where "the church is bound in chains" and where a true follower who appealed "to Christian liberty"

was "regarded a rebel." "How happy," Walther concluded, "are we, compared with our brethren in our old Fatherland!" See Henry Eyster Jacobs, *A History of the Evangelical Lutheran Church in the United States* (New York: Christian Literature Company, 1893), 404–5.

102. Mazzuchelli, *Memoirs,* esp. 185–86, 283–86, 296, 300–302. Some decades later, another Roman Catholic leader professed essentially the same belief. The American was a pragmatist, Martin Marty argued, "reasonable in his judgments," "not intolerant," one who "willingly listens and accepts things from others." He also had "freedom" and was "a lover of order, a friend of law." It thus followed that the American would appreciate the "universal worth" of Catholic principles, and "if he realizes that the Catholic Church really makes men better, he will also be a Catholic." See Martin Marty, *Verhandlungen der 32 General-Versammlung der katholischen Vereine Deutschlands in Munster i. W., 9–12 September 1885* (Munster i. W., 1885), 249, cited and trans. in Barry, *The Catholic Church and German Americans,* 39.

103. Peter Berger, Brigitte Berger, and Hansfried Kellner, *The Homeless Mind: Modernization and Consciousness* (New York: Random House, 1973), 176–77.

2

The Mercurial Nature and Abiding Power of Race

A Transnational Family Story

MARTHA A. HODES

There are many ways to expose the mercurial nature of racial classification. Scholars of U.S. history might note, for example, that the category of "mulatto" first appeared in the federal census of 1850 and then disappeared in 1930, or they might discover that immigrants who had not thought of themselves as "black" at home in the Caribbean found themselves classified as such upon passage to the United States. Such episodes serve to unmask the instability of racial systems, yet simply marshaling evidence to prove taxonomies fickle tells only a partial story. In an effort to tell a fuller story about the workings of "race"—by which I mean principally the endeavors of racial categorization and stratification—I focus here on historical actors who crossed geographical boundaries and lived their lives within different racial systems. A vision that accounts for the experiences of sojourners and migrants illuminates the ways in which racial classification shifts across borders and thus deepens arguments about racial construction and malleability.[1]

At the same time, however, the principal argument of this essay moves in a different direction. We tend to think of the fluid and the mutable as less powerful than the rigid and the immutable, thereby equating the exposure of unstable racial categories with an assault on the very construct of race itself. In a pioneering essay in which Barbara J. Fields took a historical analysis of the concept of race as her starting point, she contended that ideologies of race are continually created and verified in daily life. More recently, Ann Laura Stoler has challenged the assumption that an understanding of racial instability can serve to undermine racism, and Thomas C. Holt has called attention to scholars' "general failure to probe beyond the mantra of social constructedness, to ask what that really might mean in shaping lived experience." Hilary McD. Beckles affirms that "the analysis of 'real experience' and the theorising of 'constructed representation' constitute part of the same intellectual project." Drawing together these theoretical strands, I argue that the scrutiny of day-to-day lives demonstrates not only the muta- bility of race but also, and with equal force, the abiding power of race in local settings. Neither malleability nor instability, then, necessarily diminishes the potency of race to circumscribe people's daily lives.[2]

On one level, people who hold authority (courtroom judges, employers, even neigh- borhood gossips) impose classification on subordinates. They determine who can marry whom and how to label the children, whom to hire for which jobs and whom to deny work, with whom to socialize and whom to ostracize. But the assignment of individu- als to lesser categories can be ambiguous or transitory, and part of the abiding power of racial classification lies precisely, I argue, within this mercurial quality. To put it more concretely, that power lies within the ability of legal, economic, and social authorities to assign and reassign racial categories to oppressive ends; as Nell Irvin Painter has writ- ten, the purpose of such categorization is "to rank people and keep them in place." On another level, though, communities, families, and individuals seek to resist such authority by naming and defining themselves, an endeavor that entails the assignment of others to various racial categories. To name and define others is also to establish one's own superior station, and so these efforts on the part of rulers and subjugated alike work to create, reshape, and reinforce ideologies of race: who is worthy or superior, who is depraved or inferior. Together, these endeavors work continually to determine, destabilize, and ulti- mately to sustain racial hierarchies. No matter how chimerical we prove "race" to be, that wisdom alone remains inadequate to diminish the might of racism, for the power of race lies within the very fact of malleability.[3]

The nature of the power that lies within the capricious exercise of racial categori- zation in everyday life can best be illustrated by exploring the experiences of particular historical actors in particular geographical settings. The transnational family story to be told here centers on a journey across racial lines and national borders. Such travels, metaphorical and literal, expose both the volatility and the potency of racial classifica- tion. The geographical and temporal markers are New England and the British Caribbean in the nineteenth century, although the questions are transportable to other places and times. The protagonist is an Anglo-American working-class woman named Eunice Con- nolly. Born in 1831 to a struggling Massachusetts family, Eunice married a local carpenter at seventeen, just before her alcoholic father deserted her mother. Marriage offered no respite from labor, and, like other wage-earning women, Eunice would work in a mill, take in washing, clean other people's houses, and sell hats she fashioned out of palm leaves. In the late 1850s, Eunice's husband set out to try his luck in the booming Gulf port city of Mobile, Alabama. In 1860, Eunice joined him there, but the couple's aspira- tions collided with the Civil War, and, with luck running low, Eunice's husband joined the Confederate Army. Seven months pregnant, Eunice and her young son boarded a train for the arduous journey back to New England. Through four years of war, she eked out a living in New Hampshire, barely able to support herself and two children; she had little knowledge of her husband's whereabouts, and wartime Confederate aid did not extend to northern wives. Soon after Union victory, word arrived that Eunice's husband had died fighting for the South.[4]

Years of poverty and despair abated only with her marriage to William Smiley Connolly, the story's second protagonist. Smiley (as he was called) was born on Grand Cayman Island in 1833, just before the emancipation of slaves in the British West Indies. Of mixed African and European descent, his family settled with other freed people on the unclaimed acres of the island's eastern end. Over the next decades, Connolly men accumulated land and became successful mariners. Smiley built and captained his own schooners, engaging in the turtle, coffee, and cattle trades. He married a Caymanian woman, but at some point that union dissolved. Documents remain silent as to where or how the widow Eunice met the sea captain Smiley, but the couple wed in 1869 just outside of Lowell, Massachusetts, and swiftly sailed for Grand Cayman. For eight years, Eunice made her home there, keeping house and caring for her children, attending church and sailing on the bay, all the while sending reassuring letters back to New England. In 1877, on a voyage to the Bay Islands of Honduras, Eunice, Smiley, and their children were struck by a hurricane and drowned off the Mosquito Coast of Nicaragua.[5]

The two Atlantic World sites that provide the principal settings for this story could hardly appear more dissimilar. If northern New England stood at the center of much of nineteenth-century history-in-the-making—transatlantic capitalist expansion and industrialization, the creation of a powerful nation in the American Civil War—the Cayman Islands occupied a space on the margins of history, peripheral to the British Empire. Measuring about twenty miles long and less than a hundred miles square, Grand Cayman is the largest of three islands (with Little Cayman and Cayman Brac) situated south of Cuba and northwest of Jamaica. The islands remained under the administrative rule of Jamaica in the nineteenth century, and Caymanian men sailed to Kingston to buy and sell goods, even to collect their mail. With soil too poor to nourish a staple crop, Cayman (like Bermuda, the Bahamas, and British Honduras, among others) never supported a plantation economy. At emancipation, the thousand or so slaves who had worked on farms and as domestics constituted a majority of the population. Turtle-fishing and wrecking (the liberation of goods from shipwrecked vessels) continued as the islands' major industries, and all residents, including former slavemasters who chose to stay, worked the land without benefit of imported indentured labor. There are no records or traces of indigenous people.[6]

To nineteenth-century visitors, Cayman seemed remarkably secluded. One Scottish missionary, who arrived the same year as Eunice Connolly, described the "sequestered" islands as a "lonely" place of "extreme isolation." Yet at the same time, Cayman provides a revealing example of the ways in which one small place could be connected to a more expansive geographical arena. Many of the men were mariners who traveled not only to Jamaica and Honduras but also to Cuba, the Florida Keys, New Orleans, Mobile, New York, and Boston. In 1872, this same missionary found his church services filled with women whose husbands, fathers, and sons were "at sea or in foreign countries." Moreover, because the land was surrounded by coral reefs, frequent shipwrecks brought in both foreign goods and forever-stranded outsiders. From the seventeenth century onward, the islands witnessed an amalgam of cultures, with a flow of European pirates, settlers, and sailors, enslaved and free people of African descent, and its own seafaring population. A woman born in 1899 told how one of her grandfathers was a slave from Africa, while the other was a shipwrecked seaman from Ireland. According to one linguistic analysis, natives spoke a "mixture of an archaic form of English with fragments of Negro dialect, Spanish forms, and expressions common to the Southern United States, as well as a remarkable number of nautical words." Caymanians, an elderly resident recently agreed, have been "traveling the world from the beginning."[7]

Lives that raise questions about the day-to-day workings of racial classification and stratification across national bounds, coupled with a small body of direct evidence, warrant a certain willingness to embrace speculation. The six surviving letters that Eunice wrote from the West Indies include evidence that other communications never arrived in New England, and none of the mail that Eunice received in the Caribbean outlasted the tropical climate. Six much shorter letters survive from Smiley Connolly, including two penned in North America. But both Eunice and Smiley, along with most of their correspondents, kept ideas about race largely to themselves, and other evidence has proven scarce as well. Like hundreds of thousands of working-class women in the nineteenth century, Eunice and her family seldom appear in the historical record beyond the most commonplace documents (a birth or marriage certificate, a census listing, a muster roll). In Cayman, members of the Connolly family can be found in vital records that begin only in the 1880s, as well as in the memories of islanders born in the early twentieth century who have participated in the Memory Bank project of the Cayman Islands National Archive.

In trying to discern the lived experiences of my protagonists, then, some of my analysis necessarily relies more on context and extrapolation than on the evidence of conventional historical documentation. In particular, my own conversations with Connolly and Conolly descendants (the name is spelled both ways) have yielded scattered fragments about Smiley (a few recall hearing that he and an American woman drowned in the terrible hurricane of 1877), but have proven more fruitful concerning Smiley's father, brothers, and three sons from his first marriage. From childhood, these descendants, most of whom still reside in East End, where Eunice disembarked in 1869, listened to narratives of family, local, and island history, absorbing the ways in which parents, grandparents, and great-grandparents described themselves and others in terms of ancestry or color or local status. Thus do I at times rely openly on their language and reflections in efforts to speculate about the nineteenth-century lives of Eunice and Smiley Connolly, about the ways in which they were classified by others and endeavored to embody categories to their own satisfaction.

Ancestry, color and appearance, class status, gender, and behavior: all of these perceptions and assessments intertwined in the lives to be investigated here. Scholars of race most often contend that ancestry was the principal determinant of racial categorization in the nineteenth-century United States. In this view, the U.S. system was largely a binary one, built on the polar categories of "black" and "white," with American Indians and Asian immigrants occupying a place outside of that central duality. A system that placed all people of mixed African and European ancestry into the category of "black" worked to deny separate classifications for people of mixed descent. This feature worked also, theoretically, to erase sex across the color line and to preclude any fluidity of racial identification, since intermediate categories were subsumed within a monolithic black-ness. Whiteness in nineteenth-century North America, then, was not intended to be a description of color but rather an unfragmentable quality that marked a person off from African lineage. In 1860, a Connecticut court maintained that the phrase "per-sons of color" in its "common, ordinary and popular meaning" included "those who have descended in part" from African ancestors, and that African ancestry and whiteness were mutually exclusive. In turn, scholars have contrasted this binary structure with the non-binary system of the nineteenth-century British Caribbean that recognized categories in between "black" and "white." With greater fluidity (though with no less prejudice against darkness), class and complexion openly counted in the pursuit of racial stratification in the West Indies, and individuals of known African ancestry could move closer to the cat-egory of "white" precisely because color, and especially class status, were deeply bound up with racial rankings.[8]

Yet by drawing the distinction between the United States and the Caribbean too sharply, we miss an opportunity to understand the ways in which the largely binary North American system offered a margin of latitude: not only for those who were able to reject an imposed subordinate ranking by means of "passing" but also for authorities (whether courtroom judges or neighborhood gossips) who aimed to enforce oppression by impos-ing rankings that did not depend on a person's ancestry. The "one-drop rule" in North America was never legally firm in the nineteenth century, and although it often prevailed informally, the experiences of Eunice and Smiley Connolly in New England make clear that racial classification could be challenged by factors other than genealogy. As in the British Caribbean, class status and personal associations could affect the shadings of one's racial classification and subsequent treatment in local, daily life.[9]

Eunice's journey across racial boundaries was not simply a metaphorical crossing of the color line, rendering her a white woman married to a black man. Rather, the court-ship and marriage to Smiley Connolly set in motion circumstances that, as shall become apparent, at first denied Eunice the privileges of white womanhood in her New England neighborhood and then, as she came to be part of a community of former Caribbean slaves, brought her closer—though in a surprising way—to the embodiment of white woman-hood than she had ever been before. It was the crossing of national borders that made possible this contradictory sequence of events. This essay investigates, in turn, Eunice's status in Civil War New England, Smiley's status in the West Indies and the ways he was perceived in post-Civil War New England, and finally, Eunice Connolly's transformative experiences upon marriage to an African Caribbean captain, both in New England and the British Caribbean. Each of these episodes reveals how the malleability of racial clas-sification could work to fortify and invigorate the workings of racial hierarchy.

Eunice Stone lived in Manchester, New Hampshire, in the 1850s, a thriving mill city on the banks of the Merrimack River, where capital and cotton converged with looms and labor to build the nation's industry in cloth. Exploited and protesting wage workers in antebellum New England likened themselves to southern slaves ("Slave-driverism at the

South and Overseerism at the North is one and the same thing"); northern white families like Eunice's, who found themselves slipping down the slope of industrial capitalism—landless and struggling to find what was inevitably low-wage employment—consequently emphasized their identity as free and white. Slavery was a useful theoretical invocation, but that institution was far distant from upper New England, and native-born Protestants measured themselves most immediately against a different degraded population: foreign-born Irish Catholics. Like other mill cities, Manchester hosted an influx of Irish immigrants during the 1850s (by 1860, one-quarter of the city's 20,000 residents were Irish), and native-born Americans reacted with hostility, creating a pattern of nativist violence across northeastern cities. Over the past decade, scholars have asserted that certain historical actors of no African ancestry, most notably Irish immigrants, were nonetheless excluded from the category of "white" in the nineteenth-century United States. More recently, historians have questioned this formulation, calling for greater precision in the form of attention to "lived experience" to augment the evidence of image and representation. One scholar has suggested as well that attention to transnational contexts can better situate the workings of whiteness in U.S. history. Eunice's experiences are instructive in both of these efforts.[10]

When Eunice registered to work at Manchester's Amoskeag Mills just before she joined her husband in Mobile, she became part of an ongoing shift within New England's workplaces. During the 1830s, nearly all mill workers had been young, native-born, white women recruited from farm families, sojourning to river-bank cities like Lowell and Manchester in order to earn extra money prior to marriage. As waves of Irish families fleeing the potato famine disembarked in Boston beginning in the 1840s, the ethnic composition of that work force began to change. As industrial expansion kept pace, mill agents set out to enlist this new labor. Irish families were poor and willing to work for lower wages. Irish women and girls preferred the mills to the degradation of domestic service, just as the men and boys were satisfied to refuse hard outdoor labor such as canal digging. These same years also brought new opportunities for middling Yankee women, who began to take teaching positions or move west with their fathers or husbands. Accordingly, poorer native-born women like Eunice, who entered the mills in the 1850s and 1860s, were motivated more by economic necessity than were the earliest "mill girls." Eunice's decision to sign the employee register of the Amoskeag Manufacturing Company in March 1860, and the consequent boarding out of her young son, reflected her dire circumstances; she lived apart from her husband (he was down south) and had no father to lend interim support, nowhere even to take up residence without imposing on other straitened family members. The first generation of Yankee operatives, those who worked prior to marriage, defined themselves against women like Eunice, calling them "low class New England girls" and lumping them together with Irish immigrants, blaming them all for decreasing wages.[11]

Across the urban northeast, tensions continued to mount between native-born and newcomer. The first naturalization law in the United States, enacted in 1790, extended citizenship to all "free white persons" in the new nation. Beginning with the Irish influx of the 1840s, the unexamined inclusiveness of that phrasing began to unsettle white

Americans of British descent. While the concept of the "Anglo-Saxon" gained popularity, Anglo-Americans also began to rank different nationalities. "Celts," for example, were white, but they might also be savages. As pseudo-scientific racism found a popular audience, white Americans came to parse other white people into various subcategories, only some of which they considered fit for citizenship. In this scheme, Irish Catholics were eligible (unlike people of African descent), but native-born Americans hardly welcomed such immigrants as their equals. Beginning in the 1850s, Anglo-Americans pointed to the Celtic physique as proof of innate inferiority and immutable difference. Irish people were depicted as slothful and sensual, brutish and coarse, dark-skinned, diseased, four-legged, low-browed, and wild.[12]

Such stereotypes overlapped with racist ideas about Africans and African Americans, with political cartoons apt to depict Irish people as more simian than human. One prominent antebellum New Yorker described Irish men as bearing "prehensile paws" and likened a group of mourning Irish women to "wailing as a score of daylight Banshees." A Congregational minister in Boston referred to Irish and Negroes (along with Indians and Mexicans) as "savage, barbarous, half-civilized" populations, and another observer described "the black tint of skin" in "Celtic physiognomy." According to one Manchester newspaper in 1858, the Irish were "the offals of Europe, as little qualified to go to the ballot box as the veriest Hottentot." In 1850, the census taker for Manchester listed one Elias Haskall living in the almshouse; his place of birth was recorded as Ireland, his color as black. A faint parenthetical jotting in another hand reads, "Error no doubt," but on the bottom of the page, the clerk who totaled the numbers added the comment, "Irish 'nigger!'" Certainly the marshal may have recorded the wrong birthplace or color, or maybe Haskall had been born in Ireland of African descent. On the other hand, the enumerator may have considered this poverty-stricken Irishman no better than a black person. If so, then class status, nationality, and religion acted as the determinants of race, with little attention to proof or disproof of African descent.[13]

Eunice's family, too, defined themselves against New England's latest immigrants. "I think Manchester has altered a good deal," a sister reported of the city's landscape in a letter to Eunice and their mother. "It seems to me the morals of the place are much corrupted," she worried, explaining that "the St[reet]'s in the center of the City seem filthy and mostly inhabited by Irish." In the face of such disturbing changes, she continued, "the American families all seem to have moved to the outskirts of the city." There were probably "just as many good people here as ever, but the low Irish have increased fast and remain in the old tenements while our people have erected new buildings and taken themselves out from amongst them, leaving rather a rough set." The sister's insistence on her own American nationality ("our people") likely stemmed from the fact that her family too closely resembled the stereotypes of Irish families. For one thing, their father drank and deserted his wife and children. For another, the women of these Irish families, so disdained by the sister, worked in the Amoskeag Mills, if not alongside Eunice in the weaving and dressing rooms, then nearby in the carding and spinning rooms. Living without a husband, working in the mills, boarding out her son, standing on the edge of poverty: in 1860, Eunice was inching steadily toward a social status difficult to distinguish from that of Irish immigrant women. The sister's anxious reiteration of the family's "American" character was meant to separate them from the immorality, filth, poverty, overbreeding, and crudeness that she defined as "Irish."[14]

These kinds of deprecatory images are related to, though cannot be simply equated with, prejudice against people of African descent. Anglo-American racial thinking is illustrated by Thomas C. Holt's reading of the British writer Thomas Carlyle, who believed black and Irish people alike to be savage and indolent, although the light skin of the Irish, he maintained, made it harder to segregate them. In Holt's analysis of Carlyle on this point, the two outcast populations were not equal; rather, black people were the "emblem of degradation, of the level to which whites could sink." Importing this astute formulation to mid-century New England casts light on Eunice's experiences there. Certainly no one could claim Eunice to be an immigrant from Ireland, and yet she was descending steadily, just as the Irish in Carlyle's estimate remained white but had declined to a level of civilization equivalent to that of black people.[15]

Such classificatory blurrings were made manifest in lived experience. Eunice's fall resulted from her status as a married woman with children but without a husband to provide an adequate home for the family. In northeastern cities, the positions of servant, washerwoman, and cook were reserved for Irish girls and women, or alternatively for free black daughters and wives. (As one white woman wrote from Maine, "My colored girl has gone and I am without a servant and doing my own work.") In this way, the lives of Irish and black women intersected. In one of New York City's poorest neighborhoods, eight black women and eight Irish women worked together as laundresses, and the girls and women of Manchester's small black population who worked for wages likewise had little choice but to take jobs as domestic laborers. For their part, unskilled Yankee women like Eunice preferred the mills to domestic service, since the latter paid less for more demeaning labor. But since mills often required their workers to live on the premises, married women in need of money turned their homes into boardinghouses; Eunice had no such option, however, as she lacked a husband to buy land and build a home, or even to pay rent, and hence had no rooms to let. Next down the ladder were domestic jobs that provided room and board, but Eunice now had two children. "If I could go into the Mill this summer, I could get a long," Eunice reasoned upon her return from the South. "But if my baby lives, I cannot do much in the Mill *this* summer, and I dont know as any one would want me to do house work with so young a child." Live-in maids with children of their own would have to send their offspring away, and so working mothers often settled for live-out domestic labor, positions largely filled by Irish and black women. It was an especially bleak scenario, since day wages were no better, but they did not include shelter and meals, and it was this scenario that came to describe Eunice's circumstances as a husbandless mother of two children during the Civil War. Of course, the cotton mills stood idle for parts of the war, and Claremont, New Hampshire, where Eunice settled to be near her in-laws upon her return from Mobile, was home to few immigrants or African Americans. Still, even more than in Manchester in 1860, Eunice now slipped to near the lowest possible status a white woman could know: unskilled and without family support, caring for her children in between housecleaning and laundering for hire, vigilantly but barely keeping destitution at arm's length. All in all, it was a lowly, lonely, and onerous existence. Only prostitution or the poorhouse would have felt more degraded.[16]

Eunice's circumstances did not make her either Irish or black in the eyes of other white people; her economic and social degradation did, however, make it harder for her to define herself against either of those categories, and permitted other white people to define themselves against people like her. To families whose husbands provided for their wives and children, to Yankee women who deserted the factories when the immigrants arrived, to mistresses who were able to assign the drudgery of domestic labor to those unlike themselves, Eunice's poverty and plebeian occupations crowded her into circumstances closely resembling those of Irish immigrant and black women. As one New Hampshire newspaper put it, "Our native-born citizens hate to work by the side of an Irishman," for that aroused "the same feeling which makes it impossible for a respectable white man to labor by the side of slaves in the South." The same could be said about native-born white women, for working the same jobs as Irish and black women made it yet harder to claim the privileges of white womanhood.[17]

That is where Eunice stood just before she began to be courted by the African Caribbean sea captain. To understand the ways in which the malleability and attendant power of racial classification would transform Eunice's life, it is imperative to account for the experiences of Smiley Connolly and to consider Eunice's perceptions of her new husband. At home on Grand Cayman Island, Smiley took his place in a three-part hierarchy. The categories in Jamaica's nineteenth-century population tables were "white," "brown," and "black," and the 1855 Cayman census similarly divided the islands' population into "white," "coloured," and "black." Travelers, too, noticed these distinctions. Just as the British novelist Anthony Trollope, sojourning in the late 1850s, divided the residents of Jamaica into "black," "colored," and "white," so a shipwrecked Scottish missionary on Grand Cayman in the mid-nineteenth century described the inhabitants there as "white, black, and brown." But this three-part configuration often proved insufficient, and British Caribbean residents and visitors alike employed a wider spectrum of appellations in efforts to make sense of more informal categories in between. An observer in Jamaica during the 1840s named "sambos, mulattoes, quadroons, mestees, and mestiphinoes." According to a white Englishwoman in Antigua, also in the 1840s, "there are as many gradations in *tint* as there are in *rank*." Her inventory included "mongrel," "mulatto," "mustee," "fustee," and "dustee." Caymanians, too, contributed to this multihued taxonomy; a slave-sale record in 1829 described "a Sambo Girl," one Conolly descendant born in 1903 described her mother as "mustee," and two Conolly siblings invoked the term "quadroon" to describe their grandmother. According to an anthropologist who studied folk racial categories in Cayman in the mid-twentieth century, Europeans tended to divide the population into a dual system of "black" and "white," whereas those of African descent laid out a system bracketed by "black" and "white" but containing various grades in between, including "mulatto," "quadroon," "musty," "sambo," "half sambo," and "mustyfeno." Blue or grey eyes and brown hair moved one toward whiteness, whereas darker eyes and hair, or curls, shaded a person toward blackness.[18]

Class and race in the nineteenth-century West Indies were, as one scholar has phrased it, "impossibly entangled," and this description applied to the Cayman Islands as well. Yet Cayman's social structure differed from that of plantation colonies. Relations among Caymanian classes and colors were less violent during slavery, and so the transition to freedom also proved less explosive. It is equally true that few if any Caymanians had attained the kind of wealth known to plantation societies. One missionary described the islands' white people as "a plain, hardworking class of men" dependent on "manual labor for their daily bread"; another observed, "Since abolition, white people have either to do the work in plantation themselves" (meaning farm labor), "or hire others to do it for them, and black men are sailors as well as white." At the same time, however, Cayman's closest economic and political ties remained with Jamaica, and Smiley Connolly and his mariner brothers derived their status in part from their dealings in that major sugar colony. There, as elsewhere in the British Caribbean, the colored (or brown or mulatto) classes occupied an ambiguous middle position. In general, wealth and color were correlated, with whites benefiting the most from connections to an Atlantic market economy and blacks surviving as exploited laborers. White people treated colored people better than they treated black people, since it was in their interest as a numerical minority to keep colored people on their side. But whereas a well-to-do, educated, and mostly light-skinned faction among the colored classes allied itself with whites and was permitted entry into white society, for the most part whites did not consider colored people their equals. Tensions between the colored and black classes continued through emancipation, and caste lines persisted despite legal equality.[19]

In nineteenth-century Jamaica, where Smiley and his brothers sailed their vessels, respectable middling occupations for colored men included shopkeeping, teaching, and the ministry, and Connolly men could be found in each of these sectors. A half-brother was a mariner and a preaching church elder; three brothers were mariners; sons became mariners and shopkeepers, and one became a teacher and an island officer. At the same time, Smiley stood above the middling artisanal trades such as carpentry (he hired carpenters to build his house for him), and, as a mariner, he (and other Connolly men) belonged to the small class of Caymanians who owned land and prospered through participation in the Atlantic economy, thus drawing closer to the colored elite. In Cayman, then, Smiley Connolly was a man of color whose economic standing and partial European ancestry shaded him toward whiteness.[20]

In the United States, by contrast, African ancestry carried enough weight in the exercise of racial designation that North Americans who knew of Smiley's lineage could have called him "black." Certainly there is evidence that Eunice and her northern compatriots ascribed to a one-drop rule that would have placed Smiley in that personally unfamiliar category. When William G. Allen, a man who described himself as of "one-fourth African blood," was violently assaulted by white people upon his engagement to a white woman in New York in the 1850s, he observed, "Whatever a man may be, though, in personal appearance, he should be as fair as the fairest Anglo-Saxon, yet, if he have but one drop of the blood of the African flowing in his veins," no white woman was permitted to marry him. The African-American novelist Frank J. Webb likewise captured this axiom in his

1857 work, *The Garies and Their Friends,* which portrayed the virulent enforcement of a one-drop rule in antebellum Philadelphia. As one northern character informed the son of a slaveowner and a slave: "if you should settle down here, you'll have to be either one thing or other—white or coloured." Should the man choose to live as a white person in the North, he was advised that "it must never be known that you have a drop of African blood in your veins . . . no matter how fair in complexion or how white you may be."[21]

Yet at the same time, the term "mulatto" was familiar to nineteenth-century North Americans, and Smiley could have fit into that category as well, thereby destabilizing the black-white binary. Historians plotting the racial systems of the United States have situated the lower South, and especially cities such as New Orleans, Charleston, and Mobile, as closest to a tri-racial West Indian system.[22] Such tidy regional divisions, however, obscure apertures in the dominant binary system, beyond the well-trodden path of passing from black to white. In the face of antebellum legal rulings in the U.S. North that asserted a one-drop formulation comes contrary evidence that fractions of African ancestry could be overlooked, or even erased. In 1810, the Massachusetts Supreme Court defined "mulatto" as strictly one-half black and one-half white, ruling that the child of one mulatto parent and one white parent could not be classified as such. Although the judges offered no alternative (say, "white" or "quadroon"), the verdict nonetheless defied a one-drop system. "Who can tell the proportions and trace the mixtures of blood?" wondered a Connecticut lawyer in 1834. "Shall one half, one quarter, one twentieth, or at the least possible taint of negro blood, be sufficient to take from its possessor the citizen character?" As Massachusetts debated legalizing marriage between blacks and whites in the 1830s and 40s, one lawmaker queried, "How *far,* through how many generations, must African or Indian blood be diluted, before it can attain to respectability?" adding, "The truth is, it is extremely arbitrary."[23]

A series of court cases in antebellum Ohio affirmed that "all nearer white than black, or of the grade between the mulattoes and the whites" were entitled to the privileges of citizenship. In one suit, the court declared that ancestry ("blood"), rather than color, should be the determining factor in racial designation, yet simultaneously ruled that remote African ancestry could not dilute whiteness. Indeed, according to the justices in an 1852 inheritance case in Maine, the same laws that counted "any proportion of African blood" as nullifying whiteness, could still (however contradictorily) count people with one-eighth or less African ancestry as white—thus paralleling Jamaican law, which granted the privileges of whiteness to anyone removed a certain number of generations from African descent. The U.S. federal census of 1850 had been the first to enumerate "mulattoes," and census takers in 1870 were instructed to record as "mulatto" (as opposed to "black") all those possessing "any perceptible trace of African blood." The word "perceptible" made clear that the marshals were to rely on appearance rather than ancestry. If "African blood" was visible, it counted; otherwise, it disappeared. A system predicated on the duality of black and white, then, did not preclude an intermediate category. Nor was it possible for such a system to be based solely on genealogy. Rather, a black-white binary based on a one-drop definition of blackness coexisted with a middle category defined as much by visibility as by ancestry.[24]

Not just in law but in daily life, too, North Americans created discourses about complexion, recognizing a range of skin colors beyond black and white. For one thing, North Americans who stepped ashore on Caribbean islands in the nineteenth century were adept at rejecting a two-category system that consisted of white people and undifferentiated people of African descent. Within their own communities, African Americans often spoke in terms beyond a black-white binary, and the antislavery activist and missionary Henry Highland Garnet likewise noted the "various hues of complexion" in his Jamaica congregation in the 1850s. But white people, too, could employ a wider vocabulary. A white New England woman traveling in the West Indies during the 1860s wrote of the "mixing of black, white and yellow," describing one servant as "mahogany." A white Philadelphian on St. Thomas in the 1860s wrote of "a great concourse of people" extending "from white to ebony," and a white Northerner who sailed to the Spanish and British West Indies in the 1870s described women who were "blackest ebony, orange tawney, or café-au-lait."[25]

The spectrum of complexions was no narrower in North America, and it is possible as well to find similar enumerations of color at home. Abolitionists in New York offered examples of enslaved people who were shockingly white in appearance, describing "ruddy" or (echoing a common West Indian term) "clear" complexions. A lecturer before the Boston Society of Natural History in 1860 told of "a colored pic-nic party . . . of all hues, from the darkest black to a color approaching white." When the District of Columbia abolished slavery in 1862, masters filled out forms that required an identifying description of each former bondperson, and the notations there ranged from dark black, dark brown, and chestnut, to copper-colored and bright yellow, to pale yellow and "nearly white." When African-American men from Massachusetts volunteered to fight in the Civil War, the enlistment rolls included a column for "complexion" that carried notations of black, mulatto, colored, and dark, with occasional invocations of ebony, brown, medium, coffee, yellow, and light. Moreover, it was not only African-American soldiers whose color was evaluated and recorded, but the same officers filled in the column marked "complexion" for every man. The two most common terms for white recruits were "dark" and "light," invoked about equally, but other white men were sandy, florid, ruddy, muddy, medium, sallow, pale, swarthy, fair, and fresh. The term "dark" (and, less often, "light") notably was employed for black and white soldiers alike, and there were instances in which a volunteer for the black Fifty-fourth Massachusetts was described as "dark," followed immediately by a volunteer for a white regiment, also described as "dark."[26]

The attention to complexion in these kinds of inventories parallels the slave registration returns of the British Caribbean. Far from uniform, and rarely dependent on any precise knowledge of individual lineage, these returns recorded an array of colors, including black, brown, red, copper, yellow, light, and clear (sometimes modified by "dark," "very," "rather," or simply "-ish"), accompanied by terms such as Negro, mulatto, quadroon, sambo, mustee, mestizo, and griffe. True, the U.S. federal census at mid-century narrowed all individuals to white, black, and mulatto, but so, too, did British Caribbean censuses in the nineteenth century. The Jamaican census of 1844 pressed residents into the categories of white, brown, and black, just as Cayman's 1855 tables permitted only white, colored, and black. Scholars have most often contrasted the limited categories of the U.S. federal census with the continuum of colors found in Caribbean slave returns, but such a comparison is mismatched. A census offers a legal count, and both U.S. and British West Indian censuses during parts of the nineteenth century restricted individuals to three categories. Caribbean slave returns, with their more complicated scale of colors, are more properly compared to similar kinds of descriptive lists generated in the United States (of former slaves or Civil War soldiers, for example) that were intended, like the Caribbean slave returns, to identify particular individuals.[27]

By comparing descriptive lists from both regions, the finer gradations of U.S. color perceptions and discourses come to light. Indeed, when Eunice and her New England family exchanged information about their own coloring, they invoked vocabulary that mirrored the common West Indian descriptions of "fair" and "dark." One sister described her own son as "fair and white"; the sister's daughter, according to Eunice, had "eyes like two black coals," "hair like the ravens wing," and "skin neither to[o] dark or to[o] fair"; and Eunice's daughter from her first marriage had "very white fair skin." As for Eunice herself, a lone photograph (only as reliable as any image captured on film) portrays her as a dark-haired, perhaps olive-skinned woman. Maybe Eunice made a point of describing her newborn daughter's "very white fair skin" because she thought of herself, by contrast, as dark. Discussion of newborns' coloring might have been innocent news, but it might also point to the anxieties of white women who toiled in the same realm as Irish factory operatives and Irish and black domestics.[28]

When Smiley Connolly arrived in New England in the 1860s, then, he might have been described as "black," "mulatto," or some variation thereof, but it is also likely that in certain venues he passed for white. The column asking for "color of groom and bride" on the couple's Massachusetts marriage license remained blank, the same as for the vast majority of those on the roster, indicating that the clerk assumed both parties to be white, and that no corrections were offered. Perhaps the Irish last name helped, too. Whether Eunice believed the sea captain to be a white man when she first encountered him remains unknown, but as she stated unequivocally when commenting on the happy marriage of a sister some years later, "I would not change Husbands with her, if hers has got a white skin. I know mine has not." And that is precisely the point. Smiley may have passed on his wedding day, thereby illuminating the ways in which mutable perceptions can diminish the power of racial classification to circumscribe a person's life. Yet within the confines of the neighborhood, it was well understood that Eunice had (to put it in U.S. terms) married across the color line. Recalling a local gossip who disapproved, Eunice wrote, "I can't quite get over some of her slurs," and to her mother Eunice explained that she could not have given up Smiley "even though public opinion was against *him* and against *me* on *his* account." Some members of Eunice's family shared in that opinion. Though ardent supporters of the Union during the Civil War, the family (like most white Northerners) did not oppose slavery on moral grounds, nor did they champion racial equality. Eunice's brother Henry, who had returned to New England a celebrated Union veteran, offered the harshest condemnation. As Eunice confessed to her mother just before she sailed for Grand Cayman, "I wanted to tell Brother Henry how much I had always loved him and how his treatment had pained me." It is not difficult to imagine Henry wondering angrily why he had fought to free the "darkies" (his word), only to find one marrying his sister.[29]

Other family members, though, were more accommodating. "I have the kindest regard for your husband," another sibling told Eunice, "hope he will think of me as a sister for as such I esteam him." That kind of affection might reflect nothing more than garden-variety racism, in which a friend is set apart from all other, unknown, people of color. As one immigrant to nineteenth-century Lowell from the Caribbean island of Nevis put it, "After all the obstacles had been overcome—the obstacles of race and color, paramount objectives in the eyes of prejudice—I became very popular amongst my neighbors." Eunice's family may also have kept their fondness for Smiley confined to a private sphere. The antislavery activist Charlotte Forten noted of her Salem, Massachusetts, schoolmates in the 1850s: "I have met girls in the schoolroom—they have been thoroughly kind and cordial to me—perhaps the next day met them in the street—they feared to recognize me." Or the family's accommodation might have stemmed in part from Smiley's complexion. The division between "black" and "mulatto" codified in the U.S. (and Massachusetts) censuses also operated informally, with lighter-skinned people of African descent suffering comparatively less racial discrimination. In Boston in the 1860s and 1870s, those of mixed descent were more likely to be literate, skilled, and better off than their darker neighbors. In Smiley's case, class status likely mattered, too. Because the majority of African Americans in northern cities were poor, Eunice's family may have perceived him, with his impressive schooners and trade goods, less as a man of color than as a well-to-do foreigner with a British accent. Indeed, foreigners did not always readily divide into established racial categories, thereby working to destabilize the binary in another way. In the slave South, for example, a claim of Spanish or Portuguese nationality could erase counter-claims of blackness. For Smiley in New England, British nationality may have accomplished the same end.[30]

Mulatto, white, rich, British, foreign: just as in the Caribbean, malleable perceptions of Smiley Connolly's status and complexion could move him away from blackness. But that mutability worked just as often to oppress as to liberate, and that, again, is the point. If one day white people welcomed Smiley as a British captain conducting important business in the port, another day they scorned him as a lowly black man scandalizing the neighborhood. Within the most local terrain, Smiley suffered the slurs of neighbors and the wrath of in-laws. That treatment in the neighborhood, and even in the very home of the woman he was to marry, made palpable to him, and in turn to Eunice, the often-unyielding power of racial classification, no matter how fluid or mutable those classifications might be. Surely there were days in post–Civil War Massachusetts when Captain Connolly was startled that a man such as he should be treated so poorly, for that treatment contrasted sharply with the ways in which he had always categorized and ranked himself. In order to maintain that ranking, Smiley and his new bride had little choice but to depart North America, and in fact they set sail just one week after the wedding.

When Smiley returned to the Cayman Islands with Eunice, he again embodied the more familiar status of a West Indian colored man. Most especially within East End, Grand Cayman's darker and poorer side, the Connolly family enjoyed considerable standing. Educated and literate, they were "better" than others; they were "the important people," descendants recall. According to a great-granddaughter of one of Smiley's brothers, the Connollys "always had a big sway over here," and the couple's nineteenth-century letters bear out such memories. Upon his return with Eunice, Smiley began to build "a large House in American style," as he wrote to New England, much fancier than the common wattle-and-daub cottages, and with "an American Carpenter to do the work." (Descendants still recall that "big house" with its "big veranda," since destroyed in a hurricane.) As one East Ender recently explained, "it didn't matter what colour you were" if you were a sea captain, since discrimination took the form "more like a little class prejudice than colour prejudice." In Eunice's new West Indian home, components of class—connections to the maritime economy, the hiring of others to perform manual labor—formed key elements in the assignment of racial categories. And by bringing home a white wife (whose lowly origins likely never needed to be known), Smiley edged still closer to whiteness himself.[31]

An illuminating shard of evidence emerges from Eunice's descriptions of her domestic life on Grand Cayman, where she was entitled to household help. "I have always had a woman do my washing and ironing and washing out my house," she wrote to her mother. Eunice explained that her servant did "all that and my other work too," describing her as "a good respectable trusty girl," before adding, "I think much of her although she is a black girl." Those words expose Eunice's own racism, expressed freely to her New England relatives, but they also reveal Smiley's place in a non-binary hierarchy of color that Eunice would have learned from her West Indian neighbors. If Eunice did not think of Smiley as white in New England, neither did she think of him as black in the West Indies. Although both her husband and her servant were of African descent, her servant was "black," while her husband, the ship captain, belonged to the more elite category of "colored." None of Smiley's letters offers a hint of his own ideas, but certainly he agreed with his wife's assessment of their servant as trustworthy despite her blackness. A white New Yorker in Jamaica in 1850 observed that, whereas relations between "the whites and the colored people" were growing ever more cordial, "a very different state of feeling exists between the negroes or Africans, and the browns." This traveler elaborated, "The latter shun all connection by marriage with the former, and can experience no more unpardonable insult, than to be classified with them in any way." A Scotsman in Jamaica likewise found that many of the colored population would "scarcely stoop to shake hands with the blacks, whom they regard with disdain." The "browns," this man noted, "deem their half Saxon descent and partial whiteness reasonable grounds for treating haughtily their Ethiopian fellow-subjects." Or in the words of another observer, "the antagonism between the brown and the black is greater than that of either against the white."[32]

Smiley Connolly's respective classifications in New England and Grand Cayman set in relief the mutability of racial denomination and gradation across national borders, as well as the differences between the two systems. Speculating about Smiley, William Warren Conolly, a great-grandson of Smiley's half-brother, put it this way: "If he wasn't white, he could pass for white." That phrasing proves illuminating, coming from a man who grew up in East End, traveled the world in the American Merchant Marine, lived in New York City, and returned to Cayman, for it combines the workings of different racial systems. The rumination that Smiley's complexion permitted him to "pass for white" applied to his status in North America. As for Smiley's status in the West Indies, the phrasing implies that Smiley might have been *accepted as* white, despite the fact that one of his parents was known to be of African descent. (In this light, Smiley may not have believed himself to be deceiving the marriage clerk at all.)[33]

The descendant's formulation indicates less an emphasis on lineage than on class and color, and perceptions of other descendants shed further light. Family members recall Smiley's much younger brother Laban as a "white man" and one son from Smiley's first marriage as a "big white man." Memories of Smiley's son Cornelius (he died in 1932, a prominent mariner and East End shopkeeper) range from "darkish brown" to "quadroon" to "very white." As for Smiley himself, a descendant born in 1903 thought he was one of five "brown-skin" children. Vagaries of time and memory must be taken into account, but it is also important to understand that such descriptions could rest on class status, so that a man might be understood (or remembered) as light or white precisely because he was a successful sea captain. If Eunice's family back in New England strived to claim and prove respectability, Smiley's family in East End did the same. If Eunice's labor alongside Irish and black women made it difficult for her family to distinguish themselves from those they hoped to keep beneath them, then the upward mobility of Smiley and his brothers allowed the Connolly family to realize those same kinds of distinctions.[34]

Moreover, in all of these perceptions, "brown" and "white" could be as closely allied for West Indians as were "mulatto" and "black" for North Americans. Smiley Connolly's experiences in New England and the British Caribbean illuminate an important difference: in Massachusetts, if Smiley did not formally belong to the *category* of white, he might still pass for the *color* white. In Cayman, by contrast, he may not have been the *color* white, but that was understood to be so ambiguous a designation that he could still belong to the *category* of white. The more significant distinction between the two systems, then, lay not in a binary versus a ternary configuration but in the placement of the middle category. Whereas in the United States, "mulatto" lay closer to "black," in the British West Indies, those labeled "colored" could be counted as closer to "white." Indeed, missionary census takers on Grand Cayman in 1855 had formulated one category for "black" inhabitants and another, separate category for "white and coloured" inhabitants. No doubt unable to sort islanders' descriptions of themselves (and their neighbors) with any uniformity, the missionaries plainly noted that it was "impracticable to distinguish between the white and coloured population." As another missionary discovered, black people in Cayman were buried in segregated cemetery plots, while white and colored residents shared a final resting place. Such an arrangement stemmed as much or more from class as from complexion, evident in the observed divisions set down by a *New York Times* correspondent that beneath the planter aristocracy in the British West Indies stood "the middle class, composed alike of white and colored mechanics, and the lower orders, which are the black laborers." If within the U.S. system, generations of one family could openly shift between black and mulatto, then in the British West Indies, generations could shift between colored and white. In New England, Smiley Connolly's ancestry ultimately—that is, in a particular local neighborhood and within his new wife's family—placed him closer to blackness. In East End, Grand Cayman, his status and color ultimately placed him closer to whiteness. There, he was a respected mariner who lived in a big house, employed a black servant, and brought home a white wife.[35]

But was Eunice Connolly a white wife? Here we arrive at the part of the story in which Eunice's life intersects most starkly with the mercurial nature and abiding power of racial classification. Just as Smiley Connolly's racial designation proved mutable, so, too, did Eunice live with ambiguities of categorization following her marriage to a man of African descent. Just as Smiley experienced tensions between the ways in which others sought to label him and the ways in which he thought of himself, so, too, did Eunice resist the racialized judgments of others and seek to claim a racial status of her own. That resistance would succeed only with departure, not just from the neighborhood but from the United States altogether.

Again, much as ancestry was most often the legal and social determinant of whiteness in the nineteenth-century United States, a certain porousness nonetheless prevailed in daily life. Ideologies about class and gender came into play, since poverty could intervene to cloud the supposed or ideal immaculacy of white womanhood. A woman's behavior mattered, too. In New England, as Eunice's sinking class standing pushed her to the margins of white womanhood, that precarious status became more fragile still upon marriage to a man of color. In the words of Rainier Spencer, "What was it about blackness that allowed it to be mixed with whiteness and yet stay black? And conversely, what was it about whiteness that caused it to be corrupted irretrievably by one drop of black blood?" Such asymmetry, where it operated, rested on the ideological equation of whiteness and purity, but the notion of "purity" did not rest solely on ancestry. The idea of pure ("Anglo-Saxon") bloodlines could shade over into another, gendered meaning of purity: the idea of sexual chastity for white women, determined by those who held power to define and to sanction, whether as magistrates or as rumormongers. In tandem came the idea of blackness (or, more literally, African ancestry) as a product that tarnished purity, not only of "blood" but also of morals.[36]

In one sense, Eunice's poverty and her marriage across the U.S. color line went hand in hand: white women who married black men in the nineteenth-century North tended to be poor, indeed, often Irish. Mid-nineteenth-century visitors to one of New York City's poorest enclaves were offended by intimacy between Irish women and black men, whose liaisons and marriages can also be documented in census returns. During the New York City draft riots of 1863, an Irishman himself led a mob targeting "a nigger living here with two white women" (perhaps his wife and light-skinned daughter), threatening to "burn him" and "hang him on the lamppost." In mid-century Philadelphia, Irish rioters likewise attacked a tavern whose black proprietor had married an Irish woman. When northern Democrats coined the pejorative term "miscegenation" in 1864 (from the Latin *miscere*, "to mix" and *genus*, "race"), they caricatured such liaisons by claiming that "the white Irishwoman loves the black man," despite the fact that the Irish were "a more brutal race and lower in civilization than the negro." If Eunice's Anglo lineage did not match this stereotype, her economic circumstances placed her close enough. The outcast white woman Mag Smith (perhaps she was Irish?) who married a black man in Harriet Wilson's 1859 autobiographical novel, *Our Nig: or, Sketches from the Life of a Free Black,* earned her living the same way Eunice did: as a washerwoman.[37]

Although marriage between blacks and whites had been legal in Massachusetts since 1843, a white woman of the upper or middle classes would have much to lose by union with a man of color. As a working-class woman, Eunice had less to lose, but her decision nonetheless tarnished (in the eyes of her brother and some white neighbors) both her "blood" and her chastity. Cheryl I. Harris has written astutely about whiteness as a form of property, yet that property was not always inalienable. Recall the slurs that Eunice suffered and the "public opinion" that stood "against" her. To many New Englanders, it mattered little that Eunice had married a man who could lift her out of poverty, since he was also a man of African descent. Other northern white women who crossed the color line suffered similar social consequences. In 1795, a New Englander sneered that white women who married black men were "without exception, of the lowest class in society, both for education and morals." In 1833, Lydia Maria Child (actually writing in defense of mixed marriage) remarked, "Under existing circumstances, none but those whose condition in life is too low to be much affected by public opinion, will form such alliances." A legal commentator cited by a Connecticut court in 1834, put it this way, speaking of the "African race": "Marriages are forbidden between them and whites . . . and when not absolutely contrary to law, they are revolting, and regarded as an offence against public decorum." William Allen, the man whom white New Yorkers assaulted in the 1850s, observed that a white woman who wed a black man would be "rendering herself an almost total outcast." The character of Mag Smith in Wilson's autobiographical novel was a working-class white woman in New England who (like Eunice) improved her economic status by marrying a man of color, but she "descended another step down the ladder of infamy" in the process. "She was now expelled from companionship with white people," Wilson wrote, "this last step—her union with a black—was the climax of repulsion." It was less that a woman like Eunice (working-class and about to marry a black man) forfeited the designation of "white"; rather, the perceived purity required to partake of the privileges of white womanhood did not rest exclusively on ancestry. In standards of behavior and personal association, transgressing white women like Eunice surrendered respectability (already, for Eunice, compromised by poverty), thereby suffering expulsion from a local community, as well as from part of her family.[38]

Slippage of this sort held fewer consequences for men. When the white abolitionist William Lloyd Garrison proclaimed at the 1859 New England Colored Citizens' Convention in Boston that "nothing had gratified him so much as the reputation which he had gained of being a black man," he meant to imply the racial equality of black and white people. Although his detractors equated such rhetoric with dreaded "amalgamation," Garrison and his male allies could weather such accusations without judgments about personal purity. If white men identified themselves with black people, their enemies might pronounce them disruptive, even dangerous, but those were qualities quite different from the powerlessness of utter degradation. When Massachusetts legislators debated repealing the ban against marriages between blacks and whites, the opposition called such unions unnatural, immoral, and disgusting, warning of the dilution of white purity by animalistic people of African descent. Very occasionally, these opponents mentioned white men and black women, but mostly they reserved their warnings for "the blue-eyed daughters of the Anglo-Saxon lineage" and "the dark African" man, taking up such refrains as, "Every parent would rather follow his daughter to the grave, than to see her married to a black man." If Eunice's own mother accepted the marriage to Smiley with reservations, other New Englanders rejected Eunice entirely, for her actions had, in those minds, revoked whatever vestiges of the privileges of white womanhood Eunice had retained as a poor, laboring, husbandless, and at times homeless mother of two young children. Indeed, before the marriage to Smiley, Eunice earned her living not only the same way as Mag Smith did (as a washerwoman) but also the same way as Mag Smith's free black daughter: as a domestic servant and sewer of palm-leaf hats. Upon marriage to Smiley Connolly, Eunice saw her status in the neighborhood decline to as lowly as any she had known before, maybe worse.[39]

When Eunice Connolly accompanied her new husband to the West Indies, and moved into the freedpeople's settlement of East End on Grand Cayman Island, she experienced something quite different. If Eunice's beloved brother never spoke to her again, if New England neighbors slandered her, then as Eunice herself articulated from Cayman in a pointed reference to the hostilities of Massachusetts, Smiley was "in his own home now and feels at liberty to act all the love he feels for me without fear of disturbing anyone." Smiley's letters, too, reveal a certain ease and defiance, as when he imparted that Eunice "look[s] more beautiful to me every day" or mentioned that she was "teasing me for a kiss." Certainly Eunice and Smiley crafted letters for a family ambivalent and anxious about the marriage and departure, and certainly post-emancipation Cayman was no racial utopia. Yet the relief Eunice felt there resulted from Smiley's high local status, as well as from the fact that marriages across shades of color were common and the majority of the population openly claimed mixed European and African descent.[40]

Eunice's life in the British Caribbean would be profoundly affected not only by this widespread mixture but also by the West Indian correspondence between the categories of "colored" and "white." When asked if Eunice would have been the only white person in the freedpeople's settlement of East End in the 1870s, one descendant mentioned two other families who were "considered white" even though they had "some colored blood," asserting that Eunice would therefore not have stood out. These speculations are supported by nineteenth-century evidence. Writing about the colored majority in the West Indies in 1860, the African-American visitor J. Dennis Harris observed of whites that "the easiest way for them is to allow themselves to be peacefully absorbed by the colored race in these regions." The impression that white people could be "absorbed" by those of African descent indicates a level of racial interchangeability between "white" and "colored" that lent new meaning to Eunice's racial status in the islands. Recall that, although no one in Cayman disputed Smiley's African ancestry, he could still be classified as white, and that census takers in Cayman in 1855 had found it overly burdensome to mark off "colored" from "white." In Caribbean ideology, whiteness and African ancestry were not mutually exclusive, and virtually no one (no matter how light-skinned) was thought to be without African ancestry. Could these Caribbean ideas have served to shift Eunice toward the category of "colored" upon her passage across the water?[41]

When asked if nineteenth-century Caymanians might have thought of Eunice as a colored woman, descendants gave these answers: "I don't think that would have worried them in East End," one mused. There was "quite a lot of mix-up" at that time, and Eunice would have "fit in." Or in the words of another, "Well I guess in that time they would. I don't think it would make any difference." These responses, and others like them, nearly skipped over the question, in an effort to establish that no one would have minded that Eunice was a colored woman. Indeed, the question itself did not carry the weight it would have carried in the United States, precisely because of the proximity of "colored" and "white" in the West Indian racial system, especially when paired with high class standing. In one possible scenario, Smiley enhanced his own status by bringing home a white wife; alternatively, some East Enders may simply have assumed that Smiley had brought home a colored bride. Nor is it out of the question that Smiley had assumed that Eunice, with her dark hair and possibly none-too-fair skin, was a colored woman when he first encountered her in North America (a meeting that remains entirely obscured in the sources). In the West Indies, Eunice lived in a freedpeople's settlement, she was the wife of a man of color and of means, and she employed a black servant to keep house. Any or all of those circumstances could have marked her as a colored woman.[42]

Nor should perceptions of complexion be overlooked. Werner Sollors concludes that "the presumed superiority of the white race" meant that "what was really at stake was the whitening of blacks, and hardly the reverse." Yet white fears of black passing could be matched by the dread of a white person being mistaken for black. Years of living under the tropical sun would have altered any New Englander's skin, and white travelers to sunny climes were known to despair about such transformations. "I am so horribly tanned!" shrieked a Massachusetts native on her trip to the Gulf South in the 1830s. Decades after a German immigrant was sold into slavery, it was discovered that, "during the twenty-five years of her servitude, she had been exposed to the sun's rays in the hot climate of Louisiana, with head and neck unsheltered." (From the other side, the mixed-descent narrator of Wilson's *Our Nig* was forced to labor outdoors without a hat in order to distinguish her complexion from that of the household's white daughter.) The Caribbean was particularly troublesome, with its low, strong rays. "It ought to be inculcated on the mind of the newly arrived European," wrote a white doctor living in Jamaica in the nineteenth century, "that he should avoid exposure to the sun." No doubt Eunice did. In New England, Eunice's face and hands would have tanned from planting vegetables, gathering firewood, and walking from one workplace to the next. In Cayman, she likely, and ironically, paled under the tropical sun, given her ability to stay indoors (or at least under the shade trees) while someone else washed her clothes and gathered her fuel. In Eunice's new home, the combination of class privilege and relative lightness of complexion marked her either as a white woman or a colored woman.[43]

All of this raises the question of whether historians can accurately speak of a white person "passing." The very circumstances of racial passing depend on the distinctive U.S. construction (codified unevenly in nineteenth- and twentieth-century state laws) that someone with any African ancestry, no matter how many generations removed, must be defined as "black." Were such an inflexible and dualistic system to function perfectly, no person of African descent could ever shift into the category of white. Yet the same rigid binary would make it effortless for a person without any African ancestry to shift into the category of black. As Gunnar Myrdal phrased it, "To cross the caste line from the white side would be a comparatively easy matter, since in America a Negro is not necessarily supposed to have any Negro features at all." Or in the words of scholars St. Clair Drake and Horace R. Cayton, "any white person—including the lightest blond can, if he wishes, pass for colored."[44]

Evidence of passage from the classification of white to that of black can be found in the nineteenth-century U.S. South, where marriage across the color line was illegal. In Tennessee during the 1860s, a white woman was warned away from living with her black husband, and she appealed to the Freedmen's Bureau, hoping to prove that she was "in reality a colored woman." On the border of Virginia and Tennessee in 1873, a black man obtained a license to marry a white woman by "falsely representing to the clerk that she was a colored woman." Both parties were subsequently arrested and thrown in jail. Although these narratives allow for the possibility that the woman had been passing for white at the outset, in each case legal authorities and neighbors understood a white woman to be assuming identification as a black woman. A variation on this scenario is captured in Frank Webb's novel *The Garies and Their Friends,* when a minister (in the North), called to join a black woman and a white man in matrimony, inquired whether the man was truly white. Mr. Garie could at that moment have chosen to represent himself as a black man; although he did not do so, at his death he was buried in the graveyard of the colored Episcopal church. Another variation appears in accounts of white people who literally infused themselves with drops of blood from a person of known African descent. Millie Markham, born about 1855, told the story of her mother, a planter's daughter in Virginia, who fell in love with the family's coachman and drank a cup of whiskey mixed with his blood in order to swear that she had "Negro blood in her," so as to marry him. The federal census subsequently listed both husband and wife as "mulatto." A white North Carolinian likewise spoke of a neighborhood white woman who, before the Civil War, "had her free-negro lover bled, and drank some of his blood, so that she might swear she had negro blood in her, and thus marry him without penalty."[45]

Such shifts from whiteness to blackness cannot, however, be filed casually under the rubric of "passing," since that very concept has historically implied an escape from oppression into a world of greater privilege. Rather, those who moved from the designation of "white" to that of "black," even if voluntarily, opened themselves to more acute subjugation in a racist world (or neighborhood). And yet, in the case of Eunice Connolly, the ultimate outcome was quite different. True, by marrying a man of color, Eunice sacrificed the privileges of white womanhood in her native land, and most particularly in her own neighborhood. Like Mag Smith in Wilson's autobiographical novel, Eunice had "descended another step down the ladder of infamy" in New England. But by marrying Smiley Connolly, Eunice also married up. She moved from being a servant in New England, to having a servant of her own in the Caribbean. Transplanting the marriage from the United States to the West Indies was the key to this advancement.[46]

Ideologies of gender again prove central. In New England during the Civil War, Eunice had been, in her words, "jogging around the world so without a home," had so wanted her Confederate husband to be "spared to come home and provide for his little family" in order to "have a place to *call home*." Then, an ocean away from her mother and siblings, East End came to be Eunice's "little 'Island Home,'" "a Happy home," she wrote, complete with "an indulgent loving Husband." In one letter back to New England, Eunice wrote, "I never go any where, only when Mr. Connolly and I go out to take a walk, and in the evening we go and sit on the beach. I have no desire to go away from *my home* to take comfort. I find it there." That Eunice underlined the words "my home" (as well as the earlier words "call home") signifies the highlighting of an impressive status to her relatives. The ability to remain at home all day offered not only shelter from the Caribbean sun, it also served as a symbol of white, middle-class domesticity that Eunice had never achieved as a laborer in North America. Staying at home—in fact, having a home at all—rather than cleaning other people's houses, became a badge of Eunice's newfound white womanhood, concurrent with a blurring toward the West Indian category of "colored."[47]

After a lifetime of tenement living and unrelenting toil, Eunice could now take comfort in domesticity, and it is remarkable how closely the narration of her relationship with Smiley adhered to a model of middle-class Victorian marriage. "I am determined he shall not do more for me that way than I do for him, so far as I know how to do, to make him happy," she expounded from Grand Cayman. "So while there is a mutual desire and each one takes pleasure in making the life of the other pleasant and happy, there is nothing to fear." Nothing to fear because Smiley so well met Victorian expectations of a husband thoroughly attentive to his wife's contentment. As for running the household, Eunice added: "Mr. Connolly allows me to do as I think best about every such thing. I always go to him, but he always says You know what suits you and any thing you do suits me." (Whereas Eunice had never referred to her first husband by surname, she now routinely referred to "Mr. Connolly," a class affectation to which her sisters back in New England did not feel entitled when naming their own husbands.) Had Eunice married a well-to-do North American white man, she would have aspired to a home with a parlor, a library, a nursery—a home, too, that embodied Christian civilization and salvation. Yet married to a man of color in the West Indies, even without so many elegant accoutrements, Eunice became "a constant church goer," with her husband and children nearly as devout. Eunice married across the color line, but she married up; that upward mobility depended on departure from North America, and so Eunice followed her new husband to the West Indies to attain what would have been impossible with him in New England. Just as those who passed from black to white often lost loved ones in the process, so did Eunice suffer loss: most palpably, her brother's love, more literally, her whole family, when she set up a new life so far away.[48]

Almost certainly, Eunice never came to think of herself as a colored woman. More likely, in fact, just the opposite: she married Smiley Connolly in part to remove herself from the poverty and degraded status that had edged her away from white womanhood in New England. Smiley's status in his native land had always been greater than Eunice's in hers, and the stature and skills that Smiley possessed in Cayman changed Eunice's life from everything that had come before: life as the daughter of an alcoholic father who deserted his family, as the wife of a white man unable to find work in the depressed mill towns of the North and who failed on the southern frontier, as a mother forced to work in the mills and board out her child, as a widow forced to labor as a domestic servant. In the West Indies, Eunice became a respectable wife who enjoyed the leisure of a companionate marriage. She became a mother who sent her children to school and who left home only to attend church or stroll on the sand in the evenings. She became a lady who directed a dark-skinned maid. "As for me I jog along in a quiet easy way," Eunice boasted to her mother. "I have enough to eat & drink, & wear," she wrote, noting that in three months she had never twice donned the same dress for Sunday services. So remarkable was all of this that Eunice repeated it in another letter. "I have aplenty to eat, drink & wear," she reminded her family and herself, "and do not have to sit up nights sewing by lamp light making and trimming dresses to get it better." In a freedpeople's settlement in the British West Indies, Eunice experienced what it meant to attain white woman-hood as she had imagined that ideal in nineteenth-century New England.[49]

And so, in marrying Smiley Connolly, Eunice defied her New England neighbors and family. "My darling mother," Eunice wrote one day in 1870, "It is over four months since he took me or rather"—and here she corrected her narration to reflect her own agency—"since I sent from you to be with him." Maybe, as one nineteenth-century American traveler wrote, Eunice's prejudices began to "melt away" in a place "where people of colored blood have attained to such social consideration as to make them-selves respected." In the end, however, Eunice only transferred herself from one racial-ized system to another. Sandra Gunning, writing about the African-American traveler Nancy Prince, notes that "what is subversive in one context might not necessarily carry the same disruptive effectiveness in another." Radical choices in New England turned out to be not at all radical in the West Indies. Eunice stoically relinquished the privi-leges of white womanhood in her native land but emphatically embraced those same privileges in the West Indies, now by virtue of membership in a well-off colored family. Crossing both racial and geographical boundaries, Eunice landed, finally, at the upper end of a stratified society. When Eunice settled in East End, she contentedly took her place among the local community's elite, even if that community comprised the poor-est and darkest on an island of little wealth.[50]

If Eunice's West Indian neighbors thought of her as a colored woman, that desig-nation lay closer to whiteness than to blackness, evident in the journey from laboring New England widow to leisured West Indian wife—evident, even, in Eunice's increas-ingly pale skin despite life under the Caribbean sun. The character of Clarence Garie, in Frank Webb's 1857 novel set in the U.S. North, agonized that he could not "be white and coloured at the same time; the two don't mingle, and I must consequently be one or the other." Unlike Clarence Garie, Eunice could be both white and colored at the same time. With certainty in her own mind, and the minds of sympathetic New Eng-landers, she was a white woman, safely marked off from African ancestry in the past. To unsympathetic New England relatives and neighbors, Eunice had surrendered the sta-tus of white womanhood, not only in her economic circumstances but also in her "low" and "revolting" behavior. To her West Indian family and neighbors, Eunice was either colored—that expansive and often subdivided Caribbean category in between African and European—or maybe she was a white woman with "colored blood." Eunice and Smi-ley had two daughters of their own (never described in the letters); to New Englanders who knew the father, those children would have been labeled as "black" or "mulatto";

to Eunice's Caymanian neighbors, those children could have been "white." Or maybe it was just that Eunice's own colored blood (everyone in the islands had some, after all) had shown up in the children.[51]

In Eunice Connolly's descent into poverty and in her later elevation to ladyhood, in her journey with William Smiley Connolly across racial lines and national borders, in the face of imposed rankings and in her quest to rank herself and others, we can see the ways in which the mercurial nature of racial classification could by turns oppress and endow power. "American people don't know color," William Warren Conolly told me emphatically. Looking over a copy of Eunice and Smiley's marriage license that I had brought to Grand Cayman from the Massachusetts State Archives, the great-grandson of Smiley Connolly's half-brother pointed to the column that asked for "color of groom and bride," saying, "They put color there, but American people don't know color." Making sense of racial categorization is an elusive historical endeavor, doubly so when historical actors and their ancestors crossed racial boundaries and lived their lives across geographical borders, from Africa and Europe to North America and the Caribbean. Transnational journeys expose the malleability of racial classification and thus add an important dimension to our understanding of the constructed nature of race. Yet no matter how fickle we prove racial classification to be, knowledge of that malleability alone cannot subdue its power to circumscribe lives, to categorize, distinguish, and separate people, to subjugate some and elevate others. Transnational journeys illuminate, with equal certainty, the potency of racial malleability in local, daily lives. In the end, we may ask, if scholars have proven race so mutable, why does its might remain so great? Perhaps it is because the abiding power of race lies precisely within that mercurial nature.[52]

Notes

I thank members of the Connolly-Conolly family and of the Cushman family; Linda McCurdy and the Duke University Rare Book, Manuscript, and Special Collections Library; Jan Liebaers, Tammi Selzer, and the Cayman Islands National Archive; Martha Mayo and the University of Massachusetts Center for Lowell History; Thomas Bender and his Project on Internationalizing the Study of American History; Jeanne Masters of North Side, Grand Cayman; and Carolyn Brown, Thomas Dublin, Ada Ferrer, Cheryl Fish, Leslie Harris, Debra Walker King, Paul Kramer, Zita Nunes, Colin Palmer, Jeffrey Stewart, Margaret Vendryes, Jeffrey Wasserstrom, Craig Wilder, the anonymous reviewers, and especially Bruce Dorsey. I thank commenters and audiences at the many institutions and conferences where I have presented these ideas, and for funding, the Schomburg Center for Research in Black Culture of the New York Public Library, the Library Company of Philadelphia, and New York University.

1. I use quotation marks for racial descriptors for the sake of clarity only, with an overall understanding of the social construction of such terminology; I employ the overly reified term "race" only at particular rhetorical junctures. Following Rogers Brubaker and Frederick Cooper, "Beyond 'Identity,'" *Theory and Society* 29 (February 2000): 1–47, I have refrained from overuse of the slippery term "identity." On changing categories in the U.S. federal census, see David Theo Goldberg, "Taking Stock: Counting by Race," in *Racial Subjects: Writing on Race in America* (New York, 1997),

27–58. For a fine theoretical discussion, see Gayle Wald, *Crossing the Line: Racial Passing in Twentieth-Century U.S. Literature and Culture* (Durham, N.C., 2000), 1–24. On mobility among racial categories within a single lifetime, see Marilyn Halter, *Between Race and Ethnicity: Cape Verdean American Immigrants, 1860–1965* (Urbana, Ill., 1993); Clara E. Rodríguez, "Challenging Racial Hegemony: Puerto Ricans in the United States," in *Race,* Steven Gregory and Roger Sanjek, eds. (New Brunswick, N.J., 1994), 131–45; Jorge Duany, "Reconstructing Racial Identity: Ethnicity, Color, and Class among Dominicans in the United States and Puerto Rico," *Latin American Perspectives* 25 (May 1998): 147–72; Benjamin Bailey, "Dominican-American Ethnic/Racial Identities and United States Social Categories," *International Migration Review* 35 (Fall 2001): 677–708.

2. Barbara J. Fields, "Ideology and Race in American History," in *Region, Race, and Reconstruction: Essays in Honor of C. Vann Woodward,* J. Morgan Kousser and James M. McPherson, eds. (New York, 1982), 143–77; see also "Slavery, Race and Ideology in the United States of America," *New Left Review* 181 (May/June 1990): 95–118. Ann Laura Stoler, "Racial Histories and Their Regimes of Truth," *Political Power and Social Theory* 11 (1997): 183–206; Thomas C. Holt, *The Problem of Race in the Twenty-First Century* (Cambridge, Mass., 2001), 10; and see Holt, "Marking: Race, Race-making, and the Writing of History," *AHR* 100 (February 1995): 1–20; Hilary McD. Beckles, *Centering Woman: Gender Discourses in Caribbean Slave Society* (Kingston, 1999), xxiii. Peter Wade urges us to understand "how both flexibility and racism co-exist," in *Race and Ethnicity in Latin America* (London, 1997), 68.

3. Nell Irvin Painter, "'Social Equality,' Miscegenation, Labor, and Power," in *The Evolution of Southern Culture,* Numan V. Bartley, ed. (Athens, Ga., 1988), 48.

4. The story can be traced in the 500 or so letters in the Lois Wright Richardson Davis Papers, Rare Book, Manuscript, and Special Collections Library, Duke University, Durham, N.C. (hereafter, LWRD); some punctuation has been added for readability. The full story will be told in a forthcoming book, to be published by W. W. Norton.

5. Massachusetts Vital Records, Dracut, 1869, vol. 218, p. 166, Massachusetts State Archives, Boston, Mass. (hereafter, MSA). Genealogy in family Bible in possession of William Warren Conolly, and author's conversation with William Warren Conolly (b. 1920), East End, Grand Cayman, July 22, 1998. Tapes and transcripts of all conversations cited are in the possession of the author, unless otherwise noted. On former slaves settling in East End, see Dispatch no. 33, June 27, 1835, Public Record Office, London, England (hereafter, PRO): CO 137/199, p. 274.

6. On the marginal non-sugar colonies (which also included Anguilla, Barbuda, and the Turks and Caicos), see B. W. Higman, *Slave Populations of the British Caribbean, 1807–1834* (Baltimore, 1984), 43–44, 64–70; and Michael Craton, *Empire, Enslavement and Freedom in the Caribbean* (Kingston, 1997), 150. In the 1830s, two-thirds of Cayman's population were enslaved, almost a quarter were white, a tenth were free people of color, and most holdings of slaves were small; Higman, *Slave Populations,* 77, 102–03, 159, 584; Classified Statement, Cayman Islands, PRO: T 71/683, fol. 16; Return of Slaves, Grand Cayman, 1823–30, PRO: T 71/243, pp. 130–31A; Dispatch no. 131, October 20, 1858, PRO: CO 137/339, p. 216. On the economy, see George S. S. Hirst, *Notes on the History of the Cayman Islands* (1910; rpt. edn., Kingston, 1967), 264–76; Neville Williams, *A History of the Cayman Islands* (1970; rpt. edn., Grand Cayman, 1992), pp. 11–12, 20–21, 35–36, 42–45, 52–53, 56–57; Roger C. Smith, *The Maritime Heritage of the Cayman Islands* (Gainesville, Fla., 2000).

7. *United Presbyterian Missionary Record,* June 2, 1873, p. 530; May 1, 1872, p. 149; June 2, 1879, p. 537; June 1, 1872, p. 176; interview with Geneva Range no. 1 (b. 1899), by Heather McLaughlin, August 27, 1990, Memory Bank (hereafter, MB), Cayman Islands National Archive, George Town, Grand Cayman, British West Indies (hereafter, CINA), 2–4; Edwin Doran, Jr., "Notes on an Archaic Island Dialect," *American Speech* 29 (February 1954), 82; interview with Daniel Montague Tatum no. 2 (b. 1900) by Heather McLaughlin, October 12, 1993, MB, CINA, p. 16. On traveling Caymanians, see also Smith, *Maritime Heritage,* 112–46.

8. *Johnson v. Norwich,* 29 Conn. 407 (1860), 408–9. On different racial systems, see the enduring Winthrop D. Jordan, "American Chiaroscuro: The Status and Definition of Mulattoes in the British Colonies," *William and Mary Quarterly* 19 (April 1962): 183–200; and the more recent Werner

Sollors, *Neither Black nor White Yet Both: Thematic Explorations of Interracial Literature* (New York, 1997), 112–41. Much cited on the one-drop rule is F. James Davis, *Who Is Black? One Nation's Definition* (University Park, Pa., 1991); see also Joel Williamson, *New People: Miscegenation and Mulattoes in the United States* (New York, 1980), 1–2, 62, 73–75, 109. Eunice's brother, who prospered as a mill agent, traced his ancestry to seventeenth-century English colonists; see Courier-Citizen Company, *Illustrated History of Lowell and Vicinity, Massachusetts* (Lowell, Mass., 1897), 253.

9. Gayle Wald writes, "The one-drop rule is not the only standard of racial definition, yet it has disproportionately shaped the U.S. social and cultural imagination of race"; see *Crossing the Line,* 13. Randall Kennedy notes that "the one-drop rule has by no means exercised easy or uncontested dominance"; see "The Enforcement of Anti-Miscegenation Laws," in *Interracialism: Black-White Intermarriage in American History, Literature, and Law,* Werner Sollors, ed. (New York, 2000), 147. For important challenges to the conventional divide between the United States and British Caribbean, see Stephen Small, "Racial Group Boundaries and Identities: People of 'Mixed-Race' in Slavery across the Americas," *Slavery and Abolition* 15 (December 1994): 17–37; and *The Matrix of Miscegenation: People of Mixed Race under Slavery in the Nineteenth Century* (New York, forthcoming). On racial malleability in the U.S. South, see Martha Hodes, *White Women, Black Men: Illicit Sex in the Nineteenth-Century South* (New Haven, Conn., 1997), 96–122; Ariela J. Gross, "Litigating Whiteness: Trials of Racial Determination in the Nineteenth-Century South," *Yale Law Journal* 108 (October 1998): 109–88; Walter Johnson, "The Slave Trader, the White Slave, and the Politics of Racial Determination in the 1850s," *Journal of American History* 87 (June 2000): 13–38; Joshua D. Rothman, *Notorious in the Neighborhood: Sex and Families across the Color Line in Virginia, 1787–1861* (Chapel Hill, N.C., forthcoming), chap. 6.

10. *Voice of Industry,* October 23, 1846 ("slave-driverism"). On Manchester, see Tamara K. Hareven and Randolph Langenbach, *Amoskeag: Life and Work in an American Factory-City* (New York, 1978), 9–18; James P. Hanlan, *The Working Population of Manchester, New Hampshire, 1840–1886* (Ann Arbor, Mich., 1981); *Manchester: A Brief Record of Its Past and a Picture of Its Present* (Manchester, N.H., 1875), 267–306; Peter Haebler, "Nativist Riots in Manchester: An Episode of Know-Nothingism in New Hampshire," and "Nativism, Liquor, and Riots: Manchester Politics, 1858–1859," *Historical New Hampshire* 39 (Fall/Winter 1984): 122–28, and 46 (Summer 1991): 66–91.

Two of the finest works in the whiteness literature are David R. Roediger, *The Wages of Whiteness: Race and the Making of the American Working Class* (New York, 1991); and Matthew Frye Jacobson, *Whiteness of a Different Color: European Immigrants and the Alchemy of Race* (Cambridge, Mass., 1998). Also important are Theodore W. Allen, *The Invention of the White Race* (London, 1994); and Noel Ignatiev, *How the Irish Became White* (New York, 1995). For the reassessments, see Eric Arnesen, et al., "Scholarly Controversy: Whiteness and the Historians' Imagination," *International Labor and Working-Class History* 60 (Fall 2001): 3–92; Peter Kolchin, "Whiteness Studies: The New History of Race in America," *Journal of American History* 89 (June 2002): 154–73, including the call for transnational visions.

11. Amoskeag Manufacturing Company Employee Register, March 21, 1860, p. 47, Manchester Historic Association, Manchester, N.H.; "Rights and Duties of Mill Girls," *New England Offering* 7 (July 1849), 156 ("low class"). On Irish labor, see Thomas Dublin, *Transforming Women's Work: New England Lives in the Industrial Revolution* (Ithaca, N.Y., 1994), 77–118; and *Women at Work: The Transformation of Work and Community in Lowell, Massachusetts, 1826–1860* (New York, 1979), 132–64; Caroline F. Ware, *The Early New England Cotton Manufacture: A Study in Industrial Beginnings* (Boston, 1931), 228–32; Peter Way, *Common Labour: Workers and the Digging of North American Canals, 1780–1860* (New York, 1993), 76–104.

12. Jacobson, *Whiteness of a Different Color,* 15–90; see also Roediger, *Wages of Whiteness,* 133–63; Allen, *Invention of the White Race,* 184–99; Ignatiev, *How the Irish Became White,* 34–59. And see L. Perry Curtis, Jr., *Apes and Angels: The Irishman in Victorian Caricature* (Washington, D.C., 1971); Dale T. Knobel, *Paddy and the Republic: Ethnicity and Nationality in Antebellum America* (Middletown, Conn., 1986), 68–128, 192–93.

13. Allan Nevins and Milton Halsey Thomas, eds., *The Diary of George Templeton Strong: Young*

Man in New York, 1835–1849, 4 vols. (New York, 1952), 1: 318, 2: 348; *Collected Works of Theodore Parker,* Frances Power Cobbe, ed. (London, 1864), 64; "A Scene from Irish Life," *Harper's New Monthly Magazine* 3 (November 1851): 833; Manchester (N.H.) *Daily American,* January 26, 1858, quoted in Haebler, "Nativism," 74; U.S. federal census, Hillsborough County, N.H., 1850, p. 60, National Archives, Washington, D.C. (hereafter, NA).

14. Hattie Harvey to Lois Davis and Eunice Stone [her first husband's name], Manchester, N.H., August 5, 1865, LWRD; Dublin, *Women at Work,* 148.

15. Thomas C. Holt, *The Problem of Freedom: Race, Labor, and Politics in Jamaica and Britain, 1832–1938* (Baltimore, 1992), 280–82, 319; of the 1849 assertion in *Punch* magazine that the Irish were "the missing link between the gorilla and the Negro," Holt notes the "striking similarities between Irish and Afro-Jamaican caricatures" (319, 463 n.); and see 318–36. See also Carlyle to Emerson, August 13, 1849, in *The Correspondence of Thomas Carlyle and Ralph Waldo Emerson, 1834–1872,* 2 vols. (Boston, 1883), 2: 184; and Hilary McD. Beckles, "A 'Riotous and Unruly Lot': Irish Indentured Servants and Freemen in the English West Indies, 1644–1713," in *Caribbean Slavery in the Atlantic World,* Verene A. Shepherd and Hilary McD. Beckles, eds. (Kingston, 2000), noting that African slaves and Irish servants, both perceived as dangerous and lazy, could be "interchangeable" in the view of planters (p. 230).

16. Charlotte Vance Morrill to Emma J. Page, Augusta, Me., January 27, 1870, Page Collection, Center for Lowell History, Lowell, Mass.; Eunice Stone to Lois Davis, Claremont, N.H., March 19, 1862, LWRD. On the contours of domestic labor, see David M. Katzman, *Seven Days a Week: Women and Domestic Service in Industrializing America* (New York, 1978); Susan Strasser, *Never Done: A History of American Housework* (New York, 1982), 162–79; Hasia R. Diner, *Erin's Daughters in America: Irish Immigrant Women in the Nineteenth Century* (Baltimore, 1983), 80–94; Faye E. Dudden, *Serving Women: Household Service in Nineteenth-Century America* (Middletown, Conn., 1983), esp. 44–76; Christine Stansell, *City of Women: Sex and Class in New York, 1789–1860* (New York, 1986), 155–68; Dublin, *Transforming Women's Work,* 157–65, 193–204; James Oliver Horton and Lois E. Horton, *In Hope of Liberty: Culture, Community, and Protest among Northern Free Blacks, 1700–1860* (New York, 1997), 114–15. On domestic labor outside big cities, see Catherine E. Kelly, *In the New England Fashion: Reshaping Women's Lives in the Nineteenth Century* (Ithaca, N.Y., 1999), 27–35.

U.S. federal census, Hillsborough County, N.H., 1850, p. 99, NA; *Manchester City Directory,* 1850, p. 77 (black domestic); Graham Hodges, "'Desirable Companions and Lovers': Irish and African Americans in the Sixth Ward, 1830–1870," in *The New York Irish,* Ronald H. Bayor and Timothy J. Meagher, eds. (Baltimore, 1996), 121. On preferring mill work to domestic labor, see, for example, L. B. Demick to Clarissa Demick, Manchester, N.H., December 26, 1872, New Hampshire Historical Society, Concord; Hanlan, *Working Population,* 60. On the efforts of fiction writers to preserve the privileges of white womanhood for impoverished working women, see Mari Jo Buhle, "Needlewomen and the Vicissitudes of Modern Life: A Study of Middle-Class Construction in the Antebellum Northeast," in *Visible Women: New Essays on American Activism,* Nancy A. Hewitt and Suzanne Lebsock, eds. (Urbana, Ill., 1993), 145–65; Bruce Dorsey, *Reforming Men and Women: Gender in the Antebellum City* (Ithaca, N.Y., 2002), 85–89.

17. Concord (N.H.) *Independent Democrat,* in Johnstown (Pa.) *Cambria Tribune,* April 14, 1855, quoted in Tyler Anbinder, *Nativism and Slavery: The Northern Know Nothings and the Politics of the 1850s* (New York, 1992), 109.

18. Blue Book, Jamaica, 1869 (Spanish Town, 1870), PRO: CO 142/83; *Missionary Record,* November 1, 1855, p. 190; Anthony Trollope, *The West Indies and the Spanish Main* (London, 1860), 55–100; Hope Masterton Waddell, *Twenty-Nine Years in the West Indies and Central Africa: A Review of Missionary Work and Adventure, 1829–1858* (London, 1863), 215–16; James M. Phillippo, *Jamaica: Its Past and Present State* (London, 1843), 144; *Antigua and the Antiguans: A Full Account of the Colony and Its Inhabitants,* 2 vols. (London, 1844), 2: 164–65; Public Recorder's Records, November 18, 1829, XH/5/2, p. 59, CINA (sambo); interview with Aurellia Conolly (b. 1903), by Heather McLaughlin, February 12, 1990, MB, CINA, p. 8 (mustee); William Warren Conolly conversation, July 22, 1998, and author's conversation with Theoline Conolly McCoy (b. 1919), Bodden Town, Grand Cayman,

July 13, 1999 (quadroon); see also Hirst, *Notes,* 147, 156, 157, 169 (sambo, quadroon, quarteroon); I. R. Buchler, "Caymanian Folk Racial Categories," *Man: A Monthly Record of Anthropological Science* 290 (December 1962): 185–86. For a multi-tiered scheme on which later observers drew, see Edward Long, *The History of Jamaica,* 3 vols. (London, 1774), 2: 260–61.

19. Holt, *Problem of Freedom,* 237; E. A. Wallbridge, Kingston, September 13, 1839, Section E1/1, Mss. Brit. Emp. s. 16–24, Anti-Slavery Society Papers, Jamaica and Cayman Islands, Rhodes House Library, Oxford University, Oxford, England (hereafter, RH); *Missionary Record,* June 2, 1873, p. 531. On West Indian racial systems in the nineteenth century, see Stanley L. Engerman and B. W. Higman, "The Demographic Structure of the Caribbean Slave Societies in the Eighteenth and Nineteenth Centuries," and Gad Heuman, "The Social Structure of the Slave Societies in the Caribbean," both in *The Slave Societies of the Caribbean,* Franklin W. Knight, ed. (London, 1997), 45–104, 138–68; Kevin D. Smith, "A Fragmented Freedom: The Historiography of Emancipation and Its Aftermath in the British West Indies," *Slavery and Abolition* 16 (April 1995): 113–22; Michel-Rolph Trouillot, "The Inconvenience of Freedom: Free People of Color and the Political Aftermath of Slavery in Dominica and Saint-Domingue/Haiti," in *The Meaning of Freedom: Economics, Politics, and Culture after Slavery,* Frank McGlynn and Seymour Drescher, eds. (Pittsburgh, 1992), 147–82; Patrick Bryan, *The Jamaican People, 1880–1902* (London, 1991), 67–91; Arnold A. Sío, "Marginality and Free Coloured Identity in Caribbean Slave Society," *Slavery and Abolition* 8 (September 1987): 166–82; Gad J. Heuman, "White over Brown over Black: The Free Coloureds in Jamaican Society during Slavery and after Emancipation," *Journal of Caribbean History* 14 (1981): 46–69; B. W. Higman, *Slave Population and Economy in Jamaica, 1807–1834* (Cambridge, 1976), 139–53; Douglas Hall, "Jamaica," in *Neither Slave nor Free: The Freedman of African Descent in the Slave Societies of the New World,* David W. Cohen and Jack P. Greene, eds. (Baltimore, 1972), 193–213. David Lowenthal categorized Cayman as a society "differentiated by colour but not by class," also stating incorrectly that whites and non-whites do not marry; *West Indian Societies* (London, 1972), 77, 80.

20. Patrick Bryan, "The Black Middle Class in Nineteenth-Century Jamaica," in *Caribbean Freedom: Economy and Society from Emancipation to the Present,* Hilary Beckles and Verene Shepherd, eds. (Kingston, 1993), 284–95; Smith, *Maritime Heritage,* 76–77; interview with Phoebe Watler Spence no. 4 (b. 1907), by Heather McLaughlin, December 4, 1990, MB, CINA, pp. 28–29; will of John Jarrett Conolly, Public Recorder's Records, March 21, 1878, XH/5/5, pp. 187–89, CINA; will of Thomas Dighton Conolly, Public Recorder's Records, September 28, 1906 (orig. January 17, 1894), XH/121/1, pp. 12–18, CINA; family Bible in possession of William Warren Conolly, East End, Grand Cayman. Also on Connolly professions, see East End Births, no. 28, November 4, 1885, XH/16/1/D7; no. 103, October 13, 1887, XH/16/1/M8; no. 129, July 25, 1888, XH/16/2/B6; no. 220, February 11, 1891, XH/16/2/I5; no. 301, August 28, 1893, XH/16/3/E1; no. 275, October 5, 1892, XH/16/9/F5; and East End Deaths, no. 230, October 21, 1912, XH/203/2/O5; all CINA; author's conversation with Lou Connolly Coleman (b. 1928), West Medford, Mass., March 11, 2000; Hirst, *Notes,* 143, 311, 313, 400. One observer wrote of the "formation of a middle class of inhabitants, chiefly coloured, independent of manual labour, and occupied in various branches of commercial industry" in the British West Indies; see Herman Merivale, *Lectures on Colonization and Colonies* (1861; rpt. edn., London, 1928), 337.

21. William G. Allen, *The American Prejudice against Color: An Authentic Narrative* (London, 1853), 2, 7; Frank J. Webb, *The Garies and Their Friends* (1857; rpt. edn., Baltimore, 1997), 44.

22. On a three-tier system in North America, see Michael P. Johnson and James L. Roark, *Black Masters: A Free Family of Color in the Old South* (New York, 1984); Williamson, *New People;* Ira Berlin, *Slaves without Masters: The Free Negro in the Antebellum South* (New York, 1974), 108–32, 162–65. On the use of "mulatto" in the colonial and antebellum North, see Lorenzo Johnston Greene, *The Negro in Colonial New England, 1620–1776* (New York, 1942), 150, 207–10; James Oliver Horton, *Free People of Color: Inside the African American Community* (Washington, D.C., 1993), 122–45. Theodore Hershberg and Henry Williams found that those recorded as "mulatto" in 1850 but as "black" in 1860 had often experienced downward mobility; see "Mulattoes and Blacks: Intra-Group Color

Differences and Social Stratification in Nineteenth-Century Philadelphia," in *Philadelphia: Work, Space, Family, and Group Experience in the Nineteenth Century,* Hershberg, ed. (New York, 1981), 397.

23. *Medway v. Natick,* 7 Mass. 88 (1810); *Crandall v. Connecticut,* 10 Conn. 339 (1834), 349; *Liberator,* March 10, 1843.

24. *Parker Jeffries v. John Ankeny,* 11 Ohio 372 (1842), 375; *Williams v. School District,* Ohio Unreported Cases 1, 578 (1831); see also *Polly Gray v. Ohio,* 4 Ohio 353 (1829), 353–54; *Edwill Thacker v. John Hawk,* 11 Ohio 376 (1842); *Bailey v. Fiske,* 34 Maine 77 (1852); Carroll D. Wright, *History and Growth of the United States Census* (Washington, D.C., 1900), 147, 157. The Massachusetts state census of 1865 required a choice among white, black, mulatto, and Indian, with a presumably similar definition of "mulatto"; Oliver Warner, *Abstract of the Census of Massachusetts, 1865* (Boston, 1867), 235.

Sources disagree about the exact degree that conferred white privilege; see Long, *History of Jamaica,* 2: 261, 231, 321, 332; Bryan Edwards, *The History, Civil and Commercial, of the British Colonies in the West Indies,* 2 vols. (London, 1794), 2: 17; Matthew Gregory Lewis, *Journal of a West India Proprietor, Kept during a Residence in the Island of Jamaica* (London, 1834), 106; R. R. Madden, *A Twelvemonth's Residence in the West Indies, during the Transition from Slavery to Apprenticeship,* 2 vols. (Philadelphia, 1835), 1: 89; Matthew Gregory Lewis, *Journal of a Residence among the Negroes in the West Indies* (London, 1845), 55; Phillippo, *Jamaica,* 144. Southern state laws through the early twentieth century also varied as to the number of "generations removed" necessary to confer white privilege; see Charles S. Mangum, Jr., *The Legal Status of the Negro* (Chapel Hill, N.C., 1940), 4–17. This could render individuals legally white but socially black; see Berlin, *Slaves without Masters,* 97–99, 365–66; Williamson, *New People,* 13–14, 65, 97–98.

25. Henry Highland Garnet quoted in John McKerrow, *History of the Foreign Missions of the Secession and United Presbyterian Church* (Edinburgh, 1867), 341; Mary Gardiner Davis Journal, 1861–1863, Massachusetts Historical Society, Boston, pp. 28, 228; George Truman, *Journal of Rachel Wilson Moore, Kept during a Tour to the West Indies and South America, in 1863–64* (Philadelphia, 1867), 214; W. P. Talboys, *West India Pickles: Diary of a Cruise through the West Indies in the Yacht Josephine* (New York, 1876), 45.

26. "White Slavery in the United States," Anti-Slavery Tracts, no. 2 (New York, 1855), 6, 7; J. L. Baker, *Slavery* (Philadelphia, 1860), 9; Emancipation Papers Resulting from the Act of April 16, 1862, M433, Records of the United States District Court for the District of Columbia Relating to Slaves, Record Group 21, NA; Descriptive Lists of Recruits for Massachusetts Volunteers, 1863–64, Middlesex County and Suffolk County, 477X, MSA.

27. Higman, *Slave Populations,* 154–56, and for an extensive list of slaves' colors in St. Lucia and Berbice, see 527, 529. Holt, *Problem of Freedom,* 215; *Missionary Record,* November 1, 1855, p. 190 (censuses). As one scholar writes of Trinidad's slave registration records, "the detailed colour scale does not seem to have been employed in everyday life, but chiefly when it was necessary to describe someone with particular accuracy"; Carl Campbell, "Trinidad's Free Coloureds in Comparative Perspectives," in Shepherd and Beckles, *Caribbean Slavery,* 601.

28. Ellen Merrill to Lois Davis, Manchester, N.H., January 30, 1857; Eunice Stone to Lois Davis, Mobile, Ala., March 3, 1861; Eunice Stone to Charles Henry Richardson and Lois Davis, Claremont, N.H., December 7, 1862, all in LWRD. The photograph is also in LWRD.

29. Massachusetts Vital Records, Dracut, 1869, vol. 218, p. 166, MSA; Eunice Connolly to Lois Davis, East End, Grand Cayman, March 7, 1870; Eunice Connolly to Lois Davis, Provincetown, Mass., November 13, 1869 (part of William S. Connolly to Lois Davis), LWRD. See also Joanne Pope Melish, *Disowning Slavery: Gradual Emancipation and "Race" in New England, 1780–1860* (Ithaca, N.Y., 1998), 163–237.

30. Ann McCoy to Eunice Connolly, Dracut, Mass., February 16, 1870 (unsent), LWRD; Rachel Frances Levy, ed., *The Life and Adventures of John Levy* (Lawrence, Mass., 1871), 73; *The Journals of Charlotte Forten Grimké,* Brenda Stevenson, ed. (New York, 1988), 140; Horton, *Free People of Color,* 122–45; Elizabeth Hafkin Pleck, *Black Migration and Poverty: Boston, 1865–1900* (New York, 1979); Horton and Horton, *In Hope of Liberty,* 101–24. Willard B. Gatewood, *Aristocrats of Color: The Black*

Elite, 1880–1920 (Bloomington, Ind., 1990), 149–81, writes that post–Civil War elite African Americans based status on a combination of ancestry, color, wealth, education, occupation, and gentility, both distancing themselves from other blacks and championing civil rights. On foreigners, see Halter, *Between Race and Ethnicity;* Hodes, *White Women, Black Men,* 97, 100, 105, 119.

31. Author's telephone conversation with James T. Conolly, Brooklyn, N.Y., November 11, 1996 (untaped); interview with Cecily Pierson no. 2 (b. 1916), by Heather McLaughlin, April 3, 1991, pp. 6–7, MB, CINA; Cleopathra Conolly to author, East End, Grand Cayman, August 9, 2001; Hirst, *Notes,* 136 (on literacy). On the house, see William S. Connolly to Lois Davis, East End, Grand Cayman, October 16, 1872, LWRD; Theoline Conolly McCoy conversation, July 13, 1999. Interview with Phoebe Watler Spence no. 3, by Heather McLaughlin, December 4, 1990, MB, CINA, p. 30 (class/color).

32. Eunice Connolly to Lois Davis, East End, Grand Cayman, August 25, 1870 (part of May 16 letter), LWRD; John Bigelow, *Jamaica in 1850: or, The Effects of Sixteen Years of Freedom on a Slave Colony* (New York, 1851), 25–27; David King, *The State and Prospects of Jamaica* (London, 1850), 59–60, 65; Madden, *Twelvemonth's Residence,* 1: 145. See also Trollope, *West Indies,* 74, 81, 97; Mrs. Carmichael, *Domestic Manners and Social Condition of the White, Coloured, and Negro Population of the West Indies* (London, 1833), 70; Edward Bean Underhill, *The West Indies: Their Social and Religious Condition* (London, 1862), 192, 225.

33. William Warren Conolly conversation, July 22, 1998.

34. Interview with Elderly Residents of East End no. 1, by Anita Ebanks, 1982, MB, CINA, p. 15; author's conversation with Dorothy McLean Welcome (b. 1917, a Conolly on her mother's side), East End, Grand Cayman, July 15, 1999; Theoline Conolly McCoy conversation, July 13, 1999; author's conversation with Lou Connolly Coleman, East End, Grand Cayman, August 27, 2000; Aurellia Conolly interview, p. 4.

35. *Missionary Record,* November 1, 1855, p. 190; "A Wesleyan Missionary in Grand Cayman, 1837," acc. no. 177, CINA; William G. Sewell, *The Ordeal of Free Labor in the British West Indies* (New York, 1861), 37. In Dominica in 1845, residents protested a census that would enforce "distinctions between the whites and coloured"; *Dominica: Copies or Extracts of Despatches Relating to the Disturbances in the Island of Dominica* (London, 1845), 115. In the nineteenth-century Bahamas, "some locally acknowledged whites were of mixed descent"; Michael Craton and Gail Saunders, *Islanders in the Stream: A History of the Bahamian People,* 2 vols. (Athens, Ga., 1998), 2: 90. Ann Twinam's study of legitimation petitions in colonial Spanish America concludes that a classification of "white" could be "achieved" if not ascribed at birth; see *Public Lives, Private Secrets: Gender, Honor, Sexuality, and Illegitimacy in Colonial Spanish America* (Stanford, Calif., 1999), 25–26, 130–31, 306–11.

36. Rainier Spencer, "Race and Mixed-Race: A Personal Tour," in *As We Are Now: Mixblood Essays on Race and Identity,* William S. Penn, ed. (Berkeley, Calif., 1997), 135. On the idea of white purity, see Virginia R. Domínguez, "Exporting U.S. Concepts of Race: Are There Limits to the U.S. Model?" *Social Research* 65 (Summer 1998): 384. On Anglo-Saxonism, see Nina Baym, "Onward Christian Women: Sarah J. Hale's History of the World," *New England Quarterly* 63 (June 1990): 249–70.

37. Hodges, "'Desirable Companions,'" 112, 122–24; *People v. John Leavy and John Leavy, Jr.,* Indictments, October 28, 1863, New York City Municipal Archives; Bruce Laurie, *Working People of Philadelphia, 1800–1850* (Philadelphia, 1980), 156–57; David Goodman Croly, *Miscegenation: The Theory of the Blending of the Races, Applied to the American White Man and Negro* (New York, 1864), 30. And see Leslie M. Harris, "From Abolitionist Amalgamators to 'Rulers of the Five Points': The Discourse of Interracial Sex and Reform in Antebellum New York City," in *Sex, Love, Race: Crossing Boundaries in North American History,* Martha Hodes, ed. (New York, 1999), 199–207; James Oliver Horton and Lois E. Horton, *Black Bostonians: Family Life and Community Struggle in the Antebellum North* (New York, 1999), 22–24; Harriet E. Wilson, *Our Nig: or, Sketches from the Life of a Free Black* (1859; rpt. edn., New York, 1983), 9, 22.

38. *Acts and Resolves Passed by the Legislature of Massachusetts* (Boston, 1843), 4; Louis Ruchames, "Race, Marriage, and Abolition in Massachusetts," *Journal of Negro History* 40 (July 1955): 250–73; Cheryl I. Harris, "Whiteness as Property," *Harvard Law Review* 106 (June 1993): 1707–91; Jeremy

Belknap, "Queries Respecting the Slavery and Emancipation of Negroes in Massachusetts," *Collections of the Massachusetts Historical Society*, 1st ser., vol. 4 (Boston, 1795), 209; Lydia Maria Child, *An Appeal in Favor of That Class of Americans Called Africans* (1833; rpt. edn., Amherst, Mass., 1996), 187; *Crandall v. Connecticut*, 10 Conn. 339 (1834), 346; Allen, *American Prejudice*, 7; Wilson, *Our Nig*, 13, 15. Wilson resided in Massachusetts and New Hampshire, including Hillsborough County and Goffstown, N.H., where some of Eunice's relatives lived around the same time; Henry Louis Gates, Jr., "Introduction," *Our Nig*, xiv–xvii.

On white women, class, and purity, see Hodes, *White Women, Black Men*, 198–202; and on white womanhood constructed in relation to non-white femininity, see Hazel V. Carby, *Reconstructing Womanhood: The Emergence of the Afro-American Woman Novelist* (New York, 1987), 20–39; Louise Michele Newman, *White Women's Rights: The Racial Origins of Feminism in the United States* (New York, 1999), esp. 22–85; Amy Kaplan, "Manifest Domesticity," *American Literature* 70 (September 1998): 581–606. Joel Williamson writes of the post-Reconstruction South that "whites could easily descend into blackness if they failed in morality"; *New People*, 108. Victoria Bynum found that "many whites considered even living among African Americans grounds for being socially defined as one"; "Misshapen Identity: Memory, Folklore, and the Legend of Rachel Knight," in Hodes, *Sex, Love, Race*, 239. Ann Laura Stoler notes that European women (often lower-class) who married non-European men demonstrated, in the eyes of colonial authorities, moral degradation sufficient to deserve demotion to native status; "Sexual Affronts and Racial Frontiers: European Identities and the Cultural Politics of Exclusion in Colonial Southeast Asia," in *Tensions of Empire: Colonial Cultures in a Bourgeois World*, Frederick Cooper and Ann Laura Stoler, eds. (Berkeley, Calif., 1997), 217–22.

39. *Liberator*, August 26, 1859; Harris, "Abolitionist Amalgamators," 194. For the marriage law debates, see *Liberator*, March 10, 1843, May 21, 1831, February 25, 1842, March 15, 1839. Wilson, *Our Nig*, 124, 133; Eunice Stone to Lois Davis, Claremont, N.H., February 8, March 29, April 30, May 22, July 12, 1863, and Clarence Stone to Lois Davis, Claremont, N.H., February 1, 1863, LWRD (sewing hats). The ambivalence of Eunice's mother is apparent in Eunice's continual reassurances in the letters from Cayman. On the gendered rhetoric of "amalgamation," see Dorsey, *Reforming Men and Women*, 150–54. On the idea of intimacy across the color line as a violation of nature, see Elise Lemire, *"Miscegenation": Making Race in America* (Philadelphia, 2002), esp. 53–144.

40. Eunice Connolly to Lois Davis, East End, Grand Cayman, March 7, 1870; William S. Connolly to Lois Davis, Provincetown, Mass., November 13, 1869, LWRD. On post-emancipation racial conflicts, see "Diary of Occurrences at the Caymanas," Dispatch no. 33, June 1835, PRO: CO 137/199, pp. 286, 287; Reports of Andrew Malcolm to Mico Charity, Grand Cayman, May 3, 1839, and May 5, July 7, 1840, E1/1 and E1/2, RH. A descendant recalled that a grandmother who "didn't own a drop of coloured blood" had married a "mulatto," and another Caymanian recounted, "My father was dark, but now my mother she was clear, because my grandmother, she was a white woman"; Aurellia Conolly interview, p. 7; interview with Portia Dixon Grant (b. 1914), by Heather McLaughlin, Cayman Brac, March 14, 1995, MB, CINA, p. 4; see also Geneva Range interview no. 1, pp. 2–4; Hirst, *Notes*, 66–67. Edward Brathwaite found marriages and liaisons between colored men and white (or "reputedly" white) women in Jamaica during slavery; *The Development of Creole Society in Jamaica, 1770–1820* (Oxford, 1971), 188–91. That colored women became the mistresses of white men was widely commented on by travelers and residents alike; see Hilary McD. Beckles, "Property Rights in Pleasure: Marketing Black Women's Sexuality," in *Centering Woman*.

Of Cuba's racial continuum (defined "both phenotypically and contextually"), Rebecca J. Scott writes, "Such categorization did not preclude racism, of course, but it made strict segregation an implausible project"; see "Fault Lines, Color Lines, and Party Lines: Race, Labor, and Collective Action in Louisiana and Cuba, 1862–1912," in Frederick Cooper, Thomas C. Holt, and Rebecca J. Scott, *Beyond Slavery: Explorations of Race, Labor, and Citizenship in Postemancipation Societies* (Chapel Hill, N.C., 2000), 91. Gwendolyn Midlo Hall demonstrates that colonial Louisiana was a society both brutally racist and racially open; see *Africans in Colonial Louisiana: The Development of Afro-Creole Culture in the Eighteenth Century* (Baton Rouge, La., 1992), xv, 155.

41. William Warren Conolly conversation, July 22, 1998; J. Dennis Harris, *A Summer on the Bor-*

ders of the Caribbean Sea (New York, 1860), 132. And see Adrian Piper, "Passing for White, Passing for Black," in *Passing and the Fictions of Identity,* Elaine K. Ginsberg, ed. (Durham, N.C., 1996), 250. For people of African descent understood as white, see also Hall, *Africans in Colonial Louisiana,* 239–40, 258; Virginia R. Domínguez, *White by Definition: Social Classification in Creole Louisiana* (New Brunswick, N.J., 1986), esp. 36–55.

42. Author's conversation with William Warren Conolly, East End, Grand Cayman, July 13, 1999; Dorothy McLean Welcome conversation, July 15, 1999; also Theoline Conolly McCoy conversation, July 13, 1999, and Lou Connolly Coleman conversation, March 11, 2000.

43. Sollors, *Neither Black nor White,* 119; Melissa Russell Diary, November 1, 1835, SPR11, Alabama Department of Archives and History, Montgomery; William Craft, *Running a Thousand Miles for Freedom: The Escape of William and Ellen Craft from Slavery* (1860; rpt. edn., Baton Rouge, La., 1999), 5, told in greater detail in George W. Cable, *Strange True Stories of Louisiana* (New York, 1893), 145–91; Wilson, *Our Nig,* 39; John Williamson, *Medical and Miscellaneous Observations Relative to the West India Islands,* 2 vols. (Edinburgh, 1817), 1: 42. A German anthropologist wrote of white skin: "it is very easy for that to degenerate into brown, but very much more difficult for dark to become white"; see Johann Friedrich Blumenbach, *On the Natural Varieties of Mankind* (1775; rpt. edn., New York, 1969), 269.

44. Gunnar Myrdal, *An American Dilemma: The Negro Problem and Modern Democracy* (New York, 1944), 683; St. Clair Drake and Horace R. Cayton, *Black Metropolis: A Study of Negro Life in a Northern City* (New York, 1945), 164. For state laws, see Mangum, *Legal Status,* 1–17. The U.S. Supreme Court decision that established the doctrine of "separate but equal" also furthered the one-drop rule; Homer Plessy, who had challenged segregation on a Louisiana railroad, described himself as seven-eighths white and one-eighth black; *Plessy v. Ferguson,* 163 U.S. 537 (1896). Concerning the twentieth century, see Wald, *Crossing the Line,* 15–17, 53–81, 152–81. For an arresting literary representation, see Langston Hughes, "Who's Passing for Who?" in *Laughing to Keep from Crying* (New York, 1952), 1–7.

45. J. T. Trowbridge, *The South: A Tour of Its Battle-Fields and Ruined Cities* (Hartford, Conn., 1866), 343; Richmond (Va.) *Daily Dispatch,* February 3, 1873; Webb, *Garies and Their Friends,* 136–38; George P. Rawick, ed., *The American Slave: A Composite Autobiography,* 19 vols. (1941; rpt. edn., Westport, Conn., 1972), vol. 15, pt. 2, p. 107; 1850 Northampton County, N.C. census, p. 52, NA; David Dodge, "The Free Negroes of North Carolina," *Atlantic Monthly* 57 (January 1886): 29. In Reconstruction South Carolina, a white woman who had married a black man was recorded as black in the 1880 federal census; see Mark Jones and John Wertheimer, et al., "Pinkney and Sarah Ross: The Legal Journey of an Ex-Slave and His White Wife on the Carolina Borderlands during Reconstruction," *South Carolina Historical Magazine,* forthcoming. The most well-known literary renderings are Mark Twain, *Pudd'nhead Wilson* (London, 1894); and Edna Ferber, *Showboat* (Garden City, N.Y., 1926).

46. Wilson, *Our Nig,* 13.

47. Eunice Stone to Ann McCoy, Claremont, N.H., April 19, 1863; Eunice Stone to Lois Davis, Claremont, N.H., April 6, 1862, and East End, Grand Cayman, May 16, 1870, December 13, 1871, March 7, 1870, all in LWRD. On the idea of "home" representing a middle-class ideal of domesticity, see Stansell, *City of Women,* 41–42, 159–61, 202–03; Jeanne Boydston, *Home and Work: Housework, Wages, and the Ideology of Labor in the Early Republic* (New York, 1990), 142–63. For the ways in which this discourse resonates with discourses of empire, see Kaplan, "Manifest Domesticity."

48. Eunice Connolly to Lois Davis, East End, Grand Cayman, March 7, 1870; Karen Lystra, *Searching the Heart: Women, Men, and Romantic Love in Nineteenth-Century America* (New York, 1989), 192–258; Colleen McDannell, *The Christian Home in Victorian America, 1840–1900* (Bloomington, Ind., 1986), 20–51, 77–107.

49. Eunice Connolly to Lois Davis, East End, Grand Cayman, August 25, 1870 (part of May 16 letter), March 7, 1870, December 13, 1871, LWRD. On white people intentionally shifting toward blackness, see Susan Gubar, *Racechanges: White Skin, Black Face in American Culture* (New York, 1997).

50. Eunice Connolly to Lois Davis, East End, Grand Cayman, March 7, 1870, LWRD; Benjamin S. Hunt, *Remarks on Hayti as a Place of Settlement for Afric-Americans; and on the Mulatto as a Race for*

the Tropics (Philadelphia, 1860), 28; Sandra Gunning, "Nancy Prince and the Politics of Mobility, Home and Diasporic (Mis)Identification," *American Quarterly* 53 (March 2001): 38; and see Hilary McD. Beckles, "White Women and Freedom," in *Centering Woman,* on the complicity of white women in West Indian racist systems.

51. Webb, *Garies and Their Friends,* 323.

52. William Warren Conolly conversation, July 13, 1999.

3

Arriving, Settling In, and Surviving

German Women in the Midwest

LINDA SCHELBITZKI PICKLE

Farewell, O you dear fatherland,
To fare thee well we raise our hand;
Our gaze does grow sad, of course,
But fortune's eyes do smile on us;
At home just fear and poverty,
Typhus, starvation, and misery;
Thus a new home do we seek,
America, we turn to thee. . . .

—Christian Hansern, "Song of the Emigrants
    upon Their Departure for America"

Most of the German-speakers who came to rural areas of the Midwest seeking new homes free from the travails of their old life came as members of families. They knew that in all probability they were leaving their homeland forever. By traveling with family members, they had a bulwark against total estrangement in the new land, but they also knew that their lives would never be the same as they had been. For adult women, whose lives had revolved around the home and the kinship structures of the rural community, this must have been a daunting prospect. Would they be able to preserve their old ways, while of necessity adapting to their new environment? What strategies, conditioned by their ethnic and cultural background, could they employ to accomplish this? This chapter explores women's contributions in the process of emigration and the adaptation to the new environment. Family structure—that is, the context of power relations in the family—is one of the primary focuses.

In most cases we do not know what role German-speaking women played in the decision to emigrate. Their personal documents usually do not comment on this or why they emigrated since the writer and her audience already knew.[1] Because economic considerations usually set the emigration in motion and because most of those who eventually became Midwest farmers did so as part of families, it is likely that women, whose lives and work were centered in their families, were willing participants. Louisa Roenigk was certainly acting in her family's long-term interest when she left Thuringia with her thirteen-year-old brother, worked on a farm and then as a domestic in Madison and St. Louis before marrying, and later helped her parents and siblings come to Kansas. Other German-born women were eager to emigrate for similar reasons. Ferdinand and Augusta (Holtz) Beulke left Pommerania ten years after their marriage in 1877 because of family concerns: "due to the serious illnesses and disappointments in losing their four children they decided to leave their homeland." Katharine Ensinger Reinim, an impoverished widow, went to the Belleville, Illinois, area with her six children in response to a letter from her childless cousin, who had recently lost his wife. He made it clear he was at least as interested in gaining her three strong teenage boys for his farm as he was in marrying her. (Katharine Reinim's youngest son eventually inherited his uncle/stepfather's farm.) Mathias Blommer was grateful that his mother had been willing to migrate with him and his family to Osage County, Missouri, in 1840: "If my old mother had not decided to travel with us, we might have had to stay for a long time in poverty-stricken Germany and would have raised our children for other people and for the old sinner and misguided religious persecutor [Kaiser] Wilhelm." Blommer's mother died soon after their arrival, but, as he said, by supporting their decision to migrate, she had helped give her descendants the opportunity to make "much better progress than in poor Germany."[2]

The revolutionary idea that it was legitimate for the underclasses to seek to improve their place in society had become generally accepted by the early 1800s, leading to an easing of many regional restrictions on peasants' lives and movements.[3] The more adventurous among these groups were consequently freer as well as more willing to emigrate. This class-based change in attitude and self-image was one that women no doubt shared. More concrete political considerations lay behind the emigration of other German-speakers, particularly those of the middle class. Women, because they had so little share in public life, were unlikely to initiate emigration for political reasons. Their influence in such cases was actually based on family considerations. For example, a few, like the widow Anna Pohlman, left Europe to help their sons evade military obligations. Others exercised some influence in the timing of politically motivated emigration, as did Elizabeth Koepfi, who persuaded her Swiss physician husband to wait fourteen years, until the eldest sons were through with their education and the other children were old enough to be helpful, before settling in Illinois. Writing from St. Louis, Hermann Steines, a Dreißiger scout, warned his mother and sisters of the importance of their willing participation: "If you feel strong enough in body to endure the hardships of the journey, and buoyant enough in spirit to participate in the attempt of realizing the fond dream of your men folks, then we shall all be happy and greatly benefited. The older members of our family will not be materially benefited by coming here, but your interest in your children must be the deciding factor if you take this step. You women must have a clear understanding with your men." The next year the Steines family emigrated. The actions of other women also indicate support of their husbands' desire to leave an uncongenial political environment. Ulrike Haeger Gellhorn ran an apothecary and sandwich shop in Pommerania for a year, caring for five young children at the same time, until her husband could send the money for the family to join him.[4]

Yet because married women seldom acted as free agents in emigration, some were less supportive than others. Their unwillingness to leave familiar surroundings was common enough to generate broadsides like the following exchange between a husband and wife:

> Husband:
> O wife, how many pretty wares
> Come from there, America!
> Why should we any longer tarry,
> So good could we two have it there.
> Here's nothing but trouble, day after day
> And not enough bread to make it pay.
> How wonderful our life would be there,
> If we were in America . . .
>
> Wife:
> O husband, how can you think that?
> I want you to forget it now,
> Or if you don't I'll feel so bad,
> 'Cause I'm not goin', no way, no how.
> Now if I were to leave my friends
> And never see them again,
> I'd die a troubled death, I would
> So what good's America, tell me, what good? . . .[5]

The song ends with the husband's winning the argument. Of course, more women than we can know succeeded in keeping their families in Europe. Though we have no record of such cases, we do know that after emigration some women persuaded their husbands to return to Europe.[6] They were usually bourgeois women, whose families had the financial means to return and who probably had relatively less to gain by emigration. Their husbands might also have been less authoritarian in their families than rural men were. Other women could only acquiesce to their husbands' decision and voice their protest within the family circle. Most women, whether they were enthusiastic about emigration or not, seem to have put the best face possible on it.

The memoir of Helena Friesen Eitzen, written near Inman, Kansas, in 1919, when she was fifty-three, offers an interesting example of the motivations behind immigration and the way in which a woman could forestall it, at least for a time. Helena Eitzen came from a poor family in southern Russia. At fifteen she had begun to contribute to her family's support through her sewing. At twenty she was contracted to work for an aunt for a two-year period, during which time she was ill-treated, which might have contributed to the emotional problems she exhibited later. She then married a carpenter, who seems to have had a small farm as well. Soon thereafter she suffered a nervous breakdown and had to be nursed two months by her mother. After the birth of Helena Eitzen's first daughter in 1889, crops failed and work opportunities for her husband slowed down. He began pressing her to agree to go to America, something he had suggested as a possibility even before they married. Helena wrote later, "At the time I gave my consent, but now when the question really arose I didn't agree so readily, for it meant I would have to leave all those I loved, never to see them again." In about 1891, after the birth of a second daughter, things became even harder for the Eitzens. Helena was ill for a long time after the birth and could not take in sewing, and her husband injured his hand and could not work for twenty-six weeks. His requests that she agree to emigrate became ever more frequent and importunate. Viewing her resistance as contrary to the God-willed order, Helena began to pray: "I began to examine myself, also prayed a great deal because of this, but I could not say: 'Lord, may not my will but yours be fulfilled,' for the reason that I didn't want this."[7]

The next section of Helena Eitzen's memoir describes what led to her final acquiescence:

> I kept going into the barn to pray, that was my little room where I was alone with my God and where I poured out all my sorrow. I prayed that the dear God might show me in piety what I should do and what would be the best for me. Then I swore that I would also consent to do whatever I dreamed. But I dreamed nothing having to do with leaving until I had repeated the vow three times, and also had promised each time to do it [i.e., whatever she dreamed].
>
> Then I dreamed one night we were getting ready for the trip to America. My beloved mother was helping me, and we were singing together as we worked. Then I woke up, but, but my request had been fulfilled, I had dreamed, but now I also had to keep my promise, and right away the Tempter was at my side. He gave me the idea that no one knew what I had prayed or promised, that I shouldn't tell anyone anything about it, and I could stay there [in Russia]. I was tempted in this way for two weeks, didn't tell anyone what I had prayed and also not what I had dreamed. My husband kept asking me if I was sick, for I was very depressed. He was worried that I would again have a nervous breakdown. But I didn't stop praying and the dear Lord helped me vanquish, and may praise and thanks be to God, I have experienced this so often, if I am true, He is glad to help. Thus it was at that time, too. One morning, when we got up, I confided in my husband that I had prayed thusly, and also that I had promised to obey and that I now had conquered [myself] and was ready to comply with his desire [to emigrate].[8]

Few extant documents contain such explicit testimony about the inner processes of a woman's reconciliation to emigration. Helena Eitzen's memoir reveals the role a woman's piety and her acceptance of the divinely ordained subordination to her husband could play in this. Her statements confirm other aspects of a woman's role in the decision to emigrate. In this case, her husband had to seek her agreement before the plans to leave could go forward. It is also clear that deciding to leave was not easy, no matter how difficult the financial conditions from which people fled. Helena Eitzen's family supported her decision, and her mother even praised her for having been willing "to do what the Lord had showed [her]." When it was time to go to the train station to depart, though, Helena fainted and did not come to until they were already under way: "It was for me like the funeral day of my entire family."[9]

Helena Eitzen's memoir offers insights into what might have been typical of many poor women's motivations and experiences prior to emigration. In contrast, it is probably safe to guess that few women came to America for the same reason that Sophie Luise Weitbrecht did: to escape an unwanted marriage. More common is the second part of her story. On shipboard she met an Evangelical Lutheran minister on his way to take over a German parish in Red Bud, Illinois, and married him two days after their arrival in New Orleans.[10] Many women married just before departing for America, and others came to America to begin married life. Some of them were completing arrangements that had been made in Europe and were bringing a dowry payment that would help establish the newlyweds on a farm, much as would have happened in Europe. This was the case with Luise Rodekopp, whose fiancé Heinrich Steinwald (who had emigrated in 1881) threatened to marry a rich German-American farmer's daughter in Illinois if Luise's mother did not send a large enough dowry. Luise came to America and worked for relatives while Heinrich bargained with her mother. Eventually the money came, the two married, bought a farm, and had what was said to be a happy life together.[11] Other women had had no contact with their husbands-to-be beyond the exchange of a few letters. The pragmatic nature of arrangements like this, which was quite in keeping with what we know about marital relationships in rural German lands, is apparent in what Rosina Scwendleman Reusser said in later years about her wedding day, celebrated right after she arrived by train in Iowa: "Marriage in the forenoon, hoeing potatoes in the afternoon."[12]

Other economic aspects of the emigration of both married and single women reflect family and social structures of the day. A few women brought the money into their marriages that enabled the emigration. Some had the advantage of sharing the sale of their original family's holdings, and these women were better able to secure a good start for themselves and their families as American farmers. Others entered into work agreements that allowed them to pay off their fares and thus had lives in America much like those they would have had as hired help in Europe. Some single women had enough money to pay their own fare and the skills to find work in America.[13] Most, however, probably came with less capital than single males did, a reflection of the low status of female labor in the nineteenth century. Walter Kamphoefner found that four-fifths of the single women from Osnabrück who immigrated to St. Charles and Warren counties in Missouri between 1832 and 1858 had been agricultural workers or domestics, while a few others listed the profession of seamstress or midwife. The thirty-two women who came from the rural lower class took only 49.9 percent of the average amount of assets for all the immigrants to those counties during that period, while the twenty-five who were the daughters of propertied peasants took 88.2 percent of the average. One hundred and twenty-five other single women, who did not indicate their father's occupation, brought 62.6 percent of the average amount of assets.[14]

Nineteenth-century publications were full of advice on who should emigrate, where the emigrants should settle, what awaited them there, and what they should take along. Almost all the material directed at women assumed that they would be traveling as family members. The material intended for single women emphasized the perils of traveling alone. One leaflet warned that among the conditions awaiting women who emigrated were "the dangers of white slavery": "Houses of prostitution in foreign lands are filled with German women. Women and girls are seduced by agents under the guise of offering them good positions. Do not accept any job offer in a foreign land without consulting with emigrant advisory offices."[15] It is hard to know if this warning was justified. Virtually no information about German-speaking "fallen women" has been uncovered. The fact that Anglo-American women's associations were also concerned about the sexual vulnerability of immigrant women indicates that such warnings contained at least a kernel of truth.[16]

Publications for emigrants encouraged women in charge of setting up households to bring material that would make them self-reliant, and every woman brought as much of her household goods as possible. Bedding and linen were particularly important and were often part of a woman's dowry. A chest could supply sheets, towels, and clothing for the crucial early years, as it did for one Kansas sod house family. Featherbeds were prized so highly that one women made sure they were safe in the creek bed when a Kansas prairie fire threatened. Families usually left their furniture behind (which women sometimes sorely regretted), but silver and clocks made the transatlantic journey, as did family bibles and other keepsakes. The more valuable of such items were sometimes sold for cash in hard times, foiling women's attempts to maintain household continuity.[17] Generally, emigrants tried to anticipate their future needs and took only what they believed would be useful and not readily or more cheaply available in America. The common wisdom, especially among newly arrived immigrants, was that American goods were inferior. Letters in the first years of settlement contain requests for clothing, material, and household items that were not to be had in the United States. Emigrants traveling to farms sometimes took plant and orchard cuttings, and many women took flower, herb, and vegetable seeds to have a bit of home in their new surroundings and for their practical uses.

Women packed most of the baggage that accompanied the German-speaking emigrants. Women's help would be necessary once they arrived. No matter to what degree women had initiated and supported the decision to emigrate, their role would be central to the success of the family venture. They were therefore encouraged to foster the self-sacrificing qualities that would ensure success. An emigrant adviser declared:

> QUALITIES
> which the emigrating woman must possess:
> A strong resilient body
> Robust health
> A resilient soul
> Strong nerves
> A great lack of consideration for herself
> Friendly obligingness to others.[18]

This exhortation is, in several ways, a description of what was already expected of rural women in German lands, but in America, at least on the agricultural frontier, hard physical work would be required of all women, no matter what their background.

The power relations in the farm family of the antebellum Midwest entailed male domination and female exploitation. John Mack Faragher has used the term *patriarchy* to describe this family structure. He summarizes its features in this way: (1) the family and household operated as the basic unit of labor; (2) both sexes were involved in the family division of labor, with women playing central roles in both productive and reproductive work; (3) women bore more children than in simpler foraging societies or in more complex industrialized ones; and (4) the husband's rule in the household was legitimized by the sexually segregated public domain.[19] In other words, the rural family structure of the American premarket economy was much like that prevalent in rural areas of nineteenth-century German lands. American rural society would have seemed familiar to most German-speakers, although as the century wore on, the immigrants continued to live according to family structures that became outdated in many parts of the United States.

In objective terms, frontierswomen, no matter what their place of birth and mother tongue, faced similar conditions and did much the same kind of work. Glenda Riley has established the existence of a "female frontier" based on gender as the common experience of both prairie and plains women in the nineteenth century. Riley contends that shared experiences, life-styles, responsibilities, and sensibilities that transcended geography marked the patterns of women settlers' lives.[20] To no small extent, they also transcended ethnic and cultural differences. Many writers have noted that the unpaid labor of women and children was the resource that enabled farm families to survive hard years.[21] Others, in considering the broader picture of American agriculture, have asserted that this labor pool and the diversification of the areas of women's production made it possible for the farm family to withstand the elements of risk and heavy capital investment that characterize farm life. The cost to women was often immense, as it was to their husbands and children, but the agrarian ideology that praised the simple, independent, and physically and morally healthy life-style gained through harmonious family work undergirded this economic system and provided a social and cultural framework of support. The rural sociologists Cornelia Flora and Jan Flora have said, "The relations of production (that the same unit, the household, provided management, capital and labor to the enterprise, with little labor bought or sold) helps explain the fact that all in the enterprise were expected to contribute to the whole to make it work. Women's culture contributed to that sense of family, life style, and community—and has helped to mobilize the needed labor at key moments in the production cycle."[22] German-speaking women were culturally conditioned to be ready to participate in the family effort that made frontier success possible.[23]

The same emigrant literature that urged women's self-sacrifice also warned them of the physical travails of emigration. They would be expected to work without surcease in primitive living conditions, helping in the most difficult of frontier tasks: clearing forests, removing tree stumps and preparing virgin land, building houses, planting and weeding crops, tending animals and gardens. For these jobs, they should take sturdy shoes and work clothes, including trousers and bellybands (to help prevent rupture). They also had to be ready to provide family health care and to educate their children in the isolation of the wilderness.[24] German-speaking women in the Midwest did all of these things and sometimes more. For example, in the 1830s Margaret Blauff Hillenkamp helped her husband clear twenty *Morgen* (about forty acres) of forested land in St. Charles County, Missouri, for crops and a seven-acre peach and apple orchard, in between bearing several children. Elisabeth Beckbird Biehler-Meyer quarried all the stone and helped lay up the walls for the first house built on her family's Kansas farm.[25]

Labor such as this was difficult and out of the ordinary. Much more common and widespread was field work. In this regard, German-speakers continued work patterns established in Europe, even though some emigrant literature warned that this was not common among Americans and would bring disapproval.[26] Katharina Wolf Langendorf Tiek wrote her parents in February of 1869 from Moro in Madison County, Illinois, about an accident caused by a "wild" horse with which she had plowed a potato field the previous spring:

> As we came up a hill and I wanted to turn the horse, it knocked me over and struck me in the back with its hooves and the plow caught in my skirt and took me along. There I lay like dead in the field. My husband took me home. You can imagine what pain I suffered. Four days later I had a little girl on the first Pentecost morning. But what I had to endure until she was born! I didn't think that I could survive it. Then I got up on the third day and had been so badly hurt that I had to stay in bed for three more weeks. No one thought that I would get better.[27]

The daughter born after that accident in the spring of 1868 did not survive to be counted in the 1870 census.[28] A decade later, Katharina Tiek wrote that she was expecting her seventh child in a few weeks and that of the six children born to her, four had survived. Her hard life had taken its toll on her body, she said, and she had two ruptures. She assured her mother, however, that they "never suffered want in America and eat meat and sausage three times a day," and then she added, "But there's never a lack of work, either."[29] The details of Katharina Tiek's life are unclear. We know that she married again after her first husband's death and eventually had ten children, of whom only three survived childhood and adolescence. Scanty and inarticulate though they are, her letters confirm the harsh demands farm life made on women and the extent to which German-speaking women were willing to sacrifice themselves to meet those demands. The costs to them and their families in terms of women's health and child mortality are obvious.[30]

Childbirth was a hazardous thing in the nineteenth century, and nowhere more so than on the frontier. Friederika Oesterreich Staatz had the distinction of giving birth to the first white child in Dickinson County, Kansas. Having arrived in May 1857, she and her new husband spent the summer living in their wagon until they could prepare a home. In June a daughter was born, but the baby died in October.[31] Friederika Staatz had the help of other immigrant women, but others were not so fortunate. They gave birth alone or with the help of a husband or even a child.[32] When women died as a result of childbirth, illness, or years of exertion, other immigrant women often took their place caring for the family.

In difficult economic circumstances, women and men were frequently forced to neglect the children that survived and to drive them just as hard as they drove themselves. One young mother often left her infant and toddler locked up in the house, "guarded" by a big black dog, while she went to sew and wash for neighbors. Another helped her husband shock wheat with their one- or two-year-old son tied to the back of one of the horses.[33] Children were put out to work as early as eight, and their wages went to their parents to purchase supplies, pay taxes, or buy land. Some of these children had bitter memories of childhoods dedicated to work and the care of younger siblings. Others were matter-of-fact about these things, while still others emphasized the happy and funny things that happened. In northwest Nebraska in the 1880s, the Steinhaus boys teased their youngest brother in dangerous ways: hanging him out of the upstairs window by his suspenders, rolling him down the hill in the baby carriage, and getting him to chew tobacco at the age of five. Their mother "never knew any of this—she was so busy."[34]

None of these difficult and potentially tragic circumstances of family life was different from the experiences many rural immigrants had had in their homelands. There, too, women worked hard throughout their pregnancies and even gave birth alone on occasion. Women aged prematurely and died young. Many infants perished because they had poor prenatal and postnatal care and nutrition and because their mothers had to work and could not care for them properly. Infants and toddlers in poor rural families in German lands were sometimes left on their own while their parents worked. In all farm families, young children were often in the care of older children for most of the time, and children were put to work early and sent away to earn wages.[35]

In other words, the strategies that had been necessary for survival in Europe were still necessary for survival in America. The difference was that now a family could see that by pooling its labor and wages, family members could do more than just survive. They had a chance of advancement. A German who worked for a time on the farm of a Forty-Eighter in Illinois noted that the immigrants who had done best were those who had had family members work for others as soon as possible. After about ten years, the accumulated wages and interest enabled the family to buy a large farm, build a house, work the land with the now-grown children, and send the nonessential family members out for more wages to repeat the process. In a letter discussing the prospects for immigrants in America, Friedrich G. Hillenkamp acknowledged that he had had difficulty establishing his Missouri farm, even though he had started with a good sum of money and had had a hardworking wife who had helped him with all his work. Nevertheless, Hillenkamp believed that an impoverished relative with several children could do well in America: "His sturdy children, who are surely used to working, would be his capital." This is what Johann Diedrich Wilkens meant when he spoke of his young children (ages one month to seven years) as the future hired help (*Knechte* and *Magd*) for his farm.[36]

At the age of eighty, my grandmother wrote down a few lines about her family history that illustrate the cooperative strategy that made it possible for immigrants to get ahead. Her parents, Anton and Karolina (Miller) Krause, had been weavers and agricultural workers in Austria. They came to Nebraska in 1882, at the height of the German-speaking immigration, with six children, age twelve and under. The youngest, an infant, died soon after their arrival, and two more babies, including my grandmother, were born in Nebraska. Of their first years, my grandmother wrote:

> My parents were not among the very first settlers in this community, so therefore there was no homestead land for them left to settle upon but they thought nothing of living in a rented house and working to earn money to buy a farm and also feed and clothe themselves and family. Mrs. Krause's work consisted partly of walking

about twelve miles every day to work in the harvest field in midsummer and to shuck corn in the late fall. Mr. Krause obtained work in the town of Exeter. He applied for work on the railroad line they were laying, they found him not able to do this heavy work so he planted and cultivated gardens for the families who were working on the railroad. This job meant for him about a 20 mile walk at weekends. There was not much pleasure in those long walks in the early days as on a starless night one could very easily be walking around in circles and get nowhere. I remember Mother putting several slices of bread in her pocket and going to meet him when he had not arrived home by dark.

The older children contributed toward living expenses by working for neighbors and friends at herding cattle or minding younger children, earning their clothes, room and board. Herding cattle was assigned to youngsters as there were few fences. I remember the task in the summer when the tall grass hid numerous snakes and in the winter when the ground was cold to walk on, ofttimes covered with ice and snow.

My grandmother wrote nothing about who was doing the family's own farm work during the years (at least ten and probably more) that her parents and siblings worked away from home. The oldest child, the only son, no doubt did a great deal of it, along with his mother and older sisters, since Anton Krause's health never allowed him to do much hard labor. In her brief memoir, my grandmother wrote at greatest length about the strong musical tradition in her family and about her father's accomplishments as a musician. She mentioned Karolina Krause's "clear soprano voice" and the happy memories she had of her parents and the family singing together at their chores. In contrast, the hard work they all did to accomplish the family goal of landownership she depicted only in the matter-of-fact way seen above. She took this so much for granted, I think, that she did not linger on those more negative memories.[37]

In America, women were important as wage earners both before and after marriage. Their savings enabled them to marry and begin farming, much as had been the case in Europe. For instance, "Wieschen Schröder Swehn," the wife of "Jürnjakob Swehn," saved the money she earned as an Iowa farm worker for two and a half years. Her $200, added to her husband's $350, allowed them to start farming. Others continued the work they had trained for, if this could be done along with their domestic work. Nurses and midwives like Mary Cresence Berhalter Maichel found plenty of opportunity to practice their professions. From her homestead southwest of Lawrence, Kansas, she continued to practice the nursing she had learned in a Württemberg hospital. Margaret Hiebert Schroeder, a German Mennonite from Russia who immigrated to Kansas, is an unusual example of a rural professional immigrant woman. She studied medicine in America in fulfillment of a vow she made to God. After beginning her practice in 1900 at the age of forty-two, she presided at fifteen hundred births. Gesche Mahnken Block, one of the founders of the German Lutheran community of Block, Kansas, served as the district's midwife and general health care deliverer until her death in 1911. She was highly respected by area doctors as well as her patients. In the forty-two years of her work as midwife in the Block area, only four stillborn births were recorded. Within three years after her death, seven women were delivered of stillborn babies. A recent study by Charlotte Borst identifies European birthing traditions and the readiness with which midwifery lent itself to integration in a woman's domestic life as reasons for its prominence as a profession for immigrant wives and mothers.[38]

So many women took in washing, sewing, and boarders at one time or another that they cannot be enumerated here. A striking example worth mentioning is Maria Bayer Pelzer, who took her baby along when she worked as a domestic and field hand and then kept house for a year for a widower with seven children, as well as for a single man and her own husband and child. In some areas, women developed cottage industries to earn extra income. As had been true in Europe and for women of American parentage, as long as they had a husband, their paid activities were considered supplemental, however. On rare occasions, if their husband was unable to support them, they might seek work publicly, as did a Mrs. Glaubitz of Hillsboro, Kansas, in 1888. She wanted sewing work to tide the family over until her husband could find work.[39] Like Mrs. Glaubitz, women generally did only work that could be considered an extension of their domestic functions and that was in keeping with the female roles acceptable in their time and culture.[40]

The same was true of the domestic work their daughters did to supplement the family income. Such work was in demand, in the country as well as in the towns and cities. Hired girls in America usually did only housework, even on farms. Countless immigrants wrote home, urging sisters and other single women to come to America, where they could earn decent wages without having to do the heavy labor and live under the close personal control that was typical in German-speaking lands. Katarina Wolf Tiek's sister Maria Wolf Förschler wrote her twenty-four-year old sister, Mina, who had stayed with their parents in Germany: "Dear Mina, you write that you have to work hard. I believe you, because I was also stiff from work when I left my homeland. Here I don't need to guide the oxen and stumble around all day in the field like I had to do at home. Here it is better for you, Mina."[41] Much as they might have done in Europe, girls like Maria Wolf were learning and practicing the skills they would need someday in their own households. At the same time, they often gained language and domestic skills that would ease their and their family's adaptation to the new culture. If they gave their wages to their parents, young rural women were also ensuring their future inheritance. The comparatively high pay and reasonable working conditions, the relative lack of restrictions on behavior, and the freedom of movement from one job to another made work as servants appealing to German-speakers at a time when Anglo-Americans considered it degrading.[42]

One rare instance of illicit activity by a rural German-speaking family should be noted as an acknowledgement of the potential for variety among the immigrants. This family, the so-called bloody Benders of Kansas, included a son and a beautiful young daughter, Kate. In 1871, the family set up a grocery store and offered meals and lodging. A year later, Kate advertised her healing and spiritualistic gifts in a flyer. After the family precipitously departed by train in April 1873, nine bodies were discovered on the family premises. In a way, Kate, too, thought to be the bait attracting hapless men who were then killed and robbed and whom the early twentieth-century account paints in lurid colors as a bloodthirsty seductress, was working in traditional, if unacceptable, female ways for her family. The Benders were not, of course, typical rural residents, yet we cannot be sure that their deadly family business was not a way-station to a more respectable farm, though it is unlikely. They were never brought to justice.[43]

More typical rural German-speaking women contributed to the family economy in less colorful ways. Much of what they did was unpaid and involved production for the family's own consumption. Some spun wool for stockings and operated looms to weave linen and carpets. All of them sewed the family clothes and made quilts, blankets, and curtains. Until the latter decades of the century, women did this all by hand. Later, a sewing machine was likely to be the single mechanized piece of equipment a farm woman had. The cost of a sewing machine fell to about $30 by 1870, which made it affordable for family use (although some farm women had to pay more than twice that, perhaps because of transportation costs). When we remember that the price for a cow at that time was $18–20, however, it is not difficult to imagine that many farm families would have thought long and hard about making such a large investment.[44] Women who got this coveted item often let their neighbors use it. This could be an opportunity to visit or, at times, an imposition. Such sharing also reveals the community network of family and friends. Most German-speaking women probably loaned their sewing machines to or did sewing for other German-speakers only, as did Ulrike Gellhorn in Iowa, for instance.[45]

Some husbands gave their wives a sewing machine after a good harvest or upon the sale of livestock. Other women earned the cash for it themselves with their butter and egg money. Unless the family farm emphasized dairy or poultry production, this income was usually a woman's to manage, although it was almost always used for the benefit of the family. Butter and egg money bought the staples (flour, sugar, salt, coffee, calico, and the like) that the family could not produce, it paid the taxes in a lean year, and it made small improvements to the home possible. One woman decided to buy a dress with the money that she had saved, penny by penny, to buy tar paper for a roof for the family soddy. Another paid the bill on her husband's wedding suit.[46] This female income served as a cushion against the unpredictability of the grain market. In 1888, one woman wrote from Kansas that high egg and poultry prices would help offset the low prices the family could get for their grain harvest.[47] On a diversified farm, a woman's income could make up a substantial proportion of the family resources. This was true well into the twentieth century, as my own grandmother proved.[48]

The 1880 agriculture census offers provocative evidence that women's egg and butter income was more than mere "chicken feed." In Warren and St. Charles counties in Missouri, where many German-speakers farmed, small amounts of milk were sold to factories (144 and 30 gallons, respectively). Farm women produced large amounts of butter, however: 263,278 pounds in Warren County and 207,941 in St. Charles County. On farms in St. Charles County, women had also made 10,100 pounds of cheese. During the same year, barnyard poultry in Warren County had produced 369,167 dozen eggs, and those in St. Charles County, 430,882 dozen. The proximity to markets, geography, and other factors no doubt influenced the extent to which women and their families engaged in such production. The German-speakers in Marion County, Kansas, for instance, probably participated in that area's relatively intensive dairy production, as indicated by the 58,238 gallons of milk sold to factories in 1880 (produced by 3,086 milk cows, 2,470 fewer than in St. Charles County). At the same time, the women in Marion County must have been heavily engaged in the production of butter and cheese: 439,616 and 14,321 pounds, respectively. The same can be said of the German-speaking residents of Clinton County, Iowa, where 18,079 milk cows produced 373,026 gallons of milk sold to factories, barnyard poultry laid 491,609 dozen eggs, and farm women made 1,394,707 pounds of butter.[49]

Women's cash earnings were probably generally more important than the women, their husbands, or their children realized, although once in a while one comes across the acknowledgement that a woman's butter or egg production "kept the family from starving."[50] On occasion, the importance of women's traditional sources of income is indicated by the fact that the husband took credit for them. Friedrich G. Hillenkamp, for instance, wrote that *he* had planted an apple and peach orchard that produced enough fruit to warrant a trip to St. Louis, and when *he* took the fruit to market, *he* could take along several hundred dozen eggs, for which *he* could buy the necessary household things.[51] The language of this text reveals the power relations in some immigrant families. Everyone took for granted that women would contribute to the establishment and maintenance of the family enterprise and that this did not necessarily grant them power or even ownership of the returns on their production. The everyday, domestic nature of women's contributions also helped mask their significance. Nevertheless, some women no doubt gained some claim to autonomy through the money they earned. This might have been partly why some men thought of such earnings disparagingly as "pin money" and resented the time their wives gave to their churning and chickens instead of to field work or other livestock.[52] The traditional separation of a woman's income from a man's in rural society also helps explain why my grandmother kept her income in "female space," a crock in the cellar. Her wish to maintain control over it was probably also the reason that she kept it "hidden" from my grandfather, even though he must have known where it was and would not have been likely to take any of it from her anyway.

All farm women, with the help of children, tended large gardens, for food production was one of their most important activities. They planted, weeded, watered, and hoed the plants and then harvested the fruit and vegetables when they were ripe. Some produce was stored away as it was, but large quantities had to be preserved in some fashion. In the late nineteenth century, as the process became less expensive, women began to can much of their produce. On butchering days, women supervised the making of the sausages and headcheese that German-speaking families enjoyed.[53]

The children might take extra foodstuffs to sell in town. Women, however, often bartered among themselves and with merchants for what they wanted. One woman caught her biggest turkey and sent it to town with her son in exchange for the other groceries needed for a Thanksgiving dinner. Another traded the thirty pounds of butter and the fourteen seven-pound cheeses she had made for a wagonload of apples, a kraut cutter, a sausage cutter, and a raincoat. Louise Nickel, a milliner in Hillsboro, Kansas, declared her willingness to take eggs in payment for her work.[54] With hard work, good management, and luck, a woman could supplement her family's income and diet in important ways without leaving home.[55]

In spite of the immense amount of work they did, women in rural areas were in some ways better off than their city sisters. To judge by Dorothee Schneider's study of working-class families in New York in the early 1880s, most married German-American women in the urban areas did not earn wages, unlike the women in many other working-class families. Their families were consequently worse off than Anglo-American families. Some of the New York families who responded to a newspaper inquiry about their weekly budget were eating only somewhat better than they had in Germany, with potatoes still forming the staple of their diet.[56] In contrast, rural women could earn extra money without "going out" to work. The low percentage of foreign-born women between the ages of sixteen and thirty-four working for wages in agricultural pursuits compared with native-born women indicates that young women in this age group, when they were likely to have small children, did not willingly work outside the home. Rural German-speaking women's cash earnings through butter, eggs, and produce sales, however, gave them some autonomy and authority and helped the family progress. Rural families also benefited immediately, since they ate better for less because of this unpaid labor.

Women sometimes also played a role in the success of the family venture by acquiring or maintaining property on their own. One woman was awarded one share of the capital stock of a Nebraska town company, equal to ten average lots in the town, "in recognition of her true pioneering spirit in being the first woman to locate in Columbus."[57] More common were German-speaking women's accomplishments as independent farmers. It almost always was a widow who sought to secure or maintain a future for her family in this way. It is likely that most of the successful female farmers had spent time on an American farm before feeling confident enough to tackle one on their own. To succeed, their children, whether boys or girls, had to be old enough to help. Two such Kansas widows, women "of physical vigor and forceful will," managed to run large farms with the help of young children or daughters. After her husband had an incapacitating stroke, an Iowa woman acted as hired man and girl both" and did all the farming with a son for the next sixteen years. A few young widows with little children managed to stick it out long enough, with help from neighbors or relatives, to meet the obligations of residence and property improvements necessary "to prove up" on a homestead.[58]

After passage of the Homestead Act in 1862, single women and female heads of households could gain 160 acres of land by residing on and improving it over a five-year period. Given the attraction land had for German-speaking immigrants, we might expect that the women among them would have taken advantage of this opportunity in numbers at least proportional to their presence in rural areas and certainly proportional to those of Anglo-American female homesteaders. H. Elaine Lindgren has estimated that in the last four decades of the nineteenth century, women gained title to approximately 5 to 10 percent of the land acquired through homesteading, preemption, or timber culture in the Great Plains. The percentage increased as the century came to a close and grew to as much as 15 and even 30 percent in some areas of the Dakotas after 1900. In an analysis of several townships in North Dakota, however, Lindgren found that German-born women were unlikely to take advantage of the Homestead Act in the first two decades after it went into effect. Women in groups that immigrated somewhat later, like the Germans from Russia, were more likely to do so, unless they were Catholic. The differences among the various ethnic groups and subgroups in Lindgren's sample became relatively insignificant as time went on. Lindgren concludes that ethnicity played a complex role in these patterns and in the lives of individual women. Certainly German-speaking women shared their men's hunger for land. While some of them might have homesteaded as agents for men—their fathers or future husbands, for instance—others did it for themselves and for the family members dependent on them. More work needs to be done in this area of ethnic American women's history, as in so many others, before the cultural influences are clear.[59]

Inheritance is another fuzzy area. One woman believed her father was "unusually progressive" for having divided his property equally "among the boys *and girls,* not just among the boys as so many Germans did."[60] There is collaborative evidence that males were favored over females in inheritance in the families of German-speakers. Daughters received less land than sons, or they received cash, livestock, and household goods instead of land. For example, when the children of Claus Sieck, a Schleswig farmer, received their inheritance in Iowa in the 1870s, the sons were able to pay off twice as much on their American farms as the daughters did.[61] There is evidence to the contrary as well, though. A study of one area of Illinois has shown that German-Americans from the Frisian moorlands, where partible inheritance was traditional, continued the practice of dividing the land equally among all the siblings. To accomplish this, while at the same time perpetuating the tradition of farming within the family, the number of children was kept small after the first generation, and parents retired early. Other studies of the same area by the same author show that ethnically derived family and farming choices and goals, repeated over several generations, explain the contemporary replication of early farming patterns (i.e., relatively small, diversified farms) among German-Americans there.[62]

The Old World custom of parents' retiring early and passing on their land to heirs persisted elsewhere in America, even into the second generation, as my grandparents proved. Kamphoefner's study in Missouri showed that "only about half of all German men over 60 were still heads of households, compared to three-fourths of such Americans."[63] The Germans from Russia primarily practiced male ultimogeniture, although one source indicates that in the Black Sea colonies, men and women could inherit equally. Whether they actually did so has not been verified.[64] European traditions probably influenced inheritance among German-speakers in America, although the extent to which that was the case is unclear and no doubt varied greatly. The homogeneity of the immigrant community would have been an important factor in the perpetuation of such customs.[65]

American tradition and force of law also played a role. The American pattern of equal inheritance was, by and large, congenial to German-speakers. Whether they came from traditions of partible or impartible inheritance, the idea of attempting to treat all children equally was widespread, although in practice inequities had been the rule. Now they had the opportunity of fulfilling that ideal without having to pass on a family holding diminished by having been split into many smaller pieces. The hard work and family cooperative effort could result in the accumulation of enough land for all the children.[66]

To provide additional insight into inheritance patterns among German-speaking immigrants, I conducted a study of the wills of immigrants who came to Cooper County, Missouri, in the nineteenth century. I identified the individuals and families by searching through an early twentieth-century county commemorative history. Then I located their wills or other related documents, to the extent that such existed, in the county probate court archives.[67] I included individuals and families who had engaged in activities other than farming in the study, since the largest town, Boonville, remained an essentially rural community throughout the nineteenth century. In any case, farming, either as the main occupation or as a second family enterprise, was the dominant way of life for at least 90 percent of those included in the study. My search yielded 101 documents, dating between 1854 and 1957, of which 18 related to the estates of individuals (12 men and 6 women) who had died intestate. Of the remaining 83, 69 involved the wills of men and 14 those of women.

The higher number of men in the sample indicates the economic dominance of males, but this is somewhat deceptive. Fewer women than men wrote their own will, partly because married women in Missouri could not legally write a will until 1864. Women also had no property rights in the state until 1875. Before this, a woman could own land, but all rent and earnings from it were her husband's to control, as were her wages and any personal property she might have brought into the marriage. Not until 1889 could a married woman own and control her own real estate and be held liable for her own debts. It was therefore customary for the husband's will to be written in such a way as to dispose of the couple's property after the wife's death, should he predecease her. Thirty of the men whose wives were still living at the time the wills were written left their spouses a life interest in the estate, and many expressed confidence in their wives' ability and willingness to manage the estate to the advantage of the children. Others who divided the family property included provisions for the wife: a child's share (five), considerable sums in the form of notes or money to be put out at interest (six), or a part of the property greater than that of a child's share (two). Where the couple's personal property was mentioned, the wife inherited all or part of it in all except one case. These provisions demonstrate an intention to provide for widows. That twenty-nine of the fifty-two men still married to the mothers of their children named their wives as executors of their estates also indicates these men's confidence in their wives' administrative abilities.

Some of the wills specify how the settling of the estate was to proceed in order to clear debts owed it by children or to repay services children had performed. Many of the immigrants, however, split their property in ways that seem, at least on the surface, inequitable. One heir or more seems to be at an advantage in thirty-one of the wills men wrote and in eight of those written by women. Without doing an exhaustive study of land transfers and legal documents, however, I cannot be sure that what looks like inequities in a will are not attempts to make good on earlier advantages that other children had had in the form of loans for land purchase or sales of land (at low prices) to them. Given that caveat, however, certain patterns in these documents are reminiscent of European inheritance customs.

One man's will seems to be modeled on Old World *Altenteil* agreements, whereby the support of the retired farm couple was outlined. Georg Neff, who came to Cooper County in 1848 and died in November 1854, deeded his wife the "new house," half of the household furniture, and half of the livestock, while Jacob, the eldest of two sons, inherited the home farm and farm equipment. Jacob was also to give his mother one-third of the crops "free of expenses" and furnish and deliver her firewood and water free for the rest of her life. The similarity between this provision for Georg's widow and the typical third of the crops given the Midwest landlord indicates that German immigrants were probably often able to meet the cultural expectations and legal demands of their new society in regard to inheritance while disposing of their property according to the customs of their former homeland. Another Old World aspect of this will is the attempt to keep the family holdings intact while giving other children money or property of equal value. The will required Jacob to pay his brother half of the value of the farm and livestock when his brother came of age.[68]

The primacy of males in European peasant inheritance also shows up in the Cooper County wills. Fifteen men and four women wrote wills favoring one or more of their sons. The advantages male heirs enjoyed took a variety of forms. In a version of primogeniture, three parents encouraged the maintenance of the home place within the male line of the family by giving it outright to the oldest (or sole) son or by giving him the first option of buying it from his siblings. Therese Schmidt stated, "It is my wish and desire that my aforesaid farm, which for many years has been my homestead, shall continue to be owned by some member of my family, and therefore direct and will that in the event my said son . . . does not wish to purchase said farm as aforesaid, then a preference right to purchase said land is given to my second son." Although she also had two daughters, she did not expressly encourage them to buy the farm.[69]

Several fathers deeded land to sons but money to daughters. Sometimes the money gifts were close in value to the land given the sons, as when Wilhelm Kahle left each of his four older sons 100 to 140 acres, with the proviso that each had to pay one of his sisters $3,000. In a version of ultimogeniture, the home place was to be the youngest son's upon the death of Wilhelm's wife, Johanna, but he was to pay the youngest, as yet single, girl of the family $3,000. An additional 40 acres were given the five sons to share as they wished, while the couple's personal property was to remain Johanna's until her death, when the five daughters were to divide it. When Johanna died, however, twelve years after her husband, two of their five daughters had predeceased her. These women and their heirs therefore did not enjoy the advantage of that portion of the estate. In a similar instance, a father excluded two sons who had already received their share of the estate and divided what was left among his wife, three other sons, a daughter, and the children of a deceased daughter. The final settlement to each heir was just under $900. The excluded sons might have received more or less than this, but in any case they had had the use of their inheritance longer than their siblings had.[70]

Other documents also point to possible discrimination in favor of male heirs. Theobald Theiss deeded $5 to his married daughter, his house and personal property in the village Prairie Farm to his unmarried daughter, and 80 acres each to his two sons. Two other fathers gave their only sons large sums of money, while their four daughters shared the remaining cash or property. Another willed his youngest daughter $300 and his youngest son $600 "for their education."[71] Unequal treatment of female heirs existed in other cases but was not apparent in probate documents. One will, which on the surface appears to treat the man's three sons and two daughters equally, contains nothing about the three farms that the county history says he had sold to his sons.[72] Some women also seem to have favored their sons. One had inherited $7,000 from her husband. She left $1,000 to each of her four sons and the widow of the fifth, $500 to her daughter, and everything else to her third son and his family. Another gave her oldest son $2,000 and divided the rest of her estate equally among her children.[73]

Such documents indicate that legacy traditions tended to disadvantage women in German-speaking families in America. Their economic vulnerability is revealed in other ways as well. Four wills attempt to protect a daughter's inheritance from her husband's debts or control. Blasius Efinger specified that the cash and real estate given his oldest child, daughter Louise Friedrich, "shall be held and owned by her as her separate estate, to her sole, separate and exclusive use and benefit, free from all control of her husband and from any interest of her husband." Whether such stipulations were totally successful is another question. Blasius Efinger died in 1904. In the Cooper County commemorative history book published a few years later, his home place was said to belong to Charles Friedrich, Louise's husband.[74] This may, of course, be merely a convention of speech rather than an indication of authority and power. Charles and Louise Friedrich did not write wills, evidently having divested themselves of their property before their deaths, so we cannot know if Louise exercised some control over the family real estate she inherited. That four fathers in my survey attempted to protect family property from sons-in-law reveals women's economic subordination to their husbands and the desire to keep family holdings intact. In only one will were restrictions placed on the property bequeathed a son. In that case, too, the father apparently intended to protect the continuity of the family land. He entrusted the son's inherited property to the latter's older brother to keep the younger man, who was financially delinquent, from squandering his legacy.[75]

In other instances, daughters seem to have been favored. In seven of the nine such cases, however, their larger inheritances were probably due to their having cared for their aged parent(s). A telling example is that of Andrew Steigleder. He willed his wife $2,000 that he had gotten from her, perhaps as a dowry, as well as a life interest in his property. His three sons and four married daughters were then to share the estate after a seventy-acre farm had been set aside for his single daughter, Louvenia, "on account of her staying at home so long and keeping house for me, and having no home."[76] Another man, however, gave one of his two daughters $1 as her share in his estate: "I do this because of [sic] my daughter, Margaret, has not shown to me and to her mother during her lifetime, the love and affection that I feel a daughter should show to her parents."[77]

The wills of the women in the study tended to be somewhat more personal and idiosyncratic documents than those of the men. Whereas thirty-eight of the sixty-nine wills by men specified the equal distribution of the property or equal awards of money to all the children (although many of these were token gifts of $1 to $5 to minor children), only one of the women did so, and her estate was so diminished when she died that four of her children had to split the settlement costs.[78] Most of the women were left with only small estates of cash or personal property at the time of their death, which perhaps explains why they felt they could designate the recipients of personal items without being grossly unfair to their children. An interesting example is that of Sophia King. The terms of her husband's will had determined the disposition of most of her estate. John King had left eighty acres to each of his heirs: his son, his four daughters, and his wife, with the latter piece of property to revert to Lizzie Toellner, the only child of a deceased daughter, upon Sophia's death. Further, Sophia was to have a lifetime use of two forty-acre pieces of land, which their only son could then buy from the other heirs upon his mother's death. The legacy of one daughter, Ella Toellner, was to be kept free of her husband's debts and passed on to only her "bodily heirs."[79] Four years later Sophia wrote a will in which she specified:

> I direct that my large brass kettle and the large family bible, and all meat that may be on hand at the time of my death, shall be kept on the place I now occupy, for use of the family after my death. I further direct that all the carpets and rugs which may be on the floor of the dwelling house I now occupy, shall remain thereon after my death. I give and bequeath the two large pictures of myself and my late husband John King, dec'd, unto Ella Toellner, if she be living at the time of my death, if not, then said pictures to remain in the dwelling house I now occupy. I further direct that the pictures of my father and mother now on the wall of my said dwelling house shall remain thereon after my death. I give, and bequeath unto my said grand-daughter, Lizzie Toellner, six dozen chickens, one cow, and one hog, and sufficient feed to keep the same until she can get some feed of her own for that purpose. I further direct that all my fruit which may be in the cellar at the time of my death, shall remain therein for family use.[80]

This is certainly a much more personal listing of bequests than that in John King's will. Sophia King's desire to set her granddaughter up as a farm wife is apparent. Her directions about the family bible and the pictures of her parents show she also was concerned about family continuity on a subjective level. Her bequest of the pictures of herself and her husband to her daughter Ella Toellner might also have been a gesture of reconciliation, to soothe any ruffled feelings John King's will might have caused.[81]

The problems associated with inheritance in Europe could not be avoided in America. Strife among children was no doubt common, even with their parents' attempt at equality. For example, John Schnuck left everything to his wife, with $2,100 to be given each child when they came of age or "started in life for themselves." Some of these payments were made, but when John's wife's estate was settled, the widow of a deceased son had to sue the other heirs, his siblings, to get her husband's share.[82]

Other problems associated with property distribution also appear in this sample of wills. Even in America, where land-hungry immigrants had the opportunity to accumulate real estate, families did not always avoid the injustices and financial dangers of partible inheritance patterns. Louis Roth deeded all of his property to his wife, Mary. After her death, his oldest son was to inherit a 200–acre farm and the oldest daughter 80 acres. His two youngest sons, Frank and Fred, were to inherit the 160–acre home place, but this farm was encumbered with a $700 lien as the inheritance of Louis's second daughter and with a lien of $2,000 for his second son. The four youngest children were to divide the personal property in the estate. Mary died soon after Louis, and the couple's personal property was appraised—at $29.85. This German-born couple had lived economically to accumulate 440 acres of Missouri farmland. They had also committed their sons Frank and Fred to similar lives of frugality to pay off the debts incurred in dividing the value of the estate without dividing the real estate holdings.[83]

On the basis of this sampling, we cannot be sure to what extent German-speakers were influenced by the legacy traditions of their homeland. Probably the prevailing inheritance customs in the area in which they settled as well as the land transfer patterns they were used to in Europe affected their behavior in America.[84] It may be significant that in two cases, a mother administered her dead husband's estate for minor children and then seems to have passed it on to them intact, without taking the child's share to which she was entitled by Missouri law. In both cases, the mother had remarried. The self-sacrificing behavior encouraged in German-speaking women by their culture may be showing up here.[85] What does seem clear from the wills included in this study is that women as a group tended to be at a disadvantage when it came to inheritance. German-speaking immigrants passed on land to sons more often than to daughters and in greater quantities to male heirs. A significant number of the documents also show women's inferior legal and traditional status regarding property rights.

Studies of the agricultural Midwest have posed a variety of questions about the influence of ethnicity on concrete aspects of settlement among rural German-speakers. Were the immigrants influenced by the type of soil and the geographic lay of the land available to them? Did they come to frontier areas later than Anglo-Americans and choose improved rather than unimproved land where possible? Were they more mobile and more likely to be renters than Anglo-Americans were? Did they retain European farming practices and crop production? Were they more discouraged by the inhospitable qualities of the Great Plains environment than other groups were?[86] Generally, these studies have found few significant differences between German-speakers and other frontier settlers, except in isolated instances of communities founded by homogenous groups of religiously motivated immigrants. The following sections examine the ways in which rural German-speaking women were affected by concrete aspects of their new environment and identify areas of the frontier experience in which they and their compatriots differed from the population at large.

Like everyone else in the Midwest, German-speakers often settled on isolated farms. This was probably more difficult for women than men, since women did not come into contact with the outside world as often.[87] The German-speaking immigrants, however, made the same accommodations to this aspect of their new environment as other settlers, often locating their farmstead across the road from or at a corner of the farm close to the residence of their neighbors. In some areas, immigrants formed string villages, like those they were familiar with at home, but for the most part they responded to the constraints of land division as everyone else in the Midwest did.[88]

Similarly, German-speakers adjusted to geographic and climatic differences. Many letters comment on the discomfort those born in the cool, temperate European climate suffered during their first Midwest summer. One woman put it this way: "I was completely done in much of the time. Everyone who comes from Germany has a hard time the first summer because of the great heat."[89] The immigrants also suffered from other aspects of the Midwest climate. The spectacular lightning and thunderstorms of the prairies and plains were new and often frightening. The Swiss-born Louise Ritter wrote that "the sky looked like fire, and the thunder rumbled constantly so that we trembled all the time." An Ursuline nun on the edge of St. Louis wrote of one thunderstorm that lasted three days.[90]

Other German-speakers found the new landscape uncongenial. Swiss Benedictine sisters asked their mother convent to send a picture of the "dear mountains" of their homeland, and the same nuns complained of the constant winds on the wide-open northwest Missouri prairie.[91] Some women wept in despair upon confronting the "Great American Desert." Karoline Glass Zerfass, a Bukovinia German immigrant to Ellis County in June 1893, lay down weeping on the dry Kansas ground and rolled about in despair, crying, "Why did we leave our good home? What are we going to do here? We're going to starve!" Later, during the trip from their first home—a dugout—to their next—a dilapidated sod house—Karoline was frightened by her first sight of fireflies and cried out, "See, that's the devil! There it is! What are we doing in this country?" The Zerfasses, like most other immigrants, did not have the funds to return to the green, forested, rolling plains of their homeland.[92]

In spite of such anecdotes, German-speakers were no less willing than other ethnic groups to face these new elements. The extreme climate and geography of the Great Plains did not unduly discourage most of them. Indeed, many Germans from Russia were quite familiar with such conditions because of their long sojourn on the steppes, so they were particularly successful. They are credited with having developed in Russia and then introduced in America the hardy red winter wheat that helped make Kansas and the other Great Plains states the breadbasket of the nation. E. P. Hutchinson found that in 1920 the first- and second-generation Germans from Russia were especially heavily represented in the Dakotas (two to four times the national average for that group). Only the Scandinavian stock constituted an equally strong segment of the population in these states. The concentration of the first- and second-generation German stock was also well above the national average in the Great Plains states in 1920, except in Kansas, where it nonetheless approached the national average.[93]

On the frontier, woman's domain—the home—was likely to be a primitive log cabin or even a sod house or dugout. The cost or simple unavailability of finished building materials made other types of construction difficult if not impossible in many areas. Such living conditions were particularly discouraging for women who had been used to decent residences in Europe.[94] Others from more modest economic backgrounds were probably less taken aback by these primitive shelters. Many women of the poorer classes had lived miserably in Europe, so they probably found conditions comparable in America. Educated Germans and Anglo-Americans were often disgusted by the poor and dirty living conditions of such immigrants.[95] Most women, however, found they were generally too busy in the early years to be very concerned with careful housekeeping anyway. Nevertheless, many found it difficult to adjust to dugouts and sod houses. Louisa Bartsch, for example, first saw the family dugout during a heavy rain, when part of the roof had washed in and a foot of water stood in the recessed floor. Only after her husband had bailed out the water and settled the children did she agree "to enter, and take up the duties of a homesteader's wife."[96] Like other frontierswomen, the German-speakers complained of the creatures with whom they had to share these dwellings and the tendency of the roof to drip mud during rains. A sod house could also be a dangerous place, for sometimes large animals fell through the top or the structure would collapse in a storm. Elizabeth Ewy Hirschler's aunt was killed when the main beam supporting the sod house roof fell on her during a heavy rain, and Elizabeth herself, several months pregnant, hurt her leg badly. It is no wonder she was deeply depressed for some time after this.[97]

German-speaking women generally accepted sod houses and dugouts as necessary and temporary housing on the timberless Great Plains, though. Sometimes they even appreciated their practical qualities: dirt floors that did not warp as cottonwood planks did and cool solidity in the hot summer winds.[98] Sod houses also were warmer in winter than the tar-paper shacks or plank houses that women had thought would be an improvement. There are many stories of snow sifting through the chinks in such walls and of entire families going to bed for days at a time to stay warm. Caroline Emanuel and her mother took turns lying in bed with Caroline's first baby to keep her warm enough to survive the winter of 1870 in a drafty Nebraska wooden house. The family eventually put bricks and plaster on the inside walls of the house, and Caroline bore thirteen more children there before they moved, twenty-some years later, into a ten-room house.[99]

Accessibility to water was one of the frontierswoman's main concerns. Like Anglo-American women, German-speakers thought themselves lucky if they had reliable running water or a well close at hand. Still, carrying water for household use as well as for gardens and livestock was one of the heaviest chores women and children did. Testimony at a North Carolina Farmers Alliance meeting in 1886 indicated that a woman walked more than 150 miles a year fetching and carrying water for household use if her well or spring was sixty yards from the house.[100] Wells could also give out in dry weather. Emilie Joss-Bigler remembered a summer when all seven wells on her widowed mother's Illinois farm went dry. One night a voice awakened her: "There in the moonlight stood her mother, dressed in her Swiss national costume which she wore only for important occasions, telling God what it was like to have seven dry wells and no water. She was praying for rain."[101] Women like Elizabeth Bigler would have had at the least an ironic smile for Gottfried Duden's idyllic description of how everything, even wash day, was more pleasant in the Missouri woods: "For most of the harder work of housekeeping there are ways of making the labor easier. If, for instance, laundry is to be done, a fire is lighted next to a near-by brook and a kettle is hung over it. The bleaching ground cannot be far away either, and it is a matter of course that during the summer a shady place is chosen."[102] As one might guess, Duden was not speaking from personal experience here. He had a manservant to take care of such tasks for him.

In general, the adjustment to the prairies of Illinois, Missouri, and Iowa was not as difficult for settlers as adjusting to the Great Plains. There, in the "Great American Desert," scarceness of water, the vagaries of the weather, invasions of grasshoppers, the danger of prairie fire, and the treeless landscape posed particular challenges that not all cared to meet. Mary Wall Regier's family was finishing its frame house when a Kansas wind and hail storm struck, flattening the house and the wheat crop and injuring Mary and her brother. She remembered well that her family and others they knew would have gladly returned to Russia, had they had the means.[103] All areas of the Midwest frontier could try the mettle of farmers. Some immigrants had the support of strong religious faith to help them face setbacks. A diary kept by David and Katherine (Strohm) Ruth, members of a group of Mennonite families that settled in Iowa, contains the following passage from 1855:

> About two weeks before harvest time a small insect they called bugs (probably chinch bugs) came in millions and covered the ground, even in the houses they covered the walls and we were inclined to feel sorrowful as they reminded us of the Egyptian plague. They attacked the fine looking stand of wheat and in a few days sapped this so that it lost its strength, bleached to a deadly color and it soon was evident that only a few grains remained in the heads. This was not general through this section, our farm seemed to be one of those the most afflicted, oats too also yielded but very little, but we had a good crop of corn.
>
> About harvest time a continuous wet weather set in so that it was difficult and tiresome to harvest and take care of the grain. But thanks and praise be to the Lord, he has kept us and taken care of us and his will be done with us in the future.[104]

Other women and men had a sense of adventure or humor to help them face the difficulties of the frontier. One German-born woman prided herself on the prairie fires she had helped fight. Christian Krehbiel made his wife and family laugh about their economic woes with exaggerated assertions about their hopeful future. "Jürnjakob" and "Wieschen Swehn" joked about "not believing in" wooden corner posts anymore after one in their log cabin broke during an Iowa blizzard. After that they built a stone house.[105]

No matter what their ethnic heritage, those pioneers who settled in the Great Plains region and survived its harshness came to be marked by the culture its ecology shaped. The climate and landscape directly determined many aspects of Great Plains culture. Indirectly, the market pressures of the cash economy that evolved there early because of the restricted crop-growing possibilities also played a role. Vulnerability to these influences caused the inhabitants of this region to develop a fatalistic attitude toward their own efforts, evident in the Ruths' diary entry quoted above. At the same time, they came to redefine success in terms of perseverance and self-reliance. John Ise's *Sod and Stubble* and Mari Sandoz's *Old Jules* are great chronicles of the simple endurance immigrants (and others) found necessary to "succeed" on the Great Plains frontier.[106]

In many respects, people on the frontier responded to their environment in similar ways. What differences did exist between Anglo-American and German-speaking farmers often were due to the persistence of Old World agricultural habits and family production methods. An important study of agricultural practice in Nebraska in 1880 indicates that immigrant farmers did not hesitate to change their traditional crop production in response to new environmental demands. Differences in the extent to which Nebraska Germans and Germans from Russia raised small grains (wheat, in particular) might have been culturally determined, though.[107]

To some degree, other differences in agricultural practice between German-speaking immigrants and Anglo-Americans were due to certain patterns in women's roles. Many scholars have noted that the farms of German-speakers were generally more diversified than those of Anglo-Americans and that the tendency to cling to subsistence or yeoman farming typified these immigrants. In my view, this is connected to the centrality of women in farm production among German-speakers. A Nebraska study shows that German-American farmers had more poultry and cattle and were more likely to raise swine and sheep than were Anglo-Americans. This probably had to do with the traditional importance of female agricultural and domestic production as well as cultural and culinary preferences. Women, we should remember, were usually responsible for farm animals in German-speaking lands. A relatively large but diversified investment in livestock reflects certain expectations about women's participation in that sector of agricultural production.[108]

German-speaking women's support of the continuation of certain aspects of subsistence domestic production influenced farming practices in various ways. They wanted sheep's wool for the stockings many of them knit, for example. In some areas, they had their husbands plant flax for the production of homespun clothing. Since many German-speakers considered alcoholic beverages an inherent part of their diet, they grew the grapes necessary for their own wine.[109] No garden would have been complete without potatoes. German-speakers did not add some new foodstuffs, like sweet potatoes and native game, to their diet.[110]

The literature for immigrants, written almost solely by men and intended primarily for men and male enterprises, seldom gave women specific advice on how to accomplish the many demanding and often new tasks facing them.[111] Self-reliant, subsistence farming in the early years of settlement, without the support of the Old World village, meant a reversion to old methods of food and clothing production for many women. Some of them, wives of skilled laborers or of middle-class professionals, for example, were not familiar with these methods. All European immigrant women had to learn how to deal with new situations and new materials, either from American women or from country-women who had immigrated earlier.[112] This was sometimes difficult. The wives of the Latin farmers had to learn how to milk cows and cook over an open fire, sometimes with discouraging results. Most German-speakers found corn, that staple Midwest grain, unpalatable, but women had to learn how to use it, even in noodles and pancakes. Baking bread was also new to some women, and the "right" flour and even familiar leavening were not always available.[113] The process for making soap had to be learned, and once mastered, it became part of the activities frugal German-speaking housewives engaged in during the annual hog butchering.[114]

In their primary sphere of influence—the home—German-speaking women accommodated themselves to the pressures of their new environment through hard work and the willingness to accept what could not be altered. This strategy, which worked well for the family's general adaptation to American conditions, also helped women lead meaningful and productive lives in spite of the many changes in their domestic arrangements.

Outside of the home, however, immigrant women had less control of their new environment. This could have frightening and even dangerous aspects, though few German-speaking women in the Midwest suffered the fate of Stine Lauritzen and a young Mrs. Weichel. Stine Lauritzen was killed and scalped in a raid by Cheyenne Indians in the

Kansas Salina River valley in 1869. In the same uprising, Mrs. Weichel's husband was also killed, and she was captured, just a week after their arrival in Kansas. When the cavalry caught up with the Cheyennes a few weeks later, Mrs. Weichel was seriously wounded in the battle to free her. Although many German-speaking women (like their Anglo-American sisters) were terrified of Indians, most contacts they had with Native Americans were harmless.[115]

Conflict of a different kind had its origins in American society and politics. The Know-Nothing movement was not felt as strongly in the Midwest as elsewhere. This area was not yet heavily settled by German-speakers in the 1850s, and the movement had its most violent expressions in urban areas. Other political and social forces, however, did play an important role in the lives of German-speakers. Abolition was one of these. German-speaking immigrants were usually not slaveholders.[116] Slavery violated their basic belief in personal liberty, an ideal many associated with their immigration to America. The extension of slavery into the western territories through the 1854 Kansas-Nebraska Bill also threatened the opportunities for immigrants in that area. Most were therefore firm supporters of the Union cause, which made them particular targets of attack by rebel troops and guerrillas. Elise Dubach Isely remembered tension between Anglo-Americans and immigrants in Kansas in the 1850s because immigrants could take out naturalization papers after a six month residence, which made them voters in Kansas or Nebraska under the 1854 bill. In their Doniphan County homestead area, a friendly neighbor warned the German-Swiss Dubachs and other "Free-Soilers" to put a white cloth on their chimney to fool border ruffians into thinking they were Anglo-Americans and proslavery. Conflicts of this sort did widow some German-speaking women, and others lost their husbands, sons, and brothers in the German Union regiments that were formed in the Civil War. In one Missouri incident in 1862, a woman's English language skills helped her gain her Lutheran minister husband's release after he and several German men had been captured in a Rebel bushwhacker raid. The other Germans were shot.[117]

Two other political and social issues in the American arena were more immediately pertinent to women: woman suffrage and temperance. It has been well documented that German-speakers did not support either movement. In general, it seems that women agreed with men on these issues. In keeping with their lack of involvement in public life, they rarely addressed such topics in their personal writings, although they could read a great deal about them in German-American publications. A riddle in the 1 August 1867 edition of the Missouri Synod Lutheran biweekly, *Die Abendschule,* indicates traditional attitudes toward the franchise for women:

> If only the first and the second [syllables] are the honor of a man and of the
> house,
> As the Scripture and reason so clearly prescribe to them:
> They surely don't intend to beg for the third and fourth,
> Which are of value to the citizen, but don't suit the apron.

The answer, given in the 15 August edition, was *Frauenstimmrecht,* "women's franchise." German-language publications carried numerous articles and features that communicated in greater detail the ethnic community's opposition to suffrage for women. On 26

January 1876, for example, the *Wöchentliche Kansas Freie Presse* in Leavenworth reported on the push for the vote in Iowa, connected this movement to temperance, and declared that the legislature was henpecked by the "tyrants" at home. In July of 1881, the *Kansas Staats-Anzeiger* (Atchison) ran sarcastic stories about *die halbverrückte, Blumenkleid-tragende Frauenrechtlerin* (the "half-crazy woman's rights advocate who wears flowered dresses") who wanted to run for the New York state senate. The *Nebraska Staats-Anzeiger* opposed suffrage on the grounds that women were liable to yield to control by clergymen and thus become political tools of the churches.[118] Bourgeois German-American views about the domestic and maternal nature of women and religious teachings about their roles no doubt negatively influenced German-speaking women's participation in the suffrage movement.[119] Anecdotal evidence underscores published proof of German-speaking men's opposition to suffrage. On one occasion, for instance, a man heckled woman's rights speakers on a Nebraska street and drowned them out by ringing a large bell and shouting, "Oh! the vimmins, the vimmins! You can hear them every day. Vat you vant to hear them now for?"[120]

Women's inaction suggests they shared men's attitudes toward woman suffrage and temperance. For example, there were very few German-American woman suffrage groups, and little if any contact between these (urban) groups and the American women's movement. There are no Germanic names on the membership lists of a variety of organizations in Kansas and Nebraska that advocated woman suffrage in the late nineteenth century. Recent studies conclude that the German-American press (with the exception of a few urban socialist publications) supported traditional gender roles for both men and women and offered almost no information about the American women's movement. It probably did not help that movement gain adherents among the immigrants when in the late nineteenth century some leaders of the suffrage movement argued that the franchise was needed to combat the foreign vote.[121]

Although German-speaking women were certainly aware of the abuses of alcohol and the extent to which some women and their families suffered from men's excessive indulgence, there is little evidence that they supported temperance. The weight of custom and tradition was much too strong for this movement to take hold among German-speakers, unless they were unaffiliated with the ethnic community or were among the few ethnic immigrants who eschewed alcoholic beverages for religious reasons. Beer and wine were an inherent part of the ethnic diet and social scene, and beer halls and beer gardens were gathering places for whole families on Sundays.[122] Such behavior institutionalized the enjoyment of alcohol as part of family life and made it, in the view of the ethnic community, relatively harmless. This was, of course, a source of tension and conflict with American society, but rural women were generally isolated from such contacts and influences. They might confiscate the jug when their men were drinking to excess, but they also thought of beer and wine as dietary staples. One Iowa woman, upon hearing that her son, home on a visit from college, had not had the money to try the local beer there, brought up a bucket from the cellar as an immediate solution to his deficient diet.[123]

A common opinion among German-speaking immigrants was that women had many rights in America, perhaps even more than was good for them. One recently arrived immigrant wrote from Illinois, "This is the best land for women. It is not the custom for them to work and they have many rights here. Therefore all the Germans like it here. My wife thinks a lot about home, but she is quite healthy, for she weighs one hundred and eighty pounds."[124] The sequence of his ideas may indicate that he feared America was spoiling his wife, causing her to become fat and lazy. Many German-born immigrants commented on the laziness of American women and on the extent to which they ruled their husbands. This was not an aspect of American society German-born men wanted their women to emulate.[125] Mathias Blommer, however, seemed to think it was good that women in America could take the fathers of their illegitimate children to court and sue for monetary recompense: "It doesn't work here in America like in Germany, that the poor creatures have to bear their trouble and shame all their life long with no compensation."[126]

Women in rural areas apparently did not oppose the traditional pattern of female subordination after their arrival in America. There were exceptions, of course. In Missouri, a Mrs. Kloenne made her husband sell a good, but isolated, farm and move the family to a poorer one "on the left bank of the Osage in order to be able to visit more easily in Jefferson City and to receive company from there." It is likely, however, that this reflects not the Americanization of Mrs. Kloenne but her force of will and her bourgeois background.[127] The traditional European power relations in marriage and the family persisted in rural America. The following are typical expressions of the roles each assumed:

> Father was the breadwinner and the Supreme Court; Mother was the tutor and manager of the house. The great leavening factor between the children and their father was Anna, their mother. She was the first person they went to with any plans or everyday problems. Oftentimes Anna and the children would combine forces to get around the habits or inclinations of [their father].[128]

Sometimes male domination of women led to physical abuse. One immigrant tied his wife to a stake in the sun as punishment because, after having prepared food two days in a row for threshers who never appeared, she refused to do so again on the third day. A moral tale in the 19 January 1899 *O'Fallon Hausfreund,* a Missouri Catholic weekly, indicates that some German-speakers beat their wives in America, as they had had the right to do in Europe. In rural areas, communal pressure might have been strong enough to make this less common than in cities, but there is certainly evidence that it did occur.[129] It is unclear whether women felt emboldened by the protection of American law to complain to the authorities about such abuse. It is more likely that they used the familiar arbitrators of family and church in such cases, much as they had in Europe.

The work German-speaking women did at home and in the fields gained them some measure of authority and respect, but it did not result in true gender equality, even in work relationships.[130] It did not mean reciprocity. That is, women did men's work, but men rarely did women's. Young boys or even those past the age of puberty helped their mothers with housework, but only if no female child was present or capable of doing it.[131] It was considered very unusual and inappropriate for a married man to do housework, which was reflected in the December 1888 appeal in the *Marion County Anzeiger* (Kansas) to its readers to help Franz Voigt, whose wife's illness had forced him to be both *Hausfrau* and *Hausherr.*

The American environment called forth certain new forms of behavior in women, but this did not mean their basic attitudes changed. For example, women learned to ride horseback (and even, sometimes, to enjoy doing so), and they traveled alone to visit neighbors. Such unaccustomed behavior was necessitated by new circumstances, however, not an expression of newfound freedom. Riding *astride* was frowned upon by middle-class immigrants, who sometimes criticized farm women for such "immoral" behavior.[132] German-speaking women might work out in the fields, but they were reluctant to wear men's clothing to do so.[133] Women who were left alone on farms and homesteads for long periods while their husbands worked elsewhere for cash wages had to think and act independently as farm managers. Occasionally a woman took advantage of her husband's absence to carry out a project he would not have approved, especially when she could complete it before his return. But this, too, was probably the result of an individual woman's personality or the exigencies of the situation rather than the influence of the much-vaunted freedom of America.[134]

The following verse, written by a second-generation German-American in her daughter's autograph book, shows that the tradition of self-effacement among German-speaking women did not fade.

> Mother said
> When I asked her
> Don't always speak, when you know something
> Don't trust the friend who only calls himself such.
> Keep yourself quiet and pious and pure
> As your mother's beloved little daughter.[135]

These lines call upon the authority of a female heritage that demanded modesty, piety, propriety, and purity in women. Such precepts might have served to perpetuate patriarchal relationships, but women accepted them as valid and sought to instill them in their daughters.

Other evidence indicates rural German-speaking communities retained familiar patterns of gender relations in their new surroundings. The disapproval of public displays of affection between men and women is an example. Near the end of the century, members of a Kansas German-language immigrant church were disgusted by the first "modern" wedding celebrated there, which included a kiss at the altar. The congregation hid its laughter, but members later muttered that if the young couple had to act in such an animal-like manner, they could at least "lick each other" in private. Among the Germans from Russia, it was the custom for the wife to walk a few steps behind her husband, as a sign of deference as well as subordination. The women in this group considered the more affectionate public behavior of Americans shocking. Even the sight of married couples strolling together or holding hands in public made them cringe. As Carol Coburn has said of the families she studied at Block, Kansas, "A strong sense of family pride and privacy required that problems be kept from nonfamily members, and public displays of affection or anger were highly unusual."[136] The behavior in my Nebraska community also corresponds to this cultural demeanor of reticence and self-control, still evident in the third generation.

Lauren Kattner's study of young women in New Braunfels, Texas, indicates that general patterns of female development persisted several generations after immigration. A girl in that German-American community spent the five- to ten-year *Wartezeit* (waiting period) between her confirmation and her marriage (or career or unwed motherhood) much as she would have in Europe, by learning household and handcraft skills. The adolescent Bukovinia Germans of western Kansas ended their schooling with confirmation and helped out at home or went out to work for other farmers, as did the children of Block, Kansas. Studies of other closely knit German-American communities in the Midwest would probably reveal similar social and cultural patterns.[137]

Many immigrants were slow to change traditional ways of contracting marriages. Young people who were supporting themselves made their own arrangements, as had been the case among the rural laborers in Europe. Such couples were still concerned about the economic aspects of their union, however, and often postponed their marriage until they had earned enough cash to start farming. In other instances, a man would approach the father of his prospective bride to ask for her hand and to determine what help would be given her to marry. Or he would ask his father to speak with the young woman's father, and her acceptance would be communicated to him indirectly.[138] The role of mothers in such matters was probably important behind the scenes, just as the bride's acquiescence was often accomplished in the privacy of the home. The public role of males indicates the importance of economic considerations in these arrangements. As had been the case in Europe, men took the leading role in transactions that involved the present or future transfer of property. The ability of a woman to bring property to a marriage remained important. Among Germans from Russia, a girl who had nothing but her clothes to contribute was called *die mit den [sic] kahlen Arsch* (the girl with the bare ass).[139] Although the descendants of the immigrants gradually adopted the more individualistic patterns of marital choice of Anglo-American society, in some areas of the Midwest the land-based traditions were still evident in the latter half of the twentieth century.[140]

Residence in rural America did not cause German-speaking immigrants to alter their traditional gender relations. After all, most of them had not come to America to effect change of that sort in their lives.[141] Yet it should not be forgotten that within her sphere, a woman traditionally had power and influence. The Boonville, Missouri, German-language weekly *Central Missourier* cited the following joke in 1874: "Who advances the fastest? Answer: Women. Scarcely is the courtship over and they have already become corporals, and soon after that they are also in command."[142] Sometimes this domestic leverage indirectly extended to public matters via a woman's husband. "Jürnjakob Swehn" told the story of how a man agreed to help build the first community church after members of the congregation made it clear to his wife that building the church meant they would no longer track snow and mud into her house when it was her turn to host the services. Such stories indicate the influence women could wield in the wider community, even though their power was masked by the public actions only men could take.[143]

In their desire for continuity and conservation of their accustomed way of life, German-speakers sought the support of an ethnic community. Letters and memoirs indicate that such factors as the cost of the land and its proximity to relatives, Old World neighbors, and other German-speakers figured more prominently in the immigrants' choice of land than did soil type and its physical configuration. German-speakers were willing to rent or buy smaller and poorer parcels of land than did Anglo-Americans and live frugally on them until they could buy or rent more, especially if they were in an ethnic neighborhood. Emil Pieschl remembered this about his parents, Austrian immigrants in Kansas: "As long as there were some German families in our locality, Dad and Mom thought they should live there, buy the land and improve it for their home." Mathias Blommer's two daughters and their families decided to settle in Nebraska rather than Kansas, because Kansas had only Irish, no German-speaking, priests.[144] The ethnic community and its institutions helped determine an immigrant family's satisfaction and therefore their persistence on a particular farmstead. Studies in Iowa and Kansas confirm this connection. In areas of relatively high concentrations of German-speakers, immigrant farmers were very persistent, but they were quite mobile where they were a small portion of the rural population.[145]

In rural areas, German-speakers moved quickly to establish community institutions that would sustain ethnic life and at the same time provide frameworks for adaptation. Schools and churches were the most important. These institutions, particularly the ethnic church, played a vital role in providing a center for the immigrants' cultural and communal life. The ethnic identity and cultural cohesiveness that resulted encouraged the immigrants to send down roots to ensure their future and their children's. After the frontier era, ethnic clubs and societies also formed in some of the villages that served as market centers for German-speakers.[146] Although women participated in this institutional life, their roles in founding and supporting schools, churches, and clubs are not well documented.

It is rare that women's contributions to immigrant churches were acknowledged. Certainly they often played a role, as the story "Jürnjakob Swehn" told about the housewife who wanted to end church services in her home illustrates. Many German-speaking women took their spirituality seriously. Indeed, the church was one of the few areas in which nineteenth-century women could acceptably exercise some autonomy, as the well-known maxim about their proper domains indicates: *Kinder, Küche, Kirche* (children, kitchen, church). Yet here, too, there were limitations. Women were not allowed to take a public role in church work and life in the major German denominations until well into the twentieth century. Some German-American ministers' wives might have married their husbands to serve their church in a more direct fashion than otherwise would have been possible. One woman articulated this in 1842, as she sailed to America to marry, sight unseen, a German missionary. Julie Turnau had wanted to do missionary work in Africa, but the German Evangelical missionary societies would not accept single female workers. In her shipboard diary, she expressed the hope that she would make her husband's domestic life easier and thus provide him more time for his pastoral duties: "I am happy that I shall be able to be active in God's work through such ordinary housework, if not directly, at any rate indirectly."[147]

Because women's contributions were for the most part indirect, nineteenth-century church documents and histories rarely documented them.[148] The visits of circuit preachers and missionaries over a period of several years often preceded the establishment of a church. That women put up the traveling ministers, opened their (often primitive) homes for the services, and supplied meals for dozens of people afterwards is usually merely mentioned in passing, though.[149] The actual founding of a church was publicly attributed to the men and exceptional women (almost always widows) who had land or money to contribute.[150] The separation of women's private, domestic sphere from the public arena is again evident in this. It is likely, however, that many women played an important role in the contributions of land and money that made the immigrant church possible. The participatory nature of women in these processes comes out in their writings, for instance, when a woman comments on the land she and her husband contributed for a school or church. Barbara Strohm Kraemer's diary is an example: "On the 17th of August 1855 our new School House was dedicated. It was built upon our land in the Franklin Prairie. We donated an acre and 11 rods for the purpose of building a Mennonite Church and School. This was given as a memorial to us after we are gone." A year later the Kraemers moved from Iowa to Illinois and hosted church services every other Sunday for the next two years in a large room on the first floor of their house: "It was just the right thing for it." Friedrich and Dorothea Wegener made sure they would not do without church services in their new Thayer County, Nebraska, home in 1884. They built a twelve-room house, one room of which was for the pastor and another for church services. Women like these agreed with their husband's public stance and supported it with the domestic economy under their control, but it was improper for women to do more than this openly.[151]

These cultural attitudes kept women from taking a public role in policy-making in the rural churches. Local control was one of the things that differentiated the American immigrant church from the Old World church and that made it more appealing to men than had been the case in Europe. "Jürnjakob Swehn" wrote to his old schoolteacher that the country church's walls were closer together than the parish church back home; "on the other hand it is also fuller on Sundays than yours. We are also more interested here in church matters. We don't just have to pay here. We also have the obligation of speaking up and making decisions."[152] German-speaking women, however, did not openly take part in this aspect of American church life. Like their Anglo-American sisters, they made many other behind-the-scene contributions to the founding and support of the rural church. They did this in ways that paralleled their accepted roles as nurturers and farm wives. They kept the church property clean, cooked food for church affairs, and conducted a variety of fund-raisers for the benefit of the church. Sometimes their efforts resulted in special additions to the church: for example, the new organ that the Nebraska City First Evangelical Lutheran Church board asked the Ladies' Church Society to finance in 1879 or the crystal chandelier that Mrs. Henry Kalkmann convinced the captain of a river boat to donate to the first Catholic church in Nebraska City.[153] Certainly the immigrant churches, like the Anglo-American ones, could not have functioned or, sometimes, survived without the ongoing work women performed: the annual cleanings, the weekly altar decorating, and the numerous bake sales and soup suppers.[154]

These duties and activities were arduous, but they were also opportunities for rural immigrant women to see each other, exchange news, and maintain their female networks. Most German-speaking women had few chances to leave their farms and see others outside of their family circle, except for the Sunday church services.[155] Even church-related women's groups were uncommon at first. German-language churches in America were rather slow to authorize the founding of women's missionary groups.[156] It took time for men to relinquish control in some of these areas. Men dominated the American ethnic church, the center for community recreational life, much as they had the village pub in Europe. In some parishes in Iowa, for instance, men took part in fellowship and choral groups, but women were not allowed to participate in similar activities until the late 1920s and 1930s.[157] Nonetheless, aggressive female leadership could make a difference. When St. John's German Evangelical Church of rural Cooper County, Missouri, got its second full-time minister in 1899, it also got his dynamic wife and two grown daughters. Within two years, these three women had established a *Frauenverein* (women's club), a *Jugendverein* (youth club), and the church's first choir. They also made the parsonage into a social center for young people of the entire neighborhood.[158]

The heart of the rural community was the ethnic church. It supported the value system that emphasized the preservation of family farming as a way of life for future generations. It mirrored the roles expected of and practiced by those who attended it. As was the case in their homes and families, women were vital to its functioning, but their status and power within the church were not equal to men's. The rural school was the other important social and community institution in farm areas. Here, however, ethnic pioneers often had to accommodate their desire to maintain their native language and culture to the demands of public authorities.

Documenting women's contributions to frontier schools and the education of children is very difficult. What evidence we have is primarily anecdotal. As was the case with the founding of immigrant churches, women probably supported their husbands' donating land for a school and money to pay a teacher. Again, men are given the credit for these efforts. Indeed, a typical German-American attitude toward women taking too public an interest in their children's education is indicated by the praise given "a reasonable woman" in Iowa who declined nomination to the school board because she had family obligations and no desire to "shine in public."[159]

It was no doubt the case that in German-speaking communities, the traditional prerogatives of the father in the education of the children were transferred to America. The weak tradition of formal education among the European rural population was also transferred, with children in country areas often attending school only when they were not needed to work at home. Similarly, girls were generally not encouraged to get an education. Mothers were often no more supportive than fathers in this. Since a girl would, it was thought, marry and stay at home, an education would be wasted on her. Anna Goetsch, who had supported her eldest son's desire to go to college, did not intervene when her only daughter wanted to attend high school and the girl's father and brothers disapproved. Gottfried Walz wrote a niece from Bouton, Iowa, advising her not to undergo teacher training, for as a member of the school board he had too often seen such education go to waste among young women.[160]

German-speaking immigrants generally did not approve of female schoolteachers. They were used to the cultural and educational traditions of the Old World. The respect accorded education and the high status granted educators in German culture was not thought to be compatible with the relatively low status to which women were generally relegated. Particularly in rural areas in Europe, pastors and priests had often doubled as schoolteachers. Even where this was not the case, Old World teachers had been men, for women were not admitted to institutions of higher learning until mid-century and those trained as teachers had almost always stayed in urban areas. In America, German-speaking women were slow to enter one of the few professions open to their sex in the late nineteenth century. In 1900, first- and second-generation German-American women accounted for only 86 of the 314,269 female teachers and professors in the United States, far below the number one might expect from their share in the population.[161] Schools specializing in training German-language teachers were established by church denominations, conservative institutions that for the most part continued assumptions about the inappropriateness of women's pursuing careers outside the domestic sphere. The Missouri Synod church, which developed one of the largest systems of parochial schools and founded highly structured and demanding teachers' training schools, opposed for doctrinal reasons the training or hiring of women as teachers until after World War I. Only a teacher shortage or financial exigency induced some parochial schools to break the ban on hiring women, even as teaching assistants for the elementary grades and at a third the salary of a male teacher.[162]

Partly because of conservative German-American churches' opposition to women becoming teachers and partly because of old patterns of rural gender roles, many German-speakers thought girls did not need to learn anything more than was necessary to function adequately as a homemaker. For a few, however, teaching was a respectable alternative to working as a domestic to earn extra money for the family. Two of Heinrich and Ulrike Gellhorn's daughters, Martha and Louise, attended schools at Union and Steamboat Rock, Iowa, after their father's death in 1880 to help their crippled mother and other siblings pay off a $1,000 debt on their farm. That these young women became teachers, a relatively rare phenomenon for German-speakers at the time, was probably the result of several factors. The girls had been toddlers when they immigrated in 1868 and had thus grown up in America and in a family that had many contacts with Americans. Their parents, of the urban lower middle class, were themselves moderately well-educated. Perhaps most important, the Gellhorns lived in a neighborhood with relatively few German-speakers and attended an English-language rural school, where they had had female teachers.[163]

The Gellhorn family shows there were exceptions to German-speakers' negative attitudes toward the education of women. Another example is Ella Sillars's mother. She had gone to work at fourteen in a boardinghouse. Her own hard youth made her want her children to have an education, contrary to what "most of the other old Germans" in the neighborhood wanted.[164] Many rural immigrant women, however, probably did not share the belief in the value of general education that came to be part of the American dream as time went on. Instead, they, like their husbands, were much more supportive of the parochial schools that were often founded in association with the rural church.

Indeed, these schools competed successfully with public schools for students, money, and supplies in many parts of the Midwest.[165] The Catholics and the Missouri Synod Lutherans were particularly successful in establishing such schools. Missouri Synod Lutherans explicitly connected the use of German in the church, home, and school with *reine Lehre* (pure doctrine). Even other German-speaking immigrants saw such schools as the best way to combat the too-rapid assimilation of their children into American society. A comment by "Jürnjakob Swehn" is representative: "We founded the parish school so that our children will learn German and stay German, and so that they will become good Christians."[166] Many immigrants believed that these intertwined goals—language mastery, cultural retention, and religious education—could be met better in the parochial school than in the public school.

In the relative isolation of the countryside, German-speaking immigrants were free to develop an ethnic identity and cultural life without the constant, intense pressure toward assimilation typical of urban areas. Wherever they settled densely enough to form an ethnic church, their religious identification was central to their social lives. This affiliation was strong enough to link like-minded German-speakers from various countries. Secular clubs usually formed later. Although important in helping forge a "Pan-German-American" group ethnicity, such clubs, through their essentially American structures, gradually played a role in the acculturation of the immigrants. This acculturation proceeded slowly and indirectly at first, but as time went on, even the rural ethnic community responded to the demand that the immigrants adapt to the dominant culture. For example, the constitution of the Keystone, Iowa, *Turnverein,* founded on 21 December 1892, stated that it was an "association of men of free moral character, seeking physical and intellectual development, desirous of attaining and disseminating a social brotherly communion and upright American citizenship." Members had to be eighteen years of age or older and citizens or planning to become citizens.[167]

The most important German-American clubs in rural areas were the *Turner* (physical fitness and political awareness) societies and the choral groups. These did not exist everywhere in the Midwest, but most counties with large concentrations of German-speakers had at least one such organization. For example, to make up for the lack of music on the American frontier, Dietzenbach immigrants founded a "Musikchor" that performed in their rural Illinois area.[168] Women's direct participation in such clubs varied somewhat. They generally did not join or form choral groups until after World War I, since this was traditionally a male activity. Similarly, they usually served in an auxiliary function in the *Turner* societies, in keeping with the male-only origins of the movement. The records of the Brunswick, Missouri, *Turnverein,* for example, show that it was composed of men only; however, it sponsored family picnics and balls and on one occasion spent money for forty-three-and-a-half yards of chintz print and two spools of thread. In the same period, they paid a carpenter to build a stage in their hall. Their wives and daughters evidently sewed for the production. They might have also had roles in staged dramas and taken part in musical performances.[169]

In some of the Midwest towns and counties with heavy concentrations of German-speakers, women and children also had gymnastics classes at the *Turnverein* and formed affiliated clubs. Although it is unlikely that most rural women would have had the opportunity to travel to town to regular club meetings or gymnastic classes, they probably did come with their husbands and children to some of the dances, Christmas parties, and picnics the *Turner* societies sponsored. For example, the German-language *Leavenworth Post* contained many references to the activities of what must have been a large and very active *Turnverein* in Leavenworth, Kansas. Between 2 and 15 December 1887, it announced or reported on several events sponsored by the women's gymnastic club (*Turnschwestern-Verein*) or glee club (*Liederkranz*): a Christmas celebration for children of the German-English school, evening entertainment featuring a vocal and instrumental concert followed by a dance, and a "necktie party," at which supper was served and a hundred couples danced until four in the morning. These events were in addition to meetings of such men's groups as the glee club (*Männergesangverein*) and the Swabian Club (*Schwabenverein*). Washington, Missouri, had such an active club life that it, like St. Louis, was a seat of the City Federation of German Clubs. The Washington Turner Society (founded in 1859) produced German-language plays for more than half a century.[170] It is difficult to know to what extent women and families of peasant background participated in such activities, even as part of the audience, but similar club-sponsored events gave midwestern farm women the opportunity to come in contact with the larger society in a relatively comfortable and unintimidating environment. At the same time, the organizational structures and principles and the public and often "non-Germanic" nature of the events such clubs sponsored (neck-tie parties, for example) also contributed to the assimilative function such groups and activities had.

Much more work is yet to be done on the history of rural immigrant women's secular associations. From sketchy evidence, it seems that German-speaking farm women were unlikely to join clubs founded by native-born women. They might have profited by some of the activities those clubs sponsored, though. One example is the waiting rooms and child care facilities set up in small towns for the benefit of farm women who came to shop on Saturdays. German-American women also seem to have been slow to establish parallel groups, perhaps because they found all the social and cultural stimulation they had interest in and time for within the immigrant church. They had important and time-consuming work to do as conservators of tradition in the home and the ethnic community.[171]

Women had an especially important role in diminishing the shock of cultural adaptation. In all immigrant groups, they were traditionally the conservators of culture and language. In the home, the immigrants could preserve their old ways without coming into overt, direct conflict with the new culture around them. On the farm, the food ways, life-style, holiday customs, and language could be maintained while the immigrants accommodated their agricultural enterprise to the American economy.[172]

Many scholars and commentators have noted the linguistic conservatism of German-speaking women.[173] The children and grandchildren of German-speaking immigrants also often remarked on the inability of their female ancestors to speak English, and the manuscript census shows this as well.[174] Women themselves sometimes complained about the difficulties and bother of learning English, particularly when they had little pressing need to do so. This no doubt increased their isolation. Even residence among German-speakers was not always a guarantee against such feelings of linguistic solitude. For example, Pauline Gauß Wendt wrote to her sister-in-law eight years after arriving in Iowa from Berlin: "I am so alone here. Everyone is American. The Germans are Low Germans and gossipy so that I have no one to whom I can pour out my heart." Louise Ritter wrote of the same alienation from other immigrants who spoke different dialects: "we don't have that cozy living here and the language is different . . . they speak High German instead of Swiss-German." After twenty-eight years in Nebraska, she also wrote that she could not speak English because she lacked the opportunity to do so but that she could "get about fairly well in the shops and so." She regretted that her sons never learned to write High German and that her grandchildren knew only English because their mothers were not Swiss-German-speakers.[175] Rural German-speaking women in ethnic enclaves attempted to maintain their children's native language skills and were largely successful in this; however, this often led to women's partial or complete isolation from the Anglo-American society of which their descendants increasingly became a part.

In their housekeeping practices, German-speaking women could usually maintain traditional ways without risk of conflict with the dominant culture. Their cleanliness was legendary, and generally they deserved that reputation. Emilie Bigler remembered how her mother insisted on having her cooking kettles scrubbed until white paper rubbed on the bottoms remained white.[176] They brought featherbeds and bolsters with them and kept geese to renew their bedding. In some areas, they baked bread in the large brick outdoor ovens they knew from their homelands. Other women made European cheeses, like the "Quarkkäse" of the Luxembourgers, and stuffed sausages and put up sauerkraut.[177] Sometimes non-German-speakers objected to their ethnic culinary practices (e.g., Anglo-American schoolteachers refused to lodge with them and share their diet of pork and sauerkraut, and neighbors criticized Germans from Russia for having their children mix sauerkraut by stomping it with their feet in the crocks). In other cases, they learned from foreign-born women (e.g., a Swiss woman taught her neighbors to make cheese).[178]

The immigrants did not, of course, retain all their European household traditions. For instance, the peasant practice of family members' eating out of a large common bowl was abandoned, along with the protein-impoverished diet of the Old World. Instead of rye, German-speakers now baked white bread, in Europe the food of the wealthy. They ate together at the same table, instead of separating the children and hired help from the adult farm family members, as had been the custom in some households of larger landowners in Europe. Now there was often a tablecloth on the table, although it was no longer used to cover a loaf of bread.[179] In spite of such adaptations to American ways, food, if not always the manner in which it was served, remained an area for German-speaking women's ethnic expression.

The clothing women were used to wearing in Europe had to change in their new surroundings. Climatic changes dictated this, as did women's sense of appropriateness and fashion. Burdened by her woolen clothing, a German immigrant fashioned a cotton skirt out of a blanket during the Atlantic journey. One woman remembered her shame at American women's stares when she got off the train in Kansas in her Russian felt boots and peasant-style costume and was grateful for the "ordinary" clothing given her by kind American women. Other peasant women in rural areas, however, probably felt no need (or could not afford) to Americanize their dress. American observers sometimes noted the oddness of immigrant women's clothing, particularly their drab colors and headscarves. Regional costumes (*Trachten*), which were sometimes even institutionalized by law in the Old World, could retain special significance for immigrant women. Elizabeth Bigler kept her Bernese costume for important occasions, donning it, for example, when she gave a meditation at her husband's burial and when she prayed to God during a drought.[180] In America, the distinctions of social class and region that had been observed in European dress were not maintained. Some of the middle-class immigrants found it offensive that hired domestics could and did dress as stylishly as women from their own circles. But in America, only money and taste dictated what one wore. A general conformity to what was considered urban style shaped female fashion, and this was viewed as another (albeit superficial) indication of equality in American society.[181]

Women also made important contributions to the retention of ethnic holiday practices. In some Swiss families, the New Year began with a visit from a Ruprecht-like figure and continued the next day with gifts for the children and a big family meal of roast goose or pig. Easter was celebrated with the coloring of eggs, games, and another special meal.[182] A "Saxon-traditionalist" neighborhood of Lutherans at Cooper Hill in Osage County, Missouri, continued the pre-Christmas visits of "Belsnickels" (a threatening figure calculated to frighten children into good behavior), erected Christmas trees, and celebrated December 26 as well as Christmas Day as a holiday in the early twentieth century. The holiday and folk customs of Luxembourgian-Americans centered on their Catholic identity. Women expressed this in their homes, keeping rosaries, pictures of saints, the crucifix, and a holy water container in their parlors. They and their husbands gave their children the same saints' names they had in Europe, although distances from the church necessitated their waiting until the Sunday after the birth to baptize the baby. Luxembourgian-American wakes and baptisms were conducted more quietly than in the old country, but weddings were celebrated in the traditional exuberant fashion. Some old Luxembourgian customs had disappeared by the end of the century, however. The visits of St. Nicolas, for instance, gave way to the erection of Christmas trees, a custom imported by other German-speaking groups. Some Luxembourgian-Americans commemorated *Kirmes,* the anniversary celebration of the dedication of the immigrants' European church, with family and neighbors in America, but this often ended with the passing of the first generation. Not always though. For example, the descendants of immigrants from Dietzenbach near Darmstadt continued to celebrate "die Dietzen-bacher Kerb" (the anniversary of the founding date of the Dietzenbach parish church) during the last weekend of October for three or four generations after the main wave of settlement around Darmstadt, Illinois, which took place between 1837 and 1850. Annual mission festivals held in Lutheran parishes and similar church celebrations in other denominations were customs congenial to German-speakers used to church-based community holidays in Europe.[183]

Similar customs were common in many parts of the Midwest. Some differences due to varying European backgrounds persisted among the various immigrant groups. Generally, customs connected to religious holidays and events in the life cycle were the most common and the longest lasting. The 28 June 1876 *Wöchentliche Kansas Freie Press* in Leavenworth reported on a Pentecost celebration organized by the German settlement on Deer Creek in Douglas County. "In accordance with Swiss custom," a *Brautbitter* (wedding invitor) announced the wedding of the American-born daughter of Elizabeth Bigler. This was thirty-one years after the Bigler family had immigrated to Illinois.[184] *Brautbitter* and shivarees were also traditional practices in German-American areas in Missouri, Kansas, and Nebraska for many years after immigration. My own parents were shivareed when they moved into their farm house after World War II. German ethnic practices and rural conviviality combined on these occasions as strategies for community building. Women's concern with family and church made them important supporters and conveyors of such traditions.[185]

The midwestern states of Illinois, Iowa, Missouri, Kansas, and Nebraska were proving grounds for the ability of German-speaking immigrants to succeed economically in family-farming ventures. This area offered an appropriate environment and many of the conditions necessary for such success: arable land in large quantities at affordable prices; a growing economy that rewarded hard work and frugality with the opportunity to accumulate property and wealth; a native (white) culture that shared many of the family values and structures of the immigrants, ignored their relatively unobtrusive cultural differences, and, until 1914, tolerated their efforts to build an ethnic community as a bulwark against too-rapid assimilation. For their part, the German-speakers benefited from their habits of industriousness, thriftiness, and self-imposed moderation in personal wants that their often marginal existences in the Old World had imposed on them. The high value they placed on establishing, holding, and, if possible, enlarging the family holding also motivated them to persist in difficult frontier conditions and to take advantage of others' lack of such persistence.

Much of the credit for German-speakers' ability to maintain their presence in rural areas of the Midwest must go to women. Their culture had conditioned them to be hardworking and self-sacrificing, and they had ample opportunity to continue this pattern on the American frontier. They were willing to bear large numbers of children and to supervise their contributions to the family endeavor, even if that came at the cost of their own health and the well-being and education of their children. The household skills and the knowledge of animal husbandry many of them had developed in Europe were also put to good use. These contributions to subsistence farming often enabled their families to weather economic difficulties that might have broken others. Women's domestic economy also made immigrant farm families less susceptible to the pressures of acculturation that a more thorough integration into the growing American agricultural market economy would have caused.

These immigrant women were anxious to continue the home- and family-centered lives they had led. Isolation in the countryside enabled them to do so. Women also were important in the establishment of the immigrant community institutions that supported this isolation and simultaneously created a relatively familiar cultural sphere. Within the rural ethnic community, women's traditional place in the family, with its limited but comfortably familiar autonomy, could be continued. Rural German-speaking women were therefore unlikely to find the comparative independence of American women attractive or to bring gender conflict into the home. Moreover, they could be counted on to support the language, customs, and cultural traditions of the Old World through their domestic activities and in their daily interactions with family members. This domestic ethnic culture was a "safe space" within which the immigrants and their children could more gradually learn about and accommodate themselves to American society.

The cultural conditioning of German-speaking women generally proved beneficial for their families on the frontier. Their inclination toward self-sacrifice and hard work, toward the subjection of their own wishes to those of others and of individual desires to long-term goals, made many of them efficient and effective frontierswomen. Traditional family power structures among German-speakers, with female subordination at its center, suited the work patterns and long-term family goals of the subsistence frontier farmer. Through my research, I have come to regard my own family's success in accumulating land and passing it on to succeeding generations as fitting in the larger framework of the European peasant tradition. My grandfather's relatively early retirement from farming also fits this pattern. I now see my grandmother's character and behavior in a different light as well, and I view the contributions of the women in my family, more felt than documented, as typical rather than extraordinary.

For all the reasons discussed in this chapter, most rural German-speaking women were generally "contented among strangers," but human beings live on an emotional level as well as in the concrete world. Some immigrant women experienced their frontier lives as continuations of their old existences. For others, the familiar family structures and the creation of an ethnic community did not always make up for the inner displacement they felt.

Notes

ABBREVIATIONS

AHSOHP	Amana Historical Society Oral History Project, Amana Heritage Society Library, Amana, Iowa
BABS	Bochumer Auswanderer-Briefsammlung (Bochum Emigrant Letter Collection), Ruhr University, Bochum, Germany
CCMPC	Cooper County, Missouri, Probate Court, Archives, Boonville, Missouri
CHI	Concordia Historical Institute, Clayton, Missouri
ISHD-HS	Iowa State Historical Department, Historical Society, Iowa City, Iowa
ISHD-MA	Iowa State Historical Department, Museum and Archives, Des Moines, Iowa
ISHL	Illinois State Historical Library, Springfield, Illinois
KSHS	Kansas State Historical Society, Topeka, Kansas
LDMC	Lilla Day Monroe Collection of Pioneer Stories, Kansas State Historical Society, Topeka, Kansas
NSHS	Nebraska State Historical Society, Lincoln, Nebraska
Tms	Typewritten copy of a handwritten document or oral interview
WHMC-C	Western Historical Manuscripts Collection, Columbia, Missouri

1. Not one of the forty-seven letter writers in Lanwert's study states the reasons for immigrating to America (16). Agnes Bretting concludes, on the evidence of women's personal writings, that women's motives for emigration were probably usually a mixture of the personal and the economic ("Deutsche Einwandererfrauen im 'Land der unbegrenzten Möglichkeiten'—Wunsch und

Wirklichkeit: Autobiographische Quellen in der Frauenforschung," in *Frauen wandern aus: Deutsche Migrantinnen im 19. und 20. Jahrhundert,* eds. Monika Blaschke and Christiana Harzig [Bremen: Labor Migration Project, University of Bremen, 1990], 14).

2. Elsie B. Hass Stickney, "Hass-Stickney Family History" (1962), folder 2, box 5, Donald F. Danker Personal Papers, NSHS; Ludwig Kurz, *Wege des Schicksals* (Erbach im Odenwald: August Franz, 1926), 4–12; Mathias Blommer, letter of 2 May 1873, BABS.

3. Mark Wyman views this as one of the important reasons for the flood of German emigration after 1830 (*Immigrants in the Valley* [Chicago: Nelson-Hall, 1984], 50).

4. Sonya Pohlman, "John H. Pohlman, Nebraska Pioneer" (1962), folder 6, box 5, Danker Personal Papers; Joseph Suppiger, Salomon Koepfli, and Kaspor Koepfli, *Journey to New Switzerland,* ed. John C. Abbott, trans. Raymond J. Spahn (Carbondale: Southern Illinois University Press, 1987), xxvii; Hermann Steines, letter of 8 November 1833, in William G. Bek, trans. and comp., "The Followers of Duden," *Missouri Historical Review* 14 (October 1919): 70; Louise Sophia Gellhorn Boylan, "My Life Story" [ca. 1942], Manuscript Collection, ISHD-HS.

5. Cited in Lutz Röhrich, "German Emigrant Songs," in *Eagle in the New World,* eds. Theodore Gish and Richard Spuler (College Station: Texas A & M University Press, 1986), 63–64.

6. Prominent examples in Missouri of women who convinced their husbands to leave America are Luise Marbach of the Stephanite group of Saxon immigrants and Mrs. Nicolas Hesse of Westphalia. For a related discussion, see Linda S. Pickle, "Stereotypes and Reality: Nineteenth-Century German Women in Missouri," *Missouri Historical Review* 79 (April 1985): 302–5.

7. Helene Friesen Eitzen, "Erinnerungen aus meinem Leben" (4 April 1919), 16, 17, duplicate copy, Inman, Kans. I am grateful to Duane Kroeker of Columbia, Missouri, for permission to quote from his grandmother's autobiography. An English translation, "A Remembrance of My Life" (Tms, n.d.), also in Mr. Kroeker's possession, contains a few omissions and inaccuracies; therefore, the translations are my own.

8. Ibid., 17–19.

9. Ibid., 19, 20.

10. Sophie Luise Duensing Weitbrecht, "Neun schwere Aufbaujahre in deutschen Gemeinden der Vereinigten Staaten von Nordamerika (1848–1857)," comp. Hans-Thorald Michaelis, *Genealogie* 2 (1980): 52–63. Mary Cresence Berhalter Maichel, an orphan trained in nursing, also came to America to escape an unwanted marriage (microfilm roll 5, LDNC). More independent than Sophie Weitbrecht, probably because she had supported herself for a time, she paid her own fare, traveled with a friend, and after four years married a New York grocer. They later moved to Kansas for her husband's health.

11. "Da würdet Ihr Euch wundern . . .," *Die Zeit,* 21 May 1976.

12. J. Sanford Rikoon, "The Reusser House: A Log Structure in Iowa's 'Little Switzerland,'" *Annals of Iowa* 45 (Summer 1979): 6.

13. John Michael Kunz, an impoverished nobleman, married Christina Winegar and brought her to Illinois and then Nebraska (Mary Miller, "Cass County Settlers Who Were Ancestors of Marvin, Carol Ann, and Debra Kay Miller" [1962], Tms, folder 8, box 5, Danker Personal Papers). Regina Rückels Kessel and her brothers sold the family holdings and became prosperous farmers in Illinois (Rückels-Kessel Family Letters, 1859–92, BABS). In Kansas, an eighteen-year-old wrote her brother about working off her passage as a kitchen maid (Pauline Kull Fischer, letter of 23 April 1882, BABS). The eighteen-year-old Magdalena Schnack Fahrenbrink came to America with the family of a neighbor and worked one year to pay her transportation costs of sixty-six dollars (W. F. Johnson, 2:703).

14. Kamphoefner, *The Westfalians,* 43, 49.

15. "Was erwartet die auswandernde Frau," 4 970, D-Archiv, Institut für Auslandsbeziehungen, Stuttgart, Germany. Roebke's thesis discusses the most important material printed to advise nineteenth-century emigrants.

16. Britta Fees's recent study on prostitution in San Francisco makes no mention of German-speakers among the prostitutes and in general adds nothing to earlier studies of the subject ("Ein-

wanderinnen als Prostituierte in San Francisco, 1848–1870," in *Frauen wandern aus,* eds. Blaschke and Harzig, 65–81). Jacqueline Baker Barnhardt states that "the most likely victims [of white slave operations] were unattached young immigrant women, whose disappearance would raise no outcry from their families . . ." (*The Fair but Frail: Prostitution in San Francisco, 1849–1900* [Reno: University of Nevada Press, 1986], 71). Barnhardt adds that it is likely the large body of late nineteenth-century literature on white slavery overemphasized this phenomenon and that most women probably went into prostitution because of the lure of "easy" money, the life-style, and pleasure. Anne Firor Scott has found evidence of attempts by native-born women's associations to keep or save young immigrant women from a life of sin (*Natural Allies: Women's Associations in American History* [Urbana: University of Illinois Press, 1991], 38–43, 104).

17. Hannah Aschman Harms remembered her mother's chest of linen (microfilm roll 3, LDMC), and Barbara Graw Wahl recalled saving the family featherbeds (microfilm roll 9, LDMC). Frederick Steines wrote that his newly arrived mother missed her furniture (letter of 15 September 1834, in William G. Bek, trans. and comp., "The Followers of Duden," *Missouri Historical Review* 15 [April 1920]: 538). Matthew Hermann's bride, Mary Krausz, had brought her bedroom furniture with her (letter of October 1871, in Walter W. Hermann, "Germany to USA: Migration of the Matthew Hermann Family" [n.d.], 22, Tms, Nebraska United Methodist History Center, Lincoln). On 27 August 1869 Henry Ruegg went to St. Louis from his Highland, Illinois, farm to sell "two silver cups and the Bernese clock" (Diaries and Papers, 1848–1877, trans. Othmar Stutz, Tms, KSHS). Elizabeth Bigler's silver and copper-bottomed pots went down in a shipwreck on the transatlantic voyage, a loss she mourned "for all her days" (Ruth Harbecke Jewett, "The Story of Emilie Joss-Bigler," *Swiss American Historical Society Newsletter* 21 [November 1985]: 3, 13).

18. Auswanderung Deutschland-USA, Ratschläge zur Auswanderung, 4 971, D-Archiv, Institut für Auslandsbeziehungen, Stuttgart, Germany.

19. Faragher, "History from the Inside-Out," 550–51. Other scholars of ethnic groups in the United States also defined the basic patriarchal structure of the ethnic family in similar ways. See, for example, William L. Warner and Leo Srole, *The Social Systems of American Ethnic Groups,* Yankee City Series, 3 (New Haven, Conn.: Yale University Press, 1960), 103–4.

20. Glenda Riley, *The Female Frontier: A Comparative View of Women on the Prairie and the Plains* (Lawrence: University Press of Kansas, 1988), 2.

21. Among the studies of women's work on the agricultural frontier and in agriculture in general, the following are particularly worthy of note: Mary Meek Atkeson, "Women in Farm Life and Rural Economy," *Annals of the American Academy of Political and Social Sciences* 143 (May 1929): 188–94; Dorothy Schwieder, "Labor and Economic Roles of Iowa Farm Wives, 1840–80," in *Farmers, Bureaucrats and Middlemen,* ed. Trudy Huskamp Peterson (Washington, D.C.: Howard University Press, 1980), 152–68; Joan M. Jensen, *With These Hands: Women Working on the Land* (Old Westbury, N.Y.: Feminist Press, 1981); Corlann G. Bush, "The Barn Is His, the House Is Mine," in *Energy and Transport,* vol. 52, eds. George H. Daniels and Mark H. Rose (Beverly Hills, Calif.: Sage Focus Education, 1982), 235–59; Carol Fairbanks and Sara Brooks Sundberg, *Farm Women on the Prairie Frontier: A Sourcebook for Canada and the United States* (Metuchen, N.J.: Scarecrow, 1983); Scott G. McNall and Sally Allen McNall, *Plains Families: Exploring Sociology through Social History* (New York: St. Martin's Press, 1983); Riley, *The Female Frontier* and *Frontierswomen;* Deborah Fink, *Open Country, Iowa: Rural Women, Tradition and Change* (Albany: State University of New York Press, 1986); and Seena B. Kohl, "Image and Behavior: Women's Participation in North American Family Agricultural Enterprises," in *Women and Farming: Changing Roles, Changing Structures,* eds. Wava G. Haney and Jane B. Knowles (Boulder, Colo.: Westview, 1988). A useful bibliography for the more recent period is Colette Moser and Deborah Johnson, *Rural Women Workers in the Twentieth Century,* Central Rural Manpower and Public Affairs, Special Paper, no. 15 (East Lansing: Michigan State University Press, 1973). The best general study of women's work in the home is Susan Strasser, *Never Done: A History of American Housework* (New York: Pantheon, 1982).

22. Cornelia B. Flora and Jan L. Flora, "The Structure of Agriculture and Women's Culture in the Great Plains," *Great Plains Quarterly* 8 (Fall 1988): 197. Almost everyone who has written about the

work of women and children on the agricultural frontier has acknowledged their central role. A skeptical view of the governmental policies that supported patriarchal family structures, thereby encouraging families to place themselves in stressful frontier situations, is offered by Rosalinda Mendez Gonzales, "Commentary," in *Western Women: Their Land, Their Lives,* eds. Lillian Schlissel, Vicky Ruiz, and Janice Monk (Albuquerque: University of New Mexico Press, 1988), 102–4. Related works include John Stitz, "A Study of Family Farm Culture in Ellis County, Kansas, and the Relationship of That Culture to Trends in Farming" (Ph.D diss., University of Kansas, Lawrence, 1983); Susan A. Mann and James M. Dickinson, "Obstacles to the Development of Capitalist Agriculture," *Journal of Peasant Studies* 5 (July 1978): 466–81; Glenda Riley, "Farm Women's Roles in the Agricultural Development of South Dakota," *South Dakota History* 13 (Spring/Summer 1982): 83–121; Max J. Pfeffer, "Social Origins of Three Systems of Farm Production in the United States," *Rural Sociology* 48 (Winter 1983): 540–62; and Jan L. Flora and John Stitz, "Ethnicity, Persistence, and Capitalism of Agriculture in the Great Plains during the Settlement Period: Wheat Production and Risk Avoidance," *Rural Sociology* 50 (Fall 1985): 341–60. Rachel Ann Rosenfeld has shown that the work of contemporary farm women is as varied, important, and unremunerated as it was a century ago (*Farm Women: Work, Farm and Family in the United States* [Chapel Hill: University of North Carolina Press, 1986], 5–11).

23. Goebel noted this in his memoir of his life in early Missouri (45–48). See also R. Lee, 95; and K. Conzen, "Deutsche Einwanderer," 373.

24. This according to the leaflets "Was erwartet die auswandernde Frau" and "Gegenstände, welche die auswandernde Frau notwendigerweise mitbringen muß," Auswanderung nach USA, Liste für die Auswanderung, Institut für Auslandsbeziehungen, Stuttgart.

25. Hillenkamp, letter of 4 May 1843, Tms, BABS; Clara M. Shields, "The Lyon Creek Settlement," *Kansas Historical Collections* 14 (1915–18): 163. Women whose husbands were incapable of hard labor sometimes took over that role. Frederick W. Pehle's mother split rails for fences (Kamphoefner, *The Westfalians,* 161), and Karolina Miller Krause worked as a hired hand (Estelle Schelbitzki Freeman, "Anton and Karolina Krause" [1986], Tms, in author's possession).

26. Roebke, 89. See J. M. Jensen's discussion of the changes in agricultural economy and production that lay behind the eighteenth- and early nineteenth-century decrease in American women's participation in field work (*With These Hands,* 36–37, 46–48, 81–85). Lanwert also discusses these developments (56–59). Allan G. Bogue surmises that immigrant (German and Scandinavian) women and children in nineteenth-century Iowa took a greater part in field work than Americans did, in spite of the negative pressure of the dominant society (*From Prairie to Cornbelt* [Chicago: University of Chicago Press, 1963], 238). In confirmation of Bogue's assertion, the letters of Amalia Rückels, Regina Kessel, Wilhelmine Neumeier-Herbold, Christine Neumeier-Rock, and Friederike Neumeier-Hinkhaus (all in BABS) and the diary of Henry Ruegg (KSHS) all contain many references to such work of women and children. See also Louis H. Siekmann, "The German Element and Its Part in the Early Development of Otoe County, Nebraska" (M.A. thesis, University of Nebraska, 1930), 21.

27. Katharina Tiek, letter of 21 February 1869, Tms, BABS.

28. 1870 U.S. Manuscript Census, Madison County, Illinois, 305A, lines 8–13.

29. Tiek, letter of 18 March (1880?).

30. The children of many immigrants blamed hard work and the strain of numerous births for their mothers' poor health and early deaths. See, for an example, J. C. Ruppenthal, "Anna Barbara Immendorf, a Pioneer of Lincoln and Russell Counties, Kansas" (1925), Tms, microfilm 7, LDMC.

31. The reminiscences of Friederika Oesterreich Staatz are included in Shields, 148–50. Pearl Donnelly also wrote of Mrs. Staatz in "Pioneer Women of the Lyon Creek Settlement, Dickinson County" (n.d.), microfilm 2, LDMC.

32. Ruppenthal reported that his thirteen-year-old brother helped his mother deliver her seventh child because her husband and other children were on their second farm, eight miles away (8).

33. Hermann, 20; Tildy Kiest Heitman told this of her mother, Caroline Fette Kiest ("Notebooks," 8, ISHL).

34. Lucy Steinhaus, *I Remember When* (Sacrament: J. Rad, 1980), 74. Among the many documents

that mention children's contributions to the family income are Emil Pieschl, "My Memoirs, 1882–1976," 36–37, Tms, Manuscript Collection, ISHD-HS; Irene DeBettignies, "An Old Settler's Story" (n.d.), box I, Manuscript Collection, ISHD-HS; and Albert Parks Butts, "A Calhoune County Pioneer: Sabine Kropf" (1973), Tms, Manuscript Collection, ISHD-HS. Mari Sandoz documented best the pain of growing up in an unhappy family, beset by economic problems (*Old Jules* [Lincoln: University of Nebraska Press, 1962]). In contrast, John Ise remembered the warmth and sharing among the children in his large family (*Sod and Stubble* [Lincoln: University of Nebraska Press, 1936]). Interestingly, Ise recorded experiences from his mother's impoverished childhood in America much less positively ("Mother's Recollections of Her Early Life" [n.d.], Tms, Kansas Collection, University of Kansas, Lawrence).

35. On the treatment of children in rural Europe, see Braun, 62; R. Lee, 96–99; Sieder, 43–45; Rosenbaum, 93–95; W. R. Lee, "The Impact of Agrarian Change," 338–40; Weber-Kellermann, *Landleben*, 243–63; and Frevert, 27–28. To illustrate the low status of even the wives of relatively well-off peasants, Weber-Kellermann cites the 1857 instance of a peasant woman left to give birth alone while her husband and servants attended All Saints' services (*Landleben*, 145).

36. Carl Köhler, "Eight Weeks on a St. Clair County Farm in 1851: Letters by a Young German," ed. and trans. Frederic Trautman, *Journal of the Illinois State Historical Society* 75 (Autumn 1982): 178; Hillenkamp, letter of 8 January 1846, Tms, BABS; J. D. Wilkins, letter of 19 January 1886, Kleihauer Family Letters, BABS. The system Köhler and Hillenkamp describe was still working in the early twentieth century, as Nancy Wieck's memoir about her family's efforts to save money and accumulate land proves ("The Life of a Pioneer Girl," in *Memoirs of Pioneers of Cheyenne County, Kansas*, ed. Pendergrass, 123, 126, passim).

37. Albine Schelbitzki, untitled ms. (ca. 1967), Tms, in my possession.

38. Gillhoff, 46; Maichel, microfilm 5; Mariam S. Wiederstein, *The Pioneer Obstetrician: A Country Midwife*, ed. James Klassen (Newton, Kans.: United, 1972); Coburn, *Life at Four Corners*, 92–93; Charlotte Borst, "Wisconsin Midwives as Working Women: Immigrant Midwives and the Limits of a Traditional Occupation, 1870–1920," *Journal of American Ethnic History* 8 (Spring 1989): 24–59.

39. Ada Oliva, "The Story of My Grandmother" (n.d.), box 15, Manuscript Collection, ISHD-HS; *Marion County Anzeiger*, Hillsboro, Kansas, 21 September 1888. German immigrants in Plank Township, Keokuk County, Iowa, made baskets for extra income (Sophia Stanfield, "History of Plank Township" [1927], 40, Tms, Manuscript Collection, ISHD-HS).

40. On this, see Riley, *The Female Frontier*, 102–3, 121, passim. For the domestic production of nineteenth-century women in the eastern United States, see Joan M. Jensen, "Cloth, Butter, and Boarders: Women's Household Production for the Market," in her *Promise to the Land: Essays on Rural Women* (Albuquerque: University of New Mexico Press, 1991), 186–205.

41. Maria Wolf Förschler to Mina Wolf, n.d., Tms (1868–1908), Langendorf-Tiek/Foerschler/Freitag/Faust Letters, BABS.

42. Goebel wrote of the female and child labor in the families of poor rural immigrants that led to eventual financial security and said that the girls in such families benefited by their exposure to better housekeeping methods when they worked out (47–49). The most important study of domestics in America is David Katzmann, *Seven Days a Week* (New York: Oxford University Press, 1978). Two fine studies of domestic service have recently appeared in Germany: Karin Walser, *Dienstmädchen. Frauenarbeit und Weiblichkeitsbilder um 1900* (Frankfurt: extrabuch, 1985); and Dorothee Wierling, *Mädchen für alles* (Berlin: Dietz, 1987). See also Silke Wehner, "Auswanderung deutscher Dienstmädchen in die USA, 1870–1920," in *Frauen wandern aus*, eds. Blaschke and Harzig, 29–50; and Silke Wehner, "Auswanderung deutscher Dienstmädchen in die Vereinigten Staaten, 1850–1914" (Ph.D. diss., University of Münster, 1992). One North Dakota woman's memoir documents her premarital work for wages. After emigrating from Bessarabia with her sister's family, Mary Gellner worked as a dishwasher, harvest hand, and domestic before marriage (Mary Gellner Weisz, "Cloudy Skies: Gellner Family Saga," *Heritage Review* 18 [November 1988]: 3–13). On the quite different purposes and consequences domestic work had for third-generation German-American women, see Coburn, *Life at Four Corners*, 121–26.

43. Edith Connelley Ross, "The Bloody Benders," *Kansas Historical Collections* 17 (1926–28): 464–79.

44. Strasser gives a price of $30 (171). At the 1880 estate sale of Emma Blank in Cooper County, Missouri, her sewing machine sold for $25, while her four cows brought between $14 and $18 each (folder 2090, CCMPC).

45. Boylan, 2. See also Ise, *Sod and Stubble*, 81–82.

46. Mrs. Wayne Shaneyfelt, "Mrs. Rebecca Stege Beins," in *Sod House Memories*, ed. Frances J. Alberts (Hastings, Nebr.: Sod House Society, 1972), 205; Isernhagen, 74.

47. Pauline Greving, letter of 30 December 1888, Pauline and Henry Greving Letters, 1884–1923, Tms, BABS: "This year the harvest was quite good, but the prices are too low, except eggs and chickens now cost 2–3 dollars the dozen 20 cents. Last fall I sold 12 dozen chickens and now every week I sell eggs for $2.50."

48. Gilbert Fite points out the importance of butter as a cash crop in lean years (*The Farmers' Frontier, 1865–1900* [New York: Holt, 1966], 47). Joan M. Jensen has shown the significance of women's butter income for the family economy, especially when farm income was low ("Butter Making and Economic Development in Mid-Atlantic America, 1750–1850," in *Promise to the Land*, 170–185; "Cloth, Butter, and Boarders"). Jensen has also investigated the autonomy women gained through their role in butter making in the Brandywine valley (*Loosening the Bonds: Mid-Atlantic Farm Women* [New Haven: Yale University Press, 1986], 79–113). Fink found that women's income and domestic productivity were what supported many Iowa families during the Great Depression (57–71). In 1935, the egg and poultry sales on one Michigan farm nearly equaled that from the dairy herd (John L. Shover, *First Majority—Last Minority* [DeKalb: Northern Illinois University Press, 1976], 120).

49. U.S. Census Office, *Tenth Census, 1880: Productions of Agriculture* (Washington, D.C.: GPO, 1883), tables 9 and 14.

50. This was said of Rosa Felt and the fifty pounds of butter she made every week (Lorna Reichenberg, "History of My Ancestors" [1962], 4, folder 3, box 3, Danker Personal Papers). Bernie Zerfass, a second-generation Bukovina German in Kansas, acknowledged, "We would have starved to death if we wouldn't have had cows to milk and chickens. You'd take a can of cream and some eggs to town, and that's what you bought your groceries with" (Irmgard Hein Ellingson, *The Bukovina Germans in Kansas: A 200 Year History*, Ethnic Heritage Studies, 6 [Fort Hays, Kans.: Fort Hays State University, 1987], 36). Elise Isely remembered that her dairy and egg income "was the main reliance for household expenses" (Bliss Isely, *Sunbonnet Days by Elise Dubach Isely* [Caldwell, Idaho: Caxton, 1935], 171). Caroline Fette Kiest also paid for the family groceries with her butter and eggs (Heitman, 8). In contrast, and perhaps reflecting a male viewpoint, Gonner wrote that Luxembourgian-American women's poultry and dairy earnings contributed "to the support of minor needs of the household" (157).

51. Hillenkamp, letter of 4 May 1843.

52. J. M. Jensen has documented the power dynamics underlying such behavior (*Promise to the Land*, 181–83, 196). For a discussion of women's wage earning, see Kohl, "Image and Behavior," 94. Kohl has also analyzed the power base farm women gain through their contributions to family farm enterprise ("Working Together: Husbands and Wives in the Small-Scale Family Agricultural Enterprise," in *The Canadian Family*, ed. K. Ishwaran [n.p.: Gage, 1983], 234–43). Flora and Flora wrote of women among the Germans from Russia in Kansas having to resist their husbands' efforts to discourage their poultry and butter production (13). In Germany, also, some nineteenth-century analysts of agricultural economy found women's participation in the weekly markets unprofitable and detrimental to their proper work at home (Johann Gottfried Kinkel, "Die Heimatlosen," in *Dorfgeschichten aus dem Vormärz*, vol. 2, ed. Hartmut Kircher [Cologne: Informationspress, C. W. Leske, 1981], 275). Fink's chapter on egg production makes clear men's disdain for poultry until, during World War II, egg production became a viable market industry (135–59).

53. General descriptions of women's household production may be found in many sources. See, for example, Everett Dick, *The Sod-House Frontier* (Lincoln, Nebr.: Johnsen, 1954), 238–39; Riley, *Frontierswomen*, 64–67; Riley, *The Female Frontier*, 118–19; and Fairbanks and Sundberg, 52–55.

54. Shaneyfelt, 205; Isely, 166; *Hillsboro Post,* 25 March 1898. Roenigk wrote that in the first years of settlement, no one, including the merchants, had any money, so trade in goods was the usual form of commerce (312–13).

55. The same thing was true for Anglo-American rural women. Susan Armitage's interviews with twenty women who lived on the Colorado frontier showed that all were poor but that none went out to work for wages. Instead, they "engaged in home food production as a direct contribution to the uncertain farm economy" ("Housework and Childrearing on the Frontier: The Oral History Record," *Sociology and Social Research* 63 [April 1979]: 468). The patterns of these women's lives were similar to those already noted for German-speaking women. Barter for needed goods was common. They also made clothes for the family. They integrated child care into work, having the children help them and then leaving them on their own when the work was done.

56. Dorothee Schneider, "'For Whom Are All the Good Things in Life?' German-American Housewives Discuss Their Budgets," in *German Workers in Industrial Chicago: A Comparative Perspective,* ed. Hartmut Keil and John B. Jentz (DeKalb: Northern Illinois University Press, 1983), 145–60.

57. Francis Dischner, *The Franciscans in Nebraska* (Humphrey and Norfolk, Nebr.: Humphrey Democrat, Norfolk News, 1931), 54.

58. J. Neale Carman, "Foreigners of 1857–1865 at Schippel's Ferry, Saline County," *Kansas Historical Quarterly* 24 (Autumn 1958): 307, 310; Elvira Getzmeier, "The Story of My Grandmother" (n.d.), box 14, Manuscript Collection, ISHD-HS. Widowed Pauline Roedel Bremmer Downs's brother-in-law helped her and her two toddlers complete the five-year residency requirement under the Homestead Act and lay claim to the land she and her husband had settled on (Lester Harsch, *Grandfather Stories* [n.p, n.d.], 23–24).

59. H. Elaine Lindgren, "Ethnic Women Homesteading on the Plains of North Dakota," *Great Plains Quarterly* 9 (Summer 1989): 157–73. A German-born woman who gained land in Kansas under the Homestead Act was Nancy Moore Wieck's mother-in-law, but she probably would not have done so if she had not been left a widow. Mother Wieck used the $1,300 she received when she sold the homestead to pay for her keep with her son and daughter-in-law (Wieck, 113). Jules Sandoz's mother-in-law also invested in a homestead relinquishment, at Jules's urgings (Sandoz, 218). One German widow from Russia immigrated to Nebraska with her children, where they worked in the sugar beet fields until she could successfully homestead with them in Wyoming in 1912 (Harold D. Kauffman, "A Mother's Quest for a Better Life," *Journal of the American Historical Society of Germans from Russia* 9 [Spring 1986]: 33–38). Katherine Harris has asserted that women gained status and opportunities for self-realization through this experience, whether they participated in it as a partner in a family venture or as an independent settler ("Homesteading in Northeastern Colorado, 1873–1920," in *The Women's West,* eds. Susan Armitage and Elizabeth Jameson [Norman: University of Oklahoma Press, 1987], 165–78). She does not refer to foreign-born women among those she studied, however, and her positive evaluation of women as homesteaders is contradicted by negative information elsewhere.

60. Ise, "Mother's Recollections," 5.

61. Jacob Sieck, "Die Amerikafahrer," *Jahrbuch für die Schleswigsche Geest,* vol. 15 (Schleswig: Heimatverein Schleswegsche Gust, 1967), 144. Mark Friedberger has pointed out that monetary shares for daughters probably were inequitable, since the land was devalued when sold or given to sons ("The Family Farm and the Inheritance Process: Evidence from the Corn Belt, 1870–1950," *Agricultural History* 57 [January 1983]: 12). A variation on this pattern is recorded in Iowa. One family of nine accumulated enough land for each of the three sons to inherit 160 acres, while the six daughters got an education (three became teachers) and some cash, "so they pretty much came out the same" in the view of their descendant (Myrne Detloff Bogh, "Oral Interview," 11 July 1978, Remsen, Iowa, with Rebecca Conard and Mary Jo Wallace, Oral History Project, Earthwatch, #23, tape 1, Manuscript Collection, ISHD-HS). Given the relatively low level of education needed to become a teacher in the nineteenth century and the short time most women remained in the profession, however, we might ask how equal this inheritance was.

62. Sonya Salamon has contributed several especially pertinent studies of farming practices and inheritance traditions in communities of various ethnic heritages in central and southern Illinois ("Ethnic Differences in Farm Family Land Transfers," *Rural Sociology* 45 [Summer 1980]: 290–308; "Sibling Solidarity as an Operating Strategy in Illinois Agriculture," *Rural Sociology* 47 [Summer 1982]: 349–68; "Ethnic Communities and the Structure of Agriculture," *Rural Sociology* 50 [Fall 1985]: 323–40).

63. Kamphoefner, *The Westfalians,* 124. See also W. R. Lee, *Population Growth: Economic Development and Social Change in Bavaria, 1750–1850* (New York: Arno, 1977), 276.

64. Lindgren (173, note 22) cites the Russian-language source A. A. Klaus, "Obshchina-sobstvennik i eia iuridicheskaia organizatsiia," *Vestnik Evropy,* no. 3 (March 1870): 82, 103, trans. Liya Vinograd. Other sources indicate that in the Volga colonies, the Russian "mir" system prevailed, whereby land was apportioned according to the number of adult males in the household. In the Black Sea and Caucasus areas, ultimogeniture was the case. See Theodore Hummel, *100 Jahre Erbhofrecht der deutschen Kolonisten in Russland* (Berlin: n.p., 1936), 41–42, 64, 129; and Adam Giesinger, *From Catherine to Khrushchev: The Story of Russia's Germans* (Battleford, Saskatchewan: Marian Press, 1974), 69.

65. A. G. Roeber has examined the inheritance customs among Germans in eighteenth-century colonial America ("The Origins and Transfer of German-American Concepts of Property and Inheritance," in *Perspectives in American History,* n.s., vol. 3, eds. Bernard Bailyn, Donald Fleming, and Stephan Thernstrom [Cambridge, Mass.: Cambridge University Press, 1986]: 115–71). His study shows a great deal of variation stemming from local and regional differences, with further layers of complexity due to the several legal systems that had influenced these customs. The picture in German lands became increasingly complex in the nineteenth century, especially in areas of partible inheritance, as Sabean's study in Württemberg indicates (201–7). An example of the clear transferal of inheritance customs within a homogenous immigrant community, in this case Swedish-American, can be found in Robert C. Ostergren, "Land and Family in Rural Immigrant Communities," *Annals of the Association of American Geographers* 71 (September 1981): 400–411.

66. K. Conzen discusses the relationship between American inheritance patterns and the family economic strategies of German settlers and their descendants in Minnesota ("Peasant Pioneers," 266, 280–81).

67. W. F. Johnson, vols. 1 and 2. I am grateful to Westminster College for support in the form of a summer study grant to conduct this research in 1989 and to Kenton G. Askren, the Cooper County associate circuit judge, and Jammey Brandes and Terry Wolfe, probate clerks, for their assistance in gathering the pertinent material.

68. Georg Neff, will dated 5 August 1854, folder 690, CCMPC. Friedberger noted similar documents among the wills of second-generation Germans in Illinois (8–9).

69. Theresa Schmidt, will dated 20 August 1902, folder 3737, CCMPC. See also Neff will; and Jacob Schilb, will dated 18 December 1855, folder 785, CCMP. John Hoerl deeded his oldest son only personal property, but he had earlier sold him the home place and resided there with him (will dated 6 October 1928, folder 5573, CCMPC; W. F. Johnson, 2:674). In another case, John King gave his only son the opportunity to buy an additional eighty acres of family land (will dated 3 April 1914, folder 4394, CCMPC).

70. Wilhelm Kahle, will dated 16 October 1916, folder 4654; Ernst Wallje, will dated 6 March 1905, folder 4395, both in CCMPC.

71. Theobald Theiss, will (n.d.), folder 3798; Henry A. Renkin, will dated August 1925, folder 5221; Johann Jacob Blank, will dated 25 April 1888, folder 2741; Albert Muntzel, will dated 5 March 1902, folder 3674, all in CCMPC.

72. W. F. Johnson, "August Stegner," 1:566–67; August Stegner, will dated 17 April 1914, folder 5343, CCMPC.

73. Margaretha Brueckner, will dated 24 August 1910, folder 4392; Ida Joeger, will dated 10 February 1932, folder 6718, both in CCMPC.

74. Blasius Efinger, will dated 30 July 1897, folder 3476, CCMPC; W. F. Johnson, 2:648–49.

75. Theodore Brandes, will dated 25 May 1925, folder 5143, CCMPC; the wills that seek to protect the daughter's legacy from her husband are those of Johann Peter Huth, will dated 17 August 1892, folder 2950; John Langlotz, will dated 28 June 1909, folder 3829; and King will, all in CCMPC. Sonya Salamon and Anna Mackey Keim examined the relationship between landownership and women's power in a contemporary Illinois German-American community and concluded that "women appear to make a trade-off of lower status and less power for male management of the family enterprise which assures them a financially secure widowhood" ("Land Ownership and Women's Power in a Midwestern Farming Community," *Journal of Marriage and the Family* 41 [January 1979]: 109).

76. Andrew Steigleder, will dated 13 April 1907, folder 3854, CCMPC. Other testaments in which daughters seem to be rewarded for the care of parents are those of John Henry Quint, will (n.d.), folder 2241; Theiss will; Elizabeth Mittelbach, will dated 25 April 1907, folder 3937; Ferdinand Ohlendorf, will dated 28 April 1904, folder 3989; Elizabeth Spieler, will dated 28 May 1925, folder 5168; John J. Walther, will dated 8 February 1937, folder 6823, all in CCMPC. Anna Katharine Felton designated $400 for masses for herself, her husband, and her deceased son and daughter and $300 to "the child who shall care for and provide for me in my old age and in my last sickness and shall furnish me with such things that are necessary for my comfort" (will dated 6 August 1898, folder 3451, CCMPC).

77. Hoerl will.

78. Maria Bechtold, will dated 30 April 1938, folder 6368, CCMPC.

79. King will.

80. Sophia King, will dated 27 March 1918, folder 5001, CCMPC. Sophia King disposed of the remainder of her personal property (including money, clothes, household furnishings, an incubator, and two buggies and harnesses) equally among her children and granddaughter. Each received $1,464.94 in the final settlement.

81. Another interesting document is the handwritten will of Fannie Eppstein, who split up her jewelry, clothing, household goods, and family pictures among her daughters and granddaughters (her two sons, she said, had gotten their father's watch and sword, after all) (will dated 8 November 1903, folder 3751, CCMPC).

82. John Schnuck, will dated 1 August 1880, folder 2111; Katharine Schnuck, will dated 5 September 1911, folder 5119; Cooper County probate court record of jury trial, 24 May 1927, folder 5119, all in CCMPC.

83. Louis Roth, will dated 1 September 1899, folder 3175, CCMPC. A similar case is that of Christian Kosted, whose two farms were deeded to a son and a daughter, with the proviso that the daughter would pay her two sisters $500 each and that the son would pay off $3,100 in debt and $500 to each of his two brothers (will dated 10 September 1884, folder 2342, CCMPC).

84. Ostergren saw both influences at work in his study of seven Swedish-American communities in Minnesota ("Land and Family").

85. The estates involved are Henry Fricke, folder 848; and Henry Robien, folders 1606 and 1993, both in CCMPC.

86. In addition to Gerlach's *Immigrants in the Ozarks* and Jordan's *German Seed in Texas Soil,* the following studies are particularly relevant: Joseph Schafer, "The Yankee and the Teuton in Wisconsin," *Wisconsin Magazine of History* 6 (1922–23): 125–45, 261–79, 386–402; James C. Malin, "The Turnover of Farm Population in Kansas," *Kansas Historical Quarterly* 4 (November 1935): 339–72; Robert G. Wingate, "Settlement Patterns of La Crosse County, Wisconsin, 1850–1875" (Ph.D. diss., University of Minnesota, 1975); Douglas E. Bowers, "American Agriculture: The Contributions of German-Americans," *Journal of NAL Associates* 9, no. 1–4 (1984): 1–12; Donald L. Winters, *Farmers without Farms: Agricultural Tenancy in Nineteenth-Century Iowa,* Contributions in American History, 79 (Westport, Conn.: Greenwood, 1978); Robert C. Ostergren, "European Settlement and Ethnicity Patterns on the Agricultural Frontiers of South Dakota," *South Dakota History* 13 (Spring 1983): 49–82; and Bogue. Gonner (162–63) asserted that Luxembourgian-Americans had chosen wooded land rather than prairie in Iowa because in the old country, a piece of forest meant

the difference between a *Schibebauer* (a poor peasant in a traditional work shirt) and a *Herrebauer* (a wealthy peasant).

87. Lanwert cites a letter from a woman in Michigan, whose family had moved to a larger farm three and a half miles from their first. The woman lamented the distance from the "good neighbor ladies" in the old neighborhood and the lack of anyone but bachelors close by, saying that she had never missed her family in Germany as much as she did now. She consoled herself with the fact that they had twice as much land and a much better farm now, with "nothing lacking in the household" (128).

88. Gerlach noted typically "German" village construction in the Ozarks (*Immigrants in the Ozarks,* 83–85). The Amana and Bethel colonists had some success in re-creating rural villages in America, but in Kansas the Germans from Russia for the most part did not.

89. Anna Kroos, undated letter from near Lincoln, Nebraska, in *"So besinnt euch doch nicht lange und kommt herrüber . . ." Briefe von Amerikaauswanderern aus dem Kreis Lübbecke aus zwei Jahrhunderten,* ed. Heinz-Ulrich Kammeier (Lübbecke: n.p., 1985), 80.

90. Darlene M. Ritter, *The Letters of Louise Ritter from 1893–1925: A Swiss-German Immigrant Woman to Antelope County, Nebraska* (Fremont, Nebr.: Siegenthaler-Ritter, 1980), 25; "Letters to Landshut Ursuline Convent," German Tms, folder 2, box II H, Kirkwood, Ursuline Archives, Central Province, Crystal City, Mo.

91. Letter of 12 July 1876, in *Letters from Mother M. Anselma Felber, OSB, and Others,* trans. M. Dominica Bonnenberg (St. Louis: Benedictine Sisters of Perpetual Adoration, 1977); M. Beatrice Renggli, "From Rickenbach to Maryville: An Account of the Journey," *American Benedictine Review* 27 (Fall 1976): 266. See my comments on similar reactions of Swiss and German nuns to climatic and geographic changes in "German and Swiss Nuns in Nineteenth-Century Missouri and Southern Illinois: Some Comparisons with Secular Women," *Yearbook of German-American Studies,* vol. 20 (Lawrence, Kans.: Society for German-American Studies, 1985), 74–76.

92. Ellingson, 21, 23.

93. E. P. Hutchinson, *Immigrants and Their Children, 1850–1950* (New York: Wiley, 1956), table 14, 34–37.

94. For example, frontier ministers' wives were generally unprepared by their upbringing for such primitive living. See the experiences of Sophie Luise Weitbrecht (52–55); Adelheid von Borries-Garlich (Henry Bode, *Builders of Our Foundations* [Webster Groves, Mo.: privately published, 1940], 49–50); and Albertina and Gottlieb Eisen ("Personal Biographies, Plus Letters," comp. David Schoen, Tms, #11–1/Eis 8, Eden Theological Seminary, St. Louis). Other women responded with disbelief or tears when first seeing their future home, as did Frederica Hecker Fischer and Hannah Aschman Harms's mother (microfilm 3, LDMC).

95. See Gustorf, 131.

96. Ise, *Sod and Stubble,* 23.

97. Edward E. Hirschler, "The Story of a Pioneer Family" (M.A. thesis, Fort Hays Kansas State College, 1937), 27.

98. Ise, *Sod and Stubble,* 17–18; Wieck, 115.

99. Rose Marie Eidam, "History of Maternal Ancestors of Rose Marie Eidam" (1961), Tms, folder 20, box 1, Danker Personal Papers. Even in a sod house, the cold could be life-threatening, as Rebecca Beins discovered during the Nebraska blizzard of 12 January 1888 (*Sod House Memories,* ed. Alberts, 205).

100. Strasser, 58.

101. Jewett, 18. Emilie did not record if Elizabeth Bigler's prayers were answered that summer. Rosie Ise's might have been when her husband agreed to borrow money to buy a windmill, to save her from drawing water by hand for their cattle in the hot Kansas summers (Ise, *Sod and Stubble,* 195–97).

102. Duden, 72.

103. C. C. Regier, "Childhood Reminiscences of a Russian Mennonite Immigrant Mother 1859–1880," *Mennonite Quarterly Review* 15 (January 1941): 93. A letter written by a Kansas Mennonite

woman from Russia described the devastation settlers experienced during the 1874 grasshopper plague, when a woman could not even keep her houseplants safe from the insects (*Mennonitische Blätter,* Danzig, Germany [March 1875], cited by Melvin Gingerich, "The Reactions of the Russian Mennonite Immigrants of the 1870s to the American Frontier," *Mennonite Quarterly Review* 34 [January 1960]: 144). Gingerich's article lists a number of adjustments and difficulties the Mennonite Germans from Russia faced on the Great Plains, including prairie fires, recalcitrant oxen, and dust storms.

104. Howard Raid, "Migrations from Germany to Iowa by Mennonite Settlers, Excerpt Taken from the 'Tagebuch' Written by the Reverend David Ruth and Katherine Strohm" (1855), Tms, Manuscript Collection, ISHD-HS.

105. Ruppenthal, 10; Susanna Amalia Ruth Krehbiel, "Autobiography" (1979), 24, Tms, Mennonite Historical Library, Bethel College, North Newton, Kansas (original manuscript begun 9 January 1911 in Geary, Oklahoma); Gillhoff, 104. Nancy Wieck's humor and optimism are strong elements in her memoir, qualities she seems to have shared with her German mother-in-law (115, 125).

106. Related scholarly commentaries include McNall and McNall, 85; and Nelson, 170–71, 175, 177.

107. Bradley H. Baltensperger, "Agricultural Change among Nebraska Immigrants, 1880–1900," in *Ethnicity on the Great Plains,* ed. Luebke, 173–82. Kamphoefner notes that almost no Americans grew barley or buckwheat in 1850 in the area of his study in Missouri, but some Germans did (*The Westfalians,* 129). John C. Weaver shows the connection between the tendency of German-born farmers in southwest Illinois to grow more wheat than Anglo-Americans did and their origins in wheat-growing parts of Germany ("Changing Patterns of Cropland Use in the Middle West," *Economic Geography* 30 [January 1954]: 9). Gonner noted that the Luxembourg immigrants raised a great deal of wheat but were switching to corn and pig feeding in Iowa because it was proving more profitable (150, 156). Ostergren speculates that the greater amounts of wheat planted by Swedes and Germans than by Anglo-Americans in Isanti County, Minnesota, during the settlement period (1860–80) could be attributed to the early successes they had had with that crop (*A Community Transplanted,* 197–98). As K. Conzen has asserted, however, immigrants adopted American farming methods and crops quickly as a means to achieving their ultimate goals and saw no inherent value in their native practices ("Deutsche Einwanderer," 366).

108. Bogue's study of two Iowa counties in 1880 shows that immigrants lagged behind the native-born in animal husbandry as it grew in response to specialized market demands (211).

109. Among the many German-speaking immigrants who spun and knit their own wool were Minnie Sanders Volker in Kansas (Mrs. Henry Volker Jr., "Minnie Sanders Volker" [n.d.], Tms, microfilm 9, LDMC), and Mathilda Bortz's and Ella Hein Sillars's grandmothers in Iowa (Mathilda Bortz, "The Story of My Grandmother" [n.d.], box 13, Manuscript Collection, ISHD-HS; Ella Sillars, Oral History Interview [28–30 July, 4 August 1976], tape 5, Manuscript Collection, ISHD-HS). For further comment on this, see Boylan, 5, 12; and Stanfield, 35, 38. On flax and rye production as examples of "cultural rebound" among Germans from Russia in Nebraska, see Baltensperger, 177. Ostergren noted that immigrants in South Dakota also returned to familiar European crops after some years in America ("European Settlement and Ethnicity Patterns," 80). Brown called the wine distilled in Iowa basements "a part of the daily meal" (17). Gonner wrote about growing flax in western Iowa and sheep being kept for family use, even though they were not profitable (153, 156).

110. Kamphoefner found that 95 percent of the German-born in Warren and St. Charles counties, Missouri, listed potatoes among the crops they had planted in 1850, but only 5 percent had grown sweet potatoes (*The Westfalians,* 129). Louis Geiger, writing of rural Cooper County, Missouri, said that the German-speaking immigrants there and their children never developed a taste for roast raccoon or oppossum ("At Century's Turn, 1880–1930: Billingsville" [May 1991], 15, Tms, Collection 5051, WHMC-C).

111. Roebke, 108. See her listing of emigrant guidebooks (231–38). Among the more significant, in

addition to that by Duden already cited, are Friedrich Vulpius, *Amerikanische Erfahrungen* (Frankfurt am Main and St. Goar: Verlagsbuchhandlung zu Belle-Vue, 1847); Ottomar von Behr, *Guter Rath für Auswanderer nach den Vereinigten Staaten von Nordamerika* (Leipzig: R. Friese, 1847); Ludwig von Baumbach, *Briefe aus den Vereinigten Staaten von Nordamerika in die Heimath mit besonderer Rücksicht auf deutsche Auswanderer* (Cassel: Theodor Fischer, 1851); Gustav Struve, *Wegweiser für Auswanderer* (Bamberg: Buchner, 1866); and Gustav Struve, *Kurzgefaßter Wegweiser für Auswanderer* . . . (Bamberg: Buchner, 1867).

112. Goebel said that the wives of the Missouri Dreißiger learned handy cooking techniques from backwoods American women (68). Anna Kroos, working as a maid on a farm outside of Lincoln, Nebraska, wrote that she had had to learn to cook, bake and sew, "for here everyone does everything herself" (letter, undated, in Heinz-Ulrich Kammeier, *"Ich muß mir ärgern, das ich nicht ehr übern Großen Ozean gegangen bin": Auswanderer aus dem Kreis Lübbecke und Ungebung berichten aus Amerika* [n.p.: Mittwalddruck Espelkamp, 1988], 78). Elise Isely, whose mother died soon after the family arrived in Missouri, learned all of her frontier housekeeping skills from American neighbors (75–79). Louise Gellhorn Boylan remembered the picniclike atmosphere of molasses-making, a skill her northeast German family no doubt learned from their American neighbors (5).

113. August Rauschenbusch warned women that they would have to bake their own bread in the American backwoods (*Einige Ausweisungen für Auswanderer nach den westlichen Staaten von Nordamerika und Reisebilder,* 3d ed. [Eberfeld und Iserlohn: Bädeker, 1848], 61). Gustorf, after meeting the daughters of a German immigrant trial lawyer in Missouri, found it incredible "that women of such culture have come here to milk cows" (137). Goebel described how discouraged his mother became when her rice pudding, a special treat for which she had saved milk, spilled into the flames of the open hearth (48–49). The German-born Adorers of the Most Precious Blood in Ruma, Illinois, spoiled new foodstuffs because they did not know how to handle them properly. These nuns also disliked the morning snack of parched corn available to them and their pupils. For a further discussion of similar problems, see Pickle, "Stereotypes and Reality," 296; and Pickle, "German and Swiss Nuns," 75–76.

114. Dick describes the procedure for making soap out of lard (238–39). Women in German-American farm families in Nebraska were still making their own soap well after World War II, as I and no doubt many others can attest.

115. Roenigk, 113, 238–39, 277. The descendants of German-speaking women on the Nebraska frontier recorded different reactions to Indians on the part of their ancestors (see, for example, Catherine Ballow March, "A Story of the Ballow Family and the Heldt Family in Saunders County, Nebraska" [1962], folder 15, box 4, Danker Personal Papers; and Judy Blecher, "My Ancestors" [1961], folder 16, box 1, Danker Personal Papers). Immigrant children could find Indians attractive (Jewett, 15). Even when the frontier era was past, however, a newly arrived immigrant might still be frightened by a small group of Indians in wagons who stayed overnight on her farm (Ritter, 25).

116. In Kamphoefner's study of German immigrants in Warren and St. Charles counties in 1850, he found that 28 out of 1,000 households owned slaves, and half of these had only one slave. Many of those Germans who owned slaves were married to Americans (*The Westfalians*, 115–17).

117. Isely, 78; William Arndt, "Several Episodes from the Life of the Sainted Pastor F. J. Biltz," *Concordia Historical Institute Quarterly* 6 (July 1933): 41–50. One of the episodes in the Arndt article figures prominently in Robert Frizzell's "'Killed by Rebels': A Civil War Massacre and Its Aftermath," *Missouri Historical Review* 71 (July 1977): 369–95. German-speakers formed several home guard units in Missouri. For activities and casualties of the German-dominated Boonville home guard, see W. F. Johnson, 1:190–202. On the stance of German-speakers before and during the Civil War, see James A. Bergquist's "People and Politics in Transition: The Illinois Germans, 1850–60," Jay Monaghan's "Did Abraham Lincoln Receive the Illinois German Votes?" and Frederick C. Luebke's Introduction, all in *Ethnic Voters and the Election of Lincoln,* ed. Frederick C. Luebke (Lincoln: University of Nebraska Press, 1971). See also Steven Rowan and James Primm, *Germans for a Free Missouri* (Columbia: University of Missouri Press, 1983); and Richard J. Jensen, *The Winning*

of the Midwest: Social and Political Conflict, 1888–1896 (Chicago: University of Chicago Press, 1971), 96, 142–43, 294–95, passim.

118. Thomas C. Coulter, "A History of Woman Suffrage in Nebraska, 1856–1920" (Ph.D. diss., Ohio State University, 1967), 50. Frederick Luebke discusses Nebraska Germans' views on suffrage as well (*Immigrants and Politics* [Lincoln: University of Nebraska Press, 1969], 127–30). See also the exchange between the German-born pioneer Fred Hedde and the suffragist Harriet Brooks in the Grand Island, Nebraska, *Times,* May–September 1881.

119. Friedrich Muench, a prominent Dreißiger in Missouri, wrote that woman's "greatest perfections can only be manifested in Domestic Life" and that her nature is "love, innocence, tact, fineness, delicacy, in short, amiability" (*Spirit of the Age* 1 [3 November 1849]: 12). Wilhelm Sihler sets forth the prevailing attitude in the Missouri Synod in the late nineteenth century ("Über den Beruf des Weibes und seine Entartung," *Der Lutheraner* 28 [1 February 1872]: 65–67).

120. Margretta Stewart Dietrich, *Nebraska Recollections* (Santa Fe: Dietrich, 1957), 9.

121. I checked listings of woman's rights organizations at the Kansas State Historical Society and the Nebraska State Historical Society. Irene Häderle, however, found reference to the founding of a *Frauen-Stimmrechtsverein* (women's franchise club) in St. Louis County in June 1871 ("Deutsche Frauenvereine in den USA, 1840–1930: Ein Zwischenbericht," in *Frauen wandern aus,* ed. Blaschke and Harzig, 88). On the German-American women's press, see Monika Blaschke, "Die deutschamerikanische Presse für Frauen: Bestand, Prognosen und Probleme," in *Frauen wandern aus,* ed. Blaschke and Harzig, 98, 101–2, 107; and Christiane Harzig, "Elemente einer deutschamerikanischen Frauenkultur: Deutschamerikanerinnen in Chicago vor der Jahrhundertwende," in *Frauen wandern aus,* ed. Blaschke and Harzig, 116, 118. June O. Underwood notes only that immigrant women were the objects of philanthropic efforts by some Anglo-American women's groups ("Civilizing Kansas: Women's Organizations, 1880–1920," *Kansas History* 7 [Winter 1984–85]: 291–306). See also Luebke, *Immigrants and Politics,* 129–31, 138–41. For a related discussion of the connection between views of women's nature and attitudes toward suffrage among German-American socialists, see Ruth Seifert, "The Portrayal of Women in the German-American Labor Movement," in *German Workers' Culture in the United States, 1850 to 1920,* ed. Hartmut Keil (Washington, D.C.: Smithsonian Institution Press, 1988), 109–36. On the antiforeigner sentiments among suffragists, see Barbara Berg, *The Remembered Gate: Origins of American Feminism* (New York: Oxford University Press, 1978), 269.

122. An interesting history of one such family recreation spot is Robert Perry's *Schimmer's Sand Krog: Resort on the Platte* (Grand Island, Nebr.: Prairie Pioneer Press, 1984). See also Percy G. Ebbutt, *Emigrant Life in Kansas* (London: Swan Sonnenschein, 1886), 204. Paul Kleppner discusses various stances toward temperance (mostly oppositional) taken by German-American voters during the period of his study (*Cross of Culture: A Social Analysis of Midwestern Politics, 1850–1900* [New York: Free Press, 1970]). Luebke notes that the only German-Americans who supported temperance were those who joined American Protestant churches (Baptist, Methodist, Congregationalist, and Evangelical) and some Mennonites (*Immigrants and Politics,* 66).

123. C. Carnahan Goetsch, "The Immigrant and America: Assimilation of a German Family," *Annals of Iowa* 42 (Summer and Fall 1973): 17–27, 114–25. For a "strong-minded lady" in Plank Township, Iowa, who found and took away the jug her menfolk had taken care to hide from her, see Stanfield, 47.

124. Wiemar Stommel, letter of 24 June 1850, BABS.

125. See, for example, August P. Richter, *Geschichte der Stadt Davenport und des County Scott,* 2 vols. (Davenport, Iowa: privately printed, 1917), 1:453. Roebke noted the same disapproval in the emigrant advisers (181). A subtle warning to women is contained in an *Abendschule* piece on the Amazons (6 October 1881), who awaken admiration for their courage and bravery but at the same time give "the impression of the unnatural and the immoral."

126. Blommer, letter of 25 February 1874, BABS.

127. Frederick Steines, letter of 24 April 1835, in William G. Bek, trans. and comp., "The Follow-

ers of Duden," *Missouri Historical Review* 15 (July 1921): 677. Rural Anglo-American women also "did not mount much sustained criticism, nor much evident resistance to male rule" (Faragher, "History from the Inside-Out," 551).

128. Steinhaus, 74; Goetsch, 23.

129. J. R. Buchanan reported the incident of the recalcitrant wife in "The Great Railroad Migration into Northern Nebraska," *Proceedings and Collections of the NSHS,* 2d ser., 10 (1907): 28–29. Pleck's "Challenges to Traditional Authority" shows that in urban areas German immigrants were the worst offenders for wife beating and child abuse. See also Seller, 65. For particularly disturbing evidence of wife and child abuse among poor immigrants from Russia, see Pauline Neher Diede, *Homesteading on the Knife River Prairies,* ed. Elizabeth Hampsten (Bismarck, N.D.: Germans from Russia Heritage Society, 1983). On this score, see also Sandoz, *Old Jules,* 215–16, 230–31, 279.

130. Timothy J. Kloberdanz has said that the one place where men, women, and children were equal was in the field ("Volksdeutsche, the Eastern European Germans: Hungry for Land, Hungry for a Home; North Dakota's 'Other Germans,'" in *Plains Folk: North Dakota's Ethnic History,* eds. William C. Sherman and Playford V. Thorson [Fargo: North Dakota Institute for Regional Studies, 1988], 150).

131. See, for example, Pieschl, 35; and Ritter, 71. Rosenfeld writes that such reciprocity is still very rare on American farms today (10–11). In her study of Block, Kansas, Coburn found that the kind of work necessary at any time was more important than gender in determining what a child did in the family. She also concluded that first- and second-generation German-American men rarely helped their wives with household work (*Life at Four Corners,* 86–90, 97).

132. See the 10 June 1837 letter to the editor on this subject in the St. Louis *Anzeiger des Westens.* Similarly, the Evangelical minister Johann Gottfried Buettner was scandalized by the unkempt, blunt-speaking, bareback-riding German midwife he met in the Missouri backwoods while going to baptize the child she had helped deliver. According to Buettner, Americans held all German women in low esteem because of women like her and were prone to say, "The dutchwomen are worse than the squas." Buettner also reported having heard that the German women around Belleville, Illinois, rode to town bareback on market days. His conclusion: "It is a true disgrace!" (*Die Vereinigten Staaten von Nord-Amerika* [Hamburg: M. Geber, 1844], 1:199).

133. Stanfield, 48–49. It would be interesting to know if immigrant women in rural areas, removed from the pressure to conform to American women's fashions, retained the midcalf skirts from their homelands for field and yard work.

134. Nancy Wieck's engaging memoir contains several instances of her going against her mother-in-law's advice by making decisions and taking actions in her husband's absence that he had expressly forbidden (114–15, 121–22). Nancy, unlike her mother-in-law, was not German-born, which may partly explain her open independence and the older woman's inclination to go along with her son's wishes. Nonetheless, Nancy's German husband seems to have accepted this in her, telling her, "You say and I'll do" (118).

135. Autograph book epigram, written around 1890 by Pauline Lehner Hoffmann (born in 1855 in Ohio) in Battle Creek, Nebraska, in autograph book of her daughter Clara Hoffmann (later, Uhlmann, born in 1876), in the possession of Rachel Uhlmann Ehrman of South Amana, Iowa.

136. Isernhagen, 77–78; Kloberdanz, "Volksdeutsche," 150; Coburn, *Life at Four Corners,* 155.

137. Lauren Ann Kattner, "Growing Up Female in New Braunfels: Social and Cultural Adaptations in a German-Texas Town," *Journal of American Ethnic History* 9 (Spring 1990): 49–72; Ellingson, 27; Coburn, *Life at Four Corners,* 76.

138. "Jürnjakob Swehn" and his wife seem to have chosen each other without direct intervention from others and agreed to marry when they had $550 saved between them (Gillhoff, 46). August Raasch reported laconically in his diary of the steps taken between his father and the father of his future wife over the period of a week before he got the news that he "could have Marie, also that it was her will and that she had nothing against the whole matter" (Personal Diary, 19 November 1871, NSHS).

139. Schock, *In Quest of Free Land,* 55.

140. See Salamon, "Ethnic Differences," "Sibling Solidarity," and "Ethnic Communities."

141. Bretting rejects Seller's contention that women came to America to emancipate themselves: "Not an attempt to break away, but a wish for continuity was at the basis of their decision to emigrate" (28). The vast majority of "ordinary" immigrants did not redefine their role in family or society because of the new activities they had to assume.

142. *Central Missourier,* 24 December 1874.

143. Gillhoff, 206–7.

144. Pieschl, 36–37; Blommer, letter of 20 July 1871, BABS. Kamphoefner notes that in 1850 a higher proportion of the German immigrants in Warren and St. Charles counties owned property than did any other ethnic group, although the value of that property was less than half that owned by Anglo-Americans (*The Westfalians,* 142). See also K. Conzen, "Peasant Pioneers," 282.

145. Bogue concluded this on the basis of his study of Wapello County and Warren Township in Bremer County, Iowa (25–27). Coburn's study of the Block community in Miami County, Kansas, confirms this as well (*Life at Four Corners,* 16–23).

146. Studies that examine the significance of the rural immigrant church include August Hollingshead, "The Life Cycle of Nebraska Rural Churches," *Rural Sociology* 2 (June 1937): 180–91; Frederick Luebke, "German Immigrants and Churches in Nebraska, 1889–1915," *Mid-America* 50 (April 1968): 116–30; Doerries, "Church and Faith"; Robert C. Ostergren, "The Immigrant Church as a Symbol of Community and Place in the Upper Midwest," *Great Plains Quarterly* 1 (Fall 1981): 224–38; and Jon Gjerde, "Conflict and Community: A Case Study of the Immigrant Church in the United States," *Journal of Social History* 19 (Summer 1986): 681–970. Doerries points to the dual role the church played in providing cultural continuity and stability while also serving as a vehicle for accommodation to the immigrants' new world ("Church and Faith," 286–87), a point K. Conzen has also made (*Immigrant Milwaukee,* 155; "Deutsche Einwanderer," 369, 374). Studies noting the connection between the existence of immigrant churches and the persistence of ethnic communities include H. B. Johnson, 40; Gerlach, *Immigrants in the Ozarks,* 118; Peter A. Speek, *A Stake in the Land* (New York: Harper, 1921); Gjerde, *From Peasants to Farmers,* 163–65, 227–31; and Ostergren, *A Community Transplanted,* 210–11.

147. "Diary of Julie Wall, née Turnau, 1842" (n.d.), trans. Armin Saeger, 25, #12–1/WA 11, Eden Theological Seminary Archives, St. Louis.

148. Historical studies of German immigrant churches in the five-state region include Otto E. Kriege, Gustav Becker, Matthäus Hermann, and C. L. Korner, eds., *Souvenir der West Deutschen Konferenz der Bischöflichen Methodistenkirche* (Cincinnati: Jennings and Graham, 1906); George Eisenach, *A History of the German Congregational Churches in the United States* (Yankton, S.D.: Pioneer Press, 1938); C. E. Schneider; and Bode. Although Coburn's study of Block, Kansas, takes gender roles in rural immigrant communities into account, she, too, acknowledges the difficulty of ascertaining women's roles and contributions to immigrant church life because they were so much a part of the fabric of assumptions about women and their work (*Life at Four Corners,* 48–49). The archives of foundations of German-speaking Catholic nuns, however, contain many valuable sources on women's contributions to religious life.

149. Howard Ruede's letters contain many references to such frontier gatherings, without more than the following oblique acknowledgment of women's contributions: "It seems to be thought no imposition for fifty or more to take dinner at a place" after such a meeting (*Sod-House Days: Letters from a Kansas Homesteader, 1877–78,* ed. John Ise [New York: Columbia University Press, 1937], 32). The letters of Christian Helmreich, pastor for a time to a colony of East Frisians near Lodgepole, Nebraska, attest to the long struggle small ethnic communities faced in founding their own congregations ("Letters of Christian Helmreich [1866–1945]," ed. and trans. Ernst C. Helmreich, *Nebraska History* 58 [Summer 1977]: 175–92).

150. The records of the Smithton Methodist Church, Smithton, Missouri, recording the building of a new church in 1897, are an example of this (Smithton Methodist Church, Records, 1867–1951, 2:83–87, #C3704, WHMC-C). The 1871 articles of incorporation of the Brunswick, Missouri,

"Deutsche protestantische evangelisch-lutherische Johannes Gemeinde" list only men as signatories (German Lutheran Church, Record Book, 1869–1888, #C3825, folder 542, Benecke Family Papers, WHMC-C).

151. Raid, 3, 4; Stickney, 22. Fink stated of the mixed-ethnic area she studied in Iowa, "The church replicated the social organization of the family and, in turn, served as a model for its dual organization. Women, responsible for social reproduction, were the backbone of the church membership, and their dedication to church life kept it a vital part of the community. Although men had less overall involvement in religious life than women did, men were the public face of the church, its formal leaders" (41). Häderle also notes the behind-the-scenes importance of women in the functioning of immigrant churches (87). Arthur J. Vidich and Joseph Bensman's study of a twentieth-century rural community also shows that Anglo-American women played a vital but hidden role in church life (*Small Town in Mass Society* [Princeton, N.J.: Princeton University Press, 1968], 232–33).

152. Gillhoff, 191. Similarly, Gonner noted the intensification of church life among Luxembourgian immigrants in America (166–71).

153. Siekmann, 55; Henry W. Casper, *History of the Catholic Church in Nebraska,* 3 vols. (Milwaukee: Bruce, 1960–66), 1:136.

154. Concrete evidence of the contributions of immigrant church women's groups in the Midwest include the minutes of the Ladies Aid Society (1922–24) of the Smithton, Missouri, Methodist Church, vols. 6 and 7, WHMC-C. Louis Geiger's 1991 history of the St. Johannes Deutsche Evangelische Kirche (St. John German Evangelical Church) at Oak Grove-Billingsville in rural Cooper County, Missouri, contains much information about women's activities in this small country church ("St. Johannes Deutsche Evangelische Kirche" (10 May 1991), Tms, folder 1, Collection 5051, WHMC-C). Coburn's study of the rural Missouri Synod Lutheran community and church of Block, Kansas, also attests to the many unsung and unrecorded contributions women made to the maintenance of ethnic community through their church-related activities (*Life at Four Corners,* 49–55). Gjerde offers evidence of parallel activities by Norwegian women in the upper Midwest (*From Peasants to Farmers,* 230). Similarly, a Ladies Aid Society was the founding core of the rural Norwegian First Lutheran Church of Bruce, South Dakota (Elizabeth Hampsten, "Sterling Township Women Built a Church," comp. Janet Hovey Johnson, *Plainswoman* 8 [September 1984]: 6–7, 15).

155. This was true for a long time. The art historian Charles Van Ravenswaay, who grew up in Cooper County, Missouri, remembered the German-American farm women in the 1920s, whose isolation was broken almost solely by church attendance and family and neighborhood visits on Sunday (*The Arts and Architecture of German Settlements in Missouri* [Columbia: University of Missouri Press, 1977], vii-viii).

156. For example, the Evangelical Church Board of Missions refused to authorize the formation of a woman's missionary society until 1880 (Kriege et al., 47). In Block, Kansas, the Trinity Lutheran Ladies Aid was not formed until 1912 (Coburn, *Life at Four Corners,* 49).

157. Brown, 13.

158. Geiger, "St. Johannes Deutsche Evangelische Kirche," 13–14.

159. *Kansas Staats-Anzeiger* (Atchison), 14 July 1881.

160. Goetsch, 24–25; Gottfried Walz, letter of 12 February 1897, BABS. See also Speek, 65–66, 156–57, 203–18, passim.

161. Hutchinson, table 35b, 182–85. Speek noted that immigrants did not take seriously the typically young, single, female American teachers in rural, one-room public schools (207).

162. An example was Trinity Lutheran School at Block, Kansas, which hired its first such female teaching assistant in 1906. The fact that she was the unmarried daughter of the pastor made the school board feel it was not as bad as it might have been (Coburn, *Life at Four Corners,* 73–74). One of the most important studies of the Missouri Synod school system is August C. Stellhorn, *Schools of the Lutheran Church-Missouri Synod* (St. Louis: Concordia Publishing House, 1963).

163. Boylan, 8, passim.

164. Sillars, tape 3.

165. See Speek, 156–65; and Coburn, *Life at Four Corners,* 226. Some school districts in Kansas and Nebraska were allowed to teach in German as well as English (A. F. Buechler, R. J. Barr, and Dale P. Stough, *History of Hall County, Nebraska* [Lincoln, Nebr.: Western Publishing, 1920], 350–51). This led to complaints from state education officials about the diversion of public funds to non-English-language schools (Heinz Kloss, "German-American Language Maintenance Efforts," in *Language Loyalty in the United States,* eds. Joshua A. Fishbein and Mary E. Warschauer [The Hague: Mouton, 1966], 234–35). Luebke discusses German immigrants' opposition to compulsory school laws in Nebraska in the 1890s (*Immigrants and Politics,* 143–50). In contrast, J. Olson Anders suggests that in other regions, immigrants were eager to cooperate with public school policy so their children could become integrated into American society ("Educational Beginnings in a Typical Prairie County," *Rural Sociology* 7 [December 1942]: 423–31). On teacher training for these schools, see LaVern J. Rippley, "The German-American Normal Schools," in *Germanica-Americana, 1976: Symposium on German-American Literature and Culture,* eds. Erich A. Albrecht and J. Anthony Burzle (Lawrence, Kans.: Max Kade Document and Research Center, 1977), 63–71.

166. Gillhoff, 300. See also Dorothy Weyer Creigh's comments in *Nebraska: A Bicentennial History* (New York: Norton, 1977), 153.

167. Harley Ransom, comp., *Pioneer Recollections* (Cedar Rapids, Iowa: Historical Publishing, 1941), 262. This society, located in a small community a few miles north of the Amana colonies, endured well past World War II (Ransom, 263–65). See also Reinhard Doerries, *Iren und Deutsche in der neuen Welt: Akkulturationsprozesse in der amerikanischen Gesellschaft im späten 19. Jahrhundert,* Beiheft 76, Vierteljahrschrift für Sozial-und Wirtschaftsgeschichte (Stuttgart: Steiner, 1986), 90–91); and Wolfgang Helbich and Ulrike Sommer, *"Alle Menschen sind dort gleich . . .": Die deutsche Amerika-Auswanderung im 19. und 20. Jahrhundert,* eds. Armin Reese and Uwe Uffelmann, Historisches Seminar, 10 (Düsseldorf: Schwan, 1988), 46, 52–53.

168. According to an 1847 letter quoted by Schuster (23). For the location of secular German-American clubs, see Heinz Kloss, *Atlas of Nineteenth and Early Twentieth Century German-American Settlements* (Marburg: Elwert, 1974), map series F.

169. Brunswick Turn-Verein, 1866–69, #C3825, folder 574–82, Benecke Family Papers, WHMC-C. The Boonville, Missouri, *Central Missourier* listed three women among the nine actors performing "Ein toller Tag" on 28 January 1875 during a "Turn- und Gesang-Verein" benefit. Häderle gives a general overview of the formation of nineteenth-century German-American women's clubs (89–91). For an introduction to the history of the *Turner* movement in Germany and the United States, see Henry Metzner, *A Brief History of the North American Gymnastic Union,* trans. Theodore Stempfel Jr. (Indianapolis: National Executive Committee of the North American Gymnastic Union, 1911). Ralf Wagner discusses the increasing diversity among German-American *Turner* societies ("Turner Societies and the Socialist Tradition," in *German Workers' Culture,* ed. Keil, 221–40).

170. Ralph Gregory, *The German-Americans in the Washington, Missouri, Area* (Washington, Mo.: Missourian Publishing, 1981), 54–57, 66–74. For a study of Washington, Augusta, and Hermann, Missouri, see Karen Jean DeBres, "From Germans to Americans: The Creation and Destruction of Three Ethnic Communities" (Ph.D. diss., Columbia University, 1986). Related sources and studies of German-American secular clubs include Carl Wencker, "History of the 'Augusta Harmonie Verein'" (February 2, 1906), as told to Reinhard A. Hoffmann, Missouri History Manuscript Collection, Missouri Historical Society, St. Louis; Paul Adams, "The Topeka Turn Verein," *Bulletin of the Shawnee County Historical Society* 58 (November 1981): 87–98; Daniel Padberg, "German Ethnic Theatre in Missouri: Cultural Assimilation" (Ph.D. diss., Southern Illinois University at Carbondale, 1980); Roland Binz, "German Gymnastic Societies in St. Louis, 1850–1913: Emergent Socio-Cultural Institutions" (Master's thesis, Washington University, 1983); William Roba, *The River and the Prairie: A History of the Quad-Cities* (Davenport, Iowa: Hesperion, 1986), 78–79, 101; Siekmann, 64; and Creigh, *Nebraska,* 154. The influence of the *Turnverein* in German-American life continued among the children of immigrants (see, for example, Roba, 101; and Goetsch, 26, 118–19).

171. On the club-sponsored refuges for country women and their children, see Scott, *Natural Allies,* 145–46.

172. Kloss discusses the main factors contributing to language maintenance in the United States, most of which were more common in rural areas ("German-American Language Maintenance Efforts," 206–52). Useful discussions of women's and rural immigrants' adaptation to American culture include Alan Bayer, *The Assimilation of American Family Patterns by European Immigrants and Their Children* (New York: Arno, 1980), 135–36; and Richard Kolm, *The Change of Cultural Identity: An Analysis of Factors Conditioning the Cultural Integration of Immigrants* (New York: Arno, 1980). For related comments, see Coburn, *Life at Four Corners*, 6–7; Bogue, 278; and Grace DeSantis and Richard Benkin, "Ethnicity without Community," *Ethnicity* 7 (April 1980): 137–43.

173. See Dorothy W. Creigh, *Adams County: A Story of the Great Plains* (Hastings, Nebr.: Adams County-Hastings Centennial Commission, 1972), 333. Carman noted that "the Germans very frequently emigrated as families, a conservative linguistic trait," and linked the large number of women in German families to this conservatism (*Foreign Language Units,* 93). Dow observed as late as the 1970s that older female residents of Amana used German exclusively when among themselves, whereas elderly men used English, although the men also spoke German fluently (112). Häderle stated that the women's branch of the short-lived Deutschamerikanischer Nationalbund (founded in 1904 and dissolved in 1918) believed women to be "predestined" through their maternal role to preserve German language and culture (91). Gonner claimed that the dialect preference of the wife determined language usage in the homes of Luxembourgian-Americans (186). An unusual example of the linguistic conservativism of a male immigrant is Francis Arnold Hoffmann, who even persuaded his Anglo-American wife to learn German. The family spoke German exclusively from the time they married in 1844 until he died in 1903 (Minna Hoffman Nehrling, "Papapa" [n.d.], folder 4, Francis A. Hoffmann Papers, ISHL). Much more recently, Kurt Rain noted the conservative aspect of Hutterite women's language usage, in that they speak primarily the basic dialect of the home, not the standardized or "elevated" dialects reserved for business and church usage ("German Dialects in Anabaptist Colonies on the Great Plains," trans. Paul Schach, in *Languages in Conflict,* ed. Paul Schach [Lincoln: University of Nebraska Press, 1980], 108).

174. See, for example, Freeman, "Anton and Karolina Krause"; James A. Schelbitzki, interview with Linda S. Pickle, Columbia, Missouri, 30 December 1986; Elise Boyd, Oral History Interview, April 5, 1977, Clinton, Iowa, with Jay Naftager, tape 79, Manuscript Collection, ISHD-HS. The 1900 census for Benton Precinct, in Nemaha County, Nebraska, shows that Meta Mannott, Ihnke Kleihauer's sister, did not speak English after having lived thirty-two years in America.

175. Pauline Gauß Wendt, letter of 9 February 1897, Gauß-Rogosch Letters, 1865–1903, BABS; Ritter, 37, 149, 151, 163. Even under the most favorable conditions, language retention was difficult and often stunted. For a discussion of the factors favoring language maintenance, see Kloss, "German-American Language Maintenance Efforts," 206. Jürgen Eichhoff has noted the tendency for dialect usage to ossify upon transplantation to American rural areas ("The German Language in America," in *America and the Germans,* 2 vols., eds. Frank Trommler and Joseph McVeigh [Philadelphia: University of Pennsylvania Press, 1985], 1:234.

176. Jewett, 18.

177. On featherbeds and goose down, see Stanfield, 35, 43. Siekmann writes of the Old World brick ovens (22), as does Allie Wallace, *Frontier Life in Oklahoma* (Washington, D.C.: Public Affairs Press, 1964), 22. On retention of Old World foods, see Gonner, 156; and Goetsch, 116.

178. Speek, 51; Mela Meisner Lindsay, *Shukar Balan: The White Lamb* (Lincoln, Nebr.: American Historical Society of Germans from Russia, 1976), 180; Isely, 72.

179. According to Albine Krause Schelbitzki, her parents and their children had eaten in this communal fashion while still in Austria. Blommer also pointed out that families who had eaten with wooden spoons from a common bowl in Germany used porcelain and silverware daily in America (letter of 13 September 1874, BABS). Gonner noted the other changes in Luxembourgian peasant customs (148–49). J. J. Teten, however, reported a kind of community bread-breaking, which seems to have commemorated the end of the old life and the beginning of the new. When Teten's family arrived at his uncle's farm near Nebraska City in 1867, the entire neighborhood of

German immigrants was invited to share in the loaves of rye bread his mother had brought along, "because it symbolized old friendships" (Siekmann, 81).

180. "Diary of Julie Wall," 23; Lindsay, 138–40; Wallace, 22; Jewett, 10, 18.

181. See Plaul's comments on European preemigration dress (120–21). Roebke found that the immigrant advisers were aware of the relative equality in dress among American women and often disapproved when young German-American women, especially of the lower classes, assumed it (106, 181). For examples of German-American views of servant girls' inappropriately independent behavior in America, see Lanwert, 99–101. Elizabeth Ewen's study of Italian and Jewish women on the Lower East Side of New York offers interesting parallels in this regard (*Immigrant Women in the Land of Dollars* [New York: New Feminist Library, 1985], 67–71, 197). Rural women would not, however, have experienced the constant pressure to conform that the women in Ewen's study did.

182. Jewett, 20–21.

183. Steve Parsons, "A German-Style Ozarks Christmas: Before Santa There Was Scary Old Belsnickels," *Ozarks Mountaineer* 40 (November/December 1992): 32–35; Gonner, 149–50, 166–68, 216–17; Schuster, 23; Geiger, "At Century's Turn," 10–11. Ellingson mentions the traditional visits of *Pelzenickel* among the Kansas Bukovinia Germans and the retention of many other domestic and folkway customs. Mary Alicia Owen suggested that the Germans brought the Christmas tree to Missouri, where it was adopted by Anglo-Americans ("Social Customs and Usages in Missouri during the Last Century," *Missouri Historical Review* 15 [October 1920]: 181).

184. Jewett, 27–28.

185. On *Brautbitter* and shivarees, see Stickney, 10–12; Geiger, "At Century's Turn," 8; William G. Bek, "Survivals of Old Marriage Customs among the Low Germans of Western Missouri," *Journal of American Folk-lore* 21 (January–March 1908): 60–67; Coburn, *Life at Four Corners,* 106–7; and Adolf E. Schroeder, "The Persistence of Ethnic Identity in Missouri German Communities," in *Germanica Americana, 1976,* eds. Albrecht and Burzle, 38. Schroeder reports a variety of other holiday and folk customs that German-American communities in Missouri retained, in some cases until the 1970s (36–38). See also his "Deutsche Sprache in Missouri," in *Deutsch als Muttersprache in den Vereinigten-Staaten,* ed. Auburger et al., 125–59). A good general source on German and German-American folklore and traditions is LaVern Rippley, *Of German Ways* (Minneapolis: Dillon, 1970). See also John F. Streng, "Remainders of Superstitions among German-Americans in Nebraska" (M.A. thesis, University of Nebraska, 1929).

4

Gender Ideology and Black Women as Community-Builders in Ontario, Canada, 1850–70

SHIRLEY J. YEE

lizabeth Jackson Shadd Shreve was known to Blacks in Buxton, Ontario, as an energetic Christian woman who "travelled about, on horseback, through the bush, and over roads almost impassable at times, ministering to the sick, collecting and delivering food and clothing for the needy, and preaching the Gospel."[1] Anecdotal references to individual Black women, such as the one above, tell a great deal about the material and spiritual contributions Black Canadian women made to their communities. Although scholars of Canadian women's history have long acknowledged the need to develop the diverse histories of racial minorities in Canada, they have just begun to uncover the richness of Black Canadian women's historical experiences.[2]

The purpose of this essay is to explore the possibilities for developing a collective history of Black women in Canada, beginning with southern Ontario in the mid-nineteenth century, a critical place and time in the history of Black Canadian settlement. Black Canadian women's experiences as community-builders challenged simplistic notions of "true" womanhood as they struggled to survive and construct family and community institutions, such as churches, schools, and benevolent organizations.

The status of early Black migrants to Canada varied. Some had been born free, others had been freed by their masters or had escaped. Some traveled alone, others in small groups. In some cases, whole Black church congregations moved to Canada.[3] They set up communities at principal stops on the Underground Railroad: Chatham, Windsor, Amherstburg, and Sandwich. Some had brought with them enough capital to begin farms or businesses. The vast majority, however, were escaped slaves who had arrived destitute, a transient population in want of the basic necessities of life: food, clothing, shelter, and employment.[4] In 1850 Black educator and abolitionist Mary Bibb wrote that hundreds of fugitive slaves arrived in Sandwich every day.[5]

Between the 1830s and 1850s a number of factors facilitated the resettlement of Blacks in Canada: Britain's formal abolition of slavery in the empire in 1833, the enforcement of hitherto dormant Black codes in the northern United States, and the Fugitive Slave Act of 1850.[6] These events exacerbated growing frustration with white-led abolitionism, which had, since the 1830s, struggled unsuccessfully to abolish slavery and racism. Black leaders who supported separatism from white organizations sought to nurture the development of independent Black communities both in and outside the United States. Convinced that there was little hope for eliminating racial oppression in the United States, Blacks who already supported voluntary Black emigration to Great Britain, Canada, Mexico, and Africa stepped up their campaigns after 1850.[7]

The mobility of Black immigrants and the myths and legends that have enshrouded the Underground Railroad have made it difficult to pin down accurate population statistics on Canadian Blacks. Eyewitness accounts often exaggerated the number of Blacks who actually made it to Canada. Manuscript census reports, beginning with the first Canadian census in 1851, provide official data on Black women, children, and men.[8] Impressionistic accounts by visitors to Canada, muster rolls, letters, newspapers, and church membership records provide population estimates as well as information about daily life. Such sources reveal that until the 1860s, Black men outnumbered Black women who migrated to Canada.[9] Women were often pregnant and/or encumbered with young children, which made the trek slow and more dangerous than if men traveled alone or with other adults. Samuel Gridley Howe, agent for the United States Freedman's Inquiry Commission, noted in the 1850s that "the refugees were mostly men; and to this day, the males are most numerous, because women cannot so easily escape."[10] By 1850 the sex ratio of Black immigrants had begun to even out. The Canadian census counted 2,502 Black males and 2,167 Black females in Upper Canada in 1851, by then called Canada West. Unofficial accounts recorded significant increases in the total Black population during the next two years. In 1851 and 1852, approximately 25,000 to 30,000 Blacks resided in Canada.[11] Throughout the decade, the numbers of Blacks increased. Canadian historian Fred Landon estimated that between 1850 and 1860, the Black population grew from 40,000 to 60,000.[12] But, despite the steady flow of Blacks to Canada, they made up a small percentage of the total population.[13]

Whites sometimes exhibited hostility toward Black newcomers. Name calling, occasional riots, and public school segregation illustrated the persistence of race prejudice in North America and dismayed those Blacks who had believed in Canada as a haven for the oppressed. A white man from Chatham asserted matter-of-factly that even though the laws "know nothing about creed, color, or nationality," Blacks would always be considered inferior "because their color distinguishes them."[14] In a circular letter addressed to citizens of both Canada and the United States, Mary Ann Shadd Cary, a strong proponent of emigration, noted bitterly that it was an "indisputable fact" that the rights and privileges of Blacks under the British crown had been "very much infringed upon through prejudice of *color.*"[15] In 1861 U.S.-born Black abolitionist William Wells Brown, who had sung Canada's praises in September of that year, wrote: "The more I see of Canada, the more I am convinced of the deeprooted hatred of the negro, here."[16]

Women as well as men testified that the only reason they stayed in Canada was that British law protected them from enslavement and ostensibly provided them with legal rights as British citizens. One woman told Howe in the 1850s that although she endured more insults in St. Catharines than in her former home in New York state, "the colored people [in Canada] have their rights before the law." Another woman added, "If it were not for the Queen's law, we would be mobbed here, and we could not stay in this house." A Black man in Toronto observed that race prejudice in Canada was "equally strong as on the other side," and that the law was "the only thing that sustains us in this country."[17]

Nevertheless, Black women and men struggled to build a community. Upon arrival in Canada, they sought livelihoods. Underground Railroad connections were helpful for finding housing and jobs. Elizabeth Shadd (Williams Shreve) wrote to her sister Mary Ann Shadd Cary from Wilmington, Delaware, in the 1850s, asking her to house temporarily an escaped slave from Baltimore, a Mrs. Veasy. Shadd asked her sister to find work for Veasy, describing her as "a good seamster" who could earn a living "by her neadle [sic]." She assured her sister that Veasy would not sponge off the Cary family, for she was an "industress [sic] working woman and a very pleasant agreeable boddy."[18]

In Canada, employment opportunities for Black men and women resembled those in the United States. In both countries, Black women, married and unmarried, contributed to the economic survival of their families. Typically, Black men worked as farmers and laborers, although they sometimes found employment as waiters, barbers, cooks, teamsters, mechanics, plasterers, tobacconists, tavern keepers, ministers, and sailors. Opportunities for Black women tended to be limited to domestic-related work such as servants, nurses, housekeepers, milliners, tailoresses, and spinsters, a common term for seamstress.[19] Educated women found schoolteaching a meagre but essential source of income. Such occupations were typical for most wage-earning women in Canada during this period. For Black women, such work was no different from what they had done in the United States as slaves or as free Blacks.

Some expanded their domestic skills by establishing small businesses, such as boarding houses, restaurants, and hat and seamstress shops.[20] A few Black women who ran businesses helped build family fortunes, establishing their families as the social and financial elite of the Canadian Black community. Such was the case of the Duval family of Collingwood, Ontario. During the 1860s Mrs. Duval ran a dressmaking shop out of her home, while her husband, Pleasant, operated a successful barbershop and soft-drink parlor.[21]

While some free Blacks prospered, most struggled to eke out a living. Yet many still believed that Canada was a better place than the United States. A former slave woman reported: "Rents and provision are dear here, and it takes all I can to support myself and children. I could have one of my children well-brought up and taken care of . . . but I cannot have my child go there [the United States] on account of the laws, which would not protect her: but had I to struggle much harder than at present, I would prefer it to being a slave."[22]

The limited types of paid employment available to most Black women in Canada reflected their status as poor immigrant women. As women, in particular, such wage-earning opportunities clearly reflected prevailing gender/race ideologies, which relegated them to unskilled domestic-related labor. Other aspects of Black women's lives were less clear on the subject of gender roles and illustrate contradictions between dominant expectations and reality. The daily realities of women's lives often confounded the simplistic set of notions of "true" womanhood. Expectations of piety, purity, domesticity, and submissiveness had been widely disseminated in gift books, female magazines, newspapers, schools, and churches in the United States and Canada beginning in the 1820s.[23] Respectable women were supposed to be frail and dependent on men, and to shun physical labor. For urban middle-class white women, to whom this model was supposed to apply, such expectations were unrealistic, given their supervisory duties in the household and their social responsibilities. This model was even less realistic for working-class and poor women who toiled at low-paying, low-status jobs for long hours, seven days a week, in addition to caring for their own families.

Testimony by former slave women reveals that an appreciation for being treated like a lady coexisted with pride in the backbreaking physical labor in which they engaged in order to build homesteads. Mrs. John Little, who had escaped with her husband from Virginia and settled in Queen's Bush, proudly noted: "The best of the merchants and clerks pay me as much attention as though I were a white woman: I am as politely accosted as any woman would wish to be." Given the existence of anti-Black sentiment that many Blacks described, such kindness was probably a relief and provided hope that life would indeed improve in Canada. But, at the same time that she appreciated such treatment, Mrs. Little apparently did not adopt the full list of qualifications that supposedly accompanied "true womanhood." Clearly, she did not make any pretenses to frailty and submissiveness, for she took pride in being able to work alongside her husband in the physical construction of their homestead. On the long journey to Canada, she had learned "bushwacking" and farming, which enabled her to clear the land "so that we could have a home and plenty to live on."[24] Such participation in the establishment of homes and farms was not a new experience for most migrating Black women. Those who had been slaves had long been accustomed to hard, heavy labor. As John Little noted: "My wife worked right along with me . . . for we were raised slaves, the women accustomed to work, and undoubtedly the same spirit comes with us here: I did not realize it then; but now I see she was a brave woman."[25]

The harsh realities of frontier life tended to blur gender roles.[26] Black women who made the trek to Canada, whether alone or in groups, encountered many of the same hardships as native-born or immigrant white women who made similar journeys. Conditions often dictated that women take on so-called male tasks in order to survive. In this context, the comments of John Little and his wife make sense. As former slaves whose work often was undifferentiated according to sex and as free Blacks who struggled to establish homesteads, women contributed to the construction of the home and farm while, at the same time, they expressed satisfaction for being treated well.

In Canada as in the United States, the Black community appeared torn over how to position itself with regard to dominant sex role ideology. On the one hand, the creation of patriarchal households held a particular historical significance for free Blacks. At the very least it was a rejection of slavery, in which masters held the ultimate power to determine sex roles for the benefit of the slaveholding economy.[27] Slave fathers had been violated both physically and figuratively by the slave master, whose "laws" affected the formation of all social relations, including community among the slaves. As historians of U.S. slavery have aptly pointed out, resistance by both male and female slaves manifested itself in the creation of strong bonds between blood and non-blood kin who struggled to forge social roles among themselves that bore little resemblance to the roles dictated by the master.[28] To slave women, whose bodies had been violated as breeders and as sexual objects, advocating dominant codes of morals and manners flew in the face of equally dominant stereotypes of Black women as domineering and morally degraded.

The adoption of dominant standards of "true" manhood and womanhood, therefore, illustrated prevailing conceptions of "freedom" in nineteenth-century North America, in which men were dominant and women subordinate. Black immigrants to Canada brought with them these assumptions of "proper" gender roles. At the same time, economics helped determine whether husbands/fathers could be sole breadwinners and women the dependent caretakers of the household. Prosperous Black families had the means to create this "ideal" family structure. Yet the predominance of the working class and poor within the free Black community made it exceedingly difficult for most families to attain this ideal. It was not uncommon for free Black families to view husbands/fathers as heads of household whether or not they were sole providers.

Regardless of economic circumstances, participation in community activities was considered a part of Black women's social responsibility and illustrates the strength and adaptability of gender ideologies among migrating Blacks. The career of writer, teacher, and editor Mary Ann Shadd Cary illustrates the struggle over such expectations in the Canadian Black community. Cary was an outspoken supporter of the emigrationist movement to Canada who became one of her generation's most controversial Black women activists. Born in October 1823 in Wilmington, Delaware, she was the eldest of Abraham and Harriet Parnell Shadd's thirteen children. The Shadds were one of the leading free Black abolitionist families that had established roots in both the United States and Canada. Mary Ann's abolitionist training at home was augmented by her education at a private Quaker school in West Chester, Pennsylvania.[29] In the winter of 1851 she arrived in the village of Windsor, where she had accepted a teaching position from the American Missionary Association to run a school for fugitive slaves. Within a year, she was immersed in various community activities and in the accompanying internal political struggles over such issues as education and mutual aid.

Much of her early writings extolled the virtues of Canada, before disillusion set in by the mid-1850s. In 1852 she published a pamphlet entitled "A Plea for Emigration, or Notes on Canada West," in which she promoted Canada as a prime site for Black resettlement.[30] She expressed her allegiance to British Canada in the prospectus she wrote for the Black Canadian newspaper, the *Provincial Freeman*. In the essay she supported the editors' right "to express emphatic condemnation of all projects having for their object in a great or remote degree the subversion of the principles of the British Constitution, or of British rule in the Provinces."[31]

Her commitment to the development of the Black communities in Canada earned the respect of her activist colleagues, but her directness and willingness to criticize even the most esteemed Black male leaders threatened her reputation as a "lady." As one person observed, Mary Ann enjoyed "the confidence of the entire Canadian population of Windsor," but the wives of her opponents "respect her as much as they fear her."[32] Her well-publicized feud with Henry and Mary Bibb over whether to seek public support for fugitive schools led Henry Bibb to write: "Miss Shadd has said and writes many things we think will add nothing to her credit as a lady."[33]

Throughout her career, Mary Ann challenged expectations of "proper" female behavior. She was an outspoken woman during a time when women were supposed to be demure and submissive to men. Her career illustrates that while Black women's participation in community-building may have been considered an acceptable extension of women's domestic responsibility beyond the private household, those who did so found themselves in a delicate balancing act.

Within this context, Black women often worked with Black men in building institutions that were critical to daily life. Black women's involvement in the establishment of churches, schools, and mutual aid societies reflected a long legacy of cooperation between Black men and women. The construction of churches was one of the first activities in which Blacks engaged on arrival in Canada. An examination of women's role in the Black churches can provide a glimpse of their daily lives, although it cannot tell the whole story, since not all Blacks joined exclusively Black churches.

The Black churches in Canada, as in the United States, served not only the spiritual needs of their congregations, but also functioned as the hubs of political and social activities. It was through the churches that Blacks often organized on behalf of improved schooling, benevolence, and social reform. The Methodist, Methodist Episcopal, and Baptist denominations were the most common among Black newcomers.[34] In 1851 the Board of the Baptist Missionary Convention counted 80,000 Black members of the Baptist Church in Canada West.[35] Black religious leaders in the United States attempted to keep abreast of the activities of their Canadian brethren. As early as 1843 the Connecticut preacher J. W. C. Pennington reported that 444 African Methodist Episcopal churches had been established in Canada.[36] The Methodist church was also strong among Blacks. In Chatham, a bustling farming, mercantile, and shipping town on the Underground Railroad, most blacks belonged to the eastern or western branch of the Methodist church.

In addition to filling membership rolls, Black women helped in the construction of church edifices. Much of this work took place at night, after the day's work, and was divided by sex. A group of Black women in the British Methodist Episcopal congregation in Windsor, for example, carried water from the Detroit River for mortar, while the men mixed the mortar, held the torches, and constructed the building.[37] Women were also responsible for providing food at church functions and raising money to maintain the building, pay the ministers' salaries, and finance various church projects.[38] They played a central role in organizing the annual First of August celebrations to commemorate the abolition of slavery in the British empire. This holiday also served as an opportunity to point a shameful finger at Fourth of July celebrations in the United States, which honored independence at the same time that it condoned slavery.[39]

Women also helped shape church policy. In the First Calvinistic Baptist Church in Toronto, women constituted nearly half of the committee that, in 1855, petitioned the Provincial Parliament to defeat a bill that would have reduced church property rights and intervened in the internal management of the churches.[40] The formation of the Baptist

Sunday (also called Sabbath) School Committee and the Women's Home Missionary Society exemplified Black women's participation in the institutional development of the Black Canadian churches and its evangelical role in Canadian society. Both organizations were part of the Amherstburg Baptist Association, founded in 1841 as the Amherstburg Baptist Association for Coloured People. The purpose of the association was to unify Black Baptist churches in Michigan and Ontario in response to the racism they confronted in white churches in both the United States and Canada.[41] The establishment and maintenance of Sabbath schools was an important component of the association's work in religious education, and was overseen by the Baptist Sunday School Committee, formed in 1871.

Black churchwomen participated on several levels of the church hierarchy. As superintendent of the Sabbath schools, Elizabeth J. Shadd Shreve often delivered the committee's report at the annual association conventions. The association also encouraged the expansion of Sunday school facilities. In 1876, for example, the organization collected funds for the development of a Sabbath school library at the affiliate church in Shrewsbury, Ontario.[42] The female members organized fundraising events in order to carry out their charge "to promote the Gospel of Christ, to aid the weak churches and contribute to the Baptist Missionary Convention of Ontario." Black women's participation in fundraising for the Black Baptist churches was not new, for the association had from time to time called upon the women to raise contributions, decades before the formal establishment of the society.[43]

The formation of the Women's Home Missionary Society was a significant part of Black women's individual and collective activism within Canada's Black Baptist churches. It represented a move to consolidate women's activism within the association and to assign permanently to the women the task of keeping the association solvent and developing its missionary work into the twentieth century. The means by which members achieved the goals of the society were in keeping with traditional ways in which women, irrespective of race, participated in the maintenance of their churches.

Black women's efforts to build and sustain schools for Black Canadians also represented a long history of community activism that had its roots in northern free Black communities in the United States.[44] Black women who pursued teaching in the Canadian settlements during the mid-nineteenth century reflected occupational trends among both Blacks and whites in North America. Teaching was an occupation in transition. Throughout the century, women began replacing men in low-paying elementary school positions, while men, mostly white, moved into higher-paying administrative work within the schools. For women, teaching served multiple purposes. First, it was one of their only sources of income, besides agricultural or domestic work. Second, it fulfilled expectations of women as nurturers of the next generation.[45] Among whites, public acceptance of women teachers came slowly, while in the Black communities in Canada and the United states, teaching had long been a respectable occupation for women.

The demand for education in the Black settlements in Canada was high and writers for the rival Black newspapers, *Provincial Freeman* and the *Voice of the Fugitive,* called for more teachers and schools. In Black society, education held a symbolic as well as practical importance. To many Blacks, education was the key to freedom, a privilege denied in slavery. It served as a way to combat charges of racial inferiority and would produce a generation of skilled men and women who would, leaders hoped, foster the development of a self-reliant community. To this end, men and women with even the most rudimentary education were expected to contribute to the advancement of schooling for Blacks.[46] Mary Ann Shadd Cary once noted that she and other teachers of fugitives wanted to instill "confidence, intelligence, [and] independence," instead of "ignorance [and] servility."[47]

Some schools followed prevailing gender conventions by segregating students by sex. Spokesmen for the Buxton Mission boasted in 1856 of the existence of two schools, one for women, the other for men. Although both sexes received lessons in religion, the curriculum reflected contemporary models of male and female education. While young men took classes in "the common branches" of an English education, which included Latin, Greek, and mathematics, young women were taught domestic skills, particularly "plain sewing." Women could pursue a teaching career if they were willing to pay for additional courses in the "higher branches of female education."[48] Most schools for Black Canadians, however, were not as elaborate as the Buxton Mission School. Typically, teachers operated one-room schoolhouses or taught classes in their own homes to both sexes.

It was not unusual for Black educators in the settlements to bring with them a background in abolitionist work. Mary Ann Shadd Cary, Mary Miles Bibb, and Amelia Freeman Shadd had been active in the movement before migrating to Canada. Mary Miles Bibb was a schoolteacher and abolitionist from Boston, Massachusetts. She and her husband, Henry, were fervent emigrationists who helped establish the Black community in Sandwich, Ontario, in 1850. Henry Bibb once described his "beloved wife" as "a bosom friend, a help-meet, loving companion in all the social, moral, and religious relations of life."[49] Mary Bibb's activism also existed apart from her husband's activism. While he published the *Voice of the Fugitive*, she helped him direct the controversial Refugee Home Society at the same time that she struggled to maintain her private school, which suffered constantly from inadequate funding, supplies, and heat.[50]

During the late 1850s, Mary Ann Shadd Cary co-taught a school with her sister-in-law, Amelia Freeman Shadd, in addition to taking over the editorship of the *Provincial Freeman* in 1853. Her marriage to Thomas F. Cary in 1856 did not prevent her continued participation in these activities. While her husband stayed in Toronto to take care of his businesses, she moved to Chatham to teach, edit, and care for their growing family.[51] When her responsibilities became overwhelming, Mary Ann relied on her family for assistance. Her sisters, Amelia C. and Sarah M. Shadd, sometimes substituted for her at the school and helped care for the young Cary children.[52]

Amelia Freeman Shadd was the daughter of American Black activist Martin H. Freeman.[53] Her marriage to Isaac Shadd, a younger brother of Mary Ann and Elizabeth Shadd, represented the union of two respected Black activist families who had worked closely in the emigration movement. Like the Shadd children, Amelia Freeman had been a part of Black activist circles since childhood. Educated at Oberlin College, she taught in Pittsburgh before relocating to Canada. Observers held her in high esteem. Mary Ann Shadd described her as an "energetic Christian woman" who was "zealous in her duties as a moral and religious instructor." One Black writer called Amelia Freeman Shadd a "woman of great forebearance and integrity."[54]

Although Black leaders enthusiastically promoted education as an essential part of community-building, they faced a variety of obstacles to sustaining schools. Most teachers struggled to keep their schools open. Attendance was frequently sporadic, teaching materials were outdated and in short supply, and school buildings were poorly heated and shabby. Even at successful Buxton, attendance rates at the day school fell because of a shortage of female teachers.[55] Benjamin Drew commented on the poverty-stricken conditions of the Black schools in Amherstburg, noting that the teacher was "much troubled by the frequent absences of the pupils, and the miserable tattered and worn-out condition of the books." Although he praised her efforts in the face of such dire prospects, he was pessimistic about the future of education for Blacks, describing the school as "one more dreary chapter to the pursuit of knowledge under difficulties."[56] Economic hardship was constant throughout the 1850s and sometimes forced community leaders to hold fundraisers to help their teachers.[57]

Problems with funding and irregular attendance in the Black schools were not very different from the difficulties white schools faced in Canada before compulsory education in 1871. Canadian officials as well as American observers, however, acknowledged that racial discrimination shaped school policy in many Canadian towns. The fact that British law provided common schools for all did not mean that it guaranteed social equality. Even influential white Canadians who supported Black education could do nothing about efforts by white parents to keep their children separated from Blacks.[58] It was not uncommon for towns to build separate schools for Black and white children and, in at least one instance, the district school was abolished rather than allow Blacks to attend. Often, there were not enough schools for Blacks and the Black schools that did exist were usually inferior to the white schools. Mary Ann Shadd protested the "large and handsome school houses" built for white children compared with the "single miserable contracted wooden building" for Black pupils.[59] The unending struggle for equal education in Canada contributed to increasing disenchantment with the mythical land of Canaan. Mary Ann described the history of education for Blacks in the counties of Kent, Essex, and Lambton as "a chapter of wrong, ignorance and prejudice" that reflected badly on "the *British name*."

Not only did Blacks have to confront prejudice and discriminatory policies from without, they also had to contend with differences within the Black community. Black women participated actively in the internal politics of the community. One of the most heated debates among Black leaders concerned the funding of schools and racial segregation. Although a strong advocate of Black initiative and self-reliance, Mary Ann Shadd Cary was "utterly opposed" to segregation "under any circumstances." Whether imposed by white society, in the form of segregation laws and customs, or as a result of Black initiative, through the formation of Black organizations, made no difference to Mary Ann. Both situations, she argued, prevented the possibility of eliminating racism. She encouraged Blacks to avoid racial segregation at all costs and to create institutions that made no distinctions based on race.

Mary Ann apparently practiced what she preached. Before moving to Canada, she had joined an African Methodist Church in the United States for a brief time, but left the congregation because of its "distinctive character."[60] In 1851 she opened a school in her home for children "of all complexions." In that year she wrote to George Whipple, secretary of the American Missionary Association, expressing emphatic opposition to "the Spirit of Caste," stating that "whatever excuse may be offered in the states for exclusive institutions, I am convinced that in this country, and in this particular region (the most opposed to emigration of colored people I have seen), none could be offered with a shadow of reason."[61] She remained unshakeable on this point and, eight years later, opened a school with Amelia Freeman Shadd, advertised as a "School for All!"[62] Mary Ann's position, however, was based more upon principle than reality, for apparently only Black children attended her school. In 1855 Benjamin Drew recorded the existence of one interracial school, taught by Mary Bibb.[63]

The issue of segregation was tied to funding and placed Mary Ann at loggerheads with Mary and Henry Bibb. What began as a disagreement over policy quickly disintegrated into a highly publicized personal feud that lasted until Henry Bibb's death in 1854.[64] According to Mary Ann, the principle of self-help should be the guiding force for sustaining the schools in the Black settlements, and the community should not rely on the Canadian government for assistance. The Bibbs took a different position on the school issue. Although they, too, would have liked self-sustaining schools, experience had taught them that such a policy was untenable, given the destitute condition of fugitive slaves in Canada. In 1851 a disheartened Mary Bibb reported that the schools could not continue to exist without outside help. In fact, the private school that Bibb had opened out of her home in 1851 failed after about a year owing to lack of adequate financial support, after which she earned money as a seamstress.[65] By the time Mary Ann arrived on the scene in 1851, the Bibbs had decided to petition the Canadian government for assistance.

Under the Separate Schools Act of 1850, the Canadian government had officially recognized the existence of segregated schools. Thus, segregated 'government' and private schools coexisted for Black Canadians, but neither was funded adequately. In 1853 Mary Bibb taught at a government school, while Mary Ann persisted in her push for self-sustaining private schools that made no racial distinctions. Like Mary Bibb, however, Mary Ann encountered attendance problems and severe material shortages.[66] After Mary Ann found that most Black parents were unable to pay the tuition, she embarked upon fundraising trips to the United States. Unsuccessful attempts to raise money for her school led Mary Ann to accept assistance from the American Missionary Association.[67]

Mary Ann became embroiled in the larger question of fundraising in the Canadian Black communities. The solicitation of funds, whether for the upkeep of schools and salaries for teachers or for providing food and clothing for fugitive slaves, was the subject of intense debate between those Blacks who saw such donations as a reflection of Christian charity and those who viewed the practice as ripe for corruption and undermining to the struggle for self-reliance.[68] Black benevolent associations in Canada, in which women played an integral part, were established in order to promote self-reliance. As in the United States, the creation of these organizations resulted both from the exclusion of Blacks from white societies and from the desire to serve the particular needs of the community. Most were founded by Blacks, but at least one was established by a white woman, Ellen Abbott, for the benefit of poor Black women. Abbott, a domestic servant who emigrated to Canada in 1835, was married to a free Black man.[69]

The structures of the organizations were similar to their counterparts in the United States. Many functioned under the auspices of the church, while others were auxiliaries to male fraternal associations. Some were segregated by race, others by sex, and a few welcomed men and women of both races. For Black women, as for white women, benevolent societies were avenues through which they could participate in public activities. Typically, women were assigned the task of raising money for their churches and schools and clothing impoverished members of their community.

Perhaps the best-known Black Canadian benevolent organizations were the "true bands." In 1855 Benjamin Drew counted fourteen of these organizations in Canada West. The goal of the bands was to foster independence by raising money to improve schools, providing temporary assistance to needy Black families, and caring for the sick. A clear connection existed between the bands and the Black churches. The True Band of Chatham, Ontario, for example, pledged to "unify all churches and prevent division." Finally, the members of this band also saw the organization as a mechanism for self-government by intervening in disputes among its members.[70]

Like the true bands, the Provincial Union Association espoused a broad agenda. It had included women since its inception in 1854. The union, as it was commonly called, was spearheaded by supporters of the *Provincial Freeman* and encompassed many of the ideas Mary Ann Shadd had advocated, such as the development of interracial cooperation in an effort "to promote harmony—not based on complexional differences among her Majesty's subjects" by removing "the stain of slavery from the face of the earth—and check its progress in America by all legitimate means." Coalition-building was central to the agenda, but members of the union also promoted self-reliance through education in "literary, scientific and mechanical" fields and the maintenance of a newspaper that provided a vehicle to voice the concerns of Black Canadians. The union also pledged to support the *Provincial Freeman* and the association's thirty-five agents from the Black communities in Toronto, Chatham, Hamilton, Dresden, London, and Amherstburg. In order to accomplish these goals, a mechanism for fundraising was established through the formation of a fourteen-member Ladies Committee, which accepted the responsibility of organizing annual fairs in cities where auxiliaries could be formed. Mary Ann Shadd Cary was assigned the task of organizing local female auxiliaries.[71]

In addition to participating with Black men in community organizations, Black women sometimes formed all-female associations. The Mutual Improvement Society, established by the Colored Ladies of Windsor, for example, promoted adult education for Black residents. Mary Bibb served as president of the society. Other female organizations were designed explicitly to help fugitive slaves, such as the Ladies Colored Fugitive Association, the Ladies Freedman's Aid Society, the Queen Victoria Benevolent Society, and the Toronto Ladies' Association for the Relief of Destitute Colored Fugitives.[72]

Black women's participation in charitable societies in Canada exemplified an important type of unpaid female labor that was an essential part of community-building during the mid-nineteenth century. Such societies served an important function by bringing together the concerns of Black communities for economic self-reliance and improved education.

The reconstruction of familiar institutions in Black settlements in Ontario during the 1850s and 1860s illustrates the gendered dimensions of community-building and the important role women played in transplanting community in a new land. Black women in Canada did what women in North America had always done for the benefit of their families and community—they earned and raised money, taught school, organized relief organizations for the needy, and helped construct and sustain their churches. At the same time, their experiences reflected the particular historical experiences of Blacks: coping with racism among whites and with the internal struggles among Black emigration leaders.

As immigrants, Black women pioneers to Canada shared certain experiences with native-born and white women as well as with Black men. Black and white immigrants had viewed Canada as a land of opportunity, and they experienced the joys and frustrations of transplanting familiar values, customs, and institutions to a new environment while, at the same time, hoping to become accepted in Canadian society. Many Blacks soon tempered such idealism, however, as they came to realize that social attitudes and institutionalized racism in Canada differed little from those in the United States.

The extensiveness of Black women's activism raises questions about the degree to which dominant notions of "true womanhood" held true among Blacks, in particular, and for U.S. and Canadian society, in general, at least in the form set forth in the prescriptive literature. As they worked with and sometimes apart from Black men to sustain their new communities, Black Canadian women continually blurred the line between public and private and tailored their own notions of "true" womanhood to the realities they faced in daily life.

Clearly, a tension existed between the dominant ideal and reality. Expectations of women's "natural" duty to the nurturance of a moral home and community existed in the Canadian Black communities as they had among Blacks in the United States. On both sides of the border, the adoption of patriarchal structures that ironically symbolized freedom also illustrated the pervasiveness of sex-role ideology. The implementation of such structures, however, was interrupted by the intimate role Black women played in the social, economic, and political dimensions of Black life. Through their public activism, Black women maintained the interconnectedness of family and community, the private and the public—between which there was little distinction. Perhaps the greatest irony in this process of community-building was that however much Black women blurred the lines between the public and the private, they simultaneously constructed institutions—family, schools, churches, benevolent societies—that were founded on the ideology of separate spheres.

Notes

1. D. S. Shreve et al., *Pathfinders of Liberty and Truth: A History of the Amherstburg Regular Missionary Baptist Association, Its Auxiliaries and Churches* (Merlin, Ont.: n.p. 1940), 63; Dorothy Shadd Shreve, *The AfricCanadian Church: A Stabilizer* (Jordan Station, Ont.: Paideia Press, 1983); see also James K.

Lewis, "Religious Nature of the Early Negro Migration to Canada and the Amherstburg Baptist Association," *Ontario History* 58 (June 1966): 117–33.

2. Gail Cuthbert Brandt, "Postmodern Patchwork: Some Recent Trends in the Writing of Women's History in Canada," *Canadian Historical Review* 72 (Dec. 1991): 468; Joan Sangster, "New Departures in Canadian Women's History," *Journal of Canadian Studies* 23 (Spring/Summer 1988): 235; Adrienne Shadd, "Three Hundred Years of Black Women in Canada, circa 1700–1980," *Tiger Lily* 1, 2 (1987): 4–13; and Afua Cooper, "In Search of Mary Bibb, Black Woman Teacher in Nineteenth Century Canada West," *Ontario History* 83 (Dec. 1991): 39–54. Other recent historiographical essays on Canadian women include Margaret Andrews, "Attitudes in Canadian Women's History, 1945–1975," *Journal of Canadian Studies* 12 (Summer 1977): 69–78; Margaret Conrad, "The Rebirth of Canada's Past: A Decade of Women's History," *Journal of Canadian Studies* 23 (Spring/Summer 1988): 234–41; Eliane Leslau Silverman, "Writing Canadian Women's History, 1979–1981: An Historiographical Analysis," *Canadian Historical Review* 63 (Dec. 1982): 513–33; and Sylvia Van Kirk, ed., "Canadian Women's History: Teaching and Research," special issue of *Resources for Feminist Research/ Documentation de la recherche féministe* (July 1979): 5–13. For general surveys and anthologies on Canadian women's history see Susan Mann Trofimenkoff and Alison Prentice, eds., *The Neglected Majority: Essays in Canadian Women's History,* 2 vols. (Toronto: McClelland and Stewart, 1977, 1985); Veronica Strong-Boag and Anita Clair Fellman, eds., *Rethinking Canada: The Promise of Canadian Women's History* (Toronto: Copp Clark, 1986); Micheline Dumont et al., *Quebec Women: A History* (Toronto: Women's Press, 1987); and Alison Prentice et al., *Canadian Women: A History* (Toronto: Harcourt Brace, 1988).

3. William Pease and Jane Pease, *Black Utopia: Negro Communal Experiments in America* (Madison: State Historical Society of Wisconsin, 1963), 8.

4. Edith G. Firth., ed., *The Town of York, 1815–1834: A Further Collection of Documents of Early Toronto* (Toronto: Champlain Society for the Government of Ontario, 1966), 333–34; Daniel G. Hill, "Negroes in Toronto, 1793–1865," *Ontario History* 15 (1963): 76–77, and Daniel G. Hill, *The Freedom Seekers* (Concord, Ont.: Irwin Publishing, 1981), 168; R. Douglas Francis, *Origins: Canadian History to Confederation* (Toronto: Holt, Rinehart and Winston, 1988), 155–56, 302; Fred Landon, "Amherstburg, Terminus of the Underground Railroad," *Journal of Negro History* 10 (Jan. 1925): 2.

5. Sandwich, Ont., Gerrit Smith Papers, Mary Bibb to Gerrit Smith, 8 Nov. 1850, in Black Abolitionist Papers (BAP), reel 6.

6. Black codes varied, from state to state, but generally restricted Black immigration and denied Blacks the right to petition, vote, sit on juries, or testify against white persons. The Fugitive Slave Act made it a federal crime to aid fugitive slaves. See *Statutes at Large,* 31st Cong., 1st sess., 463–65, 1850; Leon Litwack, *North of Slavery: The Negro in the Free States, 1790–1860* (Chicago: University of Chicago Press, 1961), 69–72, 74–75; Fred Landon, "The Negro Migration to Canada after the Passing of the Fugitive Slave Act," *Journal of Negro History* 5 (Oct. 1920): 22–36.

7. Pease and Pease, *Black Utopia,* 5; Floyd J. Miller, *The Search for a Black Nationality, 1787–1863* (Urbana: University of Illinois Press, 1979), 104–33; Headley Tulloch, *Black Canadians: A Long Line of Fighters* (Toronto: NC Press 1975), 82–83; Robin Winks, *The Blacks in Canada* (New Haven: Yale University Press, 1971), 63–64; M. R. Delany, "Official Report of the Niger Valley Exploring Party," in M. R. Delany and Robert Campbell, *Search for a Place: Black Separatism and Africa, 1860* (1860; reprint, Ann Arbor: University of Michigan Press, 1969), 27–147, and *The Condition, Elevation, Emigration, and Destiny of the Colored People of the United States* (1852; reprint, New York: Arno Press, 1968), 174–75.

8. The category "People of Color, Mulattoes and Indians" on the enumeration sheets enabled census takers to identify a person's race. They marked the space if an individual was included in one of the above groups and left it unmarked if the person was white.

9. University of Western Ontario (UWO), Mary Ann Shadd Cary (MASC) Papers, series A, *Provincial Freeman,* Jan. (185? torn), E. Williams to Mary Ann Shadd Cary, Wilmington, Del., 18 Jan. 1852.

10. Samuel G. Howe, *Report to the Freedman's Inquiry Commission, 1864* (New York: Arno Press, 1969).

11. Census of Canada, 1851, cited in John K. A. Farrell, "Schemes for the Transplanting of Refugee American Negroes from Upper Canada in the 1840s," *Ontario History* 52 (1960): 245, and the *Voice of the Fugitive,* May 1851, 2; Benjamin Drew, *Northside View of Slavery or the Refugee: or the Narrative of Fugitive Slaves in Canada* (Boston, 1856), v.

12. Landon, "The Negro Migration to Canada," 22.

13. For example, 40 Blacks out of a total population of 3,000 resided in the village of Galt. In larger commercial centers such as Toronto, London, St. Catharines, and Chatham, the Black population ranged in the hundreds, but still constituted a relatively small percentage of the total. In the largest town on Drew's list, Toronto, there were approximately 1,000 Blacks out of a total population of 47,000. See Drew, *Northside View,* 14, 17–18, 94, 118, 136, 147, 234, 291, 308, 322, 341, 348, 367, 378; Howe, *Report,* 44.

14. Howe, *Report,* 44.

15. Howard University, Moorland-Spinarn Research Center, MASC Papers, Mary Ann Shadd Cary, circular, n.d.

16. William Wells Brown, "The Colored People of Canada," in C. Peter Ripley, ed., *The Black Abolitionist Papers,* vol. 2 (Chapel Hill: University of North Carolina Press, 1986), 466; Howe, *Report,* 46; *Pine and Palm,* 30 Nov. 1861, in BAP, reel 13.

17. Howe, *Report,* 45.

18. UWO, MASC Papers, series A, E. Williams to Mary Ann Shadd Cary, Wilmington, Del., 18 Jan. 1852.

19. Much of Black women's wage-earning work probably went undocumented, for census takers typically marked the occupation of men, but left the space blank for most women. *Census of Canada,* Town of Chatham, Ontario, 1861.

20. Drew, *Northside View,* 173; Prentice et al., *Canadian Women,* 82.

21. Hill, "Negroes in Toronto," 167, 171–73, and 175–77.

22. Drew, *Northside View,* 44.

23. See Barbara Welter, "The Cult of True Womanhood, 1820–60," *American Quarterly* 18 (Summer 1966): 151–74; James O. Horton, "Freedom's Yoke: Gender Conventions among Antebellum Free Blacks," *Feminist Studies* 12 (Spring 1986): 51–76; Shirley J. Yee, *Black Women Abolitionists: A Study in Activism, 1828–60* (Knoxville: University of Tennessee Press, 1992), 44–56; and Prentice et al., *Canadian Women,* 83–84.

24. Drew, *Northside View,* 233.

25. Ibid., 218.

26. See John Mack Faragher, *Women and Men on the Overland Trail* (New Haven: Yale University Press, 1979); Julie Roy Jeffrey, *Frontier Women: The Trans-Mississippi West, 1840–1880* (New York: Hill & Wang, 1979); and Susanna Moodie, *Roughing It in the Bush* (Toronto: McClelland & Stewart, 1962).

27. Gerda Lerner, ed., *Black Women in White America* (New York: Vintage Books, 1972), 15–42; Jacqueline Jones, *Labor of Love, Labor of Sorrow* (New York: Basic Books, 1985), 11–43.

28. See Eugene D. Genovese, *Roll, Jordan, Roll: The World the Slaves Made* (New York: Vintage Books, 1972), and John Blassingame, *Slave Community* (New York: Oxford University Press, 1974).

29. Abraham Shadd (b. 1801) was a delegate to the American Anti-Slavery Convention, and in 1859 was elected as the first Black representative in Raleigh Township, Ontario. See Dorothy Sterling, ed., *We Are Your Sisters: Black Women in the Nineteenth Century* (New York: W. W. Norton, 1984), 164–66; Winks, *The Blacks in Canada,* 215.

30. *Provincial Freeman,* 25 March 1854; *Voice of the Fugitive,* 3 June 1852; Mary Ann Shadd, "A Plea for Emigration, or Notes on Canada West" (Detroit, 1852).

31. Shadd worked with the Rev. Samuel Ringgold Ward, who founded the *Provincial Freeman* in 1853. It was Shadd, however, who apparently gave the paper its name. UWO, MASC Papers, Mary Ann Shadd to Samuel Ward, n.d.

32. Windsor, American Missionary Association Collection, Ontario Black History Society, box 2, envelope 4, Alexander MacArthur to George Whipple, 22 Dec. 1852.

33. *Voice of the Fugitive,* 15 July 1851.

34. The census of 1861 reveals that Blacks were affiliated with a variety of denominations. For example, in three enumeration districts in the town of Chatham, the following denominations were represented: Methodist, Baptist, Church of England, Roman Catholic, Disciple, Congregational, Episcopal, Church of Scotland, Shaker, and Quaker. *Census of Canada,* Town of Chatham, 1861.

35. *Voice of the Fugitive,* 4 Nov. 1851. This number may have been exaggerated. The Canadian census counted 45,353 Baptists in 1851. *Census of the Canadas,* 1851.

36. Speech by J. W. C. Pennington, delivered at Freemasons' Hall, London, England, 14 June 1843, in C. Peter Ripley, ed., *Black Abolitionist Papers,* vol. 1 (Chapel Hill, 1985), 110. Pennington may have overestimated the actual numbers of Black churches.

37. Hill, "Negroes in Toronto," 138.

38. *Voice of the Fugitive,* 30 July 1851; Hill, "Negroes in Toronto," 142.

39. *Voice of the Fugitive,* 16 and 30 July 1851; *Provincial Freeman,* 15 Aug. 1857.

40. *Provincial Freeman,* 3 Nov. 1855.

41. Amherstburg Baptist Association (ABA), minutes, 8 Oct. 1841; Shreve, *The AfricCanadian Church,* 47, 52–53.

42. ABA Sabbath School convention, minutes, 14–16 Sept. 1876.

43. McMaster Divinity College, Canadian Baptist Archives, ABA, minutes, 18 Aug. 1849, 14 Sept. 1871; Shreve et al., *Pathfinders,* 63.

44. For a general history of Black education in the United States see Carleton Mabee, *Black Education in New York State from Colonial Times to Modern Times* (New York: Syracuse University Press, 1979).

45. Alison Prentice, "The Feminization of Teaching," in Prentice and Trofimenkoff, eds., *The Neglected Majority,* 50–54.

46. William Still to the *Provincial Freeman,* 11 Nov. 1854.

47. Mary Ann Shadd Cary (1858?), in BAP.

48. "Sixth Annual Report of the Buxton Mission," 16 June 1856, in *The Ecclesiastical and Missionary Record* 12 (July 1856): 139.

49. Henry Bibb, *Narrative of the Life and Adventures of Henry Bibb* (1850), 190–91.

50. Pease and Pease, *Black Utopia,* 113–22; Winks, *The Blacks in Canada,* 205–8; *Voice of the Fugitive,* 13 Aug. 1851.

51. Cary may have owned the first ice company in Toronto and later owned a bathhouse and several barbershops. In 1854 he was one of the thirty-five men appointed as officers for the Provincial Union Association, a local benevolent association to aid destitute Blacks. Hill, "Negroes in Toronto," 168; *Provincial Freeman,* 19 Aug. 1854; UWO, MASC Papers, Thomas F. Cary to Mary Ann Shadd Cary, 11 June 1851.

52. Amelia Cisco Shadd was the sixth Shadd child, born 25 Oct. 1831, and Sarah Matilda Shadd was the ninth, born 1 Nov. 1839. UWO, Shadd Family Papers; "Record of the Shadd Family in America," 1905; Amelia Shadd to David T. Williamson, 25 July 1854, Toronto, in BAP; Mary Ann Shadd Cary to George Whipple, 3 Nov. 1859, in BAP; Sterling, ed., *We Are Your Sisters,* 174.

53. Martin H. Freeman was vice-president of Allegheny Institute and later president of Avery College.

54. Mary Ann Shadd to George Whipple, 3 Nov. 1859, in BAP; *Weekly Anglo-African,* 5 April 1862, in BAP.

55. "Eighth Annual report of the Buxton Mission," 21 June 1858, in *Ecclesiastical and Missionary Record,* 14 Aug. 1858, 120; *Voice of the Fugitive,* 26 Mar. 1851.

56. Drew, *Northside View,* 348; Jason H. Silverman and Donna J. Gillie, "'The Pursuit of Knowledge under Difficulties': Education and the Fugitive Slave in Canada," *Ontario History* 74 (June 1982): 98, 101.

57. Mental Feasts, gatherings that featured poetry, readings, lectures, and choral concerts, were popular fundraising events in the United States and Canadian Black communities. *Provincial Freeman,* 3 and 10 Jan. 1857, in BAP.

58. Egerton Ryerson, the superintendent of schools for Canada West, could only offer an apology to the Blacks of Amherstburg, one he claimed was "at variance with the principle and spirit of British Institutions." Egerton Ryerson to Isaac Rice and Robert Pedan, 5 March 1846, in Silverman and Gillie, "Pursuit of Knowledge," 98.

59. Silverman and Gillie, "Pursuit of Knowledge," 96; *Pine and Palm,* 30 Nov. 1861, in BAP; *Provincial Freeman,* 26 July 1856.

60. *Provincial Freeman,* 12 July 1856; Mary Ann Shadd Cary to George Whipple, 23 Nov. 1851, in BAP.

61. Mary Ann Shadd to George Whipple, 23 Nov. 1851, in BAP.

62. *Provincial Freeman,* 28 Jan. 1859.

63. Drew, *Northside View,* 321–22; *Voice of the Fugitive,* 17 June 1852, in BAP; Mary Ann Shadd to George Whipple, Boston, 3 Nov. 1859, in BAP.

64. Mary Ann Shadd to George Whipple, 28 Dec. 1852 and 21 July 1852, in BAP; Sterling, ed., *We Are Your Sisters,* 169.

65. Mary E. Bibb, "Schools Among the Refugees," *Anti-Slavery Bugle,* 12 Apr. 1851, BAP; Cooper, "Search," 47.

66. Cooper, "Search," 71; Mary Ann Shadd to Executive Committee—AMA, Windsor, 3 Apr. 1852, in BAP.

67. Mary Ann Shadd to George Whipple, 7 Feb. 1853 and 21 June 1859, in BAP.

68. Winks, *The Blacks in Canada,* 158–59, 206–7.

69. Prentice et al., *Canadian Women,* 104.

70. Drew, *Northside View,* 236–37.

71. *Provincial Freeman,* 19 Aug. 1854; *Voice of the Fugitive,* 13 Jan. 1855, 19 Aug. 1854.

72. Hill, "Negroes in Toronto," 179, and Drew, *Northside View,* 238.

5

"A Distinct and Antagonistic Race"

Constructions of Chinese Manhood in the Exclusionist Debates, 1869–78

KAREN J. LEONG

They are bringing plague and pestilence
   In fever-laden ships,
And taking gold and silver back
   On their returning trips.
They are bringing hordes of prostitutes
   To ply their trade of shame,
And breeding vice and foul disease
   Too horrible to name.
In fetid lanes and alleys
   They are like a festering sore.
They are coming, they are coming,
   Every week a thousand more.

—Sam Booth, "They Are Coming"

Throughout the 1860s, politicians and labor leaders in California and other western states sounded the alarm at the prospect of thousands of Chinese male laborers descending like a plague, a "yellow peril," upon the United States. The image of the Chinese female prostitute proved a key rhetorical device not only in Booth's poem, but also in western states' efforts to restrict the immigration of Chinese male laborers through federal legislation.[1] The Chinese Exclusion Act of 1882 denied entry to Chinese laborers for ten years. The first enacted piece of federal legislation to restrict immigration to the United States explicitly based on nationality, Chinese exclusion was symptomatic of heightened sensitivity to issues of race and citizenship as well as a depressed economy and labor conflicts after the Civil War. Depictions of Chinese prostitutes and the illicit sexuality associated with Chinese laborers implicated the Chinese male as immoral, uncivilized, and fundamentally unfit for American citizenship. The architects of the anti-Chinese movement and subsequent exclusion laws expanded this theme into a broad-ranging, gendered argument against the Chinese as a race. Proponents of Chinese exclusion would measure Chinese men against normative standards of Anglo-American masculinity and find them wanting.

The argument that Chinese men did not meet the ideal of Anglo-American masculinity and thus could not be virtuous republican citizens ideologically justified restricting Chinese immigrant labor. Scholars have examined how gendered arguments for exclusion relied on the image of the Chinese prostitute, yet largely have neglected complementary constructions of Chinese and Anglo-American working-class masculinity.[2] Gendered rhetoric circumvented the obstacles posed by federal constitutional law and diplomacy to states' attempts to enact anti-Chinese legislation on a racial basis. The anti-Chinese movement thus shifted emphasis from the racial threat posed by Chinese male laborers to the moral threat posed by "aberrant" Chinese gender relations. The reconstruction of racial difference as cultural difference suggested the inability of Chinese to maintain American cultural values as evidenced in the lack of a home, family, and "appropriate" relations between men and women. This strategy also allowed western state representatives to successfully situate their regional economic interests within the post-Reconstruction national discourse of race, gender, sexuality, and morality, which ultimately transcended the sectionalism of the antebellum period.

The anti-Chinese movement established itself nationally in the United States by the end of the 1870s, advocating the exclusion of the Chinese male laborer because of his fundamental difference from the Anglo-American male citizen. Perceptions that a majority of Chinese women immigrants had been forced into prostitution helped to justify the United States' rejection of Chinese manhood. Chinese men's alleged exploitation of women betrayed their lack of manhood—in this case, a failure to protect female virtue—and revealed their unsuitability as Americans. Describing the Chinese trade in women, Senator Higby of California declared in 1870, "That is their character. You cannot make citizens of them."[3] A poem printed in the *San Francisco Chronicle,* "How He Sold Her Short," told a tragic tale of a young Chinese woman, Ching Lee, who was courted by a young man in China and traveled to join him in the United States, only to be sold on arrival to another man. The poet ended this epic with a "MORAL. Now all you Chinese maidens who have lovers far away, / Be careful of your characters, and don't be led astray, / Don't leave your native rice fields to join a moon-eyed sport, / For fear you be, like poor Ching Lee, sold very badly short."[4] In 1878, a speaker in New York similarly distinguished Chinese from American men: "They consider the wife a slavish chattel; we consider her a sacred partner. . . ."[5] The conclusions drawn from these images of degraded women, of "female slaves," enabled American men and women to judge Chinese standards of morality as inferior to their own.

This moral argument crystallized in the national political consciousness when, in February 1878, the House Committee on Education and Labor issued a special report addressing the question of Chinese immigration. The committee provided three reasons why the Chinese male would be an "undesirable citizen": his effect on labor, his debilitating effect on society, and his inability to assimilate. The Chinese laborer was inferior to his Anglo-European counterpart because the American laborer "shall possess courage, self-respect and independence. To do this he must have a home." Exclusionists implied that Chinese workers depressed wages to the point where property ownership became impossible. Second, the Chinese evidenced peculiar moral habits in "their treatment of women" by profiting from their sexual servitude. In other words, by organizing prostitution, Chinese men reneged on their duty as providers. Chinese women faced lives full of "privation, contempt and degradation from the cradle to the tomb." Third, Chinese men failed to establish nuclear family households. Chinese males distinguished themselves from other immigrants because "[t]hey bring with them neither wives nor families, nor do they intermarry with the resident population. . . . Mentally, morally, physically, socially and politically *they have remained a distinct and antagonistic race.*"[6] All three reasons focus on the aberration of Chinese gender roles as perceived by the American public.

According to these perceptions, the Chinese male laborer failed to fulfill the gendered, cultural requirements of American citizenship. As several feminist historians have demonstrated, American citizenship relied upon and perpetuated the economic and moral dimensions of Anglo masculine identity. The American male demonstrated his independence and self-sufficiency by providing economically for his dependents—his wife and children—and upheld social morality by protecting the virtue of his dependents and others. The ability to provide for a family constituted an integral component of citizenship.[7] As Stephanie McCurry has noted in her study of antebellum South Carolina yeomen, maintaining dominance over dependents has constituted an integral yet often overlooked aspect of how republican ideology defined the independent male American citizen.[8] Increasingly after Reconstruction, citizenship was equated with a masculinity and whiteness that were maintained by policing the racial, class, and gendered boundaries of middle-class Anglo-American behavior.[9] Those males who neither formed families nor supported them thus undermined the assumed heterosexual, nuclear household basis of the national economy.

Similarly, anti-Chinese rhetoric also centered around the Chinese laborers' lack of wives, family, and homes, and the danger "inassimilable aliens" posed to the republic and its families. Without a home, a "Chinaman" had no reason to defend the country; without a family, a "Chinaman" had no reason to invest in the future well-being of the nation; without a wife, a "Chinaman" was simply barbaric and uncivilized.[10] Based on definitions of American masculinity, the "Chinaman" was no man at all. This argument developed after the mid-1870s to encompass relationships in which gender identities were central: marriage, family, and even the republic itself. In 1878, Senator Jones of Nevada succinctly explained the danger Chinese men posed by citing both their effect on wages and their responsibility for Chinese prostitutes: "They debauch our men by their virtues and our boys by their vices."[11]

Constructions of the Chinese as a race and culture alien to all things American focused upon the ways Chinese male behavior deviated from Anglo-American social norms. One magazine article described the Chinese as a "community of males, without the humanizing influences of women and children." According to this interpretation, "no such principle in the Chinese make-up as filial, connubial or any other form of affection" existed because Chinese men spent their money buying sexual favors from prostitutes as opposed to investing in their homes and families.[12] Women, as this article implies, were considered civilizing forces in American society. The lack of virtuous females offered little hope that

Chinese men would change. Without their civilizing influence, Chinese men could not be expected to become true citizens. The apparent fact that most Chinese women were immoral only amplified the extent to which Chinese men were wicked and debased.

Standards of masculinity, femininity, sexuality, and morality were central to the construction of working-class Anglo-American masculinity and also defined the working-class "Chinaman."[13] Rather than solely protecting the livelihood of the white male worker and thus maintaining the rights associated with American masculinity, anti-Chinese agitators also asserted their own masculine roles as protectors of the nation's morality and families. This paralleled a similar development in the Reconstruction South where, according to Martha Hodes, the prospects of political equality and economic mobility for freedmen were expressed in fears about sexual intimacy between black men and white women, resulting in the sexualization of politics.[14] Emerging norms of sexuality and morality, then, helped to maintain a racial division between Euro-American citizenry and "others," including African-American freedmen and Chinese immigrants, at the end of Reconstruction.[15]

Further examination of the gendered rhetoric of the movement to restrict Chinese immigration illustrates how issues of sexuality and gender became integral to projections of racial difference. At this particular moment, when many Americans sought to avoid the divisive issue of racial difference in Reconstruction politics, gender norms critically expressed and contributed to the national definition of American citizenry as male and of Anglo-European descent. The image of the Chinese female immigrant as enslaved, abused, and sexually exploited provided a key means through which Anglo-American working men on the West Coast could read gender and race onto the foreign body of the Chinese male worker. By articulating their own white, American masculinity in opposition to the Chinese foreigner, they thereby claimed their own political and moral dominance within the sphere of national politics.

The Chinese question emerged on a national level at a crucial time in U.S. history. In the aftermath of the Civil War, radical Republicans sought to reshape the nation. They envisioned an ideal society based on equal rights, free labor, and the continued civilizing of the frontier. One Republican declared, "My dream is of a model republic, extending equal protection and rights to all men. . . . The wilderness shall vanish, the church and schoolhouse will appear; . . . the whole land will revive under the magic touch of free labor."[16] Reconstruction legislated equality in terms of race and class but excluded gender.[17] Male politicians described the model republic from the very end of the Civil War and the beginnings of Reconstruction in masculine terms: the republic would include all men, who would manifest not only their destiny but also their manhood by extending the republic geographically. Women had roles in what Amy Kaplan has termed *manifest domesticity*—the civilizing efforts that accompanied the spread of free labor and government not only across the expanse of what constituted the United States, but abroad as well.[18] During radical Reconstruction, however, the gendered construction of the republic remained subordinate to the question of race that had underlain the issue of free labor during the antebellum period.

Debates over the immigration of Chinese labor during Reconstruction revived unresolved concerns about race and the specter of slavery. Proponents of restricting Chinese labor evoked the free labor argument: Chinese wage labor would have the same effect as slavery on American labor and industry, undermining the possibility of free men to provide for their families. Opponents of restrictions, on the other hand, warned against restricting a group of immigrants on the basis of race. Indeed, opponents successfully rejected an 1869 bill that restricted the entry of Chinese contract labor and Chinese women on the grounds that the bill was motivated by race and prejudice.[19] In 1869, Senator Williams proposed a bill that would deny entry to Chinese contract laborers and would require any Chinese woman immigrant to be accompanied by her husband or father.[20] Williams presented this secondary provision in Congress as a form of slavery on par with that of Chinese contract labor. During the open debate on this bill, Senator Pomeroy of Kansas quibbled with the largess of Senator Howard from Oregon. Pomeroy noted Howard's claims "that this [bill] is only to discriminate against a certain class; but the objection is that in that effort we discriminate against the whole. . . ." Pomeroy further disputed Howard's argument that his bill would prevent a type of slavery: "I am for the suppression of the slave trade . . . but I am not for discriminating against persons who propose to become American citizens, whether they are white or black; whether they are from China or from Africa."[21]

The agitation on the part of western states to exclude all Chinese based on race conflicted ideologically with attempts to transform the slave economy in the South to that of free labor based on the equality of all men. The passage of both the Fourteenth Amendment and the Civil Rights Bill of 1870 extended rights of equality before the law, in principle, to all naturalized or native-born peoples in the United States.[22] Some radical Republicans attempted to extend rights explicitly to Native Americans and Chinese, not solely blacks. By 1870, however, California Republicans recognized that supporting legislation granting rights to the Chinese would alienate voters and significantly erode their party's representation in that state. Subsequently, California politicians united across party lines as well as with other western representatives to ensure that the Fifteenth Amendment would not interfere with individual states' suffrage qualifications.[23]

However, western politicians who sought to exclude Chinese immigrants from America's shores still faced particularly formidable legal obstacles posed by the U.S. Constitution and international diplomacy. State laws could be overruled by both the federal and state court systems and Chinese immigrants successfully challenged many anti-Chinese laws in court.[24] The California Supreme Court and the Federal District Court ruled various state and San Francisco anti-Chinese laws unconstitutional, based largely on the 1868 Burlingame Treaty, which extended to Chinese the equal protection enjoyed by American citizens under the Fourteenth Amendment as part of a free trade and migration agreement between the United States and China.[25] California's right to self-protection was deemed subordinate to federal law in 1874, when the California Supreme Court struck down California's law prohibiting the importation of prostitutes. State protection could be ensured only by passing legislation that protected western interests on the federal level.

Meanwhile, the growing disparity between working men and industrialists resulted in class antagonism that in itself reflected norms of American manhood.[26] The self-made man celebrated by American liberal ideology demonstrated his self-sufficiency in part by his property. Working-class men in the western states feared that they might never attain this goal in the wake of the 1873 economic depression and increasing competition for jobs. During the Reconstruction era, however, their complaints—often phrased in terms of Chinese inferiority to whites—were dismissed on the whole as racist and self-seeking. One unidentified Californian complained, "It has even been asserted, and prominent men and journals in the East have repeated it, that the opposition to Chinese immigration in California is confined to a few demagogues and discontented communists."[27]

Western politicians and newspapers frequently expressed frustration that other states did not fully understand the effects of Chinese immigration. East Coast newspapers and journals regularly derided the West Coast as paranoid, reactionary, and ungrateful for the contributions of Chinese labor to the industrialization of California. *Scribner's* declared with exasperation, "In the East, the prejudice against our heathen brother John in California, seems a little unreasonable and we want more light."[28] California newspapers, in turn, deplored the "perverted condition of opinion in the East," where for months "the newspapers . . . have been filled with the grossest misrepresentations of every phase of the [Chinese] question, all proceedings from poisoned and interested sources."[29] Several newspapers reprinted commentaries from national papers concerning the reaction to the Chinese on the West Coast. West Coast papers and politicians often pointed out that if large numbers of Chinese were arriving on the East Coast, the easterners would react as the West had—an argument that probably contained more truth than those in the East cared to admit. The frustrated Californian suggested that the Pacific states vote on the Chinese question and that their Congressmen, "armed with these credentials, say to their brethren, of the East: 'The people of the Pacific Coast have been so far the only people exposed to Chinese immigration. They are strongly and bitterly opposed to it. . . . If they are wrong you can easily prove it. . . . Amend the treaty and confine the Chinese to the Atlantic ports. If this immigration suits you, you are welcome to it.'"[30]

What Californians perceived as an East-West polarization also involved issues of class. Newspapers outside of the West Coast frequently noted that a lower class of citizen inhabited most of California. The *San Francisco Chronicle* quoted the *Louisville Courier-Journal* claiming that the politicians were working on behalf of "the vast rabble of hoodlums in San Francisco," while the *Chronicle* itself implied that those "poisoned and interested sources" included corporations relying on cheap labor.[31] So long as they continued to dismiss the Chinese as racially inferior, laborers' demands were easily dismissed as lower-class resentment of more productive Chinese labor. By the late 1870s, however, national opinion began to accept the interpretation that the Chinese immigrating to the States were undesirables.[32] Increased attention in the national press and Congress evidenced a growing concern over Chinese immigration. This shift also reflected both the western states' greater importance in national politics and the changing rhetoric against the Chinese from issues of race to more nebulous and persuasive issues of morality and gender.[33]

West Coast representatives increasingly sought to persuade the national public that their actions were motivated not by base self-interest but by national interest. California politicians and the press consciously manipulated gendered images of Chinese in opposition to the ideal Anglo-American family unit in order to gain national sympathy and electoral support.

The policing of sexual disease, prostitution, and Chinese females proved an effective way to ultimately exclude Chinese male labor. By 1874 President Ulysses S. Grant in his annual address to Congress introduced the possibility of limiting the influx of Chinese prostitutes. Motivated by his party's viability in the western United States, Grant acknowledged the powerful images of Chinese slavery and prostitution in addressing the "problems" of the particular class of Chinese entering the United States:

> In relation to this subject I call the attention of Congress to a generally-conceded fact—that the great proportion of the Chinese immigrants who come to our shores do not come voluntarily to make their homes with us and their labor productive of general prosperity, but come under contracts with head-men who own them almost absolutely. In worse form does this apply to Chinese women. Hardly a perceptible percentage of them perform any honorable labor, but they are brought for shameful purposes, to the disgrace of the communities where settled and to the great demoralization of the youth of those localities. If this evil practice can be legislated against, it will be my pleasure as well as duty to enforce any regulation to secure so desirable an end.[34]

President Grant focused on the unfree status of both Chinese laboring men and prostitutes and its effects on American morality and productivity: unfree labor undermined the economy and political system upon which the American republic rested. If California came to rely too heavily upon Chinese contract labor, a system of unfree labor such as that in the antebellum South might result. The president implicitly appealed to the nation's conceptions of the republic, family, and female virtue. American citizens—native-born or naturalized immigrant males—constituted, protected, and perpetuated the nation; but American manhood could be weakened economically by Chinese labor and morally by Chinese prostitutes.

Western politicians, led by Horace Page and other California representatives, willingly obliged. On March 3, 1875, "An Act Supplementary to Acts in Relation to Immigration" entered the federal statues as law.[35] The bill's purpose purportedly was to end Chinese slavery and prostitution: it required "free and voluntary immigration" from "China, Japan, or any Oriental country"; increased the fine levied on those importing contract labor; made illegal any contracting of unfree labor; prohibited the "importation into the United States of women for the purposes of prostitution"; and, lastly, denied entry to criminals or "women imported for the purposes of prostitution." Any "such obnoxious person or persons" would be returned to their own country.[36] This act, commonly referred to as the Page Act or Page Law, added a new element to Chinese immigration legislation, supplementing an 1862 bill that had attempted to halt the transportation of Chinese contract labor to the United States. Whereas the 1862 bill withheld landing permits from ships transporting Chinese for "lewd and immoral purposes," the Page Act sought to directly prevent the importation of female prostitutes and refused entry to any woman suspected of immigrating for this purpose.[37] Significantly, this legislation established at the federal level the connection between unfree labor, prostitutes, and Chinese immigrants.

The president's strong endorsement of the issues covered in the Page Act left little room for dissent among his fellow Republicans, who traditionally opposed legislation that might discriminate on the basis of race. President Grant assumed that many Chinese immigrants entered the United States against their will, under contract to someone else who profited from their labor as workers and prostitutes. According to this widely held assumption, the bill's enactment would curtail most of the undesirable elements of Chinese immigration to the United States. Indeed, immigration officials' conviction that the majority of Chinese female immigrants to the United States were prostitutes, combined with the difficulty Chinese wives faced in proving otherwise, appear to have discouraged some Chinese women from even attempting to emigrate to the United States. As George Anthony Peffer has demonstrated, the lack of wives and families accompanying the Chinese males partly resulted from institutionalized discrimination against Chinese women immigrants by U.S. immigration officials and the Page Law of 1875.[38] The number of Chinese female immigrants to the United States significantly declined as a result of the indiscriminate enforcement of the Page Law.[39]

The Page Law of 1875 also effectively established grounds for further and broader exclusion legislation. By convincing the president and the people of the United States that a portion of the immigrants were undesirable based on moral grounds, the proponents of the Page Act opened the possibility that *all* Chinese immigrants could be categorized as undesirable. Within less than a year western politicians sought to exploit further the fears and prejudices of the American public in order to gain ready acceptance not only of the Page Act but also the necessity of revising the Burlingame Treaty.

In 1876 Senator Aaron Sargent of California spoke in favor of the resolution to renegotiate the Burlingame Treaty to allow for the further restriction of Chinese immigration. He contended that the ineffectiveness of the Page Law necessitated a policy of "general exclusion":

> The importation of females for immoral purposes is also forbidden by statute. But the law is a dead-letter, because of the impossibility of obtaining proof of its violation. And yet it is the almost universal conviction of Californians that nine-tenths of the Chinese male immigration is in violation of the former [coolie slavery], and ninety-nine hundredths of the female immigration in violation of the latter statute. There can be no remedy but general exclusion; and the policy, justice, and necessity of that supreme measure I purpose to discuss.[40]

Senator Sargent clearly admitted he had no proof of any violations and that his argument was based on Californians' *perceptions* of these violations. Californians opposed to Chinese immigration perceived the majority of Chinese male immigrants—90 percent—as enslaved.[41] More important, they were able to persuade national opinion that these perceptions were for the most part accurate. The image of the enslaved Chinese male preempted the condemnation of racial prejudice and appealed to free labor ideology while also calling into question the fitness of Chinese men to become naturalized citizens.

Establishing a link between Chinese male labor and female sexual servitude constituted an essential part of attempts to exclude Chinese immigrants. Comparing Chinese male and female immigrants to slaves conveyed both the economic threat posed by the Chinese men and the moral threat posed by Chinese women. Perceptions of Chinese as unfree justified Americans' desires to deny them entry. Free immigration, the exclusionists argued, should be restricted to those people who came freely. As U.S. Minister to China Benjamin P. Avery explained to a Chinese diplomat who questioned the immigration restrictions on Chinese, "This system of free immigration and equal privileges has had a large share in making the United States prosperous and strong and has been encouraged and protected by very careful laws which are strictly enforced."[42]

In his legal history of Chinese immigration, Hudson Janisch observed wryly, "If the South fought to protect white womanhood, the West fought to protect white manhood."[43] The West generously extended its protection to the nation's future generations of manhood as well. Images of the "Chinaman" and the diseased Chinese prostitute converged with national concerns about the stability of American social institutions. The amoral sexuality displayed by the Chinese threatened to pollute the virtues upon which American society and civilization rested. The Congregational Churches of America adopted a resolution urging the government to revise the Burlingame Treaty and to pass measures to "prevent the importation of Chinese prostitutes, and so relieve us from impending peril to our republican and Christian institutions."[44] Urban American masculine youth especially appeared vulnerable to this threat. Testimony before the Joint Special Committee that boys seven to twelve years old visited Chinese prostitutes shocked the national audience even more than the lurid descriptions of diseased prostitutes left to die on the streets of Chinatown. The Order of Caucasians, an anti-Chinese club, warned Congress that Chinese prostitution existed in many cities and that American male youth were "enticed thither by Chinese women—and who, for a few cents, can acquire a loathsome disease, ruin their constitutions and render themselves unfit to become the progenitors of a healthy and moral race."[45] Law enforcement officers, religious leaders, and local politicians, in their testimony before Congress, assumed that young boys were less likely to resist overt sexuality, especially at such bargain prices. The direct correlation between the constitution of American male youth and institutions of American society strikingly exemplifies the gendered basis of American national identity.

Concerns about the effects of perverse Chinese sexuality on the national body further illuminate the ideological relationships between virility and economic health, morality and industry. The dangers of sexually transmitted diseases graphically and concretely illustrated the danger embodied by Chinese immigrants to the nation's morality. Wherever Chinese settled, one editorial declared, "progress staggers and halts, industry withers, and public morals and public decency decay and die. . . . They are the embodiment of the plague, pestilence, famine and death."[46] Several San Francisco physicians quoted in the San Francisco *Medico-Literary Journal* attributed such diseases in that city to the Chinese prostitutes because they, "unlike the white women, use no preventative measures." This article further warned that Chinese women would spread a plague that could "sink this nation into effeminacy and political death."[47]

Disease and immorality were physical manifestations of corruption and vice that would not only ruin the constitutions of young men but also undermine the Constitution of the United States, which depended upon a healthy civic life of virtuous male participants. The Chinese, claimed one pamphlet, "corrupt the morals and undermin [*sic*] the framework of our social structure."[48] A California anti-Chinese convention memorial in 1886 explicitly spelled out the threat to white masculinity—and thus to the nation as a whole—posed by Chinese men. While Chinese labor thrived on low wages,

> the white laboring man, to whom the nation must, in the long run, look for the repro-
> duction of the race and the bringing up and educating of citizens to take the place
> of the present generation as it passes away, and, above all, to defend the country in
> time of war, is injured in his comfort, reduced in his scale of life and standard of liv-
> ing, necessarily carrying down with it his moral and physical stamina.[49]

Chinese working men and immoral Chinese women would erode the foundations of Anglo-American masculinity: work, self-sufficiency, and virility.

Discussions about the Chinese question relied upon constructions of gender and sexuality that supported America's implicitly masculine and heterosexual national iden-tity.[50] The virtues ascribed to Anglo-American women increased their political visibil-ity in opposition to Chinese males (working women also participated in anti-Chinese demonstrations).[51] Anti-Chinese sentiment even entertained the possibility of political franchise. If Chinese men were to gain the vote, white women's votes would be needed to "overbalance the Chinese power and give us the majority. . . . Republics and Empires have been saved through different causes, but not one yet has had the honor of having been saved by women. Well, let California have the glory of having been saved by them."[52] This appeal to American domesticity and womanhood was reminiscent of the race and gender logic expressed in the debates over the Fifteenth Amendment: when threatened by nonwhite masculinity, a common ethnic culture would transcend gender identity. Anglo-American women presumably would vote according to the same cultural values as Anglo-American men, just as Chinese men's votes would reflect their (inferior) racial and cultural identities.

Some anti-Chinese agitators sought moral protection through the American female as mother in opposition to the corrupted morality of Chinese women and the fallibility of male youth. The aforementioned article in the *Medico-Literary Journal* asked, "If it is through the Chinese women that our nation is threatened with destruction, why [do] not the American women at least raise their voices to repel them?" The article ended by appealing to mothers "to be more watchful of their sons."[53] Representing the highest virtues of Anglo-American civilization, white women had the power to protect American morality, even as their sexuality had the power to undo it.[54] The Chinese prostitute and the Anglo-American wife or mother emphasized the manhood and strength of character of American masculinity, and the "absence" of these traits in Chinese males.

By the late 1870s, anti-Chinese rhetoric shifted its primary focus from Chinese threats to morality to the ways Chinese men disrupted Anglo-American patterns of gender segre-gation in the workforce. After the completion of the transcontinental railroad in 1870, Chi-nese males increasingly competed with Anglo working men as well as women. They owned laundries and found employment as house servants. Because Chinese males apparently made few gender distinctions in the labor they performed—they did not care whether they were doing work traditionally assigned to females or males—they challenged the norms regarding accepted gendered divisions of labor in American society.

Politicians and rally speakers now warned that Chinese males threatened the economic basis of the American woman's virtue. Testimony persuaded members of the Joint Special Committee that Chinese males monopolized employment in traditionally female occupations by working for low wages, and that the "hardships resulting from these causes bear with especial weight upon women."[55] One witness testified that Anglo-American working women, who had lost their jobs at a sewing factory due to the influx of Chinese labor, could be found in places "where I presume you would not wish your sisters, mothers, or wives to be."[56] A pamphlet comparing contemporary evils to the "greatest curse" of intemperance deplored the fact that, although "the Chinaman" had once "filled a place and performed the labor which was not so agreeable to Anglo-Saxon masculinity," he now entered a domain hitherto occupied by virtuous Anglo women. As a result, "good, honest intelligent women" were forced to "decide between a short and wretched life of infamy and shame, or a life of starvation."[57] Chinese male laborers blurred the gendered division of labor in western cities, economically forcing Anglo-American women into prostitution, where their moral position would sink to that of Chinese women. The effects of Chinese labor manifested themselves in "domestic help, where the honest, virtuous and trustworthy females have been ousted and driven into dens of infamy and prostitution."[58] Thus Chinese males inevitably corrupted the female sex regardless of racial background, because they displaced Anglo-American women from the only respectable jobs available to them.

According to exclusionists, the Chinese male's ability to work for lower wages and in feminine occupations endangered American families. The congressional committee declared, "Family-life is a great safeguard of our political institutions."[59] This pervasive rhetoric indicates that the metaphor of family and home was a concept accepted as normative, and that it transcended class divisions in Anglo-American society. The Anglo-American nuclear family ensured the production of American institutions and represented a virtuous cause, one that could overshadow racist overtones. Senator Booth of California asserted that the "source of civilization in which we live, of the institutions we believe to be its highest outgrowth, is the family."[60] An article in *The Argonaut* (1877) characterized the intricate relationships among family, nation, and the economy:

> With us the family is not only the most sacred of our relationships, but is also the unit of nationality. Each family constitutes a little Republic. A collection of States, the nation. The nation is a collection of families. The "family relation" is, among our race sacredly regarded as the foundation of government. Society has been organized with reference to it. . . . The assumption that every man among us is to have a family and a house enters into all our calculations.[61]

The relationship of family, government, and private property—owning a house—found expression not only in masculinity but in the primary role assigned to males within the republic, that of citizen. Thus, the Chinese immigrants, most of whom lacked family and private property, could not be expected to enjoy the same privileges of government protection extended to Anglo-American males or even male immigrants from other European countries. Representative James G. Blaine said as much in his February 1879 speech before the Senate: "You cannot work a man who must have beef and bread, alongside of a man who can live on rice. In all such conflicts, and in all such struggles, the result is not to bring up the man who lives on rice to the beef-and-bread standard, but it is to bring down the beef-and-bread man to the rice standard."[62]

By blurring feminine and masculine roles and undermining the Anglo working male's ability to provide for his dependents, Chinese male labor threatened to expose the arbitrary division of American society into separate domains based on gender, the public, and the private, which thus far had restricted women from public political institutions, including citizenship. As leaders of the Workingman's Party complained, the Chinese "seem to have NO SEX."[63] The Chinese threat to Anglo-American manhood extended beyond economic livelihood and morality to the ideological underpinnings of American society. The Chinese laborer's willingness to do "feminine" work was perceived as unnatural, outside the gendered division of labor that reinforced masculine citizenship in American society.

As anti-Chinese rhetoric shifted to a gendered moral argument, national opinion about the Chinese question also changed. The *San Francisco Post* attributed this to a more elevated argument:

> Heretofore the anti-chinese [*sic*] agitation has been sporadic and violent in character. It assumed the tone of race antagonism—an attitude sure to arouse feeling against those who take it. When the venue was changed and the non-assimilative and aggressive attitude of this people shown towards, not only our labor, but our commerce and manufactures, our institutions and civilizations, the plane of statesmanship was reached and that of bitter race hostility abandoned forever.[64]

According to the *Post,* issues of assimilation and civilization, culture and morality, transcended racism and caste prejudice. Furthermore, the argument was framed proactively: rather than reacting to perceived racial and economic threats to the American male's livelihood, American masculinity sought to protect American institutions.

Anti-Chinese rhetoric also expressed larger social tensions regarding class status, race relations, and gender and sexual norms. Cultural definitions of whiteness and masculinity became the ideological focal point for political organization nationwide: politicians seized upon anti-Chinese sentiment to mobilize political support of the working-class electorate among the developing urban areas along the West Coast. As Mary P. Ryan demonstrates, western urban politics shared a critical transformation with other urban centers nationwide. Normative definitions of race, gender, and class increasingly circumscribed American civic participation in the post-Reconstruction era. "Gender . . . provided the sexual prohibitions, codes of segregation, and rhetorical power with which to mortar the rising wall of segregation," which replaced those sectional barriers that had hitherto dominated American politics.[65] Western politicians and union leaders succeeded in developing a refined political rhetoric and strategy with which to fit a blatantly racist exclusionary argument into the larger national political trend of maintaining social order and exploiting white middle-class fears of urban disarray.[66]

Indeed, the shift from class- and race-based arguments against the Chinese from the western states to ever more sophisticated arguments for exclusion based on gender at the national level took place through trial and error between the 1860s and 1882, when Congress passed the first exclusion act. Ryan's work suggests several avenues for further analysis of the ways in which exclusion legislation was part of larger national trends. It is apparent, however, that western politicians increasingly adapted their presentation of regional concerns to the evolving concerns of the North and South to persuade northern and southern politicians of the necessity of exclusion.

The political use of gender, and the issue of sexuality associated with gender roles, emphasized the necessity of ultimately excluding Chinese as a race from America's shores. During the era of Reconstruction, a racial argument still evoked suspicion and fears of division; a moral argument based on gender and sexuality that implicitly substantiated racial difference, however, was pursued with success.[67] The race argument, or the "caste prejudice" as it was frequently referred to in Congress, found expression and subsequent acceptance within a more positive ideology affirming Anglo-American manhood.

Presuming to protect both the Chinese and Americans from slavery, western leaders could deflect criticisms of racial intolerance. On the hierarchy of race, Californians referred to the Chinese laborer as "below the most degraded specimen of the American Indian, and but very little above the beast."[68] Chinese females were the most abject of immigrants, existing in "a state of servitude beside which African slavery was a beneficient captivity."[69] Employing these comparisons enabled other regions to comprehend the West Coast situation. Many southern politicians already supported the right of California and other western states to protect their population from a Chinese invasion. The nature of the Chinese slavery argument, however, also appealed to Republicans who had worked to abolish slavery and protect the rights of newly freed African Americans but also needed political support from California voters. The resulting strategy rephrased the Chinese question as one of assimilation. This argument encompassed the ideology of equality while addressing racial and labor tensions on the West Coast.[70] Significantly, it also reinforced white masculine superiority: the Anglo-American could continue to claim paternal benevolence toward immigrants in the name of exclusion, while protecting the national body from imagined harm.

Notes

An earlier version of this essay was presented as "Gender, Race, and the 1875 Page Law" at The Repeal and Its Legacy: Conference on the 50th Anniversary of the Repeal of Exclusion Acts sponsored by the Chinese Historical Society of America and the Department of Asian American Studies at San Francisco State University, November 12–14, 1993, and printed in the conference proceedings (San Francisco: CHSA and Asian American Studies Department, SFSU, 1994).

My thanks to Mary P. Ryan, who read multiple versions of this essay and each time offered insightful critiques, and Linda Song, Margaret Pagaduan, Kimie Arguello, Marcy Sacks, and Erika

Lee. I also thank Matt Basso, Laura McCall, and especially Dee Garceau, whose close readings and editing significantly shaped my revisions.

1. Sam Booth, "They Are Coming," in *The Chinese Invasion,* comp. Henry Josiah West (San Francisco: Bacon and Company, 1873). This is one stanza of the poem, most of which considers the effects of the Chinese on American labor.

2. Thomas Almaguer is one of the few scholars who has examined the development of a hierarchy of race, class, gender, and sexuality in California politics and society. His analysis of how whiteness and masculinity were constructed against the hypersexualized Chinese male and female, however, overlooks the critical role of the Page Act in this process. Mary P. Ryan's work also has examined how gender relations and sexuality were critical to urban political discourse. See Thomas Almaguer, *Racial Faultlines: The Historical Origins of White Supremacy in California* (Berkeley and Los Angeles: University of California Press, 1994); and Mary P. Ryan, *Civic Wars: Democracy and Public Life in the American City during the Nineteenth Century* (Berkeley and Los Angeles: University of California Press, 1997), as well as Mary P. Ryan, *Women in Public: Between Banners and Ballots, 1825–1880* (Baltimore: Johns Hopkins University Press, 1990).

3. *Congressional Globe,* February 21, 1866.

4. [D. O'C.], "How He Sold Her Short," *San Francisco Chronicle,* January 11, 1878.

5. *Daily Morning Call,* February 25, 1878.

6. *San Francisco Chronicle,* February 26, 1878 (emphasis mine).

7. See, for example, Martha Hodes, *White Women, Black Men: Illicit Sex in the 19th-Century South* (New Haven: Yale University Press, 1997); Stephanie McCurry, "Proslavery Politics in Antebellum South Carolina," *Journal of American History* 78 (1992): 1245–64; and Jacqueline Jones, *American Work* (New York: W. W. Norton, 1998).

8. McCurry, 1253 and 1259.

9. Hodes, 177.

10. This argument was popular in speeches. See, for example, *Report from the House Committee on Education and Labor,* February 25, 1878, by Senator Willis (Kentucky).

11. *San Francisco Post,* November 1, 1878.

12. "The Chinese in California," *Lippincott's Magazine* 2 (July 1868).

13. James Leroy Evans, *The Indian Savage, the Mexican Bandit, the Chinese Heathen: Three Popular Stereotypes* (Ph.D. diss., University of Texas at Austin, 1967); Lucie Cheng Hirata, "Free, Indentured, Enslaved: Chinese Prostitutes in Nineteenth-Century America," *Signs* 5 (1979): 27. Further work on nineteenth-century Chinese-American women has shown the fundamental impact of the Page Act on the formation of Chinese-American families and the community. See Judy Yung, *Unbound Feet* (Berkeley and Los Angeles: University of California Press, 1994); Sucheng Chan, "Immigration of Chinese Women under the Page Law," in *Entry Denied,* ed. Sucheng Chan (Philadelphia: Temple University Press, 1991); George Anthony Peffer, "Forbidden Families: Emigration Experience of Chinese Women under the Page Law, 1875–1882," *Journal of American Ethnic History* 6 (1986): 28–46; and Peffer, *If They Don't Bring Their Women Here: Chinese Female Immigration before Exclusion* (Urbana: University of Illinois Press, 1999).

14. Hodes, 151–71.

15. For an extended discussion of this process, see Ryan, *Civic Wars.* Ryan's ambitious comparative study of urban political culture in nineteenth-century New York, New Orleans, and San Francisco illuminates the development of each region's racial, gendered, and class politics within the larger national discourses of democracy.

16. An unidentified Republican in 1866, *Congressional Globe,* 39th Cong., 2nd sess., 118, Appendix, 78, as quoted and cited in Eric Foner, *Reconstruction: America's Unfinished Revolution, 1863–1877* (New York: Harper & Row, 1988), 235.

17. Ryan, *Civic Wars,* 297.

18. Amy Kaplan, "Manifest Domesticity," *American Literature* 70 (1998): 581–606.

19. A similar bill, proposed by James A. Johnson in 1870, also was denied because of concerns

about racial prejudice. James A. Johnson, *Chinese Immigration: A Speech Made in the House of Representatives, January 25, 1870* (Washington, D.C.: Government Printing Office, 1870). Johnson proposed a joint resolution to discourage the immigration of "Chinese laborers and debased and abandoned females," and notes that Senator Williams had introduced a similar "anti-coolie, anti-harlot bill" in December 1869.

20. *Congressional Globe,* 41st Cong., 2nd Sess., December 22, 1869, 299.

21. *Congressional Globe,* 41st Cong., 2nd Sess., December 22, 1869, 300.

22. Foner, 256.

23. Hudson N. Janisch, *The Chinese, the Courts, and the Constitution: A Study of the Legal Issues Raised by the Chinese Immigration to the United States, 1850–1902* (JSD thesis, University of Chicago, 1971), 184. Some politicians even requested the insertion of an exclusive clause declaring that the right to vote never was intended to apply to the Chinese or Mongolian races, but this was defeated 106 to 42 in the House. Senators Trumbull and Sumner each introduced an amendment allowing Chinese to become naturalized citizens in 1870. Both were rejected, with nearly half of the Senate not voting. See Stuart Creighton Miller, *Unwelcome Immigrant: The American Image of the Chinese, 1785–1882* (Berkeley and Los Angeles: University of California Press, 1969), 160.

24. See Charles McClain and Laurene Wu McClain, "The Chinese Contribution to the Development of American Law," in Chan, ed., *Entry Denied.*

25. San Francisco's Cubic Air Ordinance, for example, sought to limit the number of persons inhabiting a room based on cubic feet per person. See McClain and McClain.

26. Alexander Saxton, *The Indispensable Enemy: Labor and the Anti-Chinese Movement in California* (Berkeley and Los Angeles: University of California Press, 1971).

27. "The Chinese Question," in *Chinese Immigration Pamphlets,* Special Collections, Bancroft Library, University of California at Berkeley, 15.

28. *Scribner's Monthly,* January 1877, as reprinted in *San Francisco Daily Alta,* December 26, 1878. The "John" referred to is "John Chinaman."

29. *San Francisco Chronicle,* February 28, 1878.

30. "The Chinese Question," 16.

31. *San Francisco Chronicle,* January 14, 1878.

32. Gwendolyn Mink, *Old Labor and New Immigrants in American Political Development: Union, Party, and State, 1875–1920* (Ithaca, N.Y.: Cornell University Press, 1986).

33. See Saxton and Mink.

34. Message from the President, *Journal of the House of Representatives of the United States,* 43rd Cong., 2nd Sess., December 7, 1874, 12.

35. The Committee on Foreign Affairs originally introduced the Page Act to the House on February 18, 1875, with unanimous consent. Four days later, the House passed the bill. It then proceeded to the Senate Committee on Foreign Relations, which reported it to the Senate without amendment on March 3, 1875. President Ulysses S. Grant signed the Page Act into law that evening. The San Francisco newspapers merely mention the law's passage and comment no further. No records or reports remain from the committee that deliberated upon and produced the bill. See *Congressional Record,* 43rd Cong., 2nd sess., Mar. 3, 1875, 1454, 1599, and 2161; and *Journal of the House of Representatives of the United States,* 43rd Cong., 2nd sess., March 3, 1875, 487, 640, 652, and 679–80.

36. "An Act Supplementary to the Acts in Relation to Immigration," March 3, 1875, *United States Statutes at Large,* 477.

37. The Page Law was the first law to prevent women from entering the United States as immigrants on the explicit assumption that they may be prostitutes; only with the Immigration Act of 1907 would Congress authorize the deportation of foreign-born prostitutes of any race. For an extended discussion about the passage of the Page Law, its effects on the Chinese-American community, and its role in the debates on Chinese exclusion, see Peffer, *If They Don't Bring Their Women Here.*

38. Peffer, "Forbidden Families."

39. See Chan; and Peffer, "Forbidden Families."

40. Aaron A. Sargent, *Immigration of Chinese, Speech of Hon. Aaron A. Sargent, of California, in the Senate of the United States, May 2, 1876* (Washington, D.C.: Government Printing Office, 1876).

41. Almaguer, 160–62. Almaguer argues that Chinese males in service industries also were hypersexualized as threats to young women and girls, but, interestingly, these depictions did not take on the significant role of the Chinese prostitute (perhaps because they too uncomfortably paralleled racial tensions in the South).

42. Benjamin P. Avery to Prince Kung, May 28, 1878, Despatch no. 64, Inclosure 1, *Despatches from United States Ministers to China 1843–1906,* vol. 38, March 31–July 31, 1875.

43. Janisch, 81. He continues, "So far did this go that legislation was proposed, making seduction by a Chinese woman of a member of the California legislature or minister 'in good standing' a criminal offense."

44. *Resolutions Adopted by the General Association of Congregational Churches of California, Chinese Immigration Pamphlets,* vol. 1, Special Collections, Bancroft Library, University of California at Berkeley.

45. Petition to Congress from the Chico Encampment of the Order of Caucasians, *The Pacific,* December 1877.

46. Editorial from the *Cincinnati Enquirer* as reprinted in the *San Francisco Chronicle,* January 4, 1878.

47. "How the Chinese Women Are Infusing a Poison Fate into the Anglo-Saxon Blood," reprinted from the *Medico-Literary Journal* in the *San Francisco Chronicle,* November 21, 1878.

48. Henry Josiah West, *The Chinese Invasion* (San Francisco: Bacon and Company, 1873).

49. The memorial from the anti-Chinese convention of 1886 is quoted in Samuel Gompers and Herman Gutstadt, *Meat vs. Rice: American Manhood against Asiatic Coolieism, Which Shall Survive?* Published by American Federation of Labor and printed as Senate document 137, 1902. Reprinted with introduction and appendixes by Asiatic Exclusion League.

50. Jennifer Ting, "Bachelor Society: Deviant Heterosexuality and Asian American Historiography," in *Privileging Positions,* ed. Gary Y. Okihiro, et al. (Pullman, Wash., 1995), 271–80.

51. Ryan, *Women in Public,* 163.

52. *Sacramento Record Union,* February 23, 1879.

53. *San Francisco Medico-Literary Journal,* reprinted in *San Francisco Chronicle,* November 21, 1878.

54. Ryan, *Women in Public,* 163.

55. *Report of the Joint Special Committee to Investigate Chinese Immigration,* iv.

56. Testimony of Mrs. Sophronia Swift, *Report of the Joint Special Committee to Investigate Chinese Immigration,* 246.

57. Jennett Blakeslee Frost, *California's Greatest Curse* (San Francisco: J. Winterburn & Co., 1879), 15, 18.

58. Patrick Stephen Fox, Letter to the Editor, *San Francisco Daily Mail,* November 25, 1877.

59. *Report of the Joint Special Committee to Investigate Chinese Immigration,* viii.

60. *San Francisco Chronicle,* August 12, 1878.

61. "'Caucasian' vs. 'Mongolian,'" *The Argonaut,* October 27, 1877.

62. Excerpt from the Speech of James G. Blaine in the Senate, February 14, 1879, as quoted in Gompers and Gutstadt, 22.

63. *San Francisco Chronicle,* December 28, 1877.

64. *San Francisco Post,* June 22, 1878.

65. Ryan, *Civic Wars,* 296.

66. Ryan's description of municipal attempts, through legislation and police force, to "discipline occupants of public space" in the postbellum period highlights changing expressions of masculinity in public space as well. American masculinity thus was disciplined at the same time that Chinese masculinity was disciplined (and rejected) through the ever evolving contestation and definition of American citizenship. Ryan, *Civic Wars,* 217–18.

67. This increasingly sophisticated use of gender, race, and sexuality to justify nativism would

manifest itself yet again in justification of imperialism and racial eugenics toward the turn of the century. For example, see Kristin Hoganson, *Fighting for American Manhood: How Gender Politics Provoked the Spanish-American and Philippine-American Wars* (New Haven: Yale University Press, 1998), and Kaplan.

68. Memorial and Joint Resolution in Relation to the Chinese Immigration to the State of California, *Journals of Senate and Assembly of the 17th Session of the Legislature of the State of California*, vol. 2 (Sacramento: 1868), 3.

69. Memorial of the Senate of California to Congress of United States, April 3, 1876.

70. See Mink, esp. Chap. 3, "Meat vs. Rice (and Pasta): Discovering Labor Politics in California, 1875–85."

6

Enforcing the Borders

Chinese Exclusion along the U.S. Borders with Canada and Mexico, 1882–1924

ERIKA LEE

> There is no part [of the northern border] over which a Chinaman may not pass into our country without fear of hinderance; there are scarcely any parts of it where he may not walk boldly across it at high noon.
>
> —Journalist Julian Ralph, 1891

> There is a broad expanse of land with an imaginary line, all passable, all being used, all leading to the United States. The vigilance of your officers stationed along the border is always keen, but what can a handful of people do? It is a deplorable condition of affairs; we seem to be compelled to bear it; the Chinese do come in from Mexico.
>
> —U.S. Immigrant Inspector Marcus Braun, 1907

In September 1924 a Chinese male immigrant named Lim Wah entered the United States illegally from Mexico. His goals were to find work and to join his father, a farm laborer in northern California. Legally excluded from the United States, Lim paid an American $200 to bring him from Mexicali, Mexico, to Calexico, California. They waited until night and then crossed the border, ending up in San Francisco three days later. The Chinese exclusion laws (in effect from 1882 to 1943) greatly hindered Chinese immigration to the United States, but as Lim Wah's case demonstrates, they did not serve as the total barriers that exclusionists had hoped for. Deteriorating political and economic conditions in south China, the availability of jobs in the United States, the U.S. Bureau of Immigration's harsh enforcement procedures at regular ports of entry such as San Francisco, and the Chinese belief that the exclusion laws were unjust—all had the unintended consequence of turning illegal immigration via the borders into a profitable and thriving business.[1]

It is estimated that at least 17,300 Chinese immigrants entered the United States through the "back doors" of Canada and Mexico from 1882 to 1920.[2] The number of

Chinese entries pales in comparison with that of contemporary border migrants from Mexico, and recent scholarship has all but ignored this early history of Chinese exclusion in the northern and southern borderlands. Nevertheless, I argue that Chinese immigration to and exclusion from the United States had transnational consequences that transformed the northern and southern borders into sites of contest over illegal immigration, race, citizenship, immigration policy, and international relations. Considering Chinese immigration and exclusion from the vantage point of the borders illustrates both the racialization of U.S. immigration policy and the importance of the Chinese diaspora in the Americas. It also demonstrates how a seemingly national issue can sometimes be understood only in a wider, transnational context. Race, borders, and immigration policy in the United States, Canada, and Mexico became intertwined at the turn of the twentieth century over the issue of Chinese immigration and exclusion.[3]

Prior to the 1870s, American immigration laws were aimed at recruiting, rather than restricting, foreign immigration. The Chinese Exclusion Act (1882) marks the first time in American history that the United States barred an immigrant group based on race and class. It excluded Chinese laborers and allowed only a few select classes of Chinese merchants, students, teachers, travelers, and diplomats to apply for admission to the country. The act also represents the first time that illegal immigration was defined as a criminal offense in U.S. law. The new policy also provided for the deportation of Chinese in the country illegally. When Chinese responded to exclusion by taking advantage of legal loopholes and cracks in the government's enforcement practices, they became the country's first illegal immigrants, both in technical, legal terms and in the context of popular and political representations. Subsequent American immigration laws barred certain excludable aliens, such as contract laborers, convicts, idiots, and persons likely to become public charges or afflicted with a contagious disease. But until both illegal immigration and border enforcement changed in response to the 1924 immigration act, Chinese immigrants remained the main practitioners of illegal immigration and the main immigrant targets of government scrutiny.[4]

Chinese border crossers highlighted the weaknesses in American immigration law and tested the sovereignty of the United States in relation to immigration for the first time. They forced U.S. immigration officials to deal with two interrelated problems: stopping illegal immigration at the nation's borders and expelling illegal immigrants already residing in the country. The U.S. reaction signaled a new imperialist assertion of national sovereignty in the form of border control and the imposition of American nativism, immigration laws, and enforcement practices on both Canada and Mexico. The ways in which this played out in the north and south, however, differed. In the north, U.S. efforts centered on "border diplomacy" based on a historically amicable diplomatic relationship and a shared antipathy for Chinese immigration. In contrast, control over the southern border relied less on cooperation with Mexico and more on border policing, a system of surveillance, patrols, apprehensions, and deportation. Both methods eventually proved successful in closing the northern and southern borders to Chinese immigration. In doing so, they laid the foundations for racialized understandings of the "illegal immigrant problem" and of American border enforcement and nation building at the beginning of the twentieth century.

Border Crossings along the Northern Border

The most numerous and earliest border crossings occurred along the Canadian border. Some of the first illegal border crossers were most likely Chinese residents of the United States who had immigrated to Canada to work for the Canadian Pacific Railway Company (CPR) in the 1870s and then found themselves excluded from the United States after the 1882 Chinese Exclusion Act. Others went straight to Canada from China with the intention of eventually entering the United States. The largely unguarded boundary between the United States and Canada made such border entries feasible and relatively easy to execute.[5] Moreover, although Chinese immigrants in Canada were targets of racial hostility, Canada's Chinese immigration laws contrasted sharply with those of the United States. Instead of imitating the U.S. practice of direct exclusion of Chinese laborers, Canada's efforts to restrict Chinese immigration were indirect. In 1885 Canada's Chinese Immigration Act imposed a fifty-dollar head tax to be collected by each ship captain at the point of departure. Thus, though the United States explicitly singled out all Chinese laborers (and, for all intents and purposes, most Chinese immigrants), Canada's early measures allowed entry to every Chinese provided that he paid the landing fee.[6]

Although the intent was to restrict Chinese immigration, Canada's head tax system was not a sufficient deterrent. Canada was such a convenient back door into the United States that the tax reduced the appeal of immigration *to* Canada but did not reduce the appeal of secondary immigration to the United States *through* Canada. Other aspects of Canadian immigration laws seemed to facilitate Chinese illegal immigration across the border. Chinese immigrants destined for the United States were permitted to remain in the dominion for ninety days without paying the head tax and could presumably cross the border at will during that time. Those who had paid the head tax could also easily leave Canada.[7] The relatively lenient Canadian laws combined with the increasingly stringent U.S. Chinese exclusion laws led directly to a rise in illegal border entries. After the United States passed the Scott Act (1888), which nullified the U.S. return permits of an estimated 20,000 Chinese laborers, 773 Chinese immigrated to Canada. In 1892, 3,264 more Chinese immigrated to Canada following the U.S. passage of the Geary Act, which extended the exclusion of any additional Chinese laborers from the United States for another ten years and required those already in the country to register with the federal government. Witnesses at U.S. congressional hearings in 1890 and 1891 estimated that 300 to 2,000 Chinese entered illegally each year.[8] Even after Canada raised its head tax to $100 in 1900, American officials complained that the Canadian laws "practically nullified . . . the effective work done by the border officers."[9]

Chinese border crossers took advantage of established smuggling networks involving opium and other contraband substances along the U.S.-Canadian border. The Vancouver–Puget Sound area was known as a "smugglers' paradise" in the opium trade, and Chinese and their American or Canadian guides used the same smuggling boats and routes to make the journey to the United States. The cost of crossing the border along this route ranged from $23 to $60 in the 1890s. One decade later, border crossing through Washington State could cost up to $300.[10] Other popular entry points were along the northeastern border. The completion of the Canadian Pacific Railway, which stretched several thousand miles from Vancouver, British Columbia, to Montreal, Quebec, allowed immigrants to enter at a western seaport in Canada and then travel across the country to the east, where entry into the United States was even less guarded. Aided by Chinese already in the United States and white Americans looking for a ready profit, the business of transporting Chinese through Buffalo, New York, for example, became well organized and very profitable. In 1909 one newspaper reporter found that two to four Chinese were brought into Buffalo weekly, at a price of $200 to $600. Chinese were also commonly brought from the Canadian border to Boston and New York City in groups ranging from two to seventy-five in number. Corrupt immigration officials and judges along the border facilitated the illegal entry of Chinese by either masterminding the routes or admitting Chinese immigrants into the country in exchange for money.[11]

Thus, until 1923, when Canada passed a more complete exclusion bill, it remained a convenient route into the United States for anyone willing and able to pay the head taxes. This migration across the border prompted one Oregon magazine editor to complain that "Canada gets the money and we get the Chinamen," and reporters wrote about the growing "Chinese leak" coming in from Canada. As U.S. immigration officials began to understand the magnitude of the problem facing them along the U.S.-Canadian border, they also looked warily to the south and correctly predicted that the Mexican boundary would "undoubtedly be the next point of attack."[12]

Chinese Border Crossings from Mexico

As in Canada, in Mexico immigration policies regarding Chinese contrasted sharply with American laws, creating another back door into the United States. When the United States passed its exclusion law, both Chinese and Mexican authorities were encouraging Chinese migration to Mexico. The Chinese government believed that Mexico and other Latin American countries were convenient alternatives to the United States, where racial hostility and discriminatory laws placed Chinese at risk. Likewise, Mexican officials believed that foreign immigration was an essential ingredient in the development and modernization of the country's infrastructure during the Porfiriato, the rule of President Porfirio Díaz from 1876 to 1911. Attempts to attract Europeans— considered the most desirable immigrant group—failed. Instead, Chinese came in significant numbers and increasingly moved into local trade and commerce, meeting new demands for goods and services in the newly expanding society. After China and Mexico signed the Treaty of Amity and Commerce in 1899, Chinese immigration to Mexico increased. Like their fellow migrants in the north, the Chinese in Mexico also faced racial hostility, and an organized anti-Chinese movement developed in the early 1900s, reaching a climax during the 1930s. However, it did not result in the legal restriction of Chinese immigration. One reason was that though Mexican officials found Chinese immigrants "undesirable," they also admitted that Chinese labor was beneficial and necessary. Anti-Chinese sentiment in Mexico also did not hinder secondary migration to the United States. The open border continued to facilitate both Mexican and Chinese immigration to the United States.[13]

By 1906 U.S. government attempts to curb Chinese illegal entries along the northern border had proved effective enough that the business of illegal immigration shifted south. Soon thereafter, the Mexican border was considered the greatest trouble spot in relation to Chinese illegal immigration. One immigrant inspector went so far as to say that legitimate immigration via Mexico was "a joke, a hollow mockery." It was estimated that 80 percent of the Chinese arriving at Mexican seaports eventually reached the border. From 1907 to 1909, 2,492 Chinese were arrested by U.S. officials for illegal entry along the Mexican border. Mexican statistics on Chinese immigration also suggest that from 1,000 to 2,000 Chinese migrated illegally to the United States per year during the Porfiriato.[14]

Chinese immigrants choosing the circuitous route through Mexico usually disembarked in Ensenada, Manzanillo, Mazatlán, or Guaymas and then took either another steamer going north or the railroad, making sure to disembark well before the trains had reached the United States, where immigration officials were tracking passengers. Entry west of El Paso, Texas, was especially popular for those wishing to go to the West. In fact, the town was known as a "hot-bed for the smuggling of Chinese." Those headed to the eastern states might take a sea route to Florida, Louisiana, Mississippi, and other Gulf Coast states. Some Chinese simply walked across the line by themselves or hitchhiked a ride northward. Law Ngim, for example, found his way north, crossed the border, rested on the side of the road, and then waved down a car to take him to San Francisco in the 1920s. Others hired guides and engaged in highly organized plans. In 1903 one "band of fifteen to twenty Chinamen" was found camped out in a "safe house" about seventy-five miles southeast of San Diego. While the Chinese hid inside the building, their Mexican guides went into town to buy provisions and make further preparations. The average cost for a guide ranged from $25 to $75 in the 1890s, depending on where the crossing took place. By the 1930s, it had increased to $200.[15]

As in Canada, Chinese border migration in the south was built on an established foundation of U.S.-Mexican trade and smuggling networks that thrived in southwestern border towns. There Chinese border crossings were an "open secret," and American immigration officials along the southern boundary complained that Chinese illegal immigration was "carried on with the cognizance if not with the concealed cooperation of the local [Mexican] authorities." Chinese illegal immigration depended on those established networks, and Chinese on both sides of the border could be counted on to provide assistance. Newly arrived Chinese immigrants in Mexico were provided with American money, Chinese-English dictionaries, Chinese American newspapers, and American railroad maps. Immigrant guidebooks to Mexico also circulated, and fraudulent immigration documents manufactured in Mexico arrived at the El Paso post office "almost daily." One Bureau of Immigration report complained that both laborers and merchants in the Chinese community of El Paso "banded together as one man for the purpose of concealing . . . those Chinese coolies who have crossed the line." Rumors of hidden, underground chambers or rooms built between the ceilings and roofs of China-town businesses spread among El Paso residents and immigration officials alike.[16]

Crossings and Contact Zones in the Borderlands

The "banding together" of the Chinese of El Paso with the Chinese coming in from Ciudad Juárez, Mexico, reflects not only the transnational connections between and among Chinese immigrant communities in the United States and Mexico but also the fluidity of the border region for Chinese illegal immigrants. Indeed, much like contemporary migratory activity in the U.S.-Mexican borderlands, Chinese immigration and exclusion along both the northern and southern borders resembled "a world in motion" made up of shifting and multiple identities and relationships constructed for the purpose of illegal migration.[17]

One of the best examples of that multiplicity involves racial crossings, attempts by Chinese to pass as members of another race in order to cross the border undetected. Even though Chinese migration to both Canada and Mexico dated from as far back as the middle of the nineteenth century, Chinese were not viewed as "natural" inhabitants of the northern and southern borderlands like Mexican or Native Americans. Indeed, the mere presence of Chinese along the border could raise suspicion among government officials. Some Chinese immigrants and their guides thus learned, beginning in the early 1900s, to try to pass as Mexican or Native American as they crossed the border. Although such elaborate strategies were by no means the only way to cross the border undetected, they were indeed effective. In 1904 the *Buffalo Times* reported that it was not uncommon for white "smugglers" to disguise the Chinese as Native Americans crossing from Canada to the United States in pursuit of trade. They would be dressed in "Indian garb," given baskets of sassafras, and rowed across the border in boats.[18]

Racial crossings were common along the southern border as well. In 1907 special government inspectors reported on a highly organized, Chinese- and Mexican-run illegal immigration business headed by the Chinese Mexican José Chang in Guaymas. Chinese immigrants landed in Mexico on the pretense that they had been hired to work in the cotton fields there. Chang then brought them to his headquarters in Guaymas, where letters from the immigrants' United States relatives were distributed and further preparations for the border journey were made. One of the most important steps in Chang's operation involved disguising the newly arrived Chinese as Mexican residents. The Chinese cut their queues and exchanged their "blue jeans and felt slippers" for "the most picturesque Mexican dress." They received fraudulent Mexican citizenship papers, and they also learned to say a few words of Spanish, especially "Yo soy mexicano" (I am Mexican). As in the case of the Native American disguise, the Mexican one was supposed to protect Chinese should they be "held up by some American citizen" while attempting to cross the border. The Mexican disguise was apparently quite successful. In 1907 the immigrant inspector Marcus Braun traveled undercover to Mexico to investigate Chinese, Japanese, and European immigration through Mexico to the United States. In Mexico City he uncovered the use of fraudulent Mexican citizenship certificates and photographs by Chinese to facilitate their entry into the United States. On examination of the photographs, Braun expressed amazement that it was "exceedingly difficult to distinguish these Chinamen from Mexicans." To make his point even clearer, he included in his report two "exhibits" of the fraudulent citizenship papers as well as photographs of Chinese on a steamship, emphasizing that the Chinese in question could easily pass as Mexican without detection.[19]

Racial crossings were not confined to the northern and southern borders. One government report on the illicit entry of Asian and European immigrants via Cuba described a particularly successful strategy of "painting the Chinese black" to disguise them as part of the steamship's crew. They apparently "walked off the steamer in New Orleans without trouble." In Mobile, Alabama, an immigrant inspector reported a project to bring in newly arrived Chinese from Mexico and then "disguise the Chinamen as negroes." Mobile was apparently a popular destination point because it was home to one man—referred to by fellow Chinese as "Crooked Face"—whose specialty was disguising Chinese immigrants as African Americans.[20]

Chinese immigrants in effect traded their own racial uniforms, which elicited suspicion in the borderlands, for others that would allow them to blend into particular regional and racial landscapes. In the north, the dominant racial "others" were American and Canadian Indians. In the Southwest, they were Mexicans and American Indians, and in the South, they were African Americans. Chinese illegal immigrants learned to use the ways race marked each particular regional landscape to their own advantage in order to enter the country undetected.

If Chinese racial crossings reflected the multiple, hybrid nature of the borderlands, then the multiracial character of the Chinese illegal immigration business defined the border as a contact zone where people—mostly men—of different races, classes, and nationalities met and sometimes formed fragile alliances. The most numerous smugglers were white Americans or European immigrant men working with Chinese accomplices and organizers. Many were often already involved in illegal activities. Others apparently participated in the business on the side. Either their regular occupations or their geographical locations facilitated covert activities. In Seattle the locomotive engineer Billie Low and the fireman Bat Nelson took advantage of Low's railroad connections to bring both Chinese immigrants and opium into the United States from Vancouver. In Bay St. Louis, Mississippi, a government informant reported, "a certain ring of Greeks" who owned a store and factory were "running Chinese" through Mexico. The store and factory provided substantial housing for the newly arrived immigrants as well as cover for the illegitimate activities. Even those working in the highest levels of law enforcement were involved in the business of Chinese illegal immigration. In 1908 several witnesses and government informants came forward with evidence that the former chief of police Edward M. Fink was "the leader of one of the gangs of smugglers" in El Paso.[21]

American Indians were also known to guide Chinese into the country, especially across the northern border. In the south, however, the Papago Indians "seemed to have a natural antipathy for Chinese," according to the immigrant inspector Clifford Perkins, and thus were routinely hired as government informants to help apprehend Chinese illegals. Mexicans were often the primary guides across the southern border, and they made a handsome profit from selling provisions to Chinese and guiding them. In 1912 Luis Fernandez, Jordan Felize, and Wong Gong Huey of Mexicali joined Ethel Hall, Muy Fat, Lin Fat, and Chin Man of San Francisco in a transnational "notorious smuggling ring" that came under government scrutiny. Multiracial alliances forged in the underground business of illegal immigration, however, could be fragile. For example, Mexicans were not always working on the same side as the Chinese. Some Mexicans might be paid informants, employees of the U.S. Bureau of Immigration, or even witnesses in courts, while others refused to assist Chinese lest their actions call unwanted attention to themselves. Fragile or formal, the multiracial relationships and alliances made Chinese illegal immigration possible and profitable.[22]

"John Chinaman and His Smugglers": Constructing the Chinese Illegal Immigrant

Though the business of illegal immigration relied on an ability to function beyond and below the sight of government authorities, illegal Chinese immigration became the very public symbol of the continuing "Chinese problem" that had inspired the passage of the Chinese Exclusion Act in the first place. As a result, Chinese border crossers became the public image of a new type of immigrant—the "illegal." The American public learned about Chinese border crossings through sensationalist regional and national newspaper reports, magazine articles, and government investigations. The reportage borrowed extensively from existing racial stereotypes of Chinese, often merging the illegal aspect of their migration with coexisting charges that Chinese were either cunning criminals or "coolies" whose immigration constituted a harmful invasion of inferior and unassimilable aliens. As Robert G. Lee has illustrated, beginning in the 1850s, the racialized character of "John Chinaman" in American plays, songs, minstrel shows, and fiction created and reinforced the popular representation of Chinese immigrants as both "pollutants" who endangered American society with their alien presence and unfree, servile coolies who threatened the white working class. By the 1880s "John Chinaman" also came to be the primary image through which Chinese illegal immigration was explained in both popular magazines and political discourse.[23]

The San Francisco–based weekly illustrated journal the *Wasp* was one of the first publications to articulate and illustrate fears of Chinese illegal immigration from Canada and Mexico with a two-page, color illustration entitled "And Still They Come!" Printed in 1880, while anti-Chinese politicians were still laying the groundwork for the eventual passage of the 1882 Chinese Exclusion Act, the cartoon played on fears of future Chinese illegal immigration from the north and south. Having just failed to enact the 1879 Fifteen Passenger Bill that would have limited to fifteen the number of Chinese passengers on any ship coming to the United States, the supporters of Chinese exclusion worked tirelessly to keep the specter of an alien Chinese invasion alive and well. "And Still They Come!" articulated the Chinese exclusion message perfectly. It portrays two endless streams of slant-eyed "Johns" or Chinese coolies disembarking from overcrowded steamships and flowing into the United States. Their racial difference is clearly marked

FIGURE 6.1 "And Still They Come!"

Cartoons and illustrations dramatically portrayed the threat of Chinese illegal immigration via the "back doors" of Canada and Mexico. In this illustration, Uncle Sam is kept busy guarding the main "gateway" to the United States while floods of Chinese enter undetected and thumb their noses at ineffective U.S. immigration policies. *Reprinted from the* Wasp, *Dec. 4, 1880.*

and communicated through exaggerated racial features inscribed onto the bodies of the Chinese figures and through alien Chinese dress and hair. The dark slits that are supposed to be eyes are mere physical manifestations of the surreptitious, sneaky nature of the Chinese. Their loose-fitting garments, broad coolie hats, Chinese baskets, and shoes emphasize the alien customs that will pollute America. Finally, the long, rattail-like braided plaits of hair worn by the Chinese men represent a cultural anomaly that is both sexually and racially ambiguous and threatening. Entering surreptitiously through two back doors labeled "British Columbia" and "Mexico," the Chinese gleefully flout U.S. attempts to bar them. They easily evade an eaglelike Uncle Sam who is trying in vain to shut America's main gates to a third wave of Chinese coolies entering by sea. With his back turned toward the Chinese entering from the north and south, Uncle Sam is oblivious to the larger threats posed by the open borders and fails to notice the Chinese thumbing their noses at him, U.S. law, and the sovereignty of the American nation. As a symbol of the imminent invasion of Chinese, the two steamships docked in British Columbia and Mexico sag with the weight of countless Chinese hanging from the spars and streaming down the gangplank into the United States. On the distant horizon, dozens of Chinese vessels and even air balloons filled with Chinese leave China and make their way to the shores of the United States. Each ship and balloon is marked by the number fifteen, alluding to the unsuccessful Fifteen Passenger Bill and demonstrating how the

FIGURE 6.2 Dying of Thirst in the Desert

Much like the journeys of contemporary illegal immigrants across the southern border, Chinese border crossings at the turn of the twentieth century were risky endeavors, often resulting in death. *Reprinted from* Harper's New Monthly Magazine, *March 1891.*

cunning Chinese would undoubtedly evade and take advantage of America's ineffectual immigration and border policies through an outright invasion.[24]

Beginning in the 1890s, after Chinese border entries had indeed become a reality, the specter of the Chinese illegal immigrant received more national press coverage. Speakers before the U.S. Congress likened the influx of Chinese from Canada to the "swarming of the Huns" in early European history.[25] In 1891 *Harper's New Monthly Magazine* published an exposé written by the journalist Julian Ralph. Titling the piece "The Chinese Leak," Ralph explained in detail the strategies used by Chinese to enter the United States from Canada and Mexico. Lax Canadian laws, "wily" Chinese, and profit-hungry Canadian and American smugglers and "pilots" all figured prominently in Ralph's investigation. Four illustrations accompany the article. One, simply titled "John," portrays a young, disheveled Chinese male walking, presumably across the border. His queue trails in the wind behind him. His dress and shoes are distinctly Chinese, and the slant of his eyes is overemphasized. Here, the image of "John Chinaman" connects the standard racialized caricature of Chinese immigrants as alien coolies to the new phenomenon of illegal immigration. Ralph's text running alongside the image elaborates on the connection. Readers are told that John and other Chinamen who crossed the border were especially "impenetrable," "shrewd," and "intelligent trickster" members of their race. The inhuman conditions to which Chinese subjected themselves in order to enter the United States were also taken by Ralph to be signs of Chinese racial inferiority. In 1891 Ralph witnessed the interdiction of the *North Star*, a "tiny" smuggling boat in "desperately bad condition" that frequently carried as many as thirty Chinese males in her hold from Victoria, British Columbia, to the United States. Noting the small stature of the Chinese and their "raisin-like adaptability . . . to compressed conditions," Ralph observed that it would have been difficult, if not unthinkable, to transport "men of any other nationality" in the same fashion. A more graphic image entitled "Dying of Thirst in the Desert" accompanies Ralph's exploration of Chinese border crossings in the south and portrays an abandoned, parched, and dying Chinese male in the desolate southwestern desert. His canteen empty and his hat and walking stick abandoned on the desert floor beside him, this John crawls on his bony, clawlike hands and knees toward the U.S. border. In stark contrast to the comfortable, middle-class lives of *Harper's* readers, the shocking illustration sensationalized the phenomenon of Chinese illegal immigration. Although it could be perceived as a somewhat sympathetic image that pointed to the desperate measures Chinese were willing to take to enter the United States, "Dying of Thirst in the Desert" nonetheless reinforced racialized notions of Chinese criminality, alienness, racial inferiority, and difference and the threat of invasion with the very same depiction of desperation and tragedy.[26]

Not surprisingly, the construction of the Chinese illegal immigrant was especially strong in the American West and in the northern and southern border regions where most of the illicit migration took place. Both American and Canadian newspapers located in the border regions regularly and actively covered the smuggling of Chinese from the north into the south. All the major newspapers in Buffalo, New York, for example, covered Chinese illegal immigration in minute detail. One *Buffalo Evening News* article prominently displayed a stereotypical image of a disheveled, menacing, and subhuman Chinese male under the headline "Wily Tricks Played by John Chinaman and His Smugglers." Contending that the evasion of exclusion laws was common among the "wily" and "heathen" Chinese, the newspaper warned that the "smuggling business" would continue to "flourish and defy authorities." Explicitly connecting the new threat of illegal Chinese immigration with the standard anti-Chinese rhetoric from the 1870s, the headline was accompanied by a few lines from Bret Harte's popular anti-Chinese poem first published in 1871:

> Which is Why I Repeat (And I'm Free / to Maintain) That for Ways That / Are Dark and for Tricks / That Are Vain, the / Heathen Chinee is / Peculiar.

In another article, a Chinese immigrant who was caught trying to enter the country illegally was described as a "Chink" who used his "long, talon-like nails" in a struggle with law enforcement officials.[27]

Also significant is the persistent use of the terms "smugglers," "smuggled," and "imported" by both journalists and government officials to describe Chinese crossing the border. Such terminology invoked earlier charges that Chinese immigrants were merely "imported coolies" and furthered the racialization of Chinese as inferior immigrants under the control of powerful, clandestine organizations and individuals. The connections made between smuggled goods such as liquor and drugs and Chinese border crossers also painted Chinese immigrants as contraband commodities that did not

FIGURE 6.3 Wily Tricks Played by John Chinaman and His Smugglers

Racialized images of "John Chinaman" as an illegal immigrant built on existing stereotypes of Chinese as racially inferior, wily tricksters who could easily defeat the Chinese exclusion laws and endanger the nation. Such portrayals were especially popular in border cities where illegal immigration was relatively common. *Reprinted from the* Buffalo Evening News, *Feb. 1, 1904.*

belong in the United States and that disrupted communities. Sensationalist newspaper accounts fed the public's appetite, but while they focused attention on the Chinese and used existing racial stereotypes to explain why Chinese crossed the border, they ignored the role of U.S. immigration laws in creating and fostering Chinese illegal immigration in the first place.

Chinese immigrants may have been the first immigrants to enter the United States illegally, but by the early 1900s they were joined by a much larger number of immigrants of other origins who also chose the border as an alternative to the rigorous immigration inspection at American seaports. Syrians, Greeks, Hungarians, Russian Jews, Italians, and some "maidens" from France, Belgium, and Spain were the main groups entering through Canada and Mexico. All were suspected of having been denied entry at the Atlantic ports of entry, but the back door of Canada offered them a second chance. In the late nineteenth and early twentieth centuries Canadian immigrant inspection processes were considerably less rigorous than U.S. procedures and consisted mainly of a limited health screening. Both European and Asian immigrants quickly learned to buy steamship tickets for Canada and then attempt a border crossing into the United States. Exact statistics of those who entered the country illegally are not available. One sensationalist congressional report claimed that as many as 50,000 European immigrants entered via this route in 1890 alone, but more accurate Bureau of Immigration estimates place the figure at "several thousand" each year in the early 1900s.[28] American officials were consistently frustrated by what they deemed overly lax immigration laws in Canada. As the immigrant inspector Robert Watchorn explained in a 1902 report, "much that appears menacing to us is regarded with comparative indifference by the Canadian government." As a result, Watchorn claimed, "those which Canada receives but fails to hold . . . come unhindered into the United States." By 1909 general immigration via the Canadian and Mexican borders was so great that the U.S. Bureau of Immigration identified them as gateways second in importance only to New York.[29]

Even though both Europeans and Asians were illegally crossing the borders into the United States, the discourses concerning the immigrant groups differed sharply, reflecting an existing American racial hierarchy that viewed European immigration—even illegal immigration—as more desirable than Asian immigration. That the category of the illegal immigrant was, from its inception, a highly racialized one is clear from the differences between U.S. officials' discussion of the challenges posed by European immigrants who crossed the border and their discussion of those posed by Chinese immigrants. U.S. immigration officials were certainly concerned about the large numbers of European immigrants evading inspection at the regular ports of entry by crossing the borders. The U.S. government suspected that those immigrants were particularly likely to become diseased or public charges, and the back door European immigration from Canada caused some alarm. Nevertheless, unlawful entries by Europeans were not defined as a threat to the American nation as Chinese illegal immigration was. In 1890 Secretary of the Treasury William Windom, whose agency administered U.S. immigration laws until 1903, articulated that distinction most clearly. Illegal European immigration from Canada was noted as a potential problem, but the attitudes toward European immigration in general remained welcoming and supportive and reflected the view that Europeans—even illegal immigrants—were still future American citizens. "Our country owes too much in greatness and prosperity to its naturalized citizens to wish to impede the natural movement of such valuable members of society to our shores," Windom noted. The next year Windom merely noted an increase in the number of European aliens crossing the northern border illegally and made a general suggestion for increased border inspection. In later years, European immigrants crossing the border illegally were commonly portrayed in government reports as "forlorn," "unfortunate victims of unscrupulous agents in Europe" who were misled and overcharged in the border migration scheme. In other words, the European immigrants arriving via the borders were coming in violation of the law, but they were an exception to the generally acceptable population of European immigrants as a whole. They were not a reflection on *all* European immigrants.[30]

On the other hand, government officials characterized the threat of Chinese migration along the border in highly racialized terms that evoked an immigrant invasion, suggested threats to national sovereignty, and cast suspicion and blame on the entire race. The same year Windom praised the country's "naturalized citizens" of European immigrant heritage, he warned in alarmist terms of the "organized attempts . . . by Chinese laborers to *force* their way into the United States by way of Mexico, British Columbia, and Canada." The next year he warned that the department was "unable . . . to withstand the *great influx* of Chinese laborers along our Canadian border. . . . They are at liberty to *invade* our territory." Similarly, the commissioner-general of immigration blamed the border enforcement problem on the "difficulties inherent in the character of the Mongolian *race*," and the entries of Chinese through Mexico were characterized as an "evil, constant and systematic evasion of our laws."[31]

The racialization of Chinese immigrants as "illegal" also contrasted sharply with the government's treatment of Mexican immigrants crossing the U.S.-Mexican border. Compared to the estimated 17,000 Chinese who entered the country illegally from 1882 to 1920, approximately 1.4 million Mexicans migrated largely unrestricted into the United States from 1900 to 1930. Though some nativists argued that the large influx of "Mexican peons" entering the country in the 1920s was just as dangerous as the "Chinese invasion" of earlier years, before 1924 anti-Mexican nativism worked differently, in practice, than the anti-immigrant sentiment targeting Asians. Instead of excludable aliens, Mexicans were more often characterized as long-term residents of the Southwest or as "birds of passage" who returned to Mexico after the agricultural season ended.[32] Mexican immigration was not wholly unregulated, but it did exist in a state of "benign neglect," and "little attention" was paid to Mexicans who crossed the border into the United States. Indeed, though the immigration service began to record entries and to inspect aliens at the southern border in 1903, the procedures did not apply to Mexicans at all.[33]

The reasons behind the differential treatment are directly related to the expansion of the southwestern economy from the 1890s through the 1920s and the related need for a steady pool of labor. The curtailment of Asian and southern and eastern European immigrant labor beginning in 1882 and continuing through 1924 made Mexico a logical source for new labor. There were immigration restrictions directed against Mexicans, including the Immigration Act of 1917, which imposed a literacy test and an eight-dollar head tax on Mexican immigrants, but until the late 1920s, companies and agriculturalists were highly successful in evading those requirements. U.S. officials at the border also consistently allowed Mexican migrants to avoid the head tax and literacy test. In 1905 Hart Hyatt North, the commissioner of immigration in San Francisco, reported matter-of-factly that Mexicans and Indians were "crossing at will" at Mexicali and other points along the line without either immigration or medical inspection. But the Chinese, he warned, warranted the government's full and "most vigilant attention." In the eyes of the government and the public, Chinese were the "illegals," and they became the targets of concerted government efforts to control illegal immigration. American newspapers in the Southwest during the early 1900s reported on "Chinese wetbacks" instead of Mexican ones. In effect the border was controlled both to facilitate Mexican immigration and to restrict Chinese immigration.[34]

Identifying Chinese and not European or Mexican immigration as the dangerous illegal immigration had direct consequences for immigration officials' dealings with all Chinese immigration. The first was the government's blanket association of Chinese immigration with illegality. The mere presence of Chinese along the border was enough to raise suspicions among government officials. Chinese residents of El Paso, for example, complained to the government that they were routinely suspected of being illegal immigrants and were treated with "undue harshness and strictness." The categorization of Chinese in the northern and southern border regions as illegal immigrants also led to the dehumanization of all Chinese immigrants. Government officials described them as "contraband," as if they were the same as a banned drug or product being smuggled into the country. Investigators' reports routinely referred to the subjects of their inquiry as "this chink" or "these two chinks." The reward system offered by the government to those who gave information leading to the arrest of Chinese found in the country unlawfully also reinforced the dehumanizing categorization of Chinese as smuggled goods, rather than as individuals. In 1908 the government paid G. W. Edgar, a Seattle farmer, an established fee of "five dollars per Chinese head" or two hundred and fifty dollars for "fifty or more Chinamen" in exchange for information that would lead to the arrest of Chinese immigrants found in the country illegally.[35] Last, the categorization of Chinese as illegals gave the arguments of anti-Chinese exclusionists even more power and legitimacy and furthered the racialization of Chinese as undesirable, threatening, and now illegal immigrants. It also permeated the ideology and practice of policing, eventually closing the border to Chinese immigration. That the conflation of "Chinese" with "illegal" was embedded in border policy was made explicitly clear when the immigration service established a special department whose primary responsibility was to deal with illegal aliens. Its name was the Chinese Division.[36]

American Empire and Border Enforcement

Such sensationalist and institutionalized categorizations of Chinese as illegal immigrants highlighted grave weaknesses in American immigration law. Primarily concentrating on immigrant entry through the seaports, United States restrictive immigration legislation largely ignored the country's lack of control over its own land borders. As one Border Patrol inspector commented in 1924, the nation's immigration laws provided "locked doors," but there was no "connecting wall between them" due to the open borders. The United States responded by devising a border enforcement policy to assert its sovereignty and control over the northern and southern borders and to protect the American nation within. The assertion, I argue, was part of the larger practice of extending American laws, ideologies, and systems of control to other countries, a practice that characterized American imperialism in the late nineteenth and early twentieth centuries. Indeed, the process of Chinese exclusion, traditionally defined within the confines of domestic or U.S.-Chinese relations, spilled over many national boundaries. Border anxiety and U.S. immigration policy were directly linked to, and products of, U.S. expansionism.[37]

If we understand imperialism, as Matthew Frye Jacobson has recently suggested, to encompass both a "projection of vested interest in foreign climes . . . and overt practices of political domination," it becomes clear that restricting Chinese immigration via U.S. border enforcement was inextricably tied to the expansion of U.S. imperialism from its inception. At its very foundation, Chinese exclusion had always been justified and articulated through the language of American national sovereignty and self-preservation, American nation building and empire building. U.S. immigration law explicitly equated threats posed by Chinese immigration with threats to national sovereignty. Two Supreme Court cases, *Chae Chan-ping v. United States* (1889) and *Fong Yue Ting v. United States* (1893), asserted that the state held the same rights and duties to curb the foreign menace of immigration as it did to protect its citizens in time of war. Such Supreme Court decisions and domestic, federal immigration laws as the Chinese Exclusion Act of 1882 thus protected the American nation within and served as expressions of American sovereignty. As the American empire advanced across the Pacific Ocean, colonizing Hawaii and the Philippines in 1898, both American and anti-Chinese nativism and assertions of American sovereignty followed the flag. After the annexation of Hawaii in 1898, Congress prohibited all immigration of Chinese to the islands despite strenuous Hawaiian protests. In 1902 the final Chinese Exclusion Act included a section prohibiting Chinese immigration to the Philippines as well. In both cases the United States took the unusual step of prohibiting the free movement of certain peoples *within* the empire, as Chinese immigrants already in Hawaii and the Philippines were prohibited from entering the mainland United States. Like the export of capital, politics, religion, and culture, immigration laws and immigration control thus came to be understood and experienced as a central aspect of American imperialism. The "white man's burden" involved not only uplift and civilization of savage peoples abroad but also protection of Americans from the foreign menaces plaguing the mainland United States as well.[38]

As the cases of Canada and Mexico illustrate, the projection of American interests—in the form of anti-Chinese nativism and legislation—extended beyond the United States and its territories. Through an increasingly rigid set of Chinese exclusion laws, the United States had protected itself from the menace of Chinese immigration, yet it still remained vulnerable because of the lax supervision of immigration in Canada and Mexico. Increasingly, the United States began to assert its right to extend its immigration agenda to neighboring sovereign countries. One immigration official justified tough measures at the border by citing the "law of self-preservation." If Chinese illegal immigration through Canada was indeed "a threat against our very civilization," as the U.S. commissioner-general of immigration said in 1907, then extending the American legal reach into a foreign country to control the threat was a logical outcome.[39] Though it could control its newly annexed territories, the United States could not force its immigration agenda onto Canada and Mexico. Instead, U.S. officials employed a variety of other measures to extend U.S. immigration control into the interiors of its northern and southern neighbors and to induce both countries to cooperate with the United States by adopting compatible immigration laws. The United States achieved that through two new arms of imperialism in modern America: border diplomacy and border policing.

Border Diplomacy and Border Enforcement in the North

Northern borderland scholars write that historically the international boundary at the forty-ninth parallel was largely ignored as both people and goods (legal and illegal) crossed the border uninterrupted and without interference. After border disputes between the United States and Canada were resolved in the eighteenth century, the lack of significant geographical, racial, linguistic (except in the case of Quebec), or religious barriers between the American and Canadian populations helped construct and rein- force the notion of the Canadian-American border as "the world's longest undefended border." The success of Chinese border crossings through Canada does partially sup- port the perception that the boundary line was nothing more than an arbitrary mark in the landscape.[40] Nevertheless, recent scholarship has suggested that the Canadian border was not a racially neutral site and that it underwent a major transformation in immigration control by the 1890s.[41] Indeed, Chinese immigration and exclusion were the primary lenses through which the border was demarcated and racialized. Because Canada's immigration policies clashed with American goals of Chinese exclusion and facilitated illegal entry, the United States increasingly viewed the northern border as a site to be controlled and enforced. Initially frustrated and derisive of Canada's immi- gration policies, U.S. immigration officials eventually turned to border diplomacy. The mutual antipathy of Canada and the United States toward Chinese immigration and the historically amicable relations between the two countries fostered cooperation and finally control of the northern border.

Early border enforcement was an inherently difficult task. The number of inspectors was too small to monitor the large expanse of land. As a result, one of the government's first imperatives was to increase the number of inspectors along the border. In 1902 the total force numbered only 66 inspectors, mostly along the northern border. The next year, the number had increased to 116, again mostly along the U.S.-Canadian border. By 1909, 300 officers and other employees of the immigration service were committed to work along both borders. Another source of difficulty was that too many people and institutions benefited from the illegal immigration. They included the Canadian gov- ernment itself, which collected the revenue from the head tax imposed on Chinese but did not have to suffer the repercussions of increased Chinese immigration to its shores. From 1887 to 1891, revenues from the Chinese head tax equaled $95,500 or about $3,000 a month. Canadian officials were blunt in their opinions. They publicly recognized that the Chinese came to Canada "mainly to smuggle themselves across the border." As one prominent observer explained to an American journalist in 1891, "They come here to enter *your* country. You can't stop it, and we don't care."[42]

The U.S. government turned to three main strategies: pressuring Canada to assist the United States in enforcing the Chinese exclusion laws, moving the enforcement of immigration law beyond the border to the Canadian ports of entry where Chinese first entered, and encouraging Canada to adopt Chinese immigration laws that were more compatible with American goals. All measures reflected the new U.S. imperialist asser- tion of national sovereignty over its borders and marked the extension of American immigration control beyond its own territory. The goal, as Commissioner-General of Immigration Terence Powderly put it in 1901, was to reinforce the border to the point where it was so "airtight" that no one would be able to "crawl through."[43]

U.S. officials first suggested that all ports of entry along the Canadian border be closed to Chinese immigration, but they reluctantly conceded that such a drastic measure would interfere with free trade between the two countries. Instead, beginning in 1894, the U.S. Bureau of Immigration began to extend U.S. immigration law and control into Canadian seaports through the Canadian Agreement. The agreement, made between all Canadian transportation, steamship, and rail companies and the U.S. commissioner-general of immigration, allowed U.S. immigration inspectors to enforce U.S. immigration laws on arriving steamships and on Canadian soil at specifically designated border points. They were instructed to conduct examinations of all United States–bound Asian and European immigrants arriving in Canada in exactly the "same manner" and with the "same objectives" as in the examinations of all arrivals at American seaports. Those who passed inspection were issued a certificate of admission to present to border officers when entering the United States. Those who failed to do so were returned to Canadian railway companies, who were required to return the individual to Canada.[44]

The general 1894 agreement initiated transnational immigration control for both Asian and European immigrants along the border, but the problem of Chinese illegal immigration continued to vex U.S. immigration officials. Even with the Canadian Agreement, they remained unable to establish the same level of control over Chinese immigration through Canada that they had institutionalized for Chinese sailing directly to the United States. Chinese passengers on Canadian steamship lines, for example, were not required to undergo the rigorous predeparture physical examinations that those bound for the United States were subjected to. Nor were they automatically placed in detention and prevented from receiving mail and visitors while awaiting inspection as their counterparts in the United States were. U.S. officials believed that such gaps in enforcement made it easier for newly arriving Chinese to be coached for their U.S. immigration inspections. With study and practice, they could more easily survive the exhaustive interrogations designed to ferret out fraudulent claims of the right to be admitted into the United States.[45] Thus, because Canadian regulation of Chinese immigration remained different from U.S. procedures and prevented U.S. officials from fully controlling the Chinese immigration "problem," the U.S. government began to consider more specific and drastic remedies.

In 1903 Powderly successfully negotiated a new agreement with officials of the Canadian Pacific Railway Company, which operated both the transcontinental Canadian railway and the main line of passenger and cargo ships between China and Canada. Unlike the earlier 1894 agreement, the new initiative placed more border controls on Chinese immigrants exclusively. The agreement first required the CPR to examine all Chinese persons traveling on its steamships to determine "as reasonably as it can" that United States–bound passengers claiming to be admissible were in fact entitled to enter under U.S. law. CPR officials in effect agreed to interpret and enforce U.S. immigration law. Second, the company agreed to deliver *all* Chinese passengers seeking admission into the United States under guard *directly* to U.S. inspectors stationed at four designated ports along the Canadian border (Richford, Vermont; Malone, New York; Portal, North Dakota; and Sumas, Washington). By having the CPR hand over the Chinese immigrants directly to the U.S. government and by processing the Chinese at the designated immigration stations, the U.S. Bureau of Immigration was able to control the movements of Chinese immigrants more closely and to mirror the rigid procedures and detention conditions governing Chinese immigrants at American seaports.[46]

Believing that compliance with such an agreement would be detrimental to its profitable trans-Pacific steamship business, the Canadian Pacific Railway Company was at first reluctant to agree to the U.S. government's demands. Threats that the entire border would be closed unless the CPR agreed to the proposed terms, however, eventually led the company to sign the agreement. The Canadian government itself was not a formal party to the agreement but certainly consented to its terms and means of enforcement. Relations had been strained between the two countries over the issue of border enforcement. The agreement, American officials noted, was mutually satisfactory. The United States gained protection "from the evils of unrestricted immigration," and Canada realized "the extensive benefits" resulting from the loss of friction with its southern neighbor. The 1903 agreement was quite successful. Just one year after the agreement had been signed, the immigration service could report that "no Chinese person from China can enter the United States through Canada without submitting to an examination by Bureau officers. At present there are but a few Chinese coming to this country by way of Canada." With those results achieved, the U.S. Bureau of Immigration officials applauded their counterparts for their cooperation and "cordial spirit of friendship for us and for our exclusion policy." By 1908, inland border inspection points had been established across the boundary to regulate all cross-border migration.[47]

Another explicit goal of American border policy in the north was to "induce" Canada to adopt immigration laws similar to those of the United States. Agreements with Canadian transportation companies were effective but could only extend U.S. control to immigrants who were destined for the United States. Chinese increasingly claimed Canada as their final destination and then crossed the border surreptitiously. As a result, American officials grumbled that the relaxed attitudes toward immigration in Canada were detrimental to the United States. Full control of the borders required *transnational* efforts. American laws might become increasingly restrictive, but as the secretary of the treasury pointed out in 1891, "Any legislation looking to exclude will fail of its full purpose so long as the Canadian government admits Chinese laborers to Canada."[48] To remedy the gaps in immigration control, the U.S. Bureau of Immigration engaged in numerous negotiations with its counterpart in Canada. In 1903 both homegrown anti-Chinese sentiment and "patient and persistent" pressure from U.S. Bureau of Immigration and Department of Justice officers motivated Canada to increase its head tax on Chinese immigrants from $100 to $500. The increased head tax proved a strong deterrent to potential Chinese border crossers. In 1912 Canada also agreed to end the practice of admitting Chinese immigrants into the country if they had already been denied entry into the United States. Finally, in 1923, Canada drastically transformed its regulation of Chinese immigration to mirror U.S. law more closely. The 1923 Exclusion Act completely abolished the head tax system and instead prohibited *all* people of Chinese origin or descent from entering Canada. Consular officials, children born in Canada, merchants, and students were exempted.[49]

Unlike earlier acts, the 1923 Canadian bill was finally the effective barrier to Chinese admission that American immigration officials had supported. During the next twenty-four years, only fifteen Chinese persons were admitted into Canada. The bill was repealed in 1947. The reach of American regulation of Chinese immigration into Canada was thus made complete with the 1923 bill.[50] That Canada's 1923 exclusion law closely resembled the U.S. regulation of Chinese immigration was no coincidence. Pressure from both anti-Chinese activists within the dominion and from their neighbors to the south resulted in the convergence of American and Canadian policies. Border diplomacy based on a shared antipathy toward Chinese immigration in defense of the Anglo-American nation proved effective and finally closed the border to Chinese immigration.

Border Policing and Border Enforcement in the South

Increased Chinese illegal entries via Mexico were a direct outgrowth of successful border enforcement in the north. Much to the U.S. government's chagrin, in 1906 it found that Chinese immigrants, "having been practically defeated at every turn along the Canadian frontier," were increasingly turning their attention to the opportunities of entry via the southern border of the United States. Unlike the northern border, the southern border had always been marked by conquest and contestation between the United States and Mexico. No "'undefended' border" like the one to the north, the U.S.-Mexican border has been described by the border studies scholar Gloria Anzaldúa as an "*herida abierta*" (an open wound). Boundary disputes lasted well into the early twentieth century, and the border was routinely the site of activities that tested the relationship between Mexico and the United States: Indian raids, banditry, smuggling, and revolutionary activities. Chinese immigration and exclusion introduced further conflict as the border region became the site of U.S. immigration control and enforcement.[51]

As Chinese immigration and exclusion along the northern border did, Chinese illegal immigration through Mexico set in motion an American assertion of national sovereignty through the imposition of American nativism, immigration laws, and enforcement practices along the border and in Mexico. However, due to the different immigration goals in the United States and Mexico and the tense relations between them, the form and content of border enforcement in the south contrasted with the practices along the northern border. Unlike Canada, Mexico did not have extensive or consistently enforced immigration laws aimed at Chinese or other immigrants. Mexico also did not require any examination of aliens entering the country, and in general its immigration policies were designed to recruit, not restrict, labor. Although Chinese were targets of periodic racial hostility, they played a vital role in the economy from which both Mexican and American businesses operating in Mexico benefited. The United States could not simply "piggyback" or extend its own immigration policies onto an already existing framework in Mexico as it had in Canada.[52]

Moreover, though Canadian officials eventually complied with U.S. immigration law and prerogatives, Mexican officials were more reluctant to do so. In 1907 the U.S. government undertook initial talks with President Porfirio Díaz in the hope he would allow more American control over Chinese immigration entering through Mexico. The

American immigrant inspector Marcus Braun reported to Díaz that it was the intention of the United States to institute an agreement similar to the Canadian Agreement made with Canadian transportation companies. As in Canada, the United States wanted direct control over Chinese arrivals in Mexico. President Díaz expressed concern that American control over Chinese immigration would result in a loss of valuable labor needed in Mexico.[53]

Lower-level Mexican officials also resisted U.S. efforts to track Chinese immigrants entering from Mexico. In 1907 U.S. officers in El Paso tried to send inspectors over to Ciudad Juárez every day to meet the incoming trains. They were instructed to "take a good look at every Chinaman who arrived," so that they might be able to identify him in case he should later be caught in the United States. As one official reported in 1907, however, the surveillance of Chinese in Mexico had to be abandoned because the authorities in Ciudad Juárez "threatened our officers with arrest if they should take pictures or descriptions of any Chinamen to come through." Mexican transportation officials also showed little inclination to assist American immigration officials in the quest to bar illegal Chinese entries. One meeting with an agent for the Mexico-Canadian Steamship Company demonstrated this clearly. When asked to cooperate, the agent reportedly remarked that his next ship would carry about 300 Chinese as far north as Guaymas. "For all I know they may smuggle into the United States and if they do I do not give a d—n, for I am doing a legitimate business." After 1910 U.S. immigration officials seem to have been more successful, although they were not granted official jurisdiction in Mexico as they were in Canada.[54]

Like other cross-border interactions at the turn of the century, Mexican cooperation with American immigration officials was thus ambivalent and inconsistent at best. American goals of Chinese exclusion were seen as a threat to Mexico's own labor needs, and it was simply unclear to both the Mexican government and the transportation companies what benefit was to be gained by allowing American immigration officials to exercise so much power within their country. Moreover, Mexican reluctance may have been tied to larger concerns about the increased American presence in the country overall. The end of the nineteenth and the beginning of the twentieth centuries constituted a period of increasing American economic penetration into Mexico, especially in the northern state of Sonora. Mexican state-building activities also played up anti-American themes. Although the transnational economy benefited both regions, border relations—of which Chinese immigration and exclusion soon became a part—embodied this ambivalence.[55]

Southern border enforcement thus presented very different challenges to the U.S. immigration service than its northern counterpart did and led to an alternate approach. Instead of using border diplomacy and cooperation, the U.S. Bureau of Immigration closed the southern border to Chinese immigration through policing and deterrence. Immigration officials at the border were charged with the mission of preventing illegal entries in the first place, and of apprehending those caught in the act of crossing the border.[56] To accomplish this, they imposed a three-pronged system of transnational surveillance within Mexico and the United States, patrols at the border, and raids, arrests, and deportations of Chinese already in the United States.

Surveillance of Chinese immigrants in Mexico involved a large informal and formal network of immigration officers, train conductors, consular officials, and Mexican, Indian, and American informants. American diplomatic officers routinely warned U.S. immigration officials on the other side of the border of new Chinese arrivals in Mexico. A typical telegram came from Clarence A. Miller, stationed at Matamoros, warning of an upcoming "flood on the Mexican side" in November 1909 and urging immigration officers to "keep up their vigilance to a high point."[57] Government surveillance of Chinese immigrants in Mexico also involved elaborate undercover investigations by special immigration service agents. The immigrant inspector Marcus Braun, who surveyed the Mexican border situation, first suggested a "Secret Service Squad" charged with watching the Chinese in Mexico in 1907. By 1910 the immigrant inspector Frank R. Stone, praised as "one of the best criminal investigators" in the immigration service, went undercover as a smuggler to investigate the Chinese operations in El Paso. Stone unearthed a wealth of evidence, including fraudulent U.S. certificates of residence (that is, green cards) that Chinese in the United States were required to hold under the 1892 Geary Act. He also found counterfeit seals of two immigration officials and judges of the U.S. District Court for the Northern District of California. Stone's investigation resulted in twelve indictments for conspiracy: four against the Chinese principals and masterminds of the operation, three against Mexican "river-men" who were known for their ability to ford the Rio Grande, one against a Mexican driver, and four against Chinese immigrants holding fraudulent U.S. documents. Stone was also able to photograph the four Chinese leaders (in one photo, Stone himself posed with the suspects), the exact locations where immigrants usually crossed the border, the fraudulent immigration documents, and the adobe huts that served as safe houses. Beginning in the early 1900s, Mexican informants and government witnesses also regularly tracked the movements of Chinese immigrants within Mexico by taking photographs of potential border crossers. The photographs were then sent to the immigration offices at Tucson, Arizona, to be used to identify newly arrived Chinese as ones who had recently passed through Mexico.[58]

The burden of enforcement work along the Mexican border lay in the detection and arrest of "contraband Chinese" and the prosecution of those who assisted in their unlawful entry. The earliest attempts to control the southern border were centered on an increased number of officers along the border "maintaining a much closer patrol, night and day" and a "very vigorous policy with regard to the arrest of Chinese found in this country in violation of the law." The goal of patrolling the border was inherently difficult because of the magnitude of land to be covered as well as the paucity of officers to patrol it. As Braun complained to the commissioner-general of immigration in 1907, all the rivers, carriage roads, pathways, highways, and mountain trails needed to be patrolled. "There is a broad expanse of land with an imaginary line, all passable, all being used, all leading into the United States. The vigilance of your officers stationed along the border is always keen; but what can a handful of people do?"[59]

In response, the immigration service increased the number of immigrant inspectors every year. The first patrol officer in the south was Jeff Milton, who in 1887 resigned from the Texas Rangers and became a mounted inspector with the U.S. Customs Service in El Paso. In the early 1900s, Milton was hired by the immigration service as a U.S. immigration border guard in the El Paso district. His primary duty was to "prevent the smuggling of Chinese from Mexico into the United States." With a territory covering vast stretches of border from El Paso to the Colorado River, he was known as the "one-man Border Patrol." By 1904 there were an estimated eighty mounted inspectors patrolling the border for illegal Chinese entrants. The so-called "line riders" of the Customs Service continued to "pick up Hindus and Japanese" as well. In 1908 the special Chinese Division was established in the U.S. Bureau of Immigration, which took over the responsibility for dealing with illegal aliens, including the work of the patrol officers. From 1907 to 1909, 2,492 Chinese were arrested by U.S. officials for illegal entry along the Mexican border.[60]

Despite the strengthened border patrol, the inspectors could not catch every Chinese attempting to enter the country illegally. Indeed, it was this inability that led to the formulation and practice of the third feature of the government's border policy: extending border enforcement into the interior cities and regions of the United States and instituting a "vigorous policy" of raids, arrests, and deportations of suspected illegal immigrants. "Let it be known," Commissioner-General Frank Sargent declared in 1906, "that even thickly settled city districts will not afford, as in the past, a safe harbor for those who clandestinely enter." By 1909 a system of interior enforcement was in place, and many of the activities of the service were directed toward "ridding the country of undesirable aliens." The immigration service assigned special agents, commonly known as "Chinese catchers," to find and arrest Chinese unlawfully in the country. Those with high records of arrests and deportations were "celebrated" in the local press and transferred throughout the country to spread their expertise. The Chinese inspector Charles Mehan, for example, began his career in San Francisco, which was widely known as the most difficult port of entry for Chinese. Recognized within the service and by supporters of Chinese exclusion for his rigid interrogations and energetic enforcement of the Chinese exclusion laws, Mehan was called "one of the most celebrated Chinese catchers" in the newspapers and was transferred to El Paso to deal with the problem of Chinese border crossings from Mexico. In 1899 he was transferred to Canada.[61]

Border surveillance, policing, and deportation proved successful in stemming illegal Chinese border entries from Mexico. The numbers of Chinese arrested and deported for unlawful residence in the United States increased. In 1899 the ratio of Chinese admitted to Chinese deported was 100:4. By 1904 the ratio was 100:61.[62] Border enforcement also became more centralized. In 1907 the border states were consolidated and reorganized into the Mexican Border District, containing Arizona, New Mexico, and most of Texas. Demonstrating the importance of Chinese immigration in shaping general border enforcement, the first commissioner hired to manage the new Mexican Border District (which supervised all foreign immigration across the border) was Frank W. Berkshire, who had overseen the Chinese service along the New York–Canadian border and in New York City.[63]

At the same time, conditions in Mexico, including revolution and increasing anti-Chinese sentiment, placed additional barriers to Chinese immigration. By 1911 the border division reported that it was "no longer acting upon the defensive." Immigration officials also observed that by World War I, a decline in Chinese attempts at entry along the southern border led the immigration service to transfer its Chinese inspectors away from the region.[64] In 1917 Congress provided that aliens who entered the country by land from places other than those designed as ports of entry or who entered without inspection (as many Chinese crossing the borders had done) could be taken into custody and deported without any legal procedure. By 1926 the commissioner-general of immigration declared that "the smuggling of Chinese over the land boundaries, which was a vexatious problem in the past, has been greatly reduced."[65]

Conclusion

Different Chinese immigration goals and policies in the United States, Canada, and Mexico as well as different relationships between the United States and its neighbors led to the evolution of distinct border policies. While the northern border was eventually closed through U.S.-Canadian border diplomacy and a mutual antipathy toward Chinese immigration, southern border enforcement policies were the product of conflicting Chinese immigration policies in the United States and Mexico as well as inconsistent cooperation between the two countries. Border diplomacy thus gave way to border policing designed to deter and apprehend illegal Chinese immigrants already at the border and within the United States. By the 1920s, both the northern and southern borders were effectively closed to Chinese immigration. While Chinese border entries did not completely end, they ceased to warrant the level of attention and response within the immigration service that they had at the turn of the century.

From 1882 to 1924, however, Chinese immigration and exclusion along the U.S.-Canadian and U.S.-Mexican borders had transformed immigration policy, the border region, and American border enforcement. Chinese immigrants—racialized as perpetual foreigners—became the first group in the country marked as "illegal immigrants." The U.S. Bureau of Immigration's first division to deal primarily with illegal immigration was, after all, called the Chinese Division, making "Chinese" synonymous with "illegal" in the same way "Mexican" is racialized now. Indeed, Chinese immigration and exclusion along the northern and southern borders appears to have been an important trial run for the U.S. Bureau of Immigration's much larger efforts to control Mexican immigration in later years. In both cases, the racialization of political discourse and policy on immigration has been central to the ideological, legal, and political definitions of national membership and national identity.

In the wake of increased illegal immigration from Mexico since the 1970s, attitudes and responses to illegal immigration by both the American public and the U.S. government echo earlier responses and sentiments from the Chinese exclusion era. Metaphors or war, for example, are commonly used in contemporary border enforcement discourse as they were at the end of the nineteenth century. Words, phrases, and even political initiatives such as "invasion," "conquest," and "save our state" have been consistently deployed by xenophobes and others, revealing a highly racialized perspective on the new immigration, especially illegal immigration. Much as "John Chinaman and his smugglers" were the dominant public image of the illegal immigrant during the Chinese exclusion era, undocumented immigrants from Mexico became the nearly exclusive focus of government and public concern at the end of the twentieth century.[66]

Significant differences exist as well. The Chinese exclusion laws may have laid the foundations of U.S. border control and enforcement beginning in the late nineteenth century, but those early state efforts pale in comparison with recent campaigns to control immigration. In particular, the government's first attempts to enforce the northern and southern borders during the Chinese exclusion era have increased exponentially, turning the U.S.-Mexican border into a militarized zone designed to deter illegal immigration at any cost. Instead of "Chinese catchers" and "line riders," the government relies on surveillance in the form of night scopes, motion sensors, and communications equipment as well as jeeps and a fourteen-mile triple fence on the U.S.-Mexican border south of San Diego. With newly hired border inspectors mandated by Congress, the Border Patrol became one of the government's largest police agencies in the late 1990s. The United States currently spends $2 billion a year to build walls and manage a twenty-four-hour patrol of the border. During the Chinese exclusion era, the number of "mounted inspectors" patrolling the line was around 80. In 2001, the Border Patrol had 9,400 agents.[67]

In the wake of the terrorist attacks on the United States on September 11, 2001, issues of transnational immigration policies and border control have been pushed to the very forefront of U.S. and international policy. Several of the suspected hijackers who took control of the commercial flights that crashed into the World Trade Center in New York City and the Pentagon in Washington, D.C., spent time in Canada and allegedly entered the United States from the north. In the months following the attacks, policy makers have renewed their focus on increased border security, especially along the northern border. Like critics of Canada's allegedly lax Chinese immigration policies during the 1890s, contemporary American politicians blame Canada for allowing foreigners to enter with false or no passports, apply for asylum, travel freely, and raise funds for political activities while their asylum applications are pending. Canada's open doors, it is argued, increase the risk to American national security.[68] Likewise, the racialized categorization of Arabs and Muslims as "terrorists" follows on the heels of racialized characterizations of Chinese and later Mexicans as "illegal immigrants." Recent suggestions for increased border security also echo earlier efforts first articulated during the Chinese exclusion era. In the early twentieth century, U.S. government officials sought to induce Canada to adopt Chinese immigration policies that more closely mirrored U.S. laws. In late September of 2001, Paul Cellucci, the U.S. ambassador to Canada, publicly called for Canada to "harmonize its [refugee] policies with those of the United States." President George W. Bush sketched out a vision of a "North American security perimeter" in which transnational immigration controls would be central.[69] As of this writing, there is little agreement on what such a "harmonization" would mean. Nor is it clear how U.S. and North American border policies might change. What is certain is that in the United States' "new war" against terrorism, transnational border enforcement and immigration policies will undoubtedly remain central issues facing the United States, Canada, and Mexico in the twenty-first century, just as they were over one hundred years ago.

Notes

I would like to thank Matthew Frye Jacobson, Claudia Sadowski-Smith, Marian Smith, Patrick McNamara, Robert G. Lee, and Grace Delgado for their encouragement and suggestions. Valuable research assistance was provided by Josephine Fowler. Joanne Meyerowitz, Richard White, the editorial staff of, and the four anonymous reviewers for, the *Journal of American History* provided invaluable feedback and assistance in revisions.

1. The Chinese Exclusion Act of 1882 prohibited the immigration of Chinese laborers for a period of ten years and barred all Chinese immigrants from naturalized citizenship. Act of May 6, 1882, 22 Stat. 58; Testimony of Lim Wah, Dec. 2, 1932, file 12020/22130, Case Files of Investigations Resulting in Warrant Proceedings (12020), 1912–1950, San Francisco, Records of the Immigration and Naturalization Service, RG 85 (National Archives, Pacific Branch, San Bruno, Calif.).

2. Since illegal immigration is difficult to quantify and detect, this estimate is speculative. It is drawn from: U.S. Department of Commerce and Labor, *Annual Report of the Commissioner-General of Immigration to the Secretary of Commerce and Labor: For the Fiscal Year Ended June 30, 1903* (Washington, 1903), 102; George E. Paulsen, "The Yellow Peril at Nogales: The Ordeal of Collector William M. Hoey," *Arizona and the West*, 13 (Summer 1971), 113–28; C. Luther Fry, "Illegal Entry of Orientals into the United States between 1910 and 1920," *Journal of the American Statistical Association*, 23 (June 1928), 173–77.

3. On the northern and southern borders, see Timothy J. Dunn, *The Militarization of the U.S.-Mexico Border, 1978–1992: Low-Intensity Conflict Doctrine Comes Home* (Austin, 1996); Peter Andreas, *Border Games: Policing the U.S.-Mexico Divide* (Ithaca, 2000); and Bruno Ramirez, *Crossing the 49th Parallel: Migration from Canada to the United States, 1900–1930* (Ithaca, 2001). Studies that acknowledge the role of Chinese immigration and exclusion include George J. Sanchez, *Becoming Mexican American: Ethnicity and Acculturation in Chicano Los Angeles, 1900–1945* (New York, 1993); and Grace Delgado, "In the Age of Exclusion: Race, Region, and Chinese Identity in the Making of the Arizona-Sonora Borderlands, 1863–1943" (Ph.D. diss., University of California, Los Angeles, 2000). For studies on the northern and southern borderlands that use transnational and hemispheric frameworks, see Gunther Peck, *Reinventing Free Labor: Padrones and Immigrant Workers in the North American West, 1880–1930* (New York, 2000), esp. 1–7; and Samuel Truett, "Neighbors by Nature: The Transformation of Land and Life in the U.S.-Mexico Borderlands, 1854–1910" (Ph.D. diss., Yale University, 1997), esp. 3. See also David Thelen, "The Nation and Beyond: Transnational Perspectives on United States History," *Journal of American History*, 86 (Dec. 1999), 965–75.

4. Prior to 1875 some state laws barred the entry of foreign paupers or fugitive slaves, but the 1875 Page Law (which forbade the entry of Asian laborers immigrating involuntarily and of prostitutes) and the 1882 Chinese Exclusion Act were the first federal laws to exclude groups. The latter declared that any person who secured certificates of identity fraudulently or through impersonation was to be deemed guilty of a misdemeanor, fined $1,000, and imprisoned for up to five years. Anyone who knowingly aided and abetted the landing of "any Chinese person not lawfully entitled to enter the United States" could be charged with a misdemeanor, fined, and imprisoned for up to one year. The act declared that "any Chinese person found unlawfully within the United States shall be caused to be removed therefrom to the country from whence he came." On pre-1875 immigration law, see Gerald L. Neuman, "The Lost Century of American Immigration Law, 1776–1875," *Columbia Law Review*, 93 (Dec. 1993), 1834–38. For the provisions of the Chinese Exclusion Act, see Act of May 6, 1882, sec. 7, 11, 12, 22 Stat. 58. For post-1882 general immigration laws, see Act of Aug. 3, 1882, 22 Stat. 214; Immigration Act of 1891, 26 Stat. 1084; Act of Feb. 5, 1917, 39 Stat. 874; Act of May 26, 1924, 43 Stat. 153. On the 1924 change in immigration law, see Mae M. Ngai, "The Architecture of Race in American Immigration Law: A Reexamination of the Immigration Act of 1924," *Journal of American History*, 86 (June 1999), 67–92.

5. Resident Chinese laborers who had been in the United States at the time of the act were allowed to reenter. David Chuenyan Lai, *Chinatowns: Towns within Cities in Canada* (Vancouver, 1988), 52. The earliest reports of illegal border crossings by Chinese appear in northwestern newspapers in June and July 1883. See "Chinese in B.C.," *Port Townsend Puget Sound Argus,* June 15, 1883; "More about the Chinese," *ibid.,* July 9, 1883.

6. Act of July 20, 1885, ch. 71, 1885 S.C. 207–12 (Can.); Patricia E. Roy, *A White Man's Province: British Columbia Politicians and Chinese and Japanese Immigrants, 1858–1914* (Vancouver, 1989), 59–63.

7. Department of Commerce and Labor, *Annual Report of the Commissioner-General of Immigration . . . 1903,* 97.

8. Statistics are compiled from Canadian Royal Commission on Chinese and Japanese Immigration, *Report of the Royal Commission on Chinese and Japanese Immigration* (1902; New York, 1978), 271, as cited in Qingsong Zhang, "Dragon in the Land of the Eagle: The Exclusion of Chinese from U.S. Citizenship" (Ph.D. diss., University of Virginia, 1993), 238; and U.S. Congress, House, Select Committee on Immigration and Naturalization, *Investigation of Chinese Immigration,* 51 Cong., 2 sess., 1890, H. Rept. 4048, serial 2890, p. 1.

9. Act of July 18, 1900, ch. 32, 1900 S.C. 215–21 (Can.); U.S. Department of Commerce and Labor, *Annual Report of the Commissioner-General of Immigration to the Secretary of Commerce and Labor: For the Fiscal Year Ended June 30, 1910* (Washington, 1910), 143; U.S. Department of Commerce and Labor, *Annual Report of the Commissioner-General of Immigration to the Secretary of Commerce and Labor: For the Fiscal Year Ended June 30, 1911* (Washington, 1911), 159.

10. Lai, *Chinatowns,* 23; Julian Ralph, "The Chinese Leak," *Harper's New Monthly Magazine,* 82 (March 1891), 520–23; Roland L. De Lorme, "The United States Bureau of Customs and Smuggling on Puget Sound, 1851–1913," *Prologue,* 5 (Summer 1973), 77–88; Hyung-chan Kim and Richard W. Markov, "The Chinese Exclusion Laws and Smuggling Chinese into Whatcom County, Washington, 1890–1900," *Annals of the Chinese Historical Society of the Pacific Northwest* (1983), 16–30; Department of Commerce and Labor, *Annual Report of the Commissioner-General of Immigration . . . 1903,* 98–99.

11. U. S. Congress, Senate, *Reports on Charge of Fraudulent Importation of Chinese,* 49 Cong., 1 sess., 1886, S. Doc. 103, p. 8; James Bronson Reynolds, "Enforcement of the Chinese Exclusion Law," *Annals of the American Academy of Political and Social Science,* 34 (no. 2, 1909), 368; U.S. Department of Commerce and Labor, *Annual Report of the Commissioner-General of Immigration to the Secretary of Commerce and Labor: For the Fiscal Year Ended June 30, 1904* (Washington, 1904), 137–41. Stanford Lyman, *Chinese Americans* (New York, 1974), 106. On corrupt federal judges, see U.S. Department of Commerce and Labor, *McGettrick Certificates: List of Chinese Cases Tried before Former U.S. Commissioner Felix W. McGettrick, for the District of Vermont, from December 11, 1894, to June 24, 1897* (Washington, 1906).

12. Ralph, "Chinese Leak," 515; Department of Commerce and Labor, *Annual Report of the Commissioner-General of Immigration . . . 1903,* 101.

13. Ching-Hwang Yen, *Coolies and Mandarins: China's Protection of Overseas Chinese during the Late Ch'ing Period (1851–1911)* (Singapore, 1985), 292; Raymond B. Craib III, *Chinese Immigrants in Porfirian Mexico: A Preliminary Study of Settlement, Economic Activity, and Anti-Chinese Sentiment* (Albuquerque, 1996), 8, 22, 24; Evelyn Hu-DeHart, "Racism and Anti-Chinese Persecution in Sonora, Mexico, 1876–1932," *Amerasia Journal,* 9 (no. 2, 1982), 2–4, 13.

14. On the new threat to the Mexican border and U.S. government estimates, see U.S. Department of Commerce and Labor, *Annual Report of the Commissioner-General of Immigration to the Secretary of Commerce and Labor: For the Fiscal Year Ended June 30, 1906* (Washington, 1906), 98; "Report by Marcus Braun, U.S. Immigrant Inspector, New York, to Hon. Frank P. Sargent, Commissioner General of Immigration, Dept. of Commerce and Labor, Washington, D.C., dated Feb. 12, 1907," file 52320/1, Subject Correspondence, Records of the Immigration and Naturalization Service, RG 85 (National Archives, Washington, D.C.). U.S. government estimates are included in J. W. Berkshire to Commissioner-General of Immigration, April 16, 1910, file 52142/6, *ibid.;* Zhang, "Dragon in the Land of the Eagle," 372. For Mexican statistics, see Evelyn Hu-DeHart, "Immigrants to a

Developing Society: The Chinese in Northern Mexico, 1875–1932," *Journal of Arizona History,* 21 (Autumn 1980), 275–312, esp. 282–83.

15. Berkshire to Commissioner-General of Immigration, Oct. 17, 1907, file 52212/2, part 1, Subject Correspondence, Immigration and Naturalization Service Records (Washington, D.C.); Testimony of Law Ngim, May 17, 1931, file 12020/19153, Case Files of Investigations, Immigration and Naturalization Service Records (San Bruno, Calif.). On the organized smuggling attempts, see Charles W. Snyder to Commissioner-General of Immigration, Nov. 11, 1903, folder 22, box 2, Hart Hyatt North Papers (Bancroft Library, University of California, Berkeley). On the cost of border crossing, see "Report by . . . Braun . . . Feb. 12, 1907"; U.S. Department of Commerce and Labor, *Annual Report of the Commissioner-General of Immigration to the Secretary of Commerce and Labor: For the Fiscal Year Ended June 30, 1902* (Washington, 1902), 75; U.S. Department of Commerce and Labor, *Annual Report of the Commissioner-General of Immigration to the Secretary of Commerce and Labor: For the Fiscal Year Ended June 30, 1907* (Washington, 1907), 110; Ralph, "Chinese Leak," 524; Paulsen, "Yellow Peril at Nogales," 113–28; and Testimony of Lim Wah, Dec. 2, 1932, file 12020/22130, Case Files of Investigations, Immigration and Naturalization Service Records (San Bruno, Calif.).

16. Ralph, "Chinese Leak," 524; Department of Commerce and Labor, *Annual Report of the Commissioner-General of Immigration . . . 1907,* 111; Craib, "Chinese Immigrants in Porfirian Mexico," 8. On cross-border networks, see Department of Commerce and Labor, *Annual Report of the Commissioner-General of Immigration . . . 1907,* 110; "Digest of, and Comment Upon, Report of Immigrant Inspector Marcus Braun, dated September 20, 1907," file 51630/44D, Subject Correspondence, Immigration and Naturalization Service Records (Washington, D.C.); and Burton Parker to Secretary of the Treasury, June 5, 1909, file 52516/7, *ibid.* On Chinese in El Paso, see U.S. Department of Commerce and Labor, *Annual Report of the Commissioner-General of Immigration to the Secretary of Commerce and Labor: For the Fiscal Year Ended June 30, 1905* (Washington, 1905), 95–96.

17. Gloria Anzaldúa, *Borderlands/La Frontera: The New Mestiza* (San Francisco, 1987), preface.

18. *Buffalo Times,* Jan 18, 1902, p. 5. See also *New York Times,* Nov. 29, 1896, p. 1; *ibid.,* June 10, 1891, p. 1.

19. "Reports by . . . Braun . . . Feb. 12, 1907," 30–33; Department of Commerce and Labor, *Annual Report of the Commissioner-General of Immigration . . . 1907,* 110–11.

20. "Report of Inspector Feri F. Weiss to Commissioner-General of Immigration In re: Cuban Smugglers," April 4, 1925, file 55166/31, Subject Correspondence, Immigration and Naturalization Service Records (Washington, D.C.); Feri F. Weiss to Commissioner-General of Immigration, Feb. 25, 1925, *ibid.* My thinks to Libby Garland for these sources. P. H. Shelton to Commissioner-General of Immigration, Aug. 15, 1911, file 53161/2–A, *ibid.*

21. On the Seattle activities, see Thomas M. Fisher to Commissioner-General of Immigration, May 7, 1917, file 53788/3, *ibid.* On Chinese illegal immigration through Mississippi, see M. R. Snyder to S. E. Redfern, Feb. 2, 1911, file 53161/2, *ibid.* On the corrupt El Paso police chief, see Richard H. Taylor to Commissioner-General of Immigration, Oct. 24, 1908, file 52212/2, *ibid.*

22. On American Indians, see Clifford Allan Perkins, *Border Patrol: With the U.S. Immigration Service on the Mexican Boundary, 1910–54* (Washington, 1978), 23. On Mexicans, see Department of Commerce and Labor, *Annual Report of the Commissioner-General of Immigration . . . 1910,* 146; and Berkshire to Commissioner-General of Immigration, Sept. 19, 1912, file 53507/32, Subject Correspondence, Immigration and Naturalization Service Records (Washington, D.C.). On Mexican informants, see *Preventing Immigration of Chinese Labor from Canada and Mexico,* 1891, H. Rept. 2915, cited in Leon C. Metz, *Border: The U.S.-Mexico Line* (El Paso, 1989), 365, and Perkins, *Border Patrol,* 23.

23. On the construction of "John Chinaman," see Robert G. Lee, *Orientals: Asian Americans in Popular Culture* (Philadelphia, 1999), 9, 22, 32. Illegality became a racially inscribed category for Mexicans in the 1924 Immigration Act, according to Ngai, "The Architecture of Race in American Immigration Law," 67–92.

24. Both the Senate and the House passed the Fifteen Passenger Bill, demonstrating national and bipartisan support for Chinese exclusion. A presidential veto blocked its enactment. See Andrew

Gyory, *Closing the Gate: Race, Politics, and the Chinese Exclusion Act* (Chapel Hill, 1998), 3–6. "And Still They Come!," *Wasp,* Dec. 4, 1880, p. 280.

25. Ralph, "Chinese Leak," 516. See also U.S. Treasury Department, *Annual Report of the Commissioner-General of Immigration to the Secretary of the Treasury: For the Fiscal Year Ended June 30, 1897* (Washington, 1897), 758; U.S. Department of the Treasury, *Alleged Illegal Entry into the United States of Chinese Persons: Letter from the Secretary of the Treasury . . .,* 55 Cong., 1 sess., 1897, Sen. Doc. 167, p. 153; Zhang, "Dragon in the Land of the Eagle," 349–50; Department of Commerce and Labor, *Annual Report of the Commissioner-General of Immigration . . . 1904,* 149, 626.

26. Ralph, "Chinese Leak," 516–19, 522, 444.

27. *Buffalo Evening News,* Feb. 1, 1904, p. 9; *Buffalo Morning Express,* Jan. 29, 1901, p. 6; "Big Chinese Haul," *ibid.,* Feb. 19, 1902. On Bret Harte, see Lee, *Orientals,* 39, 68–69, 91; and Ronald Takaki, *Iron Cages: Race and Culture in Nineteenth-Century America* (New York, 1979), 223.

28. European immigrants are described in "Report by . . . Braun . . . Feb. 12, 1907." For statistics, see U.S. Congress, Senate, *Report of the Select Committee on Immigration and Naturalization,* 51 Cong., 2 sess., 1891, S. Rept. 3472, vii, cited in Ramirez, *Crossing the 49th Parallel,* 42; Treasury Department, *Annual Report of the Commissioner-General of Immigration . . . 1902,* 39.

29. Treasury Department, *Annual Report of the Commissioner-General of Immigration . . . 1902,* 40–41; U.S. Department of Commerce and Labor, *Annual Report of the Commissioner-General of Immigration to the Secretary of Commerce and Labor for the Fiscal Year Ended June 30, 1909* (Washington, 1909), 13.

30. U.S. Treasury Department, *Annual Report of the Secretary of the Treasury on the State of the Finances for the Year 1890* (Washington, 1891), lxxv; U.S. Treasury Department, *Annual Report of the Secretary of the Treasury on the State of the Finances for the Year 1891* (Washington, 1891), lxii; Department of Commerce and Labor, *Annual Report of the Commissioner-General of Immigration . . . 1902,* 40, 42.

31. U.S. Treasury Department, *Annual Report of the Secretary of the Treasury . . . 1890,* lxxvi. Emphasis added. Treasury Department, *Annual Report of the Secretary of the Treasury . . . 1891,* lxiv–lxv. Emphasis added. Department of Commerce and Labor, *Annual Report of the Commissioner-General of Immigration . . . 1902,* 71. Emphasis added. "Report by . . . Braun . . . Feb. 12, 1907."

32. This would change dramatically after 1924. As Mae Ngai has shown, Mexicans increasingly became characterized as dangerous foreigners and "illegal immigrants." Sanchez, *Becoming Mexican American,* 18–19. For the post-1924 period, see Ngai, "Architecture of Race," 91. On nativism directed against Mexican immigrants, see Frederick Russell Burnham, "The Howl for Cheap Mexican Labor," in *The Alien in Our Midst; or, Selling Our Birthright for a Mess of Pottage,* ed. Madison Grant and Charles Stewart Davison (New York, 1930), 45, 48. On Mexicans as "birds of passage," see Lawrence Cardoso, *Mexican Emigration to the United States, 1891–1931* (Tucson, 1980), 22; Sanchez, *Becoming Mexican American,* 20; and Abraham Hoffman, *Unwanted Mexican Americans in the Great Depression: Repatriation Pressures, 1929–1939* (Tucson, 1974), 30–32.

33. U.S. Immigration and Naturalization Service, "Early Immigrant Inspection along the U.S./Mexican Border" <http://www.ins.gov/graphics/aboutins/history/articles/mbtext2.htm> (Feb. 15, 2002).

34. Sanchez, *Becoming Mexican American,* 19–20; Hoffman, *Unwanted Mexican Americans in the Great Depression,* 30–32; Mark Reisler, *By the Sweat of Their Brow: Mexican Immigrant Labor in the United States, 1900–1940* (Westport, 1976), 8–13, 24–42; Hart Hyatt North to Frank Sargent, March 9, 1905, file 13618, Segregated Chinese Records, Chinese General Correspondence, Immigration and Naturalization Service Records (Washington, D.C.); Metz, *Border,* 365.

35. For Chinese complaints from El Paso, see Ng Poon Chew to Daniel Keefe, July 30, 1910, folder 1, box 3, Ng Poon Chew Collection (Asian American Studies Library, University of California, Berkeley). For a description of Chinese as "contraband," see F. H. Larned, "Memorandum for the Commissioner-General," Oct. 27, 1913, file 53371/2A, Subject Correspondence, Immigration and Naturalization Service Records (Washington, D.C.). On investigations of "chinks," see [signature illegible] to Brother Larned, April 19, 1901, file 52730/53, *ibid.* The agreement between the government and G. W. Edgar is outlined in Larned to Inspector in Charge, Seattle, Washington, Oct. 26, 1908, file 52214/1, part IV, *ibid.*

36. Perkins, *Border Patrol,* 9.

37. Mary Kidder Rak, *Border Patrol* (Boston, 1938), 1. On U.S. imperialism, see Amy Kaplan, "'Left Alone with America': The Absence of Empire in the Study of American Culture," in *Cultures of United States Imperialism,* eds. Amy Kaplan and Donald Pease (Durham, 1993), 16–17.

38. Matthew Frye Jacobson, *Barbarian Virtues: The United States Encounters Foreign Peoples at Home and Abroad, 1876–1917* (New York, 2000), 4, 6, 26–38, 93; *Chae Chan-ping v. United States,* 130 U.S. 606 (1889); *Fong Yue Ting v. United States,* 149 U.S. 698 (1893). On the extension of Chinese exclusion to Hawaii and the Philippines, see Act of July 7, 1898, 30 Stat. 750; Act of April 30, 1900; 31 Stat. 141; and Wu Ting Fang to John Hay, Dec. 12, 1898. Notes from the Chinese Legation in the U.S. to Department of State, 1868–1906, Records of the U.S. Department of State, RG 59 (National Archives, Washington, D.C.). The best account of Chinese immigration to Hawaii is Clarence E. Glick, *Sojourners and Settlers: Chinese Migrants in Hawaii* (Honolulu, 1980). See also Edward C. Lydon, *The Anti-Chinese Movements in the Hawaiian Kingdom, 1852–1886* (San Francisco, 1975).

39. "Report by . . . Braun . . . Feb. 12, 1907"; Frank P. Sargent, "Memorandum," c. 1905, file 52704/2, Subject Correspondence, Immigration and Naturalization Service Records (Washington, D.C.).

40. For descriptions of the U.S.-Canadian border as open and undefended, see John W. Bennett and Seena B. Kohl, *Settling the Canadian-American West, 1890–1915: Pioneer Adaptation and Community Building* (Lincoln, 1995), 13; Roger Gibbins, "Meaning and Significance of the Canadian-American Border," in *Border and Border Regions in Europe and North America,* ed. Paul Ganster et al. (San Diego, 1997), 315–32; Ralph, "Chinese Leak," 521; and De Lorme, "United States Bureau of Customs and Smuggling on Puget Sound," 77–88.

41. Sheila McManus, "Their Own Country: Race, Gender, Landscape, and Colonization around the 49th Parallel, 1862–1900," *Agricultural History,* 73 (Spring 1999), 168–82; Ramirez, *Crossing the 49th Parallel,* 39.

42. For statistics on inspectors in 1902, see Department of Commerce and Labor, *Annual Report of the Commissioner-General of Immigration . . . 1903,* 46. For statistics for 1909, see Marcus Braun, "How Can We Enforce Our Exclusion Laws?" *Annals of the American Academy of Political and Social Science,* 34 (no. 2, 1909), 140–42. Ralph, "Chinese Leak," 516.

43. Vincent J. Falzone, *Terence V. Powderly, Middle-Class Reformer* (Washington, 1978), 182.

44. The agreement underwent several revisions to permit additional transportation companies to become signatories and to perfect implementation of its terms. At the same time, the U.S. government began to place inspectors along the border. Inspectors were stationed at Quebec, Montreal, Halifax, Vancouver, and Victoria beginning in 1895. On threats to close the border entirely, see Department of Commerce and Labor, *Annual Report of the Commissioner-General of Immigration . . . 1904,* 137. On the original Canadian Agreement, see Marian L. Smith, "The Immigration and Naturalization Service (INS) at the U.S.-Canadian Border, 1893–1993: An Overview of Issues and Topics," *Michigan Historical Review,* 26 (Fall 2000), 127–47; "Canadian Agreement," Sept. 7, 1893, file 51564/4A-B, Subject Correspondence, Immigration and Nationalization Service Records (Washington, D.C.); and U.S. Bureau of Immigration, *Annual Report of the Commissioner-General of Immigration to the Secretary of the Treasury for the Fiscal Year Ended June 30, 1896* (Washington, 1896), 13. For amended versions, see Treasury Department, *Annual Report of the Commissioner-General of Immigration . . . 1902,* 46–48; and "Digest of . . . Report of . . . Braun . . . September 20, 1907."

45. "Digest of . . . Report of . . . Braun . . . September 20, 1907," 30–34.

46. Department of Commerce and Labor, *Annual Report of the Commissioner-General of Immigration . . . 1904,* 138; "Digest of . . . Report of . . . Braun . . . September 20, 1907," 29–30; U.S. Treasury Department, *Annual Report of the Commissioner-General of Immigration for the Fiscal Year Ended June 30, 1901* (Washington, 1901), 52; U.S. Bureau of Immigration, *Compilation from the Records of the Bureau of Immigration of Facts Concerning the Enforcement of the Chinese-Exclusion Laws: Letter from the Secretary of Commerce and Labor, Submitting, in Response to the Inquiry of the House, a Report as the Enforcement of the Chinese-Exclusion Laws* (Washington, 1906), 94.

47. On threats to close the border, see "Digest of . . . Braun . . . September 29, 1907," 32. Immigration officials cited the benefits of the Canadian Agreement in "Memorandum in re Proposed

Mexican Agreement" included in Berkshire to Commissioner-General of Immigration, Jan 15, 1908, file 51463/B, Subject Correspondence, Immigration and Naturalization Service Records (Washington, D.C.); Department of Commerce and Labor, *Annual Report of the Commissioner-General of Immigration . . . 1904,* 138; Department of Commerce and Labor, *Annual Report of the Commissioner-General of Immigration . . . 1906,* 94; and Department of Commerce and Labor, *Annual Report of the Commissioner-General of Immigration . . . 1911,* 159–60. On inland border inspection points, see Smith, "Immigration and Naturalization Service (INS) at the U.S.-Canadian Border," 127–35.

48. The term "induce" was first used in "Report by . . . Braun . . . Feb. 12, 1907." On changes in immigrants' strategies at the border, see Zhang, "Dragon in the Land of the Eagle," 323; Smith, "Immigration and Naturalization Service (INS) at the U.S.-Canadian Border," 127–30. On the need for fuller cooperation from Canada, see Treasury Department, *Annual Report of the Secretary of the Treasury . . . 1891,* lxv.

49. Act Respecting and Restricting Chinese Immigration, ch. 8, 1903 S.C. 105–11 (Can.); Department of Commerce and Labor, *Annual Report of the Commissioner-General of Immigration . . . 1904,* 138. On Canadian-U.S. negotiations, see, for example, John H. Clark to U.S. Commissioner-General of Immigration, July 16, 1912, file 51931/21, Subject Correspondence, Immigration and Naturalization Service Records (Washington, D.C.). Act of June 30, 1923, ch. 38, 1923 S.C. 301–15 (Can.); H. F. Angus, "Canadian Immigration: The Law and Its Administration," in *The Legal Status of Aliens in Pacific Countries,* ed. Normal MacKenzie (New York, 1937), 63–64.

50. Peter Ward, *White Canada Forever: Popular Attitudes and Public Policy toward Orientals in British Columbia* (Montreal, 1978), 133; Robert E. Wynne, "Reaction to the Chinese in the Pacific Northwest and British Columbia, 1850–1910" (Ph.D. diss., University of Washington, 1964), 483.

51. Bureau of Immigration, *Compilation from the Records of the Bureau of Immigration of Facts Concerning the Enforcement of the Chinese-Exclusion Laws,* 12–33; Lauren McKinsey and Victor Konrad, *Borderlands Reflections—the United States and Canada* (Toronto, 1989), iii; Anzaldúa, *Borderlands,* 3; Linda B. Hall and Don M. Coerver, *Revolution on the Border: The United States and Mexico, 1910–1920* (Albuquerque, 1988), 7.

52. "Report by . . . Braun . . . Feb. 12, 1907"; Marcus Braun to Commissioner-General of Immigration, June 10, 1907, file 52320/1–A, Subject Correspondence, Immigration and Naturalization Service Records (Washington, D.C.); Evelyn Hu-DeHart, "Coolies, Shopkeepers, Pioneers: The Chinese of Mexico and Peru, 1849–1930," *Amerasia Journal,* 15 (no. 1, 1989), 92–98; Hu-DeHart, "Racism and Anti-Chinese Persecution in Sonora, Mexico," 16.

53. Braun to Commissioner-General of Immigration, June 10, 1907, file 52320/1–A, Subject Correspondence, Immigration and Naturalization Service Records (Washington, D.C.).

54. Department of Commerce and Labor, *Annual Report of the Commissioner-General of Immigration . . . 1907,* 112; R. L. Pruett to Braun, May 11, 1902, file 52320/1–A, Exhibit "B," Subject Correspondence, Immigration and Naturalization Service Records (Washington, D.C.). For the post-1910 period, see Delgado, "In the Age of Exclusion," 241–42, 250–52.

55. "Memorandum in re Proposed Mexican Agreement"; Miguel Tinker Salas, *In the Shadow of the Eagles: Sonora and the Transformation of the Border during the Porfiriato* (Berkeley, 1997), 16, 161; Hall and Coerver, *Revolution on the Border,* 11, 15; Delgado, "In the Age of Exclusion," 241–42, 250–52.

56. Department of Commerce and Labor, *Annual Report of the Commissioner-General of Immigration . . . 1909,* 142.

57. Department of Commerce and Labor, *Annual Report of the Commissioner-General of Immigration . . . 1907,* 130. Keefe to Supervising Inspector, El Paso, Texas, Nov. 26, 1909, file 52265/6, Subject Correspondence, Immigration and Naturalization Service Records (Washington, D.C.); Berkshire to Commissioner-General of Immigration, Feb. 15, 1910, file 52142/6, *ibid.;* Clarence A. Miller to Assistant Secretary of State, Oct. 11, 1909, file 52265/6, *ibid.*

58. "Report by . . . Braun . . . Feb. 12, 1907"; Frank R. Stone to Berkshire, April 23, 1910, file 52801/4A, Subject Correspondence, Immigration and Naturalization Service Records (Washington, D.C.); Berkshire to Commissioner-General of Immigration, May 7, 1910, *ibid.;* Perkins, *Border Patrol,* 11, 23.

59. Department of Commerce and Labor, *Annual Report of the Commissioner-General of Immigration . . . 1906,* 95; Braun to Commissioner-General of Immigration, June 10, 1907, file 52320/1–A, Subject Correspondence, Immigration and Naturalization Service Records (Washington, D.C.).

60. John M. Myers, *The Border Wardens* (Englewood Cliffs, 1971), 16–17, 23; Rak, *Border Patrol,* 6; Perkins, *Border Patrol,* xii, 9; "The U.S. Border Patrol: The First Fifty Years," *I & N Reporter* (Summer 1974), 3; Immigration and Naturalization Service, "Early Immigration Inspection along the U.S./Mexican Border"; Zhang, "Dragon in the Land of the Eagle," 372.

61. Department of Commerce and Labor, *Annual Report of the Commissioner-General of Immigration . . . 1906,* 95; Department of Commerce and Labor, *Annual Report of the Commissioner-General of Immigration . . . 1909,* 132; "New Chinese Inspector," *El Paso Herald,* June 27, 1899, in box 8, Chinese General Correspondence, Immigration and Naturalization Service Records (Washington, D.C.).

62. Here deportation figures apply to those found to be in the country unlawfully. They do not include immigrants denied entry upon arrival. Department of Commerce and Labor, *Annual Report of the Commissioner-General of Immigration . . . 1904,* 148.

63. Immigration and Naturalization Service, "Early Immigration Inspection along the U.S./Mexican Border."

64. The commissioner-general of immigration reported that southern border strategies to curb Chinese illegal immigration were yielding results as early as 1905. Department of Commerce and Labor, *Annual Report of the Commissioner-General of Immigration . . . 1905,* 94. On the border conditions in 1911 and during World War I, see Department of Commerce and Labor, *Annual Report of the Commissioner-General of Immigration . . . 1911,* 146; and Perkins, *Border Patrol,* 49. On conditions in Mexico that diminished Chinese illegal immigration, see Salas, *In the Shadow of the Eagles,* 171.

65. Act of Feb. 5, 1917, sec. 19, 30 Stat. 889; Zhang, "Dragon in the Land of the Eagle," 375–76; R. D. McKenzie, *Oriental Exclusion: The Effect of American Immigration Laws, Regulations, and Judicial Decisions upon the Chinese and Japanese on the American Pacific Coast* (Chicago, 1927), 158.

66. Juan Perea, *Immigrants Out! The New Nativism and the Anti-Immigrant Impulse in the United States* (New York, 1997), 73; Kevin R. Johnson, "Race, the Immigration Laws, and Domestic Race Relations: A 'Magic Mirror' into the Heart of Darkness," *Indiana Law Journal,* 73 (Fall 1998), 1137; Claudia Sadowski-Smith, "Reading across Diaspora: Chinese and Mexican Undocumented Immigration at Land Borders," in *Globalization on the Line: Culture, Capital, and Citizenship at U.S. Borders,* ed. Claudia Sadowski-Smith (New York, forthcoming).

67. *Washington Post,* Oct. 1, 1996, p. A1; *ibid.,* April 5, 1996, p. A17; "Immigration Overhaul," *Migration News,* 3 (Oct. 1996) <http://migration.ucdavis.edu/mn/archive mn/oct 1996–01mn.html> (Feb. 15, 2002); *New York Times,* May 27, 2001, p. A14.

68. *Chicago Tribune,* Sept. 26, 2001, p. 9; *New York Times,* Oct. 1, 2001, p. B3; Dennis Bueckert, "Canadian Sovereignty Called into Question in Fight against Terrorism," Oct. 3, 2001, Canadian Press Newswire, available at Lexis-Nexis Academic Universe; *National Post* (Toronto), Oct. 4, 2001, pp. A1, A15; *New York Times,* Oct. 4, 2001, p. B1; *Seattle Times,* Oct. 10, 2001, p. A1.

69. *National Post* (Toronto), Oct. 1, 2001, p. A10.

7

When the Migrants Are Men

Italy's Women and Transnationalism as a Working-class Way of Life

DONNA R. GABACCIA

During the long era of international migration that shaped the world between the Napoleonic Wars and the First World War (1815–1914), 60 percent or more of all global migrants were men. The earliest students and theorists of migration saw this as a natural phenomenon, determined by biology.[1] Yet even in the nineteenth century and (more noticeably) today, gender ratios vary considerably, and in some shorter-distance migrations, women outnumber men.[2]

This chapter focuses on gender relations in Italy's mass migrations. The 16 million migrants who left Italy between 1870 and 1914 formed one of the most significant migrations of the modern world. About a third went to the U.S. and Canada, a quarter to Argentina and Brazil, and almost half to other European countries, notably Switzerland, France, Austria and Germany. Migration from Italy was otherwise typical of the nineteenth century in that most migrants were men—those whom one scholar has termed "the men without women."[3] Overall, two-thirds of the migrants who left Italy between 1870 and 1920 were men of rural backgrounds.[4] Not surprisingly, many of Italy's migrants were sojourners who returned to Italy or migrated repeatedly over the course of their working lives. The "women who waited"—contemporaries, and their historians in Italy have called them "white widows"—have also attracted some scholarly attention.[5]

Italy's men and women thus provide us with an early example of transnational lives, or lives shaped by time in more than one nation. Recent attention to transnationalism has changed the way we think about migration in the contemporary world by emphasizing the degree to which migrants continue to live in two places.[6] Yet transnational lives, and transnationalism itself, are by no means new phenomena, nor are they characteristic only of the contemporary world. Unlike today's migrants, however, most of whom are literate, with some urban experience prior to migration, Italy's men and women in the nineteenth century were generally illiterate, rural people. They had no telephones with which to communicate. Even writing or reading a letter was a challenge. They could not hop onto jet planes for short visits to distant relatives. It is therefore hard not to wonder why, when faced with such obstacles, so many of Italy's families opted for transnational lives. Certainly, they lived at a time when transnational life was more disruptive to the lives of migrants than it is today.

Gendered divisions of labor and of labor markets, culturally patterned family preferences and definitions of appropriate male and female behavior all influence migration. They help determine whether men and women migrate or remain immobile together, or whether they instead separate as one leaves the other behind. Many readers in the English-speaking world will assume that male-dominated migrations from countries like Italy simply reflect the peculiarities of Latin patriarchy. It is true that Latins, like many other Europeans in the nineteenth century, believed that women were best kept within the family circle. Unlike other Europeans they also feared the power of women's sexuality when released from male control. Yet the migration of sons also threatened a father's control over his family. Furthermore, Mediterranean societies have generally assigned control of women's sexuality to other women, whose day-to-day surveillance of each other was unaffected by male migration. Distinctive characteristics of Latin patriarchy are probably not the most convincing explanations for Italy's gendered patterns of migration.

Changes in local and global job markets in the nineteenth century had considerably more influence on migrants' decisions during the era of mass, international migration. After 1830, the abolition of slavery worldwide threatened the stability of European empires dependent on raw materials from their colonies, and generated new, largely Asian and male, migrations of semi-free laborers into colonial agriculture and mining. Italian men, and somewhat fewer women, participated in these migrations. At the same time, anti-imperial revolutions in the Americas created huge and new, but sparsely populated, national states that believed, along with the Argentine Juan Bautista Alberdi, that "to govern is to populate."[7] These nations sought new settlers and citizens, preferably in fertile and hard-working family groups with balanced sex ratios. Family migrations from Italy were much more important in the settlement of Argentina and Brazil than of the U.S., Canada or Australia. Finally, industrial capital spread from its earlier concentration in a few cities in northern Europe and Great Britain to other parts of Europe and the Americas and, to a lesser extent, Africa and Asia. The migratory workers—many of them Italian—who built cities and factories in Europe and the Americas, were men working in seasonal construction jobs. The Italian migrants who later migrated to work in factories included a significant female component in the Americas (but not in Europe). Factory employment in women's industries—not the demand of expanding urban middle classes for domestic servants—most often motivated women to leave Italy.[8] The majority, however, remained at home, in large part because they did much more there than merely "wait" for men to return. Transnationalism was common among Italy's residents mainly because it so often made economic sense for both men and women.

Gender and Migration from Italy

By almost any measure, migration from Italy in the nineteenth century was on an impressive scale. Overall, no other people migrated in so many directions and in such impressive numbers—relatively and absolutely—as from Italy. Furthermore, few showed such firm attachments to their home regions or returned in such large proportions—50 percent or more.[9] Still, migration varied considerably across Italy's regions, as did women's representation, and these variations provide clues to the complex interaction of gender, labor and migration.

Scholars have always known, but rarely attempted to explain, why migrations varied so much from region to region in Italy. These variations provide at least a few clues to why men and women more often separated than migrated together. While students of culture note differing attitudes toward gender and women's sexuality in northern and central Italy and in the south, migration patterns do not fall neatly into central, northern or southern patterns. Table 7.1 shows that some of the more prosperous and supposedly less patriarchal northern regions of Italy actually had very high rates of migration both before and after 1900. Migration developed somewhat more belatedly in the southern part of the country but there, too, a few regions had very high rates of migration while migration from others was negligible. Overall, 45 percent of Italy's migrants came from the north, and only a third from the south of the country. Table 7.2 shows that destinations even more than emigration rates varied with regional origin. Southern Italians generally, Sicilians in particular, and—in the north of Italy—Ligurians, showed a special preference for migration to the United States. Europe attracted mainly Italians from the north and the center, while Latin America was equally attractive to those of northern and southern origins.

As Table 7.3 shows, the supposedly more modern, less patriarchal and Europeanized north of Italy actually had lower rates of female migration—with the notable exception of Liguria—than most of the supposedly more patriarchal south. By tracing gendered work opportunities at home and abroad, we can better understand this outcome and its meaning. Work opportunities for men and women in Italy's north and south were sharply different. In much of mountainous northwest Italy, where peasant families maintained fairly firm access to their own lands, older women's work on the land freed younger women to migrate to textile factory jobs in nearby cities, such as Biella, Turin and Milan, or in foreign cities. Also freed to migrate were men, whose wages supplemented the work of older women as food-producers. Many took seasonal jobs as construction workers or seasonal agricultural laborers across the Alps.[10] In Sicily, by contrast, fewer peasants owned or controlled stable plots of land near their villages. Men traveled long distances in order to work, and they effectively excluded the competition of women wage-earners on large landowners' commercial estates by 1880. Women could not so easily feed their families, thus freeing men for migration, in southern regions like Sicily.[11]

Industrial jobs in the Americas (along with the empty lands of Brazil and Argentina) also seemed to offer southerners (and Ligurians) and women from both places far better opportunities for employment than transalpine Europe, where northern Italians were

Table 7.1 Annual rates of Italian emigration, by region, 1876–1914

Region	Province	1876–1894 (%)	1895–1914 (%)*
North	Piedmont	1.0	10.3
	Lombardy	0.6	0.9
	Veneto	20.6	30.3
	Liguria	0.5	0.5
	Emilia	0.3	10.0
Center	Tuscany	0.5	10.0
	The Marches	0.1	10.6
	Umbria	—	10.3
	Lazio	—	0.6
	Abruzzi-Molise	0.6	20.5
South	Campania	0.6	10.9
	Apulia	0.1	0.8
	Basilicata	0.2	20.6
	Calabria	0.7	20.3
	Sicily	0.2	10.6
	Sardegna	0.1	0.5

Source: *Annuario statistico della emigrazione italiana* (Roma, 1926), Table III.
* Migrants as percentage of total regional population in 1881 (for 1876–1894) or 1911 (for 1895–1914).

Table 7.2 Percentage of all Italian emigrants going to the U.S., by regional origin, 1876–1914

Region	Province	Percentage
North	Piedmont	10
	Lombardy	6
	Veneto	3
	Liguria	23
	Emilia	2
Center	Tuscany	17
	The Marches	20
	Umbria	19
	Lazio	71
	Abruzzi-Molise	59
South	Campania	64
	Apulia	57
	Basilicata	53
	Calabria	48
	Sicily	72
	Sardegna	12

Source: *Annuario statistico della emigrazione italiana* (Roma, 1926), Table III.

Table 7.3 Percentage female of all Italian emigrants, by province, 1876–1925

Region	Province	Percentage
North	Piedmont	22
	Liguria	29
	Lombardy	17
	Veneto	16
Centre	Emilia	19
	Tuscany	21
	The Marches	21
	Umbria	18
	Lazio	14
South	Abruzzi-Molise	19
	Campania	27
	Apulia	21
	Basilicata	30
	Calabria	19
	Sicily	29
	Sardegna	15

Source: *Annuario statistico della emigrazione italiana*
(Roma, 1926).

most likely to migrate and where gender ratios were heavily unbalanced. In Europe, construction jobs and unskilled and semi-skilled positions in a few male industries were open
to Italian men. The employment of foreign females in Germany, France and Switzerland's
textile industries was far more limited. By contrast, Argentina and Brazil welcomed Italians as both settler families and in their new industries. In fact, earlier Italian merchants
and craftsmen developed much of the urban industry in these two Latin countries, and
Italian employers seemed to prefer workers, both male and female, from their homeland.
In the US and Canada, construction was the main sector of male Italian employment, but
predominantly female industries like garments, cigars, textiles and shoes also employed
large numbers of Italian women.[12] Thus, a combination of good opportunities to work at
home and poor options abroad may have limited female migration from Italy's north. At
the same time, poor options at home and relatively good options abroad may explain the
higher rates of female migration from many parts of the south, especially from Sicily.

We know less about how rates of return varied from region to region. Local studies
suggest that the heavily male transalpine migrants from the north were most likely to
return. Returning men were 80 percent of those leaving from the Veneto and more than
90 percent of those departing Friuli in the 1890s.[13] But since the Italian government did
not systematically count returners from the Americas until 1905, or from Europe until
1921, even tentative conclusions are impossible. The proportion of returners from the
Americas — 49 percent between 1905 and 1920 — seems impressive at a time when travel
across the Atlantic took one to three weeks and cost more than half the yearly income
of an average peasant.[14] Samuel Baily has estimated rates of return from 44 to 53 percent
from Buenos Aires and New York around 1900.[15] Betty Boyd Caroli cites a contemporary
study that found 54 percent of southerners, 50 percent of central Italians and 40 percent

of northerners returning from the United States.[16] Temporary male migration was not exclusively a northern pattern, nor were gender-balanced migrations of family groups limited to the south. Transnationalism thus became a way of life throughout Italy during the mass migrations.

Transnational Family Economies

Separations during migration were most consistently characteristic of migration from Italy's north and from southern regions during the onset of migration. Culture certainly shaped migration patterns in both cases; and ties of family, sexual desire and sentiment all lured the men without women home to northern and southern villages. More important, whether in the north or in the south, the separation of men from women during migration proved not only economically feasible but in many cases more advantageous than transplantation in family groups. Separation seemed the most dependable strategy in a family's search for security, especially in Italy's north.[17]

Family security meant many things, of course—money, a dowry, house or land, a trade or profession, increased consumption of modern goods, the comforts of a familiar dialect, cuisine or religious rite, and the respect of friends and relatives. A description of family budgets—earnings and consumption—in both Italy and abroad uncovers the complex decision making that underlay transnationalism during this era of male migration. Unfortunately, we cannot easily compare southern and northern patterns of transnationalism. Italians saw emigration mainly as a problem of the south, directed to the U.S., and the nations of the Americas—which attracted disproportionate numbers of southerners—also focused more attention on immigrant workers than the nations of Europe. Consequently, we still have little good evidence on earnings and expenditures among migrants in Europe. My analysis focuses on transnationalism among American-bound migrants, most (although not all) of them southerners.

Transnationalism during the era of mass male migrations meant the creation of family economies transcending national borders. In these family economies, flows of cash remittances complemented the comings and goings of men.[18] Initially, family economies linked work camps populated by wage-earning Italian men and rural Italian villages housing disproportionate numbers of women and children awaiting their return. Families accepted separations to keep family members as fully employed as possible. But men and women also schemed how and when to reunite or (in the case of the unmarried) to marry. Whether to locate a family's "home base"[19] in Italy or abroad was a complex decision, emerging from a gradual process of learning about wages and prices in several places. While we cannot trace the learning process itself with any precision, the factors influencing Italians' decisions are clear enough.

Migration required families to learn what levels of security and material well-being they obtained by combining cash earned in Italy and abroad with food-raising and cloth production at home. Families also assessed the moral worth of differing work for men, women and children at home and abroad. The most important challenge was to learn the real value of cash earnings. Letters home and returning men reported on earnings abroad, and explained what those earnings meant once transformed into the moneta, scudi or lire of Italy. In Europe and in North America, unskilled sojourners from Italy typically earned wages a third lower than the wages of natives. In the U.S. that meant $1.50 a day at the turn of the century or—given seasonal unemployment—a bit less than $300 per year.[20] When translated into lire, these wages seemed generous. In the Abruzzi in the 1870s, for example, agricultural workers earned 1–2 lire a day (except during harvests, when wages rose to 15 lire). Peasant men averaged 25 to 50 lire in income monthly but worked only nine or ten months each year. By contrast, in the Americas, a male sojourner working in construction earned 117 lire a month in the spring and 170 in autumn. Even if a migrant man borrowed 100 lire to pay his passage, and paid interest of 80 to 100 additional lire to a *padrone* (labor recruiter), or suffered two or three months unemployment, foreign wages were clearly higher than in Italy.[21] A man's annual income of $300 was more than five times that of a prosperous peasant family in Italy's north, and even larger when compared to family cash incomes in the south.

Unfortunately for male sojourners, living costs abroad were also much higher than in Italy. American observers who found appalling conditions in all-male boarding houses always noted (but rarely praised) the thriftiness of the men without women. Most men struggled to keep expenses below $200 a year. Sojourners denied themselves food, sex and pleasure in order to generate a surplus, while natives fumed over migrants' un-American living standards. They recognized that Italian workers could live on their low wages because they ate little more than rice, pasta, bread and vegetables, while native workers wanted meat. In fact, native workers needed high wages in order to pay for the higher costs of meat, housing, reproduction and family security in developing economies.[22] Italian men, too, had dependents, but they chose to spend their wages on reproduction where prices were low—in Italy.[23]

Men from the Abruzzi later claimed that they could save 1,000 to 1,500 lire during a year's work in the U.S. A year of work in Europe generated about 600 lire in savings, and six months' work in Germany produced a surplus of 300 to 500 lire. Even that more modest sum equaled the cash income of a peasant family.[24] When combined with women's production of food and cloth, men's cash incomes easily sustained life and the reproduction of the next generation. Although peasants lived poorly, died young, and complained of "*la miseria*" (misery), they rarely starved. New sources of cash from abroad opened possibilities for greater security, comfort and pleasure in Italy. In 1880, a postal clerk in Picinisco saw almost 130,000 lire cross his counter—or about 150 lire for each of the 850 Europe-bound migrants from his small town.[25] Remittances to Italy soared with migration to the Americas, from 13 million lire in 1861 to 127 million lire in 1880, and then to 254 million a year after 1890 and 846 million a year after 1906. So large was the cash inflow that it ended Italy's negative balance of foreign trade by 1912.[26] American savings in particular struck peasants as extraordinary windfalls.

Still, men's remittances purchased security and comfort only if women and children at home continued to produce food and clothing. Analyses of migrant men and their wages often ignore their connection to the work of the women who waited for them at home. These women were also workers, albeit subsistence producers of food and clothing, working without wages for a family's consumption. Visitors from Europe and America noted with disgust the heavy and exhausting work of peasant women in Italy. In the north, they found women ploughing, mowing, carrying heavy loads of hay, wood, stone and water, grinding their own grains on hand mills, making their own bread, raising small animals, harvesting, gleaning, and processing food.[27] In the Val D'Aosta, a mountainous area of northwestern Italy where most men migrated seasonally to France, the investigator for a governmental inquest reported women were "the true beasts of burden" of the region.[28]

In the center and south, too, observers noted "the women work like slaves," carrying as many as 70 kg of produce on their heads, often only eight days after giving birth.[29] Emma Ciccotosto, the daughter of a peasant family in the Abruzzi, whose father was absent for most of her childhood, reported:

> Everything my mother knew she learned from her mother, and that included a lot of farm work . . . everything was done by hand. Our farm grew corn, wheat, olives, and flax, as well as vegetables and poultry. We had two sheep which my mother milked. . . . Occasionally we raised a pig which my mother would sell . . . all the animals were stabled at the far end of the house and their manure was thrown out of a small door into the yard where it piled up until we had time to collect it to spread on the ground for the next season's planting.[30]

"We" meant this woman and her young children, aided by groups of neighbors working communally at harvest times.

Spinning and weaving were other chores on Emma Ciccotosto's mother's long list of tasks. In the northern regions of Lombardy and Piedmont, women's domestic production of cloth continued alongside both silk- or wool-spinning cottage industries and the modern spinning and weaving mills developed after 1880.[31] In Italy's south, by contrast, women had begun to put aside their spindles and looms already in the 1870s, as cheap imported cloth rendered their labors unprofitable.[32]

Although women's work rates had declined from over 50 percent over the previous thirty years, especially in the south, census takers in 1901 still listed one in three Italian women as active, wage-earning workers outside their homes. (This was a higher rate of female employment than in the United States, for example.) From Naples in 1909, Oreste Bordiga reported that female day laborers actually outnumbered men in one region of heavy male emigration.[33] The working women were the lucky ones: desperate women in Sicily, with its limited options for female work, instead reasserted feudal rights to collect snails and greens on uncultivated lands.[34] "They graze like animals," a middle-class observer of women foragers noted with horror. The luckier white widows in southern areas turned to their parents, in-laws and female neighbors for support when necessary. They raised small household animals to eat or sell and they opened tiny shops to earn a few extra cents as "penny capitalists."[35] Although the culture increasingly condemned women who worked in the fields as immoral, it also harshly criticized women who did not work. They were the female "brooms" that swept away family resources through their idleness.[36] The occasional woman who lived in idleness on remittances—as some clearly did—easily fell victim to gossips' charges of "*ozio*" (laziness).[37]

The desire to establish a family on a more secure footing within existing village hierarchies—as landed peasants, rentiers, or small artisans and shopkeepers—motivated male migration, scholars agree. These represented the occupations most respected in much of rural Italy in the nineteenth century, and they defined a more comfortable and civilized way of life within reach of Italy's peasants.[38] Few scholars have systematically measured upward mobility of returners.[39] But existing evidence suggests that occupational mobility was limited, occurring largely within the peasant class, as wage-earning *braccianti* (laborers) and peasants' sons acquired leases or small plots of land. Few returners became wealthy landowners because remittances too quickly inflated the value of local land.[40] Land hunger in Italy remained intense and produced a new wave of land occupations after the First World War.[41]

By contrast, many returners purchased new housing or improved the houses they owned, guaranteeing a healthier, more comfortable and more secure if modest life.[42] Houses signaled their improved social status too, since the very poorest had no homes, and sometimes still lived as mendicants or in caves. Investment in housing was especially common where sojourners returned from the Americas. In the area around Salerno in the first decade of the century, peasants paid 1,000 lire (one to three years' savings) for houses government investigators found to be "substantial." These were freestanding, two-story dwellings, quite unlike the older one- and two-story attached houses of most villages. With plastered walls, and floors of brick, they had proper windows, a separate kitchen, an internal staircase and two upstairs rooms. Some had balconies and shutters, sturdy wooden doors, and a tiled roof.[43] In some villages, returners introduced acetylene lighting or made inquiries about obtaining an electricity supply in towns without piped water or sewage. The contrast of the homes of migrants to the "old black homes, piled on top of each other and separated only by torturous, dark little streets" impressed even moralizing middle-class observers.[44]

Cash earned abroad further transformed consumption habits among rural Italians, allowing many to enjoy a considerable sense of material improvement. Already in the 1870s and early 1880s, investigators had noticed with displeasure peasants' new-found fascination with purchasing from the local *pizzicagnolo,* or small shopkeeper who sold cheap trinkets, cloth, household equipment and pipes.[45] In many regions of the north and a few of the larger cities of the south, poor men and women had already abandoned traditional costumes before migration. Bourgeois observers complained that "homewoven cloth does not sufficiently satisfy [women's] vanity," so that the "mania for dressing up" increased daily.[46] Mass migration accelerated a transformation in consumption already under way. Poor Italians abandoned sandals and wooden clogs for shoes; men purchased suits of wool and velvet, hats, and watches. By 1910, traditional women's costumes had disappeared in the coastal areas around Naples; and even in isolated mountain villages, women no longer wore traditional costume but donned only distinctive scarves, shawls or headwear.

Cash also allowed poorer migrants to eat well, which made it possible that their children could eventually grow as tall and robust as urbanites. Nineteenth-century investigations had established that Italian peasants consumed sufficient food to survive while working hard but that many men nevertheless failed to achieve draft requirements for height. They also concluded that peasant diets—regardless of region—were monotonous, largely vegetarian and probably nutritionally insufficient.[47] Northern peasants ate as much as a kilo of cornmeal polenta daily; their evening meal was a thick soup (*minestra*) of grains, legumes and vegetables, along with a little wine and occasional cheese. The poor rarely ate wheat bread, except in Sicily and Apulia, and even southerners rarely consumed pasta, except on holidays. Southerners ate more greens, fruits and vegetables, but their only seasoning was oil and they rarely ate cheese or meat. Even on holidays, they drank wine mixed with water (*vinello*).[48]

Twenty-five years later governmental investigators found sweeping changes in the diet of southern peasants. Wheat bread increasingly replaced other grains. Peasants more often kept a pig, and they used its meat to season pasta dishes weekly rather than twice a year. From the Molise, a member of the local elite complained about inflated food prices as "the wives of the Americans arrive at the marketplace and buy up all the fresh fish newly arrived from Temoli, regardless of price."[49]

The decision to send men abroad to earn wages and to have them send remittances or return with their savings to Italy appears even more rational when we consider the costs of transplantation abroad. At least in the Americas, male sojourners could not easily support a transplanted family on their own earnings. In New York, where the typical Italian man earned $250–$350 a year in the early twentieth century, Robert Chapin estimated that a family of four to six required about $800 a year to live adequately.[50] In Buenos Aires, the discrepancy between an unskilled laborer's earnings and estimated costs of family living was equally large.[51] Settlement abroad became financially feasible only when a man could find year-round or better-paid work, when a family could count on additional sources of cash income or when it could produce its own food.

Women and children had to become wage-earners for most families to survive the move to the Americas. According to Samuel Baily, 38 percent of married Italian women in selected districts in Buenos Aires in 1895 worked for wages outside the home, while 60 to 80 percent of unmarried women did so. In New York, ten years later, about 7 percent of married women worked outside the home, and almost half of unmarried women did so. Women in Buenos Aires may have been more willing to leave home to work because they found employment in small-scale shops owned by fellow Italians, or because more were from Italy's north. Southern Italian women in New York, by contrast, had to move well beyond family circles to work for wages in garment factories owned by Jewish, German, or American employers.[52]

In New York, however, married women found industrial work to do at home. As homeworkers, they sewed trousers, cracked nuts and made artificial flowers, effectively combining wage earning with domestic chores.[53] Only a few New York census takers counted homeworkers as wage earners, but those who did found rates of wage earning among married and unmarried Italian women comparable to, or surpassing, those of Buenos Aires.[54] Although less well-studied, Italian families in France also seemed to expect some form of wage earning from married women and children alike.[55]

In Buenos Aires and in New York, immigrant women transformed domestic work into cash by taking into their homes sojourning men separated from their families. Family-based boarding was a new social relationship, and a source of income without precedent, in Italy. (This explains the use of the term "bordante" for the men who became boarders—a term used throughout the Italian diaspora.) About a third of New York's Italian wives kept boarders at any one time; in Buenos Aires, the percentage was even higher, over 40 per-cent. Boarders included relatives as well as friends and neighbors who paid small fees in exchange for meals, a bed and clean laundry. Boarders' contributions to family incomes were relatively small—scarcely a third of female wages earned outside the home—but (like home industrial work) they allowed many married women to continue working within the family circle and to fulfill domestic obligations too.[56]

Even with women and children working, and with boarders making their contribu-tions, families of unskilled workers in New York and Buenos Aires struggled to pay high housing, food and clothing costs. In New York, in 1909, Robert Chapin estimated that three-quarters of Italian immigrant families in the city earned less than the $800 needed for a family of four to six to live securely. He reported Italians spending a fifth of their income on rent, almost half on food, and 12 percent on clothing. Yet, surprisingly, 58 percent of the Italian families he surveyed also reported a budgetary surplus and some savings.[57] In Buenos Aires, where information about family budgets is scantier, Italian incomes were also well below those reformers found necessary to maintain minimum standards, yet over half of all working-class families there too reported some savings.[58] Many immigrant families obviously began saving at relatively low incomes. They did so by forgoing some of the pleasures of consumption in the modern and industrializing cit-ies of the Americas.

In neither New York nor Buenos Aires did immigrant families stint on food. Immi-grant families in New York ate more eggs, meat, cheese and milk than returners to Italy. Many reported the satisfaction they felt in eating great quantities. "Don't you remember how our *paesani* here in America ate to their heart's delight till they were belching like pigs and how they dumped mountains of uneaten food out of the window?" one woman in New York reminisced with pleasurable exaggeration.[59] In Buenos Aires, too, where beef was an important product of the nearby pampas, immigrants remembered eating well.[60] More than any other consumer choice, plentiful food and drink symbolized well-being for transplanted Italians in both North and South America.

Evidence from New York suggests that families more often skimped on clothing, housing, recreation and entertainment. Married women (and their youngest children) sometimes still went barefoot, made their own clothes and remodeled cast-offs. Men claimed only very small pleasures for themselves—notably tobacco, a coffee or a beer at a nearby café. Like their children, husbands and sons turned over their paychecks to their wives and mothers, who were the budget managers in most families.[61] Adolescent children proved the least willing to forgo the pleasures of urban consumerism. Some openly resented having to turn over "every cent"; others quietly "borrowed from mother." One girl in Rhode Island reported "I'll never forget the time I got my first pay . . . I went downtown, first, and I spent a lot, more than half of my money . . . I just went hog wild." More complied and "handed our pays in." Girls desired modern clothing, urban shoes and hats. Boys wanted to enjoy sports, shows, dancehalls or other commercial entertain-ments.[62] Somewhat reluctantly, mothers in New York relinquished control over their sons' wages, but having already accepted that their daughters left the family circle to work for wages, mothers seemed less willing to allow adolescent girls control over their own wages.

In both densely settled New York and lower-density Buenos Aires, immigrant mothers ruthlessly limited the amount they spent on rent in order to facilitate saving. In New York, families moved frequently in search of the cheapest quarters. Many families also willingly lived in very close proximity, with families of five or more in two rooms. In New York's downtown Little Italy the youngest of families with one or two children doubled up and lived in one room each, or three families to a three-room apartment. They shared a kitchen, and often housed additional boarders in what census takers called "partner households."[63] Because so many Italian immigrants crowded into small, old tenement dwellings, social reformers like Robert Chapin despaired of their ever learning or accepting American housing standards.[64]

Home ownership was even more important, for migrants had left a homeland where home ownership had been relatively common, even among quite poor peasants. Returners could purchase houses with savings from a year or two of work by one successful male migrant. In the Americas, by contrast, home ownership required a long-term struggle, and one in which the wages of growing children were crucial—but disputed—elements. Few Italians in high-density New York became home owners before the 1920s; a government investigation in 1909 found home ownership rates of only 1 percent. By contrast, in Buenos Aires, with its lower-scale housing, and its higher proportions of skilled and white-collar immigrants, 16 percent of Italian families in 1904 already lived in houses they owned. Compared to returners, however, these were shabby results.[65]

Thus, it is not at all clear that transplantation of men and women together to the Americas was the best choice for family groups pursuing short-term security. The parsimony of mother budget managers, like that of the men without women, originated in part in a desire to assist family members in Italy. But it also reflected persistent feelings of insecurity about the financial future, and a desire to hold open the possibility of return to the home village. While family solidarity clearly facilitated migration, transplantation abroad also demanded changes at the center of family life. Families who relocated abroad were peasants and artisans who had only recently severed their ties to subsistence production. In doing so, they relinquished their ideal of families working together under the leadership of the husband and father in order to benefit from women's and children's cash contributions to a consumer family economy. They faced as well the growing independence of their own children as wage-earners and consumers. Faced with complex trade-offs like these, the long-term commitment of many Italians to transnationalism is easier to understand, and to see as a sensible choice, no matter what its hardships.

Conclusion

International family economies developed out of rational, shrewd choices, but we cannot easily know whether to credit that shrewdness to the men without women or the women who waited for them. Transnationalism as a way of working-class life allowed men to earn where wages were relatively high and to spend where prices were relatively low. Prices in Italy remained low, furthermore, because so many women and children continued to be enmeshed in subsistence production and remained outside the consumer marketplace. Studies of Italy's migrations often comment on the importance of foreign labor markets in driving male migration. One male emigrant summarized his feelings about work, "My job was my *via crucia,* my misery, my hatred, and yet I lived in continuous fear of losing the bloody thing. THE JOB that damnable affair, THE JOB . . . this blood-sucking thing."[66]

"THE JOB . . this blood-sucking thing" loomed large in decisions about the location of a family home base, and in women's and children's migrations, too. Only the pampas of Argentina and the plantations of Brazil and Australia offered migrants possibilities to work together as families, and to combine wage-earning and subsistence production in familiar ways. Cities offered women better wage-earning opportunities—in domestic service and in industry—but only if women worked away from their families. The lure of female jobs was strongest when women's opportunities to work in Italy were also most limited—as they were, for example, in Sicily. Families reached different conclusions when faced with such choices. Sicily had the highest rates of female migration in part because women could better contribute to family economies abroad than at home.

At the same time, maintaining a home base in Italy typically required either repeated male migrations or very long separations of fathers and sons from their families. In the north, contract laborers might go seasonally to Europe for many years. In the south, too, Emma Ciccotosto's father left her Abruzzi home twice for short sojourns in the U.S. before emigrating again to Australia in the 1920s. Only after fifteen years of circulatory migrations to two continents did he call for his wife and children to re-establish their home base in Australia. In the lives of the Ciccotosto family one senses uncertainty, false starts and mixed reactions, not only to the hardships of separation but to prospects for achieving family security in Italy, America or Australia.

Whether they reunited in Italy or abroad, Italy's men and women generally desired security for themselves as part of family groups. Most women, and migrated men, needed to work—the question was where and under what conditions. Migrants' lives responded as much to the reproduction of families in Italy as to the exigencies of wage earning abroad. Working in different locations and at quite diverse tasks, Italian men and women seemed almost to occupy different class positions within the global economy, even as their family lives intimately entwined them. Wage-earning and subsistence production proved surprisingly compatible for both Italy's supposedly more economically and culturally advanced northerners and its supposedly more "economically backward" and patriarchal southerners alike. For surprising numbers of Italian men and women, transnationalism and male emigration provided a surer foundation for family security than female emigration and family transplantation, even to the distant magnets of the economically booming United States and Argentina.

Notes

1. E. G. Ravenstein, "The Laws of Migration," *Journal of the Royal Statistical Society* 48 (1885): 167–235.

2. D. Gabaccia, "Women of the Mass Migrations: From Minority to Majority, 1820–1930," in D. Hoerder and L. P. Moch (eds.), *European Migrants: Global and Local Perspectives* (Boston: North-

eastern University Press, 1996), pp. 90–111; M. F. Houston et al., "Female Predominance of Immigration to the United States since 1930: A First Look," *International Migration Review* 28 (Winter 1984): 908–63.

3. R. F. Harney, "Men Without Women: Italian Migrants in Canada, 1885–1930," in Betty Boyd Caroli, Robert F. Harney and Lydio F. Tomasi (eds), *The Italian Immigrant Woman in North America* (Toronto: The Multicultural History Society of Ontario, 1978), pp. 79–101.

4. *Annuario statistico italiano* (Roma: Commissariato dell'Emigrazione, 1926), pp. 241–42; S. L. Baily, *Immigrants in the Lands of Promise: Italians in Buenos Aires and New York City, 1870–1914* (Ithaca, NY: Cornell University Press, 1999), Table 2.3.

5. C. B. Brettell, *The Men Who Migrate and the Women Who Wait: Population and History in a Portuguese Parish* (Princeton, NJ: Princeton University Press, 1986); L. S. Reeder, "Widows in White: Sicilian Women and Mass Migration, 1880–1930," unpublished Ph.D. diss., Rutgers University, 1995. A useful study of women who waited in Italy's north is P. Audenino, "Le custodi della montanga: donne e migrazioni stagionali in una communità alpina," in P. Corti (ed.), "Società rurale e ruoli femminili in Italia tra Ottocento e Novecento," *Annali dell'Instituto "Alcide Cervi"* 12 (1990): 265–88. See also V. Teti, "Noti sui comportamenti delle donne sole degli 'americani' durante la prima emigrazione in Calabria," *Studi emigrazione* 24 (1987): 13–46; P. Corti, "Societés sans hommes et intégrations des femmes à Pétranger; Le cas de l'Italie," *Revue européenne des migrations internationales* 9, 2 (1993): 113–28.

6. N. Glick-Schiller, L. Basch and C. Blanc-Szanton (eds), *Towards a Transnational Perspective on Migration: Race, Class, Ethnicity, and Nationalism Reconsidered* (New York: Academic Press, 1992); L. G. Basch, N. Glick-Schiller and C. Szanton Blanc, *Nations Unbound: Transnational Projects, Postcolonial Predicaments, and Deterritorialized Nation-States* (Langhorne, PA: Gordon and Breach, 1994).

7. Quoted in J. C. Moya, *Cousins and Strangers: Spanish Immigrants in Buenos Aires, 1850–1930* (Berkeley: University of California Press, 1998), p. 49. See also Walter Nugent, "Frontiers and Empires in the Late Nineteenth Century," *Western Historical Quarterly* 20 (November 1989): 393–408.

8. For worldwide migrations, see Lydia Potts, *The World Labour Market: A History of Migration* (London: Zed Books, 1990); Robin Cohen (ed.), *The Cambridge Survey of World Migration* (Cambridge: Cambridge University Press, 1995); Robin Cohen, *Global Diasporas: An Introduction* (Seattle: University of Washington Press, 1997). See also Dirk Hoerder, *Global Migrations* (Durham, NC: Duke University Press, forthcoming).

9. R. J. Vecoli, "The Italian Diaspora," in R. Cohen (ed.), *The Cambridge Survey of World Migration* (Cambridge: Cambridge University Press, 1995), p. 114; R. Foerster, *The Italian Emigration of our Times* (New York: Russell and Russell, 1968), pp. 3–4; see also Mark Wyman, *Round-Trip to America: the Immigrants Return to Europe, 1880–1930* (Ithaca, NY: Cornell University Press, 1993) and J. D. Gould, "Emigration, the Road Home: Return Migration from the U.S.A.," *Journal of European Economic History* 9 (Spring 1980): 41–112.

10. F. Ramella, *Terra e teali: sistemi di parentela e manifattura nel Biellese dell'Ottocento* (Torino: Einaudi, 1984).

11. D. Gabaccia, "In the Shadows of the Periphery: Italian Women in the Nineteenth Century," in M. J. Boxer and J. H. Quataert (eds), *Connecting Spheres: Women in the Western World, 1500 to the Present* (New York: Oxford University Press, 1987), pp. 166–75.

12. D. Gabaccia, *Italy's Many Diasporas* (London: University College of London Press, 2000), p. 78.

13. R. Del Fabbro, *Transalpini: Italienische Arbeiswanderung nach Süddeutschland im Kaiserreich 1870–1918* (Osnabrück: Universitätsverlag Rasch, 1996), p. 4.

14. G. Rosoli (ed.), *Un secolo di emigrazione italiana, 1876–1976* (Rome: Centro Studi Emigrazione, 1978), Table 5.

15. Baily, *Immigrants in the Lands of Promise,* Table 3.4.

16. B. Boyd Caroli, *Italian Repatriation from the United States, 1900–1914* (New York: Center for Migration Studies, 1973), pp. 49–50.

17. A large scholarly literature has long debated the supposed familism of Italians, but it has focused almost exclusively on the south. See, e.g., the work of Edward Banfield, *The Moral Basis of a Backward Society* (Glencoe, IL: The Free Press, 1958). His many critics included S. F. Silverman, "Agricultural Organization, Social Structure and Values in Italy: Amoral Familism Reconsidered," *American Anthropologist* 70 (1968): 1–20; W. Muraskin, "The Moral Basis of a Backward Sociologist: Edward Banfield, the Italians and the Italian-Americans," *American Journal of Sociology* 79 (1974): 1484–96. For general historical introductions to the issues of Italian family history, see P. Macry, "Rethinking a Stereotype: Territorial Differences and Family Models in the Modernization of Italy," *Journal of Modern Italian Studies 2*, 2 (1997): 188–214; D. I. Kertzer and R. P. Saller (eds), *The Family in Italy: From Antiquity to the Present* (New Haven, CT: Yale University Press, 1991).

18. There is a large, and contentious, scholarly literature on family economies. For the evolution of the argument, particularly about the relationship of patriarchy, gender and family solidarity and decision making, see L. A. Tilly and J. Scott, *Women, Work and Family* (New York: Holt, Rinehart & Winston, 1978); P. Hilden, "Family History vs. Women in History: A Critique of Tilly and Scott," *International Labor and Working Class History* 16 (Fall 1979): 1–11; L. Tilly, "After Family Strategies, What?" *Historical Methods* 20 (Summer 1987): 123–25.

19. Basch, Glick-Schiller and Szanton Blanc, *Nations Unbound*, p. 240.

20. On wages, see Foerster, *The Italian Emigration of Our Times*, pp. 143–44, 166, 200, 378–79.

21. *Atti della Giunta parlamentare per l'inchiesta agraria e sulle condizioni della classe agricola* (Rome: Forzani Tip. Del Senato, 1883–1886), vol. 12, fasc. 1, p. 486.

22. R. Harney, "Men Without Women: Italian Migrants in Canada, 1885–1930," in B. B. Caroli, R. F. Harney and L. F. Tomasi (eds), *The Italian Immigrant Woman in North America* (Toronto: Multicultural History Society of Ontario, 1978): 79–101.

23. M. Burawoy, "The Functions and Reproduction of Migrant Labor: Comparative Material from Southern Africa and the United States," *American Journal of Sociology* 81 (March 1976): 1076–87. There is a sizeable and useful scholarly literature, inspired by feminist socialist theorists, on the reproduction of labor power. See K. Young *et al.*, *Of Marriage and the Market: Women's Subordination in International Perspective* (London: CSE Books, 1981); A. Kuhn and A. Wolpe, *Feminism and Materialism: Women and Modes of Production* (London: Routledge & Kegan Paul, 1978); C. Meillassoux, *Maidens, Meal, and Money: Capitalism and the Domestic Economy* (Cambridge: Cambridge University Press, 1981). See also J. Smith, I. Wallerstein and H. Evers (eds), *Households and the World Economy* (Beverly Hills, CA: Sage Publications, 1984).

24. *Inchiesta parlamentare sulle condizioni nelle provincie meridionali e nella Sicilia* (Rome: Tip. Naz di Giovanni Bertero, 1910), vol. 2, p. 258.

25. *Atti della Giunta parlamentare per l'inchiesta agraria*, vol. 7, fasc. 2, p. 347.

26. On remittances, see *Annuario statistico italiano*, pp. 1637–45; D. Cinel, *The National Integration of Italian Return Migration, 1870–1929* (Cambridge: Cambridge University Press, 1991), pp. 141–44.

27. Besides E. Zappi, *If Eight Hours Seem Too Few: Mobilization of Women Workers in the Italian Rice Fields* (Albany: State University of New York Press, 1991), and del Fabbro, *Transalpini*, pp. 264–65; see *Atti della Giunta parlamentare per l'inchiesta agraria*, vol. 4, fasc. 1, pp. 8–17 (on the Veneto) and vol. 8, tomo 1, fasc. 2, pp. 628–32 (on various regions of Piedmont).

28. *Atti della Giunta parlamentare per l'inchiesta agraria*, vol. 8, tomo 2, fasc. 1, p. 126.

29. Ibid., vol. 4, p. 259.

30. E. Ciccotosto and M. Bosworth, *Emma: A Translated Life* (Fremantle, Australia: Fremantle Press, 1990), pp. 22–25.

31. Besides Ramella, *Terra e telai*, see L. A. Tilly, *Politics and Class in Milan, 1881–1901* (New York: Oxford University Press, 1992), pp. 71–72.

32. Gabaccia, "In the Shadows of the Periphery."

33. *Inchiesta parlamentare sulle condizioni dei contadini*, vol. 4, p. 257.

34. D. Gabaccia, *From Sicily to Elizabeth Street: Housing and Social Change Among Italian Immi-*

grants, 1880–1930 (Albany: State University of New York Press, 1984), ch. 3; see Reeder, "Widows in White."

35. See L. Reeder, "When the Men Left Sultera: Sicilian Women and Mass Migration 1880–1920," in D. Gabaccia and F. Iacovetta (eds), *Foreign, Female and Fighting Back* (Toronto: University of Toronto Press, forthcoming 2002).

36. Giuseppe Pitrè, *Proverbi siciliani* (Palermo: "Il Vespro," 1978), orig. published 1870–1913, vol. 2, p. 92.

37. *Inchiesta parlamentare sulle condizioni dei contadini,* vol. 4, "Caserta."

38. On class relations in rural Italy, see Renzo Del Carria, *Proletaria senza rivoluzione,* 4 vols. (Roma: Sanelli, 1975); F. Della Peruta, *Società e classi popolari nell'Italia dell'Ottocento* (Siracusa: Ediprent, 1985).

39. Besides Cinel, *National Integration of Italian Return Migration,* and Caroli, *Italian Repatriation from the United States,* see the work of Francesco Paolo Cerase, "Su una tipologia di emigrati ritornati: il ritorno di investimento," *Studi emigrazione* 4, 10 (1967): 327–44; "Expectations and Reality: A Case Study of Return Migration from the United States to Southern Italy," *International Migration Review* 8 (1974): 245–62; *L'emigrazione di ritorno: Innovazione o reazione? L'esperienza dell'emigrazione di ritorno dagli Stati Uniti d'America* (Rome: Instituto Gini, 1971); G. Gilkey, "The United States and Italy: Migration and Repatriation," *Journal of Developing Areas* 2 (1967): 23–35.

40. Cinel, *National Integration of Italian Return Migration,* pp. 164–68.

41. A. Papa, "Guerra e terra," *Studi storici* 10 (1969); 3–45.

42. J. Davis, *Land and Family in Pisticci,* London School of Economics Monographs on Social Anthropology, 48 (New York: Humanities Press, 1973); Gabaccia, *From Sicily to Elizabeth Street,* pp. 32–33.

43. *Inchiesta parlamentare sulle condizioni dei contadini,* vol. 5, p. 504.

44. Ibid., vol. 2, pp. 186–87.

45. *Atti della Giunta parlamentare per l'inchiesta agraria,* vol. 5, tomo 2, p. 154.

46. Ibid., vol. 1, p. 236.

47. For an overview, S. Somogyi, "L'alimentazione nell'Italia unita," in R. Romano and C. Vivanti (eds), *Storia d'Italia,* vol. 5, *I Documenti* (Torino: Giulio Einaudi, 1973), pp. 841–87.

48. *Atti della Giunta parlamentare per l'inchiesta agraria* contains detailed notes on the diet of peasants in all of Italy's regions in the 1870s and 1880s.

49. *Inchiesta parlamentare sulle condizioni dei contadini,* vol. 2, p. 159.

50. R. C. Chapin, *The Standard of Living Among Workingmen's Families in New York City* (New York: Charities Publication Committee, 1909); see also L. B. More, *Wage Earners' Budgets,* Greenwich House Series of Social Studies, 1 (New York: Henry Holt, 1907).

51. Baily, *Immigrants in the Lands of Promise,* pp. 108–13.

52. Baily, *Immigrants in the Lands of Promise,* Table 7.7; M. Cohen, *Workshop to Office: Two Generations of Italian Women in New York City, 1900–1950* (Ithaca, NY: Cornell University Press, 1993); E. Ewen, *Immigrant Women in the Land of Dollars: Life and Culture on the Lower East Side, 1890–1925* (New York: Monthly Review Press, 1985), ch. 6; N. L. Green, *Ready-to-Wear; Ready-to-Work: A Century of Industry and Immigrants in Paris and New York* (Durham, NC: Duke University Press, 1997), ch. 6.

53. For a contemporary's report, see M. H. Willett, *The Employment of Women in the Clothing Trade,* Columbia University Studies in History, Economics and Public Law, 16 (New York: Columbia University Press, 1902); for a recent assessment, C. R. Daniels, "Between Home and Factory: Homeworkers and the State," in E. Boris and C. R. Daniels (eds), *Homework: Historical and Contemporary Perspectives on Paid Labor at Home* (Urbana: University of Illinois Press, 1989).

54. L. Betts, "Italian Peasants in a New Law Tenement," *Harper's Bazaar* 38 (1904): 804; Gabaccia, *From Sicily to Elizabeth Street,* p. 64; see also T. Kessner and B. B. Caroli, "New Immigrant Women at Work: Italians and Jews in New York City, 1880–1905," *Journal of Ethnic Studies* 5 (1978): 19–32. Louise C. Odencrantz, *Italian Women in Industry: a Study of Conditions in New York City* (New York: Russell Sage Foundation, 1919), pp. 16, 21, also found 24 percent of married Italian women working outside the home.

55. Foerster, *Italian Emigration of Our Times,* pp. 144–147.

56. Baily, *Immigrants in the Lands of Promise,* Tables 7.5, 7.6. See also R. F. Harney, "Boarding and Belonging: Thoughts on Sojourner Institutions," *Urban History Review* 2 (1978): 8–37. For general patterns in the U.S., see J. Modell and T. K. Hareven, "Urbanization and the Malleable Household: An Examination of Boarding and Lodging in American Families," *Journal of Marriage and the Family* 35 (1973): 467–79.

57. Chapin, *The Standard of Living Among Workingmen's Families,* pp. 245–50. See also State of New York, *Factory Commission Report* (1915), vol. 4, pp. 1608–1609, 1619–1620, 1668.

58. Baily, *Immigrants in the Lands of Promise,* Tables 5.5, 5.6.

59. Gabaccia, *From Sicily to Elizabeth Street,* p. 92.

60. On Argentina, see P. Corti, "Circuiti migratori e consuetudini alimentari nella rappresentazione autobiogafica degli emigranti piemontesi," in A. Capatti, A. De Bernardi, and A. Varni (eds), *L'alimentazione nella storia dell'Italia contemporanea, Storia d'Italia, Annali* (Torino: Einaudi, 1997); P. Ortoleva, "La tradizione e l'abbondanza; Riflessioni sulla cucina degli italiani d'America," *Altreitalie* 7 (1992): 31–52; A. Schneider, 'L'etnicità, il cambiamento dei paradigmi e le variazioni nel consumo di cibi tra gli italiani a Buenos Aires', *Altreitalie* 7 (January–June 1992): 71–83. On the U.S., more generally, D. Gabaccia, *We Are What We Eat: Ethnic Food and the Making of Americans* (Cambridge, MA: Harvard University Press, 1998), pp. 51–55; D. Gabaccia, "Italian-American Cookbooks: From Oral to Print Culture," *Italian Americana* 16, 1 (1998): 15–23, and C. Helstosky, "The Tradition of Invention: Reading History through 'La Cucina Casareccia Napoletana,'" in *Italian Americana* 16, 1 (1998): 7–23.

61. Gabaccia, *From Sicily to Elizabeth Street,* pp. 101–2.

62. Direct quotes are from J. E. Smith, *Family Connections: a History of Italian and Jewish Immigrant Lives in Providence, Rhode Island, 1900–1940* (Albany: State University of New York Press, 1985), p. 75.

63. Gabaccia, *From Sicily to Elizabeth Street,* pp. 75–77.

64. Baily, *Immigrants in the Lands of Promise,* ch. 6.

65. Baily, *Immigrants in the Lands of Promise,* Table 5.7; see also S. L. Baily, "Patrones de residencia de los italianos en Buenos Aires y Nueva York: 1880–1914," *Estudios Migratorios Latinoamericanos* 1 (1985): 8–47.

66. M. LaSorte, *La Merica: Images of Italian Greenhorn Experience* (Philadelphia, PA: Temple University Press, 1985), p. 61.

8

Boomers, Sooners, and Settlers

Americans in Mexico

JOHN MASON HART

We've come to work, we mean to stay.
We'll raise thy standard, win the day.

—From the official song and yell of the Juárez Academy, Chihuahua

During the late nineteenth century and the first decade of the twentieth century American immigrants entered Mexico as colonists and settlers in increasing numbers. Many of those who chose to live in the northern part of the nation believed that those provinces would soon become a part of the United States despite the fact that their economic and political leaders no longer regarded the acquisition of Mexican territory as a desirable undertaking. American financial elites, facing the demographic strength and the growing resistance of what they regarded as an inferior people, saw commercial empire as not only more desirable than the incorporation of territory, but inevitable.

As the American leadership turned toward economic control of Mexico rather than annexation, an initial wave of Americans numbering in the thousands was settling in the sparsely populated but fertile valleys of Sonora, Chihuahua, and Tamaulipas. In contrast to the politicians and financiers, many of them viewed the thin Mexican population of the far north as too weak to maintain control. They went to Mexico to fulfill personal ambitions and dreams, but they were mindful of creating an American way of life. Calling themselves "boomers," they expected the U.S. government to protect them, and they awaited the acquisition of these territories for an enlarged American union. They would be sorely disappointed.

An Influx of Immigrants

American immigrants, beckoned by economic opportunity, followed the railroads that had opened the way into Mexico, repeating the pattern of exploration, investment, and migration that had typified development on the American frontier. Just as the railroads and the telegraph and highly profitable extractive industries provided opportunity for the richest Americans, cheap land and higher-status jobs provided opportunity for those who were less affluent. The railroads brought virtually every desirable region of the north within fifty miles of modern communications and transportation, while land development companies, many of them owned by the directors of the railroads, bought large tracts for timber, mineral, agricultural, and real estate development. Other entrepreneurs and the settlers' own leadership established colonization companies. Between 1900 and 1910 about 3,000 American immigrants entered Mexico each year, swelling their numbers to almost 40,000.

The increasing number of immigrants encouraged American businessmen to offer their services. By 1902 they had opened 1,112 companies and small businesses in Mexico, apart from mines, farms, and ranches, and had invested $511,465,166. By 1910 the numbers were considerably larger. A small group of about 160 American individuals or companies held over 90,000,000 acres, or 18 percent of Mexico's area, and some 20,000 smaller farmers held tracts making up another 40,000,000 acres. They capitalized agriculture and ranching, expanded the economy, and offered employment to Mexican workers.

The Americans also stepped into the middle of the deepening dispute over the ownership of land, frequently employing Mexicans to work on land that the local folk regarded as their own. Growing portions of the Mexican rural working and middle classes, which constituted almost 80 percent of the population, and a significant number of the elite provincial landowners were positioning themselves against a majority of the large landholders, government officials, and their ever less enthusiastic allies in the middle and working classes. The Americans became engaged in the controversy by purchasing former pueblo lands that had been denounced and outbidding Mexican private interests for desirable assets, including land, mines, and other businesses. This process had provoked deep stress in much of the nation between 1856 and the early 1880s and had led to economic polarization, disenfranchisement, geographic disloca- tion, and violence. It had not led to the creation of the larger, more stable middle class that the Liberals had envisioned.

In the United States land promoters announced their offerings in newspaper and magazine advertisements and in mass mailings. Many of the ads carried wild exaggera- tions as to the quality of the soil, the nature of the crops produced, and the climate. Slick salesmen, or "sharpers," on the border near Mercedes, Texas, made their pitch to prospective buyers in the spring and fall to avoid showing them land that was dry all summer, when the region suffered from oppressive heat. Their employers, including state judge Victor L. Brooks, Houston mayor Richard Brooks, and other Texas Com- pany officers, also offered millions of acres for sale on the Mexican side of the river. The literature that attracted their clients referred to "giant ebony trees" in an area of Tamaulipas that was actually covered with mesquite and sagebrush. The land on the Mexican side, however, was cheaper than that in the United States, and it attracted Americans interested in small farms and the development of rural communities. In cities such as Colorado Springs salesmen sold land, sight unseen, in Sonora and Chi- huahua.[1]

Kent E. Peery, president of the Williams Real Estate Investment Company of Ponca City, Oklahoma, described the situation in positive terms to Díaz.

> If we could locate a desirable body of agricultural land, preferably in the central or northern part of Mexico, and get the proposition financed by Mexican or United States capital, we are in a position to settle the property with energetic Americans.[2]

The American immigrants were searching for independence or a better standard of living. Mexico offered them cheap land and employment opportunities in the burgeoning railroad, petroleum, and mining industries. Some settled in the cities or bought private tracts of land, but the great majority came to reside in enclaves that were designed to accommodate their insecurities regarding an alien culture, language, and rule of law. Of the more than 25,000 Americans who went to Mexico as farmers, between 9,000 and 12,000 of them joined these communities, usually sponsored by colonization and land development companies. Development companies dominated the colonization effort in Tamaulipas, San Luis Potosí, Oaxaca, and Chiapas, but American colonists also occupied properties in Baja California, Chihuahua, Coahuila, Durango, Jalisco, Sinaloa, Sonora, and Veracruz. Most of these Americans possessed limited financial resources. The promoters and the Mexican government called the settlements "colonies." The American newcomers called themselves "sooners" and "colonists" as well as "boomers." While most of those who settled in the north expected to be annexed by the United States, those who established towns in Chiapas, Oaxaca, San Luis Potosí, and Veracruz hoped that protection would be provided by "their" government.

The colony method of settlement made sense for many of the American small farmers. Surrounded by an alien language, culture, and customs, the majority of them were intent on retaining their language, values, and mores. In eastern San Luis Potosí, several hundred American colonists and a few American estate owners claimed most of the land covering three districts and inhabited by over 100,000 Mexicans of mestizo, Otomí, Nahuatl, and Huasteco descent. In Tamaulipas several American estate owners and two dozen oil companies joined between 2,000 and 3,000 American immigrants on the land. The same pattern of colonization and private ownership also took hold in northwestern Chihuahua, northeastern Sonora, Sinaloa, and the Isthmus of Tehuantepec.

In the less habitable areas, colonization played a minimal role. In Durango vast American holdings took shape in the timber zones and in the desert regions, where aridity required large properties for economic success. In Veracruz individual owners developed small but expensive coffee farms. In Coahuila the newcomers purchased large estates. The Seminole, Kickapoo, and Potawatomie colonists in Coahuila held large expanses only because Juárez had given them the land as inducement to settle the area and deter Comanche incursions. Under Díaz, these peasants of U.S. parentage suffered the same displacements as their Mexican counterparts.

The San Dieguito colony, situated just south of the Rascon hacienda in San Luis Potosí, typified the strategy of the American settlers who purchased lots in groups from the land development companies.

> Each member of the so-called colony owned in severalty the land purchased by him, the term "Colony" being merely a designation to indicate a community or settle-

ment composed entirely of citizens of the United States, engaged in farming, stock-raising, fruit-growing, gardening and other agricultural pursuits.[3]

The colony concentrated Americans in specific areas and minimized the assimilation of Mexican culture by giving the community a partially closed and culturally isolated character. The great majority, if not all, of the residents at San Dieguito raised sugarcane as their principal cash crop, processed it at the Rascon plantation sugar mills, and transported it via the Mexican Central Railroad. They supplemented that crop with products from vegetable gardens and citrus orchards, which also provided food for the colonists. Almost all of the colonists employed local Mexicans and used sharecropper contracts in lieu of cash. It is not clear if the small-scale American ranchers and farmers in this area used debt peonage as a labor strategy, but the practice was so pervasive that it could have existed.[4]

Mormon Colonies

Given the importance of religion and idealism to Americans at the time, it is not surprising that various sects either established or attempted to undertake the development of colonies. Members of the Church of Jesus Christ of Latter-Day Saints began their effort to establish communities in Mexico in 1885. By 1910 they had developed nine prosperous settlements. Seven were in northwestern Chihuahua. Díaz and Dublan were located on the rich lands along the Casas Grandes River, and the three mountain colonies of García, Juárez, and Pacheco were situated on the equally rich lands along the Piedras Verdes River. Cave Valley and Chuichupa enjoyed the benefits of running water from streams. The two other settlements, Morelos and Oaxaca, were in northeastern Sonora on the Río Bavispe. The Mormon colonists came from all over the western United States, but principally from Utah, Idaho, and Colorado. Over four thousand farmers inhabited their settlements. Devoutness, a sense of mission, and American patriotism led nearly all of the Mormon immigrants to cluster together.

The Mormons entered Mexico for reasons related to, and yet distinct from, those of the secular colonists. Although like other immigrants they sought a better life, they left the United States in the midst of controversy. In the aftermath of the Civil War, the American government had established its authority and rule of law in the areas occupied by the Mormons, and during the 1880s the Church of Latter-Day Saints began to send its members to Mexico to escape prosecution for polygamy. Another, almost equally compelling, reason motivated Mormon emigration. They were impressed with the achievements of the pre-Columbian Mayan and Aztec civilizations. The indigenous peoples of North America, in the Mormons' view, were descendants of the Lamanites, a tribe of Hebrews who had migrated to America in about 600 B.C. and abandoned their beliefs. The Latter-Day Saints combined their search for refuge with a deep belief in a missionary obligation to convert the Native Americans. They believed that all of "Israel's descendants" would need to be "gathered"—converted and baptized—"before Christ's second coming." Mexico's indigenous population had attracted Mormon missionary efforts for several decades before they established colonies.[5]

From the outset the Latter-Day Saints met with a mixed reception from their Mexican hosts. In 1884 the church leaders sent a delegation to Sonora to investigate resettlement outside the reach of the U.S. government. Benjamin Francis Johnston, a member of the group and later a sugar magnate in Sinaloa, reported that the "normally suspicious and resistant Yaqui received them with open arms." Some citizenry and local officials in northern Chihuahua and Sonora expressed open hostility. Yet they were well received by the governors, the president, and members of his cabinet, who were anxious to attract "hard working" American immigrants. They could see the efficacious effect of European immigration on the society and economy of the United States. The Mormons were also pleased to find their beliefs attractive to some Tarahumara "Lamanites" and mestizos in western Chihuahua.[6]

In 1885 the initial group of Mormon settlers purchased a tract of land just west of Casas Grandes, Chihuahua. Several years earlier they had been warned by Governor Antonio Ochoa of Chihuahua "to beware of fraudulent land titles and worthless land." A title dispute soon forced them to give up their new property. After living in tents and shacks and enduring the hardships of hard freezes, insufficient clothing, food shortages, smallpox, and diphtheria, the Mormon settlers established a series of colonies. The immigrants were successful in this endeavor because, like their entrepreneurial counterparts, they turned the matter over to specialists. They spurned opportunities to buy three large tracts of land in northwestern Chihuahua that included the vast Corralitos hacienda for an asking price of $800,000 because they knew the neighboring villages of Janos and Casas Grandes had challenged the titles. The Latter-Day Saints thus avoided contributing to the antagonism that was growing prevalent among the local officials and Mexican population.[7]

The Mormons made their capital at Colonia Juárez, located in the hills a few miles west of Casas Grandes. They adopted an introverted lifestyle, keeping to themselves "culturally and politically" despite trading with the Mexicans and proselytizing them. They wanted to maintain their "American" way of life, and they paid homage to the flag on Independence Day. The Mexican elites, led by Díaz and General Carlos Pacheco, openly supported them, arranging land concessions and tax exemptions. Pacheco approved several land grants on the Americans' behalf. At the same time the distrust of local Mexican authorities began to percolate upward toward the level of statewide authority. Border guards detained wagon trains and marshals refused to carry out their law enforcement duties in support of the colonists. The governor of Chihuahua unsuccessfully ordered their deportation, and a standoff between national and state officials resulted. Pacheco intervened against the expulsion order, enabling the Mormons to remain. President Díaz apologized for the governor and urged them "to stay and help develop the resources of the country."[8]

In 1887 the Mormons established the Mexican Colonization and Agricultural Company as a Mexican company in order to purchase land from private Mexican sellers and the government with less difficulty. They planned to subdivide it and sell the tracts to individual Mormon buyers. Among their many acquisitions were 50,000 acres at Piedras Verdes, Chihuahua, 60,000 acres at Colonia Díaz, north of the Corralitos hacienda, and 60,000 acres at nearby Corrales. During the remainder of the nineteenth century the Mormons gradually improved their material conditions and increased their numbers. When the church gave up polygamy in 1893, the influx of settlers slowed, but the majority of those already in Mexico chose to stay, some because they refused to accept monogamy. Their numbers increased thereafter largely as a result of large families and material prosperity.

At Colonia Dublan, which was adjacent to Nuevo Casas Grandes, the Mormons developed a civic center that included a school and an iron foundry, while farther west at Colonia Juárez they constructed a furniture factory, a gristmill, a school, a cannery for their orchard and vegetable harvests, and other factories. The colonists achieved a high degree of self-sufficiency. By the end of the century, they were showing their agricultural and industrial products at trade fairs in Mexico City. Despite the growing size and prosperity of Colonia Dublan, they retained Colonia Juárez as their capital, perhaps because of its position in the hills to the west, which reinforced the settlement's autonomy.[9] Charles W. Kindrich, a State Department official, described Colonia Juárez in 1899. To reach the settlement one had to

> cross the foothills of the Sierra Madre Mountains. The road winds through passes and defiles until the colony, nestling like a green garden in the wilderness, comes suddenly into view. . . . The gardens are fragrant with flowers, and the blossoms of the peach, apricot, and plum trees glow in the pure air. Clear water from the *acequia* along the hillside flows down the gutter of each cross street. Neat brick residences are nestled amid grapevines and pear trees. . . . The capital colony is a beautiful village comparable to any in New England.[10]

The spacious, open front yards guarded by white picket fences and the two-story wooden structures with brick chimneys stood in stark contrast to the neighboring Mexican town of adobe houses, which presented only their adobe walls to the street, hiding the patios within.

The Mormon colonies flourished. Even the smaller settlements of Morelos and Oaxaca did well. By 1910, when the revolution began, the Mormon colonies were more prosperous than ever. Five hundred Americans lived at Colonia Díaz. The communities donated clothing, household furniture, kitchen utensils, livestock, and "sometimes even land on which to build a first home" to newlyweds, enabling them to begin their life in Mexico with some financial security. As Thomas Cottam Romney put it, "We had about all we could wish for." Eliza Tracy Allred reported, "For the first time in my married life we had on hand our year's supply of bread and fruit."

The Mormon settlers achieved a complex coexistence with their Mexican neighbors. The Americans were good customers, reliable, and relatively rich—perhaps too rich. They had earned the respect of some Mexicans, including Felipe Chávez, the highest ranking government official at Colonia Juárez. Local Mexicans held mixed opinions. Some thought the Americans were arrogant. Many believed the Mormons lived on usurped land and prospered by exploiting them.[11]

Ernest V. Romney arrived in Colonia Díaz in 1890, and for the next two decades he worked hard and became prosperous. His neighbors Milton Lowry Gruwell and Peter K. Lemmon Jr. also did well. By 1910 Lemmon held a large interest in the mercantile store and served as one of its managers. He owned a two-story, eleven-room brick house with three porches, a bathroom, and lightning rods. It was "well finished throughout" and had a value of $5,000. His barn measured 60 by 120 feet and sported a corrugated iron roof. He also had a one-buggy garage, a granary, a chicken coop, a hog pen, and a six-foot-high corral that measured 100 by 150 feet. The Lemmons employed Mexicans, but they expected the workers to leave at the end of each day. Romney, Gruwell, and Lemmon regularly paid their taxes to the authorities. They had befriended some of the officials, but others remained reserved and a few were confrontational.

In 1890, at the age of thirty, J. W. Palmer left Provo, Utah, and settled at Colonia Pacheco. Palmer established a farm, ranch, orchard, and store. He fenced the properties and raised wheat, horses, cattle, and hogs. By 1910 he owned two houses of five rooms each, one made of adobe and the other of logs. His residences, occupied by his many wives and children, were completely furnished and complemented by outhouses. Palmer built a barn and a silo and a garage for his carriage. His farming assets included poultry, several carts, and blacksmith and carpenter tools. His crops grew on 129 acres of land. The orchard had 170 fruit trees, of which all but 20 were mature and bearing. His assets totaled more than $15,000. His marital practices compounded the grievances of the neighboring Mexicans, who were Catholic.

Palmer and Romney were more prosperous than most of the Mormon colonists. The two men lived in the head settlement and exercised community leadership. Lemmon typified the Mormon middle class. The living comforts of his families did not trail those of Palmer and Romney by much, but he lacked the financial capacity for luxuries and travel.

In 1876, the year Díaz became president, Hyrum Turley was born in Beaver, Utah. As a young man he helped establish the Colonia Chuichupa, which was located in a valley in western Chihuahua thirty-five miles south of the other Mormon colonies. The settlement enjoyed access to the headwaters of the Río Bavispe, which flowed into Sonora. Like many of his compatriots, Turley had only one spouse living with him in the colony. They constructed a modest house made of dried adobe bricks. The house was valued at only $200, but Turley owned a sizeable plot of land on which he farmed and raised livestock. He dedicated some forty-four acres to farming and a larger plot to the support of his cattle. He "completely furnished" the house and built a "lumber barn, granary, and other outbuildings." He stocked the establishment with the "necessary farming equipment, wagons, harness, livestock, and poultry." His most valuable assets were his crops and his cattle. Turley and his family lived a hard but rewarding frontier life. By 1910 their belongings had an assessed value of $3,537.50. They had no excess cash, but they could satisfy their basic needs. Most of the people in Chuichupa were in a comparable economic condition—they were poor but respectable.[12]

The American religious settlers were good trading partners for the Mexicans, prompt redeemers of debt, and steady taxpayers. Despite these attributes, their closed cultural attitudes and sinful practices, including polygamy, alienated many of their Mexican neighbors. By 1910 their Mexican friends were warning them of that resentment and telling them that there was a plan afoot to seize their properties and evict them from the country.[13]

In addition to the Latter-Day Saints, the Knights of Columbus prospered in Mexico. The organization was created in New Haven in 1882 by Father Michael McGivney as a mutual aid society for Catholic men. In 1905 John Frisbie Jr., the son of Díaz's noted railroad adviser, founded the first chapter in Mexico City. The more important early meetings were attended by the national leaders of the American organization. Edward Hearn, the supreme knight, appeared at the inaugural gathering and Patrick McGivney, the chaplain, followed up, conferring rank on the leaders of the chapter. The American chapter of the Knights of Columbus in Mexico City claimed thirty-five "saxon catholics" and seven affluent Mexicans who spoke English. The leaders identified their membership by ethnicity and degree of Americanization. "Their only concession to local custom came when they called it the 'Guadalupe' chapter."[14] By 1911 the Mexican membership had grown and outnumbered the "anglo saxons," but Mexican critics complained vaguely that the "Caballeros" continued to operate under statutes "adapted to the nature and needs of American Catholics."[15]

Colonies in Urban Settings

The most affluent Americans in the cities joined their less wealthy brethren of the countryside in attempting the colony method of settlement. The presence of English-speaking neighbors reassured them, and their numbers provided the basis for an active social life. The largest settlement developed in Mexico City. Smaller ones developed in Guadalajara, Monterrey, Tampico, and Chihuahua.

American venture capitalists and land developers were also interested in urban colonies. They focused on Mexico City, developing the Paseo de la Reforma, Colonia Roma, the Calzada de Chapultepec, and Chapultepec Heights. In 1883 a consortium of New York businessmen headed by architect Stephen D. Hatch, financier Andrew Mills, civil engineer Samuel Keefer, attorney William Henry Butterworth, securities and real estate broker Thomas B. Lewis, and, probably, George Baker, chairman of the First National Bank, organized the Mexico Land and Building Company. The company acquired, surveyed, and prepared lots for construction along the Paseo de la Reforma, including a luxury hotel.

The directors maintained their headquarters on the fifth floor of number 2, Wall Street, a New York City building that housed both the First National Bank and the Bank of the Republic. The directors of the Mexico Land and Building Company provided an integrated leadership that was as sophisticated in terms of the interplay of functions as the leadership of the railroads. All of the principals were connected with members of the New York banking elite, including Stillman and Morgan. From the 1880s until 1935, when the Mexican government completed the buyout of the Americans' remaining 50 percent interest in the nation's railways, the directors of First National took a leading role in the management of Mexican transportation and communications.

Hatch was an investment banker and one of the world's leading architects. He had designed the Corning, Norwell, and Roosevelt buildings and the Murray Hill Hotel in Manhattan. He took over the task of designing buildings for the Paseo de la Reforma, including an elite hotel with an estimated construction cost of 500,000 pesos. Mills came from a New York banking and railroading family that represented "old money." He served as a director of the Manhattan Life Insurance Company, the Broadway Bank, and the Stuyvesant Insurance Company and as president of the Dry Dock Savings Bank, and he mixed socially as a member of the Union League Club.[16]

Keefer, the owner of the Keefer Hotel in Manhattan, was a high-ranking civil engineer with the Morgan-backed Northern Pacific Railroad when he joined Mexican Land and Building. He had supervised the construction of the suspension bridge over Niagara Falls in 1869 and, later, the site of the Sault Sainte Marie Canals. The combined talents of Hatch and Keefer gave the firm leadership experience in architecture, engineering, finance, and management. Butterworth, a New York attorney, lent expertise in securities and international law. He served as a trustee as well as an incorporator of the firm. Lewis served as a securities broker and as the general manager of operations in Mexico City, where he took up residence. The combined talents of the firm helped make the extension of the Paseo de la Reforma and the residential zone west of Mexico City one of the most desirable areas in the capital region.[17]

In 1903 the Compañía de Terrenos de la Calzada de Chapultepec of Lewis Lamm, E. W. Orrin, and E. N. Brown undertook the development of properties west of the historic Chapultepec Castle and adjacent to the company's holdings. That year they entered into an agreement with the Díaz government to provide "paving of the streets and installing sewer systems, sidewalks, etc. in 'Colonia Roma.'" Lamm then bought haciendas in the state of Puebla, one hundred miles southeast of Mexico City, and developed a major oil field there. His Chapultepec Land Company, an American firm that controlled Compañía de Terrenos, carried out urban modernization projects for the Mexican government. Nelson Rhoades of Cleveland served as manager of operations in Mexico and as general manager of its subsidiary, the Chapultepec Heights Development Company. In that capacity he oversaw the construction of the most distinguished housing subdivision in the nation.[18]

Rhoades served as a member of one of the most prestigious law firms in the United States, James R. Garfield and Nelson Rhoades of Cleveland. The firm enjoyed close ties with members of the government in Washington, D.C., the Standard Oil Company, and the New York financial establishment. That background placed him in a strong position with Díaz, who awarded him survey contracts accessing valuable tracts of property across Mexico. He used those arrangements to become president of the Oso and Navito Sugar Companies while still managing urban development projects. By 1913 the government owed the Compañía de Terrenos 917,994 pesos in unpaid bills.

The success of the company's urban development efforts in the capital brought ever more Americans to the scene. By 1910 some 12,000 Americans had registered as residents of Mexico City, but only the richest among them could afford Chapultepec Heights, later known as the Lomas de Chapultepec. John B. MacManus figured prominently in the Chapultepec social scene. He was a member of the steel manufacturing family of Camden and Philadelphia that had been associated with Rosecrans and Scott in the ill-fated Texas and Pacific and Tuxpan railroad projects.[19]

Guadalajara, the nation's second largest city, attracted Americans because of its relatively cheap real estate and pleasant Mediterranean climate. They congregated in "Colonia Seattle," the counterpart of Chapultepec Heights. Some of the residents were Mexican, as were some residents of Chapultepec Heights. The number of Americans in the Seattle Colony is unknown. Most were financially well-off, some even powerful. For example, Charles and Adelaide Dolley lived there until revolutionary conditions forced them out in 1914. Using Guadalajara as their headquarters, the Dolleys operated a network of Mexican enterprises that included a mine in Sinaloa and plantations in Guerrero and Chiapas. Many Americans concentrated in Monterrey, where George Brackenridge held real estate interests. Brackenridge lost interest in those ventures in light of his considerable successes in San Antonio, and he sold his holdings to American, British, and Mexican investors. Tampico Alto, on the high ground above colonial Tampico, attracted a wide assortment of American oilmen and suppliers.

Promoting the Land for Colonization

Private entrepreneurs attempted to establish American settlers across the length and breadth of Mexico. George Blaylock, a real estate developer from Oklahoma and Houston, developed one of the most notable concentrations of American colonists. In 1903 he was the probable head of a consortium that bought the 174,000–acre Chamal hacienda in the southwestern corner of Tamaulipas. His position as the principal buyer is uncertain—more-powerful capitalists in New York, Chicago, and Los Angeles often emerge as the heads of such syndicates when in-depth company records become available or when a sudden death requires a full revelation of ownership of an American firm in Mexico before it can be reorganized.

The Chamal hacienda straddled the municipal districts of Antiguo Morelos and Ocampo, just west of the town of Mante (present-day Ciudad Mante). The Chamal hacienda was a rundown cattle estate with a variety of terrains: mountains, forests, chaparral, grazing lands. The Boquillas River made the low land potentially suitable for fruit orchards and farming if sufficient sums of capital could be committed to irrigation. The burgeoning port of Tampico in the new Mexican oil fields was 120 miles to the west, and its inhabitants were capable of consuming whatever produce the hacienda could provide.

By 1907 Blaylock and his associates had obtained a clear title for the land and clearance to subdivide the estate and sell it to American colonists. They developed a plat for the hacienda that divided the property into farms, ranches, orchards, and a town site. By 1910 Blaylock had sold five hundred farm, ranch, and orchard plots in 160–acre tracts to buyers in Oklahoma and Texas. The majority of the buyers came from Oklahoma, while Houston and San Antonio provided most of the others. Some of the land brought $1.00 per acre, about six times what Blaylock and his partners paid for it. Yet it was a bargain price for his buyers because comparable land in Oklahoma and Texas was selling for $1.50 an acre and more.

Many of the buyers came as families to settle and develop small farms and ranches. They bought guns and barbed wire along with their land titles. The settlers formed an association that purchased an additional 57,000 acres to augment their ranching capacity. Some of their Mexican neighbors resented them. The nearby *municipios* of Antiguo Morelos and Ocampo had been part of land disputes a mere twenty-five years earlier. Much of the violence carried out against the Americans in the area during the revolution of 1910 was committed by their former workers.

Seymour Taylor, one of the more successful settlers in the Blaylock Colony, came to make a better life for himself. He bought several of the 160–acre plots, employed a Mexican workforce, built a home, a silo, a barn, and other buildings, and fenced in his land. He planted one of his parcels with 1,500 orange trees. By 1911 that portion of his land alone grossed 18,000 pesos yearly. Taylor achieved success through wise land selection and investment. He bought land on the edge of the mountains and then diverted water from the mountains to water his crops. His orchard was the best in the colony because "the water being piped from the mountain brings his trees to bearing quicker and keeps them in better condition." His inventive strategy, however, contributed to the later demise of his estate at the hands of the revolutionaries. Mountains traditionally offered the rural populace of Mexico firewood, building materials, and water, which was divided between local estates and settlements—in this case the pueblos of La Roncha and Chamal Viejo. Taylor monopolized the water, firewood, and building materials. He either knew nothing of these arrangements or rejected them.[20]

In 1903 seventeen-year-old Flora Ellen Medlin, a native of Barton County, Missouri, came to the Blaylock Colony from Lampasas County, Texas, with her husband. Expending a considerable amount of cash for 2,000 acres of land, they built a "nice, well furnished home" of pine. They complemented the house with an American-style flower garden. Their property also included twenty-four "tenant houses." The Medlins developed a profitable combination of farming and ranching at Chamal. They owned barns, silos, and modern planting and harvesting equipment, which probably impressed the tenant farmers, who had not seen such expensive technologies applied to the land by its previous owners. Flora's husband, L. A. Medlin, performed the function of a "dealer in livestock." The couple's principal crop was corn, supplemented by sugar cane and bananas. By 1911 they had 250 acres of cultivated croplands, and they had fenced the ranch, which enabled them to raise and sell cattle and horses. To cut their labor costs, the Medlins offered some of the workers sharecropping contracts. These workers planted beans "and some other stuff as well as corn."

Americans of adequate wealth applied technologies to the land that their Mexican predecessors had not, usually because markets were too remote and the cost of transportation too high. The construction of the Mexican Central Railroad from Tampico to San Luis Potosí and the Monterrey and Gulf Railroad totally altered the profitability of such enterprises. The pattern of American success with livestock and agricultural products at the Blaylock Colony paralleled that of the mining industry. Although the successes of American farmers and ranchers were less spectacular than those of American miners, the elements of success were the same: cheap transportation to previously inaccessible markets and sufficient capitalization to provide the latest technologies.[21]

South of the Blaylock Colony other American immigrants established four settlements along the railroads that terminated at Tampico. The colonists that settled in the southwestern extreme of Tamaulipas formed the communities of Atascador and Guerrero, while their neighbors to the west in the state of San Luis Potosí established Micos and San Dieguito. The affluent colony of Altamira, largely populated by oil company employees, was located north of Tampico. There were several other American colonies in both states of comparable size and similar circumstances, but San Dieguito was exceptional because of the closeness of the settlers and their appreciation for the beauty of the place.

Early in 1903 a group of American investors bought the Hacienda de Micos, located in the heart of the Sierra Madre foothills. They divided the property, more than 50,000 acres, into tracts for farming and ranching. It was a particularly beautiful region of the Huasteca Potosína, named after the indigenous people and the state in which it was located. Technically there were separate colonies at Micos and San Dieguito—the original legal name of the latter was "Elk City, Oklahoma, Mexico Colony"—but the entire area soon came to be known affectionately as San Dieguito. A prospectus described it with reasonable accuracy as "a beautiful mixture of prairie, timber, hill, and valley." The flat valley floor comprised some 22,000 acres. One hundred and sixty Americans settled the area. They raised livestock and poultry and cultivated oranges, hay, wheat, corn, and sugar. The Río del Naranjo, filled with game fish and wildlife, bordered the San Dieguito farmlands on the northeast for twenty-five miles. The town of San Dieguito claimed at least one medical doctor.

San Dieguito lay in the heart of a prosperous zone of American enterprise. To the north, the American-owned San Luis Land and Cattle Company had constructed a sugar mill with an 800–ton daily capacity. To the west, the enormous American-owned Rascon hacienda had over 1,200 acres of sugar cane and a processing mill capable of handling 1,000 tons. Twelve miles to the southwest, alongside the Mexican Central Railroad, the American-owned Tamasopo Sugar Company plantation had "over five hundred acres of cane and one of the finest up-to-date refineries in the republic." A plethora of smaller American sugar producers, farmers, and ranchers surrounded the settlers at San Dieguito.[22]

G. E. and Augusta Fuller bought nine numbered lots totaling some 500 acres of rich, level bottomland located between the town of San Dieguito and the railroad station at Micos. They raised horses and cattle, but their primary emphasis was sugar cane. They bought carts and wagons for hauling cane, plows, machinery, and tools and erected fences, barns, and a sugar mill. The mill featured a boiler, an engine, tanks, and evaporators in an adjacent building. The industrial facilities were worth some $6,000. The Fullers built a large home, a store, and a warehouse near the railroad tracks. They soon found that the sugarcane business was more profitable than retailing and converted the store and the warehouse into sugar storage facilities for themselves and their neighbors. Three large houses, valued at $1,000, were constructed near the mill for their American employees. Nearby they constructed a dozen *chozas* for their Mexican workers. By the start of the second decade of the twentieth century, the Fullers had 170 acres of growing cane and another 80 acres ready for planting. The yearly crop brought a $9,000 net profit.[23]

Many of the San Dieguito promoters established residency there. One was O. D. Jones. He retained a mixed farming and ranching establishment with seventy-five horses.

The estate produced at least ten tons of crude sugar, known as *piloncillo,* each year. The income generated by its sales made sugar the most important crop in the region. Within a few years the settlers at San Dieguito and their neighbors were economically prosperous, and that attracted greater numbers of colonists to the scene. Jones, the president of the Tampico Real Estate Company, also held land in the American colony of Doña Cecilia, a suburb of Tampico. The realty, headed by Jones, W. A. Bowie, and Ed Williams, owned twenty-four acres, and Jones held an additional thirty acres of prime suburban land in Tampico. The three men specialized in the sale of homes that attracted American petroleum company employees.[24]

A number of individual settlers took up residence among the concentration of colonists along the border between San Luis Potosí and Tamaulipas. In 1908 Jasper Exendine, his spouse, a daughter, and two sons, all members of the Wichita Delaware Nation of Oklahoma, took up residence near Valles. They bought 2,500 acres of land known as "El Ojo de Agua" from Rinaldo del Campo, a banker and realtor in Valles, where they registered their property titles and paid property taxes. When Exendine decided to live "apart from the tribe to which he had formerly belonged," he became a citizen of the United States. The irony of becoming a citizen by leaving the United States underlines the nature of American immigration to Mexico during the Díaz regime. The newcomers came in search of opportunity, but very few gave up their U.S. citizenship. People who experienced "marginalization" in the United States became "Americans" in Mexico. The Exendines correctly regarded their citizenship as an important asset in Porfirian Mexico. They, and most of the other Americans in the eastern San Luis Potosí–Tamaulipas area, registered with the U.S. consulate at Tampico just in case they had trouble.[25]

The burgeoning oil industry and the rich potential for farming and ranching brought a larger number of American immigrants to Tamaulipas than to any other Mexican state. For the most part the immigrants came from Texas and the midwestern United States. The La Palma colony had an even larger concentration of Americans than did the colonies along the Tamaulipas–San Luis Potosí border. La Palma took root about thirty-five miles northwest of Tampico. In the first decade of the twentieth century an American development company purchased the Hacienda La Palma and "certain lands, adjacent thereto." Known to the residents of the area as the "Columbus Lands," they sold quickly because of their proximity to the port and oil refineries. American purchasers of modest means acquired lots and built homes. The La Palma settlers initially numbered about 300, but by 1913 some 600 American farmers lived there. Many of them developed truck farms to serve Tampico and the oil fields. Michael Bowes owned 40 acres, and Rueben Cox bought 20 acres. Jacob Gergen and George Graff, among the largest landholders, held 320 and 410 acres, respectively. Some of the oil company employees bought homes at La Palma for their families while they worked and lived most of the time in the oil fields.[26]

Several hundred American colonists made their way to Oaxaca and Chiapas in the far south. In Oaxaca, Frederick Stark Pearson, the magnate who owned the Mexican Northwestern Railroad in Chihuahua and various electric companies in central Mexico and South America, attempted a colonization project of his own. In 1904 Pearson and his associates bought the 58,000–acre Agua Fría tract in the jungle near the projected line of the Mexican Southern Railroad, which would run across the Isthmus of Tehuantepec from Veracruz to Salina Cruz. They had visited the site in 1903 and understood the challenge that awaited them. The tract was ideally located because crops could be exported to either coast of the United States. Pearson's group formed the Mexican Agricultural Land Company of Oklahoma and divided up the property that was adjacent to the railroad into town sites. They created a town, composed of American-style houses with streets named after heroes of the American Revolution, out of an older Mexican site named Medina. They changed its name to Loma Bonita.

Using the funds derived from land sales to colonists, they surveyed, "cleared" the jungle, and divided the property into three lots. In Lots 1 and 2 they created parcels of about 640 acres and then subdivided them. Their sales of properties from Lots 1 and 2 totaled some 18,000 acres. The purchasers included stockholders in the company, but in the great majority they were "persons of ordinary means, principally citizens of the United States, who were interested in small farms in a tropical and fertile section." Three hundred and thirty of the buyers were Americans. A few were Mexicans, who purchased 200 acres. The Mexican Agricultural Land Company kept the rest of the property for the production of tropical fruit, especially bananas, for export. In 1908 Pearson and associates sold Lot 3, consisting of 20,000 acres, to a group of farmers from Council Grove, Kansas.

Among the rush of new colonists were Henry Martin Pierce, Mary P. Pierce, and their seven children, who arrived at Loma Bonita in 1909. Pierce and his family had lived in Oklahoma. They purchased fifty-eight acres of land from the Mexican Agricultural Land Company at $10 an acre. During 1909 and 1910 the Pierces employed four or five men for six to seven months each year, clearing the place and planting banana, orange, and other fruit trees. The Pierces built a home, dug a freshwater well, and eliminated fifteen acres of underbrush. They planted a lawn in front of the house and fenced the twenty-five-acre area with barbed wire, placing the posts ten feet apart. The Pierces and their neighbors created a replica of the American dream in Oaxaca with their houses, yards, and small farms and plantations. Henry joined the American Colony and Fruit Growers' Association, which the planters had established in order to represent their interests before local, state, and federal authorities. The association also bargained with private interests over such matters as contract labor, freight rates, and shipping prices. The Americans were charmed by Oaxaca. They marveled at the colorful garb of the indigenous people, the bright flora, and the beautiful landscapes. Local male "Indians" stepped to the side, bowed, and doffed their hats to American passersby.[27]

Joanna Bogy, who settled in Durango as a colonist and established a small ranch, represents a level of wealth and educational background that stands in contrast to that of Cora Townsend, who took over the Rascon hacienda. Bogy was an intrepid woman whose story offers special insights regarding the diverse nature of the immigrant population. She is also another example of those Americans who found that they could transcend marginality by immigrating. In Mexico, Bogy was not "just a woman," she was an American woman.

Bogy gave birth to her oldest child at DeKalb, Texas, in 1887 and later moved to Sapulpa, Oklahoma, with two daughters. Her spouse had sold Sonoran real estate out of an office in Colorado Springs at the turn of the century, but his fate is unknown. In

1908 Bogy bought a 1,280–acre subdivided tract on the beautiful Santa Isabel Ranch in Durango from the American-owned Creek Durango Land Company of Oklahoma. Bogy paid $10 per acre for the land, a mixture of irrigated farmland, pasture, and high ground with timber. Her cost was at least ten times the per-acre sum expended by the operators of Creek Durango when they purchased the Santa Isabel from its Mexican owners only three years earlier. Bogy understood, however, that its beautiful locale, rich topsoil, pine timber, and running water made the purchase a bargain in comparison to prevailing land prices in the United States. Some of the property was titled to her two daughters, Annie and Lillie. Each held one 160–acre plot, probably purchased in their names by Bogy.

In February of 1909 Joanna took her daughters to Durango and established residence on the ranch. A few Americans joined her as neighboring rancho owners. Her daughter Annie was twenty-two years old, and Lillie was in her late teens. The region of Oklahoma where the Bogys had lived offered the family few opportunities for a comfortable life-style. The amount of cash that Joanna invested in the endeavor might have facilitated a small country store, at best. The family left the familiar behind when they entered Durango. The area was associated by many Texans and Oklahomans with banditry and danger, and the cultural and social expectations in rural Mexico were different from those of the midwestern United States and presented many unknown variables. Joanna was probably fulfilling plans she made with her deceased husband.

Beyond these considerations we have few facts regarding Bogy's background. She could read and write and had the know-how to negotiate with land agents, Mexican authorities, and Mexican workers. Bogy's purchase of land in her daughters' names sug-gests that she was setting an example for them as a woman who knew how to manage her affairs. She had the courage, determination, and ingenuity to leave her home, take her daughters with her, and successfully run the ranch.

Bogy's business strategy speaks for itself. In addition to buying the land, she pur-chased five mules, twenty head of cattle, and eight horses from Creek Durango. Her total investment was $15,000. The women operated the ranch as a single unit and mar-keted the corn, wheat, and cattle in the city of Durango, some forty miles distant. After establishing the rancho as a working enterprise, Bogy aggressively opposed the Mexican campesinos who, in accordance with local practice, harvested *lena,* or firewood, on her forestland. In the United States this was trespassing. In Mexico it could be a crime, but the practice was common and was provided for in written sharecropping contracts and land leases. Bogy put up fences in a vain attempt to prevent the campesinos from gath-ering the wood they depended on for heating and cooking. The conflict between Bogy and her neighbors was economic as well as cultural.

Despite their modest circumstances, the American women could afford to hire Mex-ican cowboys and farm workers by subletting plots of land to them for sharecropping. In that way they obtained inexpensive labor for the difficult farm and ranch tasks while escaping the much more expensive costs of farm machinery, which were a major obstacle to small farming in the United States. Given the Bogys' lack of capital, the enterprise they established would not have been feasible in the United States, where ranch labor was much more expensive. In Mexico not only was their operation economically rational, but it placed them above the hard work and perhaps limited independence experienced by rural middle-class women in Texas or Oklahoma in the early twentieth century. The Bogys enjoyed a lifestyle that included socializing with the elite among the farmers, ranchers, and businessmen who formed the American "colony" in Durango City.

Some of the Americans who entered Mexico at the turn of the century and established small farms and ranches were bold, as Joanna Bogy certainly was, but many Americans clustered in enclaves to protect or insulate themselves from their mysterious, "dirty," and sometimes hostile working-class neighbors. Typically, American colonists and small landholders did not understand Mexican culture, and few could speak the language. The Americans viewed the peasant's practice of gathering firewood on the estates where they worked as theft. The frequent holidays associated with Mexican Catholicism annoyed them and reinforced their stereotype of the Mexicans as "slothful and lazy." The drunken sprees of the poor frightened and repelled them.

Sometimes American "colonies" were quasi-private real estate acquisitions in which American entrepreneurs took advantage of Mexican colonization laws to obtain government support, but the "colonists" were largely Mexican sharecroppers. In 1909 John T. Cave of Alhambra and his partner R. L. Summerlin of Port Hueneme, California, purchased the 78,000–acre Hacienda del Rio in the territory of Tepic, bordering the state of Sinaloa. The site was one hundred miles south of Mazatlán by sea or rail and blessed with the waters of the Acaponeta River. The large size of the river allowed for extensive irrigation projects on the hacienda, which featured some 69,000 acres of level land on which fruit and timber grew. The river was navigable for most of the year.

Cave and Summerlin incorporated their investment as the Quimichis Colony. The advantages of incorporation included a government concession for irrigation rights and tax exemptions that were linked to the promotion of immigration and land development by foreign settlers. However, the owners did not recruit colonists like the Bogys; instead, they populated the estate with Mexican sharecroppers. The arrangement, while not fulfilling the provisions of the colonization laws, seems to have satisfied the region's federal authorities. Cash payments frequently encouraged official approval in such situations. By 1911 the sharecroppers recruited by Cave and Summerlin had successfully enlarged the cultivated area of the estate from 4,000 to 12,000 acres, which they planted in corn, beans, cotton, and tobacco. Irrigation made the cultivation of corn for the Mexican marketplace a paying proposition, since the land irrigated with water from the Acaponeta River yielded 3,600 pounds of corn per acre. The timberlands included marketable cedar and pine. By 1912, when revolutionaries invaded the estate, it was realizing healthy profits.[28]

The entrepreneurial vision of Cave and Summerlin combined with the hard work of the Mexican sharecroppers to turn a desolate land into a profitable enterprise. The notion of colonization promulgated by the Americans to gain the government concession was also the source of their undoing. The Mexican workers living in pueblos around the estate, if not those employed on it, resented the wealth and power of the Americans. In 1912 self-proclaimed "Zapatista" revolutionaries from the neighboring settlements entered the property, drove away the sharecroppers, and divided up the land for their own use.[29]

Profitable Vice and Wholesome Occupations

In contrast to the settlers who sought to develop agriculture and create colonies consistent with family life, an assortment of American businessmen chose to open bars, casinos, dance halls, and whorehouses rather than enter agricultural, industrial, or ranching endeavors. In doing so they gave the most important population centers in the border area a frivolous and even vicious stamp.

By 1901 an elite group comprising Carl Withington, Baron Long, and James Coffroth had emerged from among these Americans. Withington owned the Tivoli bar and casino, a "sporting house" in Tijuana. He paid the local authorities some $60,000 each month for "gambling rights." Known as the "Czars of the Bars," the three owned nightclubs, gambling establishments, and brothels along the border from the Pacific Ocean to Matamoros on the Gulf of Mexico. They also opened the plush Casino de la Selva in Cuernavaca, a resort and watering place for the Mexican elite some fifty miles south of Mexico City, and the swanky Foreign Club in the national capital. Withington, with Marvin Allen and Frank Beyer, also owned the notorious Tecolote Bar in Mexicali, where they paid the local authorities some $30,000 each month for operating rights.

The cost of prostitutes represented a fraction of the expenses that clubs incurred in the United States, and the promoters faced fewer restrictions for floor shows. The American bar, casino, and brothel operators in the border cities reinforced consumer preferences by dividing their prostitutes into two groups: those who entertained African Americans and Mexicans, and those who did not. The American entrepreneurs and managers in the vice clubs on the border assumed the same superior attitude toward the Mexican and American women who worked for them in the brothels as their industrial counterparts assumed toward their laborers. Their moral justifications for their undertakings, however, were quite opposite. Men such as William Dodge and John McCaughan supported Christian universities and missionary work. They equated their business enterprises with a moral mission that uplifted the Mexicans by introducing the capitalist work ethic and the virtues of individualistic Protestantism. In contrast, Withington and his cohort believed that the women they employed were degenerate. Why not, then, take advantage of what they would do regardless of circumstance?

Tijuana began to attract a cross-section of southern Californians that included Hollywood stars such as Charlie Chaplin, who frequented the track and sumptuous clubs, as well as sailors from San Diego, who patronized the less salubrious climes. Mexico's resort industry began to flourish when Rosarito Beach and the booming tropical resort of Acapulco claimed Errol Flynn, Betty Grable, Clark Gable, and Jean Paul Getty as visitors.[30]

The American organizers of sporting events such as baseball and American football openly expressed their desire to convert Mexicans from bullfighting and cockfighting to more "wholesome" American pastimes, changing their interests and behavior. Baseball and American football entered Mexico late in the nineteenth century. In 1877 American sailors disembarked at the port of Guaymas in Sonora and played a baseball game witnessed by the local citizenry. That same year the construction workers for the Mexican National Construction Company played a game at Nuevo Laredo. Presumably the American railroad workers and sailors continued to play at construction camps and port cities whenever the opportunity presented itself. Meanwhile a Mexican team at Guaymas challenged Hermosillo, and two years later a league emerged involving the townspeople of Guaymas, Hermosillo, Nogales, Cananea, and La Colorada.[31]

During the early 1880s teams made up of American railroad workers began to play in the capital, where there was already a sizeable American colony. The American editors of the *Two Republics* newspaper in Mexico City urged the residents of the colony to give their support to a league of teams made up of Mexican Central employees to ensure the successful introduction of "the American national game." The editors saw the introduction of baseball as part of their "leadership role" in bringing the Mexicans to "healthful and recreative outdoor pastimes not yet known." They believed that the wholesomeness of baseball, in contrast with the butchery of bullfights and cockfights and the gambling associated with these contests, would teach Mexicans patience, attention to detail, individual initiative, and constancy.[32]

In 1887 "large crowds"—"1,000 spectators" in one case—attended baseball games between American railroad workers in Chihuahua and Mexico City. At that point some relatively skilled Mexican players formed the "Mexico" team in Mexico City. They played two American teams and opponents from Chihuahua and El Paso in Sunday afternoon games. In 1888 the Mexican railroad workers formed their own team in emulation of the Americans. In 1889 Bernard Frisbie, another son of Díaz's American railroad adviser, captained a team of American railroad workers from Mexico City called the "Washingtons." They met another American team in a series facilitated by the secretary of the U.S. legation.

By the end of the century the sport had caught on, growing from sandlot teams to municipal leagues. In 1904 two leagues began play, one composed of amateurs, the other of semiprofessionals. In 1907 Charlie Comiskey brought his defending "World Champion" Chicago White Sox to Mexico City for a week during spring training. Ramon Corral, the vice president of Mexico, attended one of the games. A Mexican team, "El Record" of Mexico City, played the White Sox on 12 March and lost 12 to 2 because of poor fielding. The revolution of 1910 subsumed sports reporting for a full decade, but the games continued.

American football was not far behind. In 1895 George Hill from Austin, Texas, an investor in Mexican railroads and land, organized a tour by two college teams. The varsity football teams from the Universities of Texas and Missouri barnstormed the country, playing three games at Mexico City, Guadalajara, and Monterrey. Missouri won the first two encounters, and the third, played while the players suffered from "hangovers," was a scoreless tie. Small but enthusiastic crowds viewed the games.[33]

Other American sportsmen joined those associated with baseball, seeking to become part of Mexican culture. In 1894 Robert C. Pate, a Saint Louis horseman, built a racetrack at Indianilla, outside Mexico City. He introduced pari-mutuel betting and arranged for seventy-five horses, largely from Texas and Kentucky, to race against twenty-five Mexican steeds. The races, held in the fall, lasted two months, and opening day drew 4,000 patrons, including notable contingents of Americans and Englishmen. The metropolitan elite identified with the sport and its rituals. Horseracing prospered and in 1910 the Jockey Club, created by the Mexico City elite, opened its elegant Hipodromo. In 1883 Howard Conkling, a grandson of a former U.S. minister to Mexico and a relative of Edgar Conkling, made a well-publicized climb up Popocatepetl, the volcano that dominates the Mexico City landscape to the southeast. Americans took part in the introduction of boxing, bicycle riding, and even a yacht race at Veracruz. In 1891 a group led by Edward C. Butler of New York created the Lakeside Sailing Club in Mexico City. They staged regattas on Lakes Xochimilco and Chalco. In 1894 Butler became the first secretary of the U.S. legation.[34]

American intellectuals, artists, and political dissidents found Mexican culture to be an irresistibly romantic brew. They were attracted to the endless vistas of mountains and the clear air, the grand Arab-Spanish cupolas and patios, the distinctly indigenous element of the populace, the idealism expressed in art and song, and the direct contact with the past. At first they came to Mexico by the hundreds to study, photograph, draw and write, marry, live, and die. Later they came by the thousands. With them a new and richer cultural relationship came into being.

Notes

1. For examples of the land promotions, see "An Open Letter to American Farmers and other discriminating Land Buyers." Mexico American Land Co., Kansas City, n.d., bundle 40, box 14, document 734, Colección Porfirio Díaz, Universidad Iberoamericano, Mexico City (hereafter cited as CPD). Also the Rio Grande Land and Irrigation Company Papers, Shary Collection, Rio Grande Valley Historical Collection, University of Texas Pan-American, Edinburg, Texas. The Sonoran land promotions in Colorado Springs are found in Annie Stevens, Lillie Mitchell et al., agency 2132, Records of the Special Claims Commission (hereafter cited as SCC), records group 76, Washington National Records Center, College Port, Maryland (hereafter cited as WNRC) and Hart Collection, Houston (hereafter cited as HC).

2. Kent Peery, Ponca City, to Díaz, Mexico City, bundle 32, box 6, 1907, CPD.

3. Frederick Nuffer (San Dieguito Colony), agency 141, docket 14, entry 189, SCC, records group 76, WNRC.

4. Ibid.

5. F. LaMond Tullis, *Mormons in Mexico: The Dynamics of Faith and Culture* (Ogden: Utah State University Press, 1987), 4.

6. Ibid., 53.

7. Nellie Spilsbury Hatch, *Colonia Juárez: An Intimate Account of a Mormon Village* (Salt Lake City: Deseret Book Company, 1954) 14.

8. Tullis, *Mormons in Mexico,* 57 and 60; and Hatch, *Colonia Juárez,* 7–14.

9. Hatch, *Colonia Juárez,* 57–59.

10. Ibid., 59.

11. Ibid., 92 and 94.

12. Hyrum Turley, agency 5998, entry 125, SCC, records group 76, WNRC and HC.

13. J. W. Palmer, agency 5947, entry 125, SCC; and Peter K. Lemmon Jr., agency 111; and Milton Lowry Gruwell, docket 114, American Mexican Claims Commission (hereafter cited as AMCC), records group 76, WNRC and HC.

14. Randall S. Hanson, "A Day of Ideals: Catholic Social Action in the Age of the Mexican Revolution, 1867–1929," Ph.D. diss., Indiana University, 1994, 141–47.

15. Palomar y Vizcarra to Padre David Ramirez, March 9, 1924, Palomar y Vizcarra Archive, cited in Hanson, "A Day of Ideals," 147.

16. Document 2710, 1885, CPD. For the capitalists see *Who Was Who in America* (Chicago: Marquis-Who's Who 1896–).

17. See *Who Was Who* and *New York Times* obituaries.

18. Lewis Lamm, E. N. Brown, and E. W. Orrin, agency 6021, entry 125, SCC, records group 76, WNRC and HC.

19. Lewis Lamm, E. N. Brown, and E. W. Orrin, agency 6021, entry 125; and C. and A. Dolley, agency 2175, SCC, records group 76, WNRC and HC. Also document 2710, year 1885, CPD. Also see the Rosecrans Papers and "Nelson Rhoades" in the index to the Approved Agrarian Claims, AMCC, records group 76, WNRC.

20. Claims 4, 112, 174, 176, 177, 278, and 299, box 10; claims 155, 174, 254, 255, 266, and 278, box 15; and Memoranda, claims 12, 101, 118, 120, and 121 (consolidated as one claim), AMCC, records group 76, WNRC.

21. Flora Ella Medlin, agency 5279, entry 125, SCC, records group 76, WNRC.

22. G. E. Fuller, agency 2190, entry 125, SCC, records group 76, WNRC.

23. Ibid.; and Hiram Blagg, agency 2124, SCC, records group 76, WNRC.

24. Blagg, agency 2124; and O. D. Jones, agency 6054, SCC, records group 76, WNRC.

25. Jasper Exendine, agency 677, SCC, records group 76, WNRC.

26. Michael Bowes, Mrs. R. P. Cox, Jacob Gergen, and George W. Graff, agency 6173, SCC, records group 76, WNRC. Also Department of State decimal file 312.451/37, box 3812, records group 59, National Archives and Records Administration, Washington, D.C. (hereafter cited as NARA).

27. Henry Martin Pierce, agency 111, entry 125, SCC, records group 76, WNRC. See also claims listed under agency numbers 34, 47, 76, 81, 115, 118, 135, 140, 150, 172, 1992, 2135, 4546, and 4547.

28. John T. Cave and R. L. Summerlin, agencies 53 and 53a, entry 189, SCC, records group 76, WNRC and HC.

29. Ibid.

30. Ramon Eduardo Ruiz, *On the Rim of Mexico: Encounters of the Rich and Poor* (Boulder: Westview, 1998), 45–56.

31. William H. Beezley, *Judas at the Jockey Club and Other Episodes of Porfirian Mexico* (Lincoln: University of Nebraska Press, 1987), 22.

32. Ibid., 19–20.

33. Ibid., 19–22.

34. Ibid., 26–66.

9

Back to the Mountain

Emigration, Gender, and the Middle Class in Lebanon

AKRAM FOUAD KHATER

Emigrants who returned to Lebanon came back to a place in flux. As part of a modernizing Ottoman world, Mount Lebanon was experiencing many of the same bureaucratic reforms as well as political and economic changes that were underway in the rest of the imperial territories. While the language and intent of these reforms would have struck many emigrants as familiar, it was the social changes which would have given them the most profound sense of déjà vu. In Lebanon, as in many of the surrounding lands, the "modern woman," the "middle-class family," and "scientific education" were an integral part of a modernizing project that was meant to bring the Ottoman empire, Egypt, and Iran away from Asia.[1] And, as in all these areas, discussions in Lebanon were focused on the construction of the category of "woman" as a universalizing and totalizing identity; women's roles—as mothers, wives, and managers of households—were intimately linked with a newly construed private sphere. In turn, as Kumkum Sangari and Sudesh Vaid argue for the case of South Asia, this middle-class discursive production of public and private spheres was tied, either explicitly or implicitly, to the formation of this class within wider economic and political processes.[2] In other words, the constructions of family and gender were integral to the definition of a new middle class in Lebanon, which in turn further crystallized the roles that women and men of this class were to play.

To emigrants this was a familiar scene. Newspapers in the *mahjar* (all the lands abroad where Lebanese migrated) had carried the same discussions and arguments about "modernity" and "tradition." In fact, their experiences were even more intense as they took place in countries where the invention of the "modern" had been going on for a longer time and where it had come to be more deeply integrated into the fabric of society. In the *mahjar*, emigrants had grappled with a hegemonic society that demanded that they abandon their "traditional" ways and embrace "modernity" in order to be permitted entry. Hence, and on their return to Lebanon, emigrants could not but infuse the debates, arguments, and compromises that made up their most recent social history in the *mahjar* into their villages and towns. Whether they were visiting for a spell or going back for good, they crammed their trunks with the stuff of the new hybrid culture which they struggled to make in the *mahjar*. *Franji* (Western) clothes, chiming clocks, and new foods were only a few items of the "New World" which they brought along. Quaint accents, new family "traditions," and new gender roles were additional cultural baggage. As much as these things had set them apart ethnically from the "mainstream" in New York or Buenos Aires, in Mount Lebanon they came to distinguish returned emigrants as members of a middling class.

For emigrants, then, there was some confluence—if not absolute similitude—between the "modernity" they had left in the *mahjar* and the one which was being made in Lebanon. This convergence has two ramifications for the history of Lebanon. While in other parts of the Middle East the middle classes remained a small percentage in comparison with the overwhelming peasant and laboring classes, in Lebanon returning emigrants swelled the ranks of the middle class to make it far more visible and potent in the making of a "modern" Lebanon. Moreover, while this process remained centered in the major cities of most of the region, in Lebanon emigrants brought the debates and tensions surrounding the definition and articulation of "modernity" into the hinterlands. Yet, as in the *mahjar*, emigrants were not merely idle observers and adopters of these changes. Rather, they brought their own desires and experiences to bear on the process of making the "modern" in Lebanon. In other words, not only did the experiences of Lebanese emigrants greatly amplify the intensity and reach of the debates within Lebanon about "modernity," but they also helped contour and define its constituent manners and customs. This process stands out as one of the main and lasting effects of emigration on Lebanon, and we turn to it now.

"Ambiguous Numbers"

Before embarking on an analysis of the middle-class world which returning emigrants helped to construct in Lebanon, we need to establish that enough returned to make my contentions plausible. So we ask, How many emigrants ultimately returned to the Mountain? The answer is simple: we do not know. More accurately, we do not know exactly how many Lebanese returned to the Mountain before the onset of World War I. Still, as historians are prone to do, we can estimate. Our sources vary from the anecdotal to the quasi-scientific. Writing in 1903, Ravndal, the U.S. consul general in Beirut, recounted the following conversation: "H. E. Naoum Pacha, for 10 years Governor General of Lebanon, told me once, half in jest, half in earnest, that the time seemed not far-off when the whole province would become American property and all its inhabitants American citizen[s]." Ravndal went on to affirm in his report that indeed "one find[s] American citizens of Syrian birth in villages all over the Lebanon mountains."[3] In a more specific report that he made earlier, Ravndal noted that "In one 5–year period more than 330 returned emigrants have been placed on our Register as American citizens." He added, in an irritated tone, "As an instance of the disregard of the formalities required of an American citizen [upon returning to Lebanon,] I beg to cite the case of a party that landed here during the recent cut in Atlantic transportation rates. The majority of the 75 Syrians from New York onboard were stated by passengers to possess evidence of American citizenship yet not one asked for the assistance of this consulate in landing, although two did actually come to the Consulate for the purpose of registry."[4] If for every returned emigrant who registered there were thirty-seven or thirty-eight who did not, by doing a bit of arithmetic we can estimate that in the five-year period of which he spoke over twelve thousand emigrants returned. Perilously extrapolating from these numbers, we reach a rate of return of about 45 percent.[5]

Needless to say, such estimates are hardly as straightforward as the process of division and multiplication would make them to appear. For example, it is difficult to assert a constant ratio of those who registered versus those who did not—that is, the 37:1 ratio that was used in reaching the twelve thousand figure. (Although it does seem from many consular reports that indeed only an absolute minority of returned emigrants bothered to go to the U.S. consulate in Beirut for the purpose of informing Ravndal and his colleagues of their presence in the country.) Another thorny issue has to be considered: How do we know that the rate of return was constant? Records from the Ottoman customs house in Beirut are almost nonexistent, and the maritime companies did not bother to keep regular or accurate records. Moreover, it was only toward the first decade of the twentieth century that U.S. immigration officials began to record the departure of immigrants. Pushing aside such troublesome considerations for a moment, we can mine the immigration records for another set of numbers. For the three years between 1908 and 1910, the U.S. Immigration Commission reported that 3,981 "Syrians" left the United States and went to—presumably—Mount Lebanon. Over the three years, these emigrants returned at a fairly constant rate: 1,355 in 1908, 907 in 1909, and 1,058 in 1910. In other words, if these figures are any indication, the rate of return was fairly stable, albeit smaller than that calculated from Ravndal's comments. In the estimate of the Commission, these figures represent 26 percent of the Syrians who emigrated to the United States in this time period, or—put another way—the rate of return to the Mountain from the United States was one in four.[6]

To make the numbers even more ambiguous, a French report for this same time period provides a much higher rate of return. In 1927, Commandant Pechkoff reported to his superiors in the French Ministère des Affaires Étrangères that of the "9,188 Lebanese migrants who were registered at their entry into the United States between 1908 and 1909, 8,725 (i.e., 95 per cent) were reported to have returned to their homeland in the following years."[7] Although this number is certainly far too high and is clearly at odds with the figures from the U.S. Immigration Commission, it expands dramatically the range of possibilities for the rate of return migration. A fourth possible source of information is Arthur Ruppin's 1917 study of the economic conditions of Bar al-Sham (Levant). Quoting the "official" statistics for the port of Beirut, Ruppin reports that 27,868 individuals arrived there between 1912 and 1915, while 41,752 people departed during that same period.[8] Assuming that the great majority of passengers in both directions were peasants on their way out or back to the Mountain, then the rate of return would amount to 66.75 percent. To add to the puzzle, emigrants were returning to Mount Lebanon from Argentina and Brazil as well as from the United States. According to one study, the rate of return from Argentina was a little over 29 percent.[9] Of course, into all the preceding confusion we must throw the ultimate wrench in the machine: we do not know how many emigrants returned permanently to the Mountain as opposed to those who merely went back for a visit. Frustratingly, then, we are left with as many "guesstimates" as sources.[10]

So, how do we answer our original question? The truth of the matter is that exactitude in numbers is not as important for our purposes as simply knowing that "many" emigrants did return to the Mountain after spending some years in the *mahjar*. In other words, these wildly varying rates of return can still provide us with a crucial answer. If we accept the lowest of all five rates of return to be the most valid, we still end up calculating that by 1914 somewhere around 77,594 emigrants had returned to the Mountain.[11] Even at this low rate of return (and it is equally likely that the rate was higher), it should be clear that return migration added a significant number of people—with a disproportionate financial worth—to the 414,400 people in the Mountain. And most of these people began their journey back by the turn of the century, with most returning sometime toward the end of the first decade of the twentieth century. Having reached this conclusion, it behooves us to reflect, even if briefly, on the reasons for this return.

An implicit assumption in early U.S. studies of immigration was that those who returned to their country of origin were the immigrants who did not succeed in the United States. These "Fourth of July Orators"—as one historian called them—could not conceive of any other reason that would compel immigrants to leave the land of opportunity for the "old" country, with its "outdated and oppressive customs."[12] More sophisticated commentators who actually talked to emigrants decided that there were in fact two types of returning emigrants: those who succeeded and those who failed.[13] There is no doubt that some returned because they had not been able to to attain their dreams of financial wealth. However, those would have been few and far between. If they had indeed failed to accumulate money, then it certainly would have been difficult for them to afford the $40 or $50 needed to buy the return ticket on a steamer. More likely, their hesitation to go back derived from the shame factor. These folks had left their homes and—in many cases—their families only to make money. To go back as poor as they had been when they left (or even poorer) would have been rather shameful, particularly as many others returned with pockets full of dollars. Therefore, poorer emigrants would have been more likely to stay in the *mahjar* than to return empty-handed. However, many did return simply because they had attained their main goal for coming: to make money.

But money was not the only factor. Just as many reasons prompted people to emigrate in the first place, there were an equal number for their return to their villages and towns. Some emigrants returned because they were homesick. They missed their families, their homes and villages, their language and food. As the years went by, their memories of what they had left behind grew fonder and more romantic. *Zajal* (improvised poetry) rhymes buried the muddy fields and cold winters under images of grapevines laden with fruit and luxuriant summer days. As one *zajal* poet who lived in the *mahjar* Asàd Saba, lamented:

> There near the river on the hills
> In my verdant village
> Do you think I will ever go back to roof the *'irzal*
> And spend the evenings?
> Gather the figs and cluster the grapes.[14]

Another emigrant poet, Michel Trād, appealed, in the name of the "Mountain," to anonymous emigrants:

> Stay with us here in the Mountain
> I will make your bed out of jasmine
> I will cover you with clouds and roses
> I will feed you almonds and figs.[15]

In evening conversations friends in the *mahjar* recalled the good times and interspersed their recollections with *mijana'* and *'ala dal'ouna,* the trademark songs of the Mountain. All this rekindled the desire to go home. So it is not surprising that some did go back for just that reason.

Amplifying this homesickness was the fact that others did not like America. Their visions of streets laden with gold—which had attracted them in the first place—were corrected on their arrival. They saw the misery of the industrial capitalism that was fueling America's economic revival. The following words, written by a Russian Jewish immigrant in the Yiddish newspaper *Forverts,* echoed the sentiments of many other immigrants, including those from Mount Lebanon: "Where is the golden land, where are the golden people? What has happened to human feeling in such a great wide world, in such a land which is, as it is said, a land flowing with milk and honey? When in such a rich city like New York on 88 Clinton Street a woman is dying of hunger, of loneliness, and need—that can only say: 'Cursed be Columbus, cursed be he for discovering America.'"[16] In other words, many were perceptive enough to understand that in return for material comfort the United States exacted a social cost. Furthermore, the lives of immigrants were under scrutiny, if not attack, by middle-class social reformers and nativists, who sought to "Americanize" and "modernize" these "foreigners." While such attempts rarely attained their specific goals, they nonetheless took a toll on the identities and lives of immigrants. Some were willing to make those compromises. But others turned their backs on middle-class "American" society and headed home for what they hoped would be a familiar and comfortable social setting. In the end, one must add, these reasons were not mutually exclusive. Rather, financial success, homesickness, and unwillingness to accept the harsh pace of life in the United States meshed into a singular desire to go "home."

"Home"

The first glimpse of the "home" was the crowd of relatives and friends waiting for them at the port of Beirut or Tripoli eager to celebrate their return—and to see the gifts they came bearing. For emigrants of greater wealth, poets were commissioned to write panegyrics, and newspapers published news of the "happy return." In October of 1906, for instance, an article announced the return "from the American lands" of "the exalted Amir Hani Qa'adan Shihab with his family after an absence of 7 years during which he obtained his goals."[17] Qaysar Ibrahim Maalouf—"the exalted writer"—also returned that year to Zahleh "from the American lands . . . after he spent in it a long time where he was an example of energetic work and honesty."[18] Those who were not quite as prominent, financially or otherwise, were still feted, albeit in more modest and localized fashion. In either case, the celebrations went on for weeks. During the villagewide celebrations, sheep were slaughtered in honor of the returned emigrants, and feasts were laid out for the whole village. No sooner was that phase over than the emigrant was expected to return the favor—in double for good measure.

But all was not that joyfully simple or straightforward. "Home" had changed, and romanticized images were quickly dispelled. Politically, Mount Lebanon was in the midst of both continuation and change. The Mutasarrifiyya government—which had run the affairs of the Mountain since 1861—was replete with corruption and nepotism under various governors.[19] Yet beyond the government bureaucracy—which, to be fair, included many conscientious civil servants—attempts at reforms were afoot. Critics were demanding that the government be more responsive to the citizenry of the Mountain. In practical terms, this demand translated into calls for transparency in the hiring and firing of government employees and for considering merit above political connections in doling out positions.[20] Moreover, the government of Mount Lebanon had "modernized" its postal service and customs at the port of Beirut and had attempted to create a coherent and "clean" judicial system to deal with the growing number of law suits. On a civil level, political clubs (secret and public) were debating the idea of citizenship and nationality as it pertained to the Lebanese within the Ottoman Empire. Although only the radical few (such as the Arab society of al-Fatat) envisioned a separate nation, the majority of Lebanese intellectuals still wanted to safeguard and enhance the Mountain's semi-independence from the Sublime Porte.[21] One of these clubs was Harakat al-Islah, which argued for a larger degree of self-government in the Arab provinces, including Lebanon. In making their respective arguments, these intellectuals employed the language of the "modern," and particularly democracy, to justify their claims.

Debates were not always centered overtly around politics. Rather, a large number of "clubs" and societies were dedicated to exploring scientific and literary themes. Members of these various associations would meet to discuss a book authored by a European scientist or the poetry of al-Mutanabi (a fabled medieval Arab poet). They would "read" the history of the Arabs from the perspective of newly found nationalist aspirations and discuss language as a "modern" tool of self-expression. To satisfy the growing demand for knowledge and thought (which was promoted by the proliferation of institutions of higher education), a vibrant press emerged in Beirut and in the Mountain. Between 1858 and 1918 close to 350 Lebanese newspapers and magazines were published in Beirut, Tripoli, Sidon, and various parts of the Mountain.[22] While many of these periodicals lasted a year or two at most, some (like *Hadiqat al-Akhbar* and *Lubnan*) survived for decades. In addition, journals and newspapers that were established by Lebanese émigrés in Egypt were circulated widely in Beirut and the Mountain. For example, *al-Muqtataf*, which was established by

Ya'qub Sarraf and Faris Nimr, and *al-Hilal,* which was founded by Jirji Zaidan, were two commonly read magazines that published articles on "modern" knowledge of science and literature. On a larger scale, an encyclopedia was complied and published in periodical parts by Butrus al-Bustani throughout the 1870s and 1880s. Regardless of the duration of any particular publication, the sheer volume of printed issues points to a substantial and dedicated readership. And—as we will see later in this chapter—this press, like its counterpart in the *mahjar,* was regularly engaged in discussions about "modernity" by the time emigrants began steaming back into the port of Beirut.

On the economic side, some changes had also taken place. Villages and towns were prospering thanks in large part to the influx of money from the *mahjar,* which accounted for about half of the annual income of the Mountain. Beirut continued to blossom as a commercial center, and tourism was emerging as a new industry (which catered mainly to Egyptian elites), even as industry and agriculture languished because of the befuddled economic policy of the administration of the Mountain. Roads—which were meant to support the tourist trade and extend the control of the central government—had been built throughout the mountains surrounding the coastal cities. By 1917 over eleven hundred kilometers of roads snaked across the face of the mountains.[23] Coupled with faster carriage service, these roads allowed for more connections between city and village. They transported people, goods, and ideas more frequently and swiftly between the two worlds and thus brought them closer than they had been before.

But more apparent—and more familiar to emigrants—than any of these changes were those in the realm of society. By the time emigrants began their influx into the Mountain, most of these changes were visibly centered in the city of Beirut. Like other major cities in the Ottoman Empire, Beirut was undergoing a transformation in its landscape that was emblematic of the rise of a new urbanized middle class.[24] This change was easily apparent to emigrants as they came into the port of Beirut. Scanning the horizons of the city, they would have noticed that most of the roofs were gleaming red as opposed to the prevalent flat roofs that they had last seen ten or twelve years before as they departed for the Americas. Moreover, their eyes would have had to range over a larger space to see the new suburbs that had emerged in their absence. After disembarking, they would have come to know the names of these as Achrafiyeh, Ras el-Naba'a, Mazra'a, and Ras Beyrouth. The growth of these districts had come about to accommodate the swelling of the population of the city from 80,000 in 1880 to 110,000 in 1906. And these newcomers were mostly members of a middle class of professionals, artisans, clerks, and salaried employees. Thus, as May Davie argues, the city had been transformed in this process from a medieval Arab-Islamic city to a "ville bourgeoise méditerranéenne."[25] As we shall see later in this chapter, the more intimate manifestations of this process at the level of gender and family are the ones which would have struck returning emigrants as familiar.

Leaving behind the city and climbing up to their villages, the emigrants discovered that even there things were not what they had imagined them to be while in the *mahjar.* "Home" was the poverty of the place with its dirt roads and small hovels. It was the "coarse" clothes on the backs of their peasant relatives. It was the lack of running water, outhouses, and other amenities that they had encountered during their recent sojourns in New York or Rio de Janeiro. Contrasted with their fresh memories of the metropolis, these visions must have been disappointing at some level; a disappointment that was made more profound by the pastoral images they had painted of "home" while in the *mahjar*. Such feelings produced a sense of dislocation because they highlighted how much these emigrants had changed. Panama hats and shorter dresses, dangling gold watches and new coifs were signs of that change. But that was not all. The peasants who had stayed in the Mountain were also different. All had gotten older, some had married and even had children, others had passed away, still others may have gotten poorer or richer, and a few may have moved to a different village. Socially, many disputes and arguments had taken place, and the topography of power and authority had changed over time. Most certainly there would have been some element of jealousy and resentment toward the "newcomers" who flaunted their financial comfort. These feelings combined to make the meeting of returning emigrants and resident peasants far more awkward than anticipated by anyone involved in the communal celebrations. Such awkwardness meant that most returned emigrants would come at various times to the realization that they had to forge new places for themselves in the communities they left behind, just as they had to previously establish a niche for themselves in "American" society.

Although the process of defining that "place" was carried out in a great many different ways, a few stand out as common denominators among the experiences of most returned emigrants. These included the houses that emigrants built, the clothes they wore, the food they ate, the way they raised their children, and how men and women behaved. Into all these matters emigrants introduced the mannerisms and traditions that they had developed in the *mahjar* and which resonated with the elements of an emerging middle class in Beirut. Consciously or otherwise, they had brought back with them things they thought they were leaving behind. And these clearly set them apart as different. This difference was further accentuated by the mixture of disdain and envy with which many villagers and townspeople reacted to these "innovations."

Internally and externally, then, many of the returned emigrants were coming to be lumped together as a new social class that was distinct from the peasant society out of which it grew and altogether different from the upper classes of Beirut; in other words, they were drawing together into a middling class of sorts. Parts of the framework of this class were already put in place by those who previously made money within the silk industry and by those who had newly settled in Beirut. However, return emigrants greatly expanded the reach of that class as they surged back to the Mountain. Their sheer number coupled with their newly acquired wealth expanded the numbers of the middle class from a sprinkling in some towns to a ubiquitous presence in almost all the villages of Lebanon—a phenomenon that was not common at that time in Egypt, Syria, Iran, or Turkey. Moreover, in their desire to make others cognizant of their struggle overseas, they surrounded themselves with material wealth and cosmopolitan airs. These elements made the boundaries of the coalescing social class sharper than they had ever been before. In these ways the returning emigrants left their indelible mark on the middle class. To understand this process and its inherent tensions, we need to turn now to its details.

The House

Like Polish, Greek, and Italian return emigrants, one of the first and most common elements that came to distinguish those Lebanese emigrants who came back from their kinsfolk and fellow villagers was the house they built for themselves.[26] Invariably, the returnees chose to build for themselves a house that was bigger and more ornate than any other in the village—save, perhaps, for that of another, wealthier emigrant. Undoubtedly, part of the reason for such expenditure was the returnees' desire to display their financial success. In addition, having experienced—even if from visual encounters instead of actual residence—better housing, emigrants were loathe to live in the old hovel. But there were other aspects of themselves that returned emigrants, for conscious reasons or rather more submerged ones, wanted to show. In design and function their new houses were partly a reflection of their new self-images and social habits, which they had piled on top of the old ones. To illustrate this point we need to look at the house as historical artifact.

In order to fully understand the historical significance of the new "emigrant house," we have to digress a bit and look at the "traditional" house in the village. Throughout the greater part of the nineteenth century, most peasant families lived in a one- or two-room hovel whose walls were made of the local ubiquitous stone and whose flat roof was a combination of timber logs and packed dirt. One of the rooms was used to keep the animals in during the winter, and the other served as living, cooking, eating, and sleeping space. This room was sparsely furnished with a few mattresses, a portable brazier, and maybe a chest of drawers if the peasant was well-off. There were few cooking utensils; most of them were built in, and the rest were manufactured locally. Storage space for the few utensils and linens was shelves built into the walls.[27] Bread, the main ingredient in the peasants' diet, was baked on a *tannour*[28] that was located right outside the house.

Architecturally, the peasants' houses were hardly appealing. Most travelers, except for those whose eyes were clouded by thick romantic notions about the Holy Land, remarked at the misery of peasant abodes.[29] For instance, in 1860 David Urquhart described the house where he had to spend one night as a crowded hovel that contained a few "potteries" and little else. He went on to state that "the rest of the villages in this area were, if not worse, no better than the state of this village."[30] And F. Bart lamented that "these habitations [of peasants] could afford a splendid view. But practically all [of these houses] have only one room, without a window, which serves all the needs of the home."[31] Late-nineteenth-century photographs of villages (and not just individual houses) in the Mountain confirm that—to some extent—these statements did not simply express the unflattering personal views of European sojourners. Moreover, these observations are not surprising in view of the fact that a peasant's house was built by members of his family who had little if any experience in masonry. Stones were selected to fit on top of each other as tightly as possible without much shaping since the tools and expertise necessary for constructing tight-fitting walls were not readily available to the fellah. In addition, if a house was built without interior supports, the dimensions were limited to a mere twenty square meters, a space that was barely adequate for four people. To construct a larger house, peasants had to use wooden beams or pillars of stone. However, both of these materials were extremely expensive. Wood was becoming a precious commodity in the Mountain, as silk factories had consumed tons of wood to fire up their spinning machines.[32] Even when a peasant could afford it, the space added was only six square meters. And while stone pillars added much more space, the cost of constructing this larger space was much higher than most peasants could afford.[33]

Aside from being larger versions of this typical house, the homes of wealthier peasants and even of many of the *shuyukh* (notables) were only different in two ways: content and location. These wealthier homes may have contained a big iron bed, many more pillows, a cupboard or two, some wooden trunks, and a low table.[34] While a few items, like the bed, were imitations of European possessions common in Beirut, most of the other possessions were "traditional" household goods. Such contents marked their owners as rich and elite members of peasant society but hardly as "modern" in the European sense. Another distinguishing factor was the location of the house within the general layout of a particular village. The most influential members of the village occupied its central part, while poor ones lived at the periphery. For example, in the village of 'Ammatur, the two main clans of 'Abd as-Samad and Abu-Shaqra occupied the center of the village, while the lower class Druzes and Christians lived at the periphery of the village, and an outcast Christian-Muslim couple had to live at a considerable distance from the village.[35] This visual rendition of social hierarchy immediately clued visitors to the locus of power and directed them to the house where they could expect the greatest amount of hospitality.

A decade or two after Urquhart's visit to Lebanon (1870–1880), money from silk was showing up in—among other things—slightly better homes for wealthier peasants.[36] The large, single, and multipurpose living space was no longer sufficient, nor was the proximity to animals desirable. The first change in the construction of peasant houses was the adoption of two-level rectangular houses, with the lower level reserved for the animals. The physical separation of living and service areas terminated the cohabitation of human and animal. One observer saw this shift as "symbolizing man's emancipation from unremitting toil."[37] Even if we do not subscribe to such dramatic views, we can still argue that this physical elevation was meant as an indication of a social rise above the general peasantry. The way these new types of houses were constructed confirms this point. While the lower level of the house—or the reserve of animals and the *tannour* (oven)—was still a crude construction of stone walls and dirt ceiling, the second level was a different affair altogether. Reserved for people, the upper level displayed better masonry work and consisted of a bigger room with a couple of slightly larger windows. One door on that level let out to the road and another to the roof of the lower level which served in the summer as a terrace.[38] Yet, despite the larger dimensions, the living space of the family was essentially the same as that in older and poorer houses in that it was multipurpose. In other words, the same physical space served as a communal sitting room, eating area, and—at the end of the day—sleeping area. Thus, we can fairly conclude that the first eighty or so years of the nineteenth-century were marked by slow changes in the architecture, interior design, and functions of the Lebanese house.

The following thirty years were different. Emigrant money funded the most rapid and dramatic transformation of that house at every level, creating in the process the "central-hall house." This was long assumed to be the Lebanese house par excellence, and it is etched into the collective memory as a national icon whose roots derive from the "Mountain"—and to a much lesser extent from the Phoenician past.[39] In fact, rather than simply emanating from the Mountain, these houses were emigrant adaptations of the mansions of the upper bourgeoisie of Beirut. In turn, this style was an earlier extroversion of the Arab-Islamic interior, which dominated the mountain houses mixed with Italian and French material and ornamentation. Moreover, these edifices—while remaining unique in some ways—were part of a Levantine bourgeois architecture that was emerging around the same time throughout the Eastern Mediterranean.[40] For example, Zeynep Çelik speaks of similar architecture and of the integration of "western appliqué façades on traditional interiors," which was remaking the elite houses in Istanbul.[41] Put another way, the "central-hall house" was a dialectical outcome of the various cultural currents that ran through Beirut and into the Mountain villages. These came from the Ottoman *metropole,* from the peasant villages, and through Italian and French architects and builders.

Regardless of their roots, these houses stood in the villages of the Mountain as unambiguous and impressive testaments to the wealth and status of their owners—returning emigrants. As Friedrich Ragette commented rather dramatically about architecture in the Lebanese village, "Towards the end of the nineteenth century . . . the houses turned into veritable villas . . . majestically dominating their surroundings."[42] Ranging between 140 and 200 square meters (and sometimes reaching palatial dimensions with 300 square meters of floor space), these *harat* (as they were called) were larger than any of the older houses. Beyond size, the striking elevated triple-arch motif of the central hall—which included two ornate windows that framed the door—made these houses stand out among the plain façades of the older homes. Finally, the *coup de grâce* was the signature red-tiled roof, which stood out ever so dramatically against the green and brown surroundings.

Digging a little deeper, we find that from their foundations these *harat* were different from their poorer cousins. Many of these houses (some of which are still standing today) show in their details that construction was assigned to local professional masons. The stones for the walls were better dressed and arranged, and the ceiling was sometimes sealed with *trabé franjié* ("European soil"), or cement.[43] More interesting, this elaborate variation included arches within the house. Each set of arches was called *habl qanater*, or a "cord of arches," and the house could contain one, two, or three such cords depending on the wealth of the family.[44] Functionally, these arches improved the insulation of the house, which was also enhanced by the new way that the walls were constructed. These new walls, which could be as thick as one meter, were generally constructed as two separate walls with dirt filled in between them.[45] The outside wall was made of carefully selected stones, called *mdamik,* that were shaped to fit on top of each other without the need for mortar and with the joints barely apparent. Alternating sandstone and limestone (the limestone being used in façades exposed to the winter rains or in more load-bearing areas) created a most pleasing decorative effect that contrasted with the monotonous exterior of older homes.

Ornamental designs in windows, shutters, and porticos distanced this house even further from its plain cubic neighbors. Doors and their frames incorporated moldings and carvings that made them more attractive than the old doors, which consisted of pieces of wood nailed together. On a more cosmetic level, windows with paned glass as well as wooden shutters became more common, and ornamental glazed circular windows were placed near the top of walls in order to infuse the inside with a multitude of colors. In 1890 these changes were just emerging, as observed in a French report: "today the use of glass windows is being generalized very quickly."[46] Its author went on to estimate the amount of window glass imported yearly at 450,000 square feet, at an average cost of 1,400 piasters per 100 square feet.[47] By 1911 we find that the importation of window glass had surpassed the million-square-foot mark.[48] It would appear from these numbers that returning emigrants wanted the power to see and to be seen—when they chose—from within the private space of their distinct houses.

Ultimately, however, the most visually striking sign of emigrant wealth appeared on the roof. Imported brilliant red tiles covered the new slanted roofs, which contrasted strongly with the traditional flat roofs of peasant homes. These blushes of wealth became popular and common enough that while in 1887 one million red tiles were imported from France, five years later this figure had doubled, and by 1911 it had crossed the five-million mark.[49] Although many of these tiles were destined for houses being built in Beirut, a large proportion made their way to the villages of Mount Lebanon as observed by various contemporaries. For example, Ernest Weakley, a British parliamentarian who was writing in 1911 about commerce in Mount Lebanon, commented that "all new households in Beirut as well as in the villages on the Lebanon are covered with the bright red foreign article [tiles]."[50] Ravndal was more explicit in his observation of this phenomenon: "When it is considered that there is hardly a village in the most remote parts of the Lebanon that has not at least 2 or 3 new houses with tiled roofs and that even whole villages have been thus constructed—the amount of money diverted from America and permanently invested in Syria can be easily recognized."[51] These observations are all the more dramatic when one takes into account the fact that until the late 1870s "one could hardly find a single red-tiled roof in the Mountain."[52]

Changes were as dramatic—albeit less public—on the inside of these emigrant homes. Floors were covered with mosaic tiles, sanitary fixtures and equipment were added, and better heating stoves were installed. Most notably, large multipurpose space gave way to a number of smaller rooms with a specific use for each. Although there were some differences from one house to the next, in general the floor plan remained quite similar. The main door opened into an entry hall that led straight ahead to a central hall—hence the name of this design. This central hall was the main living room and reception area for guests; this much of the basic design was the same as that of "traditional" and poorer peasant homes. However, additional rooms (the number of which depended on the size of the house) branched off to the side of the entryway. These rooms dramatically altered the layout of the house by creating specialized spaces that had never really existed before. One of these was the kitchen, and the others were the bedrooms. Each of the bedrooms had a door that—when closed—effectively isolated the happenings in that room from the rest of the family life. In other words, a more distinct sense of privacy derived from the design of these houses. This privacy separated guests (in the central hall) from the occupants of the house who—for whatever reason—were in their bedrooms. Equally, the "modern" interior separated the parents' room from that of the children, and then again the boys from the girls.

Because of the enlargement and subdivision of the space, the house acquired different types of furniture. The few mattresses which seated and slept the whole peasant family were no longer enough for all of the bedrooms as well as the living room. Beds—complete with iron frames—had to be purchased for the bedrooms; cushions, a sofa, and a couple of chairs were placed in the central hall. The increased demand for Western-style furniture translated into a rise in the number of imported chairs. While in 1868 only twelve thousand items of furniture were imported, during the 1890s eighty thousand chairs *en bois courbé* (of curved, or bent, wood) alone were imported yearly to Beirut and Mount Lebanon. Iron beds were another big import item by the end of the 1890s. In 1887, for instance, more than thirteen thousand English-made iron beds were imported to Beirut, with about a third destined for the villagers in the mountains.[53] Two decades later, the figures had doubled.[54] Demand for these goods finally propelled some local companies to build *franji* furniture. Early on in the twentieth century, these companies were advertising their wares in most of the popular newspapers, like *Lubnan*. One local manufacturer of furniture placed the following advertisement:

> Al-Suyufi Factory: [We] manufacture and sell in it all kinds of furniture . . . like armoires with mirrors, sinks of all kinds, buffets, and dining tables . . . drapes and coffee tables, hall trees . . . sofas and chairs, etc.[55]

Other local stores were opened to sell a greater number of imported luxury goods. For instance, no fewer than three separate stores advertised the availability of clocks, armoires, and sofas at their various outlets in the Mountain. Since advertising was still fairly uncommon in Lebanon in the 1910s, we can appreciate that there were many other stores which did not advertise yet but were selling the same wares.

Inside the armoires emigrants hung their *franji* clothes. Gone were the days when a peasant could not don the clothes of a *shaykh* without fear of retribution.[56] By the turn of the twentieth century the Lebanese middle class bought whatever fashion they could (and in some instances, could not) afford. The styles, as one *zajaliya* (popular poem) recorded, were distinctly different from those of the peasants—and of the *shuyukh*, for that matter. For the "little ones" there was:

> a blue suit with buttons
> and each button costing sixty *misriyya*
> On the waist there must be a leather
> Belt, according to the latest in fashion
> And a straw hat with
> A band all around
> And an ironed collar
> And a tied neck-tie

Women, the poet continued in his laments, were even more "lavish."

> I want a short corset
> And two dresses that are tasteful

> I want a jeweled comb
> And I want earrings and a choker
> The hat costs four liras
> And the dress is from heavy wool
> And a raincoat that
> has no equal in the country[57]

Men wore their Panama hats, leather boots, and waistcoats with a gold watch dangling from a pocket.

Such was the demand for these luxury items that by the first decade of the twentieth century stores catering to these acquired tastes had spread throughout the larger cities of the Mountain. One of those, located in Beirut (where most of these stores were established), was Bon Marché, which advertised among its wares "parasols, pantaloons, handkerchiefs . . . perfumes and powders . . . fans . . .etc."[58] While it was rare to find similar stores with finished goods in the larger towns of Dayr al-Qamar, Jubayl, Brummana, Zahleh, and Batrun, all had *franji* tailors. For instance, by the end of the nineteenth century, there were five such tailors in Dayr al-Qamar, and, more tellingly, a provincial city like Jubayl boasted of seven tailors who catered to the surrounding villages.[59] Even smaller and more distant towns like Brummana, Bsherri, and Jezzine could count on one or two tailors in their areas.[60] All advertised themselves as capable of clothing men and women in the latest European fashion.

Amidst this "modern" wardrobe there was increasingly little room for the *sirwal* (peasant pants) and *labbada* (wool peasant hat) or for the geometric tattoos on the arms and faces of women. By wearing *franji* clothes, the rural middle class used their bodies to display their wealth, sophistication, and social difference. When this effort is considered along with the emergence of the *harat,* it should become clear that the members of this social group (dominated, as it was, by emigrants) worked hard to distinguish themselves from their poorer peasant neighbors through their novel styles of sitting, eating, sleeping, and dressing. Although these efforts at contrast stretched over years of history, they are nonetheless striking. Even as emigrants, these people had consciously and anxiously wanted to come back to their villages; once there they were equally desirous to distance themselves from the social milieu. In the *mahjar* they had elevated peasant life to romantic heights, but upon their return they shunned its "traditional" reality for their version of "modernity." This simultaneous presence in the village and distance from its poorer inhabitants was a source of tension that exaggerated the social stratification within the village, a stratification already begun in part by the commercialization of silk and the establishment of silk factories.

The growing distance between the peasants and the rural middle class becomes more apparent when we compare the social spaces of the "traditional" and the "modern" house. Before the 1890s (and even afterward in peasant houses), working and living spaces in the villages were almost indistinct visually and, for most of the year, functionally.[61] People, animals, work, and play intermeshed across the physical boundaries of the house. Women worked on raising their silkworms inside the house to add to the income of their families; lentils were spread on the flat roofs to dry them for the winter; and chickens and goats were brought in in the winter to safeguard the family's investment from the harsh weather. The roofs—built in close proximity to each other—were also a physical space; there women socialized with each other and participated in the public life of the village. Moreover, the dark and cramped interior of older peasant homes encouraged women to spend most of their time outside the house. In sum, the "traditional" house of the peasant was an integral part of the overall socioeconomic texture of the village and the fabric of daily life.

However, the *'atbeh* (threshold) of the *harat* pushed the internal life of a family into a more isolated sphere. Animals did not meander in, nor was it necessary to bring them in during the winter nights—they had their "stable" beneath the house. And while women continued to work within the house, their labors were no longer remunerated financially in any direct way. Cooking, cleaning, and raising children still went on behind the walls of the house, but *sitt al-bayt* (the lady of the house) did not need to raise silkworms. (This is ironic since many of these women had worked in the *mahjar* to help the family accumulate its money.) In addition, the new design also served to curtail *sitt al-bayt*'s social interactions in the public sphere. Women in the emigrant household no longer had to go to the *'ayn* in the village to get water; either their servants did that, or water was brought much closer to the house. Cooking, normally an outdoor activity, was brought into the added kitchen, where more complicated and time-consuming meals were prepared. Finally, the beautiful pyramid of red tiles which topped these houses made it most impractical to climb on top of the roofs. Altogether, then, and in contrast to the "traditional" peasant abode, the "central-hall house" afforded women fewer possibilities to go outside.

Isolating them further was the fact that the *'atbeh* also symbolized the division between those who owned the land and those who worked for them. One anecdote told about the wealthy Habib Doumani family from the town of Dayr al-Qamar dramatizes this separation. One day, "*Sitt* [Lady] Sa'ada [Habib's wife] was bothered when she saw tens of *shuraka'* peasants [workers on the landowner's land] entering her house with their muddied boots dirtying her white and red tiles, and she complained of the matter to her husband."[62] Not always nor in every new household was the separation so distinct. Yet the division was obvious all over the Mountain since most of the returned emigrants ceased to work on their land. It was all the more apparent as the sons (and some daughters, as we will also see later in this chapter) of these same emigrants were sent off to school while the youth of their peasant neighbors were busy tilling the fields. Thus, women of the *harat* could no longer easily intermingle with women of lesser financial stature, as all such relations had an undertow of unequal social power. One need not exaggerate the extent of this distinction to realize that it furthered the stratification of the village society even as—and because—it pushed middle class women into a more distinguishable private sphere.

Womanhood

Affirming this "modern" ideal of an insular life for middle class women—a model that the emigrants had encountered and engaged in the *mahjar*—was a localized cult of domesticity which had been, and was still being, enunciated in Beirut. From the 1880s onward, numerous newspapers and magazines and the authors of various books and speeches were engaged in the project of inventing a universal "woman." Readers and listeners were instructed that "all that is inside the house is relegated in its administration to the woman just as all external affairs are the domain of the man."[63] Such a created "tradition" needed ideological underpinnings to justify its existence and to make it appear as old as time and as natural as the air. Thus, it was infused with the utmost importance. One author, in highlighting that importance, wrote that women are the moral pillar of the family—and by extension the nation—because "there are none like them in organizing society and safeguarding its order and morals, because they are the *goddesses of their families and homes*."[64] This deification is quite startling when it was still common at the time for male peasants to refer to their wives as "The House" or "Our Paternal Cousin"[65] and when mentioning a woman's given name sent the husband into apologetic contortions for fear of offending the listener.

As the host of articles in women's magazines and newspapers constantly reminded their readers, women were not quite to the point of being "goddesses of their families and homes." One woman wrote, in an open letter to her bride-seeking son, "You asked me to find you an appropriate girl to be a partner in your life . . . for you want a rational, energetic and capable wife, and these qualities I have not found in an Eastern young woman."[66] In this one paragraph the writer created the model of "womanhood" to which "Eastern" women must aspire. Injecting the division of the world into two distinct spheres of "East" and "West" into her discourse on womanhood, this writer deftly linked "modernity" and the "woman" through the general qualities of knowledge, energy, and capability. And in every instance she found the "Eastern" young woman wanting.

To rise to these levels, the middle-class woman had to follow numerous novel ways. From breastfeeding children to setting a table, from using antiseptic hygiene to different social manners, and from comforting her husband to speaking at appropriate times, the "modern" woman had to jump through many hoops in order to reach her social peak. Advice in all these matters was abundant. For example, Ibrahim Bayk al-Aswad dedicated ten pages in his almanac—which ran through four editions between 1906 and 1910—to the act of breastfeeding. Shunning the "outmoded and unscientific" methods of yesteryear, *he* recommended the following regimen: "While breastfeeding her baby a mother should remain seated while supporting her back with a pillow . . . and for her [the mother's] comfort and that of her infant she needs to organize the times of breastfeeding in the first few weeks so that [she breastfeeds] once every two hours for 10 to 12 minutes only, and at night . . . she should give him the breast around 4 o'clock in the afternoon and allow him to eat enough and not breastfeed him again till the morning."[67]

Undaunted by the prospects of engorged breasts and crying hungry infants at night, the same author goes on to provide equally "scientific" advice for weaning a baby. At nine months, he wrote, a baby should be weaned according to the following formula:

> 7 A.M. — 12 tablespoons of milk and one tablespoon of cream and teaspoon of sugar mixed with 3 tablespoons of water;
> 10:30 A.M. — milk, sugar and water as in the preceding and 2 teaspoons of "mellin" food dissolved in warm water and added to the milk
> 2 P.M. — as was fed at 10:30 A.M.

6 P.M. — as was fed at 10:30 A.M.

7 P.M. — as was fed at 7 A.M.[68]

He proceeded to detail the feeding schedule for infants from ten to fourteen months, fourteen to eighteen months, and finally from eighteen months to the end of the second year. Variations of such demanding schedules were also recommended in articles published in women's magazines.[69] No doubt they were intended to reduce infant mortality and to produce healthier children. Nonetheless, they placed a great burden on the mother—and the mother alone—to attend to the welfare of her child.[70]

One woman's magazine, *al-Hasna'*, expounded at large on the "principles in raising children." One of its articles listed eight ways to ensure the health of a child:

1. Children are to be given the best room in the house
2. The room has to be large with many windows so that it will allow sun and air to come in easily
3. They must sleep early and they need no less than 10 hours of sleep
4. They have to spend two hours outside the house to get fresh air and they must never be exposed to cold air unless they are wearing clothes that protects them from it
5. They must be encouraged [to engage] in athletic [activity] that strengthens the body and to practice . . . regularly and in an orderly fashion
6. They need to eat at a table special for them until they reach the age of 10, and food should be heavy at lunch and light for dinner
7. They should refrain from eating sweets and doughy foods and unripe fruits and all that badly affects digestion
8. They must not be exposed to exciting subject matter such as murder, wiliness and other very dangerous events[71]

To implement such rigorous rules necessitated access to money and facilities that only the middle class could hope to have. But, more important, these rules presented a radically different approach to raising children. Unlike their peasant cousins, these children were to be protected as much as possible from the roughness of life. While peasant boys and girls started working in the fields from the age of six, children of the *harat* were to be spared deleterious exposure to work, cold weather, damp air, and violence. A "good" mother would also attend to her children's education. She needed—according to the same "experts"—to sit beside them every evening to help them with their homework and to read to them. In sum, the middle-class mother's task was to shelter and guide her children so that they would grow up to be healthy young men and women who could then contribute better to society. This is the same enthusiastic sentiment that was concurrently running through the discourse of social reformers in Iran and Egypt. For example, in his *Murshid al-amin lil-banat wal-banin,* Rifa'a al-Tahtawi stated that educating Egyptian women was important because it "prepares [them] to raise their children well. . . . That children should be given a sound . . . *tarbiyya* [education/upbringing] is of enormous social consequence."[72]

This process of defining women within the context of a household—albeit a gilded one—was not limited to their role as "modern" mothers. Additionally, a middle-class woman was expected to manage her house properly. *Al Hasna'* editorialized that "a lady must know the principles of this art [management of the house] and work according to them because she is…the manager of its affairs. And it [the home] is the mirror of her works and proof of her taste, her hard work, and the guide to her emotions;…this is particularly important because home life influences the morals and shapes the personalities."[73] *Al-Hasna'* subsequently dedicated close to a third of its pages to ensuring that its women readers approached these ideals of "modern" femininity. One article, for example, spoke about the new ways of washing clothes; another expounded on the effects of kohl, eyeliners, and powders ("heavy make-up is deleterious for the health of your skin"); and a three-page article described the "scientific" method for cleaning ("to rid the house of germs and vermin").[74]

Under the title "Managing the House," the same magazine instructed:

> Put a little ammonia in a bowl and immerse in it a piece of soft cloth and rub the jewelry with it vigorously then dry it with another piece of cloth and polish it well. Ammonia also cleans leather gloves and silk textiles from spots and removes from black silken and woolen clothes the reddishness which is caused when citric liquids falls upon them. . . . Silver utensils and dinnerware which are used during mealtimes must be washed with water and pure white soap and dried very well with an old soft towel and polished twice a week with white soft *esfidaj* mixed with alcohol . . . and if the silver has black spots that are not removed by rubbing with *esfidaj* then rub it with piece of flannel cloth wetted with citric acid and then polish it. If you want another way . . .[75]

Fatat Lubnan, another women's magazine, went further in stating the importance of such laborious tasks. It preached that "the proper management of the house is not limited [in its benefits] to the comfort of the family, but goes beyond it to the happiness of the nation, its wealth, dignity, and sovereignty."[76]

Finally, a woman's role—women were told, mostly by male writers—included catering to the needs and desires of the "man of the household." Many writers argued that women could do so only if they avoided such "trivialities" as reading romance novels and attending parties, and paid greater attention to the more "meaningful" things in life. Among these consequential matters they listed cooking proper meals, setting a good table, carefully managing expenses, and making sure the children were clean and well kept. In taking care of all these matters, a woman would simply be acting out her proper role as a helpmate for her husband because "she and she alone can . . . help him in his business and affairs even if she did not have a direct hand in them or knowledge about them." If she performed these "duties" with a smile, and if she did not complain or "gripe," the house would be a source of contentment and rejuvenation for the husband.[77] Even more liberal commentators listed similar conditions for a happy home. Elias Tweyni, who expounded at length and in several articles about giving women respect and rights, wrote, "It is important to give a woman the rights that support her elevated status within the family because she [the woman] is the real helper for it [the family] and her husband, for God has created her for this purpose and she is capable of helping her husband and supporting him in his work."[78]

In an article entitled "The Woman's Kingdom: A Discourse on Domestic Politics," one author summed up these various elements of a "modern" middle-class woman's life. "Making husband and child happy must be the main purpose behind the efforts of every woman who deserves to be described as feminine. . . . Yes, ladies, this [longing looks from the husband and kisses from the children] is the only thing that brings us happiness, we women; . . . and it does not come easily and without trouble . . . but rather it comes through a path full of exertion and difficulties, [where we] deny ourselves and shun our interests in favor of the welfare of those around us."[79] It all amounted to a large sacrifice of a woman's individuality in order to nurture that of her husband and children. This ideal was notably different from the sacrifice of peasant women, who were not quite so alone in subsuming their own interests to that of the family. Although the level of sacrifice among rural families was hardly distributed equally among their members, husband and wife and children all worked for the survival of the family. The possibilities for individual self-expression were limited by the dearth of financial and educational resources. Across the class divide, the "goddesses" of the house stood far more alone and shouldered the greater burden of life's sacrifices. Like middle-class women in Istanbul or Teheran, these women were asked to forego the homosocial life which had sustained their grandmothers and mothers because it was threatening to the new social order in which women were the "special, almost exclusive agents of what has been called the relations of social reproduction."[80] Making this isolation more poignant was the fact that these middle-class women gazed on a larger spectrum of alternative lives across the growing distance between "private" and "public." They knew about those possibilities and were expected to help their husbands and children attain them, at the same time that they were expected to recede further into a lonely existence. In that sense their sacrifice was as mentally painful as the hardships which peasant women lived with every day were physically painful.

Education

But women had to accept this trying shift in responsibilities, and they had to be prepared to accomplish all the tasks that it entailed. Even if some women embraced these new duties, others who had traveled to and worked in the *mahjar* would have been loathe to being shunted so readily into what must have appeared to be an isolated and stilted lifestyle. This reluctance is apparent to us from the recurring complaints by middle-class reformers about women's insistence on "frivolous" socialization and from the innumerable articles that were meant to make women "better" mothers, wives, and managers of their households. Because of this reluctance, many contemporaries argued that constructing the "new woman" required the education of the younger generation of women. On this premise, they engaged the debate about this issue, a debate that began in the 1870s and was still going strong by World War I. Hence, we have the emphatic and very "motherly" statement by one contemporary who wrote, "Breastfeeding them [women] the milks of science is as important a duty as breastfeeding an infant, and as necessary as water is for plants."[81] And another expressed the same idea in a few lines of poetry:

> Teach her she will be succor of happiness
> Succor of family and children
> Let her know she is the source of good
> The basis of wealth and happiness[82]

Less poetic, but more direct, was the affirmation in 1909 by the editor of a woman's magazine:

> Rearing [children] is the primary duty of a woman, given that God has singled her
> out with natural inclination [toward child raising] and what social traditions dictate.
> . . . So that she can perform this primary duty . . . she needs to be prepared for that
> with learning and schooling and to continue to follow the latest opinions . . . and
> these are the most important necessities for every mother who wishes the well-being
> of her children, and there is not a mother in the world who does not.[83]

These ideas meandered from the pages of magazines and newspapers into the ideological foundations of girls' schools. For instance, during the dedication of the Friends' School for Girls in Brummana, the principal, Eli Jones, "spoke for one and a quarter hours on the subject of female education—and was translated into Arabic."[84] His talk centered around the notion of providing women with an education to make them better companions for men.[85]

The content of girls' education was geared toward that function. One writer expounded on this matter by stating that "among the most important of the sciences that women must learn is the art of managing the house because she needs to know how to organize her home and its affairs and its needs such as cooking, baking, cleaning the furniture and setting a proper table." In addition, along with rudimentary knowledge of geography and history, it was deemed necessary to teach a woman to read so that she could peruse literary books and newspapers, "in order to amuse herself during the long idle hours and to benefit her children with knowledge," as well as to provide better companionship for her husband.[86] A few writers even thought it of the utmost importance to teach women about hygiene, nursing, and "even physiology" so that they could take better care of their children's health. Finally, women were to learn proper "home economics" in order to make their husbands' income stretch further. Quoting Benjamin Franklin, one self-appointed arbiter of women's tasks wrote, "Fear spend-thriftiness for the smallest holes sink the largest ships."[87]

Al-Hasna' and other women's journals dedicated page after page to this same subject.[88] But *Fatat Lubnan* was the most adamant in its pronouncements about this issue. In one of many articles the editor, Salima Abi Rashid, proclaimed that the cause for the "great gap between the peoples of the West and the peoples of the East [is the relative knowledge of] home economics. Their learning has made them dominate everything and our ignorance has made us dominated by everything, so they have power over truths and fantasies have power over us." Such a "sorry state of affairs" could be resolved only by imitating the curriculum which young girls in Europe were receiving in their schools. At length she wrote,

> In elementary schools girl students receive lessons in the art of cooking . . . as well
> as in washing clothes and ironing it according to the most modern of ways, and

managing the house and cleaning it, and in avoiding the ill-effects of toilets and chimneys and in disinfecting it, and other lessons in the principles of safeguarding health and caring for children, and in the ways of treating illnesses and dealing with sudden emergencies [until] the doctor arrives, and lessons in the science of home economics, and in correlating between income and expenditures.[89]

She concluded her critique of Lebanese society by pleading that "[our] life has become corrupted to such an extent that it is feared that out social structure will descend to such a stage as to make it impossible to ever rise again. And this corrupted life cannot be changed except by educating the girl."[90] Articles in other magazines agreed—albeit in a less passionate and dramatic tone—that "proper" young girls must be prepared to play the roles of middle-class wives and mothers within the boundaries of middle-class houses.

This circular construction, where gender roles define class, and class implies particular gender roles, was given urgency through links to the wider political spectrum of "nation" and its confrontation with a dominating "West." Thus, making a "nation" was inextricably linked with producing good mothers; one could not be attained without the other—at least according to some. This strategy was similar to the one that was employed by other middle classes of colonized "nations," be they in China, South Asia, or other parts of the "Orient." For example, Tani Barlow argues that female writers in China presented the same argument in demanding changes in the status of women in the 1890s and 1910s. One of these writers asked, "Why isn't China strong? Because there are no persons of talent. Why are there no persons of talent? Because women do not prosper."[91] Similarly, and around the same time, some Iranian intellectuals situated the need for women's education within the political struggle between an "East" and a "West." Arguing that education is necessary for the preparation of the "woman" for her role as a manager of the household, one writer noted that "even in household management women of Europe and America have surpassed those of Asia. . . . Nations that have mothers like European women can conquer other lands and rule over other nations."[92] So it was in Lebanon, as in these other places, that the "modern woman" became essentialized into an ideal type whose role in bringing up children and serving her husband was a prerequisite for an independent nation that would be equal to the "West" and able to repel its domination.[93]

The evangelical emphasis on the role young women had to play in lifting Lebanese society—and neighboring ones, as other scholars have pointed out—from its corruption was made all the more impressive by the absence of any such a role for boys. For them there were no lessons in "home economics," table manners, sewing, or anything of the sort. Rather, as told by H. J. Turtle, in Protestant schools, "boys are trained in all the useful branches of education, and some to trades. They go out as teachers . . ., and also as clerks and apprentices in merchants' offices and factories in Beirut."[94] Catholic schools (which were concerned about "losing" Lebanese boys to other missionaries) also changed their curriculum to provide a more practical education, greatly deemphasizing religious instruction in the process. Writing in 1866, the director of the Jesuit school in Ghazir observed that 'Aintoura—a rival school run by the Lazarists—"is a *nursery* [i.e., school] for young men who want to take up commercial or industrial careers."[95] The

Jesuits soon followed suit in providing such a new curriculum, which was implemented in all the schools under their direction.[96] Finally, one finds that all the institutions for higher education catered to young men—of good social means—and produced doctors and lawyers who added to the ranks of the professional middle class. (The Université Saint Joseph and its rival, the Syrian Protestant College—later known as the American University of Beirut—were two such institutions, and it was not until the aftermath of World War I that women were allowed to enter their hallowed halls.) Boys were, then, educated to work outside the home, in the ever-expanding "public sphere." In this manner, education was of the essence in constructing the "private" and "public" sides of the middle-class society and in ensuring their separation according to gender.

As seen in the dramatic change in the number of girls attending schools in Mount Lebanon, members of this class seem to have heeded calls for educating girls. Numbers tell part of this tale. As late as the first quarter of the nineteenth century, girls' education was considered inappropriate and even immoral by peasants and *shuyukh* alike, for it was thought to promote licentious behavior.[97] The first to break this "tradition" were Protestant missionaries, who set up schools for girls in Beirut and nearby villages. The American Presbyterians led the way as early as 1826 by providing some basic education—mostly in subjects like knitting and sewing—for about thirty girls who were in "occasional attendance" at six schools.[98] Most of these "schools" were located in the residences of the missionaries, and the wives of the missionaries carried out the instruction. It was not until 1835 that a separate room on the mission's ground was set aside for girls' education. This came to be known as the Female School, and it was headed by an American mistress and a Lebanese assistant who taught on average about twenty-five girls. However, this and other girls' schools established by the American missionaries remained limited to a few well-off Christian girls.[99] Then, in 1846, these missionaries established a boarding school for girls in Beirut and another in Suq al-Gharb in 1858, both of which offered subsidized liberal education in the arts and sciences.[100] The popularity of both schools induced the British missionaries to set up the Girls Training School in Shimlan a few years later.

Although credit must be given to the American missionaries for their early dedication to the concept of female education, the lead in that matter soon passed to the Catholic and Maronite nuns. The Sisters of St. Vincent de Paul, who arrived in Lebanon in 1849, were the first Catholic missionaries to set up schools for girls. By 1869, the sisters—twenty-eight from France and twenty-eight from Lebanon—had built a hospital in Beirut and an orphanage that took in young girls who were deprived of their parents by the civil war in 1860.[101] In addition, the sisters established a school for young girls in 1863 which had forty-three boarding students. The high cost of the school—400 francs or 1,600 piasters per year—made it accessible only to the daughters of well-off families from Beirut and the surrounding mountains. At the same time, the sisters established eight schools in Mount Lebanon, concentrated within twenty miles of Beirut except for two that were established in the Kisrawan region. All the schools taught the same curriculum—French, Arabic, arithmetic, history and geography—in addition to providing religious instruction, and education in the eight institutions outside Beirut was free for all 569 students.[102]

Indigenously, two associations of Lebanese nuns in cooperation with the Jesuits were established in 1853 to further female education in Lebanon in the "proper"—that is, Catholic—direction. One of these was the Association of Mariamiyyat, established in Bikfaiya, and the other was the Association of the Heart of Jesus in Zahleh. The first association opened schools in the areas of Kisrawan, Metn, Futuh, Jubayl, and Batrun, while the second opened schools in the Biqa'a valley and Damascus region. Yet, despite these efforts, the number of girls attending schools remained minimal. For example, Constantin Petkovich, the Russian consul general to Beirut, reported in 1885 that all the schools in Mount Lebanon tutored no more than 1,598 girls.[103] Of these, almost a third were girls from the nascent Protestant community in Lebanon, and the remainder came from the other Christian communities. He further noted—in a disappointed tone—that while a mere 135 girls were Maronite, and another 155 were Greek Catholic, none came from the Greek Orthodox community.[104]

Matters began to change fairly rapidly by the turn of the century. Within the span of two decades (1893–1914), the number of girls' schools in the Mountain mushroomed. Beginning in 1893 various orders of Catholic nuns opened schools in the Mountain. For example, the Nuns of Love established a total of twelve new schools—spread all over the mountain—in the span of fourteen years. Nuns from the St. Joseph order followed suit with four boarding schools for girls, while the Besançon nuns established another four schools in Bikfaiya, Jounieh, Ba'abdat, and Baskinta.[105] While we do not know the exact number of girls who were enrolled in these schools, we can get a glimpse of the dramatic rise in enrollment from the few examples we have available. For instance, by 1914 nuns from the Association of the Hearts of Jesus and Mary were undertaking the education of 6,000 girls in over thirty schools.[106] In 1894 Jesuit schools were educating a total of 2,130 girls in twenty schools spread over the Mountain. Similarly, by the end of the nineteenth century, the British Syrian mission alone was educating 4,000 pupils—at all levels—in Mount Lebanon, and of these a third were girls.[107] Beyond these specific numbers, we know that other Protestant missionary schools were educating another thousand or so girls around the Mountain, and the remainder of the Catholic schools enrolled at least another two or three thousand girls in their various institutions. In total, then, we can safely estimate that at least ten thousand girls were attending schools in the Mountain, as compared to the sixty thousand students who were boys.

The magnitude of this change can be brought into greater relief when we compare these numbers with numbers from surrounding regions within the Ottoman Empire. Geographically, the closest to Mount Lebanon of these regions was the *caza* of Sidon. By the last decade of the nineteenth century that *caza* had a total of five secondary schools, mostly located in the city of Sidon, with a total of 470 students; 200 of them went to two Protestant schools, and just a handful were girls.[108] Even less educationally developed was the region of Sūr, slightly further south than Sidon. In that whole region there were no secondary schools, and for a population of about thirteen thousand there were only seven elementary schools catering mainly to boys.[109] In the Jabal 'Amil district where one hundred thousand people—mostly Shi'ites—lived, formal schooling was almost nonexistent as late as the middle of the twentieth century.[110] Casting our glances even further across the Ottoman Empire, we find similar contrasts. Consider, if you will, that in the province of Aleppo only 4,150 girls out of a population that totaled 921,345 went to school.

Further to the northeast, in the province of Ankara—which included over one million people—even fewer girls (3,650) were sent to school. In fact, of the thirty-six provinces listed in the official Ottoman statistical books, none had more girls per capita attending school. To put it another way, while girls attending schools in Mount Lebanon amounted to 2.35 percent of the *total* population, the closest any other Ottoman province came to this figure was that of Sivas, where girls attending school equaled 1 percent of the population at large; most other provinces did not come close to even half a percent.[111] Another perspective is provided by the percentage of girls making up the total school population. While in Mount Lebanon it was almost 17 percent, it rarely broke the 6 percent mark in the remaining Ottoman regions.[112]

However, the weight of the changes in education in the Mountain transcends the issue of numbers. Out of the geographical distribution of these schools over the landscape of the Mountain, we can tease another fact pertinent to the story we are telling. What quickly emerges when the locales of the new schools are plotted is the fact that most were being built further away from the main cities and closer to the villages. This was hardly a matter of happenstance. Rather, we find that in many cases these schools were established in response to the demands of the local population. Take, for example, the village of Bishmizeen—a village of many emigrants. Around 1892 the people of Bishmizeen decided that it was important for their children to obtain an education. Thus, a delegation of village elders approached the Greek Orthodox bishop in Tripoli with a request to establish a school in Bishmizeen. The bishop vacillated and recommended that the villagers send "their children to the Russian mission school in the neighboring village of Amyoun."[113] This solution was not acceptable to the delegates from Bishmizeen, who deemed their village important enough to warrant its own school. The bishop then responded by saying that the people of Bishmizeen were enough trouble as it was and with an education they would become unbearable. Such a tactless argument only roused the delegates to proclaim that if the Greek Orthodox Church could not supply its parishioners with an education, then they would have to resort to the "American Missionaries."[114] The bishop upped the ante by obliquely hinting that such a move might threaten their children's religious well-being—that is, they might be excommunicated. Not to be deterred, one of the delegates replied, "Your Holiness, we don't mean that our children should change their faith; we want them to be educated as your Holiness was at a mission school. Your Holiness did not change your faith, and our children need not change theirs."[115] The delegates then went back to the missionaries and asked them to open a school, which they did.

Ba'abdat, Bayt Shabab, Bikfaiya, Baskinta, Zahleh, and Jubayl were all towns like Bishmizeen where schools were built to accommodate the growing demand for education. What is also interesting in all of these—and other—cases is that a third to a half of the townspeople were returned emigrants. Without assuming that those who did not emigrate had no desire to educate their children, we can still argue that returned emigrants pushed this trend more than others did. We can make that statement because returned emigrants—more commonly than other Lebanese—were able to afford the relatively high cost of schooling in the predominantly private institutions of the Mountain. At the St. Joseph school in Bikfaiya, for example, the cost of education in the early 1900s averaged around 220 French francs for boarders and 80 francs for nonboarders.[116] Costs aside, their experience abroad made it more likely that emigrants would accept educating their children as a "normal" part of raising them. While they were in the *mahjar,* many of these emigrants had grown accustomed to sending their children to public schools, if for no other reason than the fact that the law required it. Beyond the arm-twisting laws, emigrants had encountered the debates that raged across the pages of Arab-American newspapers about women's education and status within society. They had carried those discussions into their coffeehouses and living rooms and had gone back and forth between the pros and cons of educating girls. These various factors accounted for the large percentage (76.7 percent) of emigrant children who were attending schools (public and otherwise) in New York, for example. Similar high rates existed as well among the emigrant community in Argentina and Brazil.[117] Therefore, in addition to the fact that they had the financial wherewithal, exposure to education made returned emigrants more prone to send their girls to school than were those who had stayed behind.

But there was a far more utilitarian and, perhaps, compelling reason for families to provide their daughters with an education: "marriageability." Preparing a young woman through education to be a "goddess" of the house was considered more and more of a necessity to enhance her chances of betrothal to a man of good social standing. Here we find the remainder of the cycle which tied class with gender. Young women needed to be educated in order to be better wives and to be able to marry well; doing so would guarantee them—and, by extension, their families—a place within the middle class. As the Maronite Monsignor Emmanuel Pharès argued in 1908, young women should be taught (according to the "American" model) how to run the household economy and contribute to it by better management of their time in order to attract returning emigrant men.[118] A more popular remark, common in the early 1900s, affirmed that "she is a school girl now; we cannot hope to have her marry our [poor] son!"[119] Underlying these and many other similar statements is the keen awareness that the institution of marriage, itself, was in the process of changing. Within the ranks of this emerging rural middle class, marriage was being transformed—however slowly and incompletely—from a mechanism for solidifying the patrilineal bonds of a clan into one that reinforced relations within the same social class. To fully comprehend this transformation we need to cast a glance at marriage traditions that predated the emigration movement.

Marriage

As far back as the seventeenth century, the process of marriage among Maronite peasants followed a common path, with few occasional and minor variations. Generally, at the age of sixteen or seventeen a young boy was considered ready for marriage, and "the parents would search for a companion worthy of their son and of the family."[120] Marriage had to be contracted between *majaweez,* or "marriageables."[121] These were families whose heritage and lineage were considered by other families honorable enough to allow for intermarriage. More likely than not the "companion" would be a close paternal cousin from within the extended clan.[122] This tradition cut across the social classes and religious boundaries to apply to everyone who resided on the Mountain.

For instance, William Polk, in his study *The Opening of South Lebanon: 1788–1840*, found that of 189 marriages in the Druze family 'Abd as-Samad of 'Ammatur, 171 were contracted between paternal cousins. Similarly, the Abu Shaqra clan favored patrilineal cousin marriage in 149 of 184 marriages.[123] Among the Maronite families in the village of Bsus before 1873, only 6 percent of all marriages were contracted with members of different clans.[124]

The pressure to marry cousins was at times so extreme as to pit son against parents. For instance, in 1870 in the town of Dayr al-Qamar a young man from the Basilius clan wanted to marry a young woman from the Kik clan. His parents, however, insisted that he marry one of his cousins, and when he persisted in his refusal, they locked him up in "one of those vaults specially assigned to those who commit an offense or go against the opinion of his parents in family matters." Finally, the young man succeeded in escaping and eloping with his lover to Turkey.[125] If this tradition of eloping—well established as it was in the Mountain—provided a safety valve for the social system, it was also the exception to the rule: most young people submitted to their parents' opinion in marriage matters.

If not every young man married his cousin, the rest tended to marry from within the same village. Endogamous marriage was much preferred to exogamous marriage as practice and tradition verbalized in proverbs show. For example: "He who marries from a distant area is like that who drinks from a jar [i.e., he does not know what is in the water], and he who marries from his village is like that who drinks from a glass [i.e., he knows whether the water is clean or dirty.]"[126] Another was more explicit: "The daughter of your village will carry through good and bad."[127] Available statistics show these proverbs to be descriptive of reality. In the town of Bsus, in the Shūf region, the number of endogamous marriages between 1873 and 1882 amounted to about 87 percent of the total nuptials.[128] In the village of 'Ammatur—also in the Shūf region—only 16 out of 189 marriages in the 'Abd as-Samad clan were contracted with families from other villages. Similarly, in 187 marriages in the Abu Shaqra clan, only twenty-four brides were from a village outside 'Ammatur. Even in the few cases where the bride and the groom were from separate villages, the distance that separated them was rarely more than ten miles.[129] Finally, in the Greek Orthodox village of Munsif, no exogamous marriages were recorded before 1890.[130]

The overwhelming predominance of cousin marriage—common to most Mediterranean societies—arose from the economic conditions in Mount Lebanon. As Jane Schneider argues for the case of southern Italy and Greece, fragmentation of the land in an area where resources are limited meant a reduction in the power of the family. It also multiplied the boundaries which a family had to defend and increased the potential for conflict over encroachments by one person on another's patrimony.[131] Cousin marriage thus kept the land in the same clan and established social ties between its members in a way that defused most disagreements over land. And when conflicts arose, they were kept within the boundaries of the clan, whose elders would act as judges in such matters to limit any divisive interference from the outside. A more positive reason for the predominance of lineage endogamy among Lebanese peasantry derives from the nature of the land itself. As Robert Creswell argues, land could only become capital for the peasants if it was terraced for farming. Therefore, the lineage that had the most sons and that practiced lineage endogamy could, "by putting more and more land into cultivation, increase its capital at each succeeding generation."[132]

However, the financial prowess of the new rural middle class—which consisted largely of returned emigrants—made these issues less important. Specifically, by the end of the nineteenth century, returned emigrants were relying on their financial capital (and not their human capital) to increase their landholdings. *Al-Mashriq* magazine lamented this fact while noting that emigrants, who had spent many years toiling in some part of the Americas, were investing in land that returned no more than 1.5 percent rather than in projects with higher returns.[133] Examples of investment in land abound. A woman and her husband from Hadeth el-Jobbeh returned from Mexico to the village and bought about 200 *dirhems* of land when the three main notables of that village collectively owned 248 *dirhems*.[134] In 1898 Assaf Khater returned to his native village of Lehfed after a seven-year stay in Uruguay and invested a good part of his savings in large plots of land.[135] In total, of the estimated $8 million that came back from the *mahjar*, close to half was invested in land. In short, many returned emigrants had the money to buy land and thus did not need to depend on a large family to carve it out of the mountain. This made cousin marriage less pertinent to them as gentlemen farmers. What had become more critical was the articulation and preservation of an elevated social status. Thus, many rural middle-class families moved away from relying primarily on lineage in assessing the "marrigeability" of a potential groom or bride and began to place more emphasis on wealth (the crass definition of social class). But, here again, it would be far too simple to assume that only money mattered. Equally, the changed expectations of emigrant men helped transform the meaning of marriage. In the *mahjar*, most of them were exposed, to one extent or another, to a more cosmopolitan life where many women were educated and more liberated in their social milieu. In the cities of Boston and Buenos Aires, they saw—from the doorways—the ideal middle-class home: the woman beautifying that haven while waiting for her husband to return from his daily encounter with a tumultuous world. In the Arab-American press they read (or listened to someone reading) essays about the virtues of an educated bride and companion and about the vices of arranged cousin-marriages. They themselves, as a result of their peddling activities, had learned enough of a foreign language and arithmetic to at least assume greater sophistication and knowledge. Thus, their experiences during years of peddling in cities, their exposure to a more urbane life-style, and the education they acquired combined to change their social attitudes and expectations. One commentator back in Lebanon summarized the metamorphosis by saying of these emigrant men that they had a difficult choice because "the young woman of their class [is] lamentably lacking intellectually."[136] Thus, they wanted a more educated woman of a better class to equal their individual achievements, be they real or imagined.

By the 1910s, this change in attitudes and the emergence of a middle class launched a trend—reflected in marriage records—toward exogamous marriages in Mount Lebanon. Returning to the village of Bsus, we find that while only 13 percent of marriages were exogamous between 1873 and 1882; that percentage leapt to 34 percent in the years between 1893 and 1902.[137] In Munsif, the percentage of exogamous marriages went from zero—between 1860 and 1889—to 12.5 percent by 1914 and to 33 percent by 1930.[138] Even in the remote village of Hadeth el-Jobbeh, exogamous marriage had taken hold by the beginning of World War I, at which time 11 percent of all marriages were exogamous.[139] When compared with marital trends among Muslims (who rarely emigrated), this shift becomes even more pronounced. In the Muslim village of Haouch el-Harimi, 86 percent of the 283 contracted marriages in 1963 were endogamous, and the 40 who did marry someone from outside the village chose the spouses from close by.[140] And as late as 1980, 50 percent of Muslim marriages in Lebanon were contracted among cousins, whereas among Christians this figure was only 22 percent.[141]

If these numbers tell us anything, it is that marriage was in a state of flux by the first decade of the twentieth century. "Traditional" cousin-marriages, which were arranged by families, persisted alongside a "modern" type of marriage where lineage was but one consideration, at best. Wealth, education, and even premarital love were added, in various portions, to the formula of marriage. Rather than creating a "modern" and singular tradition of betrothal, these factors simply made for greater uncertainty as to the meaning and purpose of this institution within the middle-class society under construction. Was marriage solely the means to bring forth children and populate the society, or was it a culmination of the love between two people? Or both? If cousins should not necessarily be wedded, then how were people to select their spouses? Was money more important than schooling, or was it the other way around? How was beauty to be measured? Should love conquer religious and social boundaries?

Answers were not easy to come by, but many tried to arrive a some definitions. One of the most comprehensive of these attempts was a serialized essay by Elias Tweyni entitled "The Philosophy of Marriage." In trying to introduce his readers to a new meaning of marriage, Tweyni began by describing the history of marriage among various peoples (Persians, Romans, Greeks, Gaels). His purpose for such a circuitous journey to "modern" marriage was to affirm that throughout many times and places "a man cannot be a man and neither the woman a woman . . . except in marriage." Yet, he also argued that marriage is not static but changes with times and place. Therefore, for Lebanese society on the cusp of the twentieth century, he provided a "model" notion of marriage. He emphasized that marriage is a union of two individuals, one that should be based on "compatibility in morals, characteristics and interests." A peasant woman and a middle-class man, or the reverse, would be hard-pressed to share any of these elements. Without excluding the family from playing a role in arranging this confluence of two individuals, Tweyni reminded his readers that in the end the man and the woman decide such crucial matters. Beyond a shared culture, Tweyni counseled, "no rational person can deny that a poor educated woman is better [as a wife] than a rich ignorant one."[142] It was not that he considered money unimportant but that an ignorant woman would squander her "husband's wealth" while an educated one would certainly add to the financial well-being of the family by being frugal and not as inclined toward "senseless" expenditures on "make-up and clothes." Finally, Tweyni contended that for marriage to work properly "the man must not abuse his authority over her, and the woman must not demean his rights."[143] In other words, it must be based on "true love," whereby the man treats his wife as his equal "not only because she is a woman but because she is his wife," and the woman supports her husband and listens to his counsel. Tweyni concluded his treatise by stating, "If the husband and wife understand all of this then they will live happily ever after."[144] Tweyni was expounding the same ideology as various reformers in Egypt, Iran, and Turkey. In place of supposed awe of wife for husband, he proposed a friendship. In other words, he was intent on redirecting the attention of the woman and the man from their homosocial spheres toward a heterosexual sociability that unites them in a familial unit isolated from kin and directed toward the "nation."

Conclusion

Tweyni and others were writing against the backdrop of what they understood of peasant "traditions" of marriage and gender relations. Equality, love, and mutual individual interests were posited in sharp contrast to inequality, arranged betrothal, and the interests of the clan. This opposition—along with the juxtaposition of the *harat* with peasant homes and of education with "ignorance"—was necessary and integral to the process of defining the boundaries of the middle class. Central to this process was gender and its "modern" articulation into two separate "but equal" spheres. Ideally, one was the private and serene domain of the "home," where women were supposed to reign as "goddesses" who created an earthly haven for the family and trained the children of the nation. The other was the harsh "public" world of commerce, government, and trade, where men toiled in endless competition to gather money and support their families.

This cultural process gained a particularly vigorous social momentum in Lebanon because its ideological contents overlapped with the practical desires of a large group of Lebanese who had returned from the *mahjar* with new money and manners. Over the span of three decades (1890–1920) these emigrants employed their money to build new houses, to buy land, and to educate their children. Their actions were meant both to distinguish them from the peasants surrounding them in the villages of their birth and to allow them to live in greater comfort. To give meaning to their departures, returned emigrants sought to associate themselves with the "modern" as they had experienced it in the *mahjar* and as they read about it in the newspapers of Beirut. From both sources, they articulated their own notions of the "modern," and they applied them to their own lives. In this regard, new ideas about gender, family, love, and marriage became metaphors for "modernity." *Franji* clothes on the backs of rural middle-class women were a distinctive sign of the "modern"; education of girls was a boundary that separated the lot of peasants from a refined middle-class life; and the circumscribing of women's homosociality was deemed to be "progress." In other words, many emigrants displayed their "modernity" by embracing and helping to define a new meaning of "womanhood." To inculcate this "natural" state of being into their daughters, they sent them to schools which taught them the art of managing a household and which prepared them to be better wives and mothers. They would also be prepared to marry into a better social status and thus continue the cycle of producing and reproducing a middle class. However, not all were happy with this new state of being.

Notes

1. A whole host of studies on "modernity" in the Middle East—especially as it pertains to the construction of the category "woman"—have come out. The publication of Abu-Lughod's edited book *Remaking Women: Feminism and Modernity in the Middle East,* with eight contributors, is a sign of the maturing of this area of studies. For specific examples, see Najmabadi's *The Story of the Daughters of Quchan,* or Pollard's dissertation, "Nurturing the Nation."

2. Kumkum Sangari and Sudesch Vaid, *Recasting Women: Essays in Indian Colonial History* (New Brunswick: Rutgers University Press, 1990), 10–11.

3. National Archives, dispatches from the U.S. Consuls in Beirut, U.S./143, Ravndal, "Naturalized Americans of Syrian Origin," 14 October 1903.

4. Ibid., U.S/256, Ravndal, "Report on Emigration," 12 September 1903.

5. This hypothetical number was arrived at in the following manner. If we assume a constant rate of return of 12,000 individuals every five years (an unsubstantiated guess, to be sure), then between 1894 and 1914 we can calculate that 48,000 individuals returned to the Mountain. (Although emigration started around 1887, it would have been at least seven years before any appreciable numbers started the journey back.) In this same time period about 106,715 emigrants arrived in the United States. This estimate leads us (by dividing 48,000 by 106,715) to 45 percent.

6. Immigration Commission, *Reports of the Immigration Commission: Statistical Review of Immigration, 1820–1910,* 61st Cong., 3rd sess., 1911, S. Doc. 756.

7. *Rapport du Commandant Pechkoff,* Archives du Ministère des Affaires Étrangères, vol. 410, p. 59, 19 May 1927; quoted in K. Hashimoto's "Lebanese Population Movement 1920–1939," in A. H. N. Shedadi (ed.), *Lebanese in the World: A Century of Emigration* (London: The Centre for Lebanese Studies and I.B. Tauris, 1993), 66.

8. Arthur Ruppin, *Syrien als Wirtschaftsgebiet* (Berlin: E. S. Mittler & Sohn, 1917), 19.

9. Nabil Harfush, *al-Hūdūr al-Lubnani fi al-'alam,* vol. 1 (Beirut: Matabi' al-Karim al-Hadithah, 1974), 49.

10. Our only solace is that this is a fairly common state of affairs for all studies of returning emigrants. Gabaccia discusses the problem with official Italian and American statistics in her study *Militants and Migrants: Rural Sicilians become American Workers* (New Brunswick: Rutgers University Press, 1988), 177–79. A Finnish scholar concluded his survey of Finland's official statistics on return migration by describing them as "incontrovertibly extremely deficient"; Reino Kero, "The Return of Emigrants from America to Finland," *Publications of the Institute of General History* (University of Turku, Finland No. 4, 1972), 11–13. On the problems of German statistics for the pre-1880 era, see Walter D. Kamphoefner, "The Volume and Composition of German-American Return Migrations," in *A Century of European Migrations, 1830–1930,* ed. Rudolph J. Vecoli and Suzanne M. Sinke (Urbana: University of Illinois Press, 1991), 296–99. Even the editor of a volume of papers from a European conference on international return migration (mainly since World War II) could conclude only that "returns are quite difficult to assess with any statistical accuracy"; Daniel Kubat, ed., *The Politics of Return: International Return Migration in Europe; Proceedings of the First European Conference on International Return Migration* (Rome, November 11–14, 1981) (New York: Center for Migration Studies, 1983), 4.

11. The calculations for this number were based on the fact that, by 1914, 136,060 Lebanese had emigrated to Argentina, another 55,954 had arrived in Brazil, and 106,424 had come to the United States. Sources for Argentina: *La Siria nueva: Obra historica, estadistica y comercial de la colectividad Sirio-Otomana en las Republicas Argentina y Uruguay* (Buenos Aires: Empressa Assalam, 1917), 19; for Brazil: *Revista de Imigração e Colonização* (Rio de Janeiro: Ministério das Relaçes Exteriores, July 1940); for the United States: Immigration and Naturalization Service, *Annual Report 1914,* 63rd Cong., 3rd sess., 1915.

12. Mark Wyman, *Round-Trip to America: The Immigrants Return to Europe, 1880–1930* (Ithaca, N.Y.: Cornell University Press, 1993), 4.

13. Edward Steiner, *On the Trail of the Immigrant* (New York: Revell, 1906), 334–35.

14. Quoted in Abdel Nour Jabbour, *Étude sur la poésie dialectale au Liban* (Beirut: Publications de l'Université Libanaise, 1957), 159.

15. Quoted in ibid., 176.

16. *Forverts,* 24 November 1902, quoted in Zosa Szajkowski, "Deportation of Jewish Immigrants and Returnees before World War I," *American Jewish Historical Quarterly* 67 (June 1978): 305.

17. *Lubnan,* 1 October 1906.

18. *Lubnan,* 13 September 1906.

19. See Lahad Khatir's *'Ahd al-mutasarrifin fi Lubnan* (Beirut: Catholic Press, 1962) and Asad Rustum's *Lubnan fi 'ahd al-Mustasarrifiyya* (Beirut: Publications de l'Université Libanaise, 1954).

20. See Salim Hassan Hashi, *Yawmiyyāt lubnani fi ayām al-Mutasarrifiyya* (Beirut: Lahad Khater, 1983).

21. See Paul Jouplain's *La Question du Liban: etude d'histoire diplomatique & de droit international* (Paris: Rousseau, 1908; reprint, Beirut: alAhliyah lil-Nashr wa-alTawzi, 1995) for a treatise on an independent Christian Lebanon.

22. Yusuf As'ad Daghir, *Qamus al-sahafa al-lubnaniyya (1858–1974)* (Beirut: al-Jami' ah al-Lubnaniyya: al-Tawz'i, al-Maktabah al-Sharqiyah, 1978), 5.

23. Isma'il Haqqi, *Lubnan: Mababith 'ilmiyya wa ijtimā'yya wa siyāsīyya* (Ba'abda: al-Matba' al-'Uthmaniya, 1913) 2: 222.

24. By the end of the nineteenth century, new Cairo had expanded north of the old city and then west to include the "modern" quarters of Zamalek. Damascus was also expanding into new urbanized areas for the middle classes up the slopes of Jabal Qasiyun. For Heliopolis, a modern, middle-class neighborhood of Cairo, see Robert Ilbert, *Héliopolis: le Caire, 1905–1922: Genèse d'un ville* (Paris: Editions du centre National de la Recherche Scientifique, 1981), or Trevor Mostyn, *Egypt's Belle Époque: Cairo: 1827–1952* (New York: Quartet, 1989). One of the best studies of Istanbul, which documents the demographic growth of the city as well as the changing habits of its emerging middle class is Alan Duben and Cem Behar, *Istanbul Households: Marriage, Family, and Fertility, 1880–1940* (New York: Cambridge University Press, 1991), esp. 87–121, 148–58, 194–248.

25. May Davie, "Beyrouth et ses faubourgs: 1840–1940," in *Les Cahiers du Centre d'Etude et de Recherche sur le Moyen-Orient Contemporain,* no. 15 (Beirut: Centre D'Etude et de Recherche sur le Moyen-Orient Contemporain, 1996), chs. 1, 2. This same phenomenon was taking place in Algiers, Rabat, and Tunis, where the new *villes* were growing outside the boundaries of the old ones and where the middle-class merchants, bankers, clerks, doctors, lawyers, journalists, and government employees lived along with a sizable foreign community.

26. This phenomenon was not limited to Lebanon. "The American house" was a common sight across the European landscape. As Italy's statesman Francesco Saverio Nitti observed, "In tiny villages, the pick-axe strikes down the filthy hovels . . . and the new homes of 'Americani' began to rise." Quoted in Francesco Paolo Cerase, "From Italy to the United States and Back: Returned Migrants, Conservative or Innovative?" (Ph.D. diss., Columbia University, 1971), 111–12. One finds similar observations in Julianna Puskás, *From Hungary to the United States (1880–1914),* tr. Eva Palmai (Budapest: Akademiai Kiado, 1982), 79–80; Dino Cinel, *The National Integration of Italian Return Migration, 1870–1929* (New York: Cambridge University Press, 1991), 163–64; Immigration Commission, *Report of the Immigration Commission: Statistical Review of Immigration,* 61st Cong., 3rd sess., 1911, S. Doc. 747.

27. For a detailed description of this house, see Michel Feghali, "Notes sur la maison libanaise," in *Mélanges René Basset* (Paris: Publications de l'Institut des Hautes-Études Marocaines, 1923), 1: 163–86.

28. A *tannour* is a half-domed metallic surface where thin, pizzalike crusts of dough are placed to cook. It sits on top of a ring of stones and is heated from underneath with wood.

29. Most notable of those with clouded notions was Alphonse de Lamartine, whose book, *A Pilgrimage to the Holy Land; Comprising Recollections, Sketches, and Reflections, Made during a Tour in the East* (New York: D. Appleton, 1848), was naive in its observations to say the least, full of precon-

ceived romantic images that had little to do with reality. Even contemporaries were aware of that bias. Another French romantic observer was the Vicomtesse d'Aviau de Piolant, who recorded her highly impressionistic recollections about Mount Lebanon in a book entitled *Au pays des Maronites* (Paris: Librairie H. Oudin, 1882). Lebanese folklorists provided equally romantic images of the Lebanese house and of village life in general, but for more political reasons. Most of these writers tended to be Maronite Christians, who were loathe to admit any relationship between the surrounding Arab culture and that of the Maronite community. Thus they argued, with a great stretch of the imagination at times, that the Maronites had safeguarded their Aramaic, Syriac, Phoenician, *marada*, or even European heritage. For example, Feghali, in his article "Notes sur la maison libanaise," wrote, "The conclusion which we can reach is that on this point in particular, as with many others, the Arab and Turkish civilization did not succeed, at any moment, to impose itself in Lebanon. The Lebanese, in addition to having kept their vocabulary in large part Syriac, still exist in the same way as their ancestors from the early Christian centuries. . . . It is for this that we still find today a striking similarity between the actual inhabitants of Lebanon and the ancient peoples of Syria: Arameans, Canaanites and Hebrews" (185–86).

30. David Urquhart, *The Lebanon (Mount Souria): A History and a Diary.* 2 vols. (London: Thomas Coutley Newby, 1860), 1: 233–34.

31. F. Bart, *Scènes et tableaux de la vie actuelle en Orient—Mont Liban* (Paris, 1883), 42.

32. Wood was becoming a rare commodity in Lebanon as early as the 1860s and 1870s. "Because of the unchecked logging and herding of goats in the mountains Lebanon has lost the great majority of its wood resources." Haqqi, *Lubnan*, 2: 94.

33. A nice house of this type with six pillars would have measured about eighty-eight square meters.

34. For a list of the household possessions of one of the Khazin *shuyukh*, see Dominique Chevallier's "Que possédait un cheikh Maronite en 1859? Un document de la famille al-Khazin," *Arabica* 7 (1960): 80–84.

35. William Roe Polk, *The Opening of South Lebanon, 1788–1840: A Study of the Impact of the West on the Middle East* (Cambridge, Mass.: Harvard University Press, 1963), 184.

36. John Gulick notes that "none of the existing examples of it [this new style of house] in Munsif is probably more than a hundred and fifty years old [1800], and some are probably as little as sixty years old [1890]," *Social Structure and Cultural Change in a Lebanese Village* (New York: Wenner-Gren Foundation for Anthropological Research, 1955), 34. In the village of Lehfed, local informants indicated the late 1800s as the time when this new style of house appeared in the village (personal interviews with the priest and the mayor of the village).

37. Friedrich Ragette, *Architecture in Lebanon: The Lebanese House during the 18th and 19th Centuries* (Delmar, N.Y.: Caravan Books, 1980), 45.

38. Jacqueline des Villettes, *La Vie des femmes dans un village Maronite libanais, Ain el Kharoubé* (Tunis: Impr. N. Bascone and S. Muscat, 1964), 9.

39. See, for example, Soraya Antonius's *Architecture in Lebanon* (Beirut: Khayat's, 1965) and Ragette's *Architecture in Lebanon*.

40. See, for example, Robert Saliba's *Beirut 1920–1940: Domestic Architecture between Tradition and Modernity* (Beirut: Order of Engineers and Architects, 1998), esp. ch. 4.

41. Zeynep Çelik, *The Remaking of Istanbul: Portrait of an Ottoman City in the Nineteenth Century* (Seattle: University of Washington Press, 1986), 137.

42. Ragette, *Architecture in Lebanon*, 92.

43. Feghali, "Notes sur la maison libanaise," 178.

44. Ibid., 169.

45. Gulick, *Social and Cultural Change in a Lebanese Village*, 34.

46. AE CC, Correspondance commerciale, Beyrouth, July 29, 1890.

47. Ibid.

48. Ernest Weakley, "Report on the Condition and Prospects of British Trade in Syria," *Parliamentary Accounts & Papers*, Cd. 5707 (1911).

49. AE CC, Correspondance commerciale, Beyrouth, vol. 10, report entitled "Situation de l'industrie et du commerce de Beyrouth en 1892," April 7, 1888; and vol. 13, May 13, 1905. Weakley, "Report on the Condition and Prospects of British Trade in Syria."

50. Weakley, "Report on the Condition and Prospects of British Trade in Syria," 157.

51. National Archives, dispatches from the U.S. consul in Beirut, U.S./256, Ravndal, "Report on Emigration," 12 September 1903.

52. AE CC, Correspondance commerciale, Beyrouth, February 1890, and dispatch no. 135, 1892.

53. Ibid., vol. 9, 1868; vol. 11, 1895; and vol. 13, 1905. The number of chairs is calculated on the basis of the statistics supplied by the French consulate general in its annual report, which stated that 200,000 francs worth of wooden furniture was imported, with a dozen costing between 25 and 35 francs. The number of imported iron beds is based on statistics supplied by the French consulate general in its commercial correspondence of April 1888 (vol. 10). According to the French consul, the British shipped about 5,178 metric tons worth of iron products to Beirut. Of this, 1,250 tons were steel bars intended for construction, and there were 500 more tons of miscellaneous items. The other 3,428 tons were primarily "English beds that cost about 660 piasters each." Assuming an average weight of 250 kilograms per bed, we arrive at an approximate number of 13,172 sold in one year.

54. Weakley, "Report on the Condition and Prospects of British Trade in Syria," 169.

55. *Lubnan,* 10 June 1907, 1.

56. Khatir, *Al-'Adāt wal-taqālid al-lubnaniyya,* 26, 96.

57. Elias Masabki, "Imitation and Us, Where Is the End," *al-Mashriq* (1913): 636–37.

58. *Lubnan,* 10 June 1907, 4.

59. Shukri al-Bustani, *Dayr al-Qamar fi akhir al-qarn al tasi' 'ashar* (Beirut: Lebanese University Press, 1969), 78–113. Also, interview with author's father with regard to father's childhood.

60. Shakir al-Khuri, *Majma' al-masarrat* (Beirut: Al-Ijtihad Press, 1908), 43.

61. During the summer, the blending of the two spaces achieved its epitome when the family constructed on its plot an *'arzal,* which is a hut made of dried tree branches. Many of the family, especially the men, stayed in their *'arzal* throughout most of the summer.

62. al-Bustani, *Dayr al-Qamar fi akhir al-qarn al tasi' 'ashar,* 67.

63. Ibrahim Bayk al-Aswad, *Daleel Lubnan* (Ba'abda: al-Matba' al-'Uthmaniya, 1906), 359.

64. Ibid., 357.

65. Henri Guys, *Rélation d'un séjour de plusieurs années a Beyrout et dans le Liban* (Paris: Comptoir des Imprimeurs, 1850), 98, 102.

66. *al-Muhazab,* 21 December 1907, 1.

67. Ibrahim Bayk al-Aswad, *Daleel Lubnan* (Ba'abda: al-Matba' al-'Uthmaniya, 1906), 336.

68. Ibid., 329–30.

69. For example, *al-Hasna'* had two articles, in one year, on the proper manner of breastfeeding (vol. 1, 1907, 187 and 191). Another magazine, *Fatat Lubnan,* also dedicated regular space on its pages to this subject. However, being more of a feminist journal, it advocated that girls be breastfed as long as boys.

70. Among peasants the task of caring for an infant was not as complex. Generally, a baby was swaddled tightly and placed in a crib for the first few months of life. More relevantly, the task of breastfeeding the child was considered communal. The tradition was for nursing mothers of the village to visit a new mother shortly after the arrival of her baby and for each of them to suckle the baby at her breast. This was a symbolic gesture of their willingness to be responsible for the baby, but in fact the practice of exchanging nursing continued until the baby was weaned a year later.

71. *al-Hasna'* 1 (January 1910): 380.

72. Rifa'a Tahtawi, *Murshid al-amin lil-banat wal-banin,* vol. 2 of *al-'Amal al-kamila li-Rif'a Rafi' al-Tahtawi/ Dinrasā t wa-tahqīq Muhammad Imarah* (Beirut: al-Muassasa al-'Arabiyya lil-Dirasāt wa-al-Nashr, 1973), 369–78.

73. *al-Hasna'* 1 (June 1909): 26.

74. *al-Hasna'* 2 (March 1911): 381; 1 (January 1910): 214; 1 (September 1909): 123–25.

75. *al-Hasna'* 1 (January 1910): 381.

76. *Fatat Lubnan* 1 (January 1914): 15.

77. al-Aswad, *Daleel Lubnan,* 360, 358.

78. Elias Tweyni, "The Woman," *Lubnan,* 1 October 1895.

79. Ester Muyal, "The Woman's Kingdom: A Discourse on Domestic Politics," *al-Hasna'* 1 (July 1909): 52–55.

80. Mary P. Ryan, *The Empire of the Mother: American Writing about Domesticity, 1830–1860* (New York: Institute for Research in History and the Haworth Press, 1982), 17–18.

81. Quoted in ibid., 358.

82. *Fatat Lubnan* 1 (January 1914): 10.

83. *al-Hasna'* 1 (20 June 1909): 20.

84. H. J. Turtle, *Quaker Service in the Middle East: With a History of the Brummana High School, 1876–1975* (London: Friends Service Council, 1975), 37.

85. This kind of argument was common among early advocates of female education in most areas. For instance, in Egypt, Qasim Amin wrote in his *Tahrir al-mar'a* (Cairo: Maktabat al-Taraqqi, 1899) that educating women was an essential part of improving society and providing suitable partners for educated middle-class men.

86. Ibid., 358.

87. al-Aswad, *Daleel Lubnan,* 362.

88. A list of women's journals that were published in the first decade of the twentieth century includes the following magazines:

Title of Magazine	Editor
al-Fatat (The Young Woman)	Hind Nawfal
Miriat al-Hasna' (Mirror of the Beautiful)	Miriam Mazhar
al-'Aila (The Family)	Ester Muyal
al-Mar'a (The Woman)	Anisa 'Atallah
al-Sa'ada (Happiness)	Rogina 'Awad
al-Zahra (The Flower)	Mariam Mas'ad
Majalat al-Saydat wal-Banat (Magazine for the Ladies and the Girls)	Rosa Antoun
al-Moda (The Fashion)	Salim Khalil Farah
al-Hasna' (The Beautiful)	Jurji Nqula Baz
al-'Arus (The Bride)	Mary 'Ajmi
al-'alam al-Jadid (The New World)	'Afifa Karam
Fatat Lubnan (Lebanon's Girl)	Salima Abi Rashed

89. *Fatat Lubnan* 1 (December 1914): 15–17.

90. Ibid., 17.

91. Quoted in Tani Barlow, "Theorizing Woman: Funu, Guojia, Jiating (Chinese Women, Chinese State, Chinese Family)," in *Feminism and History,* ed. Joan Wallach Scott (Oxford: Oxford University Press, 1996), 204.

92. "An Essay Devoted to Education of Girls (*Maqalah-'i makhsus dar ta'lim-i 'awrat*)," *Habl al-matin* 9, no. 12 (6 January 1902): 16. Quoted in Afsaneh Najmabadi, "Crafting an Educated House-wife in Iran," in *Remaking Women: Feminism and Modernity in the Middle East,* ed. Lila Abu-Lughod (Princeton, N.J.: Princeton University Press, 1998), 104.

93. This intertwining of a strong "nation" and the new "woman" derived in part from the similarity in the nature of European imperial and colonial projects across the globe. Whether in South Asia, China, Egypt, West Africa, or North Africa, colonialists underscored the "need" for their occupation and domination through the argument of cultural superiority and the notion of "lifting the lesser peoples." This need was nowhere more "evident" to the Europeans than when it

came to the position of women in these colonized societies. Thus sati, purdah, foot-binding, and harem became signifiers of the supposed backwardness of the colonized and—in reverse—of the superiority of the colonizer.

94. Turtle, *Quaker Service in the Middle East,* 42.

95. H. Jalabert, *Un montagnard contre le pouvoir: Liban 1866* (Beirut: al-Machreq, 1978), 134.

96. *Les Pères Jesuits à Ghazir 1844–1944* (Jounieh: Kaslik University Press, 1944), 56.

97. Khatir, *Al-'Adāt wal-taqālid al-lubnaniyya,* 371.

98. Papers of the American Board of Commissioners for Foreign Missions, Houghton Library, Harvard University, series ABC: 16.6, vol. iii, document 217, "Schedule of Schools in Syria 1826."

99. Ibid., series ABC: 16.8.1, vol. iv, report on the Syrian Mission dated 31 December 1835.

100. Haqqi, *Lubnan,* 2: 192.

101. AE CC, Correspondance commerciale, Beyrouth, vol. 8, annex to dispatch no. 39, March 22, 1870.

102. Ibid.

103. Constantin Petkovich, *Lubnan wal-Lubnaniyun,* Tr. Yusuf 'Atallah (Beirut: al-Mada, 1986 [1885]), 150.

104. Ibid., 135–37.

105. Haqqi, *Lubnan,* 2: 200.

106. Ibid., 2: 572.

107. J. D. Maitland-Kirwan, *Sunrise in Syria: A Short History of the British Syrian Mission, from 1860–1930* (London: British Syrian Mission, 1930), 40–44.

108. Cited in Vital Cuinet, *Syrie, Liban et Palestine: Géographie administrative, statistique, descriptive, et raisonnée* (Paris: Lerous, 1896), 72–73.

109. Ibid., 83.

110. Mūnzer Jaber, "Pouvoir et société au Jabal 'Amil de 1749 à 1920," Ph.D diss., University of Paris IV, 1978, 184.

111. All the preceding comparative figures were collated from Kemal H. Karpat's *Ottoman Population, 1830–1914: Demographic and Social Characteristics* (Madison: University of Wisconsin Press, 1985), Tables IV.3 (Population Distribution) and IV.12 (Pupils Attending Schools), 211 and 219, respectively.

112. Ibid., Table IV.12 (Pupils Attending Schools), 219.

113. Afif Tannous, "Trends of Social and Cultural Change in a Lebanese Village: Bishmizeen." Ph.D Diss., Yale University, 1939, 178.

114. Ibid.

115. Report of the Presbyterian Mission at Tripoli, Lebanon, in Presbyterian Church in the United States, Board of Foreign Missions, *Fifty-fifth Annual Report of the Board of Foreign Missions of the Presbyterian Church in the United States* (New York, 1898).

116. AE CC, Correspondance commerciale, Beyrouth, vol. 12, "Rapport sur l'état économique, sociale et politique du Mont Liban," 1901.

117. Rates for the United States: Lucius Hopkins Miller, *Our Syrian Population: A Study of the Syrian Communities of Greater New York* (San Francisco: Reed, 1969 [1905]), 23; for Brazil: Clark Knowlton, "The Social and Spatial Mobility of the Syrian and Lebanese Community in São Paulo, Brazil," in *The Lebanese in the World: A Century of Emigration,* edited by Albert Hourani and Nadim Shehadi (London: Centre for Lebanese Studies and Tauris, 1992), 298; for Argentina: Ignacio Klich, "*Criollos* and Arabic Speakers in Argentina: An Uneasy *Pas de Deux,* 1888–1914," in *The Lebanese in the World,* 264.

118. Mgsr. Emmanuel Pharès, *Les Maronites du Liban.* Lille: n.p., 1908, 28.

119. Quoted in Afif Tannous, "Social Change in an Arab Village," *American Sociological Review* 6 (1941), 657.

120. Ibid. To marry a boy off at such an early age guaranteed two things. First, his economic dependence and young age made him more susceptible to his parents' will. Second, and perhaps more important, was the issue of sexuality. In a close living environment—within the tiny houses

as well as within the small village—sexuality had to be tightly controlled in order to safeguard the social structure from the upheaval that might be set loose by premarital sex.

121. This term was quite common in the villages during the nineteenth century, but its use has lapsed to the point that today not many would understand the reference. See Anis Furayha, *Hadara fi tarīq al-zawāl: al-Qarya al-lubnaniyya* (Beirut: n.p., 1957), 152.

122. See Robert Creswell, "Lineage Endogamy among Maronite Mountaineers," in *Mediterranean Family Structures* (London: Cambridge University Press, 1976), 101.

123. Polk, *The Opening of South Lebanon,* 175–89.

124. Joseph Abu-Najm, "Recherche ethnologique sur le mariage dans un village libanais: Bsus" (Ph.D. diss., Université de Paris III, 1984), 122.

125. al-Bustani, *Dayr el-Qamar fi akhir al-qarn al-tasiʿʿashar,* 118.

126. Khatir, *Al-ʿAdāt wal-taqālid al-lubnaniyya,* 246.

127. Anis Furayha, *A Dictionary of Modern Lebanese Proverbs* (Beirut: Libraire du Liban, [1974]), 196.

128. Abu-Najm, "Recherche ethnologique sur le mariage dans un village libanais," 147.

129. Polk, *The Opening of South Lebanon,* 175–89.

130. Gulick, *Social Structure and Culture Change in a Lebanese Village,* 130.

131. Jane Schneider, "Of Vigilance and Virgins: Honor, Shame, and Access to Resources in Mediterranean Societies," *Ethnology* 10, no. 1 (January 1971): 1–24.

132. Robert Creswell, "Lineage Endogamy among Maronite Mountaineers," in *Mediterranean Family Structures* (London: Cambridge University Press, 1976), 111.

133. A. Cheikho, "Lubnan: Nathra," *al-Mashriq* 10, no. 9 (1907): 398.

134. Toufic Touma, *Un village de Montagne au Liban (Hadeth el-Jobbé)* (Paris: Mouton, 1958), 107, 110.

135. Personal interview with Najibé Ghanem, daughter of Assaf Khater, 1998.

136. Pharès, *Les Maronites du Liban,* 27.

137. Abu-Najm, "Recherche ethnologique sur le mariage dans un village libanais," 176.

138. Gulick, *Social Structure and Culture Change in a Lebanese Village,* 130.

139. Touma, *Un village de Montagne au Liban,* 83, 87.

140. Judith Williams, *The Youth of Haouch el-Harimi: A Lebanese Village* (Cambridge, Mass.: Center for Middle Eastern Studies of Harvard University, Harvard University Press, 1968), 96.

141. Joseph Chamie, *Religion and Fertility: Arab-Christian-Muslim Differentials* (Cambridge: Cambridge University Press, 1981), 33.

142. Elias Tweyni, "The Philosophy of Marriage," *Lubnan,* 26 September 1895, 3.

143. Ibid., 1.

144. Elias Tweyni, "The Philosophy of Marriage," *Lubnan,* 3 October 1896, 1.

Reinventing Free Labor

Immigrant Padrones and Contract Laborers in North America, 1885–1925

GUNTHER PECK

In the spring of 1911, fifty Greek copper miners from Bingham Canyon, Utah, wrote an angry letter to the governor of Utah, William S. Spry, demanding his intervention against their padrone, Leon Skliris, nicknamed Czar of the Greeks.

> Do you think this is right for Skliris to sell livelihoods to the poor workman at extortion 20 dollars and to thus suck the blood of the poor laborer? Where are we? In the free country of Amerika or in a country dominated by a despotic form of government? . . . Hoping you will liberate us from this padrone, who is ravaging the blood of the poor laborer.[1]

For these highly mobile young men, the American West, region of free land and free labor, had become instead a mocking backdrop to their suffering, a place whose oppressions seemed even worse than what they had recently escaped under the Turks. Their questions to Governor Spry underscore just how profoundly Skliris had turned their expectations of free labor in "Amerika" upside down: In signing Skliris's work contracts, Greek workers found, instead of freedom, endless deductions from their wages. In seeking the best prices on Bingham's "free" market, Greeks faced a grim choice: exorbitant prices at the Panhellenic Grocery store, run by Skliris's brother, or unemployment and another round of job fees should they stay in Bingham. When Greek workers quit their jobs and left Bingham, they encountered, not freedom, but more job fees as Skliris controlled access to nearly all mining and railroad jobs in Utah. In short, rather than finding freedom and democracy in the American West, Greek workers found bondage and "despotism."

This essay explores how padrones such as Leon Skliris used hallmarks of "free" labor relations—the wage contract and the right to quit—to create an expansive system of coercive labor relations in the North American West between 1885 and 1925.[2] It extends the insights of critical legal studies scholars, such as Amy Dru Stanley, William E. Forbath, and Robert Steinfeld, who have explored how aspects of a free-labor legal system sometimes sanctioned coercive labor relations in the late nineteenth century.[3] But this essay moves beyond the confines of critical legal studies, which remain focused primarily on the meanings of particular laws and legal doctrines. Instead, it explores the geographic and cultural contexts in which diverse immigrant workers and their padrones defined and redefined notions of voluntary contract and free labor.[4] Not only did padrones use contracts and the legal system to create coercive labor relations, but much of their power grew without *any* formal legal sanctions. Padrones controlled immigrant workers primarily by exploiting their geographic mobility and the family networks that sustained it. Paradoxically, they transformed workers' freedom to move and to quit into building blocks of padrone power.

The essay focuses on three individual padrones and the immigrant workers they imported to the North American West. Antonio Cordasco, an Italian immigrant, was based in Montreal, Quebec, but he sent Italian workers vast distances across the Canadian plains to British Columbia as railroad workers for the Canadian Pacific Railway. Roman Gonzalez, a Mexican American, lived in El Paso, Texas, but from there he sent Mexican workers to railroad jobs throughout the southwestern United States and to sugar beet fields in Minnesota and North Dakota. Leon Skliris, a Greek immigrant, lived on the top floor of the Hotel Utah in Salt Lake City and sent Greeks to jobs in coal and copper mines and railroads throughout Utah, Colorado, Nevada, and Idaho. These three men were not the most conspicuous padrones on the continent, but their locations on the borders of the three North American countries highlight the importance of boundaries—cultural, political, and geographic—in the creation and significance of padronism.[5]

By examining how these three padrones exploited the mobility of immigrant workers through space, this essay unravels the paradox that bedeviled Greek workers—why the spacious West could become a place of bondage.[6] It aims to broaden where historians look for class struggles and how they conceptualize them, moving beyond the shop floor and the legal system as sites of working-class resistance and ideological contest.[7] The quest to control labor mobility by padrones, corporate managers, and immigrant workers became crucial to these groups' comprehension of class relations and of free labor in the North American West. During their sojourns, immigrant workers quickly realized how political their mobility was, how connected it was to their identities as men, ethnics, workers, and citizens. In so doing, they learned to control their mobility and discovered strategic advantages in their ability to move and to quit, reinventing the meaning of free labor on terms quite distinct from those of their padrones and corporate bosses.

Although middle-class American reformers defined the padrone as a primitive progenitor of unfree labor relations between 1885 and 1925, padrones possessed close ties to the modern corporation. While reformers at the beginning of the twentieth century described a great variety of immigrant entrepreneurs as padrones, the most successful padrones worked directly for North American corporations, helping them meet their expanding needs for unskilled labor.[8] In 1901, Antonio Cordasco was one of many Italian labor agents competing for corporate business in Montreal, but his success in breaking a major strike on the Canadian Pacific Railway's (CPR) western lines that summer soon earned him the valuable position of "sole Italian labor agent." His ensuing monopolistic choke hold on the importation, hiring, and firing of Italians for Canada's biggest corporation led him to seek even greater glory by being crowned "Re de la lavoratori" (King of the workers) in front of CPR managers in spring 1904. Leon Skliris likewise competed with other Greek labor agents for corporate contracts in the intermountain West until 1910, when he became the Utah Copper Company's salaried labor agent, a position that made him the most powerful padrone in the region. And when Roman Gonzalez secured jobs for three thousand of his compatriots on the Gulf, Colorado, and Santa Fe Railroad in 1907, it appeared he would soon become the critical labor broker among Mexicans in El Paso. Reformers' rhetoric aside, which defined the padrone as an archaic and primitive creation of the Old World, padrones were among the first modernizers of the unskilled labor market, directly linking isolated rural hamlets around the globe with the fluctuating but growing unskilled labor needs of corporations in North America.[9]

Padrones were not the only people stimulating unskilled workers to come to North America, nor the only ones trying to control the migrations. As immigration historians have documented, chain migrations, whereby a pioneering immigrant generates a self-sustaining flow of immigrants by sending passage money to his or her relatives, shaped the timing, direction, and scale of most population movements to North America in the late nineteenth century.[10] Padrone power did not exist in opposition to such networks, however, but rather helped reorganize and stimulate chain migrations. In 1901, for example, Cordasco recruited all two thousand of the CPR's Italian strikebreakers from the unskilled labor markets of Boston and New York. But at the peak of his power in the spring of 1904, fully 65 percent of his contract workers came directly from villages in northern Italy. Skliris likewise initially recruited all of his workers from existing pools of Greek sojourners in North America, but by 1912 he was importing over two hundred of his compatriots to Utah directly each month from villages scattered throughout the southern Peloponnese and the island of Crete. In neither case did padrone power originate in the Old World village or even in the "preindustrial" culture that immigrants left behind. Rather, Cordasco and Skliris gained power first as labor market entrepreneurs in North America and only subsequently reached back to the villages in Europe to organize new chain migrations to North America.[11]

Padrones were at their most modern, however, in the adept use of the forms and rhetoric of free labor to their economic and political advantage. Cordasco required all Italian workers to sign contracts in Italian that legitimated his power to deduct "tributes" from their wages. Cordasco was proud of these contracts, boasting to one of his new agents in Italy that "each man gets a contract in Italian, containing the clear conditions under which they will have to work, in which is specified the length of time, salary, etc. In one word there will be no tricks or schemes." Like an apostle of the doctrine of liberty of contract, Cordasco equated his contracts with truly free labor relations. When the Canadian government investigated his business practices in the summer of 1904, Cordasco acknowledged to government investigators that Italian workers paid him tributes to receive work, but he did not deem them excessive, "unfair," or "unfree." They were, he asserted, part of a contractual exchange that benefited both immigrant workers and himself. When questioned about the fees, he claimed simply, "I took what was right." Cordasco insisted to his agents in New York and Italy that immigrant workers came to Montreal only "by their own free will." Pressed further, he stated without irony, "They forced me to take their money."[12]

Leon Skliris likewise used both the forms and rhetoric of free labor to his advantage. His Greek workers in Utah all signed a contract stating, "I do hereby irrevocably authorize, empower, and direct said Company to deduct one dollar a month out of wages earned . . . and pay same to L. G. Skliris."[13] It is especially noteworthy that the contracts were adapted to any employment the Greek worker sought in Utah or its surrounding industrial enclaves, suggesting just how pervasive Skliris's tribute system was in the region. The contracts were printed only in English, highlighting their dual purpose: to sanction Skliris's deductions and to persuade American companies of the contractual and thus legitimate nature of his dealings with immigrant workers.

But if Skliris succeeded in using contracts to cast himself as a defender of free labor relations, he was equally skilled as the purported Czar of the Greeks in playing the role of outlaw, rising above the law's penalties even when he occasionally lost his battles in court. One of his cleverest triumphs occurred in 1908 when Skliris sued the Giles American Mercantile Agency, a debt collection company, for having wrongfully garnished $198.36 out of his salary as a labor agent for the United States Mining Company in Bingham Canyon in 1906. According to his complaint, Leon Skliris had been confused with a man named Louis Skliris, whom Leon claimed he had never seen or met. Leon conceded that the imposter, Louis, had indeed purchased $198.36 worth of services at St. Mark's Hospital in 1905 in the interest of six injured Greek workers, but he insisted that "his name is not Louis Skliris." Circuit Judge C. W. Morse was persuaded by Leon's case, rewarding him his full judgment plus costs. In point of fact, Louis and Leon Skliris were the same person, as subsequent oral histories and newspaper stories made abundantly clear. To Skliris's closest friends, he was Louis; but to a larger American public, he was Leonidas G. Skliris. To certain of his business associates, Skliris went by the given name of his father, Gust, the name he put down on his petition to become a naturalized American citizen in 1905.[14] Skliris not only exploited the indeterminacy of contracts and notions of free labor, he literally made himself an indeterminate legal subject, capable of transforming himself at the drop of a hat from Louis to Louie to Leon to Gust.

Like Skliris, Gonzalez sought to turn the United States legal system to his financial advantage. His career as a labor contractor began in 1901, when he became El Paso's first Hispanic policeman. Gonzalez's primary task was to enforce the city's newly passed vagrancy laws, which authorized him to "arrest any and all persons . . . obstructing the streets." Using his discretion to define who was or was not a vagrant in El Paso's Mexican barrio, Chihuahuita, Gonzalez rounded up hundreds of new Mexican arrivals and sent them out of town. It was here as a kind of municipal bouncer that Gonzalez learned to mobilize immigrants into a work force. This skill served him well when he quit the police in 1905 and opened a labor agency, following in the footsteps of his police chief, James White, who likewise became a labor agent on retiring in 1905. In contrast to Skliris and

Cordasco, Gonzalez did not require his workers to sign contracts. None needed to: As a former policeman with a keen insight into the workings of vagrancy law, Gonzalez still wielded the coercive sanction of the legal system.[15]

But the success of padrones in manipulating the legal system is perhaps most dramatically manifest in the way they capitalized on legislative attempts to control their influence among immigrant workers. Between 1874 and 1924, the United States Congress tried to eliminate the padrone system. Its most significant attempt to curtail the power of padrones was the Foran Act, passed in 1885 to "prohibit the importation and migration of foreigners and aliens under contract or agreement to perform labor in the United States." For those immigrant workers who already possessed jobs on entering the United States, the Foran Act represented a hurdle. But friends, family, or padrones could instruct them in the proper responses to give immigration authorities. By creating hurdles for new immigrants, the Foran Act actually increased the need for an immigrant middleman to help guide workers across the border. The more rigorously the Foran Act was enforced, the more stature padrones gained in the eyes of American corporate officials by their demonstrated ability to circumvent the law's requirements.[16]

The symbiotic relationship between the contract labor law and padrone power was dramatically apparent in the careers of Cordasco and Skliris, whose migration businesses circumvented immigration laws in three countries. The Italian immigrant's journey began with an overland trip to Chiasso, Switzerland, a town just across the Italian border that served as the major staging ground for organizing illegal shipments of contract workers out of Italy, which possessed its own laws forbidding contract labor. Here immigrants met Frank Ludwig, Cordasco's chief overseas agent, who prepared and drilled them on the proper answers to questions they would encounter. Marcus Braun, special investigator for the United States Bureau of Immigration in 1903, described Ludwig as among those who "laugh at the measures adopted against the transportation of their people. . . . [He] has the labourers instructed so well as not to entertain any fear of . . . deportation." Schooled by Ludwig, Italian immigrants boarded boats in Marseilles, France, and left for New York where they quickly passed by the immigration inspectors at Ellis Island, stating that they had no jobs but were not paupers. Here they were met by Cordasco's agent Anthony Aiello, who gave them instructions and tickets for reaching Montreal.[17] Once there, they were quickly outfitted for work and were soon speeding across the Canadian plains on their way to work laying railroad ties in British Columbia.

Skliris and his agents were equally skilled in teaching Greek workers the proper requirements of the Foran Act. Like Cordasco's Italians, Greek contract laborers indicated to immigration officers at Ellis Island that they did not have jobs lined up in Utah. All of them also had "show money" of between thirty and fifty dollars to prove that they were not potential paupers. They thus circumvented immigration laws enacted by Congress in 1882 that excluded "the vicious, the criminal, and the pauper." But Skliris faced a greater challenge than did Cordasco in evading the conflicting requirements of United States immigration law. United States immigration officials usually asked the immigrant's final destination to ferret out large importations of contract workers to one common address in the United States. By listing Montreal, Italian immigrants quickly placed themselves outside the attention of most Ellis Island inspectors; consequently, they could arrive in New

York in large shipments. In May 1904, for example, one ship held over seven hundred Italian contract laborers, all of them headed to Montreal. Greek immigrants, by contrast, had to travel in small batches of three or four because of the scrutiny of immigration inspectors. Skliris possessed numerous discrete addresses for Greek workers to give immigration officials: 531, 533, 535, 537, and 539 West Second Street South in Salt Lake City looked like distinct residences, but all designated the same place: Skliris's labor agency office. So too, for all practical purposes, was the address R-3–23 in Bingham Canyon, Utah, twenty miles southwest of Salt Lake City, where Skliris's brother Evangelos ran the Panhellenic Grocery Company.[18]

While the Foran Act proved no match for the sophisticated strategies of Cordasco and Skliris, it nonetheless played an important role in the evolution of their businesses. The Foran Act discouraged both American and Canadian corporations from directly recruiting unskilled workers overseas. As Charlotte Erickson, a historian of immigration, has correctly observed, "industry did not formally organize the immigrant labor market." But North American companies did indirectly organize it by seeking to import immigrants, often as strikebreakers, through the padrone's services. Corporations adopted indirect methods largely because the political and financial price for doing the work themselves was too high. The padrone's ability to circumvent the contract labor law increased his prestige and marketability to hiring managers of North American companies. When asked by a government investigator why he had chosen Cordasco to be the CPR's *sole* Italian labor agent in 1901, special agent George Burns of the CPR acknowledged that Cordasco seemed to have "the least trouble" in controlling his men and to be the most adept in traversing the legal, political, and geographic obstacles to the recruitment of transient workers.[19]

Where the contract labor law was weakly enforced, by contrast, less opportunity existed for the immigrant padrone to make money from the commerce of migration. Although officials of the United States immigration service in El Paso tried to enforce the Foran Act, the geography of the Mexican border frustrated their best attempts. One agent, Patrick Bryan, in 1907 barred fifteen Japanese workers as contract laborers only to run into ten of the same workers on his way home that afternoon. According to immigration inspector Marcus Braun, immigrants flagrantly violated the Foran Act in El Paso "by simply wandering or being carried a few miles off our examining stations and crossing the border."[20] As Braun pointed out, the nation's immigration laws were designed for seaports, not for an often invisible two thousand–mile boundary policed by a few border agents.

At first glance, Gonzalez seems not to have been hindered by the open United States–Mexican border. Like Skliris and Cordasco, he was adept at circumventing the Foran Act. According to special immigration investigator Frank Stone in 1910, Gonzalez was "open to the severest criticism, having been the most pernicious violator of our law" on the entire United States–Mexican border. Not only did Gonzalez hire agents to recruit workers from villages and haciendas throughout the Mexican provinces of Chihuahua and Jalisco, he also colluded with municipal authorities in Ciudad Juárez, Mexico, El Paso's sister city across the Rio Grande. Every worker who sought help from the city-run emigration office in Ciudad Juárez was given Gonzalez's cards by a representative of the mayor, who told him how to get into the United States and how to find Gonzalez's office in El Paso. Gonzalez also excelled where Cordasco and Skliris never even attempted to recruit workers: finding jobs for compatriots denied admission to the United States. In February 1910, Gonzalez used his connections with the Mexican National Railroad to find jobs for over seven hundred workers in the interior of Mexico in a rare moment when the Foran Act was enforced.[21]

And yet, despite such impressive legal dexterity, Gonzalez never became a czar or king to Mexican workers. In 1910, one of his very best years, he found jobs for some fifty-eight hundred Mexican workers. But that represented just 13 percent of all Mexicans who contracted for work out of El Paso that year. Instead of becoming a king, Gonzalez experienced repeated business failures between 1905 and 1928, the year he went bankrupt for the last time and became a night watchman to pay his rent. To understand Gonzalez's failures, we need to consider the impact of the open border on his business. Gonzalez struggled financially because such American companies as the Southern Pacific Railway (SP) did not need immigrant middlemen. The SP, like all other railroads in the Southwest, operated its own labor agency in El Paso, the Holmes Supply Company, and it hired agents in Ciudad Juárez to recruit its labor supply directly.[22] The SP likewise managed its own commissary system, the Norton-Drake dry goods store, between 1895 and 1920. Because of the lax enforcement of the Foran Act and the abundance of Mexicans in Ciudad Juárez, the Southern Pacific had little need for an ethnic middleman to help recruit and organize unskilled workers.

Consequently, Gonzalez never acquired Cordasco's or Skliris's monopolistic control over sites of labor supply and labor demand, but instead faced a situation of extreme and debilitating competition. When twelve laborers crossed the bridge from Juárez to El Paso in 1907, for example, they were met by no fewer than eleven labor agents. As the *El Paso Times* reported:

> Each agency seized on his victim. One tried to pull his laborer one way and another another. One had a laborer by the coat, another by the sleeve, and another by his hair, each voicing in loud tones, with a noise like a rough house, the advantages of his particular agency.

Gonzalez lost out in this and many other competitions when "reinforcements" from the SP's Holmes Supply Company arrived on the scene and escorted all twelve men to its office. Such competition was responsible for the remarkably high turnover among both Mexican and American labor agents in El Paso, two-thirds of whom went out of business within a year of opening.[23] By this yardstick, Gonzalez was quite successful, managing to stay in business almost continuously for twenty-three years, a reflection of his intimate knowledge of municipal officials in Ciudad Juárez, Mexico, the border, and El Paso's vagrancy laws.

Yet if Skliris, Cordasco, and Gonzalez sought to capitalize on aspects of a free-labor legal system, it was not the primary source of padrone power. Skliris's contracts specified only that "one dollar a month" be deducted from the wages of each worker, with no mention of the ten-dollar fee each paid to get a job, or of the requirement that he shop at the Panhellenic Grocery store. The contracts that Italian workers signed similarly made no mention of Cordasco's commissary system, perhaps the most lucrative part of his tribute system. To understand how the power of individual padrones grew in scope over time, we need to consider the key element of their success: an ability to control and commodify the geographic mobility of immigrant workers and to mediate the family networks that sustained their migrations. It was here, in struggles over labor mobility, that workers initially contested the padrone's definitions of voluntary contract and free labor and eventually succeeded in subverting their power.

Cordasco made his fortune, not by evading the Foran Act, but by collecting tributes at every phase of the Italian immigrant's long journey from an Italian village to the Canadian Northwest and back again. In addition to exacting between five and seven dollars for each Atlantic crossing, Cordasco charged each compatriot three dollars to get a job and another two dollars to get to the work site. Once on the job, Italian workers continued paying Cordasco tribute by purchasing their food from his traveling commissary service. Charges for all supplies consumed by these mobile men were immediately deducted from their wages and paid to Cordasco at the end of the work season. The more his compatriots traveled along Canadian Pacific Railway lines, the more goods they consumed, and the more Cordasco profited.[24] For this entrepreneur of the international labor market, every distance between Italy and Canada was monetized: space, not time, was money.

But the mobility of Italian workers by itself did not guarantee Cordasco a profit. If Italian workers had been more inclined to quit their positions on the CPR, as so many French Canadian, Ukrainian, and Irish track workers had done before them, Cordasco's earnings would have been greatly reduced. Mobility had to be controlled to be profitable. There were several reasons why Italians did not usually quit their jobs. Cordasco's practice of withholding the wages of Italian workers until they returned to Montreal discouraged many, as did the isolation of railroad work on the CPR. Where, after all, would a worker go once he had quit his job in the Canadian Rockies? Equally important, however, were the domestic commitments that these sojourning men carried with them. In 1901 most Italian track workers were not single men, but married fathers intent on making money for their dependents in Italy.[25] Jumping jobs would not only eliminate income vital to the family's survival but also greatly reduce their chance of returning to Italy after the work season ended. Precisely how Cordasco exploited these domestic obligations is evident in the frustration of one Italian worker who threatened his Italian foreman when he injured himself on the job: "Are we slaves, beasts, or men, sir?," the bloody worker demanded after picking himself up. When the foreman responded that he was "free" to quit, the Italian worker hesitated, then muttered to himself, "God if I did not have wife and children in Italy."[26] Cordasco's ability to mediate the international family relations of married Italian sojourners kept the men literally on track.

Gonzalez also sought to capitalize on the mobility of Mexican workers by charging workers fees for their jobs and for journeys to and from isolated work sites. But he was profoundly unsuccessful in profiting from that mobility. Unlike Italian workers in Canada, Mexicans frequently jumped their contracts on their way to sugar beet fields in Minnesota or railroad jobs in the Southwest and East. G. A. Hoff of the Manning Labor Agency, with offices in El Paso and Tucson, Arizona, told the sociologist Paul Taylor in 1928 that "forty-six to forty-seven percent of our shipments on the average desert us without paying for transportation." Mr. Soots, of a Kansas City labor agency, observed the same year that "the Mexicans will jump the job. Fifty percent of them use it as a means of securing transportation." Railroad workers were the most likely to jump. In 1928 another labor agent stated, "We ship about 500 Mexicans a month for the Pennsylvania Railroad. . . . Out of every 100 we bring, only about 20 stay on the job more than a few weeks."[27]

The ability of Mexican track workers to jump their jobs did not reflect any great disrespect for contracts, but Mexican family relations and geography. Unlike Italian track workers, the vast majority of Mexican immigrants were young, single men, "solos" in the jargon of labor agencies, without dependents relying on their paychecks. Single Mexican immigrants remained very much a part of their individual family economies, but they risked much less than married Italian men in quitting their jobs. Solos also possessed numerous transportation options for returning to their home villages in the off-season, including competing train lines and by the 1920s buses and automobiles. Consequently, they were not dependent upon their padrones for making these travel arrangements.[28] Rather than keeping Mexican men "on track," Mexican family obligations and the railroad lines fomented remarkably high job turnover, to the detriment of padrone power.

American corporations fared little better than individual padrones in exploiting the mobility of Mexican workers. Consider, for example, the efforts of the Pennsylvania Railroad to control the mobility of its hired Mexican workers. Former track worker Gregorio Diaz recalled that in 1908 "they used to lock the doors on the trains and have a piece of lumber screwed on the outside of the windows" to prevent contract laborers from climbing out when the train stopped. But as Diaz explained, "The Mexicans used to buy sandwiches and coffee or cigarettes. These were the pretexts for jumping the train. Even the illiterates used to know when to jump from the descriptions that had been given to them."[29] One crucial reason so many Mexican solos jumped their work contracts was the knowledge of other job opportunities. Their remarkable success in frustrating the efforts of railroad officials suggests that even had Gonzalez procured the commissary privileges of the SP railroad, he would have had difficulty becoming a powerful padrone like Cordasco. Mexican solos simply possessed too many skills and advantages as transients to have their mobility controlled or commodified for very long.

The mobility of Greek workers in the intermountain West paralleled the footloose pattern among Mexican immigrants and might seem a hindrance to the development of a powerful padrone system. Most Greek sojourners were single men like Harry Mantos, an eighteen-year-old who traveled over thirty thousand miles in the West between 1908 and 1912, bounding between four jobs in two or three states each year.[30] But such mobility did not hinder Skliris. To the contrary, high job turnover helped him become the most powerful padrone in North America between 1906 and 1912. To understand why, we need to consider the different kinds of mobility that padrones exploited. If Cordasco made money from the continuous mobility of Italian workers through geographic space, Skliris became rich from the mobility of Greek workers between jobs. His ability to do so was not contingent on his monopolistic control over the labor supply, but rather on his control over most sites of labor demand in Utah. In 1971 the Greek immigrant Jack Tallas recalled the relationship between job turnover and Skliris's power:

The biggest trouble was Louis Skliris. He charge them $10 to get job. . . . And he put you to work about twenty days and then he fire you and hire somebody else. In other words just to make money. And you couldn't get a job unless through Skliris.[31]

As long as one stayed in Utah and its surrounding industrial enclaves, there was no place to hide from Skliris's tributes. "Protesting with your feet" by quitting, an effective strategy of individual resistance for Mexican workers, only fattened Skliris's profits.

Given how effective padrones were in turning the legal system, immigrant family relations, mobility, even geography itself to their advantage, how could immigrant workers resist padrones' power? No single strategy worked for all contract laborers, but as they gained experience and skills as migrant workers, they managed to use labor mobility and the legal system to resist their padrones.[32] Mexican workers chose flight from the padrone's exactions as their best solution. Although individuals chose to stay or to jump their jobs, these decisions in practice were not individualistic, for they grew out of collective networks of kin and adopted kin. Consider, for example, the plural voices that Mexican contract laborers used to describe their experiences on the move: "We live here like birds of the air," one track worker told the sociologist Paul Taylor in 1928. "When the steady work closes down, we are away to any place we can hear of steady work. . . . I have no other outlook than to keep working until I die." Other track workers found confidence in the mutualistic ties that facilitated their movement. Another seasonal track worker informed Taylor, "If things are good here in the United States, we come here to work. If they are better in Panama, or Colombia, or Peru, tomorrow or the next day we will go down there. We are only here for a short time." For the Mexican American track worker Jesus Garza, these networks made survival possible and transcended the power even of traditional family ties. "My pal was a Mexican and we cared for each other more than brothers," recalled Garza. "When one didn't have money the other did and we helped each other in everything."[33]

Yet if these fraternal networks made it difficult for Gonzalez or any other labor agent to profit from Mexican mobility, the workers nonetheless needed individuals who could mediate the political and cultural chasms separating them from American culture. One glimpses sojourning Mexicans fashioning an alternative to the padrone system in their dealings with Mrs. W. E. Duffy, an Anglo grocer in Fort Madison, Iowa, who was "adopted" by a group of Mexican lumber workers in 1923. According to a former labor department investigator, George L. Edson, the Mexican workers "come to her for everything—to call the doctor, priest, or undertaker, to arrange for births, marriages, and funerals, to talk to lawyers, bankers, and policemen." Others brought her their paychecks to cash, while "never questioning her reliability." Like many other padrones, Duffy, nicknamed Benita, mediated the diverse cultural, political, and economic boundaries separating migrant workers from American society. She was not exactly an entrepreneur, however, for she had been chosen by Mexican men to do this work. As Duffy recalled, "Some years ago some Mexicans came into my shop and the ringleader informed me that they wished me to learn Spanish, explaining that their heads were hard and that English was out of the question for many of them."[34] Benita was their creation, their "padrone," a figure who underscores how padrones were products of particular North American contexts. A great variety of people could become padrones in North America, not only immigrant entrepreneurs with aspirations to royalty, but American women with quick language skills.[35]

But although Mexican contract laborers such as Benita's clients could sometimes create their own mediators of American culture, they remained deeply ambivalent about the United States legal system. Contracts, in particular, remained a double-edged feature of the Mexican solo's experience between 1890 and 1930. On the one hand, mutual obligation and informal contract—between sojourners and kin, adopted and inherited—were crucial to the Mexican solo's survival, constituting ties that could weaken the power of labor agents and company managers and could even help the migrants create their own padrones. But many Mexican contract laborers remained skeptical of the promises of contracts and free labor in the United States. One Mexican railroad worker in Texas expressed the disillusionment of many when he recalled that his first contract in 1908 left him a prisoner in a train with "nothing to eat except crackers and sardines." His subsequent question, "Is this the land of liberty?," anticipated the anguished cry of Greek workers in Utah three years later. Juan Castillo, a Mexican American contract laborer in Texas, put it more directly in 1928: "There is a law for the Americans but none for the Mexicans."[36]

By the 1920s, however, increasing numbers of Mexican contract laborers began turning to written contracts and the United States legal system to achieve the promises of free labor. While Mexican workers continued to jump their contracts in droves and to seek alternatives to padrone influence, many also began insisting that padrones live up to their promises and demanded written rather than oral agreements with them. Patricio Shutter, an American cotton rancher in Texas, commented in 1928, "Most Mexicans now won't work without written contracts." The shift in preference from oral to written contracts had a dramatic effect on Gonzalez's own migration business in the 1920s. In 1923 Gonzalez stood on the brink of financial success: The closing of European immigration and the creation of a closed border with Mexico promised for the first time to give him a niche in the labor contracting business he had so long sought to control. But just as business was beginning to boom, he was sued by Will Kimble and two other contract workers, who demanded a full refund of their job fees and "exemplary damages" of two thousand dollars each to compensate them for finding no jobs when they reached their desert destinations. Although an El Paso judge ruled that Gonzalez had to refund each worker only his three-dollar job fee, his fortunes plummeted as the Gulf, Colorado, and Santa Fe Railroad refused to do any more business with him. Gonzalez watched his business drop from five thousand workers shipped in 1923 to two thousand a year later and fewer than six hundred by 1926. By 1928 Gonzalez was bankrupt and looking for work as a night watchman.[37]

Like Mexican workers, Italian contract laborers sought to limit padrone power by taking control of the family connections and mobility patterns that Cordasco had briefly exploited. Many Italians hoped to accomplish this simply by returning to Italy after the work season was over and remaining there, having satisfied their original goals in migrating. Such was certainly the Italian sojourner's hope, though few realized these dreams after all of Cordasco's deductions and tributes had been removed. Those who did remigrate, moreover, often returned to the very conditions that had first propelled them to North America; conditions that led them to make another seasonal migration the following spring, if not to North America, then to northern Europe or perhaps South America. Such remigration in no way hindered the power of Cordasco and other entrepreneurs of space, but rather fueled it.[38]

More threatening to Cordasco, however, was the increasing tendency by 1904 for Italian immigrants to bring their families to Canada permanently. Rafaele di Zazza, one of Cordasco's most trusted foremen of six years, for example, decided in the fall of 1903 to send for his wife and family, thus ending Cordasco's ability to mediate his kin connections to Italy. The full implications of such individual decisions were more clearly manifest by 1907: in 1904 fewer than half of all Canada-bound Italians possessed relatives already in Canada, but by 1907 fully three-quarters did. The growing strength of these family migrations helped rupture Cordasco's control over the migration to Canada. In 1904, when Cordasco was crowned "King of the workers," some 83 percent of all Canada-bound Italians at Ellis Island listed Montreal as their final stop, many of them using Cordasco's address at 375 St. Catherine's Street. By 1907, just 7 percent listed Montreal as their final destination. The vast majority of new Italian arrivals in Montreal no longer looked to him for employment or paid him transportation fees; they traveled to their work sites directly, relying on their own kin connections.[39]

Yet before we conclude that immigrant family connections by themselves caused Cordasco's downfall, we must first consider the political context that produced these dramatic changes in the Italian migration to Canada. Italian resistance to the padrone system was far more collective and explicitly political than Zazza's sending for his family. Few would have predicted Cordasco's downfall in the weeks following his triumphant coronation, when all sixty of his foremen and some two thousand Italian workers marched through the streets of Montreal chanting, "Viva Le Canada, Viva Antonio Cordasco, Viva C. P. R., Viva l'Italia." Within five months, however, those same Italian workers had succeeded in toppling his crown and nearly putting him out of business. Trouble began when a late thaw delayed the start of the work season, even as thousands of additional Italian workers, lured by promises of steady work, continued to pour into Montreal with no place to stay except the city's streets and parks.[40] Cordasco's ability to dominate his countrymen by exploiting their continuous mobility through space had, in the passing of a snowstorm, abruptly vanished.

The only place Cordasco controlled by the end of May 1904 was his labor agency office. But even here he found headache and frustration as first a few, then dozens, and finally hundreds of Italian workers visited him daily, demanding immediate employment or their money back. Cordasco's response to their requests exposed the coercive nature of his allegedly contractual relations with Italian workers. When laborer Giovanni Morillo asked why there was no work available, Cordasco stated, "If you do not get out of my office, I will kick you out." When foreman Michele Cilla had the courage to ask for a refund of job fees for himself and his forty-member work gang, Cordasco pulled out a gun and threatened "to pull forty drops of blood" from his forehead. And when another foreman, Vincenzo Sciano, demanded his "rights," Cordasco stated bluntly but revealingly, "You have no rights at all."[41]

Such dialogues not only clarified the emptiness of Cordasco's contractual promises to Italian workers but also galvanized increasing numbers of them to demand their "rights" as free laborers in North America. When the Canadian government opened an investigation into the "alleged fraudulent activities" of labor agents in summer 1904, dozens of Cordasco's still-idle "subjects" testified, producing devastating evidence against their former king. Indeed, just two days after the investigation ended, the CPR fired Cordasco as their sole Italian labor agent.[42] Perhaps most damaging, thirteen Italian workers and foremen sued him for their unrecovered job fees and the pay they had lost while waiting for promised jobs in 1904. Each case stated the same basic facts: Cordasco had violated his written contracts by not providing them jobs and thus had also swindled them out of their job fees.[43] When Cordasco finally lost these court cases a year later, his choke hold over Italian migration had been shattered. Not only had he lost control over where his compatriots migrated, but his power to influence the legal system and the meaning of contracts had waned. In 1905, Cordasco sued the CPR for civil damages, complaining bitterly that his firing and the company's breach of contract meant he "was now unable to earn a living." But Cordasco lost that case too and spent the next decade, his last, trying to regain his once regal form.[44]

Greek workers in Utah faced a far greater challenge in resisting Skliris. Attempts to use the strategies favored by Mexican workers—quitting their jobs or jumping contracts—actually increased Skliris's profits. Attempts to turn the United States legal and political system against Skliris also proved futile. Greek workers' impassioned complaint to the governor of Utah, William Spry, produced only a letter in which he suggested they go to the management of the Utah Copper Company for a "fair and impartial hearing." Attempts to sue Skliris and his subagents likewise bore little fruit, even when American political leaders agreed to cooperate. In fall 1911, former Idaho governor William McConnell became a "special immigration inspector" and launched an investigation into the activities of William Caravelis, labor agent for the Oregon Short Railroad Line and one of Skliris's former business partners. Unlike Governor Spry, Governor McConnell promised Greek workers strict confidentiality and succeeded in securing "signatures to a number of affidavits by Greek workers." But Caravelis and Skliris survived the threatened conviction under federal peonage laws by calling in their debts from local legal officials in Pocatello. Two days after McConnell announced his plan to convict Caravelis of peonage, Bannock County attorney William Terrell announced that the case was "premature" and would not be prosecuted. Local papers praised Caravelis as a fine leader "who stands high among the businessmen, officers, and officials of the railroad."[45]

One reason Greek workers looked to United States government and legal channels for help against the padrone system was that efforts to challenge Skliris's power using ethnic and mutual aid societies had already failed. Although in Montreal the Italian Emigration Aid Society figured prominently in efforts to help Italian foremen and workers bring forward their testimony against Cordasco during the Canadian government's 1904 investigation, among Greeks in Utah, such philanthropic and fraternal organizations were dominated by allies of Skliris. The most conspicuous Greek nationalist organization in Utah, the Kanaris Society, was founded by Leon Skliris himself and obviously proved poor soil for nurturing resistance to his tribute system. Skliris also had close ties to the official "Greek community of Utah," which built the Holy Trinity Greek Orthodox Church of Salt Lake City in 1907. His brother, Evangelos, served on the community's board of directors, while its vice-president, Nicholas Stathakos, worked as Skliris's banker. Given Skliris's ties to official ethnic leadership in Utah, it is hardly surprising that few Greek workers turned to the church for help in fighting the padrone system. Indeed, only one out of twenty Greeks in Utah was a member of the official community in 1910.[46]

What, then, were Greek workers to do? They answered this question decisively by exploiting one of the most effective aspects of Skliris's padrone system: its unintended success in encouraging workers to remain at one job site to avoid additional job fees. By remaining in Bingham Canyon for as long as possible, Greek workers not only began developing collective strategies for resisting Skliris—sending petitions and letters to the governor of Utah—but also looked more carefully at the local chapter of the Western Federation of Miners (WFM), an American-led organization that had recently made overtures to Greek and other new immigrants working in Bingham. In August 1912 the organizers got more than they bargained for when nearly one thousand Greek and Italian miners joined the WFM local and promptly voted to go on strike, over the protests of the American membership. On September 18, 1912, all twelve hundred Greek employees of the Utah Copper Company walked off their jobs and began arming themselves with rifles, stockpiling dynamite, digging breastworks, and even constructing a makeshift cannon, in a remarkable display of military power and solidarity. Joining them were almost two thousand Italian, Slavic, and Japanese immigrants, who demanded the immediate dismissal of Skliris, the abolition of the padrone system for all ethnic groups in Bingham—Italian and Japanese included—and the recognition of their new union, the Western Federation of Miners.[47]

What began as an attempt by Greek workers to break Skliris's choke hold over their mobility had become a militant class struggle by over a dozen nationalities against the Utah Copper Company and the padrone system. The paths of worker mobility that Skliris had formerly exploited were now turned against him, as immigrants developed a regional movement to resist Skliris's power. Two weeks into the strike, six hundred Greek copper miners in Ely, Nevada, led a sympathy strike against a subsidiary of Utah Copper, the Nevada Consolidated Copper Company, echoing the demands of Bingham's strikers for the abolition of the padrone system and union recognition.[48] In the face of such dramatic regional militancy and the sensational publicity surrounding the strike, Skliris resigned his position as chief labor agent for the Utah Copper Company, to the delight of Greek strikers, who nonetheless pressed their demands for union recognition. Greek strikers were unsuccessful in this struggle, as Skliris performed one last service for the Utah Copper Company. Two weeks after he resigned, his subagent Gus Paulos imported one hundred newly arrived Greek strikebreakers into Bingham Canyon, undermining the solidarity of the strike's most conspicuous participants. With tempers at a boiling point, Skliris feared for his life and left Salt Lake City, legend has it, dressed as a woman.[49] There were no boundaries, it would seem, that Skliris could not cross.

For Skliris, Gonzalez, and Cordasco, both the legal system and the mobility of immigrant workers represented sources of tremendous power and profit. All three padrones manipulated aspects of the law to create far-flung networks of coercive labor relations. But if the legal system helped them establish their migration businesses, control over the mobility of their compatriots remained central to whatever economic success they enjoyed. Of the three, Cordasco most successfully exploited the largest expanse of geographic space, acquiring tributes at every step of the Italian track worker's journey from northern Italy to British Columbia and back again. But the sheer size of such space did not guarantee him a profit. Different kinds of worker mobility—through space and between jobs—each based on distinct family networks among immigrant workers, played important roles in determining a padrone's relative power. Skliris was remarkably effective in commodifying Greek workers' mobility between jobs, a far more lucrative practice than Cordasco enjoyed. Gonzalez, by contrast, had difficulty exploiting either form of worker mobility. The openness of the border dramatically reduced the geopolitical space he could commodify, while the passion single Mexicans exhibited for jumping their work contracts made it difficult for Gonzalez or anyone else to exploit Mexicans' mobility between jobs in North America.

Understanding how padrones succeeded in making different kinds of worker mobility profitable illuminates why the North American West became a bastion of coercive labor relations in the early twentieth century. With its vast expanses of sparsely populated geographic space and enduring labor scarcities, the region presented remarkable potential to middlemen who could traverse those spaces and regulate the mobility of workers through space and between jobs. While workers in eastern cities changed jobs just as frequently, they could remain in one city: western track workers and miners, by contrast, often had to travel hundreds of miles to remain employed. The isolation of work, in other words, increased workers' geographic mobility. The ability of padrones to make money from these conspicuous forms of transience did not make the West and its labor history exceptional. What Skliris and Cordasco accomplished was not fundamentally different from what padrones did in the migrant labor camps of upstate New York, where they remained "all powerful" according to municipal authorities in 1912.[50] The exploitation of workers' mobility through space and between jobs was not exceptional to the North American West, but it was unique in its intensity and visibility.

If the coercions that Greek, Italian, and Mexican contract laborers experienced were not exceptional, their predicaments highlight just how double-edged their experiences of free labor relations were. Quitting a job may have been a path to freedom for Mexican solos, but it left Greek workers even more dependent on Skliris. Greeks harnessed mobility to their advantage during the strike by creating a regional labor movement, but mobility also proved the strike movement's undoing, as footloose Greeks imported by Paulos broke the strike. The labor contract too could serve conflicting purposes. While Skliris's and Cordasco's contracts established their authority over immigrant workers, they also became bases for challenging that power. It is perhaps not surprising, then, that no single, unified interpretation of free labor and the wage contract emerged from workers' interactions with the legal system and the labor movement. Even in Bingham Canyon, where Greek workers demonstrated remarkable solidarity during the 1912 strike, a variety of views about the merits of contracts flourished. For the Greek striker Louis Theos and a small but increasingly vocal minority of Greek workers, Skliris's tyranny discredited the legitimacy of all contracts, unmasking the coercion inherent in every agreement with the capitalist class, a message that Theos spread far and near as an organizer for the Industrial Workers of the World after 1912. But for the majority of Greek strikers, the quest for a union contract continued as they scattered across the industrial West.[51]

Although immigrant contract laborers succeeded in overthrowing their padrones, their stories provide few whiggish comforts about the progressive status of contractual, wage labor relations. Rather, their struggles highlight just how unstable and contested such labor relations remained throughout the Progressive Era. Indeed, struggles to control labor mobility continue to be crucial but neglected arenas of class conflict for today's migrant workers, whose experiences of free labor have likewise been shaped and transformed by entrepreneurs of space—be they Mexican coyotes or Asian American and African American labor contractors. Consider, for example, the case of migrant worker George Smith of South Carolina, who in the spring of 1994 signed a contract with a man named Willie Bonds to pick peaches. Bonds gave Smith "free" transportation to an isolated labor camp and food, alcohol, and drugs once he got there. But when payday rolled around two weeks later, Smith discovered that he owed Bonds eight hundred dollars and was forbidden to leave without first paying his contractual debts. Smith and several coworkers resisted with two weapons familiar to immigrant workers eighty years earlier: their feet and the legal system. "We took to the woods," Smith recalled, and when he reached Raleigh, North Carolina, forty miles later, he filed a lawsuit against Bonds that eventually put him out of business.[52] Though George Smith has probably never heard of Leon Skliris, Roman Gonzalez, and Antonio Cordasco, his struggle to reinvent free labor and his small victory in so doing would have made Greek strikers in Bingham, Will Kimble of El Paso, and Giuseppe Teolo of Montreal both sad and proud.

Notes

I would like to thank the following individuals for their critical comments on various drafts of this essay: Susan Armeny, Eric Arnesen, Jonathan Brown, William Cronon, Pete Daniels, Leon Fink, William Forbath, Faulkner Fox, Julie Greene, Reeve Huston, Howard Lamar, Bruce Laurie, David Montgomery, Sylvie Murray, Robert Steinfeld, David Thelen, David Waldstreicher, and the anonymous reviewers for the *Journal of American History*. The essay was also enriched by the collective wisdom of my colleagues at the University of Texas, where I presented it for a faculty seminar entitled "Race and Slavery in the Americas," organized by Jim Sidbury and Richard Graham. Special thanks are due Helen Papanikolas, Allan Bogue, and David Zonderman for their early support and encouragement.

1. "Fifty Greek and Crete Men to Utah Government," petition, Feb. 2, 1911, File "G," box 10, William S. Spry Papers (Utah State Archives, Salt Lake City).

2. Although differences between chattel slavery and free waged labor have been portrayed as transparent and self-evident, these distinctions have in social practice been murky. It would be more accurate to describe a continuous spectrum of coercion between free and unfree labor. A

variety of coercions thrive within many ostensibly free wage labor relations, just as many slaves maintained degrees of control and limited autonomy as workers. On coercion in free labor relations, see Jonathan A. Glickstein, *Concepts of Free Labor in Antebellum America* (New Haven, 1991); Robert J. Steinfeld, *The Invention of Free Labor: The Employment Relation in English and American Law and Culture, 1350–1870* (Chapel Hill, 1991); and Christopher L. Tomlins, *Law, Labor, and Ideology in the Early American Republic* (Cambridge, Eng., 1993). See also Julie Saville, *The Work of Reconstruction: From Slave to Wage Laborer in South Carolina, 1860–1870* (New York, 1994); and Christopher Waldrep, "Substituting Law for the Lash: Emancipation and Legal Formalism in a Mississippi County Court," *Journal of American History,* 82 (March 1996), 1425–51.

3. See Amy Dru Stanley, "Beggars Can't Be Choosers: Compulsion and Contract in Postbellum America," *Journal of American History,* 78 (March 1992), 1265–93; William E. Forbath, "The Ambiguities of Free Labor: Labor and the Law in the Gilded Age," *Wisconsin Law Review* (no. 4, 1985), 767–817; William E. Forbath, *Law and the Shaping of the American Labor Movement* (Cambridge, Mass., 1991); and Robert J. Steinfeld, "Law in the Construction of Wage Labor and Peonage: A Critical Legal History," paper delivered at the annual North American Labor History Conference, Detroit, Oct. 1993 (in Gunther Peck's possession).

4. For varied criticism of the alleged radicalism of critical legal studies, see Peter Karsten, "'Bottomed on Justice': A Reappraisal of Critical Legal Studies Scholarship Concerning Breaches of Labor Contracts by Quitting or Firing in Great Britain and the U.S., 1630–1880," *American Journal of Legal History,* 34 (July 1990), 213–61; and Eugene Genovese, "Critical Legal Studies as Radical Politics and World View," in *Legal Studies as Cultural Studies: A Reader in (Post)modern Critical Theory,* ed. Jerry Leonard (Albany, 1995), 269–98.

5. This essay is drawn from Gunther Peck, "Reinventing Free Labor: Immigrant Padrones and Contract Laborers in North America, 1880–1920" (Ph.D. diss., Yale University, 1995). On Antonio Cordasco's career, see Robert Harney, "Montreal's King of Italian Labour: A Case Study of Padronism," *Labour/Le Travail,* 4 (Summer 1979), 57–84. On Leon Skliris's career, see Helen Papanikolas, "Toil and Rage in a New Land: The Greek Immigrants of Utah," *Utah Historical Quarterly,* 38 (Spring 1970), 100–204. On Roman Gonzalez's early career, see Mario T. Garcia, *Desert Immigrants: The Mexicans of El Paso, 1880–1920* (New Haven, 1979), 53–56; and Camille Guerin-Gonzales, *Mexican Workers and American Dreams: Immigration, Repatriation, and California Farm Labor, 1900–1939* (New Brunswick, 1994), 38–41.

6. On the coexistence of a great range of coercive labor systems in the West, see Howard Lamar, "From Bondage to Contract: Ethnic Labor in the American West, 1600–1890," in *The Countryside in the Age of Capitalist Transformation: Essays in the Social History of Rural America,* ed. Steven Hahn and Jonathan Prude (Chapel Hill, 1985), 293–324.

7. Among many studies examining the role of community and the shop floor in working-class mobilization, see Herbert Gutman, *Work, Culture, and Society in Industrializing America: Essays in American Working-Class and Social History* (New York, 1977); David Montgomery, *Workers' Control in America: Studies in the History of Work, Technology, and Labor Struggles* (Cambridge, Eng., 1979); Richard Oestreicher, *Solidarity and Fragmentation: Working People and Class Consciousness in Detroit, 1875–1900* (Urbana, 1987); James R. Barrett, *Work and Community in the Jungle: Chicago's Packinghouse Workers, 1894–1922* (Urbana, 1987); and Dorothy Sue Cobble, *Dishing It Out: Waitresses and Their Unions in the Twentieth Century* (Urbana, 1991). On the importance of space and labor mobility to conceptualizing class formation, see David Harvey, *The Urbanization of Capital: Studies in the History and Theory of Capitalist Urbanization* (Baltimore, 1985), 33–35; and David Harvey, *The Limits to Capital* (Chicago, 1982), 415–17. For case studies that consider the relationship between labor mobility and class, see Donna Rae Gabaccia, *Militants and Migrants: Rural Sicilians Become American Workers* (New York, 1987); Sarah Deutsch, *No Separate Refuge: Culture, Class, and Gender on an Anglo-Hispanic Frontier in the American Southwest, 1880–1940* (New York, 1987); and David Montejano, *Anglos and Mexicans in the Making of Texas, 1836–1986* (Austin, 1986).

8. In 1870, middle-class reformers and writers such as Horatio Alger portrayed the padrone as a Fagin-like villain who exploited Italian boys, teaching them to play the fiddle while forcing them

to give up all their "earnings." By 1900, however, the term had become largely ascriptive, referring to Italian bankers, Greek labor contractors, Mexican railroad bosses, Japanese foremen, and
Bulgarian bootblack proprietors. See Horatio Alger Jr., *Phil, the Fiddler, or, the Story of a Young Street
Musician* (Boston, 1872); and Robert Harney, "The Padrone and the Immigrant," *Canadian Review
of American Studies,* 5 (Summer 1974), 101–18.

9. For definitions of the padrone as an archaic figure, see John Koren, *The Padrone System and
Padrone Banks* (Washington, 1897), 1; and Frank J. Sheridan, *Italian, Slavic, and Hungarian Unskilled
Laborers in the United States* (Washington, 1907), 435. In the 1920s corporations began to hire and
train their own "padrones," better known as "personnel managers," who accomplished many of the
padrone's former tasks. See Peck, "Reinventing Free Labor," 148–53; and Sanford M. Jacoby, *Employing Bureaucracy: Managers, Unions, and the Transformation of Work in American Industry, 1900–1945* (New
York, 1985), 137–40. On Cordasco's business history, see the Canadian government's investigative
report, *The Royal Commission appointed to inquire into the Immigration of Italian Labourers to Montreal
and the Alleged Fraudulent Practices of Employment Agency* (Ottawa, 1905), 88. On Skliris's business
career, see *Walker Bros. v. Caravelis,* case 1938, Supreme Court, Case Files (Utah State Archives, Salt
Lake City); and *Eastern Utah Advocate,* April 9, 1915, p. 1. For a ruling on the case, see *Walker Bros.
v. Skliris,* 98 P. 114 (1908). On Gonzalez's business dealings with the Gulf, Colorado, and Santa Fe
Railroad Company, see *El Paso Times,* Feb. 6, 1907, p. 5.

10. See Charles Tilly, "Transplanted Networks," in *Immigration Reconsidered: History, Sociology,
and Politics,* ed. Virginia Yans-McLaughlin (New York, 1990), 79–95; and Gabaccia, *Millitants and
Migrants,* 79–90. Immigration historians frequently juxtapose family migrations and "middlemen"
as competing factors in shaping regional migrations. One writes that "families invariably superseded labor agents and 'middlemen' in influencing the entry of newcomers." John Bodnar, *The
Transplanted: A History of Immigrants in Urban America* (Bloomington, 1985), 68. But Skliris and Cordasco gained fame as padrones only after chain migrations of kin became well established. In 1901,
when Cordasco came to power, 46% of Montreal-bound Italians possessed family ties in Canada;
in 1907 almost two-thirds of Utah-bound Greeks possessed such ties there. See Peck, "Reinventing Free Labor," 295–98; and Steamship Manifest Lists, March 1901, March 1907, Records of the
Department of Immigration and Naturalization, RG 85 (National Archives, Washington D.C.).

11. Testimony of Antonio Cordasco, in *Royal Commission,* 101, 128. In March 1904, just 6 Greeks
passed through Ellis Island with final destinations in Utah, while 216 passed through in March 1912.
Steamship Manifest Lists, March 1904, March 1912, Records of the U.S. Department of Immigration and Naturalization.

12. Antonio Cordasco to Antonio Paretti, March 1, 1904, in *Royal Commission,* 80; Cordasco,
ibid., 76; Cordasco to Angelo de Santis, Feb. 19, 1904, *ibid.,* 130; Cordasco, *ibid.,* 120.

13. Unsigned labor contract of L. G. Skliris, straight numerical file 161414, box 1384, Central
Files, Records of the Department of Justice, RG 60 (National Archives, Washington, D.C.).

14. See *Leonidas G. Skliris v. Giles American Mercantile Agency, a Corporation, C. Frank Emery, Sheriff
of Salt Lake County,* 1909, case 8080, Records of the Third District Court, Salt Lake County (Utah
State Archives); Naturalization Records of Gust Skliris, Aug. 11, 1905, Salt Lake County, microfiche
2, Naturalization Files, *ibid.*

15. El Paso City Council, Minutes, May 23, 1901, p. 181, Southwest Collection (El Paso Public
Library, El Paso, Tex.); *ibid.,* Jan. 30, 1902, p. 511; *ibid.,* Oct. 17, 1906, p. 562; *El Paso City Directory,*
1905, *ibid.*

16. The first federal legislation directed against padrones was passed in 1874 and stated that "who-
ever shall bring into the United States . . . any person inveigled or forcibly kidnapped in any other
country, with intent to hold such person in confinement or to any involuntary service . . . shall be
deemed guilty of a felony." *Congressional Record,* 43 Cong., 1 sess., June 1, 1874, p. 4443. See Foran Act,
23 Stat. 332–33 (1885); Charlotte Erickson, *American Industry and the European Immigrant, 1860–1885*
(Cambridge, Mass., 1957); Gwendolyn Mink, *Old Labor and New Immigrants in American Political
Development: Union, Party, and State, 1875–1920* (Ithaca, 1986), 98.

17. U.S. Department of Justice, "The Braun Report," file 52320/47, Immigration Subject Cor-

respondence Folder, Records of the Department of Immigration and Naturalization; Harney, "Montreal's King of Italian Labour," 63; Cordasco, in *Royal Commission,* 88.

18. For the language of the 1882 Immigration Act, see Edith Abbott, ed. *Immigration: Select Documents and Case Records* (Chicago, 1924), 186. Testimony of Antonio Sicari, in *Royal Commission,* 36; Steamship Manifest Lists, Port of New York, March 1912, Records of the Department of Immigration and Naturalization.

19. Erickson, *American Industry and the European Immigrant,* 11; testimony of George Burns, in *Royal Commission,* 41–42. Many corporations possessed their own labor recruiters between 1885 and 1930. Padrones had the special advantage, however, of being able to reach beyond national boundaries to Old World villages, something fewer corporations were willing to do after the Foran Act made such practices illegal. On exceptions to this pattern, see the corporate recruitments of Mexicans by the Southern Pacific and the Atchison, Topeka and Santa Fe railroads and of French Canadians by companies in New England through the same Canadian "back door" that Cordasco used. See Tamara K. Hareven and Randolph Langenbach, *Amoskeag: Life and Work in an American Factory-City* (New York, 1978), 19–20. On corporate recruitment of unskilled workers within national boundaries, see Walter Licht, *Getting Work: Philadelphia, 1840–1950* (Cambridge, Mass., 1992). On companies that imported European immigrants, see Erickson, *American Industry and the European Immigrant,* 19–29. On Chinese companies, see Sing-wu Wang, *The Organization of Chinese Emigration, 1848–88* (San Francisco, 1978); Kil Young Zo, *Chinese Emigration into the United States, 1850–1880* (New York, 1979); and Sucheng Chan, *This Bittersweet Soil: The Chinese in California Agriculture, 1860–1910* (Berkeley, 1986), 7–31. On Japanese companies, see Alan Takeo Moriyama, *Imingaisha: Japanese Emigration Companies and Hawaii, 1894–1908* (Honolulu, 1985); and Yuji Ichioka, *The Issei: The World of the First Generation Japanese Immigrants, 1885–1924* (New York, 1987).

20. Charles L. Babcock to Frank P. Sargent, commissioner general of immigration, Jan. 10, 1908, p. 5, file 51748/11A, box 78, Records of the Department of Immigration and Naturalization; Marcus Braun to Sargent, Feb. 12, 1907, p. 14, file 52320/1, box 95, *ibid.* On the openness of the United States–Mexican border in this period, see Alejandro Portes, "From South of the Border: Hispanic Minorities in the United States," in *Immigration Reconsidered,* ed. Yans-McLaughlin, 160–63; and Lawrence Cardoso, *Mexican Emigration to the United States, 1897–1931: Socioeconomic Patterns* (Tucson, 1987).

21. Frank R. Stone to Sargent, June 30, 1910, pp. 38, 35, 19, table B, file 52546/31, box 125, Records of the Department of Immigration and Naturalization. See Oscar Martinez, *Border Boom Town: Ciudad Juárez since 1848* (Austin, 1979).

22. Zarate-Avina Employment Office personnel interview by Paul S. Taylor, 1928, Field Notes 17–189, BANC-MSS-74/187c, Paul S. Taylor Papers (Bancroft Library, University of California, Berkeley).

23. *El Paso Times,* Sept. 14, 1907, p. 1. Between 1905 and 1920, 9 Mexican and 26 Anglo employment agencies opened in El Paso. Of these 35 agencies, 24 folded within their first year and just 4 stayed in business longer than three years. *El Paso City Directory,* 1905–1920, Southwest Collection.

24. Testimony of John Skinner and Salvatore Mollo, in *Royal Commission,* 24, 34. Cordasco cleared $3,800 from his commissary service to Italian and Chinese track workers in 1903. Skinner, *ibid.,* 166.

25. Fully 66% of all Canada-bound Italians who entered the continent through the port of New York in March 1901 were already married. Steamship Manifest Lists, Port of New York, March 1901, Records of the Department of Immigration and Naturalization. Although Italian workers remained on the job longer than single Irish and Ukrainian track workers, their employment with the CPR was brief, lasting one summer work season. On their job turnover, see Bruno Ramirez, "Brief Encounters: Italian Immigrant Workers and the CPR, 1900–1930," *Labour/Le Travail,* 17 (Spring 1986), 9–27.

26. Cesidio Simboli, "When the Boss Went Too Far," *World Outlook* (Oct. 1917), in *A Documentary History of the Italian Americans,* ed. Wayne Moquin with Charles Van Doren (New York, 1974), 147. On legal connections between labor and marriage contracts, see Amy Dru Stanley, "Conjugal Bonds and Wage Labor: Rights of Contract in the Age of Emancipation," *Journal of American His-*

tory, 75 (Sept. 1988), 471–96; and Sara L. Zeigler, "Wifely Duties: Marriage, Labor, and the Common Law in Nineteenth-Century America," *Social Science History,* 20 (Spring 1996), 63–96.

27. G. A. Hoff interview by Taylor, 1928, Field Notes 46–556, BANC-MSS-74/187c, Taylor Papers; Mr. Soots interview by Taylor, 1928, Field Notes 44–216, *ibid.;* Manager of the Peterson Employment Agency interview by Taylor, 1928, *ibid.*

28. In 1920, 97% of all Mexicans who found jobs through private employment agents in Texas were male. See Texas Bureau of Labor Statistics, *Sixth Biennial Report, 1919–1920* (Austin, 1921), 18. On the role of single migrant Mexican men in family and village economies, see Deutsch, *No Separate Refuge,* 35–40; and Robert R. Alvarez Jr., *Familia: Migration and Adaptation in Baja and Alta California, 1800–1975* (Berkeley, 1987).

29. Gregorio Diaz interview by Taylor, 1928, Field Notes 113–117, BANC-MSS-74/187c, Taylor Papers. On the "crisis of labor turnover," see Sumner Schlicter, *The Turnover of Factory Labor* (New York, 1919); Jacoby, *Employing Bureaucracy,* 133–65; and Alexander Keyssar, *Out of Work: The First Century of Unemployment in Massachusetts* (New York, 1986), 123–60.

30. Harry Mantos interview by Louis Cononelos, Dec. 9, 1974, Greek Oral History Collection, American West Center (Marriott Library, University of Utah, Salt Lake City).

31. Jack Tallas interview by Helen Papanikolas, Jan. 18, 1971, *ibid.*

32. Historians of transient workers have typically viewed them through the lens of a "culture of poverty," defining mobility as evidence of cultural impoverishment. In so doing, historians have not considered how transiency and community could nurture each other or how transiency itself could be a skill used for collective and communal ends. See Melvyn Dubofsky, *We Shall Be All: A History of the Industrial Workers of the World* (New York, 1973), 5; Peter Way, *Common Labour: Workers and the Digging of North American Canals, 1780–1860* (Cambridge, Eng., 1993), 104; and Peter Way, "Evil Humors and Ardent Spirits: The Rough Culture of Canal Construction Laborers," *Journal of American History,* 79 (March 1993), 1397–1428.

33. Paul Taylor, *Mexican Labor in the United States,* 3 vols., (Chicago, 1928–1934), II, 257, 275; Jesus Garza interview by Manuel Gamio, 1928, in *The Mexican Immigrant: His Life Story,* ed. Manuel Gamio (Chicago, 1931), 18.

34. George L. Edson, "Mexicans at Fort Madison, Iowa," March 8, 1927, "Interviews with Labor Contractors" file, BANC-MSS-74/187c, Taylor Papers.

35. The history of "Benita" also highlights the importance of gender ideology in shaping the creation of padrone power. To view padronism as an embodiment of literal male power obscures the experience of Benita and her clients by conflating gender and biological sex as historical categories. On the role of gender ideology in both constituting and undermining padrone power, see Peck, "Reinventing Free Labor," 346–68. On distinguishing between the categories of male and masculine, see Joan Wallach Scott, *Gender and the Politics of History* (New York, 1988), 53–67.

36. Jose of Old Mexico, "The Future of Mexican Immigration: A Story on the Outside Looking In," 1929, box 1, BANC-MSS-Z-4R, Taylor Papers; Juan Castillo interview by Taylor, Field Notes 284–454, BANC-MSS-74/187c, *ibid.*

37. Patricio Shutter interview by Taylor, 1928, Field Notes 147–736, BANC-MSS-74/187c, Taylor Papers; *Will Kimble v. R. G. Gonzalez,* case 22567, Records of the 65th District Civil court (El Paso County Courthouse, El Paso, Tex.); *Will Johnson v. R. G. Gonzalez,* case 22568, *ibid.; Earnest Young v. R. G. Gonzalez,* Case 22569, *ibid.;* J. R. Silva interview by Taylor, 1928, Field Notes 106–10, BANC-MSS-74/187c, Taylor Papers, *El Paso City Directory* (El Paso, 1928), Southwest Collection.

38. Calculating the precise percentage of Italians who remigrated to Italy in the off-season is difficult given the paucity of sources on individuals leaving the United States or Canada. For an estimate that 46% of Italian immigrants and 54% of Greek immigrants remigrated, see Thomas J. Archdeacon, *Becoming American: An Ethnic History* (New York, 1983), 139. On the global context of labor migration in this period, see Edna Bonacich and Lucie Cheng, "Introduction: A Theoretical Introduction to Labor Migration," in *Labor Immigration under Capitalism: Asian Workers in the United States before World War II,* ed. Lucie Cheng and Edna Bonacich (Berkeley, 1984); Dino Cinel, "The Seasonal Emigration of Italians in the Nineteenth Century: From Internal to International

Destinations," *Journal of Ethnic Studies,* 19 (Spring 1982), 43–69; and Donna R. Gabaccia, "Worker Internationalism and Italian Labor Migration, 1870–1914," *International Labor and Working-Class History,* 45 (Spring 1994), 63–79.

39. Testimony of Rafaele di Zazza, in *Royal Commission,* 35; Peck, "Reinventing Free Labor," 292–303; Passenger Manifest Lists, Port of New York, March 1901, March 1904, March 1907, Records of the Department of Immigration and Naturalization.

40. Cordasco, in *Royal Commission,* 167; testimony of John Rodier and Hormisdas Laporte, *ibid.,* 89, 133.

41. Testimony of Giovanni Morillo, in *Royal Commission,* 67; testimony of Michele Cilla, *ibid.,* 37; testimony of Vincenzo Sciano, *ibid.,* 32.

42. See *Cordasco v. Canadian Pacific Railway Corporation,* case 2195, Records of the Superior Court of Montreal (National Archives of Canada, Montreal).

43. The amounts demanded ranged from $134 by a laborer to $350 by a foreman, and together totalled almost $4,000 in lost job fees and wager. See *Giuseppe d'Abramo v. A. Cordasco,* case 2787, Records of the Superior Court of Montreal; *Pietro Bazzani v. A. Cordasco,* case 1359, *ibid.; Michele Cilla v. A. Cordasco,* case 2575, *ibid.; Fillip D'Allesandro v. A. Cordasco,* case 2357, *ibid.; Alfredo Folco v. A. Cordasco,* case 2223, *ibid.; Nicola Fondino v. A. Cordasco,* case 3127, *ibid.; Giuseppe Mignella v. A. Cordasco,* case 503, *ibid.; Benvenuto Missiti v. A. Cordasco,* case 1420, *ibid.; Salvatore Molla v. A. Cordasco,* case 2135, *ibid.; Donato Olivastro v. A. Cordasco,* case 2198, *ibid.; Domenico Poliseno v. A. Cordasco,* case 572, *ibid.; Giuseppe Teolo v. A. Cordasco,* case 990, *ibid.;* and *Michelle Tisi v. A. Cordasco,* case 2513, *ibid.*

44. On judgments against Cordasco, see March 3, 1909, Registre des Jugements de la Cour Superieure, vol. I, p. 577 (National Archives of Canada, Montreal); May 11, 1906, *ibid.,* vol. II, p. 515.

45. "Fifty Greek and Crete Men to Utah Government," petition, Feb. 2, 1911, File "G," box 10, Spry Papers; Mike Lakis et al. to Gov. William Spry, Aug. 1, 1911, *ibid.;* Spry to Lakis et al., Aug. 17, 1911, *ibid.; Pocatello Tribune,* Dec. 3, 1911, p. 8; *ibid.,* Dec. 8, 1911, p. 8. As a county official, William Terrell had no authority to dismiss a federal investigation, but William McConnell was acting along with no official status or backing. Frustrated by Terrell's public rebuke, McConnell sent his file to the Department of Justice in Washington, hoping to generate a more formal federal investigation. Nothing came of his efforts and the Justice Department did not save his affidavits, no doubt because McConnell was not a United States attorney or federal investigator.

46. Testimony of Charles Catelli, president of the Italian Emigration Aid Society, in *Royal Commission,* 126; *O Ergatis,* Oct. 26, 1907, p. 1; *By-Laws of the Greek Community of Utah,* arts. 12, 19, 25 (Salt Lake City, 1905). On Stathakos's business dealings with Greeks, see *Thrassyvoulos Koliopoulos v. Nicholas P. Stathakos,* case 21002, Records of the Third District Court, Salt Lake County; Minutes of the Greek Community of Utah, 1910 (Holy Trinity Greek Orthodox Church, Salt Lake City, Utah). Translated from Katharevousa Greek by the author with the help of Mrs. Lena Nikolaou.

47. *Salt Lake Evening Telegram,* Sept. 18, 1912, p. 1. On the strike and the race, ethnic, and class relations that it dramatized, see Gunther Peck, "Padrones and Protest: 'Old' Radicals and 'New' Immigrants in Bingham, Utah, 1905–1912," *Western Historical Quarterly,* 24 (May 1993), 157–78.

48. *Ogden Evening Standard,* Oct. 2, 1912, p. 1; *Salt Lake Tribune,* Oct. 2, 1912, p. 1.

49. George Lamb interview by Papanikolas, Sept. 3, 1972, Greek Oral History Collection.

50. Morris L. Ernst, *Public Employment Exchanges: Report of the City Club of New York on Public Employment Exchanges* (New York, 1914), 12.

51. Papanikolas, "Toil and Rage in a New Land," 122. Many of these Greeks ended up in the coal fields of Colorado, where they embraced the message of Greek organizer Louis Tikas, martyr of the infamous Ludlow massacre in 1914. On connections between the Bingham strike and the Ludlow massacre, see Zeese Papanikolas, *Buried Unsung: Louis Tikas and the Ludlow Massacre* (Salt Lake City, 1982).

52. *Raleigh News and Observer,* March 13, 1994, pp. 1, 3.

Race, Labor, and Citizenship in Hawaii

EVELYN NAKANO GLENN

Hawaii has often been portrayed as a racial paradise, a tolerant multicultural society in which natives and immigrants have freely intermingled. Visitors to the islands since the nineteenth century have described their fascination with the diversity of the population and the exotic beauty of the many people of mixed descent. Novelists, journalists, and academics have all contributed to the idealization of Hawaii's race relations, broadcasting glowing descriptions of Hawaii as a "racial melting pot" and trumpeting the absence of racial hostility and overt discrimination. At the same time, however, scholars and journalists have been struck by the degree to which race has served as an organizing principle in the social, political, and economic institutions of the islands. They have described an overarching racial hierarchy in which land and capital wealth, social privilege, and political control are concentrated in the hands of a small white elite, while arrayed below in a kind of political-economic pecking order are diverse nonwhite groups, including Native Hawaiians, Asians, and Pacific Islanders.[1]

These seemingly contradictory pictures of Hawaii as racially harmonious and as racially stratified both capture parts of a complex whole. This complexity makes Hawaii an especially rich source for insights into the intricacies of how race, gender, and class relations and meanings are formed and contested at the local level, even while being influenced by institutional structures and cultural forces at the national level.

Racial tolerance has often been viewed as a legacy of indigenous (pre-European contact) Hawaiian values of openness and generosity. The openness of Native Hawaiians to outsiders in the early post-contact period set the tone for widespread acceptance of interracial unions. Such unions occurred not just among ordinary people but also among Native Hawaiians of the *alii* (chieftain) class. The tradition of forging political and economic alliances through intermarriage had been utilized by King Kamehameha I, who unified several independent and quasi-independent entities into the Kingdom of Hawaii by 1795. Later he offered the hands of royal Hawaiian women in marriage to European and American missionaries and merchants whom he trusted and used as advisors.[2]

One measure of Hawaii's racial attitudes is that, unlike other areas of the United States with large proportions of "nonwhite" population, Hawaii never had any laws against miscegenation, nor was there any notable sentiment in favor of such legislation. The reasons for the absence of anti-miscegenation laws may be more complex than simply a culture of tolerance. Even in Hawaii, interracial unions followed certain gender patterns which contributed to a willingness by Europeans and Americans to sanction interracial marriages. Peggy Pascoe has pointed out that anti-miscegenation laws in many parts of the United States were adopted to prevent men of color from having access to white women, not to prevent white men from having access to women of color. Hence such laws were most prevalent in areas, such as the South, where men of color were seen as posing a threat to white womanhood. The imbalanced sex ratio among Asian groups in Hawaii might have created such a threat. However, the scarcity of white women and the availability of Native Hawaiian women directed Asian men toward Hawaiian women. Almost all interracial unions in Hawaii before 1940 involved Native Hawaiian, Asian, or mixed-race women. As in the Southwest, domestic unions between dominant-group women and subordinate-group men were exceedingly rare.[3]

The frequency of interracial unions meant that from the mid-nineteenth century there was a substantial and growing mixed race population in all parts of local society. By the beginning of the twentieth century part-Hawaiians made up one-fourth of the Native Hawaiian population, and by 1930 they outnumbered pure Hawaiians.[4] As part-Hawaiians further intermarried, the mixtures became increasingly complex, involving various fractions of Asian, European, Anglo American, and Native Hawaiian ancestry. The resulting heterogeneity within many extended kin networks, including some elite *haole* (European and Anglo American) families, helped forestall the kind of race- or color-based Jim Crow laws and practices that prevailed in the South and the Southwest.

The absence of blatant color barriers did not, however, mean an absence of racial hierarchy. Indeed, the growth and elaboration of race-based stratification was integral to Hawaii's development as a colonial dependent economy. Hawaii was incorporated into the world capitalist system initially as a trading center, and then as a producer of agricultural staples, particularly sugar, for the U.S. market. Although formally an independent nation before annexation by the United States in 1898, first as a kingdom (1795–1893) and briefly as a republic (1895–1898), it was in effect part of the U.S. economy from the mid-nineteenth century on.[5] The pathway to Anglo American hegemony was paved by American and European traders and New England lay missionaries who arrived in the early 1800s. They quickly established themselves economically and politically, assuming roles as advisors and agents for the Hawaiian royalty. They implanted Anglo American institutional forms in the areas of religion, government, law, language, and education. Under their influence, the Hawaiian monarchy instituted a system of private ownership of what had been communally held land.[6] Also, as in the Southwest, where in-migrating Anglo men gained control of estates through marriage to the daughters of landed Mexicanos, European and American businessmen and descendants of missionaries solidified their claims to land through marriage with Native Hawaiian women of the chieftain class.[7]

Privatization of land enabled the nascent Anglo American oligarchy to establish a plantation-based economy relying at first on Native Hawaiian labor and later on imported

Asian labor. Sugar cultivation began early in the nineteenth century but did not dominate the economy until after the Civil War, when the demand for sugar caused prices to soar. A reciprocity treaty was signed in 1876, allowing Hawaiian sugar to be imported to the United States free of duty in exchange for the United States having rights to Pearl Harbor for a military and commercial base.[8] Sugar production grew by 2,000 percent over the next two decades. Planter and financial interests further consolidated their rule in 1893, when they seized control of the government and deposed Queen Liliuokalani. They established a republic in 1895 and then engineered annexation in 1898, making Hawaii a U.S. territory and permanently exempt from all U.S. tariffs.[9]

As in the South, planters saw cheap and tractable labor as the key to profitability. Prior to 1876 Native Hawaiians were the main source of plantation labor. However, with explosion of sugar production, there were not enough Native Hawaiians to fill labor demand. The native population, by some estimates 300,000 at the time of contact, had fallen to 47,528 by 1878 and to 39,504 by 1896.[10] Moreover, Native Hawaiians could not be easily tied to wage labor because they could still live off the land and the sea. Planters briefly considered importing black labor, but discarded the idea on the grounds that, slavery having been abolished, freedmen would not be sufficiently docile. Instead they turned to male contract labor, most of it from Asia. From 1850 to 1930 over 400,000 workers were imported. The first recruits were men from China (an estimated 40,000–50,000, mostly between 1876 and 1885); after the flow from China was cut to a trickle by Hawaiian government restrictions, planters turned to Japan (around 180,000 arrivals, mostly between 1886 and 1924); and, after 1924, when immigration from Japan was cut off by U.S. law to another U.S. colony, the Philippines (about 120,000 between 1907 and 1931). Of these Asian immigrants, only among the Japanese was there a significant number of women, 40,000 of whom arrived between 1907 and 1923. Portuguese, mostly from the Azores and Madeira, the largest non-Asian group (17,500), were recruited in two waves, from 1878 to 1887 and from 1906 to 1913. Smaller numbers of workers came from Korea, Puerto Rico, Spain, Germany, Russian, Norway, and other Pacific islands.[11]

The pattern of organization for sugar was repeated in the production of pineapple, cultivation of which began on a small scale in 1900 and which grew to become the second-largest export product by 1920. The same Anglo American corporations controlled land and financing, and much the same labor force was employed. Together, sugar and pineapple dominated the Hawaiian economy from 1876 to the mid-1930s. At the peak of the plantation economy in the 1930s, over half of the population of Hawaii was made up of sugar and pineapple workers and their dependents.[12]

Outside observers were struck by the extreme concentration of economic and political power in the hands of the local oligarchy. Economic activity, from banking to cultivation to processing and shipping, was controlled by thirty to forty corporations tied together by interlocking directorates. Individual directors, drawn disproportionately from a handful of families descended from early missionaries, sat on numerous boards. This network of local corporations held an iron grip on financing, transportation, public utilities, plantations, factors, and construction industries. Most critical to the oligarchy was control of the land on which to grow the sugar and pineapple. By 1909 over half of private land was owned by haole corporations; of the remainder, one-third was controlled by individual haoles; one-third by the haole directors of the Bishop Estate, a giant land trust; and the last third by individual Native Hawaiians, part-Hawaiians, and Asians.[13]

With land and capital heavily concentrated, Hawaii offered few opportunities for small producers. Consequently, Hawaii never experienced a major influx of agrarian white settlers. The absence of a white "yeomanry" simplified the race and class structure. Aside from the severely reduced Native Hawaiian population, the main division was between a small white planter and business elite and a large group of imported Asian laborers. The relative paucity of white small producers and laborers precluded the kind of "race warfare" that raged between white and Asian workers in California.[14]

Relations between haoles and Japanese in Hawaii provide a localized example of the contestation over labor and citizenship in the United States in the period 1870–1930. In the beginning of the period the Japanese consisted of male workers concentrated in field work, seen as and seeing themselves as temporary residents, and lacking a stake in or membership in the society. By the end of the period the Japanese were permanent settlers, made up of families, and at nearly 38 percent of the population the largest racial ethnic group in Hawaii. A substantial generation born in Hawaii and therefore entitled to U.S. citizenship, the "nisei," had reached adulthood; many had moved out of plantation labor and into trades, small businesses, and urban employment. The haoles still held political and economic control, but the Japanese had achieved considerable educational and occupational mobility.

This relationship unfolded within a larger context of shifting multicultural relations, but the conflict and contestation between haole and Japanese was the most prominent in this crucial sixty-year period. Because of their numbers, the Japanese were seen as genuine competitors and threats to haole domination. Also, compared with other groups, haoles and Japanese had low rates of out-marriage, thus retaining more or less distinct communities and identities. Other groups, particularly Native Hawaiians, were active in struggles over resources and status, but the Japanese (as the predominant workforce) and the haoles (as the predominant owner/manager class) positioned themselves in particularly oppositional ways. Japanese and haole representation of self and other, "us" and "them," were interdependently constructed, as was the case with whites and blacks in the South and Anglos and Mexicans in the Southwest. Haoles defined themselves as "Americans" or "we" in contrast to the Japanese as "other" or "foreign"; they constructed Japanese as "not-American" or "un-American." Japanese were forced to confront haoles as the dominant other; through their organizations and vernacular press, Japanese in Hawaii countered haole representations, sometimes rearticulating dominant concepts and values to assert their identities as simultaneously "Japanese" *and* "American."

Hierarchy and Control in the Labor System

In setting up the labor system, planters designed an elaborately stratified structure to maintain white privilege and facilitate control over work and workers. White privilege was manifested in two principles: that Europeans and Americans should not have to work as equals or subordinates of non-Europeans/Americans; and that skill and authority were the purview of "higher races." Accordingly, planters recruited mainland whites and Europeans to fill managerial and skilled positions rather than promoting "Oriental" assistants. Surveys found that management positions were filled by white Americans, English, Germans, and Scots, and skilled and supervisory positions by Europeans (such as Germans and Norwegians). The largest category, unskilled laborers, was made up overwhelmingly of Chinese, Japanese, and later Filipinos, with smaller numbers of Puerto Ricans, Koreans, and others. Planters' control over this mass of lower-level field workers was mediated by the employment of "middlemen minorities" in field-supervisory positions. Thus jobs as field foremen (*luna*) as well as middle-level semiskilled positions were given to Native Hawaiians and Portuguese. This practice shielded elite haoles from the dirty work of disciplining workers; it deflected field workers' hostility onto other groups; and it kept field workers in the fields by cutting off avenues of mobility. A 1902 survey of 55 plantations showed that Japanese and Chinese made up 83 percent of the plantation workforce but held only 18 percent of the superintendencies. In contrast, "Portuguese" and "Other Caucasians" made up 6.3 percent and 2.4 percent of the workforce respectively but held 24 percent and 44 percent of the superintendencies. This basic structure was still in place in 1915, when another survey showed that 89 percent of the mill engineers and 83 percent of the overseers were of European descent.[15]

Wages were similarly stratified, with separate pay scales that ensured that Anglo Americans and northern Europeans received higher pay for equivalent work. The abovementioned 1902 survey revealed that "American" blacksmiths averaged $3.82 a day, "Scotch" $4.33 a day, Portuguese $2.61, Native Hawaiian, $2.12, and Japanese $1.63. On these same plantations, "American" carpenters received $4.38 a day, Portuguese $1.98, Chinese $1.56, Native Hawaiians $1.49, and Japanese $1.17. White American overseers received 57 percent more than Portuguese overseers and 100 percent more than Japanese overseers. The wage differentials continued in 1915, with American overseers earning 73 percent and 107 percent more than Portuguese and Japanese overseers.[16]

Recruiting practices and perquisites also differed. Asian workers were treated strictly as laborers, not as settlers and potential citizens. At first the policy for Asian workers favored single men—sojourners free of family ties. In the words of a U.S. official, the sugar interests sought "cheap, not too intelligent, docile unmarried men."[17] Wages could be kept low and housing costs and perquisites minimized if men were not supporting families. Indeed, early plantation camps afforded Asian and Native Hawaiian male workers only the most primitive shelter, usually hastily constructed shacks and barracks. Lacking adequate sanitation, workers' housing harbored rats and insects, which set off periodic epidemics of typhoid and bubonic plague. Plantation owners rationalized the conditions by citing the Oriental's low standard of living and primitive notions of hygiene.[18]

In contrast, Portuguese, Germans, and other Europeans were from the outset recruited as family groups or couples, in order to encourage them to become permanent settlers. European men were treated as family heads and potential citizens. Unlike Asian immigrant workers, Spanish, Portuguese, and Russians had their passage paid and were accorded better housing, plots of land to homestead, and free medical care. Plantation owners acknowledged a higher standard of living for European workers.[19]

Only when faced with continuing labor shortages after 1905 did planters rethink the policy of favoring single men for the Japanese workforce. The absence of attachments that made single male workers cheap and malleable also made them mobile. By the first decade of the twentieth century plantation owners concluded that women stabilized the workforce. They began to provide cottages for families, often with small subsistence plots to grow food. Motivated by these incentives and the opening provided by the 1907–8 Gentleman's Agreement, which cut off immigration of laborers from Japan but allowed entry to spouses, Japanese men began sending for brides. Between 1907 and 1923 over 40,000 Japanese women immigrated to Hawaii. Women constituted only 19.2 percent of the Japanese population aged twenty and older in 1900; by 1920 they were up to 38.3 percent and by 1930 to 42.9 percent.[20]

Although plantation owners now encouraged family formation, they did not adjust men's wages to meet the greater consumption needs of families. For example, in 1910 the estimated cost of food alone for two adults was $12–$14 per month, while the low-est-paid male workers received only $18 per month. Wives had to make up the income gap by engaging in subsistence farming and wage-earning activities. While Hawaiians, Portuguese, German, Norwegian, and a few Chinese women were drawn into mill operations, Japanese women were pulled into field labor. There they were concentrated in the back-breaking jobs of hoeing weeds and stripping dry leaves off the cane stalks. They were also employed in so-called men's jobs of cane cutting and cane loading. Women field workers typically worked a sixty-hour week (six ten-hour days), the same as the men; they earned about two-thirds of the pay of Japanese male field workers, who in turn earned less than Portuguese or Native Hawaiian male workers.[21]

The planters developed elaborate racial theories to justify the stratification of labor. Racial-ethnic stereotyping was rampant as planters and managers debated labor problems and the advantages and disadvantages of employing one group or another. Stereotypes made racial or ethnic stratification of occupations seem natural by portraying specific groups as suited to particular types of work by their physical, moral, or psychological attributes. A 1902 U.S. Labor Department report on the "present plantation labor supply" presented extensive descriptions of the supposed characteristics of major ethnic groups. The report recognized the non-haole status of the Portuguese, noting that they "form a class apart": "This is probably because the 'white man' has always been a sort of aristocrat in the islands, and a large body of immigrants who live in ordinary plantation quarters and work with hoes could hardly aspire to that rank in public estimation." Nonetheless, in the authors' opinion, the Portuguese were the most "hopeful" element of the population, as they rapidly Americanized, made good citizens, were "industrious and frugal," and raised enormous families of "bright, sturdy children—the most desirable crop of all in a country like Hawaii." Planters described them as more individualistic than either the Chinese or the Japanese. Apt to disagree with fellow workers, they were not inclined to strike against the employer.[22]

Native Hawaiians were described as desirable as teamsters, plowmen, ranch hands, wharf men, and porters because of their superior strength. They were said to be good workers and "almost perfectly honest" unless corrupted by city influences. However, they lacked industrial discipline and were "indisposed" to occupations of a monotonous character. They were thus ideally suited to jobs involving irregular employment, such as wharf men and porters.[23]

For unskilled labor, most managers felt that an ideal labor force would be equally divided between Chinese and Japanese. The report notes: "The two people in spite of their kinship, have marked dissimilarities. The Chinaman is usually the more steady and reliable but the less energetic laborer of the two, and is preferred for irrigation and cane cutting. The Japanese has greater physical strength, and is the better man for loading or for general roustabout work in the mill." This report was made only two years after a series of strikes following the Organic Act which had made Hawaii a U.S. Territory. Planters' attitudes toward Japanese had soured, while those toward Chinese (whose immigration was halted when Hawaii was annexed) had mellowed. The planters reported: "In matters of business honor, the Chinaman is considered vastly more reliable. He seldom deserts a contract, even though he loses heavily, while a Japanese will walk off and leave a manager in the lurch if he fails to get what he considers a profitable bargain." The Chinese were praised for being more constant in domestic relations and raising their children in strict accord with their ethical ideals. The report is particularly critical of Japanese "private morals," citing the practice of picture marriages. It describes the wives as having been "practically purchased by friends or agents." Consequently wives "promptly desert the men if they do not meet with their approval. Much looseness in the sex relations results."[24]

By 1926 Stanley Porteus, an Australian who was a professor of psychology and director of the Psychology and Psychopathology Clinic at the University of Hawaii, was translating racial stereotypes into the then-popular science of "race and temperament." On the basis of his observations and psychological tests, he concluded that while the temperaments of Native Hawaiians and Chinese harmonized with those of the ruling whites, "between white and Japanese there was an inevitable clash of temperaments. The latter was too adaptable and too ready to seize and turn the white man's own weapons against him." Summing up, he wrote: "The outstanding traits of Japanese character as these have been brought to attention during their stay in the Islands, we may say that collectively they are intensely race-conscious, ready to combine for any purposes of group advancement, aggressive and rather untrustworthy when self-interest is in question. Individually they are extremely adaptable, ambitious and persistent and emotionally self controlled."[25]

Prior to annexation by the United States, most plantations relied on a quasi-slave system based on penal contracts. Under the Master Servant Act of 1850 employers could "bind" workers for fixed terms of up to ten years, with penal provisions allowing for fines, imprisonment, and doubling the length of the contract for desertion or absence from work. The original act declared a contract void upon the death of the employer and banned inheritance of servants, thus avoiding one key feature of chattel slavery. However, transfer of contracts was common.

Starting in 1864 an agency of the Kingdom, the Hawaii Bureau of Immigration, took charge of recruiting workers, making contracts with them, and assigning them to plantations upon arrival. Many Asians signing "labor contracts" did not understand that they were selling themselves into quasi-slavery; the shock of discovering their true status led many contract laborers to resist abusive treatment and thus to incur imprisonment or physical punishment. Planters found ways to evade the prohibition of sale or transfer of labor contracts by forming companies to hire contract workers. A court ruled in 1876 that contracts could be written with a company and that a change of partners did not invalidate a contract. Moreover, throughout the contract period, employers were allowed to unilaterally assess fines and penalties. Workers' only recourse was desertion or refusal to serve, which brought down the forces of the law against them. In 1877 the Hawaii Supreme Court further hemmed in workers by ruling that matters regulated by the Master Servant Act were civil and not criminal matters. Workers were left with no recourse, since they lacked legal representation to bring suit in civil court. Workers under penal contracts were also subjected to types of physical abuse, such as whipping, used by white slaveholders in the South.[26]

Edward Beechert notes that throughout the 1880s and 1890s, despite some amendments designed to increase protections for workers, for example by limiting time served to the length of the contract, overall there was a further drift toward peonage: "The legal situation as it developed in Hawaii before annexation placed the workers in a category *outside* the law. For those under a penal contract, there was only the flimsy reed of appeal to the provisions against physical abuse, failure to pay wages, or transfer of contracts."[27]

Annexation by the United States meant that Hawaii law was replaced by U.S. law and jurisprudence barring penal contracts and upholding "liberty of contract." Planters in Hawaii thus faced similar problems as landowners of the South in maintaining coercion within an ostensibly free labor system. Without the existence of penal contracts, Chinese and Japanese workers could no longer be legally bound. Nonetheless, many planters continued to impose the old harsh methods of discipline. They granted overseers considerable leeway to chastise workers, and some overseers still made use of the black snake whip.

Workers responded to miserable living conditions and harsh treatment by desertion, malingering, and other forms of individual resistance, as well as by organized protest. In response, planters employed police to ferret out deserters and used a passbook system to prevent workers from moving from one plantation to another. Even after penal contracts ended, planters claimed that workers were incapable of governing themselves and attempted to regulate all aspects of their lives from diet to waking hours. In Miriam Sharma's words: "People who wished to enter the plantation needed passes. This was supposed to protect the 'gullible' and 'childlike' workers from confidence men, extortionists, and others of their ilk." Elaborate lists of rules established fines for infractions ranging from insubordination to drunkenness. Suspecting workers of malingering, overseers denied ill workers permission to take time off. Owners attempted to overcome forms of resistance such as self-pacing, soldiering, malingering, and absenteeism by keeping regular wages low and offering substantial year-end bonuses for those who averaged more than twenty days of work a month. They deducted payments for housing, food, and supplies purchased at the company store, and even dues for community center membership.[28]

Perhaps the most common response of workers was to leave plantation work as quickly as possible. They moved to town or city, fled to the mainland, or returned to their homelands. Turnover was a continuous problem. Over the years planters tried numerous methods to bind workers to their jobs and to motivate them to work longer hours.

After 1900 many planters sought to keep workers on the plantation by bettering conditions. They improved housing and recreational facilities and expanded perquisites such as hospital and medical benefits. The 1902 U.S. Labor Department report stated that workers were comfortably housed and well treated and that sanitary conditions were uniformly good, with regular cleanup and pickup of trash. Most plantations had special facilities for laundry, bathing, and cooking. Workers were encouraged to improve their quarters. Managers furnished them with plants and flowers for yards and awarded prizes for the most attractive quarters. Still, paternalism, not equality, was the goal; owners preferred to dispense charity rather than allow workers' autonomy.[29]

Many workers chafed at the overarching control by plantation management and preferred to forgo the amenities and convenience of plantation housing in order to live more independently. A manager expressed his perplexity that many of the workers "insisted on moving down into the squalid town, paying money for their house, buying their own fuel and walking an unnecessarily long distance to work in the morning."[30]

To further discourage movement to nonplantation jobs, in 1903 the planter-controlled territorial legislature passed a law banning the employment of Japanese in public works jobs on the grounds that their labor was needed on the plantations. Less formally, business firms in Honolulu were implored not to hire Japanese. Such measures had a limited effect as turnover accelerated. One unintended consequence of annexation was to open up Hawaii as a source of labor for the mainland. Labor agents soon arrived to lure workers to fill jobs in agriculture and railroads at wages that plantations could not or would not match. Over 1,000 Japanese workers left Hawaii for the mainland in 1902. By 1904 the number of annual departures was 6,000 and by 1905 more than 10,000. To stem the mass exodus planters sought to impose penalties on outside labor agents, but there was only so much they could do to restrict freedom of movement. They would not succeed in getting the federal government to cut off migration of Japanese from Hawaii to the mainland until 1907. Hawaii officials also continued to look for replacements for Japanese labor. Their representatives in Washington lobbied unsuccessfully for a special exemption to the Chinese Exclusion Act to allow planters to recruit workers from China.[31]

In response to workers' mobility, plantation owners increasingly moved from a straight wage system toward various forms of subcontracting and tenancy. One type of short-term arrangement was similar to a piece-rate system: workers were offered short-term contracts in which they were paid for accomplishing a given task, such as irrigating a field or cutting a field of cane, rather than for time worked. Under one type of long-term contract a group of workers under a headman was allotted acreage and given seed, cane, water, fertilizer, and tools. The group performed all the tasks needed to bring the field to harvest and were paid at the end. In another type of long-term contract owners made tenancy agreements with heads of households similar to southern sharecropping arrangements. By 1929 half of all plantation workers were employed as short- or long-term contractors.[32]

Like sharecropping in the South, subcontracting was adopted in response to perceived recalcitrance and withholding of labor by "free" workers. As in the South, contracts were designed to tie workers down while reducing any risks on the part of the landowner. Beechert observed, "The contracts, although elaborate in detail, were principally one-sided instruments." They contained clauses that allowed for re-writing the terms if the price of sugar fell or rose, and many contained provisions that required contractors to perform additional work desired by the employer. In a revised "uniform cultivation contract" drafted by the sugar producers in 1922, the contractor was required to give two months' notice to cancel the contract while plantation owners could cancel at will. Like tenant farmers in the South, contract workers in Hawaii seldom realized much of a profit after settling their debts. Beechert found that for the period 1915–1917 Japanese day workers could earn a maximum of $36.32 a month including bonuses, while cultivating and cutting contractors could receive $38.23 for a slightly shorter work month. However, "the vicissitudes of agriculture—a drought, pests, such as the leafhopper, or too much rain—might reduce his harvest to a point below the amount advanced for living expenses and fertilizer."[33]

Racialized and Gendered Citizenship

For much of the late nineteenth and early twentieth centuries the usefulness of Chinese and Japanese labor for the planter class was closely tied to their exclusion from citizenship. Their noncitizen status helped mitigate one potential problem for the planters: how to ensure an abundant supply of labor and at the same time retain their political dominance despite their small numbers. During the contract-labor period Asian men were taxed but were not allowed to vote. The 1887 Hawaii Constitution set substantial property requirements for voting and restricted suffrage to "male residents of Hawaiian, American, or European birth or descent." When the planters and the haole elite seized control of the government in 1893, they wrote a new constitution that continued to disfranchise Asian workers (as well as many Native Hawaiians): it required that a voter be a citizen by birth or naturalization *and* be able to speak, read, write, and explain the constitution in English.[34]

Disfranchisement for Asians continued after annexation. Unlike Mexicans following the Treaty of Guadalupe Hidalgo and blacks after the Fourteenth Amendment, who were at least technically accorded national citizenship, Asian immigrants were formally excluded. The applicable law was the 1790 Naturalization Act as amended in 1870, which limited the right to become a naturalized citizen to "white persons" and persons of African nativity or descent. In key cases involving Asian applicants, the U.S. courts created a separate legal status for Asian immigrants as "aliens ineligible for citizenship." Thus not only were most plantation workers not citizens, their special status as "ineligible for citizenship" differentiated them from other noncitizens. They could be singled out for discriminatory treatment and deprived of protections accorded noncitizens who were eligible for naturalization. In California and Oregon "aliens ineligible for citizenship" were barred from owning agricultural land. In Hawaii the Hawaii Sugar Planters Association (HSPA) adopted a resolution in 1904 stating that skilled jobs should be limited to "citizens" and those "eligible for citizenship."[35]

Ineligibility for citizenship underlined the position of Asians as temporary workers, not permanent settlers. As noted earlier, in contrast to policies aimed at encouraging

Europeans to settle as families, initial policies toward Asians were aimed at recruiting single males and discouraging the entry of women. Because of the scarcity of Japanese women, the population remained extremely gender imbalanced well into the 1930s, and the growth of an American-born generation entitled to citizenship by birthright, and therefore eligible for suffrage, was considerably delayed. As late as 1905, more than twenty years after the Japanese started immigrating, not a single Japanese resident of Hawaii was registered to vote. In 1910, when the Japanese population was 79,675, only 0.2 percent of the adult Japanese population had been born in Hawaii and therefore were citizens. At this time, Japanese constituted 41.5 percent of the population—the largest ethnic group in Hawaii—but were a minuscule 0.4 percent of adult citizens and 0.1 percent of registered voters.[36]

Citizenship status and race were so closely intertwined that planters and officials often used the contrasting terms "citizen labor" and "noncitizen labor" interchangeably with "white" and "nonwhite" ("Oriental" or "Asiatic"). The reports of labor officials refer frequently to the problem of "noncitizen labor" rather than referring to race or nationality. As noted, in 1904 the HSPA barred Japanese from skilled positions not by making reference to race but by referring to citizenship status. Seven years later, perhaps owing to an increasing influence of mainland racial discourse, the HSPA adopted a resolution that recommended restricting semiskilled and skilled jobs to Native Hawaiians and "whites."[37]

According to the U.S. Labor Department report of 1902, planters believed that the Japanese would not be desirable citizens because of their "inherited reverence for authority" (presumably Japanese authority). Not only was their allegiance suspect, they lacked the independence necessary for true American citizenship. While granting that the Japanese were clean and tidy and apt to adopt "the superficial tokens of Caucasian civilization" (such as wearing European clothing and carrying a watch), the report continued, "His white employers consider him mercurial, superficial and untrustworthy in business matters." Japanese were seen as good imitators; thus their adoption of Western cultural ideals betokened only surface change.[38]

Territorial status opened Hawaii to great scrutiny, both from mainland critics and from Republicans in control of the national government. One observer, the Progressive journalist Ray Stannard Baker, who investigated economic conditions in Hawaii in 1911, was moved to compare the position of the Anglo American elite to that of the white planter class in the "Old South." According to Baker, domination in both situations was based on control of the most fertile land, the machinery of production, and the labor supply: "Control is made easier in Hawaii, as it was in the old South, by the presence of a very large population of non-voting workmen. . . . Fully three quarters of the population of Hawaii have no more say about the government under which they are living than the old slaves."[39]

Annexation also heightened concerns on the mainland about maintaining both white supremacy and the semblance of political democracy. Visiting officials raised worries about the sheer number of "non-whites" in the population and the absence of a substantial class of "white yeomen" who could be allies of the tiny planter and business elite. By 1901, when the Japanese made up nearly 40 percent of the population, a mainland official was fretting about the consequences of Japanese becoming permanent settlers and their incorporation as citizens. He conceded that the Japanese adopted "occidental habits" but added that they were "intensely alien in their sympathies, religion and customs." Regarding the sharp increase in Hawaii-born Japanese, he noted the embarrassment that would be created "should this oriental population ultimately get control of the local government, by means of institutions established by Americans, and employ their racial solidarity to maintain themselves in power in the Territory." Since the Caucasian population was unlikely to increase through voluntary immigration, he urged special legislation to allow planters to import European field hands and families through civil contracts without penal provisions.[40]

In his 1905 report on Hawaii, the Commissioner of Labor blamed some segments of the planter class for stifling the growth of a white yeomanry. He said the planters' "democratic impulses were blunted by long years of being feudal lords" and suggested that what was good for the planters' profits might be bad for a democratic civic community. For the planters, the problem was one of securing a sufficient and stable labor force. For citizens of the Territory and people of the United States, the problem was one of "securing a working population with the civic capacity necessary to an upbuilding of a self-governing American commonwealth." He expressed concern over the harm done to democratic self-government by the presence of a large "Oriental labor population excluded from citizenship by law and apparently indifferent to citizenship as a matter of fact." Echoing prevailing Republican sentiments, he noted that such a situation bred no community of thought, feeling, or sympathy. Assimilation into American ideals "cannot be expected in a community in which only a very small percentage of the population are even descendants of people who have known representative government and have long had traditions of free institutions." He recommended efforts to increase the population of small producers and citizen residents. Such residents should not be "soft-handed" and should be suited for the physical hardships of Hawaii. Portuguese from the Azores, Spaniards, Italians from Sicily, and even Finns were suggested as candidates. The Commissioner added hopefully: "The fair-haired Portuguese of the Azores, whose descendants are now growing up in the Territory, are said to have been originally of Saxon stock."[41]

In response to these concerns about the lack of a significant "citizen population," the territorial government created a Board of Immigration in 1905 to recruit immigrants from Spain and Portugal, subsidizing their passage with subscriptions from the Planters' Association and then with a special income tax. Later the Hawaii Board of Immigration paid for passage of thousands of Russians from Siberia. These recruitment programs were intended only in part to fill labor needs. They were designed primarily to increase the white population. As the U.S. Labor Commissioner reported, "the fear of an oriental electorate had much to do with the adoption of this policy."[42]

Despite the inducements of wages one-third higher than those paid to Asians and land on which to homestead, most of these potential "white citizens"—with the exception of a significant number of Portuguese—left as soon as they saved enough money to flee. In 1911 a mainland journalist observed Portuguese and Russian families "living in utmost squalor and misery in Honolulu waiting for the men of the family who had gone to California to earn enough money to send for them." The Hawaii Board of Immigration also employed recruitment agents in California and New York City, but attempts to attract immigrants from the mainland proved "fruitless."[43]

Interdependent Lives and Identities

The plantation has been called the central "race making experience" by Andrew Lind, a dean of race-relations scholars of Hawaii. It was race making in two senses. First, it forged culturally and linguistically disparate immigrants into larger "nationality" groups. Laborers from the main islands of Japan (so-called Naichi) and from Okinawa, who considered themselves to be ethnically distinct, were lumped together as "Japanese." Workers recruited through Canton as culturally and linguistically diverse as the Hakka and the Punti became "Chinese." Lind notes, "A comparable growth in nationalistic or what is called racial unity, as a consequence of the planters having dealt with their workers as if they were culturally and linguistically alike, occurred among the more sharply differentiated Tagalogs, Visayans, and Ilocanos recruited from the Philippines."[44] Thus new ethnic identities were encouraged by the practice of assigning workers to ethnically homogenous housing compounds and work groups.

Second, and most significantly, the plantation system created the racial-class category of haole to which all others were counterpoised. The word "haole" in the Hawaiian language originally denoted "stranger," that is, someone without family and therefore without ties to the land. It referred to status as an outsider and did not designate race. A black sailor and a white missionary, for example, were both haoles. The term took on a more specific meaning as English and Anglo Americans acquired positions of prestige and influence in the government, starting in the reign of King Kamehameha I and accelerating thereafter. The European/American came to represent the "stranger" or haole, in contrast to the Native Hawaiian. The consolidation of haole as a racial category occurred with the development of the plantation and the need for the small proprietorial and managerial class to distinguish itself from workers. According to Lind, this class's influence "appeared to depend in some instances on their ability to keep the workers at a distance through the barriers of race. Hence even groups which in the strict biological interpretation of race were akin to the promoting groups, such as the Germans, Norwegians, Poles, Russians, and Spanish, who came to Hawaii as laborers, were designated as separate racial groups while on the plantation, and it was not until they moved into the less class conscious atmosphere of the city, or the plantation developed to its later stage, that they were able to become associated with the haole community."[45] Thus the term "haole" came to have a specific class as well as racial meaning in contrast to an ethnically diverse laboring class.

Within the stratified plantation system, the racial-class category of haole was constructed and preserved through a contrast schema that drew a sharp distinction between haoles and non-haoles. Social distance, materially and symbolically, was central to this distinction. With regard to the distance in material circumstances, Lawrence Fuchs observes, "By 1910, many managers were making $1,000 a month in addition to extensive perquisites, a fantastic sum in Hawaii, where the field hands were getting less than seventy-five cents a day." The huge disparity in earnings enabled the managerial class to enjoy an opulent colonial lifestyle unknown on the mainland. Letters and diaries of nineteenth- and early twentieth-century visitors to Hawaii are replete with references to "the open handed hospitality of [haole] residents, which was dispensed by the ever-present maids and houseboys."[46] The plethora of servants in the households of plantation owners, managers, and supervisors was a natural outgrowth of the race- and class-structured plantation system.

Employment of household staff to maintain gardens and grounds, run stables, prepare and serve meals, clean, run errands, and care for infants and children was necessary to the standard of living appropriate to haole status. The employment of servants was also symbolically important as a marker of social distance between haoles and others. Mainland and European whites recruited to fill managerial and skilled positions on plantations were encouraged to consider themselves members of the privileged class. These newcomers became haoles by adopting the accoutrements and rituals of haole status, and the employment of domestic servants was one important sign. Mainlanders who came from modest backgrounds were initially startled by their newfound status. A public school teacher who arrived from the mainland to teach in a plantation school found that she was to be housed in a cottage with four other mainland teachers. The principal had engaged a maid, and each teacher was to pay her four dollars a month. "A maid! None of us had ever had a maid. We were all used to doing our own work. . . . Our principal was quite insistent. Everyone on the plantation had a maid. It was therefore, the thing to do."[47]

Houseboys, gardeners, stable hands, cooks, and maids could be drawn from the very groups that supplied field laborers. While the general patterns of dominant and subordinate group relations in domestic service did not differ from those in the Southwest and the South, one peculiarity of Hawaii was the scarcity of subordinate-group women. Unlike the situation in the rest of the country, the majority of domestic servants in Hawaii were men until well into the twentieth century. In the late nineteenth century Chinese men predominated among household servants; by the beginning of the twentieth century Japanese men had succeeded the Chinese. Only with the arrival of Japanese women in substantial numbers after 1907 did domestic service gradually become feminized. It was not until the late 1920s that women finally outnumbered men in household service.[48]

Managers were made to feel like monarchs, for there were few checks on their power. As Fuchs puts it:

> The manager was king. He lived in a superb house, usually on the highest hill in the area. His court consisted of other haoles—assistant managers, section *lunas,* book-keepers, and engineers. . . . His every word was followed with excitement by the plantation community and even in the small villages beyond. He might speak graciously at the sixth or eighth-grade commencement of the village school and give out prizes on behalf of the plantation; he might ungraciously fire and punish employees according to his whims. It was up to him whether gambling and drinking would be sanctioned or prostitutes permitted to visit the camps. It was his decision whether movies would be shown or primitive recreational facilities be built. His word determined whether workers could leave camp for weekends in Hilo or Honolulu.[49]

Despite their luxurious style of life, women from missionary families can be said to have lost power relative to men in the transition to a plantation economy. In the earlier period men and women were considered partners in missionary work, concentrating on instructing Native Hawaiians of their own sex. According to Joyce Lebra, who collected oral histories, an elite haole woman "would enjoy the perquisites of the colonial life-style . . . But she has no direct or immediate role in the political and economic mechanisms that sustained her privilege." While haole men ran the plantations and businesses of Hawaii along paternalistic lines, their wives, much like their elite sisters in the South and the Southwest, were expected to play a complementary "maternalistic" role managing the household and engaging in charitable activities.[50]

As to life before marriage, in stark contrast to daughters of Japanese plantation workers, who often had to start working at an early age, young unmarried haole daughters were conspicuously unengaged in any gainful pursuits. As explained by Margaret Catton, a prominent haole social worker:

> In that era it was the exception, rather than the rule, for island [haole] girls to go to college, and unless they needed money, they did not take jobs. It was a period, too, when domestic help was both plentiful and cheap, and girls of the leisure class had little responsibility in the way of household duties. Until they married, girls graced their parent' homes and drove their mothers by horse and carriage to market or to make formal calls. They gave parties—riding, swimming, tennis, and dancing. Taking their sewing, embroidery or crocheting, the young ladies of Honolulu would spend an afternoon or day with one another. They had picnics, card parties, and tea parties.

Catton adds, "Girls of that time, brought up with a sense of noblesse oblige, also gave many hours in volunteer service to church or community."[51]

For workers, clustering according to haole-perceived race/ethnic categories encouraged the formation and maintenance of old and new ethnic identities among the diverse plantation workforce. Planters housed workers in ethnically specific housing compounds and assigned them to ethnically homogeneous work gangs. This grouping made it possible for some workers to sustain native languages, prepare food in native style, and modify living quarters into some semblance of homes they had left, and as mentioned previously, submerged groups such as Okinawans into broader ethnic categories.

For Japanese workers, a Japanese-style bath—an *ofuro*—for nightly bathing was the most basic necessity. As they became more settled the Japanese began to build community institutions, forming sumo and sports clubs, sponsoring entertainers, and establishing Buddhist temples and Japanese-language schools. Some planters contributed funds to help build temples and foreign-language schools, even though these institutions might seem contrary to Americanism, because they were seen as pacifying the workers. Although planters resisted the imposition of taxes to pay for public schools, they viewed donations to ethnic institutions as consistent with their roles as benevolent patrons.[52]

Ethnic clustering and donations to community institutions were not just for the workers' comfort, however. Plantation managers also wanted to encourage separation among groups and play them off against one another. Concerned that reliance on any one group gave it too much leverage, managers continually sought to "diversify" the workforce. A labor commissioner report of 1902 details a number of such attempts and concludes, "Hardly a locality in the world exists where there is a surplus of unskilled labor that has not been visited and investigated by Hawaiian labor agents."[53]

Despite planters' efforts to play groups off against one another, and workers' own efforts to build distinct cultural communities, the shared experience of plantation life forged a sense of commonality among workers. Whatever their cultural differences, all were subordinate to the haole. Plantation workers developed a local culture that drew on their various traditions and on the daily practices of plantation life, including a distinct local cuisine that drew on techniques and foods from all groups, often adapted to make use of available foodstuffs. They developed a common dialect, derived from the pidgin English used by overseers and traders to deal with Asian traders and workers. This local dialect had a distinctive syntax, intonation, and accent, with words borrowed from all of the languages of the plantation camp. Use of this "local" dialect marked off plantation workers from the haoles, who spoke standard English. John Reinecke commented that the "sharpest racial and social line drawn between haoles and non-haoles is thus to a considerable extent reinforced by the linguistic line between them." For local youth "it is considered snobbish and presumptuous to speak without the Island intonation, accentuation, and other peculiarities. This is being a 'black haole.'"[54]

The lives of "local" women, including the Japanese, contrasted sharply with those of haole women. Especially within Japanese American families, economic provision was an expected aspect of wives' duties. Edna Oshiro reported that ten days after her mother arrived in 1922 she "went to work in the sugar cane fields. She did all kinds of work, including *hanawai* (irrigation of the fields), cutting grass (commonly referred to as *hoe hana*), planting cane slips, flume cane (sending cane to the mill in the water flumes), and *pula* (cutting cane slips) . . . despite the hard work, Mother kept right on working until a month before her first child was born in August, 1924. In November, 1925 a second daughter was born. But Mother did not stay home for long. When the baby was four months old, Mother went back to work for six months, because of some family reverses."[55] Oshiro does not mention whether her mother took her infants to the fields, but contemporary observers saw mothers carrying infants on their backs in the fields. A mainland journalist described working mothers making tents of cloth and placing their babies in them on the ground, where they attracted swarms of flies.[56] Despite the fact that they worked the same hours as men, women remained responsible for childcare and housework, which had to be fit around their work schedules.

Mothers who did not work in the fields often earned income by providing domestic services to bachelor workers: taking them in as boarders, cooking their meals, and laundering and ironing their clothes. There were ethnic differences in the economic role of mothers. In Japanese families, mothers were more likely to work to enable children to attend school, while among the Portuguese, children were more likely to be employed to enable mothers to stay at home. A 1901 survey to 225 families of various nationalities found that among the Japanese "the wife was almost without exception engaged in work outside the home," but that in all other nationality groups, including the Portuguese and Native Hawaiians, wives were for the most part "engaged solely in home duties." However, the data table shows that while 51 out of 62 of the Japanese families reported "income from wives," a large proportion of the European and Native Hawaiian families reported income from "boarders and other sources." The authors of the report ignore the fact that keeping boarders requires considerable labor—cleaning, washing, and cooking—which almost certainly was performed by wives. We may infer that many European and Native Hawaiian women reported as "engaged solely in home duties" were actually contributing to family income through their labor. Inclusion of these women would lead to the conclusion that a substantial proportion of wives in all worker groups were bringing in income.[57]

The degree to which Japanese women were engaged in field labor is nonetheless striking. By 1910, out of 43,917 Japanese field workers, 24,093 were women and children. Of all female field workers, Japanese women constituted 80 percent. Japanese women were clearly not thought to be subject to physical limitations due to sex. Haoles apparently included Asian women in their notion that some races were inherently suited to labor that would have broken most white men. Officials of the U.S. Department of Labor responsible for monitoring labor in Hawaii reported extensive employment of women and children, but did not advocate special protections for them.[58] In any case, federal laws regulating hours and working conditions for women in most industries specifically exempted agriculture and domestic service.

Domestic service continued to be an important area of employment for immigrant Japanese and their daughters both on the plantation and in town. Because it was one of the few situations in which dominant and subordinate groups interacted in the private sphere of the household, it allows us to look at the way race/gender identities and meanings were created and contested in daily interactions. The availability of women for domestic service was ensured by the feudal system of dependence and paternalism which gave owners and managers considerable sway over workers and their families. Lind observes:

> It has been a usual practice for a department head or a member of the managerial staff of the plantation to indicate to members of his work group that his household is in need of domestic help and to expect them to provide a wife or daughter to fill the need. Under the conditions that have prevailed in the past, the worker has felt obligated to make a member of his own family available for such service if required, since his own position and advancement depend upon keeping the good-will of his boss. Not infrequently, girls have been prevented from pursuing a high school or college education because someone on the supervisory staff has needed a servant and it has seemed inadvisable for the family to disregard the claim.[59]

Even when they moved to town from the plantation, Japanese women found that the most readily available jobs were positions as maids, nursemaids, laundresses, cooks, and housekeepers. Many Japanese high school students spared their families from having to support them by working as live-in "school girls" (servants). Students from other islands who wanted to attend high school or college on Oahu had to come to Honolulu and take domestic positions as babysitters, housekeepers, and maids to pay for their room and board.

Relations between mistresses and female employees retained the feudal character of plantation relations. The servant was intimately involved in the household, and her status was tied to the status of the family she served. In many cases workers reported feelings of affection for the employing family, particularly for children. Some mistresses reciprocated by showing an interest in the schoolgirl's studies and friends. The more usual pattern was one of asymmetry. The servant saw all the intimate details of daily life and the employers' faults and foibles and sometimes petty meanness. In contrast, employers knew little about (and often did not care to know about) the servant's personal life, which existed only as a vague aspect outside the boundaries of their concerns.[60]

Some haole women felt entitled to the services of Asian women, who presumably existed to serve them. They viewed quitting a job as a form of betrayal. An interviewer reported that a Japanese woman and her mother were working as full-time maids for a haole woman who kept piling on more and more work until the daughter became distressed at her mother being so overworked. When her complaint about this went unheeded for some weeks, the two women decided to quit. The mistress became infuriated at this announcement, shouting: "You Japs speak of loyalty, you make me sick! None of you can be depended upon! I knew this was going to happen when the 'sneaking' mama-san [another Japanese maid] next door first started visiting you."[61]

Despite haole women's beliefs about the natural subservience of Japanese girls and women, nisei schoolgirls reported feeling resentment at being treated like servants. One student wrote about this in detail: "Never in my life did I have such a 'cooped-up' feeling; as if I were bound to something. My independent spirit seemed to gradually [be] taking wings, and I felt as though my individuality was propped on top of those wings." Another domestic worker reported: "The foremost thing that hit me was an inferiority complex . . . I felt this unpleasant feeling when guests came to the house where I was working in. I was nothing but a housemaid, not to be seen or heard. I felt as if the sons, who were younger than I am, of these two families looked down at me."[62]

Contestation and Resistance

Haole efforts at control of workers were in some sense responses to resistance from those being controlled. Planters frequently complained that the Japanese were "difficult" to deal with compared to Chinese, Native Hawaiians, and Portuguese. Though their characterizations of the Japanese were colored by their own interests, we can still look at haole complaints as evidence of Japanese resistance, especially smaller-scale cases of face-to-face and hidden resistance that would otherwise be difficult to document. Many themes that recur over and over in various documents and reports are encapsulated in the following uncited report quoted by Porteus:

> "From the outset," says Coman in her review of the labour situation, "they were difficult to deal with, proving to be restless and self-assertive to a degree hitherto

unknown in the canefields of Hawaii. They were moreover remarkably clannish, clubbing together for the championship of their common interests in a way that was distinctly embarrassing. They showed no disposition to marry Hawaiians and while readily adopting American dress and ways, cherished allegiance to their native land with peculiar tenacity. They found their way into skilled trades even more rapidly than the Chinese."[63]

Thus, from the perspective of the haole, the Japanese were being difficult when they did not accept their subordinate place and when they attempted to "better themselves," as well as when they persisted in maintaining a distinct cultural community and did not marry out and when they stood up for their rights and fought back, whether individually or collectively.

Despite the planters' view of the Japanese as clannish, within the Japanese community itself, class, ethnic, and political schisms fostered a certain amount of tension and conflict. As Eileen Tamura points out, the Japanese came from a hierarchical society. Those with more education and from "better families" tended to look down on others. There was also division between Japanese from the home islands (the Naichi) and those from Okinawa, which had been a separate entity until annexed by Japan in 1879. Okinawans, who made up about 14 percent of the immigrant population, had their own language and a distinct culture. Their differences made them targets of Naichi discrimination.[64] Okinawans recall being taunted by Naichi children, who called them unclean and pig eaters. Naichi parents forbade their sons and daughters to marry Okinawans, while Okinawan parents warned their children that if they married Naichi they would be subject to degradation by their in-laws.[65]

BUILDING SEPARATE SPACES

The building of formal and informal organizations and institutions was important as a defense against the cultural oppression experienced by the Japanese. Ethnic associations connected immigrants with their home country and with one another and offered a more expansive identity and more respect than could be gotten at work. Through leadership in an organization, donation to a community fund, or contribution of labor to a building project, ordinary workers could gain status and recognition. Tamura describes the plethora of "spaces" the issei (those of the immigrant generation) built and the nisei (the Hawaii-born children of immigrants) continued:

> [They] organized Buddhist and prefectural associations, held bon dances to honor their ancestors, celebrated the emperor's birthday with sumo wrestling matches, and welcomed the new year in the Japanese way. As among Japanese on the mainland, a strong sense of group solidarity enabled Hawaii's issei to look to their ethnic community for social and economic support. One example of this was the practice of tanomoshi, or rotating credit associations adapted in Japan from the Chinese hui. Like the Chinese hui, and the Filipino hulugan, the tanomoshi helped immigrants finance expenses they could not otherwise afford, and its effectiveness depended on trust, honor and community solidarity.[66]

One major formal institution was the Buddhist temple, a central site of community life. Despite opposition from Christians, plantation managers initially supported the building of temples. According to the U.S. Labor Commissioner's report for 1902, managers believed "the moral and social influence of the priests among the laborers to be good." The first temple was established in 1889, and by 1909 there were 33 temples of the two main sects, Hongwanji and Jodo Mission. Buddhism continued to attract adherents; by 1937 there were 107 temples representing 12 sects and enrolling some 39,719 registrants.[67] The issei generation also established Shintoism, the ancient religion of Japan, building shrines throughout the islands. While there were converts to Christianity, they remained a tiny minority, perhaps 2–3 percent of the Japanese in Hawaii through the 1920s.[68]

As anti-Japanese sentiment waxed in the wake of a 1909 strike and as the size of the American-born generation grew, Buddhist leaders began adapting Buddhism toward more American forms by emulating Christian churches. Temples installed pews and organs and held Sunday services, which included sermons and the singing of *gathas,* religious songs patterned after Christian hymns. Temples also conducted Sunday schools and sponsored Young Women's and Young Men's Buddhist Associations, patterned after the YWCA and YMCA. The YWBA and YMBA (later merged into the Young Buddhist Association or YBA) sponsored lectures, classes in arts and crafts and martial arts, oratorical contests, and social events. They were important training grounds for nisei leadership and provided forums for discussion of social and political issues. Island-wide and inter-island conferences helped forge ties among nisei in different plantation communities.[69]

A second major community institution was the Japanese-language school. The early issei pioneers expected to eventually return to Japan and wanted their children to be prepared for life there. The first such school was established in 1892 on Maui, and by 1900 there were 10 schools enrolling 1,500 students. A decade later 140 schools were teaching over 7,000 students. Some schools were sponsored by Christian churches and Buddhist temples, others by parents. As with the temples, plantation managers considered the schools a stabilizing influence and supported them with free land and financial help. Funding was provided by student tuition and by donations from members of the community. By 1920 close to 20,000 students, 98 percent of all Japanese children attending public schools, were enrolled in Japanese-language schools. The percentage dipped in the 1920s as a result of attacks by Americanists, but rebounded in the 1930s. As the orientation of the Japanese shifted to being permanent settlers, the schools were no longer viewed as preparing children for living in Japan but as helping retain Japanese culture in Hawaii. Schools were central sites for marking Japanese holidays. Until the 1920s children were kept home from public schools on those days and entire families gathered to celebrate holidays at the schools.[70]

A third important institution was the Japanese-language press. When they arrived in Hawaii, issei men had an average of four to six years of schooling and women two to five years. They were functionally literate and valued learning regardless of their occupational status. They read and kept afloat an amazing number of newspapers. Between 1900 and 1941 a total of eighty-six Japanese-language publications appeared, nineteen of which survived ten years or more. At the midpoint, in 1920, there were thirteen newspapers and journals. Like other immigrant publications, the Japanese-language press kept the community informed about events in the homeland and preserved a sense of connection there; however, it also helped acculturate immigrants by "informing them of American ways, interpreting events around them, and encouraging integration in the larger community." Although taking varied, often conflicting positions on issues, the press encouraged community discussion by editorializing about working and living conditions on the plantations. During World War I the newspapers unanimously endorsed the Liberty Bond campaign and urged the nisei to give up dual citizenship, and after the war the major papers, led by the *Nippu Jiji,* began publishing English-language sections to reach a wider audience.[71]

WORKPLACE RESISTANCE

Plantation laborers, whether Chinese, Japanese, Native Hawaiian, Puerto Rican, Portuguese, or Filipino and whether male or female, were far from docile. Under the brutal and relentless conditions, Japanese laborers, like other plantation workers, sometimes resorted to violence, especially against overseers. Chinzen Kinzo reports being stopped just in time from delivering a fatal karate chop to a luna who had whipped him. In 1900 striking Japanese workers wielded hoes to fight lunas trying to evict them. Setting fire to sugar mills or cane fields was another form of revenge, one that was particularly potent because of the cost exacted.[72]

The more common forms of resistance, however, were indirect, aimed at slowing down work and evading the constant surveillance of the lunas. Managers and overseers complained about the slowness of workers, their taking of frequent breaks, smoking, and gossiping. Workers became experts in deception. Jack Hall, a haole luna, recorded in his diary his frustration at trying to supervise women workers on a Kohala plantation:

> Hoeing was more pleasant and would have been all right except for the fact that the gangs on this work were largely composed of Japanese wahines [women] and it always seemed impossible to keep them together, especially if the fields were not level. The consequence was that the damsels were usually scattered all over the place and as many as possible were out of sight in the gulches or dips in the field where they could not be seen, where they would calmly sit and smoke their little metal pipes until the luna appeared on the skyline, when they would be busy as bees.[73]

Malingering was another classic strategy, as workers feigned illness or invented a death in the family or some other problem to get excused from work. Ronald Takaki notes that some Japanese laborers resorted to drinking shoyu (soy sauce) to raise their temperatures.[74]

Like their counterparts on plantations in the South who sang while working, issei workers composed folk songs (called *hole hole bushi*) while toiling in the fields. *Hole hole,* from the Hawaiian for "peeling," refers to stripping cane, a job done primarily by women, and *bushi* is Japanese for "tune." Hole hole bushi expressed the workers' sorrow and pain, while lyrics also allowed workers to comment critically on the plantation system and the lunas.

> Wonderful Hawaii, or so I heard.
> One look and it seems like Hell.
> The manager's the Devil and
> His lunas are demons.[75]

The only reason I'm doing
This tough and painful hole hole work
Is for the sake of my wife and children
Who live back home.

Those who curry favor and spur us to work
For mere extra ten cents
Better be bitten by a dog
And killed.

Two contract periods
Have gone by
Those who do not return
Will end up as fertilizer
For the cane.[76]

Women's hole hole bushi were especially apt to comment on their exploitation and double day:

My husband cuts the cane
I do the hole hole
By sweat and tears
We get by.[77]

It's starting to pour
There goes my laundry
My baby is crying
And the rice just burned.[78]

Why settle for 35 cents
Doing *hole hole* all day,
When I can make a dollar
Sleeping with that *pake*.[79]

Perhaps the most common form of resistance was "voting with one's feet." During the era of contract labor, many workers fled before the end of the contract period. Planters employed agents to track down and bring back "deserters" and instituted passbooks that any worker found away from the plantation would have to show. Once the contract era ended, Japanese workers could move to the city or migrate to the mainland. Between 1898 and 1907 an estimated thirty to forty thousand issei—one out of every five—departed for the mainland. The flow was stemmed in 1907, when President Theodore Roosevelt, at the behest of anti-Japanese forces in California, issued an executive order barring entry to the mainland United States by Japanese workers from Hawaii, Mexico, and Canada.[80]

PROTESTS AND STRIKES

When given the opportunity, Japanese workers demonstrated a willingness to confront employers to register their grievances. The very first group from Japan, who were recruited by labor agents in 1868, began lodging complaints with the Hawaii Bureau of Immigration within a month of their arrival. Of the 149 emigrants, 40 returned to Japan before the end of their contracts, 39 of whom signed a complaint charging the planters with violation of contracts and cruelty. This early experiment was deemed a failure and immigration was not resumed until the mid-1880s under agreements secured by Robert Walker Irwin, Hawaiian consul general and immigration agent in Japan. Irwin arranged for the importation of some 29,000 workers between 1885 and 1904. The first group of 676 men, women, and children arrived in 1885, and again there were "incidents" that had to be mediated by a Japanese "inspector" of labor employed by Irwin. In 1886, 50 of 92 workers on Koloa plantation were jailed for refusing to work, and in 1890, 170 workers on Heeia plantation rebelled against the lunas.[81] Between 1890 and 1899 the major Hawaiian newspapers reported 30 "disturbances" by Japanese workers, including marches and strikes, and many more incidents must have gone unreported.[82]

Japanese workers expressed their pent-up frustration and hopes for the future by engaging in demonstrations for several days when Hawaii became a U.S. territory in June 1900. Workers understood well that annexation meant the end of the hated contract-labor system. At a mass march in Honolulu demonstrators carried a banner declaring, "We are a Free People." All plantation activity was brought to a halt. U.S. officials chose to interpret these actions not as real strikes, "as no real demands were made by the laborers regarding their employment. It was merely a pause, during which the laborers seemed to expect some sort of readjustment in their relations with employers." In fact, there had been three major strikes—at Pioneer Mill, Olowalu plantation, and Spreckelsville plantation (all on Maui), in the months before the Organic Act took effect. In each of these strikes workers made specific demands for higher payment for accident victims, shorter workdays, and higher wages. In the remaining six months of 1900, Japanese field hands and cane workers engaged in at least 18 further strikes, the largest of which involved 1,350 strikers.[83]

The walkouts in celebration of annexation signaled growing worker militancy, as protest began to take more organized forms. Six major strikes, each involving more than a thousand workers, occurred between July 1904 and January 1906. The involvement of women in these protests is seen in some of the demands. In a December 1904 strike on the Waialua plantation, one of the demands was "that the white overseer of the women's gang be discharged upon the ground that he favored the pretty girls in assigning work."[84]

The first cross-plantation strike was an island-wide action by Japanese workers in Oahu in 1909. This strike differed from previous more limited actions in that it was spearheaded by an educated elite and supported by an inter-island network of voluntary organizations, newspapers, temples, and business associations. In stating their demands, leaders of the new movement (the Higher Wages Association) displayed a full command of Americanist labor movement discourse. Leaders called for "full fledged" manhood and the workers' right to a "just reward for their labor." In a letter to the Hawaii Sugar Planters Association, they demanded a rise in wages from $18.00 to $22.50 per month, the amount paid to Portuguese and Puerto Rican workers. Declaring that "the Japanese here are not coolies," the HWA proclaimed the Japanese the "equal of any man before the law" and thus deserving "the same consideration as any other labor." Echoing the larger labor movement, the HWA called for a "living wage" to maintain families and dependents in "a decent respectable manner."[85]

Instead of agreeing to negotiate, planters conducted a propaganda campaign through the press. As positions hardened, Japanese workers on Kauai, Maui, and Hawaii as well as business and social organizations pledged support for the HWA. In May, when workers from individual plantations presented their own petitions and were rebuffed, the strikes began, eventually encompassing all of the major plantations on Oahu and involving some seven thousand workers.

Planters quickly mounted a counteroffensive. The HSPA trustees signed a compact to share the cost of any losses from strikes on individual plantations. Plantation owners began mass evictions from plantation housing, using police to turn workers out. More than five thousand adults found shelter in Honolulu in vacant buildings, theaters, or private homes or camped out in A'ala Park. Mass outdoor kitchens were set up to feed thousands of evictees. Yasutaro Soga recalled: "The city of Honolulu was like a battlefield. . . . Women volunteers turned out in full force and helped in caring for [the strikers]." Planters hired Chinese, Portuguese, Native Hawaiian, and Korean workers to replace the Japanese, paying more than twice the rate the HWA had asked for. They also had strike leaders arrested and jailed on conspiracy charges. The strikers held out for four months but were finally exhausted by the prolonged encampment and the separation from their leaders. In early August representatives of the HWA met and voted to end the strike.[86]

Four months later the planters quietly raised the wage rate and abolished wage differentials by nationality. Observers of Hawaiian labor history conclude that the results of the strike were both discouraging and exhilarating for the workers: it accelerated both the move of Japanese out of plantation labor and simultaneously the movement up into more skilled and white-collar positions for those who stayed on the plantation. It also helped politicize and further Americanize the participants.[87]

A second major island-wide strike, in 1920, united Japanese and Filipino workers. Sparked by inflation and the worsening standard of living in the aftermath of World War I, it took place in the context of rising trade unionism by longshoremen, fishermen, telephone operators, and ironworkers and molders. Unlike the 1909 strike, which had been led by educated professionals and the vernacular press, the 1920 strike was instigated by leaders indigenous to the plantations. The Japanese Federation of Labor brought together worker associations from each of the plantations. The Federation grew out of the organizing activities of the Young Men's Buddhist Associations, whose membership consisted of young men from plantations. Filipino workers were organized under a separate union, the Filipino Federation of Labor.[88]

Overall, 8,300 workers representing 77 percent of the plantation labor force on Oahu went on strike. As in the 1909 strike, women were active and visible, not just as supporters, but as strikers. In addition to higher wages, an eight-hour day for field workers and ten for millhands, overtime pay, old age insurance, and a greater share of the crop price for tenant growers, the union demanded an eight-week paid maternity leave for women.[89]

Two weeks after the start of the strike, planters evicted all strikers and their families, some 12,020 adults and children. The union quickly set up tent cities, rented buildings, and opened kitchens. The mass encampment occurred in the midst of a raging influenza epidemic that eventually killed an estimated 55 Japanese and 95 Filipinos. Planters again employed scabs of varying ethnicity and carried out a vigorous anti-Japanese campaign in the press. Despite pressure from the planters, Governor Curtis Iaukea, a Native Hawaiian, stoutly refused to call out any troops. In April, responding to the anti-Japanese propaganda orchestrated by the planters, the Japanese Federation of Labor voted to change its name to the Hawaii Laborers' Association and applied for membership in the American Federation of Labor. The union mobilized support throughout the Islands, collecting and disbursing a strike fund of $600,000 and raising another $300,000 of in-kind donations. Still, it could not hold out indefinitely, and on July 1 the leaders finally capitulated. Afterward the owners quietly raised wages by 50 percent, began paying bonuses on a monthly rather than yearly basis, and expanded recreational and welfare benefits. However, strike leaders were blacklisted and participants denied promotion to higher jobs. One outcome of the strike, then, was to spur the exodus of more politicized workers out of plantation labor.[90]

Education and Americanization

By the mid-1920s, with immigration from most of Asia cut off and the U.S. Congress contemplating measures to stem immigration from the Philippines, the planters had to rely more heavily on native-born, and therefore citizen, labor of Asian descent. In 1927, for the first time, the number of native-born youth was sufficient to meet the needs for agricultural labor. Confronted with these shifting demographics, planters had to rethink their strategies for securing and maintaining labor. The realization that there was a rising generation of Hawaii-born Japanese who were citizens by birthright also changed the dominant discourse on race. During most of the nineteenth century and into the 1910s, the haole elite had subscribed to a belief in the natural inferiority of the Oriental. This belief justified their rule and also excused such practices as flogging and the enforcement and sale of labor contracts. By the 1920s, as haoles observed Japanese "invad[ing] the social and political life of the islands," some haoles began to worry that, far from being inferior, the Japanese had a greater capacity of hard work and study than Caucasians. Some haoles advocated restricting the mobility of Orientals to curb this unfair "racial superiority." A significant minority, led by descendants of missionaries, saw the problem as one of culture and sought to "uplift" the Oriental population by "haolifying" or "Americanizing" it.[91]

The shift in emphasis from controlling noncitizen immigrant labor to Americanizing the nisei generation marked the transition from categorical exclusion to stratified citizenship. The nisei could not be denied citizenship, but perhaps they could be molded to occupy a permanent subordinate position. They were already rapidly acculturating on their own, although not in the ways that the haoles wished, by joining labor unions, engaging in strikes, pursuing education, starting businesses, and entering the professions. In Fuchs's view, the Americanizers did not agree precisely on what Americanization meant, but at the least it meant "attending Christian churches, playing American sports, and eating apple pie; there was nearly complete accord that it did not mean labor unions, political action, and criticism of the social order of the Islands." According to Tamura, some haoles talked about inculcating the ideals of democracy and representative government and freedom, but such views were in the minority: "What Americanizers really wanted was for the nisei to give undivided loyalty to the United States and discard all vestiges of Japanese culture. They also insisted that the nisei read, write and speak Standard English, become Christians, obey the law, and be good plantation workers."[92] Accordingly, Americanization efforts were three-pronged: first, wiping out all vestiges of foreign and nondominant local culture; second, inculcating American culture and values; and third, constraining nisei ambitions and keeping the nisei in agricultural labor.

Efforts to eliminate alien influences focused on "cutting off fresh supplies of Asiatic immigrants," suppressing foreign languages, and discouraging forms of nonstandard English. Haole planters who had earlier supported the building of Buddhist temples and foreign-language schools now viewed them as subversive. Indeed, schools and temples had become sites for organizing resistance. During the 1920 island-wide sugar workers' strike, Japanese-language schools and the vernacular press came under attack by the major Honolulu newspapers, the *Star-Bulletin* and the *Advertiser.* The *Star-Bulletin* accused the "priests of Asiatic Paganism," made up of foreign-language teachers, editors of Japanese newspapers, and Buddhist priests, of seeking to gain control of Hawaii's industry. It declared that Hawaii must remain "in the hands of Anglo-Saxons whose brains and means have made the Territory what it is."[93] Tellingly, Filipinos, who were equally active in the strike but not seen as a major political threat, were not subject to this kind of racist attack.

Soon after the strike was broken, the territorial legislature passed laws to hobble foreign-language schools by requiring tests of teachers' knowledge of American culture, forbidding the enrollment of children before they had completed three years in an American school, limiting the hours of instruction to six per week, and directing that the courses and texts be selected by public school officials. It also passed legislation requiring Japanese-language newspapers to publish translations of all articles, a requirement which would have bankrupted the vernacular press. The restrictions on language schools exacerbated divisions within the Japanese community between those who favored accommodation and those who supported a more militant position. In the end, a group of Japanese challenged the restrictions in court, and the laws were found to be unconstitutional by the U.S. Supreme Court in 1927.[94]

On another front, there were concerted attacks on the local dialect. Pressure was exerted on the schools to discourage the speaking of Hawaiian Creole (pidgin). Separate "English Standard" schools were established in the 1920s as a response to haole objections to their children being educated in schools with Asian majorities. Entrance to English Standard schools was based on examination in English skills. Ostensibly their purpose was to encourage Americanization, but their actual result was segregated schooling. Virtually all "Caucasians" in the public schools were enrolled in the English Standard schools, while only a small number of Japanese were able to gain entrance into them. The *Hawaii Hochi* newspaper attacked the segregated system, calling the school board a "Jim Crow" board.[95]

Related to the establishment of English Standard Schools were efforts to inculcate American culture, values, and lifestyles. Although these efforts were influenced by Americanization programs on the mainland, there were two significant differences. First was a difference in the timing and duration of Americanizing fever. On the mainland, Americanization efforts targeting eastern and southern Europeans had begun in the 1910s, peaked in the mid-teens, and died out by the mid-1920s when immigration from these regions slowed to a trickle. While the Southwest received federal support for Americanization of Mexicans, Hawaii was not included in the federal programs. Americanization efforts in Hawaii were locally organized; they began later, starting in the early 1920s and continuing until World War II. As on the mainland, the timing of Americanization efforts in Hawaii was related to anxieties about perceived threats to the dominant cultural system. In Hawaii the threat loomed in the 1920s as the nisei generation grew to adulthood and was projected to become a plurality in the electorate.[96]

A second difference was in the targets of Americanization. Mainland programs, including efforts in the Southwest, targeted women in their role as mothers, but Japanese women were not the focus in Hawaii, possibly because they were seen as inassimilable aliens. Instead, efforts were directed at the Hawaii-born children through the public schools. Curricula were fashioned to focus on American history, civics, and literature, as well as music, drawing, and vocational work. Science and mathematics were not stressed because they did not inculcate patriotism. A nisei teacher in rural Oahu recalled: "We always had patriotic programs. In the morning the whole school assembled and we used to have the pledge to the flag and we used to sing patriotic songs—everyday."[97]

The focus on Americanization through schools was consistent with the missionary heritage of a substantial portion of the haole elite, who supported education for the masses as a form of racial uplift. According to Fuchs, the haole plantation oligarchy did not favor public education but did not actively attempt to prevent its development. Too busy to get involved, they left it to "do-gooders," often women descendants of missionaries, to run school committees. These haole women, like their mainland counterparts, engaged in charitable and educational efforts. For example, Mrs. Baldwin, the wife of the "Lord of Maui," established the Baldwin House, which ran a kindergarten, a library, night school classes, a high school, and a language program. She also helped organize the Maui Aid Association, which set up "American Citizenship Evening Schools."[98]

Also aiding the growth of public education was the local elite's sensitivity to mainland views of Hawaii as backward. They were eager to prove that Hawaii was civilized and truly American. Thus, when a U.S. Department of Education survey of the Hawaii schools in 1920 called for extensive reforms, local officials quickly acted to carry out the recommendations. They increased liberal arts education, following the precepts of the then-influential progressive education movement of John Dewey. Mainland educators were recruited to administer and teach in the public schools, and many fine schools, including the first public high school, McKinley in Honolulu, provided liberal arts education to the children of immigrants.[99]

Despite these strides, public schools remained seriously underfunded. Haoles and others who could afford the fees sent their children to private schools. For the entire period prior to 1941, Hawaii had the highest proportion of children enrolled in private school of any U.S. state or territory. Since the haole elite did not make use of public schools, they were loath to support them with their taxes. Also, as the nisei eagerly pursued education, including high school and college, some segments of the planter group began to declare that too much education would spoil them for plantation labor. These planters lobbied to limit education beyond the eighth grade. In 1928 the Department of Public Instruction, responding to criticisms by plantation industry leaders, ruled that beginning in 1930, 20 percent of junior high school graduates would be denied entry into high school. The effect, much to the chagrin of the planters and the dismay of public school educators, was to swell private secondary enrollments. Haole planters and property owners also complained about paying the lion's share of taxes for educating "Orientals," whose parents did not for the most part own property. During the 1920s proposals to charge tuition for high school were advocated by the Hawaii Chamber of Commerce, representatives of the Planters Association, and even a former president of the University of Hawaii. In 1933 the State Education Board did institute a $10 tuition for attending public high school, a considerable sum for poor families.[100]

Some haole educators and business leaders expressed concern that the nisei were overly ambitious when it came to education and aspiring to white-collar and professional employment. In a parallel with the conflict between Booker T. Washington and W. E. B. Du Bois over black education and aspirations, the Reverend Takie Okumura, a Congregationalist minister, and Fred Kinzaburo Makino, a newspaper publisher, clashed over Japanese educational aspirations. In 1921, in the aftermath of the bitter sugar strike and in the midst of the assault on the Japanese schools, Okumura, backed by sugar plantation interests, began a six-year campaign to Americanize the issei and nisei. He admonished the Japanese to "go more than halfway" to dispel suspicions and improve their relations with the haoles. He organized meetings of plantation workers to urge them to "adopt American ways, become Christians, remain on the plantation, and encourage their children to do likewise." While urging nisei to be 100 percent American, Okumura advised them to hold on to the Japanese values of duty, responsibility, and loyalty, which he saw as compatible with Americanization. He also opposed legal challenges to the territorial restrictions on foreign-language schools. Starting in 1927 Okumura organized a series of New American Conferences, at which haoles and Japanese businessmen and leaders spoke to nisei men and women delegates of community organizations about issues related to Americanization. The general tenor of the messages can be gauged by the address delivered at the first conference by David Crawford, president of the University of Hawaii (and older brother of the territorial superintendent of schools). He opined that "too many young people of Japanese and Chinese ancestry consider agriculture beneath them—they want white collar jobs," when it was "obvious" that they "must go into agricultural industry—sugar, pineapple, coffee and general farming." Three years later he admonished the delegates, "do not count too much on education to do too much for you, do not take it too seriously."[101]

Okumura's main critic was Makino, who had vigorously taken up the cause of the Japanese in their struggles against discrimination and labor exploitation. Among other actions, he had helped lead the sugar strike of 1909, headed the legal challenge to the territorial laws aimed at destroying the Japanese-language schools, and editorialized in his newspaper against injustice and discrimination against the Japanese. Makino agreed that the Japanese should retain aspects of Japanese culture while adopting American values, but stressed the importance of justice and fair play. Subscribing to the dominant discourse of white manliness, Makino noted: "Americans bow to no master and cringe to no superior. They are straight shooters and are very apt to say exactly what they think, because they are not afraid of anyone." He urged the nisei not to be obsequious: "When the young Japanese are able to look their white brother squarely in the eye and tell them to 'get out of the way,' they will find out whether there is any race discrimination that can hinder them or keep them from success." In a later critique of the New American Conferences, Makino said the conferences were attempts at "mental grooming" of the nisei through speeches in which "selected 'pap'" fell from the "lips of big shots" to plant the "right views."[102]

While the debate was roiling the Japanese community, haole public officials were taking action to allay the concerns of haole educators and businessmen who felt that too many nisei students were pursuing liberal studies. Using newly available federal funds, the Department of Public Instruction expanded vocational training programs aimed at instilling respect for the dignity of manual labor. Auto mechanics, machine shop, carpentry, and electrical work were offered for boys, and dressmaking, cafeteria and restaurant service, and lauhala weaving for girls. "Homemaking" programs for girls were actually intended to train them as maids, "the rationale," as one official put it, "being that many students worked as maids while attending school and would continue to do so after graduation." The greatest emphasis was on vocational agriculture. In one program boys over fourteen attended classes for half the day and spent the other half in the sugar fields. In another program high school boys studied coffee production, poultry and hog raising, and gardening.[103]

Nisei responses to these agricultural education programs paralleled the reactions of Mexican American girls to domestic work training programs in the Southwest: although the programs were offered in some twenty schools, they were under-enrolled. The nisei disputed the notion that their futures lay in plantation labor. From their perspective, issei parents had put up with plantation work so their children could live a better life. Moreover, nisei students were already familiar with manual labor. Many of them had done field work while going to school and wanted no part of it. A young nisei woman enrolled in normal school said about her experience of field work: "I shed my tears secretly. I thought if I only had the chance, I'll never come back to the fields."[104]

Portents of Things to Come

Young nisei understood all too well the lack of opportunities in plantation labor and aspired to enter skilled crafts and white-collar employment, despite admonitions by haole leaders that such aspirations were unrealistic. The number of Japanese employed in the plantation sector fell from a peak of 31,029 in 1902 to 16,992 in 1922 and to 9,395 by 1932. They also moved up the occupational ladder: Japanese classified as laborers fell from 33,871 in 1916 to 12,754 in 1930.[105]

As the American-born children of immigrants reached adulthood, they added to the citizen population. By 1930, 16 percent of adult Japanese were citizens. The haole oligarchy did not cede control of the political realm without a struggle. The haole-controlled Republican party tried to curb Japanese voting by making registration difficult. Nisei registrants had to "prove" their citizenship by furnishing sworn statements from midwives or other witnesses that they had been born in the Islands. The haole-controlled legislature sought to curtail Japanese political activity by passing a bill requiring any material on politics written in a foreign language to be translated and submitted with the names, residences, and businesses of the authors to the attorney general for approval.[106]

Haoles persisted in their belief that the Japanese, despite Americanization, did not act independently. Just as Mexican workers in the Southwest were accused of being in the thrall of bosses, Japanese laborers in Hawaii were suspected of being controlled by others—in this case the government of Japan. Testifying before members of a U.S. Senate Committee on Immigration in 1920, Hawaii Governor Charles J. McCarthy speculated that Hawaiian-born Japanese were not registering to vote on instruction from the Japanese government. He noted that a thousand Japanese were eligible and surmised that if the policy of the Japanese government changed "and they were all instructed to register and vote, we might be swamped."[107]

Japanese in Hawaii pressed the case for inclusion by demonstrating their civic virtue and displayed their Americanization by fighting for their rights. They subscribed heavily to World War I bonds, published broadsides asserting their patriotism, and lobbied officials. They also engaged in walkouts and strikes, hired lawyers to challenge discriminatory legislation, took officials to court for violating their rights, and lobbied to gain the ears of influential mainlanders. Senator William H. King of Utah, at the U.S. Senate hearing of the Committee on Immigration, told of his fact-finding visit to Hawaii two years previously. He said he had visited homes and found that Japanese women were devoted to their homes and children and kept their households in good condition. He reported that Japanese in good standing complained that not enough attention was given to their Americanization, "but rather there was an effort made to isolate them and to make them feel that they were not welcome as American citizens, and they begged me to use what influence I might have—of course I have none there, not being a resident—to induce the people of Hawaii to extend to them in their schools and in their businesses and other relations a more generous welcome, to the end that they might—those who were Americans who were entitled to American citizenship—they might feel they were a part and trifle of this American Republic."[108]

In the meantime the nisei were becoming aware of the importance of suffrage. As early as 1915 some Japanese leaders were decrying the lack of an electoral voice and urging those eligible to vote to do so. They saw voting as a mark of first-class citizenship and first-class citizenship as the only way to gain respect. In an article entitled "Get Your Right to Vote" in the Japanese-language *Maui Shimbun,* the writer opined: "Treatment by authorities and ordinary individuals differs greatly on whether one has the right to vote or not . . . people with the right to vote are respected among *gaijin*. . . . Sometimes even white people who look down on Japanese treat those with the right to vote as first class citizens and try not to treat them shamefully." Makino and other leaders organized a movement, which they publicized in Makino's newspaper, *Hawaii Hochi,* to assist nisei to have their citizenship certified. In an editorial headlined "Citizenship! Citizenship! Reporting to Those Obtaining Citizenship," the writer warned that the territorial government was "posturing" to stop accepting applications, and declared: "The movement to gain citizenship is a pressing task and we cannot let our guard down for even one day. We must rally those of us who have the right to citizenship and walk together toward our goal through legal means."[109]

As the nisei generation grew to maturity in the 1920s and 1930s, the number of nisei registered voters rose dramatically. In 1920 only 658 of the 26,335 registered voters in Hawaii were nisei. One factor exacerbating the low numbers was that only 57 women were registered, a much smaller proportion than in other ethnic groups. Nonetheless, by 1930 nisei made up 7,017 out of a total of 52,149 registered voters, and by 1936 they made up about a quarter of the registered electorate, the largest voting bloc in Hawaii.[110]

By the end of the 1930s the fears of the haole elite were being realized. It was clear that U.S. citizens of Asian descent would make up the majority of the labor force and citizenry of Hawaii in the future. The U.S. Labor Commissioner reported that citizen labor on plantations had risen from 12 percent in 1930 to 45 percent in 1939. Overall, four-fifths of the population were citizens. The Commissioner warned that conditions that had been "acceptable" to illiterate alien labor would not be so to citizen labor. His 1939 report noted some improvement in material conditions, in wage levels, housing, recreation, medical care, and mechanization. Less satisfactory was the continuation of paternalistic policies and arbitrary methods of determining wages and benefits. Such practices made workers too dependent on the goodwill of managers. In sum, the Commissioner reported: "The complete dependence of employees upon the plantation in respect to every aspect of the life of the working community makes them less independent than farm laborers on the mainland."[111] Not until the decline of the sugar plantation economy after World War II would the assumed "dependence" of Japanese and other Asians be shattered and the majority Asian population come to dominate politics.

In Hawaii, despite the frequent blurring of racial boundaries and the absence of widespread legalized segregation, race was a central organizing principle in the labor system and other social institutions. As in the South and the Southwest, the labor market was stratified by race and gender, and workers were subject to coercive and abusive controls common to colonial labor regimes. There was also considerable spatial and social separation between haoles and Asians, and patterns of interaction underscored racial difference and social hierarchy. Racializing discourse was also rampant as planters constructed elaborate portraits of each group's "racial temperaments" and gender "characteristics."

In terms of citizenship status, blacks in the South were excluded as anti-citizens (enemies of the social compact) and Mexicans in the Southwest were excluded on grounds of nationality (including those born on the U.S. side of the border). The excuse used against the Japanese in Hawaii was based on supposed lack of allegiance. The Japanese were not merely "aliens," like other immigrant groups, they were "aliens ineligible for citizenship," incapable of voluntary allegiance to the United States. Ordinary signs of assimilation, such as the adoption of Western dress, were seen as superficial; inside these clothes the Japanese were seen as forever alien. Even second-generation Japanese born in Hawaii were suspected of acting under the direction of the Japanese government.

For the Japanese in Hawaii, as for blacks and Mexicans, education was a central arena of struggle. Planters' resistance to publicly funded education for children of immigrant plantation workers retarded the development of public education beyond the elementary years. During the 1920s the white elite shifted its efforts toward Americanization programs, which involved the closing down of Japanese-language schools, the teaching of patriotic Americanism in public schools, and the expansion of vocational education designed to track Japanese boys into agriculture and girls into domestic work. Like blacks and Mexican Americans, Japanese in Hawaii strove to acquire education despite the barriers. Community activists disputed the notion that maintaining their language and culture was incompatible with Americanism. In this belief they were conjoined with blacks and Mexicans, and indeed other nonwhite Americans, in arguing for a pluralistic nation in which being a true American did not require "whiteness."

Notes

1. See Glen Grant and Dennis Ogawa, "Living Proof: Is Hawaii the Answer?" *Annals of the American Academy of Political and Social Sciences* 530 (Nov. 1993), 137–54; Jonathan Okamura, "The Illusion of Paradise: Multiculturalism in Hawaii," manuscript, n.d.; Jonathan Okamura, "Aloha Kanaka Me Ke Aloha 'Aina: Local Culture and Society in Hawaii," *Amerasia* 7, no. 2 (1980), 119–37. Some observers have found rampant ethnic stereotyping, albeit often expressed in humorous form and including one's own group. See, e.g., Jitsuichi Masuoka, "Race Attitudes of the Japanese People in Hawaii: A Study in Social Distance" (Master's Thesis, University of Hawaii, 1931).

2. Romanzo Adams, "Race Relations in Hawaii: A Summary Statement," *Social Process in Hawaii* 2 (1936), 56–60; Romanzo Adams, *Interracial Marriage in Hawaii* (New York: Macmillan, 1937), 47–48.

3. Peggy Pascoe, "Race, Gender, and Intercultural Relations: The Case of Interracial Marriage," *Frontiers* 12, no. 1 (1991), 5–18; Adams, *Interracial Marriage,* 49–54.

4. Andrew W. Lind, *Hawaii's People,* 4th ed, (Honolulu: University Press of Hawaii, 1980), table 3, 34. There is substantial contention over who should be called "Hawaiian." The term has at various times been used to describe any person who is primarily (usually 50 percent) descended from the people who lived in the Hawaiian Islands prior to contact by Captain Cook in 1778; any person who can trace any ancestor to the pre-contact period; any person born in the Hawaiian Islands at any time regardless of current residence; or any current citizen of the state of Hawaii. (Issues of "Hawaiianness" were dealt with by the U.S. Supreme Court in *Rice v. Cayetano,* decided in March 2000.) In this book I describe persons who consider themselves or most likely would have considered themselves to be descended from pre-contact Hawaiians as "Native Hawaiians."

5. Hawaii was a territory until 1959, when it became the forty-ninth state. See Gavan Daws, *Shoal of Time: A History of the Hawaiian Islands* (Honolulu: University of Hawaii Press, 1968), 264–320.

6. In the Great Mahele of 1848 King Kamehameha III divested the crown of its feudal entitlement and divided up the islands' 4 million acres: two-fifths was allotted to some 250 *alii* (chiefs), while most of the remainder was divided between crown land (the private property of the king) and public land to be controlled by the legislature and its agents. Less than 30,000 acres was set aside for the common people. Over the next decades two-thirds of the public land and much of the land held by the crown and the chiefs was sold or leased to European and American individuals and corporations. The Great Mahele represented the triumph of a European and American

conception of land as a commodity, whereas Hawaiians viewed land as part of the sacred domain. See Robert H. Horwitz, "Hawaii's Lands and the Changing Regime," *Social Process in Hawaii* 26 (1963), 67; Lawrence Fuchs, *Hawaii Pono: A Social History* (New York: Harcourt, Brace and World, 1961), 15–16.

7. Fuchs, *Hawaii Pono,* 38, reports that as many as 30 early white residents married *alii* women.

8. Edward D. Beechert, *Working in Hawaii: A Labor History* (Honolulu: University of Hawaii Press, 1985), 79–80, 122.

9. Ibid.; Daws, *Shoal of Time,* 270–92.

10. These figures include part-Hawaiians. Lind, *Hawaii's People,* 20 and table 3, 34. Estimates of the population at the time of contact range from 100,000 to well over a million. See, e.g., David E. Stannard, *Before the Horror: The Population of Hawaii on the Eve of Contact* (Honolulu: Social Science Research Institute, University of Hawaii, 1989).

11. Statistics on Chinese are from Eleanor Nordyke, *The Peopling of Hawaii* (Honolulu: East West Center/University of Hawaii Press, 1977), 4, 27, 37–38; on Japanese and Filipinos from Eileen H. Tamura, *Americanization, Acculturation and Ethnic Identity: The Nisei Generation in Hawaii* (Urbana: University of Illinois Press, 1994), 5, 27; on Portuguese from Lind, *Hawaii's People,* 32, 35, 36. A group's actual population at any time was less than half of the total who immigrated because of return migration and remigration to the mainland United States.

12. Andrew Lind, *Hawaii: The Last of the Magic Isles* (London: Oxford University Press, 1969), 22.

13. Fuchs, *Hawaii Pono,* 251–53.

14. Edna Bonacich, "Asian Labor in the Development of California and Hawaii," in Lucie Cheng and Edna Bonacich, eds., *Labor Immigration under Capitalism: Asian Workers in the United States before World War II* (Berkeley: University of California Press, 1984), 130–86, 179–82.

15. U. S. Commissioner of Labor, *Report of the Commissioner of Labor on Hawaii, 1902* (Washington: Government Printing Office, 1903), calculated from tables on 84–85; U.S. Bureau of Labor Statistics, *Labor Conditions in Hawaii: Fifth Annual Report of the Commissioner of Labor Statistics on Labor Conditions in the Territory of Hawaii, 1915* (Washington: Government Printing Office, 1916), calculated from table B, 120–53, 132, 135–36, 143. Virtually all of the white/European field workers were Portuguese or Spanish.

16. U.S. Commissioner of Labor, *Report, 1902,* 152–55, 170–71; U.S. Bureau of Labor Statistics, *Report, 1915,* 143.

17. U.S. Bureau of Labor Statistics, *Report, 1915,* 40.

18. Ibid., 40, 33–35.

19. U.S. Bureau of Labor Statistics, *Fourth Report of the Commissioner of Labor on Hawaii, 1910* (Washington: Government Printing Office), 52–58; U.S. Bureau of Labor Statistics, *Report, 1915,* 35–37.

20. Calculated from Nordyke, *Peopling of Hawaii,* table 4b.3, 144–45.

21. U.S. Bureau of Labor Statistics, *Report, 1910,* 21 and table 6, 227; U.S. Bureau of Labor Statistics, *Report, 1915,* table A, 96.

22. U.S. Commissioner of Labor, *Report, 1902,* 23.

23. Ibid., 23–24.

24. Ibid., 35, 37. Picture marriages were ones in which overseas male migrants who could not afford to return home used go-betweens in Japan to select prospective mates and arrange for the exchange of photographs. The marriage was legally registered in Japan without the groom being present, after which the bride would leave to join the husband in Hawaii.

25. Stanley D. Porteus and Marjorie E. Babcock, *Temperament and Race* (Boston: Richard G. Badger, 1926), 49, 52.

26. Fuchs, *Hawaii Pono,* 19; Beechert, *Working in Hawaii,* 42–57.

27. Beechert, *Working in Hawaii,* 56.

28. Miriam Sharma, "Labor Migration and Class Formation among the Filipinos in Hawaii, 1906–1946," in Cheng and Bonacich, eds., *Labor Immigration,* 588.

29. U.S. Commissioner of Labor, *Report, 1902,* 55–56.

30. Ibid., 211.

31. Fuchs, *Hawaii Pono,* 209; Ray Stannard Baker, "Wonderful Hawaii, Part 2: The Land and the Landless," *American Magazine* 73 (Dec. 1911), 211.

32. C. J. Henderson, "Labor: An Undercurrent of Hawaiian Social History," *Social Process in Hawaii* 15 (1951), 44–55.

33. Beechert, *Working in Hawaii,* 138–39; Andrew Lind, *An Island Community: Ecological Succession in Hawaii* (Chicago: University of Chicago Press, 1938), 230–321.

34. Daws, *Shoals of Time,* 240–52, 281.

35. Ian F. Haney López, *White by Law: The Legal Construction of Race* (New York: New York University Press, 1996), 44; Ronald Takaki, *Pau Hana: Plantation Life and Labor in Hawaii, 1835–1920* (Honolulu: University of Hawaii Press, 1983), 76.

36. Data from Lind, *Hawaii's People,* table 3, 34, table 17, 99, table 18, 100, and table 19, 102.

37. Takaki, *Pau Hana,* 76.

38. U.S. Commissioner of Labor, *Report, 1902,* 23.

39. Ray Stannard Baker, "Wonderful Hawaii," *American Magazine* 73 (Nov. 1911), 32.

40. U.S. Commissioner of Labor, *Report, 1902,* 119.

41. U.S. Bureau of Labor Statistics, *Third Report of the Commissioner of Labor on Hawaii, 1905* (Washington: Government Printing Office, 1906), 19, 57, 79.

42. U.S. Commissioner of Labor, *Report, 1902,* 42–46; U.S. Bureau of Labor Statistics, *Report, 1915,* 10.

43. Ray Stannard Baker, "Human Nature in Hawaii," *American Magazine* 73, no. 3 (Jan. 1912), 330. See also U.S. Bureau of Labor Statistics, *Report, 1910,* 53–58, 61, 99.

44. Henry Toyama and Kiyoshi Ikeda, "The Okinawan-Naichi Relationship," *Social Process in Hawaii* 14 (1950), 51, 54–55; Lind, *Hawaii,* 44.

45. Lind, *Hawaii,* 45–46.

46. Andrew W. Lind, "The Changing Position of Domestic Service in Hawaii," *Social Process in Hawaii* 15 (1951), 73.

47. Ibid., 78.

48. Ibid., 74.

49. Fuchs, *Hawaii Pono,* 62.

50. Joyce Chapman Lebra, *Women's Voices in Hawaii* (Niwot: University Press of Colorado, 1991), 76; Margaret M. L. Catton, *Social Service in Hawaii* (Palo Alto: Pacific Books, 1959), 9–13, 15–21, 33–41, 63–77, 163–65.

51. Catton, *Social Service in Hawaii,* 30–31.

52. U.S. Commissioner of Labor, *Report, 1902,* 36–37.

53. Ibid., 22.

54. John Reinecke, "The Competition of Languages in Hawaii," *Social Process in Hawaii* 2 (1936), 7–10, 9. The use of the term "local" to refer to a certain race-class segment of the population seems to have appeared in the 1930s. At the most general level, "local" designated those born and raised in Hawaii or residing long enough to be steeped in the distinctive lifestyle of the Islands. Beneath this meaning, however, lie several other registers, whose significance varies by context and period. Eric Yamamoto, citing Lind, notes that the term "local" first was used in reports of the Massie Trial of 1931 to distinguish the island-bred alleged rapists (two Native Hawaiians, two Japanese, and a Chinese-Hawaiian) from their white military accusers. In this usage the emphasis was on differentiating locals from "outsiders." However, there was also a racial register, in that locals were nonwhites, while Massie and the military officers in charge of the case were whites. In the latter sense, "local" is counterposed against "haole." Thus, in the eyes of many "locals," haoles born and bred in the islands are "kamaaina," a term that distinguishes them from mainland haoles, but they are not "local." Finally, there is a class register to the term "local," which may or may not exclude all haoles. According to Jonathan Okamura, "locals" see themselves as embodying certain values and character traits that include being "easygoing, friendly, open, trusting, humble, generous, loyal to family and friend, and indifferent to achieved status distinctions." These traits are viewed as

consonant with idealized Native Hawaiian culture and as discordant with haole or American values and ideals of individualism, competition, achievement, and contractual relations. Yamamoto, "From Japanese to Local: Community Change and the Redefinition of Sansei Identity in Hawaii" (Undergraduate thesis, Sociology Department, University of Hawaii, 1974), 105; Okamura, "Aloha Kanaka Me Ke Aloha 'Aina,'" 127–28.

55. Edna Oshiro, "The Americanization of My Mother," *Social Process in Hawaii* 18 (1954), 30.

56. Baker, "Human Nature in Hawaii," 334.

57. Takaki, *Pau Hana,* 78–80; U.S. Commissioner of Labor, *Report of the Commissioner of Labor on Hawaii, 1901* (Washington: Government Printing Office, 1902), 101, tables V and VI, 141–253.

58. U.S. Bureau of Labor Statistics, *Report, 1915,* table B; U.S. Bureau of Labor Statistics, *Report, 1910,* 48–50.

59. Lind, "Changing Position of Domestic Servants," 77.

60. Ibid.

61. Document MA hl 27m, 2, Romanzo Adams Papers, Department of Sociology, University of Hawaii–Manoa.

62. Document MA 15 I, 4–5, Romanzo Adams Papers; Document MA 18–I 3, Romanzo Adams Papers.

63. Porteus and Babcock, *Temperament and Race,* 46. The idealization of the Chinese and Native Hawaiians as less assertive and more agreeable was nostalgic nonsense; when these groups were the main labor force, they also resisted control, ran away, and engaged in violence, arson, and strikes, prompting bitter complaints from managers and overseers. See Takaki, *Pau Hana,* 127–52.

64. Henry Toyama and Kiyoshi Ikeda have characterized the relationship between the Naichi and the Okinawans as analogous to that between the British and the Irish, with feelings of superiority on one side and defensiveness on the other. This analogy has some aptness because of a colonial relationship between Japan and Okinawa. Okinawan culture had been influenced by cultures from the south such as from Taiwan and the Philippines, and its language, though belonging to the same family as Japanese, had become separated sometime before the sixth century A.D. After annexation and conversion into a prefecture, Okinawans were subject to government policies aimed at assimilating them into the dominant Japanese culture and language. In Hawaii, Okinawans were set apart not only by culture and language but also by their arrival after the Naichi had already established themselves. See Toyama and Ikeda, "Okinawan-Naichi Relationship," 51, 54–55; and the following articles, all in Ethnic Studies Oral History Project, *Uchinanchu: A History of Okinawans in Hawaii* (Honolulu, 1981): Mitsugu Sakihara, "History of Okinawa," 7–10; Tomonori Ishikawa, "A Study of the Historical Geography of Early Okinawan Immigrants to the Hawaiian Islands," 82; Mitsugu Sakihara, "Okinawans in Hawaii: An Overview of the Past 80 Years," 110–12.

65. Dorothy Ochiai Hazama and Jane Okamoto Komeji, *Okage Sama De: The Japanese in Hawaii, 1885–1985* (Honolulu: Bess Press, 1986), 71–76.

66. Tamura, *Americanization,* 27.

67. Ibid., 15, 17, 208.

68. U.S. Commissioner of Labor, *Report, 1902,* 37; Louise H. Hunter, *Buddhism in Hawaii: Its Impact on a Yankee Community* (Honolulu: University of Hawaii Press, 1971), 71–73; Tamura, *Americanization,* 51, 17, 208; U.S. Bureau of Labor Statistics, *Report, 1910,* 72.

69. Tamura, *Americanization,* 205; Beechert, *Working in Hawaii,* 197.

70. Tamura, *Americanization,* 146–47.

71. Ibid., 205, 146, 71–72.

72. Takaki, *Pau Hana,* 127–29.

73. Ibid., 130–31.

74. Ibid., 131.

75. Franklin S. Oda and Harry Minoru Urata, "Hole Hole Bushi: Songs of Hawaii's Japanese Immigrants," *Mana* (Hawaii ed.) 6, no. 1 (1981), 72.

76. Yukio Uyehara, "The Horehore-Bushi: A Type of Japanese Folksong Developed and Sung among the Early Immigrants in Hawaii," *Social Process in Hawaii* 28 (1980–81), 115, 116.

77. Ibid., 114.

78. Gary Y. Okihiro, *Cane Fires: The Anti-Japanese Movement in Hawaii, 1865–1945* (Philadelphia: Temple University Press, 1991), 32.

79. Odo and Urata, "Hole Hole Bushi," 74. *Pake* is the local term for Chinese.

80. Tamura, *Americanization*, 19–20.

81. Masaji Marumoto, "First Year Immigrants to Hawaii and Eugene Van Reed," in Hilary Conroy and T. Scott Miyakawa, eds., *East across the Pacific: Historical and Sociological Studies of Japanese Immigration and Assimilation* (Santa Barbara: ABC Clio, 1972), 33; Hilary Conroy, "The Japanese Frontier in Hawaii, 1868–1898," *University of California Publications in History* 46 (1953), 30, 65; Okihiro, *Cane Fires,* 22, 23–26; Ernest Katsumi Wakukawa, *A History of the Japanese People in Hawaii* (Honolulu: Toyo Shoin, 1938), 28, 39.

82. Fuchs, *Hawaii Pono,* 113–14.

83. Takaki, *Pau Hana,* 148–49; U.S. Commissioner of Labor, *Report, 1901,* 17, 112–15, table 7, 254–57.

84. U.S. Bureau of Labor Statistics, *Report, 1905,* 140; Beechert, *Working in Hawaii,* 163–69.

85. Takaki, *Pau Hana,* 154; U.S. Bureau of Labor Statistics, *Report, 1910,* 64, 65–75.

86. Quoted in Takaki, *Pau Hana,* 160; Okihiro, *Cane Fires,* 51–53.

87. Okihiro, *Cane Fires,* 55–57.

88. Beechert, *Working in Hawaii,* 196–97, 199–201; Okihiro, *Cane Fires,* 68.

89. Okihiro, *Cane Fires,* 71; Beechert, *Working in Hawaii,* 199.

90. Beechert, *Working in Hawaii,* 204–8; Okihiro, *Cane Fires,* 80; Fuchs, *Hawaii Pono,* 225.

91. Beechert, *Working in Hawaii,* 240–42; Fuchs, *Hawaii Pono,* 51.

92. Fuchs, *Hawaii Pono,* 50; Tamura, *Americanization,* 59.

93. U.S. Bureau of Labor Statistics, *Report, 1915,* 41; Fuchs, *Hawaii Pono,* 219.

94. Tamura, *Americanization,* 73–74, 147–50.

95. Ibid., 112. Tamura (113) notes that until World War II "Caucasians" constituted half of all students in the English Standard schools but only 2.5 percent in non-Standard schools. Japanese made up 3–8.5 percent of the students in English Standard and 55 percent in non-Standard public schools. Native Hawaiian, Portuguese, and Chinese students were more equally represented in proportion to their numbers in the public schools.

96. John Higham, *Strangers in the Land: Patterns of American Nativism, 1860–1925,* 2d ed. (New Brunswick: Rutgers University Press, 1994), 234–61; John F. McClymer, "Gender and the 'American Way of Life': Women in the Americanization Movement," *Journal of American Ethnic History* 10 (Spring 1991), 3–20; Gayle Gullett, "Women Progressives and the Politics of Americanization in California, 1915–1920," *Pacific Historical Review* 64 (Feb. 1995), 71–74. The Hawaii delegate to the U.S. House of Representatives, a native Hawaiian, complained that Hawaii was not included in federal funding of Americanization programs. U.S. Congress, Senate Subcommittee on Immigration, *Japanese in Hawaii* (Washington: Government Printing Office, 1920), 42.

97. Tamura, *Americanization,* 60.

98. Fuchs, *Hawaii Pono,* 266, 269–70.

99. Ibid., 271–88.

100. Fuchs, *Hawaii Pono,* 291; Tamura, *Americanization,* 133–35.

101. Tamura, *Americanization,* 62; Okihiro, *Cane Fires,* 142, 144.

102. Tamura, *Americanization,* 63, 64.

103. Ibid., 135–37.

104. Ibid., 137–39, 140.

105. Lind, *Hawaii's People,* 82, 99.

106. Ibid., 99; Fuchs, *Hawaii Pono,* 177.

107. U.S. Congress, *Japanese in Hawaii,* 9–10.

108. Ibid., 10.

109. *Maui Shimbun* (newspaper) "Get Your Right to Vote," Feb. 9, 1915, trans. Wesley Ueunten; *Hawaii Hochi* (newspaper), "Citizenship! Citizenship! Reporting to Those Obtaining Citizenship," June 11, 1915, trans. Wesley Ueunten.

110. Romanzo Adams, *The Peoples of Hawaii* (Honolulu: American Council, Institute of Pacific Relations, 1933), 18; Fuchs, *Hawaii Pono,* 135. The ratio of female to male voters remained low.

111. U.S. Bureau of Labor Statistics, *Labor in the Territory of Hawaii, 1939* (Washington: Government Printing Office, 1940), 79.

12

Turning the Tables on Assimilation

Oglala Lakotas and the Pine Ridge
Day Schools, 1889–1920s

THOMAS G. ANDREWS

Ambitious, numerous, and controversial, boarding schools comprised the primary front in the federal government's campaign to assimilate Indian children into the American mainstream. Yet all too often, popular memory and historical scholarship alike have isolated residential schools from the larger educational context in which they operated.[1] Boarding schools represented the largest and most heavily publicized component of the government Indian school system, but they hardly comprised the sum total of government efforts to educate Native American children. Federal officials built more than a hundred day schools throughout the Indian reservations of the American West in the late nineteenth century. Moreover, in regulations first promulgated in 1894 and frequently reinforced in the following three decades, the Office of Indian Affairs carved out a crucial niche for day schools in the federal Indian education system. According to these rules, Indian children were to begin their formal education at local day schools, progress to reservation boarding schools around the age of ten, and leave their tribal homelands for further schooling only after they had exhausted their reservation's educational resources, usually around the age of sixteen. The scheme proved difficult to implement on many reservations; nonetheless, roughly 15–20 percent of the Indian children attending school in any given year between the late 1880s and the 1920s received their education not at residential institutions, but at local day schools. Just as importantly, at least as many more children likely arrived at boarding school only after years of day schooling.[2]

Despite the appearance in recent years of dozens of fine monographs and articles on Indian education, the story of these important institutions nonetheless remains practically untold.[3]

The history of the most extensive system of Indian day schools in the nation—the thirty or so little schoolhouses of southwestern South Dakota's Pine Ridge reservation—thus promises to provide an illuminating counterpoint to the better-known tale of deculturation, abuse, and resistance at residential institutions during the assimilation era. In this essay, I explore the important, but heretofore overlooked, story of the cultural contests that occurred at federal day schools on the homeland of the Oglala Lakota. I begin by examining the ideological lenses through which policymakers, teachers, and Oglalas conceptualized day schools. Then, I analyze how these agendas shaped academic instruction, manual training, and community work. In contrast to the fundamentally authoritarian nature of power at boarding schools, I find more dispersed power relations at play in the day schools. Neither policymakers, teachers, nor Oglalas could ever fully exercise their will upon each other. Thus, day schools became important sites of cultural contact and negotiation where Oglala people struggled to subvert and resist the federal project of destroying their culture and changing their lifeways. Government officials envisioned day schools as weapons in their war against tribalism. The story of the Pine Ridge day schools, though, demonstrates that Oglalas managed to blunt the blow of assimilationist education. Moreover, it suggests how the people of Pine Ridge turned the tables on federal policy, refashioning day schools designed to eviscerate their culture into tools of individual and collective survival.

The day schools of Pine Ridge educated more Oglalas than any other component of the Indian school system.[4] In many ways, these schools resembled little red schoolhouses elsewhere in rural America. Blackboards and portraits of Washington and Lincoln graced the walls. Desks stood in neat rows. Windows offered distraction. Children of many ages crowded into single classrooms to recite readings from primers, master new lessons, play, and fight. Teachers maintained order, delighted at students' progress, and frowned upon their failings. But, in other ways, the Pine Ridge day schools represented another world altogether, because the men and women who created them endowed them with a singular purpose: to transform Indian children into Americans. Moreover, teachers at Indian day schools wrestled with unusual challenges. Finally, the Indian objects of the government's designs had notions of their own about schools and the role they could play in the tribe's future. Before we can understand what happened in the Pine Ridge day schools, then, we need to examine the varied and often conflicting agendas government bureaucrats, teachers, and Oglalas brought to the reservation's schoolhouses.

Literally and figuratively, policymakers, bureaucrats, and philanthropists were the architects of the day school system. They drafted plans for the schools, hired contractors to construct the buildings and instructors to teach in them, and supervised operations. A sense of mission guided them in all these arenas. An enlightened federal government, they believed, had to save Indians from extinction by dissolving tribal cultures and incorporating Indian individuals into the American nation. As Commissioner of Indian Affairs T. J. Morgan argued in 1889, the government had to liberate Indians from the ancient lifeways that would doom them "either to destruction or to hopeless degradation."[5]

Allotment and education comprised dual fronts in this campaign to save individuals by destroying tribalism.[6] Assimilationists intended the Dawes Act of 1887 to dismantle Indian patterns of communal land ownership in order to create a yeoman class tilling privately-owned lands. Removed from damaging tribal ties, made to embrace the plow instead of the gun, and rescued from dependence on government aid, individual Indians would become self-sufficient agriculturalists, archetypal Jeffersonian citizens invigorating the nation instead of profligate wards enfeebling it.[7]

Allotment would help assimilate Indians into the nation's economy and polity, while education would teach them how to speak, think, and work like other Americans. From the founding of the first Indian schools in the 1600s, Indian education lay within the bailiwick of Christian missionaries, but after the Civil War, the federal government increasingly assumed responsibility for educating Native children. In treaties signed with the Oglala and other Indian nations, the federal government promised to build schools for Indian children.[8] These schools sought, as Morgan phrased it, "the disintegration of the tribes" and the instruction of Indian students "not as Indians, but as Americans."[9]

The assault on tribalism began with moral training to inculcate mainstream American values, particularly Protestant Christianity, Anglo-Saxon civility, and republican virtue. Morgan urged that the whole course of study for the schools "should be fairly saturated with moral ideas, fear of God, and respect for the rights of others; love of truth and fidelity of duty; personal purity, philanthropy and patriotism."[10] Moral training would teach students to respect the superiority of America's belief system and to disparage the hopeless primitivism of Indian cultures, supplanting the cultural norms of the tribe with those of the nation.

The academic portion of Indian instruction, meanwhile, focused on replacing supposedly doomed Native languages with English, the cornerstone of Anglo-Saxon civilization and the *lingua franca* of the American Melting Pot. To Richard Henry Pratt, founder of Carlisle Indian School and one of the most influential educators of the era, language constituted the "first great barrier to be thrown down in all work of assimilating and unifying our diverse population."[11] Before students could progress to arithmetic, geography, history, or other subjects, they would first need to master English. The attack upon Native languages in Indian schools had broad cultural repercussions, for these languages were the creations and representations of Native epistemologies: they were the symbolic forms Indians used to conceptualize and communicate their ideas of the physical, social, and spiritual realms. By eradicating Indian languages, reformers hoped, they could begin to unravel what they considered the destructive bonds of culture that shackled Indian individuals to savage and doomed ways of life.

Equipped morally and linguistically to take their place in the mainstream of American society, Indian students were now ready, as Pratt put it, to be "wrought into shape and then sent to work on the great ocean of . . . industry and thrift."[12] Eastern reformers and government officials alike argued that manual training would impart skills Indians would need to support themselves. Though Indian schools provided instruction in traditional trades as well as modern industrial occupations such as printing and machining, agriculture formed the core of the manual training curriculum. "The Indians' capital is very largely land," proclaimed Commissioner of Indian Affairs Francis Leupp, "and their environment and every natural circumstance make it peculiarly necessary that the great majority of them should become farmers and stock raisers."[13] Yet the benefits of vocational instruction transcended mere economics. Superintendent of Indian Education W. Hailmann explained that so-called "industrial training" instilled "a keen sense of duty, self-control, persistence of will power, and all the other things that go to make up a strong, reliable character."[14] Having acquired the virtues of honest industry, Indian scholars would graduate to positions as independent farmers or wage-earning laborers. In 1889, Treaty Commissioner William Warner advised the Oglalas that "the Great Spirit helps those who help themselves," and believed that if they followed his advice, Indians would stop draining the federal treasury, start producing wealth, and begin paying taxes.[15]

The architects of assimilation were confident that this program of moral indoctrination, linguistic instruction, and manual training would turn Indians into Americans. Although assimilationists agreed on the message they wanted to impart, they argued strenuously about what medium would best convey "civilization" to the nation's Indian wards. Initially, most assimilationists felt that off-reservation boarding schools were best-suited for turning Indians into Americans. In the face of well-publicized reports that Indian boarding school graduates failed to flourish upon returning to their reservations, though, enthusiasm for off-reservation institutions began to wane by the early 1890s.[16] Returned students had trouble conversing with relatives and neighbors who spoke only tribal languages, adjusting to tribal lifeways they had been taught to despise, and applying knowledge and skills learned in school to reservations blighted by poverty and underdevelopment. "Honest and truly," wrote one Sioux graduate. "I can't live among these Indians out here. Even I couldn't eat the food they cook." "I gave up trying to farm for myself," complained another, "for I didn't have the farm implements nor horses . . . [a] fellow can't get out and farm with nothing."[17] As more returned students struggled to apply lessons imparted by Indian boarding schools, more educators began to sing the praises of on-reservation schools.[18]

Reservation schools promised two benefits. First reservation schools—particularly day schools—could accommodate more students for less money than off-reservation institutions.[19] Secondly, reservation schools could spread the assimilationist gospel to entire Indian communities instead of reaching only the young. Off-reservation schools molded Indian children into American citizens much more quickly, Superintendent of Indian Education Daniel Dorchester admitted, but "simply educating a few pupils at the East" would do little to diffuse the "leaven of civilization" to "the dark haunts which we are most anxious to enlighten and transform." To destroy the tribe and assimilate the Indian, he argued, "the lever of uplift must be applied nearer to the base of Indian life— directly on the reservations." Dorchester and his allies believed that every reservation school would serve as a fulcrum for "lifting the whole reservations" to "avoid a large and irretrievable loss and furnish a ground of hope for the future of the Indian masses."[20] Leupp later echoed Dorchester's argument. Residential institutions, he claimed, were "educational almshouses" that fostered dependence and laziness. Leupp advocated planting day schools on the reservations to "carry civilization to the Indian." Every school sown in Indian country would sprout into a "sphere of influence" that would indoctrinate Indian children in American ways and even "bring the older members of the race" into the national fold. From the day schools of the western reservations, the commissioner argued, "there should radiate into the Indian world all that is good and suitable for the Indians' advancement."[21] Leupp, Dorchester, and their allies believed reservation schools would stretch tight federal dollars further and bridge the gap between school and reservation that returning students found so difficult to navigate.

Policymakers and reformers felt confident that academic, manual, and moral training in the Pine Ridge day schools would destroy the tribal bonds that held Oglala culture together and seamlessly transform Oglalas into Americans. Conceiving of Indian lifeways as time-trapped and monolithic, they assumed Lakotas would offer little resistance before capitulating and blending into the advancing tide of American progress. Subjected to the teachings of the most civilized and powerful nation in the world, how could the Oglalas fail to see the wisdom of abandoning their doomed ways of life and embracing the superior practices and beliefs America had to offer?

At each of the Pine Ridge day schools, the architects of assimilation entrusted a teacher and a housekeeper with educating the Oglalas. They preferred these emissaries of civilization to be white married couples, and they expected the men to teach and the women to keep house. Indian couples or pairs of white women ran a few schools, but most were headed by white couples from the states of the Old Northwest.[22] A number of factors motivated couples to leave the comforts of home to teach on the reservation. Many "had come for a salary," claimed Luther Standing Bear.[23] Others answered a humanitarian or missionary calling to guide the benighted Indians of the West towards the light of civilization.[24] Though their motivations differed, most white teachers nonetheless shared the assimilationists' faith that the Oglalas' best chance in the future lay in English instruction, manual training, and moral indoctrination.[25] But their assimilationist zeal soon evaporated as they discovered the isolation of their posts and their vulnerability as outsiders in Oglala settlements. In the cultural contests that pervaded the Pine Ridge day schools, white teachers could never forget that they were not on home ground.

Consider the story of Albert and Edith Kneale. In his 1950 memoir *Indian Agent,* Albert provides little sense of what led him and his wife to abandon a comfortable teaching post in upstate New York for the remote, hard living of Pine Ridge. The Indian Service held an exam in Rochester. Kneale took the test and a few months later accepted a teaching post in Pine Ridge. Never having ventured farther west than Buffalo, the young couple found the train ride to Pine Ridge "all new, all exciting, all most wonderful." As they encountered for the first time what Elaine Goodale Eastman eloquently termed the "strange, uncouth landscape" of the Great Plains, Albert noted in spare language how "the distances between towns and habitations" grew as the train traveled westward. "Trees and streams became more scarce. Fences disappeared. Occasionally we noted a strange structure of which we could make but little." At Rushville, Nebraska, the closest rail depot to the reservation, the Kneales disembarked and boarded a stage for the twenty-five mile drive to the agency through "utter desolation—no habitations, no trees, . . . not a fence or stream."[26] Frederick Jackson Turner famously declared that the American frontier had closed in 1890, but almost a decade later Pine Ridge remained a geographically and culturally isolated Oglala homeland, undeveloped and virtually unsettled by non-Natives.

Like most Anglo teachers, the Kneales had little or no personal experience with Native people. They were ecstatic when they reached the agency and got their first chance "to study at close range some of these wards of Uncle Sam," but the famous chief, Red Cloud, proved a disappointment. The Kneales expected Oglalas to act like the Indians they had encountered in captivity accounts, newspapers, and novels. "I had read Cooper's *Leatherstocking Tales,*" lamented Kneale, "and had notions of how a chief should look." But Red Cloud "had none of these earmarks" and "looked much like the others."[27] As Albert Kneale discovered, his preconceptions of Indians squared poorly with reservation reality.

The confused cultural encounters at the agency were but a prelude to the challenges that pervaded the Kneales tenure at No. 10 Day School. Albert and Edith found their four-room cottage poorly built and sparsely furnished, while the shoddy school building next door contained a single room with windows on three sides. On the fourth wall hung a blackboard, a map of the United States, and a clock, which "served little purpose as there was seldom an opportunity to set it." The Kneales had crossed beyond the margins of an American society and economy inextricably dependent upon the minute division and measurement of time. "It was well nigh impossible to keep track of the days of the month," Albert lamented, "or even the week."[28]

The isolation of their new post sank in even more deeply that afternoon when the Kneale's neighbors visited. Albert and Edith shook hands, looked around a roomful of Oglala faces, and smiled uncomfortably as their neighbors asked questions in a language they could not understand. The teachers became acutely aware of their status as the only white residents of a Lakota community. Like other Anglo teachers, they lived in isolation from other whites and depended on Oglala neighbors for assistance, companionship, and security. The architects of assimilation imagined that day schools would sow the seeds of civilization in the "dark haunts" of Indian Country, but day-school teachers like Albert and Edith Kneale found themselves in no position to impose their worldview on their Indian neighbors. Teachers' weakness in the community counterbalanced their power in the classroom, while their success, as Albert Kneale discovered soon after arriving at No. 10, rested upon their ability and willingness to compromise.

One night, Kneale "was endeavoring to inveigle" an old Oglala man "into cutting his hair" to comply with American norms. After the teacher implored the Indian with every argument he could muster, the Oglala replied, "So it is not right for a man to wear his hair long?" Thinking the man had finally conceded his point, Kneale eagerly reaffirmed that men indeed should cut their hair short. But the teacher had stumbled into a trap the Oglala had sprung "with Socratic cleverness." Raising a finger to a portrait of Jesus upon the wall, the man asked mischievously "Whose picture is that?" Knowing he was "sunk," Kneale sullenly replied that it was Christ. "Well," replied the Indian, "Christ was a good man, so I have heard you say, and I note that he wore his hair long. I fear you are speaking lies, for either Christ was not a good man or else it is not wrong for a man to wear his hair long." Kneale could press the point no further, for his Lakota "vocabulary was not equal to the occasion." Not long after the incident, he and Edith "talked things over and decided we had better learn the Indian language." Tenacious and creative people who thrived on challenge, the Kneales stuck it out for three more years of such compromises and negotiations, but ultimately "the isolation was too great" and they transferred to a boarding school in Oklahoma.[29] Most of their colleagues did not even last that long before the hardships of reservation life overwhelmed them.[30] Like "Paph" Julian and his wife, many teachers "were not the least elated with" teaching on Pine Ridge, recalled Kneale. "The country itself frightened them, and the Indians terrorized them."[31]

Though evidence is scarce, Oglalas clearly had their own ideas about education, and they invested schools like the one in which the Kneales taught with their own hopes and fears. The Oglala voices preserved in treaty minutes and letters to government officials express a shared belief that federal schools could provide the tribe's next generation with important skills that would protect the tribe's interests. Yet education, like most other thorny issues confronting the people of Pine Ridge during the reservation era, also exposed deep rifts within Oglala society.[32]

Oglala children had attended federal schools for over a decade when a three-man commission arrived on Pine Ridge in the summer of 1889 seeking the tribe's consent to disband the Great Sioux Reservation. While many Lakota continued to harbor doubts about sending their children to school, Oglala leaders argued before the commission that children educated in American schools would serve as the tribe's best defense against the misunderstandings and errors of translation that had plagued the tribe in previous negotiations with the United States. High Wolf had "put [his] children out to different schools," but he knew "very well that they are not capable of doing any work for us yet." He wanted the commissioners to "wait until our children are advanced far enough and educated and return back home, . . . and then we can speak about it and decide." White Cow Killer also saw Indian school graduates as protectors of tribal interests. He wanted to leave the crucial question of allotment "to the children that is [sic] off to school." The Oglalas, he claimed, had "lost a great deal and we are to blame for it, and I don't want to go ahead and lose anything more."[33] These headmen may have simply been trying to delay unwelcome and divisive negotiations, yet their remarks indicate a sincere belief that schools would make young Oglalas conversant in English and familiarize them with American customs and culture. Thus trained, the next generation could counsel their people and pilot them through the shoals of the reservation era.

On an 1891 visit to Pine Ridge, Daniel Dorchester found "a great willingness" among "all classes of Indians . . . to have their children educated," and "even a demand for schools."[34] But if Oglalas agreed that education would shield the tribe from further mistreatment, they disagreed bitterly over whether boarding or day schools would best meet the tribe's needs. No Flesh complained, "I don't care how many years those schoolhouses may be there and our children goes to school, they will never learn to read and write and talk English." Boarding school was the "only" place where his children could "learn anything." American Horse claimed that children learned more in four years of boarding school than in eight years of day school. He compared building day schools to "throwing money away for nothing."[35]

While boarding school supporters stressed the superior education residential institutions provided, day school advocates emphasized the benefits of local schooling. "We can't send them here to this boarding-school," pleaded Little Wound at the 1889 negotiations. Because of the perils young children faced when they ran away from boarding school, he demanded "schools on the different creeks of the reservation." Oglalas such as Little Wound felt that day schools provided an antidote to the heart-breaking separation of parents and children that boarding entailed, not to mention immunity from the contagious diseases that brought many Oglala children home from distant institutions in caskets. As Red Cloud and Young Man Afraid of His Horses argued in an 1892 council with the Rosebud Sioux, their people did not want their children sent to schools in the East. "It does them more harm than good. The schools at the agencies are alright and they learn more."[36]

Such disagreements over schooling reflected deeper conflicts between Oglalas about how best to cope with conquest and its legacies. American Horse and other so-called "progressives" felt that the Oglalas should change their ways and become more like other Americans. They advocated boarding schools because they wanted their children to learn the language, values, and technology of the dominant society as quickly as possible.[37] "Traditionalists," on the other hand, tended to be cultural conservatives wary of sending their children away to be immersed in a foreign culture.[38] Some tried to keep their children out of school altogether, but most preferred day schools. Compulsory attendance laws punished parents for keeping their children home.[39] More importantly, many Oglalas realized the possibilities day schools provided. Not only did the little schoolhouses feed and clothe the impoverished people of Pine Ridge but they seemed to promise a middle path. By blending newly acquired skills from American culture with the influences of the family home and the Oglala community, many Oglalas hoped that day schools could give their children the best of both worlds.

Each fall when the school bells of Pine Ridge pealed out across the reservation, another cycle of negotiation began between the architects of assimilation, teachers, and Oglalas. Each brought their own hopes and fears to the day schools, and each tried to use the schools for their own purposes. Assimilationists divided the school day into three segments embodying their trinity of detribalization: morning academic instruction, afternoon industrial training, and evening moral edification and community work. They defined the shape of the school day, but they mostly left the daily operation of the schools to teachers. Teachers like the Kneales, meanwhile, felt like strangers within the borders of their own country, the sole white folks in communities where Lakota language and lifeways endured. The Oglalas, for their part, brought troubles of their own to the schools. They realized that education could safeguard their future, but it also threatened to further erode their cultural distinctiveness. Not everyone could have their way, and thus the school day became the venue for ongoing bargaining and subtle struggles.

Starting with two rituals that ushered in the school year, granting school names and remaking students' physical appearance, Oglala day school pupils learned to straddle two worlds: the schoolhouse community where they spent their mornings and afternoons and the Lakota community in which they spent their evenings and nights. Albert Kneale recalled how he excitedly prepared for the first day of school. He and Edith watched in their Sunday best as students arrived on horseback. After all the pupils had taken their seats, the New Yorker asked them to identify themselves. His repeated requests met with only blank stares and silence. Finally, Kneale "handed a paper and pencil to one of the larger boys and told him to write his name." The boy scribbled his name, then passed the paper on. After the sheet had traveled around the room, Kneale discovered that "[e]very child in the room, with the exception of the very smallest" had signed "his or her name in beautiful 'copybook' hand": Frank White Horse, Sarah Looks Twice, George Charging Bear, and others.

Kneale found the combination of Anglicized Lakota surnames with English Christian names intriguing, but he soon learned that these were just school names, "and no more than that." Kneale and his fellow teachers gave new names to Oglala children by compounding a popular American first name with a last name formed by Anglicizing the Lakota name of the child's father. Kneale claimed that children "were not known by these names to the Indians of the camp, nor even by their own parents." School names served as superficial markers of identity that most Oglala children left in the classroom at the end of the day. The ritual of naming, then, not only expressed the power teachers possessed; more importantly, it demonstrated how Oglala agency persistently circumscribed this power.[40]

Names represented but the first form of Indian identity that day school teachers set out to change. After Kneale recorded the names he and his predecessor created, he began to transform the physical appearance of his pupils. The kids had been out of school for several months. The dust of summer covered their bodies, while lice riddled their long, unkempt hair. As Edith brought washtubs outside and told the girls to bathe, Albert handed clippers, shears, and combs to two of the "brightest-looking boys" and indicated that he wished them to go to work. When Kneale returned, he found the boys earnestly shearing other pupils' tresses. When one student pointed to the lice and nits infesting another child's hair, Kneale brought out kerosene and discovered to his delight that "the boys seemed to know what to do with" this common lice treatment.[41] By the end of the day, Albert and Edith had made over the students at No. 10 to resemble poster children for the assimilationist cause: bodies scrubbed, scalps deloused, and hair cut to comply with the gendered norms of the dominant society. Like the famous before-and-after photos contrasting wild-haired braves in buckskins to immaculately groomed Victorians in starched collars and neat suits that Richard Henry Pratt used to illustrate the metamorphosis Carlisle Indian School effected, day school teachers sought to turn Oglalas into Americans by first making them look the part.

Though Kneale claimed that students acquiesced with these makeovers, his comments belie the trauma such physical transformations probably inflicted. Most Oglalas, for instance, considered long hair an important symbol of Indian masculinity, as Kneale learned in his Socratic dialogue with the old Indian not long after he arrived at No. 10.[42] A few years later, the Oglala father Makes Enemy petitioned the commissioner of Indian affairs, asking permission for his son to wear long hair at school. "I have long since adopted the ways and customs of civilization in every particular," claimed the Oglala, "except that I have not yet cut off my hair." Makes Enemy did not understand why the way his son "[wore] his hair [would] have any thing to do with his learning, or living according to what they may teach at the school." Makes Enemy not only questioned the connection between physical appearance and education, but pointed out the hypocrisy of forcing Indian boys to wear their hair short. "I have been among the white people," he wrote, "and have seen that they are permitted to wear their hair as they choose, and have seen boys, and even men among the whites that wear their hair long. Cutting the hair does not make us Indians like they [*sic*] ways of the white man any better," concluded the defiant father, "and it does not keep us from being Indians."[43]

Albert Kneale noted no rage or sadness as the boys' locks fell to the classroom floor, but perhaps his students shared Makes Enemy's view that short hair did not prevent them from "being Indians." Day school teachers imposed American names and American norms on their pupils, but these superficial modifications did little to alter what it meant to be Indian. From the first day of school, students became adept at adopting a dual identity. Externally, they took on school names, scrubbed skin, and short hair while internally resisting incursions into the deepest recesses of self-identity. The transformations day school teachers tried to enact at the beginning of the school year proved only skin deep.

Changing names and appearances proved but a prelude of things to come. Having renamed their pupils in the manner of American children and made them over to fit the part, teachers next endeavored to teach Oglala schoolchildren English and the manual skills they would need to succeed in the perilous currents of the American mainstream. Despite the designs of teachers and assimilationists, though, Oglalas managed to use morning classroom instruction and afternoon manual training in the day schools to navigate a route of their own.

The architects of assimilation devoted the morning academic program to teaching students English, but this often proved an agonizing process for the majority of Oglalas to whom it remained a foreign tongue. William Fire Thunder recalled that on his first day of school he knew exactly one word: "Yes"—one more word of English than any of his peers could speak.[44] Like Calvin Jumping Bull, many students had only heard English spoken a few times before starting school, often by ranch-hands or immigrant farmers who could not speak it "that well."[45] Given students' lack of exposure to English, it took "[p]atient and laborious effort," to teach Oglala children the language, according to longtime day school teacher E. M. Keith.[46] Having a sympathetic teacher helped. As his first year at No. 10 wore on, Kneale realized "that the children did understand a smattering of English." If he scorned or rushed them, they bit their tongues, but if he gave them time, "they could and would express themselves—however broken and faltering such expression might be." Pupils worried that they sounded silly, and teachers had to disarm these fears if they wanted their students to speak like Americans. Students always possessed considerable power—to refuse to articulate the English they already knew or to refuse to learn the language altogether. As Albert Kneale learned, most Lakota pupils could speak and understand English; "it just depended upon whether it was *I* that wanted something or *they*."[47]

The teacher-student dynamic changed significantly in classrooms led by Indians. Take the case of Clarence Three Stars, a voracious learner, superb teacher, and tireless advocate for his people whose remarkable teaching career spanned three decades.[48] Though Three Stars began his formal schooling late and thus could not finish his studies at Carlisle, he compensated for his lack of training with boundless enthusiasm. "Always on the lookout for further advantages and improvement," he "always advised" other "returned students to subscribe for good papers and buy good books and read them over and over until they [had] acquired some knowledge." "Read! Read! Think! Think!," Three Stars exhorted, "and practice what you have learned, and add to it and be somebody! Be a man and stand your ground! Then you will be respected . . . by your friends and enemies." Improvement through education constituted Three Stars' "motto."[49] Through a staunch advocate of learning about the wider world beyond the reservation, Three Stars championed the selective incorporation of those aspects of American culture that would ensure the Oglala's individual and collective survival.

An accommodationist rather than an assimilationist, Three Stars performed a tight rope act throughout his twenty years of day school teaching. On the one hand, he had to convince his skeptical supervisors that an Oglala could succeed as a day school teacher. Early assimilationists emphasized the importance of training Indians to spread the gospel of civilization on their home reservations, but such sentiments foundered in the growing racism of the 1890s. To make matters worse, Pine Ridge officials enacted a general prohibition against Oglala teachers in 1896. "There is nothing of which I feel more certain," wrote the day school inspector, "than this[,] that Oglala teachers, full bloods, or nearly so, cannot make a success of Day School work."[50] While Three Stars survived the inspector's purges to become the only Indian teacher on the reservation, the hostility of some agency personnel to Oglala instruction placed his job in constant jeopardy. In evaluations, reservation officials bemoaned that he "couldn't pass a civil service examination to save his neck" and backhandedly complimented him as "one of the most interesting of teachers, though taking it all around not the best."[51] On the other hand, Three Stars felt compelled to use whatever methods he could to accomplish what he viewed as his most vital task: helping his students become proficient English speakers. In order to teach Oglalas to talk like Americans, however, Three Stars developed a uniquely Lakota approach, employing bilingual, bicultural techniques that contrasted radically with those of his non-Lakota colleagues. Instead of forcing English upon his students, Three Stars developed more nuanced techniques that drew from the local physical environment and traditional Lakota pedagogy. Given his tenuous position as an Oglala in the day school teaching corps, Three Stars risked his job by employing such methods, but supervisors could not quibble with his results. While other teachers had trouble getting beginning students to speak English at all, Three Stars had them "express[ing] themselves readily" in English before the onset of winter.[52]

Three Stars believed that in order to learn English, students first had to learn how to connect objects with spoken words, then organize these words into narratives. He began by drawing stick figures on the blackboard to represent new vocabulary. Instead of deriving these words from the tales of cities and seashores that filled American primers, Three Stars taught words drawn from everyday life on Pine Ridge. Referring to a common teaching tool of the era, Three Stars admitted that it was "all right to have a sand table [similar to a sand box?] to describe and lay out invisible places and things that the pupils" had learned about from teachers and books, he conceded. He felt that it was much more effective pedagogy, though, to employ "the surroundings near the school and many many many real happenings occur daily." Teachers could use these objects and events "as original lessons in English." Students "could look out of the windows or go out and see the teams passing by" and make links between real objects and the words "hills, dam, bridge, cows, ditch, horses, chickens, garden, trees, etc." Three Stars believed Oglala children learned English more quickly when they could link words to their everyday experience. Students, he noted, seemed "to like more the real things than a table."[53] Practical and relevant to reservation life, "real things" could move, collide, and interact to make stories on the ground and in students' minds.

Three Stars encouraged his pupils to craft stories out of new vocabulary words. "This is competition in talking," he explained, "it is comical sometimes how they wish to express themselves, they would try to imitate older pupils in language but I do not allow them, they must get the idea of thought themselves and express themselves, this, they do after a few lessons."[54] Telling stories spurred pupils' imaginations and encouraged them to experiment with speaking English.

At the same time, making stories reinforced Oglala modes of thought in ways that helped students bridge Indian and American worlds. Once students had created a story, Three Stars asked them to illustrate it. Rose Catches, a former student of Three Stars's, remembered: "If we had something in our mind, the meaning of the thoughts we had, we draw it on the paper. So we don't just scratch on the paper."[55] In encouraging his students to read and write through drawings, Three Stars drew upon a long tradition of Oglala pictorial representation. For centuries, each Oglala band had designated an artist/historian who recorded important events in tribal life by painting or drawing on hides, tipis, ledger sheets, and other media. "The picture," these men liked to say, "is the rope that ties memory solidly to the stake of truth."[56] Though clearly inspired by Oglala traditions, Three Stars had students draw pictographic narratives in order to transcend language. Stories remained the same, after all, whether one used Lakota or English to narrate them. Three Stars staked his students' memories to a distinctly bicultural and bilingual "truth."

Three Stars incorporated other Lakota traditions into his teaching as well. Oglalas in the pre-reservation era used games to teach children hunting, housework, and other crucial skills.[57] To help his students learn English, Three Stars altered the content of one such game, entitled The Bear and the Children, to provide continuity between past and present and smooth the gulf between the Lakota and English words. The game brought out "vividly to the childrens' [*sic*] minds that they would answer readily the questions: What do you see? Taku wan-la-ka he? What is this? Le-taku-he?" As in the pre-reservation days, such games taught children the skills they would need to cope in a difficult world. For Three Stars, speaking English had supplanted bison-hunting, hide-tanning, and Crow-fighting to become the new technology of survival.[58]

White teachers tried to immerse their students in English. Three Stars, on the other hand, sought to build bridges between the Oglala and American tongues. Telling stories, drawing pictures, and playing games all helped students tie English to their own experience and make the language their own. Three Stars creatively drew upon the reservation environment and refashioned traditional pedagogical methods, but he also frequently taught in Lakota. "He gave us one day *wasicu* [English] lessons," Rose Catches remembered, "and the next day he turned around and he interpreted everything he teach us in *wasicu* way, in Indian." Three Stars "talked Indian" in the classroom and even taught the written Dakota language developed by American missionaries. He used "three kinds of books," Catches recalled. "One is drawing, one is Lakota language book. And one is *wasicu*."[59] Three Stars designed remarkable teaching methods to prepare students for life in a dual society. In the home and tribal community, Lakota would remain dominant, but beyond Pine Ridge loomed another world that could no longer be ignored or wished away. Like the Oglala headmen who spoke at the 1889 negotiations, Three Stars saw speaking English as a critical weapon in the struggle against American encroachment.

Through his innovative teaching methods, Clarence Three Stars took English fluency, one of the central tenets of the assimilationist program, and recast it into a tool of Oglala survival.[60] The architects of assimilation and most Anglo teachers envisioned linguistic instruction as a way to obliterate antiquated tribal languages and replace them with the keystone of Anglo-Saxon civilization. Three Stars, in contrast, and perhaps other Indian teachers, as well, imagined a bilingual future in which Lakota and English would co-exist. They agreed that Oglala children needed to learn how to talk like Americans, but they turned assimilationist logic on its head: They emphasized English proficiency not because it allowed Indian children to be incorporated into the American mainstream, but because it gave them the strength to remain apart and persist as Oglalas in a nation controlled by whites. The school bell did not have to be the death knell of Oglala culture.

Few Anglo teachers could muster the energy, creativity, or dedication of Clarence Three Stars, nor could they have run a bilingual, bicultural classroom.[61] Like Albert Kneale, many undoubtedly found the morning sessions frustrating, for "there seemed to be nothing gained through knowing that 'c-a-t' spells cat; arithmetic offered no attraction; not one was interested in knowing the name of the capital of New York, nor in the name of the stream into which the Missouri discharges its waters." At least the afternoons, Kneale consoled himself, "made up for" the humdrum mornings.[62] Many pupils shared their teachers' relief at the end of the academic portion of the day, oral historian Jeanne Smith discovered. Outdoor chores provided "a break from the school routine, a chance to get outside, stretch their muscles and get away from the books for awhile." Calvin Jumping Bull explained that some students "really wanted to be out there because some of them were having a hard time with school."[63]

Teachers and students alike craved a reprieve from the tensions and misunderstandings that pervaded day school mornings, but cultural contests often spilled over into the afternoon vocational lessons. The architects of assimilation included manual training in the Pine Ridge day school curriculum because they wanted to replace the nomadic hunting ways of the Lakotas with sedentary American agrarianism. But as in the remaking of student appearances and the teaching of English, Oglalas managed to selectively adapt only those aspects of the manual training curriculum that helped them meet the exigencies of reservation life. The case of school gardens suggests how the people of Pine Ridge picked and chose from what day schools had to offer, subverting assimilationist education and even recasting it into a means for cultural preservation.

Agriculture represented a central tenet of assimilation policy, yet environmental, economic, and cultural obstacles hampered teachers' efforts to convert Oglalas into farmers. Government parsimony denied schools the implements, draught animals, and seeds they needed to conduct agricultural programs.[64] Student labor might have been plentiful, but the manual tasks necessary to support the school (cutting wood, cooking lunch, sewing clothes, and so forth) already consumed most pupils' afternoons.[65] Moreover, Pine Ridge possessed poor soil and an extreme, unpredictable climate.[66] Irrigation might have helped. Building dams and digging ditches required capital no Oglalas could muster, however, and federal water projects tended to benefit non-Indian farmers instead of tribal members.[67] Most importantly, Oglalas knew farming would not work on their reservation, while the deep-seated prejudice of Oglala men that agriculture was an unmanly, un-Lakota pursuit compounded resistance.[68]

Gardening, on the other hand, provoked no such qualms. The environmental constraints that crippled farming made gardening difficult, but the location of most reservation day schools near narrow, well-watered bottomlands easily accommodated small garden plots. Vegetables—particularly hardy root crops—fared much better in the harsh South Dakota climate than row crops like wheat and corn. Gardens required minimal capital, and though labor-intensive, schools could usually spare enough students to tend the plots. Most importantly, Oglalas embraced school gardens as fervently as they opposed farming. Their intimacy with the plains reassured them that produce could flourish in the fertile bottomlands along the reservation's creeks, while gardening seemed not to threaten their self-conception.[69] And who could quibble with the results? Pupils, teachers, and parents alike eagerly anticipated harvest time. "When everything's good, nice and ripe," Rose Catches remembered, the Oglala community around No. 27 descended on the little school plot to help pick, clean, and can their share of the harvest.[70] As the fruits of the day school gardens found their way into Oglala mouths via school lunches and home pantries, each crunch of carrot or bite of potato provided tangible, edible proof that the time and effort Oglala children put into the soil had been worthwhile. Gardens succeeded within the limits of the reservation environment and the bounds of Lakota identity. Just as importantly, they provided young Oglalas with a skill that supplemented and enlivened meager government rations. Inspired by the success of day school gardens, Oglalas soon started to raise vegetables of their own. So prolific had these plots become that a U.S. Department of the Interior official boasted in 1913 that "in the home of every child attending a day school at Pine Ridge Agency there is a garden of greater of [sic] less extent."[71] Instead of American farmers, the children of Pine Ridge became Oglala gardeners.

When the day ended, the community of the schoolroom disbanded. Children buttoned their cumbersome government-issue coats, then melted back into the Oglala communities from which they had come. What had they learned that day, relatives might have asked. Not much, the children might have shrugged before enunciating a few English words and bragging about the seeds they had planted. As the days turned into weeks, months, and years, these small lessons accumulated, gained momentum, and rolled in surprising directions. The architects of assimilation expected that Indian children would abandon their ties to tribal cultures, learn to talk and work like Americans, and disappear into the mainstream. But this is not what happened on Pine Ridge. Instead, the people of the reservation engaged in an ongoing struggle to resist assimilationist schools and turn them into vehicles for cultural survival. Oglalas, they demonstrated, could talk and work like Americans without becoming American. In 1906, Makes Enemy had written that cutting the hair of Indian boys did not stop them from "being Indians." He could have said the same about speaking English or planting gardens. Knowing the language, Oglalas protected themselves against American encroachment. Growing their own food to supplement government rations, they ate better. Changing in small ways, the Oglala shielded themselves from the fundamental transformations assimilationists tried to enact.

After the pupils left, schoolhouses became, once again, two-person communities encircled by Lakota communities of hundreds. Though outnumbered and isolated, day school teachers nonetheless sought to meet assimilationist expectations by making their day schools "centers of usefulness" for the "advancement" of Lakotas young and old.[72] Just as the Oglalas of Pine Ridge turned the tables on assimilationism within the school room, however, they adroitly blunted the cultural blow that assimilationists expected schools to administer during their evening community work. Instead of allowing the schoolhouses of the reservation to become the beacons of assimilation Leupp imagined radiating into every corner of the reservation, Oglalas transformed them into institutions that reinforced communal ties and eased the hardships of reservation life.

Day schools, for example, fortified bands or *tiyospaye,* helping these traditional band structures survive the transition to reservation life.[73] Apart from the day schools at the agency, most schoolhouses stood in settlements of 100 to 300 Indians located along the creeks of Pine Ridge. Most of these communities developed when Oglalas slowly abandoned their nomadic ways to establish fixed communities with fellow band members.[74] Kin ties remained so central in these settlements that Oglalas continued to call them simply *tiyospaye.* By keeping children within the *tiyospaye* instead of tearing them away, day schools strengthened the overlapping bonds of kinship and community. Rose Catches, for example, remembered that her mother told her to befriend her schoolmates, "but of course I knew most of them. . . . All these people along here used to be my relations from my mother's and my father's side." Rose found herself surrounded by cousins, "so we're all together all the time. Here, at home, or at school."[75] Numerous interviews with Oglalas like Catches led Jeanne Smith to conclude that the day schools' compatibility "with traditional Oglala social organization" helped to make them "highly successful from a community standpoint."[76]

Over time, the reservation's schoolhouse not only buttressed *tiyospaye* ties, they also became valuable community assets that Oglalas used to ameliorate the difficulties of reservation life. Day schools not only educated children, but fed, clothed, and cared for them as well. Adults benefited just as much. Many teachers kept their doors open after school, and Oglalas asked them for help without hesitation. As one instructor put it, Pine Ridge teachers possessed a "broad" job description, one that included the duties of "minister, farmer, gardener, cook, literary teacher, etc." Other teachers added "acting as nurse to sick Indians," "doing the janitor work," "trying to impress upon [the Indians] a higher standard of living," "home nursing, sanitation work," and "agricultural activities" to the list. Teaching on Pine Ridge, summarized another teacher, entailed an enormous amount of "general community work."[77]

Oglalas pestered teachers constantly as they sought to employ day school instructors as cultural brokers who could help them make sense of the confusing complexities of the dominant society. A single doctor covered the entire reservation until the hiring of a second physician in 1906, and traditional healers were losing influence in the face of Euro-American diseases, so Oglalas often turned to teachers when *tiyospaye* members became ill.[78] The local teacher, claimed F.C. Heckart, was "about the only friend the Indian has that he relys [*sic*] upon for help in sickness or other trouble." In the face of such virulent maladies as scrofula or tuberculosis, teachers could offer little but solace and comfort, but some did learn to treat broken bones, cuts, and colds, as well as to "administer simple remedies."[79] American law and bureaucracy proved just as baffling as the diseases whites brought to Indian Country, and Oglalas frequently asked day school teachers for advice on topics ranging from settling estates to securing veterans' benefits.[80] The people of Pine Ridge, in short, cultivated strategic alliances with day school teachers, relying upon them for help in their struggles with the medical, legal, and bureaucratic difficulties reservation life presented.

The architects of assmimilation envisioned day schools as "spheres of influence" that would apply the "lever of uplift" to the "dark haunts" of Pine Ridge, but Oglalas had different plans. They did what they could to reshape day schools from agents of Americanization to bulwarks of Lakota community. Federal officials could craft blueprints for the Oglalas' future, but they could not keep the people of Pine Ridge from subverting these assimilationist designs and building histories of their own.

Why do Indian peoples and cultures, Indian lifeways and languages, Indian nations and worldviews survive and even thrive in the United States despite five centuries of deculturation, disease, and dispossession? No question is more central in understanding America's Native peoples and their complex histories. Yet given the number and diversity of Indian cultures, as well as the almost unfathomable variations in time, space, and culture that have shaped different pasts for different peoples, any attempt to address what Patricia Limerick has termed "the persistence of natives" in general or synthetic terms risks elliding more than it illuminates.[81]

As scholars seek to solve this larger puzzle, the case of the Pine Ridge day schools provides small yet suggestive clues. In *Indian Agent,* day school teacher Albert Kneale tells a seemingly apocryphal tale that nonetheless provides an apt metaphor for the process of selective adaptation one important Indian group, the Oglalas of Pine Ridge, engaged in as they sought to rebuff American dominance. Approaching a tree-shrouded ford on Wounded Knee Creek with a new shotgun in hand and visions of roast duck in his mind, Kneale heard "a string of oaths that would do credit to the vocabulary of a seasoned mule skinner," the most notoriously foul-mouthed figure of the frontier. "Both surprised and interested," Kneale heard not the "broken, hesitating" English he usually heard in classroom and *tiyospaye,* but rather "clear and ringing and well enunciated" English. Convinced that no Oglala could speak the American tongue so adeptly, the young teacher wondered what could have brought a white man so far from home. But as he approached the crossing, Kneale discovered neither a mule skinner nor a wayward traveler, but rather an Indian whose stock had become mired in the mud.

Why did the young Indian speak such profane English so well? Having heard white men using the same language when their animals had foundered in a similar predicament, Kneale reasoned, the young Oglala must have figured "that these magical words added strength to the team." As he lashed his horses with whip and curses, then, the teacher thought the Oglala must have been deploying "the only English he knew" in order to free his horses from the creek's soggy grasp. Like most Oglalas, Kneale later discovered, the Indian "was familiar with every last bit of profanity to be found in the English language," though he "knew not another word of the tongue." The Oglalas had no idea what the foul words coming out of their mouths meant, Kneale claimed, yet they nonetheless "seemed to recognize the occasions that called for their use." In the vast majority of situations, Indians deployed the language they already had. Why say "horse" instead of "tasunke," or "white man" instead of "wasicu"? Sometimes, however, the occasion demanded something more, something different. So Oglalas made pragmatic additions to their vocabulary, incorporating into their lexicon the English expletives that Kneale delicately omitted from his account.[82]

Whether the encounter Kneale relates ever occurred or not, the teacher's explanation of the incident nonetheless conveys a key insight about the Oglalas with whom Kneale worked and lived. In the period between the creation of the reservation and the wavering of assimilationist sentiment in the 1920s, the people of Pine Ridge acted not unlike the character in Albert Kneale's story. Like him, the Oglala children, parents, teachers, and community members who turned the tables on assimilationist education represented the continuation of an enduring theme in Oglala history: the integration of alien customs into Lakota lifeways. From embracing the horse and gun in the seventeenth and eighteenth centuries, to embarking on the great Teton migration westward in the eighteenth and nineteenth centuries, to adapting the day school curriculum to meet their own needs between 1889 and the 1920s, the Oglala people evinced a remarkable ability to incorporate new technologies and modes of thought. Indeed, this capacity had underpinned the tribe's survival for more than three turbulent centuries. In the end, then, the little schoolhouses that dotted the Pine Ridge Reservation presented what assimilationist educators might have called an object lesson: Not the lesson in detribalization and assimilation these architects of the day school system so earnestly desired, but rather a lesson in how native peoples have struggled to balance cultural change with cultural continuity in order to persist in the face of overwhelming odds, unconscionable violence, and heart-rending loss.

Notes

1. The most comprehensive treatment of Indian boarding schools is David Wallace Adams's excellent book, *Education for Extinction: American Indians and the Boarding School Experience, 1875–1928* (Lawrence, KS, 1995). See, among others, Scott Riney, *The Rapid City Indian School, 1898–1933* (Norman, OK, 1999), John Milloy, *"A National Crime": The Canadian Government and the Residential School System, 1879 to 1986* (Winnipeg, 1999), K. Tsianina Lomawaima, *They Called it Prairie Light: The Story of Chilocco Indian School* (Lincoln, NE, 1994), Clyde Ellis, *To Change Them Forever: Indian Education at the Rainy Mountain Boarding School, 1893–1920* (Norman, OK, 1996), and Brenda J. Child, *Boarding School Seasons: American Indian Families, 1900–1940* (Lincoln, NE, 1998).

2. For day school attendance, see the *Annual Reports of the Commissioners of Indian Affairs* (Washington, DC, 1880s–1920s) [hereafter *ARCIA*]. The three-tiered system of federal Indian education is explained in *ARCIA* (1894), 343, 349. Later directives undercut day schooling, but boarding schools generally declined in favor as the assimilation era wore on. Circular #58, 10 October 1901, Entry 718, Records of the Education Division, Records of the Bureau of Indian Affairs, RG 75, National Archives–Washington, DC (hereafter, NA-DC).

3. Exceptions are Susan Elaine Gray, "Methodist Indian Day Schools and Indian Communities in Northern Manitoba, 1890–1925," *Manitoba History* 30 (Autumn 1995): 2–16; Laura Woodworth-

Ney, "The Diaries of a Day-School Teacher: Daily Realities on the Pine Ridge Indian Reservation, 1932–1942," *South Dakota History* 24 (Fall/Winter 1994), 194–211; and Katherine Jensen, "Teachers and Progressives: The Navajo Day-School Experiment, 1935–1945," *Arizona and the West* 25 (Spring 1983), 49–62.

4. For day school attendance figures, see J. J. Duncan to unknown, n.d., 1901, Box 946, Pine Ridge Agency Records, Records of the Bureau of Indian Affairs, RG 75, National Archives—Central Plains Branch, Kansas City, MO [hereafter PR-KC]; W. W. Coon, "Inspection Report on the Twenty-nine Pine Ridge Day Schools," 12 December 1914 and H. C. Calhoun, "Inspection Report," 15 May 1928, Education Files, Pine Ridge Agency, General Classified Files, Records of the Bureau of Indian Affairs, RG 75, NA-DC [hereafter all Pine Ridge Agency files located at the National Archives in DC will be labeled PR-DC].

5. Thomas J. Morgan, *Education of American Indians: A Paper Read before the Mohonk Conference* (Carlisle, PA, 1889), 2.

6. Francis Paul Prucha periodizes federal Indian policy in his magisterial *The Great Father: The United States Government and the American Indians* (Lincoln, NE, 1984). In *A Final Promise: The Campaign to Assimilate the Indians, 1880–1920* (1984; reprint New York, 1989), Frederick E. Hoxie reexamines what Prucha treated as a unified era of assimilationism, claiming that policy makers became increasingly pessimistic after 1900 about the ability of Indians to melt into the American mainstream. Wilbert H. Ahern's study of Indian employees in federal schools supports Hoxie's thesis. Wilbert H. Ahern, "An Experiment Aborted: Returned Indian Students in the Indian School Service, 1881–1908," *Ethnohistory* 44 (Spring 1997): 263–304.

7. On allotment, see Janet A. McDonnell, *The Dispossession of the American Indian, 1887–1934* (Bloomington, IN, 1991) and Emily Greenwald, "Allotment in Severalty: Decision-Making during the Dawes Act on the Nez Percé, Jicarilla Apache, and Cheyenne River Sioux Reservations," (Ph.D. diss., Yale University, 1994).

8. For overviews of Indian education policy, see Margaret Connell Szasz, *Indian Education in the American Colonies: 1607–1783* (Albuquerque, 1988) and David H. DeJong, *Promises of the Past: A History of Indian Education in the United States* (Golden, CO., 1993).

9. Morgan, *Education of American Indians,* 3.

10. Thomas J. Morgan, *Indian High Schools: Further Details of the Proposed New Indian School System* (Carlisle, PA, 1889), 2.

11. Richard H. Pratt, "The Indian No Problem," *Proceedings of the Delaware County Institute of Science* 5 (1909), 6.

12. Ibid., 5.

13. *ARCIA* (1911), 8. As historian David Adams puts it, reformers viewed the Indian's "ability and willingness to adopt the ways of agrarian existence" as "the natural yardstick for measuring the degree of his civilization." David Adams, "The Federal Indian Boarding School: A Study of Environment and Response, 1897–1918," (Ph.D. Diss., Indiana University, 1975), 151–52.

14. *ARCIA* (1895), 344–45.

15. U.S. Senate, *Message from the President of the United States Transmitting Reports Relative to the Proposed Division of the Great Sioux Reservation, and Recommending Certain Legislation,* 51st Cong., 1st sess., 1889, S. Ex. Doc. 51, serial 2682 [hereafter 1889 Minutes], 84.

16. Herbert Welsh, *Are the Eastern Industrial Training Schools for Indian Children a Failure?* (Philadelphia, 1886) and Charles C. Painter, *Extravagance, Waste, and Failure of Indian Education* (Philadelphia, 1892). See also Adams, *Education for Extinction,* 273–306.

17. Matthew Ishkahula to Annie Beecher Scoville, 16 July 1896, folder 1081 and Samuel H. Baskin to Annie Beecher Scoville, folder 778, Correspondence of Annie Beecher Scoville, Beecher Family Papers, Yale University Manuscripts and Archives, New Haven, CT.

18. Several factors motivated the turn towards day schooling. Later advocates such as Francis Leupp, for example, were motivated more by thrift and their low conception of Indian intelligence, as Hoxie argues in *Final Promise,* 241–44. Nonetheless, many so-called "friends of the Indian" first

embraced day schools in the late 1890s as a solution to the gulf between transformed students and largely unchanged reservation milieux.

19. *ARCIA* (1890), 278. Day schools, claimed Elaine Goodale Eastman, educated students at half the cost of boarding schools. Elaine Goodale Eastman, *Sister to the Sioux: The Memoirs of Elaine Goodale Eastman, 1885–91,* ed. Kay Graber (Lincoln, NE, 1978), 118.

20. *ARCIA* (1890), 265–66; (1891), 493–94; (1892), 588.

21. *ARCIA* (1907), 21–22; (1908), 21; (1909), 26; Pine Ridge *Oglala Light,* December 1907. As noted earlier, Hoxie posits a discontinuity in federal Indian policy around 1900, after which assimilationists toned down their rhetoric and lowered their expectations of Indian peoples. Leupp's comments, however, demonstrate an essential continuity in the role bureaucrats assigned day schools on both sides of Hoxie's divide. Moreover, it is unclear how the shift in policy Hoxie identifies on the national level actually played out on the reservations of the West, where the ideologues and actions of local Indian Office personnel often proved more important than those of their distant superiors.

22. "Too many of the teachers were middle-aged men," complained Elaine Goodale Eastman of the reservation teaching force in the late 1880s, "not only incompetent but totally unadaptable." Eastman, *Sister to the Sioux,* ed. Graber, 126. On the regional background of teachers and housekeepers, see Susan Peterson, "'Holy Women' and Housekeepers: Women Teachers on South Dakota Reservations, 1885–1910," *South Dakota History* 13 (Fall 1983): 256.

23. Luther Standing Bear, *Land of the Spotted Eagle* (1933; reprint, Lincoln, NE, 1978), 241.

24. Most teachers likely agreed with Lewis Lincoln's pragmatic assertion that "The function of education is to fit people to earn a living." Lincoln to Charles Burke, 26 March 1922, PR-DC. As Marion McLaughlin put it, "We are not idealists but when we see the difference here today from the past we cannot but think that there may yet in the future be something still better for those most concerned, the Indians." Reports of School Surveys, 1922, Entry 1392, Records of the Board of Indian Commissioners, RG 75, NA-DC (hereafter, Reports of School Surveys, 1922).

25. For evidence on teachers' attitudes towards education, see Reports of School Surveys, 1922.

26. Eastman, *Sister to the Sioux* ed. Graber, 107. Albert H. Kneale, *Indian Agent* (Caldwell, ID, 1950), 18–23.

27. Ibid., 25–29. Standing Bear likewise agreed that most teachers' "knowledge of Indians was book knowledge." Standing Bear, *Land of the Spotted Eagle,* 241. On American attitudes towards Native peoples, see Robert F. Berkhofer, Jr., *The White Man's Indian: Images of the American Indian from Columbus to the Present* (New York, 1978) and Philip J. Deloria, *Playing Indian* (New Haven, 1998).

28. Kneale, *Indian Agent,* 32–36. For another telling description of the contents of a day school classroom, see Will H. Spindler, "Early Day School Employees Pioneered on South Dakota Indian Reservations," in *Tragedy Strikes at Wounded Knee and Other Essays on Indian Life in South Dakota and Nebraska* (1955; reprint Vermillion, SD, 1972), 89.

29. Kneale, *Indian Agent,* 41–43, 78.

30. Several schools had ten or more teachers within a twenty-year period. Quarterly School Reports, 1910–1930, Pine Ridge, Entry 745, Records of the Education Division, RG 75, NA-DC.

31. Kneale, *Indian Agent,* 66. By "terrorized," Kneale referred to teachers' fears of savage Indians, not actual harassment by Oglalas.

32. The best account of nineteenth-century Oglala factionalism is Catherine Price, *The Oglala People, 1841–1879: A Political History* (Lincoln, NE, 1996). See also Joseph Agonito, "Young Man Afraid of His Horses: The Reservation Years," *Nebraska History* 79 (Fall 1998): 116–32 and Mark R. Ellis, "Reservation *Akicitas:* The Pine Ridge Indian Police, 1879–1885," *South Dakota History* 29 (Fall 1999): 185–210.

33. 1889 Minutes, 105, 109.

34. *ARCIA* (1891), 492.

35. 1889 Minutes, 104, 222. More than twenty years later, Oglala pupil Charlie Twiss echoed the

arguments of No Flesh and American Horse. "I don't want to go to the day school. I could learn nothing . . ." quoted in Scott Riney, "'I Like the School So I Want to Come Back': The Enrollment of American Indian Students at the Rapid City Indian School," *American Indian Culture and Research Journal* 22, no. 2 (1998): 173.

36. 1889 Minutes, 109. The commitment to education of a chief called "Ta opi (wounded)," was memorialized by Oglala Philip F. Welles in 1909. James A. Finley to Omaha *Night Press-Bee,* "Account of a Council of Pine Ridge and Rosebud Sioux, 1892," Box 779, PR-KC. *Oglala Light,* October 1909, 12–13. Fed up with sending their children to distant boarding schools, parents even circulated petitions asking that the government "give our Children a proper education" and "establish an Indian day school in our midst." Petitions from Spring Creek and Red Shirt Table, 4 March 1911, PR-DC and 27 October 1915, Box 1147, PR-KC.

37. American Horse would implore students at the Oglala Boarding School "to be industrious and obedient and not to run away," *Oglala Light,* June 1902, 4.

38. As David Rich Lewis persuasively argues, the terms "traditionalist" and "progressive" often obscure more than they illuminate, polarizing complicated political stances into two camps. David Rich Lewis, "Reservation Leadership and the Progressive-Traditional Dichotomy: William Wash and the Northern Utes, 1865–1928," *Ethnohistory* 38 (Spring 1991): 124–48. Nonetheless, the concepts are useful for understanding how Oglala attitudes towards day schools differed.

39. Attendance lingered at around 80 percent of enrollment. This was due to the scandalously poor health of many Oglala children and the necessity of many impoverished Oglala families to travel seeking wage work, as well as the refusal of some parents to place their children in school. Tidwell to Malcolm McDowell, Reports of School Surveys, 1922. Evidence is contradictory on the role coercion played in enforcing school attendance. Eastman claimed that "it was rarely necessary to compel, or even to urge, attendance at day schools," but Tidwell complained: "Half of the work of the police of this reservation is devoted to keeping students in school." Eastman, *Sister to the Sioux,* ed. Graber, 123 and Tidwell to CIA, 5 May 1923, PR-DC. See also File on Reports of Police Visits to Day Schools, Box 1147, PR-KC.

40. Kneale, *Indian Agent,* 39–42.

41. Ibid., 42.

42. A 1906 survey found that just 25 out of 391 fathers of Pine Ridge day school students wore short hair. *ARCIA* (1907), 355.

43. Makes Enemy to Commissioner of Indian Affairs, 4 September 1906, Box 780, PR-KC. Peter Catches, an Oglala student at Holy Rosary Mission in the 1920s echoed Makes Enemy's argument that hair-cutting was designed "to curb everything that was Indian in us." Peter Catches transcript, MSS 459, South Dakota Oral History Center, Institute of American Indian Studies, University of South Dakota, Vermillion, SD. As Makes Enemy and Catches knew, Agent John Brennan had inaugurated a concerted campaign against the wearing of long hair on the reservation in 1902. *ARCIA* (1902), 337–38.

44. Quoted in Emily H. Lewis, *Wo'wakita Reservation Recollections: A People's History of the Allen Issue Station of the Pine Ridge Indian Reservation of South Dakota* (Sioux Falls, SD, 1980), 86.

45. Quoted in Jeanne Smith, *Teaching on the Reservation: Reflections on the Period between the Wars* (Kyle, SD, 1985), 13. The Dull Knife family communicated with nearby German families using improvised sign language. Joe Starita, *The Dull Knifes of Pine Ridge: A Lakota Odyssey* (New York, 1995), 187–88.

46. Eli S. Ricker Papers, Records of Interviews with Indians 1904–1909, Western History and Genealogy Department, Denver Public Library, Mss Microfilm 69, Reel 3, Tablet 29, 37.

47. Kneale, *Indian Agent,* 44, 48. For positive assessments of English usage on the reservation, see *Oglala Light,* May 1906, 4 and Report of Special Superintendent R. E. L. Newberne, 13 September 1913, General Classified File, PR-DC. On English language instruction in Indian schools, see Amy Goodburn, "Literacy Practices at the Genoa Industrial Indian School," *Great Plains Quarterly* 19 (Winter 1999): 35–52 and Laura E. Donaldson, "Writing the Talking Stick: Alphabetic Literacy as

Colonial Technology and Postcolonial Appropriation," *American Indian Quarterly* 22 (Winter/Spring 1998): 46–62.

48. Three Stars is first mentioned in 1895 as teacher of No. 20. By 1916, he had left the Indian School Service to become active in the Bennett County political system, serving as treasurer of the school board and visiting Washington on official business for the county. *ARCIA* (1895), 292; *Oglala Light,* November 1912, 14 and May 1913, 26–7; School Report, No. 14 Day School, 31 December, 1912, Quarterly School Reports, 1910–1930, NA-DC; Public School Contract with District 2, Bennett County, 23 December 1916, Entry 745, PR-DC.

49. Letter from Clarence Three Stars to Carlisle Indian School, reprint in *Oglala Light,* April 1902, 10. See also the verse Three Stars penned when his daughter Louisa died from a "sickness" she had caught at Pierre boarding school. "You and I seek for education," the two stanzas begin, before concluding with the refrain "We endure it all altho/We die; that is what we/Did, Louisa, I know it." *Oglala Light,* March 1908, 25.

50. On Indian teachers generally, see Ahern, "An Experiment Aborted." On the prohibition, see J. J. Duncan to John Brennan, n.d. 1901, Box 946, PR-KC.

51. Reports of 10 May 1910 and 11 October 1912 on Clarence Three Stars, Box 752, PR-KC.

52. *Oglala Light,* April 1907, n.p.

53. "Teaching Indian pupils to speak English in the Day School work," 10 March 1905, Box 1154, PR-KC.

54. Ibid.

55. Quoted in Smith, *Teaching on the Reservation,* 51.

56. Mari Sandoz, "Introduction," in *A Pictographic History of the Oglala Sioux,* Amos Bad Heart Bull and Helen H. Blish, (Lincoln, NE, 1967), xx–xxi. See also Dorothy Dunn, *American Indian Painting of the Southwest and Plains Areas* (Albuquerque, 1968), 147–83 and Hartley B. Alexander, *Sioux Indian Painting, Part 1, Paintings of the Sioux and Other Tribes* (Nice, FR, 1938).

57. "Games and the Education of Children," Black Elk interview with John Neihardt, in *The Sixth Grandfather,* ed. Raymond J. DeMallie (Lincoln, 1984), 323–25.

58. "Teaching Beginners to Talk English," *Oglala Light,* April 1907, n.p.

59. Quoted in Smith, *Teaching on the Reservation,* 50–51.

60. Though field supervisors tended to frown on bicultural teaching practices, Francis Leupp supported the use of "Indian music and other arts, customs, and traditions, provided they are innocent in themselves and do not clash needlessly with the new social order into which we are inducting our aboriginal race." Circular #175, 3 December 1907, Entry 718, NA-DC.

61. See, for example, Ralph Julian's "Object Teaching and Education," *Oglala Light,* September 1909, 10–15 and Rebecca Brigance's "My Method of Teaching English to Beginners," *Oglala Light,* June 1913, 15–16.

62. Kneale, *Indian Agent,* 52.

63. Smith, *Teaching on the Reservation,* 8–9.

64. See, for instance, teacher Ray Schultz's lament in Reports of School Surveys, 1922.

65. On common day school tasks, see Coon, "Inspection Report," 7 and the quarterly school reports from No. 15 day school, 31 March and 30 September 1919, 31 December 1920, and 31 March 1921, PR-DC.

66. Agents' reports habitually refer to poor growing conditions. See, for example, *ARCIA* (1897), 292.

67. *ARCIA* (1907), 353.

68. R. Douglas Hurt, *Indian Agriculture in America: Prehistory to the Present* (Lawrence, KS, 1987), 230; Gordon Macgregor, "Changing Society," in *The Modern Sioux: Social Systems and Reservation Culture,* ed. Ethel Nurge (Lincoln, NE, 1970), 95; and Raymond J. DeMallie, "Pine Ridge Economy: Cultural and Historical Perspectives," in *American Indian Economic Development,* ed. Sam Stanley (The Hague, NL, 1978), 241.

69. On gardening in Sioux culture, see Herbert T. Hoover, "Ankara, Sioux, and Government

Farmers: Three American Indian Agricultural Legacies," *South Dakota History* 13 (Spring/Summer 1983): 29.

70. Quoted in Smith, *Teaching on the Reservation,* 53.

71. *Oglala Light,* June 1913, 34. See also the 1925–1926 survey of every family on Pine Ridge, which found that nearly all Oglalas kept a small garden. Entry 762, PR-DC.

72. C. E. Hawke to John Brennan, 4 December 1914, General Classified File, PR-DC.

73. Raymond J. DeMallie identifies allegiance to a band chief, the construction of dance halls, and the expression of "the common identity of belonging to a certain named community" as the main bonds which held *tiyospaye* together, but the role day schools played should not be underestimated. DeMallie, "Pine Ridge Economy," 269–70.

74. In 1888, for example, the Plenty Bears, Hollow Heads, and Hunts Horses families broke away from the No Flesh Community to found Potato Creek Community, while four years later a mixed-blood *tiyospaye* comprised of the Pourier, Patton, and Mesteth families established the Wakan Community on Wounded Knee Creek. Spindler, "Potato Creek Indian Village," in *Tragedy Strikes at Wounded Knee,* Spindler, 100; "School History of No. 12 Day School," n.d., Box 1157, PR-KC. On the context of settlement, see DeMallie, "Pine Ridge Economy," 269 and Macgregor, "Changing Society," 98. For the location of day schools, see Office of Indian Affairs, "Map of the Pine Ridge Indian Reservation, South Dakota" (Washington, DC, 1914).

75. Quoted in Smith, *Teaching on the Reservation,* 49.

76. Ibid., 23–24.

77. "Report of the 10th Annual Institute of Pine Ridge Agency, S.D.," 3–5 October 1905, Box 1154, PR-KC; statements from questionnaires used to compile the Meriam Report, Box 752, PR-KC, and Reports of School Surveys, 1922.

78. *ARCIA* (1905), 339 and (1906), 357.

79. Kneale, *Indian Agent,* 43 and Reports of School Surveys, 1922.

80. Jesse Tyler to Malcolm McDowell, 8 March 1922, in Reports of School Surveys, 1922.

81. Patricia Nelson Limerick, *The Legacy of Conquest: The Unbroken Past of the American West* (New York, 1987), 179–221.

82. Kneale, *Indian Agent,* 46.

13

Confronting "America"

Mexican Women and the Rose Gregory Houchen Settlement

VICKI L. RUIZ

As a child Elsa Chávez confronted a "moral" dilemma. She wanted desperately to enjoy the playground equipment close to her home in El Paso's Segundo Barrio. The tempting slide, swings, and jungle gym seemed to call her name. However, her mother would not let her near the best playground (and for many years the only playground) in the barrio. Even a local priest warned Elsa and her friends that playing there was a sin—the playground was located within the yard of the Rose Gregory Houchen Settlement, a Methodist community center.[1]

While one group of Americans responded to Mexican immigration by calling for restriction and deportation, other groups mounted campaigns to "Americanize" the immigrants. From Los Angeles, California, to Gary, Indiana, state and religious-sponsored Americanization programs swung into action. Imbued with the ideology of "the melting pot," teachers, social workers, and religious missionaries envisioned themselves as harbingers of salvation and civilization.[2] Targeting women and especially children, the vanguard of Americanization placed their trust "in the rising generation." As Pearl Ellis of the Covina City schools explained in her 1929 publication, *Americanization Through Homemaking*, "Since the girls are potential mothers and homemakers, they will control, in a large measure, the destinies of their future families." She continued, "It is she who sounds the clarion call in the campaign for better homes."[3]

A growing body of literature on Americanization in Mexican communities by such scholars as George Sánchez, Sarah Deutsch, Gilbert González, and myself suggest that church and secular programs shared common course offerings and curricular goals. Perhaps taking their cue from the regimen developed inside Progressive Era settlement houses, Americanization projects emphasized classes in hygiene, civics, cooking, language, and vocational education (e.g., sewing and carpentry). Whether seated at a desk

343

in a public school or on a sofa at a Protestant or Catholic neighborhood house, Mexican women received similar messages of emulation and assimilation. While emphasizing that the curriculum should meet "the needs of these people," one manual proclaimed with deepest sincerity that a goal of Americanization was to enkindle "a greater respect . . . for our civilization."[4]

Examples of Americanization efforts spanned the Southwest and Midwest from secular settlements in Watts, Pasadena, and Riverside to Hull House in Chicago. In addition, Catholic neighborhood centers, such as Friendly House in Phoenix, combined Americanization programs with religious and social services. Protestant missionaries, furthermore, operated an array of settlements, health clinics, and schools. During the first half of the twentieth century, the Methodist Church sponsored one hospital, four boarding schools, and sixteen settlements/community centers, all serving a predominately Mexican clientele. Two of these facilities were located in California, two in Kansas, one in New Mexico, and sixteen in Texas.[5] Though there are many institutions to compare, an overview, by its very nature, would tend to privilege missionary labors and thus, once again, place Mexican women within the shadows of history. By taking a closer look at one particular project—the Rose Gregory Houchen Settlement—one can discern the attitudes and experiences of Mexican women themselves. This chapter explores the ways in which Mexican mothers and their children interacted with the El Paso settlement, from utilizing selected services to claiming "American" identities, from taking their babies to the clinic for immunizations to becoming missionaries themselves.

Using institutional records raises a series of important methodological questions. How can missionary reports, pamphlets, newsletters, and related documents illuminate the experiences and attitudes of women of color? How do we sift through the bias, the self-congratulation, and the hyperbole to gain insight into women's lives? What can these materials tell us of women's agencies within and against larger social structures? I am intrigued (actually obsessed is a better word) with questions involving decision making, specifically with regard to acculturation. What have Mexican women chosen to accept or reject? How have the economic, social, and political environments influenced the acceptance or rejection of cultural messages that emanate from the Mexican community, from U.S. popular culture, from Americanization programs, and from a dynamic coalescence of differing and at times oppositional cultural forms? What were women's real choices and, to borrow from Jürgen Habermas, how did they move "within the horizon of their lifeworld"?[6] Obviously, no set of institutional records can provide substantive answers, but by exploring these documents through the framework of these larger questions, we place Mexican women at the center of our study, not as victims of poverty and superstition as so often depicted by missionaries, but as women who made choices for themselves and for their families.

As the Ellis Island for Mexican immigrants, El Paso seemed a logical spot for a settlement house. In 1900, El Paso's Mexican community numbered only 8,748 residents, but by 1930 this population had swelled to 68,476. Over the course of the twentieth century, Mexicans composed over one-half the total population of this bustling border city.[7] Perceived as cheap labor by Euro-American businessmen, they provided the human resources necessary for the city's industrial and commercial growth. Education and economic advancement proved illusory as segregation in housing, employment, and schools served as constant reminders of their second-class citizenship. To cite an example of stratification, from 1930 to 1960, only 1.8 percent of El Paso's Mexican workforce held high white-collar occupations.[8]

Segundo Barrio or South El Paso has served as the center of Mexican community life. Today, as in the past, wooden tenements and crumbling adobe structures house thousands of Mexicanos and Mexican Americans alike. For several decades, the only consistent source of social services in Segundo Barrio was the Rose Gregory Houchen Settlement House and its adjacent health clinic and hospital.

Founded in 1912 on the corner of Tays and Fifth in the heart of the barrio, this Methodist settlement had two initial goals: (1) provide a Christian roominghouse for single Mexicana wage earners and (2) open a kindergarten for area children. By 1918, Houchen offered a full schedule of Americanization programs—citizenship, cooking, carpentry, English instruction, Bible study, and Boy Scouts. The first Houchen staff included three Methodist missionaries and one "student helper," Ofilia [sic] Chávez.[9] Living in the barrio made these women sensitive to the need for low-cost, accessible health care. Infant mortality in Segundo Barrio was alarmingly high. Historian Mario García related the following example: "Of 121 deaths during July [1914], 52 were children under 5 years of age."[10]

Houchen began to offer medical assistance, certainly rudimentary at first. In 1920, a registered nurse and Methodist missionary Effie Stoltz operated a first aid station in the bathroom of the settlement. More important, she soon persuaded a local physician to visit the residence on a regular basis and he, in turn, enlisted the services of his colleagues. Within seven months of Stoltz's arrival, a small adobe flat was converted into Freeman Clinic. Run by volunteers, this clinic provided prenatal exams, well-baby care, and pediatric services and, in 1930, it opened a six-bed maternity ward. Seven years later, it would be demolished to make way for the construction of a more modern clinic and a new twenty-two-bed maternity facility—the Newark Methodist Maternity Hospital. Health care at Newark was a bargain. Prenatal classes, pregnancy exams, and infant immunizations were free. Patients paid for medicines at cost and, during the 1940s, $30 covered the hospital bill. Staff members would boast that for less than $50, payable in installments, neighborhood women could give birth at "one of the best equipped maternity hospitals in the city."[11]

Houchen Settlement also thrived. From 1920 to 1960, it coordinated an array of Americanization activities. These included age and gender graded Bible studies, music lessons, campfire activities, scouting, working girls' clubs, hygiene, cooking, and citizenship. Staff members also opened a day nursery to complement the kindergarten program. In terms of numbers, how successful was Houchen? The available records give little indication of the extent of the settlement's client base. Based on fragmentary evidence for the period 1930 to 1950, perhaps as many as 15,000 to 20,000 people per year or approximately one-fourth to one-third of El Paso's Mexican population utilized its medical and/or educational services. Indeed, one Methodist from the 1930s pamphlet boasted that the settlement "reaches nearly 15,000 people."[12]

As a functioning Progressive Era settlement, Houchen had amazing longevity from 1912 to 1962. Several Methodist missionaries came to Segundo Barrio as young women and stayed until their retirement. Arriving in 1930, Millie Rickford would live at the settlement for thirty-one years. Two years after her departure, the Rose Gregory Houchen Settlement House (named after a Michigan schoolteacher) would receive a new name, Houchen Community Center. As a community center, it would become more of a secular agency staffed by social workers and at times Chicano activists.[13] In 1991 the buildings that cover a city block in South El Paso still furnish day care and recreational activities. Along with Bible study, there are classes in ballet folklorico, karate, English, and aerobics. Citing climbing insurance costs (among other reasons), the Methodist Church closed the hospital and clinic in December 1986 over the protests of local supporters and community members.[14]

From 1912 until the 1950s, Houchen workers placed Americanization and proselytization at the center of their efforts. Embracing the imagery and ideology of the melting pot, Methodist missionary Dorothy Little explained:

> Houchen settlement stands as a sentinel of friendship . . . between the people of America and the people of Mexico. We assimilate the best of their culture, their art, their ideals and they in turn gladly accept the best America has to offer as they . . . become one with us. For right here within our four walls is begun much of the "Melting" process of our "Melting Pot."[15]

The first goal of the missionaries was to convert Mexican women to Methodism since they perceived themselves as harbingers of salvation. As expressed in a Houchen report, "Our Church is called El Buen Pastor . . . and that is what our church really is to the people—it is a Good Shepherd guiding our folks out of darkness and Catholicism into the good Christian life." Along similar lines, one Methodist pamphlet printed during the 1930s equated Catholicism (as practiced by Mexicans) with paganism and superstition. Settlement's programs were couched in terms of "Christian Americanization" and these programs began early.[16]

Like the Franciscan missionaries who trod the same ground three centuries before, Houchen settlement workers sought to win the hearts and minds of children. While preschool and kindergarten students spoke Spanish and sang Mexican songs, they also learned English, U.S. history, biblical verses—even etiquette a la Emily Post.[17] The settlement also offered various after-school activities for older children. These included "Little Homemakers," scouting, teen clubs, piano lessons, dance, bible classes, and story hour. For many years the most elaborate playground in South El Paso could be found within the outer courtyard of the settlement. Elsa Chávez eventually got her playground wish. She and her mother reached an agreement: Elsa could play there on the condition that she not accept any "cookies or koolaid," the refreshments provided by Houchen staff. Other people remembered making similar bargains—they could play on the swings and slide, but they could not go indoors.[18] How big of a step was it to venture from the playground to story hour?

Settlement proselytizing did not escape the notice of barrio priests. Clearly troubled by Houchen, a few predicted dire consequences for those who participated in any Protestant-tinged activities. As mentioned earlier, one priest went so far as to tell neighborhood children that it was a sin even to play on the playground equipment.

Others, however, took a more realistic stance and did not chastise their parishioners for utilizing Methodist child care and medical services. Perhaps as a response to both the Great Depression and suspected Protestant inroads, several area Catholic churches began distributing food baskets and establishing soup kitchens.[19]

Children were not the only ones targeted by Houchen. Women, particularly expectant mothers, received special attention. Like the proponents of Americanization programs in California, settlement workers believed that women held a special guardianship over their families' welfare. As head nurse Millie Rickford explained, "If we can teach her [the mother-to-be] the modern methods of cooking and preparing foods and simple hygiene habits for herself and her family, we have gained a stride."[20]

Houchen's "Christian Americanization" programs were not unique. During the teens and twenties, religious and state-organized Americanization projects aimed at the Mexican population proliferated throughout the Southwest. Although these efforts varied in scale from settlement houses to night classes, curriculum generally revolved around cooking, hygiene, English, and civics. Music seemed a universal tool of instruction. One Arizona schoolteacher excitedly informed readers of *The Arizona Teacher and Home Journal* that her district for the "cause of Americanization" had purchased a Victrola and several records that included two Spanish melodies, the "'Star Spangled Banner,' 'The Red, White, and Blue,' 'Silent Night,' . . . [and] 'Old Kentucky Home.'"[21] Houchen, of course, offered a variety of musical activities beginning with the kindergarten rhythm band of 1927. During the 1940s and 1950s, missionaries provided flute, guitar, ballet, and tap lessons. For fifty cents a week, a youngster could take dance or music classes and perform in settlement recitals.[22] Clothing youngsters in European peasant styles was common. For instance, Alice Ruiz, Priscilla Molina, Edna Parra, Mira Gómez, and Aida Rivera represented Houchen in a local Girl Scout festival held at the Shrine temple in which they modeled costumes from Sweden, England, France, Scotland, and Lithuania.[23] Some immigrant traditions were valorized more than others. Celebrating Mexican heritage did not figure into the Euro-American orientation pushed by Houchen residents.

In contrast, a teacher affiliated with an Americanization program in Watts sought to infuse a multicultural perspective as she directed a pageant with a U.S. women's history theme. Clara Smith described the event as follows:

> Women, famous in the United States history as the Pilgrim, Betsy Ross, Civil War, and covered wagon women, Indian and Negro women, followed by the foreign women who came to live among us were portrayed. The class had made costumes and had learned to dance the Virginia Reel. . . . They had also made costumes with paper ruffles of Mexican colors to represent their flag. They prepared Mexican dances and songs.[24]

Despite such an early and valiant attempt at diversity, the teacher did not think it necessary to include the indigenous heritage of Mexican women. Indeed, stereotypical representations of the American Indian "princess" (or what Rayna Green has termed "the Pocahontas perplex"[25]) supplanted any understanding of indigenous cultures on either side of the political border separating Mexico and the United States.

Like Americanization advocates across the Southwest, Houchen settlement workers held out unrealistic notions of the American dream as well as romantic constructions of American life. It is as if the Houchen staff had endeavored to create a white, middle-class environment for Mexican youngsters complete with tutus and toe shoes. Cooking classes also became avenues for developing particular tastes. Minerva Franco, who as a child attended settlement programs and who later as an adult became a community volunteer, explained, "I'll never forget the look on my mother's face when I first cooked 'Eggs Benedict' which I learned to prepare at Houchen."[26] The following passage, taken from a report dated February 1942 outlines, in part, the perceived accomplishments of the settlement:

> Sanitary conditions have been improving—more children go to school—more parents are becoming citizens, more are leaving Catholicism—more are entering business and public life—and more and more they taking on the customs and standards of the Anglo people.[27]

Seemingly oblivious to structural discrimination, such a statement ignores economic segmentation and racial/ethnic segregation. Focusing on El Paso, historian Mario García demonstrated that the curricula in Mexican schools, which emphasized vocational education, served to funnel Mexican youth into the factories and building trades. In the abstract, education raised expectations, but in practice, particularly for men, it trained them for low-status, low-paying jobs. One California grower disdained education for Mexicans because it would give them "tastes for things they can't acquire."[28] Settlement workers seemed to ignore that racial/ethnic identity involved not only a matter of personal choice and heritage but also an ascribed status imposed by external sources.[29]

Americanization programs have come under a lot of criticisms from historians over the past two decades and numerous passages in the Houchen collection provide fodder for sarcasm among contemporary readers. Yet, to borrow from urban theorist Edward Soja, scholars should be mindful of "an appropriate interpretive balance between space, time and social being."[30] Although cringing at the ethnocentrism and romantic idealizations of "American" life, I respect the settlement workers for their health and child care services. Before judging the maternal missionaries too harshly, it is important to keep in mind the social services they rendered over an extended period of time as well as the environment in which they lived. For example, Houchen probably launched the first bilingual kindergarten program in El Paso, a program that eased the children's transition into an English-only first grade. Houchen residents did not denigrate the use of Spanish and many became fluent Spanish speakers. The hospital and clinic, moreover, were important community institutions for over half a century.[31]

Settlement workers themselves could not always count on the encouragement or patronage of Anglo El Paso. In a virulently nativist tract, a local physician, C. S. Babbitt, condemned missionaries, like the women of Houchen, for working among Mexican and African Americans. In fact, Babbitt argued that religious workers were "seemingly conspiring with Satan to destroy the handiwork of God" because their energies were "wasted on beings . . . who are not in reality the objects of Christ's sacrifice."[32] Even within their own ranks, missionaries could not count on the support of Protestant clergy. Reverend Robert McLean, who worked among Mexicans in Los Angeles, referred to his congregation as "chili con carne" bound to give Uncle Sam a bad case of "heartburn."[33]

Perhaps more damaging than these racist pronouncements was the apparent lack of financial support on the part of El Paso area Methodist churches. Accessible records reveal little in terms of local donations. Houchen was named after a former Michigan schoolteacher who bequeathed $1,000 for the establishment of a settlement in El Paso. The Women's Home Missionary Society of the Newark, New Jersey, Conference proved instrumental in raising funds for the construction of both Freeman Clinic and Newark Methodist Maternity Hospital. When Freeman Clinic first opened its doors in June 1921, all the medical equipment—everything from sterilizers to baby scales—were gifts from Methodist groups across the nation. The Houchen Day Nursery, however, received consistent financial support from the El Paso Community Chest and later the United Way. In 1975, Houchen's Board of Directors conducted the first community-wide fund-raising drive. Volunteers sought to raise $375,000 to renovate existing structures and build a modern day care center. The Houchen fund-raising slogan "When people pay their own say, it's your affair . . . not welfare" makes painfully clear the conservative attitudes toward social welfare harbored by affluent El Pasoans.[34]

The women of Houchen appeared undaunted by the lack of local support. For over fifty years, these missionaries coordinated a multifaceted Americanization campaign among the residents of Segundo Barrio. How did Mexican women perceive the settlement? What services did they utilize and to what extent did they internalize the romantic notions of "Christian Americanization?"

Examining Mexican women's agency through institutional records is difficult; it involves getting beneath the text to dispel the shadows cast by missionary devotion to a simple Americanization ideology. One has to take into account the selectivity of voices. In drafting settlement reports and publications, missionaries chose those voices that would publicize their "victories" among the Spanish speaking. As a result, quotations abound that heap praise upon praise on Houchen and its staff. For example, in 1939, Soledad Burciaga emphatically declared, "There is not a person, no matter to which denomination they belong, who hasn't a kind word and a heart full of gratitude towards the Settlement House."[35] Obviously, these documents have their limits. Oral interviews and informal discussions with people who grew up in Segundo Barrio give a more balanced, less effusive perspective. Most viewed Houchen as a Protestant-run health care and after-school activities center rather than as the "light-house" [sic] in South El Paso.[36]

In 1949, the term Friendship Square was coined as a description for the settlement house, hospital, day nursery, and church. Missionaries hoped that children born at Newark would participate in preschool and afternoon programs and that eventually they and their families would join their church, El Buen Pastor. And a few did follow this pattern. One of the ministers assigned to El Buen Pastor, Fernando García, was a Houchen kindergarten graduate. Emulating the settlement staff, some young women enrolled in Methodist missionary colleges or served as lay volunteers. Elizabeth Soto, for example, attended Houchen programs throughout her childhood and adolescence. On graduation from Bowie High School, she entered Asbury College to train as a missionary and then returned to El Paso as a Houchen resident. After several years of service, she left settlement work to become the wife of a Mexican Methodist minister. The more common goal among Houchen teens was to graduate from high school and perhaps attend Texas

Western, the local college. The first child born at Newark Hospital, Margaret Holguin, took part in settlement activities as a child and later became a registered nurse. According to her comadre, Lucy Lucero, Holguin's decision to pursue nursing was "perhaps due to the influence" of head nurse Millie Rickford. According to Lucero, "The only contact I had had with Anglos was with Anglo teachers. Then I met Miss Rickford and I felt, 'Hey, she's human. She's great.'" At a time when many (though certainly not all) elementary schoolteachers cared little about their Mexican students, Houchen residents offered warmth and encouragement.[37]

Emphasizing education among Mexican youth seemed a common goal characterizing Methodist community centers and schools. The Frances De Pauw School located on Sunset Boulevard in Los Angeles, for example, was an all-girls boarding school. Frances De Pauw educated approximately 1,800 young Mexican women from 1900 to 1946 and a Methodist pamphlet elaborated on its successes. "Among [the school's] graduates are secretaries, bookkeepers, clerks, office receptionists, nurses, teachers, waitresses, workers in cosmetic laboratories, church workers, and Christian homemakers." While preparing its charges for the workaday world, the school never lost sight of women's domestic duties. "Every De Pauw girl is graded as carefully in housework as she is in her studies."[38] With regard to Friendship Square, one cannot make wholesale generalizations about its role in fostering mobility or even aspirations for mobility among the youth of Segundo Barrio. Yet it is clear that Houchen missionaries strived to build self-esteem and encouraged young people to pursue higher education.

Missionaries also envisioned a Protestant enclave in South El Paso; but, to their frustration, very few people responded. The settlement church, El Buen Pastor, had a peak membership of 150 families. The church itself had an intermittent history. Shortly after its founding in 1897, El Buen Pastor disappeared; it was officially rededicated as part of Houchen in 1932. However, the construction of an actual church on settlement grounds did not begin until 1945. In 1968, the small rock chapel would be converted into a recreation room and thrift shop as the members of El Buen Pastor and El Mesias (another Mexican-American church) were merged together to form the congregation of the Emmanuel United Methodist Church in downtown El Paso. In 1991, a modern gymnasium occupies the ground where the chapel once stood.[39]

The case histories of converts suggest that many of those who joined El Buen Pastor were already Protestant. The Dominguez family offers an example. In the words of settlement worker A. Ruth Kern:

> Reyna and Gabriel Dominguez are Latin Americans, even though both were born in the United States. Some members of the family do not even speak English. Reyna was born . . . in a Catholic home, but at the age of eleven years, she began attending the Methodist Church. Gabriel was born in Arizona. His mother was a Catholic, but she became a Protestant when . . . Gabriel was five years old.[40]

The youth programs at Houchen brought Reyna and Gabriel together. After their marriage, the couple had six children, all born at Newark Hospital. The Dominguez family represented Friendship Square's typical success story. Many of the converts were children and many had already embraced a Protestant faith. In the records I examined, I found only one instance of the conversion of a Catholic adult and one of the conversion of an entire Catholic family.[41] It seems that those most receptive to Houchen's religious messages were already predisposed in that direction.

The failure of proselytization cannot be examined solely within the confines of Friendship Square. It is not as if these Methodist women were good social workers but incompetent missionaries. Houchen staff member Clara Sarmiento wrote of the difficulty in building trust among the adults of Segundo Barrio. "Though it is easy for children to open up their hearts to us we do not find it so with the parents." She continued, "It is hard especially because we are Protestant, and most of the people we serve . . . come from Catholic heritage."[42] I would argue that the Mexican community played an instrumental role in thwarting conversion. In a land where the barrio could serve as a refuge from prejudice and discrimination, the threat of social isolation could certainly inhibit many residents from turning Protestant. During an oral interview, Estella Ibarra, a woman who participated in Houchen activities for over fifty years, described growing up Protestant in South El Paso:

> We went through a lot of prejudice . . . sometimes my friends' mothers wouldn't let them play with us. . . . When the priest would go through the neighborhood, all the children would run to say hello and kiss his hand. My brothers and I would just stand by and look. The priest would usually come . . . and tell us how we were living in sin. Also, there were times when my brother and I were stoned by other students . . . and called bad names.[43]

When contacted by a Houchen resident, Mrs. Espinosa admitted to being a closet Protestant. As she explained, "I am afraid of the Catholic sisters and [I] don't want my neighbors to know that I am not Catholic-minded." The fear of ostracism, while recorded by Houchen staff, did not figure into their understanding of Mexicano resistance to conversion. Instead, they blamed time and culture. Or as Dorothy Little succinctly related, "We can not eradicate in a few years what has been built up during ages."[44] Their dilemma points to the fact historians Sarah Deutsch and George Sánchez have noted: Americanization programs in the Southwest, most of which were sporadic and poorly financed, made little headway in Mexican communities. Ruth Crocker also described the Protestant settlements in Gary, Indiana, as having only a "superficial and temporary" influence.[45] Yet even long-term sustained efforts, as in the case of Houchen, had limited appeal. This inability to mold consciousness or identity demonstrates not only the strength of community sanctions, but, more significant, of conscious decision making on the part of Mexican women who sought to claim a place for themselves and their families in American society without abandoning their Mexican cultural affinities.

Mexican women derived substantive services from Friendship in the form of health care and education; however, they refused to embrace its romantic idealizations of American life. Wage-earning mothers who placed their children in the day nursery no doubt encountered an Anglo world quite different from the one depicted by Methodist missionaries and thus were skeptical of the settlement's cultural messages. Clara Sarmiento knew from experience that it was much easier to reach the children than their parents.[46] How did children respond to the ideological undercurrents of Houchen programs? Did

Mexican women feel empowered by their interaction with the settlement or were Methodist missionaries invidious underminers of Mexican identity?

In getting beneath the text, the following remarks of Minerva Franco that appeared in a 1975 issue of *Newark-Houchen News* raise a series of provocative questions. "Houchen provided . . . opportunities for learning and experiencing. . . . At Houchen I was shown that I had worth and that I was an individual."[47] Now what did she mean by that statement? Did the settlement house heighten her self-esteem? Did she feel that she was not an individual within the context of her family and neighborhood? Some young women imbibed Americanization so heavily as to reject their identity. In *No Separate Refuge*, Sarah Deutsch picked up on this theme as she quoted missionary Polita Padilla: "I am Mexican, born and brought up in New Mexico, but much of my life was spent in the Allison School where we had a different training so that the Mexican way of living now seems strange to me." Others, like Estella Ibarra and Rose Escheverría Mulligan, saw little incompatibility between Mexican traditions and Protestantism.[48]

Which Mexican women embraced the ideas of assimilation so completely as to become closet Mexicans? As a factor, class must be taken into consideration. In his field notes housed at the Bancroft Library, economist Paul Taylor contends that middle-class Mexicans desiring to dissociate themselves from their working-class neighbors possessed the most fervent aspirations for assimilation. Once in the United States, middle-class Mexicanos found themselves subject to racial/ethnic prejudice that did not discriminate by class. Due to restrictive real estate covenants, immigrants lived in barrios with people they considered inferiors.[49] By passing as "Spanish," they cherished hopes of melting into the American social landscape. Sometimes mobility-minded parents sought to regulate their children's choice of friends and later marriage partners. "My folks never allowed us to go around with Mexicans," remembered Alicia Mendeola Shelit. "We went sneaking around, but my Dad wouldn't allow it. We'd always be with white." Indeed, Shelit married twice, both times to Euro-Americans.[50] Of course it would be unfair to characterize all middle-class Mexican women immigrants as repudiating their mestizo identity. Working in a posh El Paso department store, Alma Araiza would quickly correct her colleagues when they assumed she was Italian.

> People kept telling me, 'You must not be Mexican.' And I said, 'why do you think I'm not?' 'Well, it's your skin color. Are you Italian?' . . . I [responded] 'I am Mexicana.'[51]

Or, as a young woman cleverly remarked to anthropologist Ruth Tuck, "Listen, I may be a Mexican in a fur coat, but I'm still a Mexican."[52]

The Houchen documents reveal glimpses into the formation of identity, consciousness, and values. The Friendship Square Calendar of 1949 explicitly stated that the medical care provided at Houchen "is a tool to develop sound minds in sound bodies; for thus it is easier to find peace with God and man. We want to help people develop a sense of values in life." Furthermore, the privileging of color—with white as the pinnacle—was an early lesson. Relating the excitement of kindergarten graduation, Day Nursery head Beatrice Fernandez included in her report a question asked by Margarita, one of the young graduates. "We are all wearing white, white dress, slip, socks, and Miss Fernandez, is it alright if our hair is black?"[53] Sometimes subtle, sometimes overt, the privileging of race, class, culture, and color taught by women missionaries had painful consequences for their pupils.

Houchen activities were synonymous with Americanization. A member of the settlement Brownie troop encouraged her friends "to become 'an American or a Girl Scout' at Houchen." Scouting certainly served as a vehicle for Americanization. The all-Mexican Girl and Boy Scout Troops of Alpine, Texas, enjoyed visiting El Paso and Ciudad Juárez in the company of Houchen scouts. In a thank-you note, the Alpine Girl Scouts wrote, "Now we can all say we have been to a foreign country."[54]

It is important to remember that Houchen provided a bilingual environment, not a bicultural one. Spanish was the means to communicate the message of Methodism and Christian Americanization. Whether dressing up children as Pilgrims or European peasants, missionaries stressed "American" citizenship and values; yet, outside conversion, definitions of those values or of "our American way" remained elusive. Indeed, some of the settlement lessons were not incongruous with Mexican mores. In December 1952, a Euro-American settlement worker recorded in her journal the success of a Girl Scout dinner. "The girls learned a lot from it too. They were taught how to set the table, and how to serve the men. They learned also that they had to share, to cooperate, and to wait their turn."[55] These were not new lessons.

The most striking theme that repeatedly emerges from Houchen documents is that of individualism. Missionaries emphasized the importance of individual decision making and individual accomplishment. In recounting her own conversion, Clara Sarmiento explained to a young client, "I chose my own religion because it was my own personal experience and . . . I was glad my religion was not chosen for me."[56]

In *Relations of Rescue,* Peggy Pascoe carefully recorded the glass ceiling encountered by "native helpers" at Protestant rescue homes. Chinese women at Cameron House in San Francisco, for example, could only emulate Euro-American missionaries to a certain point, always as subordinates, not as directors or leaders. Conversely, Mexican women did assume top positions of leadership at Methodist settlements. In 1930, María Moreno was appointed the head resident of the brand new Floyd Street Settlement in Dallas, Texas. Methodist community centers and boarding schools stressed the need for developing "Christian leaders trained for useful living."[57] For many, leadership meant ministering as a lay volunteer; for some, it meant pursuing a missionary vocation.

The Latina missionaries of Houchen served as cultural brokers as they diligently strived to integrate themselves into the community. Furthermore, over time Latinas appeared to have experienced some mobility within the settlement hierarchy. In 1912, Ofilia [sic] Chávez served as a "student helper"; forty years later Beatrice Fernandez would direct the preschool. Until 1950, the Houchen staff usually included one Latina, during the 1950s, the number of Latina (predominately Mexican American) settlement workers rose to six. Mary Lou López, María Rico, Elizabeth Soto, Febe Bonilla, Clara Sarmiento, María Payan, and Beatrice Fernandez had participated in Methodist outreach activities as children (Soto at Houchen) and had decided to follow in the footsteps of their teachers. In addition, these women had the assistance of five full-time Mexican laypersons.[58] It is no coincidence that the decade of greatest change in Houchen policies occurred at a time when Latinas held a growing number of staff positions. Friendship Square's greater sensitivity to neighborhood needs arose, in part, out of the influence exerted by Mexican clients in shaping the attitudes and actions of Mexican missionaries.

So, in the end, Mexican women utilized Houchen's social services; they did not, by and large, adopt its tenets of Christian Americanization. Children who attended settlement programs enjoyed the activities, but Friendship Square did not always leave a lasting imprint. "My Mom had an open mind, so I participated in a lot of clubs. But I didn't become Protestant," remarked Lucy Lucero. "I had fun and I learned a lot, too." Because of the warm, supportive environment, Houchen Settlement is remembered with fondness. However, one cannot equate pleasant memories with the acceptance of the settlement's cultural ideals.[59]

Settlement records bear out Mexican women's *selective* use of Houchen's resources. The most complete set of figures is for the year 1944. During this period, 7,614 people visited the clinic and hospital. The settlement afternoon programs had an average monthly enrollment of 362 and 40 children attended kindergarten. Taken together, approximately 8,000 residents of Segundo Barrio utilized Friendship Square's medical and educational offerings. In contrast, the congregation of El Buen Pastor included 160 people.[60] Although representing only a single year, these figures indicate the importance of Houchen's medical facilities and Mexican women's selective utilization of resources.

By the 1950s, settlement houses were few and far between and those that remained were run by professional social workers. Implemented by a growing Latina staff, client-initiated changes in Houchen policies brought a realistic recognition of the settlement as a social service agency rather than a religious mission. During the 1950s, brochures describing the day nursery emphasized that while children said grace at meals and sang Christian songs, they would not receive "in any way indoctrination" regarding Methodism. In fact, at the parents' request, Newark nurses summoned Catholic priests to the hospital to baptize premature infants. Client desire became the justification for allowing the presence of Catholic clergy, a policy that would have been unthinkable in the not too distant past.[61] Finally, in the new Houchen constitution of 1959, all mention of conversion was dropped. Instead, it conveyed a more ecumenical, nondenominational spirit. For instance, the goal of Houchen Settlement was henceforth "to establish a Christian democratic framework for—individual development, family solidarity, and neighborhood welfare."[62]

Settlement activities also became more closely linked with the Mexican community. During the 1950s, Houchen was the home of two LULAC chapters—one for teenagers and one for adults. The League of United Latin American Citizens (LULAC) was the most visible and politically powerful civil rights organization in Texas.[63] Carpentry classes—once the preserve of males—opened their doors to young women, although on a gender-segregated basis. Houchen workers, moreover, made veiled references to the "very dangerous business" of Juárez abortion clinics; however, it appears unclear whether or not the residents themselves offered any contraceptive counseling. During the early 1960s, however, the settlement, in cooperation with Planned Parenthood, opened a birth control clinic for "married women." Indeed, a Houchen contraception success story was featured on the front page of a spring newsletter. "Mrs. G — — —, after having her thirteenth and fourteenth children (twins), enrolled in our birth control clinic; now for one and one half years she has been a happy and non-pregnant mother."[64] Certainly Houchen had changed with the times. What factors accounted for the new directions in settlement work? The evidence on the baptism of premature babies seems fairly clear in terms of client pressure, but to what extent did other policies change as the result of Mexican women's input? The residents of Segundo Barrio may have felt more comfortable expressing their ideas and Latina settlement workers may have exhibited a greater willingness to listen. Indeed, Mexican clients, not missionaries, set the boundaries for interaction.

Creating the public space of settlements and community centers, advocates of Americanization sought to alter the "lifeworld" of Mexican immigrants to reflect their own idealized versions of life in the United States. Settlement workers can be viewed as the narrators of lived experience as Houchen records reflected the cognitive construction of missionary aspirations and expectations. In other words, the documents revealed more about the women who wrote them than those they served. At another level, one could interpret the cultural ideals of Americanization as an indication of an attempt at what Jürgen Habermas has termed "inner colonization."[65] Yet the failure of such projects illustrates the ways in which Mexican women appropriated desired resources, both material (infant immunizations) and psychological (self-esteem) while, in the main, rejecting the ideological messages behind them. The shift in Houchen policies during the 1950s meant more than a recognition of community needs; it represented a claiming of public space by Mexican women clients.

Confronting Americanization brings into sharp relief the concept I have termed cultural coalescence. Immigrants and their children pick, borrow, retain, and create distinctive cultural forms. There is no single hermetic Mexican or Mexican American culture, but rather permeable *cultures* rooted in generation, gender, region, class, and personal experience. Chicano scholars have divided Mexican experiences into three generational categories: *Mexicano* (first generation), Mexican American (second generation), and Chicano (third and beyond).[66] But this general typology tends to obscure the ways in which people navigate across cultural boundaries as well as their conscious decision making in the production of culture. However, people of color have not had unlimited choice. Race and gender prejudice and discrimination with their accompanying social, political, and economic segmentation have constrained aspirations, expectations, and decision making. By looking through the lens of cultural coalescence, we can begin to discern the ways in which people select and create cultural forms. In El Paso's Segundo Barrio, Mexican women acted, not reacted, to the settlement impulse. When standing at the cultural crossroads, Mexican women blended their options and created their own paths.

Notes

1. Interview with Elsa Chávez, April 19, 1983, conducted by the author. *Note:* Elsa Chávez is a pseudonym used at the person's request.
2. Recent scholarship on Americanization programs aimed at Mexican communities includes

George J. Sánchez, "'Go After the Women': Americanization and the Mexican Immigrant Woman, 1915–1929," in *Unequal Sisters: A Multicultural Reader in U.S. Women's History*, 2nd ed., eds. Vicki L. Ruiz and Ellen Carol DuBois (New York: Routledge, 1994), pp. 284–97; Sarah Deutsch, *No Separate Refuge: Culture, Class and Gender on the Anglo-Hispanic Frontier in the American Southwest, 1880–1940* (New York: Oxford University Press, 1987), pp. 63–86; Gilbert González, *Chicano Education in the Era of Segregation* (Philadelphia: Balch Institute Press, 1990), pp. 30–61; Ruth Hutchinson Crocker, "Gary Mexicans and 'Christian Americanization': A Study in Cultural Conflict," in *Forging a Community: The Latino Experience in Northwest Indiana, 1919–1975,* eds. James B. Lane and Edward J. Escobar (Chicago: Cattails Press, 1987), pp. 115–34; Susan Yohn, *A Contest of Faiths: Missionary Women and Pluralism in the American Southwest* (Ithaca: Cornell University Press, 1995); Vicki L. Ruiz, "Dead Ends or Gold Mines?: Using Missionary Records in Mexican American Women's History," *Frontiers: A Journal of Women's Studies,* 12:1 (1991): 33–56.

3. Pearl Idella Ellis, *Americanization Through Homemaking* (Los Angeles: Wetzel Publishing Co., 1929), preface [no page number].

4. *Ibid.,* p. 13.

5. M. Dorothy Woodruff, "Methodist Women Along the Mexican Border" (Women's Division of Christian Service pamphlet, ca. 1946) [part of an uncatalogued collection of documents housed at Houchen Community Center, El Paso, Texas; heretofore referred to as HF for Houchen Files]. This pamphlet provides brief descriptions of each of the twenty-one "centers of work" operated by Methodist missionaries. For a celebratory overview of Methodist women's missionary endeavors throughout the United States, see Noreen Dunn Tatum, *A Crown of Service* (Nashville, Tenn.: Parthenon Press, 1960).

6. Steven Seidman, ed., *Jürgen Habermas on Society and Politics: A Reader* (Boston: Beacon Press, 1989), p. 171.

7. Oscar J. Martínez, *The Chicanos of El Paso: An Assessment of Progress* (El Paso: Texas Western Press, 1980), pp. 6, 17.

8. Martínez, *Chicanos,* pp. 10, 29–33. Mario García meticulously documents the economic and social stratification of Mexicans in El Paso. See Mario T. García, *Desert Immigrants: The Mexicans of El Paso, 1880–1920* (New Haven: Yale University Press, 1981). *Note:* In 1960, the proportion of Mexican workers with high white-collar jobs jumped to 3.4 percent. [Martinez, *Chicanos,* p. 10.]

9. "South El Paso's Oasis of Care," *paso del norte,* Vol. 1 (September 1982): 42–43; Thelma Hammond, "Friendship Square," (Houchen Report, 1969) [HF]; "Growing with the Century" (Houchen Report, 1947) [HF].

10. García, *Desert Immigrants.* p. 145; Effie Stoltz, "Freeman Clinic: A Resume of Four Years Work" (Houchen Pamphlet, 1924) [HF]. It should be noted that Houchen Settlement sprang from the work of Methodist missionary Mary Tripp who arrived in South El Paso in 1893. However, it was not until 1912 that an actual settlement was established. ["South El Paso's Oasis of Care," p. 42].

11. Stoltz, "Freeman Clinic"; Hammond, "Friendship Square"; M. Dorothy Woodruff and Dorothy Little, "Friendship Square" (Houchen Pamphlet, March 1949) [HF]; "Friendship Square" (Houchen Report, circa 1940s) [HF]; *Health Center* (Houchen Newsletter, 1943) [HF]; "Christian Health Service" (Houchen Report, 1941) [HF]; *El Paso Times,* October 20, 1945.

12. "Settlement Worker's Report" (Houchen Report, 1927) [HF]; Letter from Dorothy Little to E. Mae Young dated May 10, 1945 [HF]. Letter from Bessie Brinson to Treva Ely dated September 14, 1958 [HF]; Hammond, "Friendship Square"; Elmer T. Clark and Dorothy McConnell, "The Methodist Church and Latin Americans in the United States" (Board of Missions pamphlet, circa 1930s) [HF]. My very rough estimate is based on the documents and records to which I had access. I was not permitted to examine any materials then housed at Newark Hospital. The most complete statistics on utilization of services are for the year 1944 in the letter from Dorothy Little to E. Mae Young. *Note:* Because of the deportation and repatriation drives of the 1930s in which one-third of the Mexican population in the United States were either deported or repatriated, the Mexican population in El Paso dropped from 68,476 in 1930 to 55,000 in 1940. By 1960 it had risen to 63,796. [Martinez, *Chicanos,* p. 6]

13. *El Paso Herald Post,* March 7, 1961; *El Paso Herald Post,* March 12, 1961; "Community Centers" (Women's Division of Christian Service Pamphlet, May 1963); *Funding Proposal* for Youth Outreach and Referral Report Project (April 30, 1974) [Private Files of Kenton J. Clymer, Ph.D.]; *El Paso Herald Post,* January 3, 1983; *El Paso Times,* August 8, 1983.

14. Letter from Tom Houghteling, Director, Houchen Community Center to the author December 24, 1990; Tom Houghteling, telephone conversation with the author, January 9, 1991.

15. Dorothy Little, "Rose Gregory Houchen Settlement" (Houchen Report, February 1942) [HF].

16. *Ibid.;* "Our Work at Houchen" (Houchen Report, circa 1940s) [HF]; Woodruff and Little, "Friendly Square"; Jennie C. Gilbert, "Settlements Under the Women's Home Missionary Society" (pamphlet, circa 1920s) [HF]; Clark and McConnell, "Latin Americans in the United States."

17. Anita Hernandez, "The Kindergarten" (Houchen Report, circa 1940s) [HF]; *A Right Glad New Year* (Houchen Newsletter, circa 1940s) [HF]; Little, "Rose Gregory Houchen Settlement"; "Our Work at Houchen"; Woodruff and Little, "Friendship Square." For more information on the Franciscans, see Ramón Gutiérrez, *When Jesus Came, the Corn Mothers Went Away: Marriage, Sexuality, and Power in New Mexico, 1500–1846* (Stanford: Stanford University Press, 1991).

18. Settlement Worker's Report (1927); Letter from Little to Young; letter from Brinson to Ely, *Friendship Square Calendar* (1949) [HF]; interview with Lucy Lucero, October 8, 1983, conducted by the author; Chávez interview; discussion following presentation, "Settlement Houses in El Paso," given by the author at the El Paso Conference on History and the Social Sciences, August 24, 1983, El Paso, Texas [tape of presentation and discussion is on file at the Institute of Oral History, University of Texas, El Paso].

19. Chávez interview; discussion following "Settlement Houses in El Paso." *Note:* The Catholic Church never established a competing settlement house. However, during the 1920s in Gary, Indiana, the Catholic diocese opened up the Gary-Alerding Settlement with the primary goal of Americanizing Mexican immigrants. The bishop took such action to counteract suspected inroads made by two local Protestant settlement houses. See Crocker, "Gary Mexicans," pp. 123–27.

20. "Christian Health Service"; "The Freeman Clinic and the Newark Conference Maternity Hospital" (Houchen Report, 1940) [HF]; *El Paso Times,* August 2, 1961; *El Paso Herald Post,* May 12, 1961. For more information on Americanization programs in California, see George J. Sánchez, "'Go After the Women,'" pp. 250–63. *Note:* The documents reveal a striking absence of adult Mexican male clients. The Mexican men who do appear are either Methodist ministers or lay volunteers.

21. Sánchez, "'Go After,'" pp. 250–83; Deutsch, *No Separate Refuge;* "Americanization Notes," *The Arizona Teacher and Home Journal,* 11:5 (January 1923): 26. *Note:* The Methodist and Presbyterian settlements in Gary, Indiana, also couched their programs in terms of "Christian Americanization." [Crocker, "Gary Mexicans," pp. 118–20]

22. "Settlement Worker's Report" (1927); *Friendship Square Calendar* (1949) [HF]; letter from Brinson to Ely; Chávez interview.

23. "News Clipping from *The El Paso Times*" (circa 1950s) [HF].

24. Clara Gertrude Smith, "The Development of the Mexican People in the Community of Watts" (M.A. thesis, University of Southern California, 1933), p. 104.

25. Rayna Green, "The Pocahontas Perplex," in *Unequal Sisters,* pp. 15–21.

26. Sánchez, "'Go After the Women,'" p. 260; *Newark-Houchen News,* September 1975. I agree with George Sánchez that Americanization programs created an overly rosy picture of American life. In his words: "Rather than providing Mexican immigrant women with an attainable picture of assimilation, Americanization programs could only offer these immigrants idealized versions of American life." [Sánchez, *loc. cit.*]

27. Little, "Rose Gregory Houchen Settlement."

28. García, *Desert Immigrants,* pp. 110–26; Paul S. Taylor, *Mexican Labor in the United States,* Vol. 1 (Berkeley: University of California Press, 1930, rpt. Arno Press, 1970), pp. 79, 205–206. [Quote is from Taylor, *Mexican Labor,* p. 79.]

29. Margarita B. Melville, "Selective Acculturation of Female Mexican Migrants," in *Twice a*

Minority: Mexican American Women, ed. Margarita B. Melville (St. Louis: C. V. Mosby, 1980), pp. 159–60; John García, "Ethnicity and Chicanos: Measurement of Ethnic Identification, Identity, and Consciousness," *Hispanic Journal of Behavioral Sciences,* Vol. 4 (1982): 310–11. For an insightful, brief overview of Mexican-American ethnic identification, see David Gutiérrez, *Walls and Mirrors: Mexican Americans, Mexican Immigrants, and the Politics of Ethnicity in the Southwest, 1910–1986* (Berkeley: University of California Press, 1995), pp. 1–11.

30. Edward Soja, *Postmodern Geographies: The Reassertion of Space in Critical Social Theory* (New York and London: Verso Press, 1989), p. 23. Gracias a Matthew García for bringing this text to my attention.

31. "Settlement Worker's Report" (1927); Hernandez, "The Kindergarten" [HF]; *A Right Glad New Year;* Little, "Rose Gregory Houchen Settlement"; "Our Work at Houchen"; Woodruff and Little, "Friendship Square"; "South El Paso's Oasis of Care," *loc. cit.; El Paso Herald Post,* March 7, 1961; *El Paso Herald Post,* March 12, 1961; *El Paso Herald Post,* May 12, 1961.

32. C. S. Babbitt, "The Remedy for the Decadence of the Latin Race" (El Paso: El Paso Printing Company) (Presented to the Pioneers Association of El Paso, Texas, July 11, 1909, by Mrs. Babbitt, widow of the author), p. 55. Pamphlet courtesy of Jack Redman.

33. George J. Sánchez, *Becoming Mexican American: Ethnicity, Culture, and Identity in Chicano Los Angeles, 1900–1945* (New York: Oxford University Press, 1993), p. 156; Robert McLean, *That Mexican! As He Is, North and South of the Rio Grande* (New York: Fleming H. Revell Co., 1928), pp. 162–63, quoted in E. C. Orozco, *Republican Protestantism in Aztlán* (Santa Barbara: The Petereins Press, 1980), p. 162. *Note:* Immigration has frequently been linked with food from the "melting pot" of assimilation to the "salad bowl" of cultural pluralism. McLean's metaphor of Uncle Sam as a diner at the immigration cafe follows:

> Fifty and one hundred years ago Uncle Sam accomplished some remarkable digestive feats. Gastronomically he was a marvel. He was not particularly choosy! Dark meat from the borders of the Mediterranean or light meat from the Baltic equally suited him, for promptly he was able to assimilate both, turning them into bone of his bone, and flesh of his flesh—But this chili con carne! Always it seems to give Uncle Samuel the heartburn; and the older he gets, the less he seems to be able to assimilate it. Indeed, it is a question whether chili is not a condiment, to be taken in small quantities rather than a regular article of diet. And upon this conviction ought to stand all the law . . . as far as the Mexican immigrant is concerned.

34. *Account Book for Rose Gregory Houchen Settlement* (1903–1913) [HF]; Hammond, "Friendship Square"; "Growing with the Century"; *El Paso Times,* September 5, 1975; Stoltz, "Freeman Clinic"; Woodruff and Little, "Friendship Square"; *El Paso Times,* October 3, 1947; "Four Institutions. One Goal. The Christian Community" (Houchen pamphlet, circa early 1950s) [HF]; Houghteling conversation; "A City Block of Service" (Script of Houchen Slide Presentation, 1976) [HF]; *El Paso Times,* January 19, 1977; "Speech given by Kenton J. Clymer, Ph.D." (June 1975) [Clymer Files]; *El Paso Times,* May 23, 1975; *Newark-Houchen News,* September 1975. It should be noted that in 1904 local Methodist congregations did contribute much of the money needed to purchase the property on which the settlement was built. Local civic groups occasionally donated money or equipment and threw Christmas parties for Houchen children. [*Account Book; El Paso Herald Post,* December 14, 1951; *El Paso Times,* December 16, 1951]

35. Vernon McCombs, "Victories in the Latin American Mission" (Board of Home Missions pamphlet, 1935) [HF]; "Brillante Historia De La Inglesia 'El Buen Pastor' El Paso," *Young Adult Fellowship Newsletter,* December 1946 [HF]; Soledad Burciaga, "Yesterday in 1923" (Houchen Report, 1939) [HF].

36. This study is based on a limited number of oral interviews (five), but they represent a range of interaction with the settlement from playing on the playground to serving as the minister for El Buen Pastor. It is also informed by a public discussion of my work on Houchen held during an El Paso teachers' conference in 1983. Most of the educators who attended the talk had participated, to some extent, in Houchen activities and were eager to share their recollections

[Cf. note 13]. I am also indebted to students in my Mexican-American history classes when I taught at the University of Texas, El Paso, especially the reentry women, for their insight and knowledge.

37. Woodruff and Little, "Friendship Square"; Hammond, "Friendship Square"; *Greetings for 1946* (Houchen Christmas Newsletter, 1946) [HF]; Little, "Rose Gregory Houchen Settlement"; Soledad Burciaga, "Today in 1939" (Houchen Report, 1939) [HF]; "Our Work at Houchen"; "Christian Social Service" [Houchen Report, circa 1940s) [HF]; Interview with Fernando García, September 21, 1983, conducted by the author; *El Paso Times,* June 14, 1951; Lucero interview; Vicki L. Ruiz, "Oral History and La Mujer: The Rosa Guerrero Story," in *Women on the U.S.-Mexican Border: Responses to Change* (Boston: Allen and Unwin, 1987), pp. 226–27; *Newark-Houchen News,* September 1975.

38. Woodruff, "Mexican Women."

39. *Spanish-American Methodist News Bulletin,* April 1946 [HF]; Hammond, "Friendship Square"; McCombs, "Victories"; "El Metodismo en La Ciudad de El Paso," *Christian Herald,* July 1945 [HF]; "Brillante Historia"; "The Door: An Informal Pamphlet on the Work of the Methodist Church Among the Spanish-speaking of El Paso, Texas" (Methodist pamphlet, 1940) [HF]; "A City Block of Service" (script of slide presentation); García interview; Houghteling interview. *Note:* From 1932 to 1939, services for El Buen Pastor were held in a church located two blocks away from the settlement.

40. A. Ruth Kern, "There Is No Segregation Here," *Methodist Youth Fund Bulletin* (January-March 1953): 12 [HF].

41. *Ibid.;* "The Torres Family" (Houchen Report, circa 1940s) [HF]; interview with Estella Ibarra, November 11, 1982, conducted by Jesuista Ponce; Hazel Bulifant, "One Woman's Story" (Houchen Report, 1950) [HF]; "Our Work at Houchen."

42. Clara Sarmiento, "Lupe" (Houchen Report, circa 1950s) [HF].

43. Ibarra interview.

44. Bulifant, "One Woman's Story"; letter from Little to Young.

45. Deutsch, *No Separate Refuge,* pp. 64–66, 85–86; Sánchez, "Go After the Women," pp. 259–61; Crocker, "'Gary Mexicans,'" p. 121.

46. Sarmiento, "Lupe." In her study, Ruth Crocker also notes the propensity of Protestant missionaries to focus their energies on children and the selective uses of services by Mexican clients. As she explained, "Inevitably, many immigrants came to the settlement, took what they wanted of its services, and remained untouched by its message." [Crocker, "Gary Mexicans," p. 122.]

47. *Newark-Houchen News,* September 1975.

48. Deutsch, *No Separate Refuge,* pp. 78–79; Ibarra interview; Interview with Rose Escheverría Mulligan, Vol. 27, *Rosie the Riveter Revisited: Women and the World War II Work Experience,* ed. Sherna Berger Gluck (Long Beach: CSULB Foundation, 1983), p. 24.

49. Paul S. Taylor, "Women in Industry," field notes for *Mexican Labor in the United States,* Bancroft Library, University of California, Berkeley, Box 1. *Note:* Referring to Los Angeles, two historians have argued that "Mexicans experienced segregation in housing in nearly every section of the city and its outlying areas." [Antonio Ríos-Bustamante and Pedro Castillo, *An Illustrated History of Mexican Los Angeles* (Los Angeles: UCLA Chicano Studies Research Center, 1986), p. 135.]

50. Interview with Alicia Mendeola Shelit, Vol. 37, *Rosie the Riveter Revisited,* p. 32; Mulligan interview, p. 14. Anthropologist Ruth Tuck noted that Euro-Americans also employed the term "Spanish" to distinguish individuals "of superior background or achievement." [Ruth Tuck, *Not with the Fist* (New York: Harcourt, Brace and Co., 1946; rpt. Arno Press, 1974), pp. 142–43.]

51. Interview with Alma Araiza García, March 27, 1993, conducted by the author.

52. Tuck, *Not with the Fist,* p. 133.

53. *Friendship Square Calendar* (1949); Beatrice Fernandez, "Day Nursery" (Houchen Report, circa late 1950s) [HF].

54. "Friendship Square" (Houchen pamphlet, circa 1950s) [HF]; letter to Houchen Girl Scouts from Troop 4, Latin American Community Center, Alpine, Texas, May 18, 1951 [HF].

55. *A Right Glad New Year;* News clipping from the *El Paso Times* (circa 1950s); "Our Work at

Houchen"; Little, "Rose Gregory Houchen Settlement"; "Anglo Settlement Worker's Journal" (entry for December 1952) [HF].

56. *Newark-Houchen News,* September 1975; Sarmiento, "Lupe."

57. Peggy Pascoe, *Relations of Rescue: The Search for Moral Authority in the American West, 1874–1939* (New York: Oxford University Press, 1990), pp. 112–39; Woodruff, "Methodist Women."

58. *Datebook for 1926* (entry: Friday, September 9, 1929) (Settlement Worker's private journal) [HF]; "Brillante Historia"; "Report and Directory of Association of Church Social Workers, 1940" [HF]; "May I Come in?" (Houchen brochure, circa 1950s) [HF]; "Friendship Square" (Houchen pamphlet, 1958) [HF]; Mary Lou López, "Kindergarten Report" (Houchen Report, circa 1950s) [HF]; Sarmiento, "Lupe"; "Freeman Clinic and Newark Hospital" (Houchen pamphlet, 1954) [HF]; *El Paso Times,* June 14, 1951; "Houchen Day Nursery" (Houchen pamphlet, circa 1950s) [HF]; *El Paso Times,* September 12, 1952.

59. Chávez interview; Martha González, interview with the author, October 8, 1983; Lucero interview; *Newark-Houchen News,* September 1974.

60. Letter from Little to Young; "The Door"; Woodruff and Little, "Friendship Square."

61. "Houchen Day Nursery"; "Life in a Glass House" (Houchen Report, circa 1950s) [HF].

62. *Program* for First Annual Meeting, Houchen Settlement and Day Nursery, Freeman Clinic, and Newark Conference Maternity Hospital (January 8, 1960) [HF]. It should be noted that thirty years later, there seems to be a shift back to original settlement ideas. Today, Houchen Community has regularly scheduled bible studies. [Letter from Houghteling to the author.]

63. *Program* for Houchen production of "Cinderella" [HF]; letter from Brinson to Ely. For more information on LULAC, see Mario T. García, *Mexican Americans: Leadership, Ideology, and Identity, 1930–1960* (New Haven: Yale University Press, 1989).

64. Bulifant, "One Woman's Story"; *News from Friendship Square* (Spring newsletter, circa early 1960s) [HF].

65. My understanding and application of the ideas of Jürgen Habermas have been informed by the following works. Jürgen Habermas, *Moral Consciousness and Communicative Action,* trans. Christian Lenhardt and Sherry Weber Nicholsen, introd. Thomas McCarthy (Cambridge: MIT Press, 1990); Seidman, ed. *Jürgen Habermas on Society and Politics;* Nancy Fraser, *Unruly Practices: Power, Discourse, and Gender in Contemporary Social Theory* (Minneapolis: University of Minnesota Press, 1989); Seyla Benhabib and Drucilla Cornell, "Introduction: Beyond the Politics of Gender," in *Feminism as Critique,* eds. Seyla Benhabib and Drucilla Cornell (Minneapolis: University of Minnesota Press, 1987).

66. As an example of this typology, see Mario García, *Mexican Americans,* pp. 13–22, 295–302. Richard Griswold del Castillo touches on the dynamic nature of Mexican culture in *La Familia: Chicano Families in the Urban Southwest, 1848 to the Present* (Notre Dame: University of Notre Dame Press, 1984).

14

Partly Colored or Other White

Mexican Americans and Their Problem with the Color Line

NEIL FOLEY

"R ace relations," until very recently, has usually meant relations between blacks and whites. Since the 1960s, however, the rising number of Asian and Latin American immigrants to the United States has challenged the abiding and historically important black-white binary. In Miami, Florida, tensions exist between the black and Cuban communities. Throughout the Southwest, conflicts between Anglos and Mexicans predate the War with Mexico in 1846. English-only initiatives, continued physical violence against Mexican immigrants, and the 1994 Californian proposition to deny medical, educational, and other benefits to undocumented workers attest to these ongoing conflicts. In Los Angeles, Koreans and blacks have longstanding grievances against one another; in Houston, Mexicans and Guatemalans struggle for low-paying jobs while many blacks and whites call for immigration restriction and tougher border controls.

In seven of the ten largest cities in the United States—New York, Los Angeles, Houston, San Diego, Phoenix, Dallas, and San Antonio, in that order—Latinos now outnumber blacks. In Los Angeles, Houston, Dallas, and San Antonio, Latinos outnumber Anglos, or non-Hispanic whites, as well. Latinos in Chicago now account for twenty-seven percent of the population, and their votes determine the outcome of most elections. To view the browning of America in other terms, in eighteen of the twenty-five most populous counties in the United States, Latinos now outnumber blacks. Where regions are concerned, both the Pacific Northwest and New England now have larger Spanish-surname populations than black populations. Already U.S. Latinos comprise the fifth-largest "nation" in Latin America, and in fifty years only Mexico and Brazil will exceed the number of Latinos living in the United States. Put another way, the United States will be the third-largest

"Spanish-language-origin" nation in the world.[1] In short, we live in a multiracial society that can no longer be viewed in black and white, because it has always been much more racially diverse than one encompassed by the stark simplicity of the black-white racial paradigm. Yet the black-white binary stubbornly continues to shape thinking about the racial place and space of Latinos in the United States who are often compared to, and sometimes equated with, either whites or blacks.

It must be stated from the outset that blacks themselves have been exasperated by the idea that their ethnic backgrounds—as Irish, Mexican, German, etc.—are obliterated by the necessity to maintain "blackness" as the unalloyed touchstone for determining who is white and who is not. In other words, anyone with any African ancestry is automatically "black"—a racial default sometimes referred to as the "one-drop" rule. In U.S. society, according to the racial formula by which mixed-race persons of African descent are denied any identity other than black, it would be impossible for a black woman to give birth to a white baby. By the same cultural rule, it is as impossible for an African American to claim to be "part Irish" as it is for a white person to claim to be "part black." Historian Barbara Fields relates the insightful, though probably apocryphal, anecdote of a white American journalist who asked the late Papa Doc Duvalier of Haiti what percentage of the Haitian population was white. Duvalier had answered that it was about ninety-eight percent white. The journalist assumed that Duvalier had misunderstood the question and put it to him once again. Duvalier assured the journalist that he had not misunderstood the question and repeated his answer. The journalist then asked, "How do you define 'white'?" Duvalier answered this question with one of his own: "How do you define 'black' in your country?" The journalist obligingly explained that anyone in the United States who has any black blood was considered black. Duvalier nodded and responded, "Well, that's the way we define white in my country."[2]

Historically, the one-drop rule of black racial construction fulfilled the need of white southerners to maintain the color line between white slave owners and black slaves even as the South, and the nation, had become a highly polyglot, miscegenated society in which both "whiteness" and "blackness" were cultural fictions, however devastatingly real were the social and political consequences of the "color line." Thus after 1920 "mulatto" ceased to be a racial category in the U.S. census as part of a larger racial project to maintain the color line between monolithic whiteness and blackness.

The dyadic racial thinking of white southerners and northerners encountered some challenges in the mid-nineteenth century as European whites began their westward march across the continent. In the trans-Mississippi West whites encountered Mexicans in the present-day states of Texas, New Mexico, and California. From their first encounters, Anglos (the term used by Mexicans for white Americans) did not regard Mexicans as blacks, but they also did not regard them as whites. Neither black nor white, Mexicans were usually regarded as a degraded "mongrel" race, a mixture of Indian, Spanish, and African ancestry, only different from Indians and Africans in the degree of their inferiority to whites. Indeed, many whites considered Mexicans inferior to Indians and Africans because Mexicans were racially mixed, a hybrid race that represented the worst nightmare of what might become of the white race if it let down its racial guard. Where whites encountered groups who were neither black nor white, they simply created other racial binaries (Anglo

Mexican; white Chinese, and so forth) to maintain racial hierarchies, while the quality that made whites superior—their "whiteness"—assumed a kind of racelessness, or invisibility, as they went about reaping the spoils of racial domination.

The persistence of the black-white binary has had some bizarre and unfortunate consequences for the shape of early Mexican American civil rights struggles. The period roughly from the 1930s to 1970 represented a particular strategy of civil rights activism among middle-class Mexican Americans who stressed the importance of assimilation and Americanization. But they also sought to construct identities as Caucasians by asserting their Spanish and "Latin American" descent. These second-generation Mexican Americans were reacting to the racial ideology, forged mostly between 1830 and 1930, that Mexicans constituted a hybrid race of Indian, African, and Spanish ancestry incapable of undertaking the obligations of democratic government. This chapter explores how Mexican Americans, beginning around 1930, when the census counted more U.S.-born Mexicans than Mexican immigrants, sought to overcome the stigma of being Mexican by asserting their Americanness. In the process, they equated Americanness with whiteness and therefore embarked on a strategy of dissociating themselves from African Americans as potential coalition partners in their early civil rights struggles. They came to the realization that being a U.S. citizen did not count nearly as much as being white, the racial sine qua non of Americanness.

Yet understanding the ways in which Mexicans have pursued the privileges of whiteness is not enough. In 1980 the U.S. census officially adopted the term "Hispanic," and many Mexican Americans and other Latinos have accepted the use of this term. As demographers and government officials sought to distinguish Anglos from Hispanics identifying as whites in the census, they have conceived the phrase "non-Hispanic whites" which implies the opposite category of "Hispanic whites," or simply Hispanics. This positioning of Hispanic as an ethnic subcategory of any race, and particularly its deployment as a separate class of whites, poses questions. How did Mexicans, a group historically racialized as nonwhite, arrive at their present status as ethnic whites, not unlike Italian or Irish Americans? As Hispanics continue to identify themselves as whites, what are the implications for African Americans and the continued dismal state of U.S. race relations, especially as the percentage of African Americans declines in proportion to the population of Latinos? Although this chapter does not fully answer those questions, in uncovering the Mexican American response to the black-white racial binary, it reveals the contradictions and ambiguities in the limiting vocabulary of race in our nation. Moreover, the experience of Mexican Americans in twentieth-century racial politics reflects how the long history of black-white racial thinking has not only impinged upon the freedom of Mexican Americans and other Latinos, but it has also stifled the ability of all Americans to reconsider and reconfigure racial discourses in new and productive ways.

The earliest and most persistent debates on race in the United States centered not on "the Negro problem" but on the boundaries of "whiteness"—who was white and who was not. The 1790 naturalization law was enacted to ensure that only "free white" persons—not Indians or Africans—could become U.S. citizens. However, the flood of immigrants from Ireland in the mid-nineteenth century—and later Jews, Slavs, Mediterraneans and other non-northern Europeans—altered the boundaries of whiteness to exclude all but those from northwestern Europe, the so-called Nordics. Whiteness thus fissured along *racial* lines, which culminated in the Immigration Act of 1924. This act established immigration quotas according to the national origins system, which greatly curtailed immigration from eastern and southern Europe. Asian immigrants were ineligible to become citizens, because they were not members of the "Caucasian race"; moreover, their immigration had been curtailed by the Chinese Exclusion Act of 1882 and the so-called Gentleman's Agreement with Japan in 1908 to limit Japanese immigration.[3]

Mexicans, however, continued to pose a problem to immigration restrictionists because the national-origin quotas of the 1924 immigration act did not apply to immigrants from the Western Hemisphere. Industry and large-scale agricultural farms throughout the American Southwest had so thoroughly relied on Mexican labor that immigration restriction would have meant nothing less than economic disaster for the entire region. As Mexicans continued to pour across the international border with Mexico in unprecedented numbers during the boom years of the 1920s, restrictionists argued that most Mexicans crossed the border illegally, often did not return to Mexico, took jobs from white people, and, most significantly, constituted a threat to the purity of the white race. For many Anglos in the Southwest, Mexicans were not whites and could not be assimilated into white American society.[4]

By the middle of the 1930s it was clear in Texas and other parts of the American West that African Americans did not constitute the number one race problem, as they had historically in the states of the South, including East Texas. In the West the threat to whiteness came principally from Latin America, particularly Mexico, not from Africa or African Americans. African Americans, after all, were not "alien" or foreign, and whites had a long history of dealing with blacks. In Texas and other southern states, whites and blacks had grown up together in the same towns, even if Jim Crow laws prevented them from sitting at the same lunch counters or attending the same schools. Blacks, for their part, shared much of southern culture with whites, whether on cotton farms or in Baptist churches. Indeed, African Americans in Texas shared with whites the experience of being displaced from their farms by Mexican immigrants whose language, religion, and customs differed from those of both blacks and whites.

Blacks, whatever else they might be to whites, were therefore not "alien," a word reserved by nativists to describe immigrants. Although many Mexicans had lived in Texas long before Stephen Austin established the first Anglo settlement in 1822, Anglos still regarded Mexicans as alien culturally, linguistically, religiously, and racially. Their status as racially in-between, as partly colored, hybrid peoples of mixed Indian, Spanish, and African ancestry, made them suspect in the eyes of whites, who feared that Mexicans could breach the color line by marrying both blacks and whites. Although laws existed against race mixing for whites and blacks, no such laws prevented the mixing of Mexicans with both blacks and whites.[5]

Most Anglos in the Southwest did not regard Mexicans as white, but they also did not consider them to be in the same racial category as "Negro." Before 1930 many Mexicans themselves simply thought of themselves as "Mexicanos"—neither black nor white. In 1930 a sociologist, Max Handman, commented: "The American community has no social technique for handling partly colored races. We have a place for the Negro and a place for the white man: the Mexican is not a Negro, and the white man refuses him an equal status."[6] As Handman explained, "The Mexican presents shades of color ranging from that of the Negro, although with no Negro features, to that of the white. The result is confusion."[7] No one has been more confused than whites themselves over the racial status of Mexicans, because some Mexicans look undeniably "white," while others look almost as dark as—and sometimes darker than—many blacks. "Such a situation cannot last for long," wrote Handman, "because the temptation of the white group is to push him down into the Negro group, while the efforts of the Mexican will be directed toward raising himself to the level of the white group." Mexicans, according to Handman, would not accept the subordinate status of blacks and instead would form a separate group "on the border line between the Negro and the white man."[8] Indeed middle-class, mostly urban Mexican Americans would invent themselves as a separate group after 1930, but it would not be "on the border" between black and white. They would come to insist that all Mexicans, citizens and non-citizens, were whites or Caucasians, albeit of Latin American descent.

Anglos, for their part, had long recognized that not all Mexicans were equally inferior. Immigrant Mexicans who were poor, non-English speaking, uneducated or illiterate, and often dark-skinned were inferior to a small class of Mexicans—U.S. citizens, English-speaking, educated, and often, but not always, light-skinned—who could be accorded certain privileges extended to other whites, such as voting, holding public office, sending their children to white schools, and even allowing for intermarriage, although usually in the case of an Anglo man desiring to marry a Mexican woman. Intermarriage was possible precisely because Anglos had "de-mexicanized" a privileged class of Mexicans who had been transformed into "Spanish Americans" or "Latin Americans"—into, in other words, a separate class of whites.[9]

Mexican Americans sought to have their status as whites recognized socially and politically in a region that had practiced Jim Crow segregation of both Mexicans and African Americans. They challenged attempts by state and federal governments to classify Mexicans as nonwhite and to maintain segregated schools in the aftermath of *Plessy* v. *Ferguson* (the 1896 Supreme Court decision that helped to entrench legal segregation throughout the South).

The first legal attempt to determine the racial status of Mexicans occurred in 1896 in Texas federal court when Ricardo Rodríguez, a long-time resident of San Antonio and legal Mexican immigrant, applied for U.S. citizenship. Anyone born in the United States is automatically a citizen, but immigrants who desire citizenship status must become "naturalized," a bureaucratic process by which immigrants fulfill residency requirements and forswear allegiance to their homelands. Two white politicians in San Antonio worried that Mexican immigrants might become citizens and exercise their right to vote. Consequently, they filed a law suit against Ricardo Rodríguez on the grounds that he was "Indian Mexican" and therefore not "white." The naturalization law, enacted in 1790 and amended in 1870, stipulated that only "free white persons" and "persons of African ancestry" were eligible for citizenship. Because Native Americans and all Asians were barred by naturalization law from becoming U.S. citizens, the lawyers hoped to prove that Rodríguez, a dark-skinned Mexican who freely admitted he was probably of Indian descent, was racially unfit for citizenship. In one of the many briefs filed in the year-long case, one of the attorneys opposed to granting citizenship to Rodríguez cited, as evidence, the findings of a French anthropologist who compiled a classification of race according to the variety of human skin color. It was impossible to distinguish with any degree of certainty between Indian Mexicans, African Mexicans, and "Spanish" or white Mexicans; therefore, the attorneys essentially argued that the boundary of whiteness be drawn on the basis of skin color. Rodríguez was, according to the attorneys, a "chocolate brown" Mexican. The judge in the case conceded, "If the strict scientific classification of the anthropologist should be adopted, [Rodríguez] would probably not be classed as white." Nevertheless, the court ruled that all citizens of Mexico, regardless of racial status, were eligible to become naturalized U.S. citizens. The fact that Mexicans, unlike Chinese immigrants or American Indians, could become naturalized citizens of the United States, however, rested less upon the assumption that they were white than on the obligations imposed upon the United States by Article VIII of the Treaty of Guadalupe Hidalgo. The treaty that ended the U.S. war with Mexico, signed in 1848, stipulated, among other things, that Mexicans could become U.S. citizens. From the legal standpoint, Mexican immigrants who were primarily "Indian" in appearance and ancestry could thus be granted U.S. citizenship, although Indians born in the United States were not eligible for citizenship, at least not until the Indian Citizenship Act of 1924.[10]

Second, *Plessy v. Ferguson* did not apply to Mexicans, inasmuch as they were officially recognized as "white." In Texas, for example, the legislature passed a law in 1893, six years before the Supreme Court mandated "separate but equal" facilities for blacks and whites, that required separate schools for the state's white and "colored" children. The statute defined colored as "all persons of mixed blood descended from Negro ancestry."[11] Thus Mexicans in the state were segregated by custom rather than by law, and school districts defended the practice on the grounds that Mexican children did not speak English and spent part of the school year with their families as migrant agricultural workers. When Mexican American civil rights activists were able to show that Mexican children were arbitrarily segregated, regardless of English-language facility, the courts generally ruled in favor of the plaintiff Mexican Americans.[12]

Third, the U.S. census had always counted persons of Mexican descent as whites, except in 1930, when a special category was created for "Mexicans." The question of Mexican racial identity became especially acute during the immigration restriction debates of the 1920s. This broad exemption from immigration quotas led to the historic congressional debates in the 1920s by restrictionists determined to close the door to Mexicans. The Bureau of the Census decided that beginning with 1930 it would establish a new category to determine how many persons of Mexican descent resided in the United States, legally or illegally. Before 1930 all Mexican-descent people were counted simply as white persons, because the racial categories at that time included Negro, White, Indian, Chinese, and Japanese. The 1930 census created, for the first time in U.S. history, the separate category of "Mexican," which stipulated that "all persons born in Mexico, or having parents born in Mexico, *who are not definitely white,* negro, Indian, Chinese, or Japanese, should be returned as Mexican." This meant that census workers determined whether to record a particular Mexican household as "white" or "Mexican." About ninety-six percent of Mexican-descent people were counted under this new category of Mexican;

only four percent were counted as white.[13] Mexicans had, for the first time in U.S. history, been counted as a nonwhite group. The government of Mexico as well as numerous Mexican Americans protested this new classification. Bowing to pressure, the U.S. government abandoned the category of Mexican in the 1940 census but sought other means of identifying the Latino population, by identifying those with Spanish surnames or households whose dominant language was Spanish.

Although Mexican Americans were accorded de jure white racial status in naturalization law, school segregation statutes, and in the census, they nevertheless endured de facto discrimination in their everyday lives: they lived in segregated neighborhoods or *barrios,* their children attended segregated schools, and they were prohibited from using some public facilities, such as swimming pools, or sitting in the white section at movie theaters, eating in white-only restaurants, or staying in white-only hotels. Nevertheless, Mexican Americans remained vigilant in monitoring local laws, customs, and racial protocols that might limit their claims to the rights and privileges of whiteness. Whenever local officials challenged their claim to whiteness, Mexican American civil rights activists sought redress from the federal government—sometimes through the courts—to prevent officials from classifying, categorizing, or otherwise consigning them to the nonwhite side of the color line.

In 1936, in El Paso, Texas, white city officials challenged the traditional classification of Mexicans as whites in the city's birth and death records. The county health officer, T. J. McCamant, and Alex K. Powell, the city registrar of the Bureau of Vital Statistics, adopted a new policy of registering the births and deaths of Mexican-descent citizens as "colored" rather than "white."[14] Both McCamant and Powell claimed that they were simply following the regulations established by the Department of Commerce and Bureau of the Census and that officials in Dallas, Forth Worth, Houston, and San Antonio used the same classification system.[15] McCamant also acknowledged that changing the classification of Mexicans from white to colored automatically lowered the infant mortality rate for whites in a city where Mexicans comprised over sixty percent of the population, most of whom were poor and suffered higher rates of infant mortality than did whites. Because the El Paso Chamber of Commerce had hoped to market El Paso as a health resort for those suffering from tuberculosis and other ailments, it became necessary to disaggregate Mexicans from the white category on birth records and to move them into the colored category, thereby automatically lowering the infant mortality rate for "non-Hispanic whites."

The Mexican American community of El Paso, as well as Mexicans across the border in neighboring Juarez, became furious over this racial demotion and mobilized to have their whiteness restored. Members of the El Paso council of the League of United Latin American Citizens and other community leaders immediately filed an injunction in the Sixty-fifth district court. Cleofas Calleros, a Mexican American representative of the National Catholic Welfare Council of El Paso, wrote to the attorney representing the twenty-six Mexican Americans who had filed the injunction, "Is it a fact that the Bureau [of the Census] has ruled that Mexicans are 'colored,' meaning the black race?"[16] Calleros argued that classifying Mexicans as "colored" was not only incorrect but illegal. Texas civil and penal codes classified Mexicans as "white," because "colored" referred only to those persons of "mixed blood descended from negro ancestry." He added that Mexicans "as a race are red if they are Indians and white if they are not Indians," essentially negating the historical presence of African ancestry among Mexicans.[17] An editorial in a Spanish-language newspaper argued simply that a Mexican who is not "pure Indian" is of the "Caucasian race," thereby implying that a "one-drop" rule applied to Mexicans: any amount of white blood rendered an Indian or a mestizo white, an interesting inversion of the one-drop rule of the U.S. South that rendered all those with the smallest African ancestry as black.[18] While praising the high civilization of the Aztec, Maya, Olmecs, and Toltecs, often as a defense against frequent Anglo insinuations that Mexicans were little more than mongrelized Indians, Mexicans nonetheless began to insist that they belonged, according to one Spanish-language editorial, "to the racial group of their mother country, Spain, and therefore to the Caucasian race."[19]

Alonso Perales, president of LULAC, writing to Cleofas Calleros to congratulate him for his "virile stance" on the classification issue, explained that he never protested the fact that Mexicans had their own category in San Antonio because "we are very proud of our racial origins and we do not wish to give the impression that we are ashamed of being called 'Mexicans.' Nevertheless," he continued, "we have always resented the inference that we are not whites." If Mexicans had to have their separate category for statistical purposes, he believed that the category of white ought to be subdivided into "Anglo American" and "Latin American."[20]

The campaign to restore their status as whites in the birth and death records in El Paso did not end with local classification schemes. Mexican Americans also learned that the U.S. Department of the Treasury and Internal Revenue Service had instructed applicants for social security cards to check either the "white" or "negro" box on the application forms. If applicants were neither white nor Negro, they were instructed to write out the "color or race" to which they belonged and gave as examples: "Mexican, Chinese, Japanese, Indian, Filipino, etc."[21] Once more Mexican Americans in El Paso and elsewhere in Texas wrote indignant letters to the Treasury Department complaining bitterly that Mexicans were white and should not be included in the same category with nonwhite groups like the Chinese and Japanese. The storm of protest led federal officials to acknowledge the error and to promise to reprint new forms. Tens of thousands of the old forms had already been mailed to numerous states, however, and could not be recalled. The commissioner of Internal Revenue suggested that Mexicans could simply check the "white" box. One Mexican American attributed the confusion surrounding the racial status of Mexicans to the influx of "white trash" into Texas who were ignorant of the fact that the "first white explorers and settlers in the State of Texas were Spanish speakers." Long-term Anglo residents of the region, he seemed to imply, knew better.[22]

The real issue over racial classification was clearly as much about Mexican racial pride as it was about fear over discrimination. In Texas, Mexicans endured the injuries of discrimination daily. Middle-class Mexican Americans needed to believe that segregation stemmed from Anglo ignorance of Mexico's history and the fact that many middle-class Mexican Americans, like their Anglo counterparts, actually believed that whites were superior to both Indians and Africans. Mexican Americans did not necessarily acquire a belief in white racial supremacy in the United States, although it was certainly reinforced whenever one encountered blacks and Indians in the United States.[23]

These mostly middle-class Mexican Americans were not simply content to deny any "negro ancestry." For many Mexicans and Mexican Americans, "colored" meant racial inferiority, social disgrace, and the total absence of political rights—in short, the racial equivalent of Indian and Negro.[24] In their injunction against the El Paso city registrar, for example, they cited an Oklahoma law that made it libelous to call a white person "colored."[25] Mexican Americans in San Antonio, who joined the campaign to change the classification scheme, sent a resolution adopted by various LULAC councils to U.S. representative Maury Maverick, a liberal Texas Democrat, to register their "most vigorous protest against the insult thus cast upon our race."[26] Maverick wrote to the director of the Census Bureau in Washington, D.C., that "to classify these people here as 'colored' is to jumble them in as *Negroes,* wich [*sic*] they are not and which naturally causes the most violent feelings." He urged the director to include another category called "other white," and argued that the classification of Mexicans as "colored" was simply inaccurate, because "people who are of Mexican or Spanish descent are certainly not of African descent."[27] An irate Mexican American evangelist wrote that if Mexicans were colored, then Senator Dennis Chavez of New Mexico, who was the first U.S. senator of Mexican descent, "will have his children classified as Negroes. Then Uncle Sam can hang his face in shame before the civilized nations of the world."[28]

Amidst all the protests that classifying Mexicans as "colored" insulted Mexicans on both sides of the border, little was heard from the African American community of El Paso, which, although small (less than two percent), could not have appreciated the Mexican community's insistence that being classified in the same racial category as "negro" was the worst possible affront to Mexican racial pride. However, one El Pasoan, J. Hamilton Price, who was either African American or posing as one, wrote a long letter explaining how both blacks and whites in El Paso were roaring with laughter over the Mexicans' exhibition of wounded dignity.[29] Price wrote that local blacks did not consider Mexicans white, nor did they consider them to be superior to blacks. Furthermore, if Mexicans considered themselves superior to blacks, he wanted to know why Mexicans in El Paso ate, drank, and worked with people considered racially inferior. He went on to list the numerous ways in which Mexican behavior departed radically from Anglo-white behavior with respect to blacks. "One sees daily in this city," he wrote, "Mexican boys shining the shoes of Negroes. If Mexicans are racially superior to Negroes," he continued, "they shouldn't be shining their shoes."[30] It is worth listing all the behaviors Price described to indicate how ludicrous he found the Mexican claim to whiteness:

* Some of the Mexican men had their hair made wavy to look more like the curly hair of Negroes.
* In local stores Mexican clerks addressed Negro clients as "Sir" and "Ma'am."
* In local streetcars Mexicans occupied the seats reserved by law for Negroes.
* Many Mexicans in El Paso preferred Negro doctors and dentists to those of their own race.
* Many Mexicans were employed on ranches and in the homes and commercial establishments of Negroes.
* Mexican boxers competed with Negroes in Juarez and would compete with them in El Paso, if it were permitted.

* Mexican soccer players avidly played against Negroes, and many of the players on the Mexican teams were Negroes.
* In some of the Mexican bars and small restaurants Negroes were as well received as Mexicans themselves.
* Four out of five clients of Negro prostitutes were Mexicans.
* In El Paso and Juarez many Mexican women were married to Negroes.

Price wrote that the offspring of Mexican and black marriages were so numerous in El Paso that they were called "negro-burros," literally, "black donkeys." In Mexico, according to Price, many of these mixed-race persons were considered Mexican and occupied important positions in Mexican social circles. They often frequented the best theaters, restaurants, and Mexican hair salons, married Mexican women, and, if Democrats, were able to vote in the Democratic primaries in Texas, which otherwise barred blacks from voting. His point was that the vast majority of El Paso Mexicans, who were not of the middle class, did not think of themselves as white and that El Paso blacks also did not regard Mexicans as white. Price, angered by the manner in which Mexicans objected to being labeled as "colored," ended his long letter with some racial invective of his own: "Though once pure Indians," he wrote, "Mexicans had become more mixed than dog food—undoubtedly a conglomeration of Indian with all the races known to man, with the possible exception of the Eskimo."[31]

Price's letter brought a series of angry rebuttals from Mexicans who denounced Price as a coward for using a pseudonym—they could not find his name in the city directory. One writer, Abraham Arriola Giner, accused Negroes of deserving their inferior status for having tolerated oppressive conditions that no Mexican ever would. He boasted of the high level of culture attained by his Indian ancestors and belittled Negroes as descendants of "savage tribes" from Africa where they practiced cannibalism and did nothing to improve their lives. He reminded Price that American Negroes, as former slaves, did not have their own country or flag and that there was no honor for those who did not understand the meaning of liberty. In a final stroke of racial arrogance, Arriola Giner wrote that Mexicans would never tolerate any race claiming to be superior to Mexicans because "such superiority does not exist."[32]

These middle-class Mexican Americans in El Paso sought to eliminate once and for all the ambiguity surrounding Mexican racial identity. First, they recognized that any attempt to define them as "nonwhite" could easily come to mean "noncitizen" as well, because many Anglos did not regard Mexicans, particularly of the lower class, as truly American or fit for American citizenship. Second, middle-class Mexican Americans themselves drew distinctions between themselves and lower-class Mexicans whom they often regarded as "Indios" or "Indian Mexicans" and used terms like "mojados" ("wetbacks") and other terms of class and racial disparagement. Hamilton Price, the black El Pasoan, pointed out as much when he reminded El Pasoans about the close, even intimate, relations that existed between blacks and lower-class Mexicans in El Paso, from Mexican men shining the shoes of African American men to African American men marrying Mexican women.

Many middle-class Mexican American elites in El Paso, men like Cleofas Calleros, immigration representative of the National Catholic Welfare Conference; LULAC president Frank Galván; Lorenzo Alarcon, "presidente-supremo" of United Citizens' Civic League, and many others were well connected to the white elites of the city and drew their power, in part, from being representatives of "their people." They believed that any act of discrimination against any member of their community, or any attempt to deny full citizenship rights to any Mexican American, constituted a threat to all Mexican Americans. They understood that basic citizenship rights—such as the right to vote, sit on juries, hold public office, and so forth—depended less on their citizenship status, important to them as this was, than on their right to claim status as white citizens of the United States.

Virtually the only groups that could not lay claim to white racial status were African Americans, Native Americans, and Asian Americans, whom the government classified as separate and distinct races for purposes of census enumeration. Therein lies the beauty of a word like "white" or Caucasian: it is broad enough to include Jews, Italians, the Irish, and Greeks, so why not Mexicans as well? It was not the color line per se that was the problem in American life and culture, many Mexican Americans reasoned, but the way in which they were consigned to the nonwhite side of the line. In short, Mexican American civil rights organizations sought to expand the civil rights of Mexicans by expanding the boundaries of whiteness to include, to use their own phrasing, "the Spanish speaking people," Americans of Spanish-Speaking descent, and Latin Americans.

As whites of a different culture and color than most Anglo whites, many middle-class Mexicans learned early on that hostility to the idea of "social equality" for African Americans went right to the core of what constituted whiteness in the United States. Whether or not they brought with them from Mexico racial prejudice against blacks—and certainly many Mexicans did—middle-class Mexican leaders throughout the 1930s, '40s, and '50s went to great lengths to dissociate themselves socially, culturally, and politically from the early struggles of African Americans to achieve full citizenship rights in America.

A few years after World War II ended, another Mexican American civil rights organization was founded, the American GI Forum. Significantly, the name of the organization did not include any reference to its being an organization for Mexican American war veterans. Hector García, a medical doctor who founded the American GI Forum, achieved a degree of national attention in 1949 when he challenged the Anglo owner of a funeral home near San Antonio for refusing the use of the chapel to the Mexican American family of a deceased veteran, Private Felix Longoria. Dr. García organized a statewide protest that attracted the attention of U.S. Senator Lyndon Baines Johnson who offered to have Private Longoria buried in Arlington National Cemetery in Washington, D.C., with full military honors, which the family graciously accepted. The incident established the American GI Forum as an effective civil rights advocate for Mexican Americans, even though Dr. García himself insisted, years after the Longoria incident, that the American GI Forum was not a civil rights organization but rather a "charitable organization." As late as 1954 Dr. García claimed, "we are not and have never been a civil rights organization. Personally I hate the word." What did Dr. García have against the phrase "civil rights"?[33]

Here it is worth noting that the phrase "civil rights" was so firmly linked in the post-World War II imaginary to the civil rights struggle of African Americans that Dr. García perhaps thought it best not to acknowledge too forcefully the American GI Forum's own civil rights agenda. He was in good company, if one includes the Kennedy bothers in the pantheon of civil rights advocates. In 1960, Robert Kennedy, who at the time was the campaign manager for his brother's presidential race, told campaign aides, who were in charge of efforts to secure the votes of black Americans, to change the name of their campaign section, which they had called the "office of civil rights." Robert Kennedy believed that making Negro civil rights a central concern of the Kennedy presidential campaign would alienate white voters in the South. He also asked them to change the name of a Harlem conference on civil rights to a conference on "constitutional rights."[34] Robert Kennedy, like Dr. García, did not wish to alienate whites in Texas—or anywhere else—by appearing to join the struggle of black people for civil rights.[35]

By the early 1950s the American GI Forum, while still denying that it was a civil rights organization, sought to end discrimination in Texas schools, in employment, and in the use of public spaces. The core strategy depended on educating Anglos that "Americans of Spanish-speaking descent" or Latin Americans were Caucasians and that to identify them as anything but white, whether on birth certificates or traffic citations, was illegal. Making any distinction between Latin Americans and whites, he wrote, was a "slur," an insult to all Latin Americans of Spanish descent.[36]

A decade later, Vice President Hubert Humphrey made the mistake of writing the American GI Forum to announce the government's new program to offer summer jobs for teenagers, especially, he wrote, for "the nonwhite teenagers." The AGIF Auxiliary chairwoman, Mrs. Dominga Coronado, rebuked the vice president: "If everyone in the government takes the position emphasized in your letter ([that Mexicans are] nonwhite), then it is understandable why the Mexican American is getting 'the leftovers' of the Federal programs in employment, housing, and education."[37] White people, she seemed to imply, do not eat leftovers.

Educating Anglos to acknowledge the white racial status of Mexican Americans represented a major political goal of the American GI Forum. To become white—and therefore truly American—required members to distance themselves from any association, social or political, with African Americans. When the AGIF *News Bulletin,* for example, printed an article in 1955 titled "Mexican Americans Favor Negro School Integration," Manuel Avila, an active member of AGIF and close personal friend of Hector García, wrote to state chairman Ed Idar that "Anybody reading it can only come to the conclusion [that] we are ready to fight the Negroes' battles . . . for sooner or later we are going to have to say which side of the fence we're on, are we white or not. If we are white, why do we ally with the Negro?"[38] Mexicans were learning to act like white people in Arizona, he reported, where Mexican restaurant owners, who normally served Negroes, had recently placed signs in the windows that Negroes would not be served. If Mexicans refused to serve Negroes, Avila wrote, Anglo restaurants might begin serving Mexicans. Mexican Americans, he argued, must say to Negroes, "I'm White and you can't come into my restaurant."[39]

A sympathetic white woman from rural Mississippi, Ruth Slates, who owned a store that served many Mexican and Mexican American cotton pickers, wrote to Dr. García in 1951: "My blood just boils to see these farmers . . . trying to throw the Spanish kids out of the schools . . . and into negro schools." She pointed out that although some of the "Spanish kids" "hate negroes," others, unfortunately, "mix with them." She then advised

Dr. García that Mexicans needed a strong leader to teach them "right from wrong," because some "even marry negros and some white girls." Slates was giving Dr. García a quick lesson in southern racial protocol: if Mexicans want to be white, then they cannot associate, much less marry, black folk, and she also implied that marrying white girls, in Mississippi at least, might not be a prudent thing to do.[40] Ruth Slates liked "Spanish kids" and hoped that Dr. García would provide the kind of leadership required, as it is now fashionable to say, to perform whiteness.

The American GI Forum thus faced a major dilemma: if it acknowledged that it was a civil rights organization rather than a patriotic veterans organization or a charitable organization, whites might regard it as part of the ideological and political struggle of African Americans for equal rights. How could the American GI Forum argue that Mexicans were white if its agenda included the struggle for civil rights, including, presumably, those of blacks? Put another way, if Mexican Americans were white, why did they need a civil rights organization in the first place? If being white meant anything, particularly in a state like Texas that once belonged both to Mexico and the Confederacy, it meant being not Mexican and not black. Both LULAC and the American GI Forum eliminated the word "Mexican" from their vocabularies precisely for this purpose. In seeking to equate the word "Mexican" with nationality and not race, members of LULAC and the American GI Forum asserted their identities as white Americans, although of Mexican ancestry.

The American GI Forum became the principal source of financial and political support in the only civil rights case involving Mexican Americans to reach the U.S. Supreme Court. This case highlights the irony of a civil rights strategy that is rooted in a claim that Mexicans are members of the Caucasian race. In 1954, the U.S. Supreme Court handed down a ruling that acknowledged the white racial status of Mexicans at the same time that it ruled that Mexicans represented a "separate class" of whites who had been systematically prevented from exercising their constitutional rights. An all-Anglo jury convicted the defendant, Pete Hernandez, of murder. AGIF and LULAC challenged the ruling on the grounds that Hernandez had been denied his constitutional right to be tried by a jury of his peers, because not a single Mexican American had ever been selected for jury service in the last twenty-five years in a county that was twelve percent Mexican American. The Texas Court of Appeals, however, agreed with the lower court that the "equal protection" clause of the Fourteenth Amendment to the constitution applied to "negroes and whites" and that, because Mexican Americans were legally white, Hernandez was indeed tried by a jury of his peers. The Texas courts basically reasoned that Mexican Americans could not have it both ways: they could not insist that they were white and, at the same time, that an all-white jury constituted an violation of the "equal protection" clause of the Fourteenth Amendment forbidding discrimination on the basis of race.[41]

The Mexican American attorneys appealed the decision to the Supreme Court in *Hernández* v. *the State of Texas*. Two weeks before the historic decision *Brown* v. *Board of Education* the Supreme Court ruled that Mexican Americans had been discriminated against as a "separate class" of white people, acknowledging, in effect, the differential treatment accorded to whites and Hispanics in Texas and elsewhere in the Southwest. Even the county courthouse, where the original trial was held, had segregated public bathrooms, one for whites and one for Negroes and Mexicans. This decision was a major triumph for Mexican Americans who had argued in other cases that Mexicans constituted a separate class of white people, in effect, "Hispanic whites."[42]

The American GI Forum, like LULAC, represented a narrow band of educated, English-speaking Mexican Americans that recognized that racial status counted more than citizenship in achieving full citizenship rights as Americans, as white Americans. For the masses of working-class Mexicanos, however, many of them first generation, the idea that they were members of the white race would have struck them as somewhat absurd. Anglos were white; mexicanos were, well mexicanos—raza, and later, chicanos. Perhaps that is why Manuel Avila was so upset about the American GI Forum *News Bulletin* article favoring Negro school integration. The article reports, "Whether it is because they know what segregation of their own children means or because traditionally people of Mexican and Spanish descent do not share in the so-called doctrines of white supremacy and racial prejudice, the Mexican-American population of Texas . . . is in favor of doing away with the segregation of Negro children in the public schools."[43] It seems that the lure of whiteness, and all it implies, did not exert as powerful a hold on the majority of Mexican Americans as it did on the civil rights strategists of the American GI Forum.

The claim that Mexican Americans constituted a "separate class" of whites—a kind of "separate but equal" whiteness—formed the basis of the legal strategy of Mexican American civil rights activists from 1930 to 1970 and culminated in the creation of the "Hispanic" category in the 1980 census, replicating once again the part federal policy has played in Mexican American racial politics. Significantly, the extension of "other whiteness" to Mexican Americans and other Latino groups is deeply implicated in the maintenance of blackness as the racial touchstone for determining who is white and who is not, as well as the maintenance of blackness as the racial barrier impeding the advancement of African Americans in white, mainstream society.

In 1980 the U.S. census created the official category of Hispanic, but not as a racial category on par with the category of white, black, Asian, and Native American. The census bureaucrats and politicians were aware of the sensitivity of Latinos to being regarded as nonwhite, and consequently they made the category of Hispanic an ethnic subcategory of race. In other words, one can be of any race, including black or white, and still be Hispanic. As a census category and ethnoracial identity, it has thus come to signify a whiteness of a different color, a darker shade of pale, a preference for salsa over ketchup. Many identifying themselves as white and Hispanic, whether consciously or not, are implicated in the government's erasure of the Indian and African heritage of Mexicans. The journey of mixed-race Mexicans thus ends at the doorstep of Hispanic whiteness where no blacks or Indians are free to enter.

African Americans, for their part, have sometimes been guilty of playing the "citizenship card" in their dealings with Mexicans. During the 1920s many African Americans enthusiastically endorsed immigration restrictions aimed at Mexican Americans, believing that Mexicans took jobs from African Americans and lowered the standard of living. Black Texans in Houston, for example, expressed their bitterness in 1934 over a municipal decision to set aside a ten-acre tract of land for recreational purposes for the growing population of Mexicans in Houston. Black civic leaders had purchased property from the city a year before to serve the recreational needs of African Ameri cans in Houston and complained bitterly that the city had not appropriated any money either for its purchase or upkeep. According to one complaint, "Mexicans are aliens who swear their allegiance to a foreign power. But when it comes to spending a little money for recreation purposes, it seems to be all for aliens and nothing for citizens."[44] More recently, nearly half of all African Americans in California voted for Proposition 187 to deny educational and health benefits to undocumented Mexican workers and their families.

Tensions clearly exist today in the United States between the growing Latino population and African Americans, whose percentage of the total population continues to decline in many states with each census, particularly in key electoral states. For many blacks, hard-fought gains won during a century of struggle and suffering are now being overshadowed by the prospect of majority Latino populations in major urban areas and large states, like Texas and California. For example, the Latino population in California will increase from thirty-two percent today to about forty-three percent in the next twenty-two years, while the population of blacks in the state will go from the present seven percent to just over five percent. Their percentage of the population will actually be declining over the next twenty-two years. In Texas the Hispanic population will increase from the present thirty-two percent to about thirty-seven percent in 2025, or well over one-third of the state's population, while the percentage of African Americans will increase only about two percent over the same period.

The declining percentage of African Americans in major urban areas has already led to some bitter disputes in Dallas between black and Latino members of the school board. Dallas Independent School District board meetings during the 1997–98 school year degenerated into angry accusations between Hispanics and blacks over filling the post of school superintendent. The warring factions settled on Bill Rojas, a black man of Puerto Rican descent. The source of the tensions between blacks and Latinos in Dallas and in other cities is that while the Latino population surpasses that of blacks, African Americans still retain control of school boards, local politics, and other levers of power. In Dallas, for example, blacks hold more teaching and administrative jobs than Hispanics, although slightly more than fifty percent of the students are Hispanic, compared to thirty-nine percent for black students.[45]

In Los Angeles' Watts district, blacks and Latinos constantly feud over staff hiring at the county-operated Martin Luther King, Jr.–Drew Medical Center. The hospital was built in the late 1960s in response to blacks' complaints that they were medically underserved in Watts, which was predominantly black. Now, however, Latinos outnumber blacks in Watts and are demanding that the hospital hire Latino doctors and administrators. Blacks, of course, believe that they are being pushed out by recent immigrants, who demand the rights and privileges that blacks have won only after decades of civil rights struggles.[46] Tensions are not limited to competition between the two groups. In 1995 in Lubbock, Texas, two Hispanics and a white were convicted of a federal hate crime for driving around the town shooting black men with a shotgun, leading many blacks to wonder on whose side Latinos are.[47]

The rapid increase in the Hispanic population has not, however, complicated the black-white binary of U.S. race relations to the extend one might have expected. In part, this is because middle-class Hispanics—with the assistance of the Census Bureau in 1980—have redrawn the boundaries of whiteness to include both Hispanics and "non-Hispanic whites." Mexican Americans, like other Hispanic groups, are at a crossroads: one path, slouching toward whiteness, leads to racial fissures that harden the color line between blacks and whites. Hispanic whites express their new sense of white entitlement often by supporting anti-affirmative action laws, English-only movements, and other nativist ideologies on the backs of immigrants and African Americans. Another path welcomes the shared responsibility of defining and bringing into existence a transnational multiracial identity that acknowledges the Indian and African heritage of Latinos and their ancient ties to the Western Hemisphere, an identity that author Richard Rodriguez calls simply "brown."[48] By examining how whiteness constructs and maintains racial boundaries, often in conflicting and contradictory ways, we can better begin to understand the ways in which the black-white racial paradigm masks the liminal spaces and racial places that are home to increasing numbers of Americans.

Notes

1. Mike Davis, *Magical Realism: Latinos Reinvent the U.S. City,* revised edition (London and New York: Verso, 2001), pp. 2–16.

2. Barbara J. Fields, "Ideology and Race in America," in *Region, Race, and Reconstruction: Essays in Honor of C. Vann Woodward,* ed. by J. Morgan Kousser and James M. McPherson (New York: Oxford University Press, 1982), p. 146. On the legal construction of whiteness in the United States, see Ian F. Haney López, *White by Law: The Legal Construction of Race* (New York: New York University Press, 1996); and Cheryl I. Harris, "Whiteness as Property," *Harvard Law Review* 106 (June, 1993): 1709–91. See also Thomas C. Holt, "Marking: Race, Race Making, and the Writing of History," *American Historical Review* 100 (Feb., 1995): 1–20.

3. See Mathew Frye Jacobs, *Whiteness of a Different Color: European Immigrants and the Alchemy of Race* (Cambridge: Harvard University Press, 1998); and Neil Foley, *The White Scourge: Mexicans, Blacks, and Poor Whites in Texas Cotton Culture* (Berkeley: University of California Press, 1997).

4. The debate can be traced through the numerous congressional hearings by the Immigration and Naturalization Committee during the 1920s. See, for example, U.S. Congress, House Committee on Immigration and Naturalization, *Immigration from Countries of the Western Hemisphere,* 70th Cong., 2nd sess., 1930; idem, *Immigration from Countries of the Western Hemisphere,* 1928; idem, *Immigration from Mexico,* 71st Cong., 2nd sess., 1930; idem, Naturalization, 71st Cong., 2nd sess., 1930; idem, *Restriction of Immigration,* 68th Cong., 1st sess., 1924, Serial 1–A; *Seasonal Agricultural Laborers,* 1926; *Temporary Admission;* and idem, *Western Hemisphere Immigration,* 71st Cong., 2nd sess., 1930. For scholarly analysis of the immigration debate, see David Gutierrez, *Walls and Mirrors: Mexican Americans, Mexican Immigrants, and the Politics of Ethnicity* (Berkeley: University of California, 1995); and Mark Reisler, *By the Sweat of Their Brow: Mexican Immigrant Labor in the United States, 1900–1940* (Westport, Conn.: Greenwood Press, 1976).

5. Peggy Pascoe, "Miscegenation Law, Court Cases, and Ideologies of 'Race' in Twentieth-Century America," *Journal of American History* 83 (June 1996): 44–69. Mexicans, who were legally "white," were rarely prosecuted for marrying blacks. For the only case in Texas of a Mexican brought to trial for marrying a black, see *F. Flores v. the State,* 60 Tex. Crim. 25 (1910); 129 S. W. 1111. I am indebted to Julie Dowling for bringing this case to my attention. See her paper, "Mexican Americans and the Modern Performance of Whiteness: LULAC and the Construction of the White Mexican," presented at the American Sociological Association annual conference, Anaheim, Calif., August, 2001.

6. Max Sylvius Handman, "Economic Reasons for the Coming of the Mexican Immigrant," *American Journal of Sociology* 35 (Jan., 1930): 609–10.

7. Handman, "The Mexican Immigrant in Texas," *Southwestern Political and Social Science Quarterly* 7 (June, 1926): 27.

8. Ibid., p. 40.

9. See David Montejano, *Anglos and Mexicans in the Making of Texas, 1836–1986* (Austin: University of Texas Press, 1987); and Foley, *The White Scourge.*

10. *In re Rodríguez,* 81 Fed. 337 (W.D. Texas, 1897); Arnoldo De León, *In Re Ricardo Rodríguez: An Attempt at Chicano Disfranchisement in San Antonio, 1896–1897* (San Antonio, Tex.: Caravel Press, 1979), p. 8; Tomás Almaguer, *Racial Fault Lines: The Historical Origins of White Supremacy in California* (Berkeley: University of California Press, 1994), pp. 162–64; Fernando Padilla, "Early Chicano Legal Recognition, 1846–1897," *Journal of Popular Culture* 13 (spring, 1980): 564–74; Martha Menchaca, "Chicano Indianism: A Historical Account of Racial Repression in the United States," *American Ethnologist* 20 (Aug., 1993): 583–601; Haney López, *White by Law,* p. 61; Gary A. Greenfield and Don B. Kates, Jr., "Mexican Americans, Racial Discrimination, and the Civil Rights Act of 1866," *California Law Review* 63 (Jan., 1975): 693. See also Mae M. Ngai, "The Architecture of Race in American Immigration Law: A Reexamination of the Immigration Act of 1924," *Journal of American History* 86 (1999): 88, 93. For an analysis of the legal decisions that barred numerous groups from claiming white racial status, see Stanford M. Lyman, "The Race Question and Liberalism: Casuistries in American Constitutional Law," *International Journal of Politics, Culture, and Society* 5 (winter, 1991): 183–247. For a fascinating personal history involving the legal and cultural complexities of racial identity, see Ernest Evans Kilker, "Black and White in America: The Culture and Politics of Racial Classification," *International Journal of Politics, Culture, and Society* 7 (winter, 1993): 229–58.

11. C. H. Jenkins, *The Revised Civil Statutes of Texas, 1925, Annotated* (Austin: H. P. N. Gammel Book Co., 1925), vol. 1, p. 1036.

12. See Guadalupe San Miguel, Jr., "The Origins, Development, and Consequences of the Educational Segregation of Mexicans in the Southwest," in *Chicano Studies: A Multidisciplinary Approach,* ed. by Eugene E. García, Francisco Lomeli, and Isidro Ortiz (New York: Teachers College Press, 1984), pp. 195–208.

13. See Gary A. Greenfield and Don B. Kates, Jr., "Mexican Americans, Racial Discrimination, and the Civil Rights Act of 1866," *California Law Review* 63 (Jan., 1975): 700.

14. *Herald-Post,* Oct. 6 and 7, 1936; *La Prensa* (San Antonio), Oct. 10, 1936; and *New York Times,* Oct. 21, 1936, in Cleofas Calleros Collection, University of Texas at El Paso, hereafter cited as CCC. All references from this collection are from box 28, folder 1 ("Color Classification of Mexicans"). See also Mario García, "Mexican Americans and the Politics of Citizenship: The Case of El Paso, 1936," *New Mexican Historical Review* 59 (Apr., 1984): 187–204. García, who based his article on the same file from the Calleros collection, argues that Mexican American leaders used the controversy over racial classification of Mexicans "to show Anglo leaders that Mexicans would not accept second-class citizenship." (p. 201). While that is no doubt true, García mistakenly argues that Mexican Americans used the politics of citizenship rather than race in forging racial identities as whites. As Caucasians, Mexican Americans asserted their own racial superiority over African Americans and other "people of color."

15. Mr. Calleros to Mr. Mohler, memo, Oct. 9, 1936, p. 1, CCC.

16. Ibid., p. 2.

17. *Herald-Post,* Oct. 7, 1936, CCC.

18. *El Continental,* Oct. 6 and 25, 1936, CCC.

19. Ibid., Oct. 25, 1936, CCC. Author's translation.

20. *La Prensa,* Oct. 12, 1936, CCC.

21. Form SS-5, Treasury Department, International Revenue Service, instructions for filling out form, item number 12, CCC; *Herald-Post,* Oct. 8, 1936, CCC.

22. *Herald-Post,* Oct. 8, 1936, letter of M. A. Gomez; *El Continental,* Oct. 8, 1936, CCC.

23. García, "Mexican Americans and the Politics of Citizenship," p. 189.

24. *El Continental,* Oct. 18, 1936, CCC.

25. *Collins* v. *State,* 7, A. L. R., 895 (Okla.) in petition presented to the District Court of El Paso, *M. A. Gomez et al.,* v. *T. J. McCamant and Alex Powell,* Oct., 1936, CCC.

26. LULAC Resolution, San Antonio Council no. 16 and Council no. 2, Oct. 14, 1936, CCC.

27. Maury Maverick to William L. Austin, Oct. 15, 1936, CCC; see also Calleros to Mohler, Oct. 9, 1936, CCC.

28. *Herald-Post,* Oct. 8, 1936, CCC.

29. *El Continental,* Oct. 14, 1936, CCC. An editorial appearing opposite Hamilton's letter stated that the letter appeared to be written "por un negro" and that although vulgar ("grosera"), the editor decided to publish the letter to express a different point of view.

30. *El Continental,* Oct. 14, 1936, CCC.

31. Ibid.

32. Ibid., Oct. 16, 1936.

33. Hector García to Gerald Saldana, Mar. 13, 1954, box 141, folder 13, Hector P. García Papers, Texas A&M University, Corpus Christi, hereafter cited as HPG.

34. Taylor Branch, *Parting the Waters: America in the King Years, 1954–63* (New York: Simon and Schuster, 1988), p. 341.

35. While not promoting the American GI Forum as a civil rights organization in 1949, García nevertheless wrote to the Texas governor that "Texas is in immediate need of a Civil Rights Program," Hector P. García to Allan Shivers, Dec. 4, 1949, HPG.

36. Hector P. García to Editor, *Lubbock Morning Avalanche,* July 18, 1956, HPG.

37. Hubert Humphrey to Dominga Coronado, June 12, 1967; Dominga Coronado to Hubert Humphrey, June 26, 1967, HPG.

38. Manuel Avila, Jr., to Ed Idar, Feb. 7, 1956, box 26, folder 28, HPG; *News Bulletin* 4, nos. 1 and 2 (Sept.-Oct., 1955): 1, HPG.

39. Manuel Avila, Jr., to Ed Idar, Feb. 7, 1956, box 46, folder 28, HPG; See also Isaac P. Borjas to Hector P. García, June 2, 1940; Newspaper clipping, *Caracas Daily Journal,* [1960?], box 114, folder 22; and Ruth Slates to Dr. Hector García, Mar. 23, 1951, box 59, folder 33, HGP.

40. Ruth Slates to Dr. Hector García, Mar. 23, 1951, box 59, folder 33, HGP.

41. *Hernandez* v. *State,* 251 S. W. 531 (1952); *Hernandez* v. *Texas,* 347 U.S. 475 (1954). For an extended analysis of the legal construction of racial identity in the Hernandez case, see Ian F. Haney Lopez, "Race, Ethnicity, Erasure: The Salience of Race to LatCrit Theory," *University of California Law Review* 85 (1997): 1143–1211.

42. Neil Foley, "Becoming Hispanic: Mexican Americans and the Faustian Pact with Whiteness," in *Reflexiones: New Directions in Mexican American Studies,* ed. by Neil Foley (Austin: University of Texas Press, 1988). See also Carlos M. Alcala and Jorge C. Rangel, "Project Report: De Jure Segregation of Chicanos in Texas Schools," *Harvard Civil Rights—Civil Liberties Law Review* 7 (Mar., 1972). Carl Allsup, *The American G. I. Forum: Origins and Evolution* (Austin: University of Texas, Center for Mexican American Studies, Monograph 6, 1982).

43. *News Bulletin* 4 (Sept.-Oct., 1955): 1.

44. Houston *Informer,* May 5, 1934, cited in Arnold Shankman, "The Image of Mexico and the Mexican-American in the Black Press, 1890–1935," *Journal of Ethnic Studies* 3 (summer, 1975): 52.

45. *USA Today,* Sept. 10, 1999.

46. Ibid.

47. Bill Piatt, *Black and Brown in America* (New York and London: New York University Press, 1997), p. 9.

48. Richard Rodriguez, *Brown: The Last Discovery of America* (New York: Viking, 2000).

15

Was Mom Chung a "Sister Lesbian"?

Asian American Gender Experimentation and Interracial Homoeroticism

JUDY TZU-CHUN WU

Margaret Chung (1889–1959), reputedly the first American-born woman of Chinese descent to become a physician, achieved recognition during the 1930s and 1940s for her patriotic activities on behalf of China and the United States. As part of her efforts to support the Allied cause, she "adopted" over one thousand "sons," most of whom were white American military men. Known as "Mom Chung," she entertained, corresponded with, and inspired her sons to fight against the Japanese invasion of China. Newspaper articles consistently noted two seemingly contradictory aspects of her character: First, Chung, then in her forties and fifties, was a successful doctor who never married or bore children. Second, she was a devoted mother to her adopted sons, who called themselves "Fair-Haired Bastards," because of their racial background and her status as an unmarried woman. Her respectability, premised on her professional success and asexuality, allowed her to be identified, in a humorous fashion, with such sexual improprieties as childbirth outside wedlock and miscegenation. Chung's unpublished autobiography and papers, which contain scant evidence of her romantic desires, behavior, or attitudes, help maintain this image of asexuality.[1]

Chung cultivated this asexual persona to protect her public image. In a letter to singer and actress Sophie Tucker about Tucker's autobiography, Chung expressed the belief that certain experiences should not be discussed publicly: "What a good girl you are! You *did* take my advice after all, you *did* delete the paragraph about 'doubling' up with [Frank] Westphal, and I appreciate the love and the friendship that prompted you to take that advice! As the book now stands, it is a terrific inspiration which any youth may read and emulate your life—you see, Boss—I love you deeply—I care very much what people say about you! I can't bear it if people criticize you—and that one little paragraph which is *not* essential to the interest of the book draws the censure of the blue noses and the ignorant."[2] Although Chung is discussing Tucker's autobiography, the opinions expressed in the letter most likely reflected Chung's strategy toward her own autobiography, which she began writing during this period. Her concern about self-image is understandable, considering that both her professional and political success depended on public trust in her character. Being a single, professional woman in San Francisco's Chinatown, and one of the few widely recognized Chinese American spokespersons for the war, placed her under heavy scrutiny. To attract patients and serve as a role model, she needed to exemplify and follow high moral standards.

Recognizing Chung's desire for privacy reinforces the need to explore carefully her personal relationships and attitudes toward sexuality. Her significance as a historical figure stems not only from her accomplishments in the public realm of work and politics but also from her choices in the private realm. She chose not to marry or have children during a time when the social pressure for Chinese American women to do both was considerable. Due to immigration exclusion acts, the number of Chinese American men outnumbered women by an average of eight to one from the years 1910 to 1930.[3] During this same period, antimiscegenation laws in California forbade interracial marriages between people of color and white Americans. Instead of marrying, Chung developed erotic relationships with other women, especially white women, thereby transgressing heterosexual norms and racial boundaries. She also experimented with gender presentation throughout her life, adopting a masculine or androgynous persona during the early part of her professional career and then a glamorous, feminine identity beginning in the 1930s.

Chung's transgressiveness encouraged writer Elsa Gidlow, a self-identified lesbian, to regard her as a "sister lesbian."[4] However, describing Chung as a lesbian, a woman who constructed her identity based on a desire to seek romantic and sexual relationships with other women, is inadequate for two reasons. First, the designation ignores Chung's efforts to define her own identity. Second, the concept of lesbianism, which developed during the turn of the century, does not embody the historical variety of gender identifications and expressions of homoeroticism.[5] Analyzing the evolution of Chung's gender personas and interracial relationships from the late Victorian era to the modern era provides an opportunity to explore the ways in which Asian American women negotiated shifting gender, sexual, and racial norms of both mainstream American society and their own ethnic communities. Chung was a liminal figure who not only transcended social barriers but also lived through a historical period in which these boundaries were destabilized and reformulated. Because norms were in flux, she developed strategies that challenged restrictive roles for women of color yet also deflected social criticism of her behavior.

Chung's life provides an opportunity to complicate the existing understanding of Asian American sexuality.[6] Most studies in Asian American history have focused on racial, economic, and, more recently, gender oppression and resistance. Discussions of sexuality provide incidental examples in these studies of inequality and cultural conflict. For example, the gender imbalance among Chinese immigrants and the prevalence of prostitution in these "bachelor societies" have been viewed as indicators of the detrimental impact of immigration exclusion and antimiscegenation laws on family formation. Conversely, the entry of women and the creation of conjugal families, two indicators of the "settlement" phase of community development, have demonstrated the resilience of an oppressed minority in overcoming racial discrimination.[7] These discussions of sexuality in relation to structural inequalities are important for understanding how social values and institutions influence private attitudes and behavior. However, lack of critical analysis of the category of sexuality leads scholars to make assumptions concerning the nature of sexual behavior and attitudes among Asian Americans. The condemnation of bachelor societies, combined with the celebration of conjugal family formation, naturalizes intraracial heterosexuality.

To illustrate the complexities of Chung's gender personas and interracial homoerotic desires, this article will focus on her relationships with two women, writer Elsa Gidlow and singer/actress Sophie Tucker. These two relationships, one in the late 1920s and early 1930s and the other in the 1940s and 1950s, reveal Chung's willingness to experiment with modern gender identities as well as her unwillingness to accept a modern lesbian sexual identity. Furthermore, her preference for white women as potential romantic partners demonstrates how evolving notions of race and ethnicity shaped definitions of desirability.

Masculine Dress, "Mannish" Desires, and Oriental Eroticism

Elsa Gidlow's relationship with Margaret Chung, told from Gidlow's perspective, was one of unconsummated but not unrequited love. When they first met in the late 1920s, Chung was a recently established physician in her late thirties, and Gidlow was a struggling writer in her late twenties. Born in Santa Barbara, California, in 1889, Chung was raised and educated in agricultural areas and small towns in southern California, "where there were hardly any other Chinese people."[8] Influenced by her family's Presbyterian background, she chose to become a medical missionary among the Chinese. After graduating from the University of Southern California in 1916 and completing her internship and residency in Illinois, she established one of the first Western medical clinics in San Francisco's Chinatown in the early 1920s. During the early years of her medical career, Chung adopted a Western masculine persona, an identity that symbolized her efforts to transcend traditional racial and gender barriers. Her liminal cultural and gender identity attracted the interest of Gidlow, a British-Canadian who moved to San Francisco in 1926.[9] Because no cohesive, visible lesbian community existed at the time, she and her female lover, Tommy, relied on personal networks to identify and socialize with other lesbians. Gidlow interpreted Chung's gender persona as an indication of her sexuality. Furthermore, Gidlow's orientalist fascination with Chinese culture fueled her interest in the Chinese American doctor.[10] The relationship between the writer and physician reveals Chung's disobedience to gender and racial restrictions in the social and professional realms. At the same time, she distanced herself from the modern sexual identity of lesbianism; she also upheld more traditional notions of Chinese culture as mysterious and exotic. This mixture of transgressiveness and traditionalism in Chung's strategies reflects the opportunities as well as the constraints that women of color faced during the early twentieth century.

When they first met, Gidlow recalled that she was immediately attracted to Chung's androgyny and liminal cultural background: "By this time, Margaret Chung became Tommy's and my doctor and our friend. She was Chinese, but American-born and educated, western in her general medical practice and in surgery at which she excelled. . . . Her office was a couple of blocks down the steep Sacramento Street hill where we lived. As I walked home from work, I would see her sleek blue sports car. She was a striking woman in her late thirties, smartly dressed in a dark tailored suit with felt hat and flat-heeled shoes. . . . With my increasing interest in Chinese people, their philosophy and literature (and suspecting she might be a sister lesbian) I was immediately attracted."[11] Gidlow's fascination with Chung's intermediate status between Asian and Western cultures as well as between male and female genders resonates with feminist scholar Marjorie Garber's analysis of transgenderism: "The blurring of gender binaries evoked desire through its association with transcendence of other forms of racial, class, and cultural dualisms."[12]

At the time, Chung practiced partial cross-dressing.[13] While her female identity was publicly known, she adopted Western masculine clothing and a male persona. One of her professional mentors, physician Bertha Van Hoosen, recalled that Chung "never wore Chinese clothes, but on all occasions appeared in a thin black tailored suit, a white silk shirtwaist, and when on the street, a black sailor hat. This costume would have been very inconspicuous had she not always carried a short sport cane."[14] Chung's choice of dress could be understood partly as a uniform for the medical profession. Photographs from her medical school annuals make it difficult to determine her sex on the basis of her attire.[15] Her hair is either short or pulled back, and she wears a dark suit with a tie. While some women dressed in male clothing as a protective measure that allowed them to assimilate into the existing professional culture, Chung apparently enjoyed adopting a masculine persona.[16] Van Hoosen's comment about the ostentatious sport cane suggests that Chung did not mind attracting attention to her appearance. One of Chung's favorite photographs during her early professional career featured her with slicked-back hair, dark-rimmed glasses, and a dark suit. She sent autographed versions of the photo to friends and chose to identify herself as "Mike."

The choice of Western masculine attire and nickname symbolized Chung's desire to enter the professional and social world on an equal basis with white men. In her autobiography, she noted that members of the opposite sex rarely treated her with gallantry. As a young girl working on a farm pitting apricots, she noticed that attractive girls received favored treatment from boys: "I was a homely little child, and there were always some pretty teenage girls around whom the boys liked. The boys would give them the large ripe apricots which they could simply run a knife through and slip the pit out; whereas they would give me the small green ones. . . . Needless to say, I did not make very much money pitting apricots."[17] Instead of emphasizing her femininity to gain favors from men, Chung participated in traditionally masculine activities as an equal companion. While she was in medical school, she used various strategies to finance her education: "When I was too broke to pay the carfare to and from the County Hospital and the Medical School I would borrow a penny or two from some of the boys, shoot craps with them until I won about thirty-five or forty cents which would be enough to buy a half a pie, a sandwich, and assure me of carfare for the next day."[18] In addition to gambling, Chung was also fond of drinking and swearing. As many of her surrogate sons attested, "Mom, she's a great guy!"[19] By dressing like a man, Chung claimed opportunities traditionally denied to women.

Chung's efforts to transcend social and professional barriers, visually represented by her Western masculine dress, took on additional significance because of her racial status. Chinese American women during the early twentieth century were popularly viewed as either exploited prostitutes or secluded wives with bound feet.[20] The former's access to the public arena was associated with heterosexual deviance, while the latter's respectability was associated with crippled confinement to the private realm.[21] Chung's adoption of Western masculine clothing symbolized her efforts to claim social freedom and professional opportunities for Chinese American women.[22]

Chung's attempts to transcend gender and racial boundaries resonated with the goals of other second-generation Chinese Americans. For example, Bessie Jeong, a physician who began practicing in the 1930s, echoed Chung's desire to participate as an equal in a white, masculine world. Born in San Francisco Chinatown, across from the Chinese Hospital, Jeong ran away to the Presbyterian Mission Home, when she feared that her father might arrange a marriage for her. Instead of returning to China as her father intended, Jeong sought the assistance of the Mission Home to gain an education. She became the first Chinese American woman to graduate from Stanford University and eventually attended the Women's Medical College in Philadelphia. Jeong explained that her desire to study biology and medicine stemmed from an early childhood interest in "boys' games," which were much more challenging to her than "girls' games." Medicine, to her, was a "man's game," and she believed she had a "man's mind."[23] Similar to Chung, Jeong accepted existing gender divisions, which associated certain abilities and privileges with male identity, even as she sought to transcend those boundaries.

Jeong distinguished between women, like herself, who sought opportunities in traditionally male professions, and women, like Chung, who extended their challenge to include dress and behavior. While in medical school, Jeong observed that two sororities existed: "[In] one of them, the girls smoked and drank a little. They wore those gloves and wore suits and acted mannish. They'd sit down and put their legs this way. They were the mannish type. The men don't like them and the girls don't like them. The other group was more socially acceptable—real girls."[24] Jeong's comments suggest that while Chung was certainly not alone in her practice of cross-dressing, "mannish" women faced social censure for their choice in dress and mannerism.

During the late nineteenth and early twentieth centuries, medical and social attention increasingly focused on the topic of "gender inversion," linking cross-dressing with mental and sexual degeneracy.[25] While scholars have debated the social significance of these medical theories, Chung's adoption of partial cross-dressing was interpreted as an indication of her sexuality. Not only did Gidlow think of Chung as a "sister lesbian," but members of the Chinese American community also questioned her sexual orientation. When Jeong was asked whether she and Chung shared a sense of camaraderie, she exclaimed defensively: "Oh, no! Margaret and I were as different as [pause] She was a homo, a lesbian."[26] One Federal Bureau of Investigation agent also reported that within the Chinese American community "there were rumors that she was a Lesbian."[27] Such comments suggest that Chung's sexuality, signified by her masculine dress, was socially unacceptable.

Although prevailing social attitudes and medical literature equated Chung's gender identity with her sexual orientation, the connections between the two were more complicated.[28] Evidence suggests that she participated in physical, possibly sexual, relationships with women early in her professional career. When Chung served as an intern at the Mary Thompson Hospital in Chicago in 1916 and 1917, she was banned from sharing a bed with other women. Van Hoosen, her supervisor there, commented that Chung "was a favorite with nurses and interns to the degree that the hospital, for the first time, made a ruling that two people must not sleep in a single bed."[29] The regulation of sleeping arrangements and omission of this passage in the final version of Van Hoosen's autobiography suggest that Chung's interactions with women were viewed by others as socially suspect. The hospital's censure most likely encouraged Chung to be more circumspect in her relationships with women. While her emotions are difficult to gauge given the lack of sources from her perspective, Gidlow's accounts of their flirtatious friendship suggest that Chung reciprocated emotionally but had greater reserve about expressing her desires publicly or acting upon them.

Gidlow, who had a nonmonogamous relationship with Tommy, courted Chung. Gidlow invited the doctor to her apartment for dinner and regularly visited Chung in her office, sometimes bringing her flowers. Gidlow even wrote poetry about Chung and gave her a copy of "Teasedale's Anthology of Women's Love Lyrics."[30] According to Gidlow, Chung understood the nature of these advances. Gidlow recalled one particular house call that Chung made: "Observing Tommy's and my domestic scene, [she] smiled a knowing smile."[31] A turning point in their relationship occurred when Gidlow departed for Europe to attempt a writing career. Chung invited Gidlow to a speakeasy in North Beach, the Italian community bordering Chinatown, for a farewell luncheon. Drinking bootleg liquor helped Chung reveal more about herself.[32] The growing intimacy of their relationship was sealed two days later by an exchange of good-bye presents and a kiss. Gidlow wrote: "I believe she was really sorry to see me go and heaven knows she is one of the few I part from with a pang. She gave me a pint bottle of bourbon, Government sealed, 160 proof and—what I value many times more, a spontaneous kiss on the mouth. I had never dared to hope she would kiss me."[33]

Chung made no apparent attempts to contact Gidlow while the writer lived in Europe. However, when Gidlow returned to San Francisco the following year and became dangerously ill, Chung finally expressed her growing feelings. Gidlow composed poems about Chung while under her care at the Chinese Hospital. After reading one of the poems, Chung was moved to kiss Gidlow again.[34] In and out of consciousness following an operation, Gidlow recalled two conversations she had with Chung: "I took her hand and would not let it go. How long she stayed I do not know, nor whether it was there or while still on the operating table that I heard myself say: 'Do you love me?' Her answer seemed to come after a long time: 'yes—if it will make you feel better.'"[35] Hours later, Gidlow and Chung conversed again: "The door opened and M[argaret]. came in 'I have been thinking about you all afternoon,' I heard myself say. Then I begged her to stay with me for a little while and she said she would. . . . Was it then that M said: 'You gave me hell this morning for

operating on you; and then you asked me if I loved you. There were people around too,'
I felt a vague concern for her. Had I put her in an awkward position? 'Was I very inde-
screte?' [*sic*] I asked her? 'No, no,' she assured me. . . . For a while—I remember it as a long
while—my mind was a blank, yet I was aware, with the curious comfort, of Ms presence
and thought of her constantly. Suddenly I asked: '*Do* you love me?' This time she said 'Yes'
immediately and quietly."[36] Chung apparently never acted on her declaration of love. After
Gidlow's recovery, Chung avoided contact with her. Gidlow wrote, "M. denies herself to
me almost completely."[37] A few months after the operation, Gidlow's journal reported
Chung's engagement to a wealthy man: "M is going to get married. It is bald, but it is a
man and it has half a million—another sacrifice to the twin gods, manners and respectability."[38] Although Chung did not marry her fiancé, she and Gidlow never resumed the
intimacy of their former relationship.

The interactions between the two women revealed that Chung felt romantic attraction toward Gidlow but also ambivalence about lesbian sexuality. The meals, gifts, and
kisses that they exchanged demonstrated the eroticism underlying their professional
relationship as doctor and patient. Despite this attraction, Chung's reluctance to express
her feelings initially, her refusal to act upon them, and then her engagement to a man,
soon after her declaration of love to a woman, confirmed that she was retreating from
her homoerotic desires.

Chung's decision to distance herself from a lesbian relationship reflected her efforts
to negotiate not only sexual norms but also cultural and racial boundaries in mainstream
society as well as her own ethnic community. Gidlow's orientalist fascination with Chinese
culture fueled her attraction to Chung. Although Chung embraced Western science and
culture, she also evoked the mysteriousness and exoticness of Asian culture for Gidlow.
In her journal, Gidlow reflected, "One of her fascinations for me is perhaps the ambiguity
of this blend in her of East and West."[39] She viewed Chung as someone wise, who could
perhaps explain life's mysteries: "There is no one to whom I can talk. . . . I want someone
neutral, and someone with a special sort of maturity and wisdom. M seems to me the one
person. . . . More, far more than I want to possess M physically, I want to understand her;
but she eludes me continually."[40] Gidlow's poems about Chung also demonstrate how
Western perceptions of Chinese culture as exotic and mysterious could be transferred
to people of Chinese descent. In "For a Gifted Lady, Often Masked," the author claimed
to see past the professional persona of the physician: "Matter-of-fact manner, / Brusque
speech, / Expert hands—These are not *you*." Instead, Gidlow posited the doctor's real
identity as evocative of lush, tropical lands. "Your soul is a cool tuberose / Drowsy with
perfume, / Languorous, dreaming. . . . Its fragrance wafts me / To far-off times and lands."[41]
Chung's liminal status between Western and Chinese cultures allowed Gidlow access to
the mysteries of a foreign civilization.

Gidlow's fascination with cultural difference and her perception of Chinese culture
as exotic resonated with emerging liberal notions regarding race. As historian Henry Yu
has pointed out in his study of interracial sexuality, cultural pluralists of the 1910s and
1920s argued "for an inclusive vision of America that maintained the stark differences
of various immigrant communities" and propagated "theories of culture that stressed
understanding different communities from the inside or 'native' perspective."[42] Cul-

tural pluralist views both reinforced and challenged more conservative racial thinking, which emphasized the biological and cultural inferiority of "Mongolians." Both ideologies assumed fixed cultural differences. However, conservatives denigrated these differences as inherently inferior, while cultural pluralists "placed a value on the exotic."[43]

Chung understood the attention that her liminal cultural status granted her. In some ways, she resisted Gidlow's orientalist image of her. Chung described Gidlow as an "old soul," therefore having a greater affinity with the "Orient." In contrast, she positioned herself as a Westerner: "I am Chinese, yes, but I am a new soul."[44] On the one hand, Chung suggested that Gidlow's fascination with her and Asian culture originated less from her actual identity and more from the writer's interest in orientalist difference. On the other hand, Chung accepted the dichotomous perception of Eastern and Western culture and used this juxtaposition to gain opportunities for herself. The physician who never wore Chinese clothing decorated her medical office in Chinatown with "furnishings in Oriental artistry."[45] Her choice in furniture reflected a pride in her ancestral culture. At the same time, the use of "oriental" decorations suggested that she staged her office as a tourist site for her increasing white clientele. Other Asian American women used this strategy of using their "otherness" to gain economic opportunities. Yung notes that few second-generation Chinese American women during the early twentieth century found positions outside of Chinatown. The few openings used these women as "exotic showpieces," requiring them to "wear oriental costumes" to add "atmosphere" for "teahouses, restaurants, stores, and nightclubs."[46]

Although Chung cultivated an orientalist image to attract interest from mainstream Americans, she was reluctant to pursue an explicitly lesbian relationship with a white woman. Her vigilance regarding her personal reputation dovetailed with her efforts to gain professional recognition in Chinatown. That the intimate conversations between Gidlow and Chung took place at the Chinese Hospital is significant. As a relative newcomer to the community, she had to guard her personal image carefully to protect her professional reputation, especially because her initial efforts to establish herself had met with mixed results. In her autobiography, Chung cited her limited Chinese language skills as the main reason for her sense of isolation. However, her status as a single, professional woman who adopted masculine dress also contributed to her marginalization. Questions concerning her sexual orientation created an additional social barrier. While homophobia existed within broader American society as well, Chung very likely felt more vulnerable about her status in the close-knit Chinatown community.

Chung's engagement and subsequent rejection of marriage also reflected her concerns regarding respectability and social status. Her intended marriage partner was probably white. Her sister-in-law, Lucile, remembered that Margaret was engaged to an "American" doctor.[47] Chung's Chinese American friends and family expected her to marry someone of her own class status, and few eligible candidates existed within the Chinatown community because of the scarcity of educated professionals. Although her fiancé's racial background could have contributed to Chung's marginalization in Chinatown, his class status would have assisted her efforts to gain social acceptance and recognition from both the Chinese American and white American communities.[48] According to Lucile, Chung sought her fiancé's assistance in financing her sisters' education and eventually declined to marry him because he refused to provide the economic support she requested. If this interpretation of Chung's decision not to marry was correct, marriage without a corresponding increase in social status held few attractions.

Chung's experimentation with racial crossings, gender identities, and homoeroticism during her early medical career reflected her efforts both to challenge restrictions placed upon Chinese American women and deflect criticisms directed toward marginalized individuals. Her adoption of a Western masculine persona symbolized her efforts to gain social and professional opportunities traditionally denied to women and Chinese Americans. At the same time, her incorporation of "orientalist" forms of identification reflected an interest in capitalizing on mainstream fascination with Asian culture. Just as Chung negotiated cultural expectations, she also navigated conflicting sexual norms. The decisions in her personal life reflected both romantic interest in other women and a desire for respectability. Her retreat from Gidlow suggests Chung's inability to reconcile a lesbian identity with her professional and social goals. Her simultaneous rejection of marriage, however, also indicates her desire to seek an alternative to heterosexuality.

Maternal Homoeroticism and Interethnic Alliances

Chung's relationship with Sophie Tucker, which occurred more than a decade after her relationship with Gidlow, demonstrated another approach to negotiating her private desires and public image. During the intervening years, Chung had crafted a new gender persona. Instead of dressing and behaving as a man, she embraced a glamorous maternal identity. Her new public image assisted her efforts to affiliate with the white upper middle class. Following Japan's invasion of Manchuria in 1931, Chung began to socialize with and adopt white men in the military, entertainment industry, and political arena as an expression of her patriotism for China. Her new persona also provided her with a language to express her feelings for Tucker and allowed their relationship to be perceived as co-mothering the war effort. Their ages—both women were in their fifties—contributed to their maternal image. Instead of the more explicit lesbian relationship that Gidlow offered, Chung's relationship with Tucker could be characterized as a romantic friendship. Chung expressed sensual desire for Tucker, yet their relationship could have been perceived by others, and possibly Chung herself, as nonsexual. Although her interest in Tucker might have been viewed as part of her effort to assimilate into the white social elite, the strength of their relationship also stemmed from a mutual recognition and appreciation of ethnic differences.

Tucker first met Chung in 1913 on a vaudeville tour in the West.[49] Always a self-publicist, the singer kept lists of people she met in various cities and sent postcards to remind them of her return performances. Their relationship did not become more personal until World War II. Just as Chung adopted aviators into her organization of "Fair-Haired Bastards," she also adopted musicians and actors, whom she frequently called "Kiwis" for the bird that does not fly. By January 1943, Tucker had become Kiwi number 107.

Chung's increasing fascination with entertainers and celebrities during the 1930s and 1940s undoubtedly spurred her interest in Tucker and inspired her own adoption of a more glamorous, feminine image. Chung's sisters recalled that her "clothing changed from almost mannish suits to more frivolous attire under the influence of 'stars.'"[50] Her favorite photograph during this time period featured her in an evening gown and white ermine cape, with coiffed hair and makeup. Apparently, the image accurately represented Chung's attire, as Bessie Jeong recalled that "Margaret used to drape herself in ermine and jewelry."[51] Chung's growing identification with female roles was not just inspired by her adoption of a public maternal persona but also by commercialized images of women from movies and theater. Beginning in the 1930s, Hollywood increasingly focused on the lives of "strong, autonomous, competent, and career oriented" women.[52] Even the physical appearance of female movie stars changed. Instead of the waif-like look of Mary Pickford, the movie industry favored such larger women with "more flesh and physical strength" as Mae West.[53] It must have been gratifying for Chung to emulate the desirable image of these celebrities, considering her memories of herself as a "homely little child."

The transformation of Chung's gender identity paralleled the evolution of Tucker's stage persona. When Tucker began performing in vaudeville, she was billed as a "world-renowned coon shouter" and performed in blackface. A large woman, she was viewed as lacking the sex appeal to perform in whiteface. Similar to Chung, Tucker was treated by men as a friend, not a potential love interest. In her autobiography, she recalled, "I wasn't the type of girl the boys like to play around with on tour. But they liked me as a pal, a good egg."[54] Tucker struggled to gain the opportunity to perform in whiteface and eventually became known for her sexually charged stage persona. The experiences of Chung and Tucker suggest that the ability to assume or perform a feminine role represented a privilege that not all woman could attain. A woman's racial identity, economic resources, and physical characteristics shaped her ability to assume a feminized gender image.

Chung's adoption of a glamorous identity held racial, class, and gender implications. Her new persona both resonated with and departed from the experiences of other Chinese American women. As historian Judy Yung has argued, the Great Depression ironically created new economic and social opportunities for the Chinatown community. The expanding entertainment industry during the 1930s encouraged Chinese American women to find work as performers in Hollywood and in newly established Chinatown nightclubs.[55] Individuals who associated with this glamorous industry, however, continued to be somewhat marginal to the Chinese American community. Chung's ability to purchase expensive clothing and patronize these clubs, often in the company of white Americans, separated her from both the working class and respectable merchant families of San Francisco's Chinatown. The possession of glamorous clothing, necessary for attending operas, elegant restaurants, and other forums of urban sociability, demonstrated her entry into mainstream middle-class realms of leisure.

Chung's new maternal identity both deflected criticisms regarding gender-appropriate attire and allowed her to maintain social freedoms previously associated with masculine dress.[56] Her new persona did not signal growing dependence on men, but rather symbolized her status as an independent woman. In contrast to marriage, in which a woman expressed love and commitment to one man, her voluntary maternal status allowed her to select as many sons as she desired to befriend. Instead of being a helpmate, she became the center of the network. In contrast to the pattern of attractive women receiving favors from men, Chung was often in the superior economic position, hosting parties and mailing care packages to her sons.

The asexual quality of Chung's feminine persona reinforced her autonomy. In contrast to the heterosexual image of celebrities, her age, physical presence, and maternal identity projected a predominantly nonsexual quality. Letters from her sons, many of whom were half her age, demonstrate that they did not view her as a potential romantic partner. She also took great care to protect her reputation. Although she entertained extensively in her home, only female or married friends were allowed to spend the night. The mixture of femininity without heterosexual allure perfectly suited Chung's lifestyle. She could enjoy the excitement of nightclubs and late-night card games with her sons with minimal damage to her reputation as a single woman.

Ironically, as Chung's gender image became more modern and commercialized, her erotic desires were expressed in traditional and circumspect language. She and Tucker became close companions when the singer returned to San Francisco for nightclub appearances in 1943. Chung regularly drove Tucker to her evening performances, attended shows in company with large groups of her sons, and then stayed up late into the night playing cards with Tucker.[57] During the performer's stay in San Francisco, the two spent so much time together that a local gossip columnist referred to them as "me and my shadow."[58] Their relationship continued in intensity, even after Tucker left San Francisco. Chung traveled to attend Tucker's performances. They also telephoned one another and corresponded regularly.

Chung's letters and actions revealed the depth of her feelings. While she expressed love for all her adopted children, her relationship with Tucker was laced with romantic undertones. When Tucker returned to San Francisco in January 1945, she became a regular houseguest of Chung. Mutual friends recalled that the doctor reserved for Tucker a special bedroom with a large, pink, satin bed.[59] During her stay, Chung wrote affectionate notes, using romantic and comical endearments to Tucker, known by her nickname "Boss":

> Ah Boss—I surely do love you—and I'm so happy you are with me (13 January 1945);
> Goodnight Sweet Heart (14 January 1945);
> Peek-a-boo—I love you (14 January 1945);
> Hi, Angel! Love You (14 January 1945);
> Hi—Stinky—Love You! (14 January 1945);
> Love & Kisses Nightie Night (17 January 1945);
> You are the most wonderful Pal in the whole world—and I adore you (19 January 1945).[60]

The content and frequency of these notes suggest an infatuation on Chung's part that blurred the boundary between platonic and romantic friendship.

While Chung's correspondence tended to express emotional intimacy with Tucker, a desire for physical intimacy occasionally emerged. Unable to spend Christmas together in 1947, Chung sent Tucker a series of presents and commented on the meaning of the gifts: "The silver shell, I want you to keep with you always—on your desk to keep your little candle in—and to remind you of my shining love—Please wear the blue nightgown—Christmas night because it will be *close* to you—as I will be."[61] By describing her emotional closeness to Tucker as comparable to the physical sensation of wearing a nightgown, Chung revealed the connection between emotional and sensual intimacy.

Chung more commonly expressed her feelings of love through maternal and religious language. In one good-night note, she, as the mother, promised to care for all of Tucker's needs: "Angel, it's wonderful having you to come home to! If you'll stay—I'll always draw your bath and cook for you and wait on you forever!"[62] The relationship was sometimes reversed, with Tucker as mother and Chung as child. In addition to describing herself as Tucker's "Baby," Chung also compared herself to the Biblical figure of Ruth, devoted daughter-in-law of Naomi: "Boss, I don't want to be sent home with all the rest of your junk to be put away in storage!! *I want to go with you*—wherever you go—to be *your shadow*—Can't I ride with your music in the music case? Cause I want to go where you go—do what you do—then I'll be happy!—and you want your baby to be happy don't you? Remember what Ruth said to Naomi? 'Whither thou goest, I will go—and thy people shall be my people—and thy god, my god.'"[63]

Chung's reference to Ruth and Naomi provides insight into her negotiations of sexual, racial, and ethnic boundaries. The Old Testament story demonstrates the love and loyalty between women of different national and religious backgrounds. Ruth, a Moabitess, married into a Hebrew family. When she became a widow, Naomi entreated Ruth to stay in Moab and find another husband for herself. However, Ruth refused to abandon her widowed mother-in-law, choosing instead to follow her into the land of Judah and care for her.[64] The expression of Chung's desires through maternal and religious language both highlighted her passionate commitment to Tucker and masked the eroticism of her feelings. By comparing her love to maternal and religious devotion, Chung emphasized the power of her feelings. At the same time, her expression of a lifelong commitment to Tucker could be interpreted as spiritually and idealistically, not *sexually*, motivated. As scholar Martha Vicinus has argued, this "transference of sexual tensions into the language of the family (and sexual love into the language of religion) . . . [helped] conceal the physical basis of so much . . . love."[65] The practice of "transference" was more characteristic of female romantic relationships during the Victorian era than the lesbian relationships of the modern era.

Given Chung's ambivalence about pursuing a romantic relationship with Gidlow, her expressions of maternally and religiously inspired love could be interpreted as a conscious attempt to reconcile her homoerotic desires with her rejection of a modern lesbian identity. Her strategy resonated with the experiences of other middle-class women who came of age during the turn of the century. As historian Estelle B. Freedman has suggested, the subjective sexual identities of these women stemmed from their liminal historical positions. They represented "individuals raised with the sexual categories of an earlier culture" who then "partake in the social changes that redefine their behaviors" in a later era.[66] While one should caution against exaggerating the acceptability of romantic friendships during the Victorian era, Chung's choice of erotic expression suggests that the nineteenth century notion of female "passionlessness," reinforced in this particular case by her class status, maternal persona, and use of religious language, continued to provide some protection from social and perhaps even personal recognition of lesbian sexuality well into the twentieth century.[67]

Chung's religious and maternal language also provides insight into the significance of racial and ethnic identity in her intimate relationships. Ruth's abandonment of her native land of Moab could be interpreted as a rejection of her own culture. Similarly, Chung's preference for white Americans as romantic partners and friends could be explained by internalized racism. Her statements and behavior indicate her idealization of white definitions of beauty. Karen Garling Sickel, whose father was one of Chung's surrogate sons, recalled a startling remark from her adopted grandmother: "She turned to me one time and said, 'I wish I could wake up one morning and be blonde-haired and blue-eyed. All my troubles would go away.'"[68] Chung's apparent desire to alter her physical appearance, based on an awareness of the social advantages of achieving normative ideas of beauty, may have encouraged her enthusiasm for befriending white Americans. In fact, the two groups that she most adored, actresses and military heroes, epitomized mainstream cultural standards of femininity and masculinity.

Chung's attitudes and behavior suggest the power of mainstream racial thinking in shaping definitions of beauty and sexual desire. At the same time, her experiences reveal that conceptions of race, which shifted over the course of her lifetime, represented just one of many factors that shape identity formation and explain attraction.[69] Although Chung's romantic partners may not have shared a common racial background, they did have similar gender, class, and ethnic affinities. Chung, Gidlow, and Tucker were independent women who lived outside traditional family structures. In addition, both Gidlow and Tucker came from working-class, immigrant backgrounds. Like Chung, Gidlow grew up in a poor, large family in a rural community. Tucker, a Russian Jew, spent her childhood years working to contribute to the family income. Like Chung, she expressed a sense of obligation to her ethnic community and contributed time and effort to social causes.

Chung's reference to an Old Testament story to compare her relationship to Tucker suggests that she sought a common cultural reference to bridge their religious and cultural differences. As an American-born Chinese Christian, she tried to identify similarities with Tucker's Jewish immigrant background. While they spent Christmas together, they also celebrated Jewish holidays. Separated during one Passover, Chung sent a telegram to wish: "Happy Holidays to you and your family. Wish I were having matzofry with you in the kitchen. Am nostalgic with many beautiful and happy memories of seder and passover spent with you and yours. I cherish your friendship above all else and love you."[70] Chung's interest in developing personal connections across ethnic and racial lines paralleled the formation of political alliances during World War II. She sought not to erase race and ethnicity entirely but rather to craft possibilities for recognizing and uniting individuals of different backgrounds. Her adoption of a maternal persona and the creation of surrogate network translated the Allied political agenda into familial language.

Chung's negotiation of racial and ethnic identities reflects broader transformations

of social attitudes during the first half of the twentieth century, when the incorporation of European ethnic groups into the racial category of whiteness intensified.[71] Yu
noted that "what began in the 1910s and 1920s as a fascination with the exotic became
by the 1940s and 1950s a desire to erase the exotic. . . . The 1950s were marked by a
belief in America as potentially homogeneous, and . . . the desirability of the 'melting
pot.'"[72] As European ethnic groups viewed themselves and became viewed as "white,"
they also struggled to maintain a sense of ethnic identity. Chung's efforts to assimilate
into the white middle class and yet maintain her affiliation with the Chinese community paralleled this transformation. Her relationships with "white" individuals from
immigrant, ethnic backgrounds reflected a mutual desire for, as well as sense of anxiety
about, incorporation.[73]

Chung's relationship with Tucker reveals her efforts to redefine her gender, class,
racial, and sexual identities. Her adoption of a glamorous, maternal persona in the 1930s
through 1950s fulfilled multiple functions. She responded to social pressure to adopt
appropriate gender attire and behavior by crafting a feminine identity that nevertheless emphasized her financial independence and social autonomy. While her maternal
performance indicated her growing identification with the white middle class, she continued to express political commitment to the Chinese in the United States and China.
Her preference for white Americans as friends and romantic partners demonstrated her
internalization of racial attitudes as well as her desire for companionship from women
of similar ethnic and class backgrounds. Finally, her new persona helped redefine her
homoerotic longings as maternally and religiously, not sexually, inspired. Chung's new
maternal identity expressed her conflicting desire to balance respectability and independence.

Conclusion

Chung's relationships with Gidlow and Tucker offer insight into her attempts to define
an acceptable self-identity while negotiating the shifting gender, sexual, racial, and class
boundaries of the first half of the twentieth century. Perhaps because Chung felt isolated at times due to her personal choices, she created alternative family and community networks. Among her acquaintances and "sons" were individuals, such as Tallulah
Bankhead, Anna May Wong, Tyrone Power, and Liberace, who became known as or were
rumored to be homosexual or bisexual.[74] The coexistence or comingling of heterosexuals
and nonheterosexuals in Chung's circle of friends shared similarities with middle-class
lesbian communities during the middle decades of the twentieth century. During the
1930s, gay bars such as Mona's and the Black Cat Cafe opened in San Francisco, attracting a predominantly young, working-class clientele. Lesbians from middle- and upper-
class backgrounds, however, continued to socialize privately in homes with their own
networks of homosexual and heterosexual friends. The middle-class lesbian subculture
rejected the butch masculine roles that were performed in working-class bar culture.
Instead, middle-class lesbians sought integration into the existing heterosexual culture
and emphasized dressing "appropriately" and behaving with "sufficient, though never

excessive, femininity."[75] This pattern of coexistence, which continued through the war and into the 1950s, provided middle-class women who pursued same-sex relationships with a degree of protection from social persecution.

Although Chung developed her community of friends mainly with white Americans, she was not the only Chinese American living an alternative private life. Author Russell Leong recalled a conversation with his uncle regarding homosexuality in San Francisco's Chinatown: "I ask him about growing up in San Francisco Chinatown in the 1930s and 1940s before World War II. I ask him about gays and lesbians before I was born. He laughs. He says that there were many white homosexuals in North Beach 'who had a thing for Asian and Black boys,' at the time. But that there were also many spinsters and unmarried sisters in the families he knew about."[76] In addition to these "spinsters and unmarried sisters," at least one wife and mother, and probably many more, formed romantic and sexual relationships with other women. In a poem entitled "Chinatown Talking Story," novelist and poet Kitty Tsui described her grandmother, a Chinese opera singer who traveled to the United States in 1922:

> my grandfather had four wives
> and pursued many women
> during his life.
> the chinese press loved
> to write of his affairs.
>
> my grandmother,
> a woman with three daughters,
> left her husband
> to survive on her own.
> she lived with another actress,
> a companion and a friend.[77]

Chung's experimentation with gender identities and her participation in interracial homoerotic relationships provide insight into how other individuals with alternative sexual desires may have negotiated racial, gender, and class boundaries during the first half of the twentieth century. Her decisions to adopt masculine as well as feminine identities, express her erotic feelings through religious and maternal language, and engage in romantic friendships with white women revealed her efforts to contain transgressive behavior and feelings through normative forms of expression. Chung's ability to maneuver within social barriers stemmed from her liminal position between historical eras. During her lifetime, American society witnessed the transformation from the Victorian to the modern world. While her adoption of masculine dress and identity expressed discontent with the separation of gender spheres that characterized the Victorian era, her creation of a glamorous, feminine persona embraced the opportunities available for middle-class women within a commercialized society. While her choices in gender scripts exhibited an enthusiasm for change, her rejection of lesbianism, of same-sex sexuality as the basis of identity, indicated a desire to uphold Victorian notions of homosociality and asexuality as forms of protection. Her desire for companionship with white Americans called upon emerging notions of liberal equality to challenge social beliefs and practices of racial segregation. At the same time, those interracial relationships mirrored the persistence of ethnicity and social hierarchy within modern America. Chung's textured strategies reflected the challenge of crafting identities that foster social acceptance yet allow for transcendence.

Notes

1. This article has benefited from the comments of my advisors, colleagues, students, and friends. I particularly want to thank Estelle Freedman, Gordon Chang, Mary Louise Roberts, Leila Rupp, Birgitte Søland, Marc Stein, Nan Alamilla Boyd, Henry Yu, Evelyn Nakano Glenn, John Kuo Wei Tchen, Pamily Paxton, Kira Sanbonmatsu, Stephanie Gilmore, Heather Lee Miller, Kristina de los Santos, Jeong-eun Rhee, and Oona Besman. Chung's papers, held at the Asian American Studies Library, University of California, Berkeley, contain little correspondence from Tucker, although they wrote to one another. There is also no reference to Gidlow in Chung's writings or collection. I accidentally discovered their relationship by browsing through Susan Stryker and Jim Van Buskirk, *Gay by the Bay: A History of Queer Culture in the San Francisco Bay Area* (San Francisco: Chronicle Books, 1996), 21–23, which published a photograph of Chung and identified her as Gidlow's friend.

2. Chung to Tucker, 29 March 1945, Sophie Tucker Scrapbook Collection, 10,957, New York Public Library, Performing Arts Branch, New York City. From the passage, it appears that Tucker and Westphal, her second husband, lived together or "doubled" up before they were married.

3. See Judy Yung, *Unbound Feet: A Social History of Chinese Women in San Francisco* (Berkeley: University of California Press, 1995), 293.

4. Elsa Gidlow, *Elsa: I Come with My Songs* (San Francisco: Booklegger, 1986), 207.

5. I situate Chung's sexuality historically by differentiating between the concept of lesbianism that developed during the turn of the century and other forms of homoeroticism. See Leila J. Rupp, "'Imagine My Surprise': Women's Relationships in Mid-Twentieth Century America," in *Hidden from History: Reclaiming the Gay and Lesbian Past,* ed. Martin Bauml Duberman, Martha Vicinus, and George Chauncey, Jr. (New York: New American Library, 1989): 395–410; and Estelle B. Freedman, "'The Burning of Letters Continues': Elusive Identities and the Historical Construction of Sexuality," *Journal of Women's History* 9, no. 4 (1998): 181–200.

6. See *Amerasia Journal: Dimensions of Desire* 20, no. 1 (1994); David L. Eng and Alice Y. Hom, eds., *Q & A: Queer in Asian America* (Philadelphia: Temple University Press, 1998); Chris Friday, *Organizing Asian American Labor: The Pacific Coast Canned-Salmon Industry, 1870–1942* (Philadelphia: Temple University Press, 1994); Russell Leong, ed., *Asian American Sexualities: Dimensions of the Gay and Lesbian Experience* (New York: Routledge, 1996); Jennifer Ting, "Bachelor Society: Deviant Heterosexuality and Asian American Historiography," in *Privileging Positions: The Sites of Asian American Studies,* ed. Gary Y. Okihiro, Marilyn Alquizola, Dorothy Fujita Rony, and K. Scott Wong (Pullman: Washington State University Press, 1995), 271–80; and Jennifer Ting, "The Power of Sexuality," *Journal of Asian American Studies* 1, no. 1 (1998): 65–82.

7. Brett de Bary and Victor Nee use the phrases "bachelor society" and "family society" to characterize the development of San Francisco's Chinatown community. See Brett de Bray and Victor Nee, *Longtime Californ': A Documentary Study of an American Chinatown* (Stanford, Calif.: Stanford University Press, 1972). For overviews of Asian American history, see Ronald Takaki, *Strangers from a Different Shore: A History of Asian Americans* (Boston: Little, Brown, 1989); and Sucheng Chan, *Asian Americans: An Interpretive History* (Boston: Twayne, 1991).

8. Gidlow, *Elsa,* 207. For more information about Chung, see Judy Tzu-Chun Wu, "Mom Chung of the Fair-Haired Bastards: A Thematic Biography of Doctor Margaret Chung (1889–1959)" (Ph.D. diss., Stanford University, 1998); and Yung, *Unbound Feet.*

9. In 1923, Gidlow published *On a Grey Thread,* considered the first collection of explicitly lesbian poetry in North America. For more information about her life, see Gidlow, *Elsa;* and Stryker and Van Buskirk, *Gay by the Bay.*

10. In Edward W. Said's study *Orientalism,* he argues that the West historically has imaged the Orient as its "contrasting image." While the West is associated with progress, rationality, science, and normativity, the East represents "a place of romance, exotic beings, haunting memories and landscapes, [and] remarkable experiences." Because of this juxtaposition, the East holds an exotic allure for the West. At the same time, the contrast between the Occident and the Orient situates the West in a superior position in relation to non-European cultures. Orientalism thus represents "a Western style for dominating, restructuring, and having authority over the Orient." Edward W. Said, *Orientalism* (New York: Vintage, 1979), 1–3. For studies of American forms of orientalism, see John Kuo Wei Tchen, *New York before Chinatown: Orientalism and the Shaping of American Culture, 1776–1882* (Baltimore, Md.: Johns Hopkins University Press, 1999); and Robert G. Lee, *Orientals: Asian Americans in Popular Culture* (Philadelphia: Temple University Press, 1999).

11. Gidlow, *Elsa,* 207.

12. Marjorie Garber, *Vested Interests: Cross-Dressing and Cultural Anxiety* (New York: Routledge, 1992).

13. Vern L. Bullough and Bonnie Bullough define cross-dressing as a "symbolic incursion into territory that crosses gender boundaries." Because dress represents a visible marker of gender differences, cross-dressing challenges the naturalness of masculinity and femininity. See Vern L. Bullough and Bonnie Bullough, *Cross Dressing, Sex, and Gender* (Philadelphia: University of Pennsylvania Press, 1993), viii. For discussions of gender and performativity, see Judith Butler, "Performative Acts and Gender Constitution: An Essay in Phenomenology and Feminist Theory," in *Performing Feminisms: Feminist Critical Theory and Theatre,* ed. Sue-Ellen Case (Baltimore, Md.: Johns Hopkins University Press, 1990), 270–82; and Judith Halberstam, *Female Masculinity* (Durham, N.C.: Duke University Press, 1998).

14. Bertha Van Hoosen, *Petticoat Surgeon* (Chicago: Pelligrini & Cudahy, 1947), 219.

15. *El Rodeo* 9 (Los Angeles: University of Southern California, 1915), 221, 233.

16. While some professional women adopted masculine dress to symbolize their entry into traditionally male occupations, others viewed male dress as "protective coloring." See Bullough and Bullough, *Cross Dressing;* and Lillian Faderman, *Odd Girls and Twilight Lovers: A History of Lesbian Life in Twentieth-Century America* (New York: Columbia University Press, 1991), 21.

17. Margaret Chung autobiography, Margaret Chung Collection, Box 1, folder 1, Asian American Studies Library, University of California, Berkeley. The autobiography is not paginated.

18. Ibid.

19. "'Mom, She's a Great Guy' to Her 465 Flying 'Sons': Dr. Margaret Chung, Chinese American, Keeps Close Watch over Brood: Each Wear Buddha," Chung Scrapbook, Chung Collection, Box 10.

20. Judy Yung provides a richer depiction of Chinese American women's lives in San Francisco during this time period. See Yung, *Unbound Feet;* and Peggy Pascoe, *Relations of Rescue: The Search for Female Moral Authority in the American West, 1874–1939* (New York: Oxford University Press, 1990).

21. Ting, "Bachelor Society."

22. Around the turn of the century, women in China also adopted masculine clothing to challenge the existing gender order and to proclaim their support for the emerging republican nation. For a discussion of the possible sexual connotations of adopting masculine clothing, see Vivien Ng, "Looking for Lesbians in Chinese History," in *The New Lesbian Studies: Into the Twenty-First Century,* ed. Bonnie Zimmerman and Toni A. H. McNaron (New York: Feminist Press, 1996), 160–64.

23. Bessie Jeong, interview by Suellen Cheng and Munson Kwok, 17 December 1981, 17 October 1982, Southern California Chinese American Oral History Project, Special Collections, Univer-

sity of California, Los Angeles. For biographical information about Jeong, see Yung, *Unbound Feet,* 131–33.

24. Jeong, interview.

25. See Garber, *Vested Interests;* San Francisco Lesbian and Gay History Project, "'She Even Chewed Tobacco': A Pictorial Narrative of Passing Women in America," in *Hidden from History,* 183–94; and Carroll Smith-Rosenberg, "Discourses of Sexuality and Subjectivity: The New Woman, 1870–1936," in ibid., 269–71.

26. Jeong, interview.

27. L. B. Nichols to Tolson, memorandum, 9 October 1940, Federal Bureau of Investigation file on "Dr. Margaret Jesse Chung," Department of Justice, Washington, D.C.

28. Given the difficulties of uncovering past sexual lives, scholars have focused on the figure of the "mannish" woman as a signifier of the sexually assertive lesbian. In contrast, romantic friendships, characterized as erotic but nongenital relationships, are associated with the homosocial world of the Victorian era. Elizabeth Lapovsky Kennedy has noted that this framework tends to portray nonmannish women as lacking sexual initiative and experience. For discussions of the methodological approaches of lesbian/sexuality studies, see Lisa Duggan, "The Trials of Alice Mitchell: Sensationalism, Sexology, and the Lesbian Subject in Turn-of-the-Century America," *Signs* 18, no. 4 (1993): 791–814; Martha Vicinus, ed., *Lesbian Subjects: A Feminist Studies Reader* (Bloomington: Indiana University Press, 1996); and Elizabeth Lapovsky Kennedy, "'But we would never talk about it': The Structures of Lesbian Discretion in South Dakota, 1928–1933," in *Inventing Lesbian Cultures in America,* ed. Ellen Lewin (Boston: Beacon Press, 1996), 15–39.

29. Bertha Van Hoosen, "Manuscript of Autobiography," 403, Bertha Van Hoosen Papers, Box 3, folder 1, Bentley Historical Library, University of Michigan, Ann Arbor.

30. Gidlow journal, 13, 25 January, 30 August 1928, Elsa Gidlow Collection, Box 1, Gay and Lesbian Historical Society of Northern California, San Francisco. The poems that Gidlow wrote about Chung include "Chinese Lotus," "For a Gifted Lady, Often Masked," "Miracle," and "Surgeon's Hands," Gidlow Collection, Box 11.

31. Gidlow, *Elsa,* 208.

32. Gidlow journal, 28 August 1928.

33. Ibid., 30 August 1928.

34. Ibid., 12 May 1931.

35. Ibid., 28 May 1931.

36. Ibid.

37. Ibid., 4 July 1931.

38. Ibid., 13 August 1931.

39. Ibid., 10 November 1928.

40. Ibid., 4, 13 July 1931

41. Gidlow wrote and published various versions of this poem. The earliest typed version was entitled, "An Exercise in Free Verse, Dashed off for Doctor Margaret Chung," 22 September 1927, Gidlow Collection, Box 11.

42. Henry Yu, "Mixing Bodies and Cultures: The Meaning of America's Fascination with Sex Between 'Orientals' and 'Whites,'" in *Sex, Love, Race: Crossing Boundaries in North American History,* ed. Martha Hodes (New York: New York University Press, 1999), 444–65, quotation on 446–47. Although Yu's article focuses on the racial ideas of social scientists, his findings also reflect changes in popular culture.

43. Ibid., 447.

44. Gidlow journal, 10 November 1928.

45. Shirley Radke, "We Must Be Active Americans," *Christian Science Monitor* (3 October 1942).

46. Yung, *Unbound Feet,* 136.

47. Lucile Chung, interview by author, Vista, California, 28 January 1996.

48. Although antimiscegenation laws in California forbade interracial marriage, some local officials overlooked the state laws. Some couples also traveled to states that allowed interracial

unions. See Karen Isaksen Leonard, *Making Ethnic Choices: California's Punjabi Mexican Americans* (Philadelphia: Temple University Press, 1992).

49. Michael Freedland, *Sophie: The Sophie Tucker Story* (London: Woburn, 1978), 211.

50. Mariko Tse, "'Made in America': Project for East West Players and CBS," 12 June 1979, Research Project for East West Players on Chinese in Southern California, in possession of author.

51. Jeong, interview.

52. Elaine Tyler May, *Homeward Bound: American Families in the Cold War Era* (New York: Basic, 1988), 42.

53. Ibid.

54. Sophie Tucker, *Some of These Days* (1945), 58.

55. Yung, *Unbound Feet,* 200–201.

56. In her study of female athletes, Susan K. Cahn argues that women who threaten the gender hierarchy by excelling in traditionally masculine activities are pressured to emphasize their femininity. Susan K. Cahn, *Coming on Strong: Gender and Sexuality in Twentieth-Century Women's Sport* (New York: Free Press, 1994).

57. Chung described their daily interaction in a series of letters to Tucker. See Chung to Tucker, 4, 5 January 1944, Tucker Scrapbooks, 10,950.

58. Untitled clipping, *San Francisco Call-Bulletin,* 17 November 1943, Chung Scrapbook.

59. Barbara Bancroft, "Creating Homes for Real Living: Dr. Chung's Decorative Furnishings Express Her," newspaper clipping provided by Betsy Bingham Davis.

60. Chung to Tucker, 13, 14, 17, 19 January 1945, Tucker Scrapbooks, 10,955. These notes were most likely attached to a series of birthday presents.

61. Chung to Tucker, [25 December] 1947, Tucker Scrapbooks, 10,980.

62. Chung to Tucker, 17 January 1945.

63. [Chung] to Tucker, n.d., Tucker Scrapbooks, 10,950.

64. I thank Pamela Paxton for pointing out the ethnic and religious implications of Ruth's decision to follow Naomi.

65. See Martha Vicinus, "Distance and Desire: English Boarding School Friendships, 1870–1920," in *Hidden from History,* 212–29, quotation on 224.

66. Freedman, "'Burning of Letters Continues,'" 185.

67. The use of religious and maternal language to express romantic longing represents a different strategy than the concept of "private lesbianism" suggested by Kennedy. She has argued for the possibility of women who "considered themselves lesbians but were completely private . . . about their erotic love for women." In contrast, Chung may not have embraced a lesbian identity, even in private, but instead fashioned alternative means to express her romantic desire for women. See Kennedy, "'But we would never talk about it.'"

68. Karen Garling Sickel, interview by author, Palo Alto, California, 17 September 1996.

69. Yu's study of interracial sexuality ("Mixing Bodies and Cultures") influenced my effort to contextualize historically the conception of race. See also Colleen Fong and Judy Yung, "In Search of the Right Spouse: Interracial Marriage among Chinese and Japanese Americans," *Amerasia Journal* 21, no. 3 (1995): 77–98. For an overview of social science literature on interracial marriage, most of which focused on heterosexual relationships during the post-World War II and post-1965 eras, see Timothy P. Fong, *The Contemporary Asian American Experience: Beyond the Model Minority* (Upper Saddle River, N.J.: Prentice Hall, 1998), 224–33.

70. Chung to Tucker, 10 April 1955, Tucker Scrapbooks, 15,850.

71. Karen Brodkin, *How Jews Became White Folks and What That Says about Race in America* (New Brunswick, N.J.: Rutgers University Press, 1998); and Matthew Frye Jacobson, *Whiteness of a Different Color: European Immigrants and the Alchemy of Race* (Cambridge, Mass.: Harvard University Press, 1998).

72. Yu, "Mixing Bodies and Cultures," 447.

73. Because Chung was of Chinese ancestry, she was less likely to be perceived as "white" compared to individuals of European ancestry.

74. Neil Okrent, "Right Place Wong Time," *Los Angeles Magazine* (May 1990), 84.

75. Faderman, *Odd Girls,* 181. For histories of the San Francisco gay and lesbian communities, see Stryker and Buskirk, *Gay by the Bay,* 22–27; and Faderman, *Odd Girls,* 107, 175–87.

76. Russell Leong, "Home Bodies and the Body Politic," in *Asian American Sexualities,* 1–20, quotation on 11.

77. Kitty Tsui, "Chinatown Talking Story," in *The Words of a Woman Who Breathes Fire* (Iowa City, Iowa: Spinsters Ink, 1983). Tsui is writing a historical novel based on her grandmother's experiences. Kitty Tsui, "*Bak Sze,* White Snake," in *Asian American Sexualities,* 223–26, quotation on 223.

16

Intraethnic Conflict and the
Bracero Program during World War II

MATTHEW GARCÍA

nitiated in response to acute labor shortages in agriculture during World War II, the *bracero* program quickly developed into a cornerstone of citrus associations' new system of employment. In 1942 Mexico and the United States signed an agreement that brought thousands of temporary Mexican workers to harvest crops on farms throughout the West and Midwest. Although the governments planned to terminate the program once potential workers returned from the war front, U.S. agribusiness acquired an addiction for the low-cost foreign laborers. By the passage of a series of public laws, agribusiness lobbyists extended the contract system through 1964.[1]

The agreement had a particularly significant impact on agricultural labor in California. Although totals of contract workers varied according to the season and crop, California growers consistently attracted the highest number of *braceros* of all the states participating in the program. For example, among the twenty-four states involved between 1943 and 1947, California drew an average of 54 percent of the total *braceros* that came to the United States.[2] These numbers continued to grow in the postwar period, increasing to 456,000 by 1957, well above the wartime high of 76,184 in 1943. During the 1950s, Mexican nationals represented better than 10 percent of the total seasonal workers hired, but these figures masked many California growers' dependence on *bracero* labor. According to one contemporary observer, "in working certain crops in California . . . braceros represented more than 75 percent of the labor force."[3] *Citrograph* articles and studies of the citrus industry bear this out. "Of 4,203 brought into the country in 1942," a Berkeley researcher observed, "around 1,000 were transferred from sugar beet fields to pick oranges and lemons in the Fillmore (Ventura County), Whittier, Redlands, and Los Angeles districts." *Citrograph* authors confirmed the importance of the program to the industry, reporting that Mexican nationals performed 60 percent of all picking in 1945. By 1946, *braceros* constituted around 13,000 of the workforce in California citrus groves, or 80 percent of all pickers.[4]

According to the bilateral agreement, employers guaranteed Mexican nationals a wage of 30 cents per hour and were required to pay at or above the standard wage in a given region, a restriction adopted to prevent the replacement of local workers. In practice, *braceros* routinely earned less than what their contracts promised, but more than what they received for the same work in Mexico. For example, in the citrus orchards of Cucamonga, the prevailing wage averaged 70 cents per hour during the war years. By 1958, the hourly wage for Mexican American workers rose slightly to between 80 cents and $1, depending on the season, but employers often paid *braceros* between 10 and 15 cents less than their local coworkers. By the end of the season, local workers earned an average weekly gross income of $43.20 compared with $38.40 for *braceros*. Interviews with twenty-five *braceros* conducted by Claremont Graduate School student Daniel Martínez during the mid-1950s revealed that Mexican nationals worked at a piece rate instead of an hourly rate and did not earn the standard wages for local employees until late in the season. With deductions for room and board included, *braceros* stood to earn a net total of $20.10 per week in 1940. Although low by U.S. standards, earnings compared favorably to the average annual income of the typical worker in Mexico. During the same year, a Mexican laborer earned approximately 340 pesos per year, which amounted to roughly $40. Given the wide discrepancy between wages in Mexico and the United States, Mexican nationals rarely complained of the exploitative conditions on California farms.[5]

In spite of better wages in the United States, *braceros* incurred many expenses that cut substantially into their profits. In particular, Mexican nationals resented the bribes or *mordida* (literally meaning "bite") many had to pay Mexican officials to be considered for the program. Although illegal under the formal agreement, standard practice dictated that potential *braceros* render between 150 and 300 pesos to agents in Mexico to initiate the process. Once they arrived, Mexican nationals had to purchase clothing and equipment and pay rent with the more expensive U.S. currency. *Braceros* living in the Cucamonga camp, for example, paid $12.50 per week for room and board, and had approximately 10 percent of their earnings deducted from each paycheck for nonoccupational insurance negotiated for them by the Mexican government. At the conclusion of their contracts, *braceros* could recoup some of this money, though the Mexican government required them to return to Mexico to collect their checks.[6]

Many *braceros* supported their families back in Mexico at a much lower cost than local Mexican American workers. During World War II, a Mexican national could support his entire family in Mexico with as little as $10 a month. Conversely, monthly expenditures for local Mexican Americans averaged $20 for rent, $13 for utilities, $10 for transportation, $10 for clothing, $10 for leisure time, $5 for medical care, and $10 for miscellaneous items. Moreover, increases in food prices during World War II pushed the monthly cost of maintaining a family of seven children from $40 at the beginning of the war to $80 by its end. The exorbitant cost of living also provided added incentive for married Mexican women to break with tradition and enter the workforce. Furthermore, Mexican nationals enjoyed the security of a guaranteed full-time job under the agreement while Mexican American workers could be laid off at a moment's notice.[7]

Wage differentials and unequal competition for jobs resulted in strong feelings of resentment toward *braceros* among Mexican American men. Interviewing local men from the Cucamonga barrio "Northtown" in 1957, Daniel Martínez found that a majority "strongly opposed the bracero program and any additional program of [its] type." Martínez observed, "[Mexican American men] felt that the braceros took jobs away from them, as well as lowered wages in the area, or at least kept them at the same level year after year."[8] Donato Bustos described the intraethnic tension, recalling that "[Mexican American men] didn't like us because we came to take the jobs away from them." Working alongside *braceros* in the La Verne orange groves, Frank Hernández recalled that Mexican Americans and Mexican nationals occasionally "tangled" over the best picking assignments and methods of picking. "Braceros were difficult," remembered Hernández, "because they picked it their way [and] they were not careful." He added, "Braceros would get a bike and start picking before the sun came up." Angry Mexican American pickers objected to such behavior since early-rising *braceros* got to the highest-yielding trees first and made locals look lazy. Similarly, Julia Salazar commented that her husband, Roman, a foreman for the College Heights Lemon Association, routinely settled conflicts between Mexican Americans and *braceros* in the groves. "Once in awhile," Salazar recalled, "Roman would say that [a bracero] would get irritated because the one from here [Mexican American] would be telling him that he was [picking] wrong." Occasionally, fights erupted into violent confrontations. "Sometimes [braceros] would pull out knives!" Salazar recalled. She added, "my brother-in-law, Cuco, told Roman that one time [a *bracero*] even chased him with a knife because he was backing the one from here [a Mexican American]."[9]

Former *bracero* Donato Bustos, however, objected to characterizations of Mexican contract workers as a burden on the Mexican American community. "We made the wages go up," Bustos asserted, "because when I started in Redlands picking oranges, they paid us 6 cents a box." Unable to pay their rent, Bustos and his fellow *braceros* initiated a strike to improve wages for all workers in the groves. He recalled:

> I picked twenty-eight boxes the first day [and] I couldn't pay my rent! And then, pretty soon we started a strike. . . . One day we didn't want to pick, they took us to the grove and we didn't pick. We went out of the grove and told the other guys [Mexican Americans] to go out to raise the price. They [said they] didn't want to walk out because of the Depression and they wouldn't give us our jobs [back] and this and that. . . . So, we told the driver to take us to the camp and he [a Mexican American] didn't want to. So we walked all day to the camp.[10]

Despite the lack of solidarity among Mexican Americans and Mexican nationals, the *bracero* strike forced the local growers association to boost the rate per box to 14 cents by the end of the 1943 navel season. Although such a strike made some employers question the use of potentially militant *braceros,* for the most part, wage differentials between Mexican nationals and locals encouraged many growers to continue to support the program.[11]

Bustos also claimed that Mexican Americans, not *braceros,* initiated most intraethnic conflict between the two groups. "[Mexican Americans] didn't like [*braceros*] because they were outsiders," he recalled. "Braceros usually went out in a group," Bustos added, "because otherwise . . . sometimes they beat us."[12] The doctor for the Cucamonga and San Antonio *bracero* camps, Walter W. Wood, reported that during the height of the program, he treated from eight to ten *braceros* weekly for injuries received in fights with locals. Work conditions informed much of the intraethnic conflict; however, contemporary observers also noted another source of tension: competition for Mexican American female companions in the local *colonias*. Citing the report of local judge William B. Hutton, Daniel Martínez summarized, "during the period from 1944 to 1946 eight to twelve men, braceros and locals, appeared before the Cucamonga District Court every Monday morning on knifing or shooting charges resulting from friction over local girls or employment."[13] This conflict became particularly acute after World War II when Mexican American male populations increased with the return of soldiers.

Conditions of life and labor in the *colonia* and the structure of the *bracero* program also contributed to the tension. The fluidity of *braceros'* lives, traveling back and forth between Mexico and the United States, raised Mexican American suspicions about the intentions of Mexican nationals. For example, Alfonsa Bustos commented that initially her family did not like her dating Donato because, as she explained, "they thought he was going to take me to Mexico." Alfonsa put their fears to rest by informing Donato that she would not live in Mexico under any circumstances. Others worried that Mexican nationals courted Mexican American women for sexual gratification and casual relationships that lasted only as long as their contracts. For example, the Mexican and U.S. governments inadvertently intervened in many interpersonal relationships when the program temporarily withdrew Mexican nationals at the end of World War II. Although lacking a precise number, Martínez reported, "many of these local girls were left with children," a situation, he claimed, outraged their families and confirmed Mexican American misgivings about *braceros*.[14]

Many Mexican American parents objected to marriages between Mexican nationals and their Mexican American daughters because they believed that *braceros* entered into such unions for the sole purpose of attaining U.S. citizenship. "Some [Mexican American women] would not be so lucky. They would find out that [their *bracero* husbands] were married in Mexico and all [*braceros*] wanted was to get their visas or whatever."[15] Martínez found similar attitudes among seven Mexican American women who married or had lived with Mexican contract workers in Cucamonga's Northtown barrio. "All seven," he reported, "shared the opinion that the braceros were just opportunists seeking a way to remain in the United States and marriage was the easiest way for them to gain this end." One woman who failed to give her name reported that she had had three children with a *bracero* as his common law wife. Despite having eventually married, the couple was separated when the U.S. government deported her husband once he finished his contract. She then spent her life savings on lawyers to prove that they had, in fact, married and that he should be allowed to return to the United States. After two months of living with the family, her husband left them for a high-paying job in downtown Los Angeles. Although she attained a court order requiring him to pay child support, at the time of the interview the woman had not received any money from her estranged husband for over six months.[16]

Selling work clothes to *braceros* for the local retailer Miller's Outpost and hosting weekend dances at local ballrooms during the 1950s, Candelario Mendoza witnessed exchanges between Mexican contract workers and Mexican American women. He explained: "[Brace-

ros] would talk to some of the chavalas (young Mexican American women) that they used to see around the barrio here, and I think that was part of the animosity. The fact that they were wooing some of the available gals—perhaps already involved with somebody else or someone was looking at them—and these guys [*braceros*] were pretty glib."[17]

According to Mendoza, Mexican American men resented Mexican nationals since *braceros* performed their "verbal love-making" in Spanish, an ability that many acculturated locals no longer possessed. Julia Salazar concurred, recalling "at dances, [Mexican American men and *braceros*] used to fight." Many conflicts began when *braceros* approached wives and girlfriends of Mexican American men for a whirl on the dance floor. "Some of the men from here don't like just anyone to go get [their] wife and pull her out to dance," Salazar commented. She added, "[*braceros*] thought anybody could dance, you know, with anybody here." For Salazar and other married local women, "braceros were too forward; they thought they were a gift to women from god!"[18]

Often, however, romance between *braceros* and Mexican American women did not result in the tragic endings feared by parents of Mexican American youth. Julia Salazar and Candelario Mendoza recalled a number of these marriages that survived the initial culture shock and stood the test of time. Donato Bustos, for example, respected the wishes of his fiancée, Alfonsa, to remain in the United States, and "skipped" his contract to start a new life. Soon after their wedding, the Bustos rented a house for Alfonsa's entire family. Eventually, the couple purchased a house in the La Verne barrio where they have lived since 1945.

The relative autonomy of a new generation of Mexican American women provided them the freedom to make their own decisions about whom they should and should not date. When asked whether women from the barrios courted *braceros,* Mendoza commented "oh yeah . . . I think love supersedes almost any obstacles!"[19] Donato Bustos concurred, recalling that some wives of servicemen began dating *braceros* in their husband's absence. "When they were left alone," he recalled, "they got with *braceros.*"[20] As Douglas Monroy has argued, employment "facilitated greater freedom of activity and more assertiveness in the family for Mexicanas." Similarly, Vicki Ruiz and Mary Odem have demonstrated how employment provided Mexican American women the means and confidence to participate in an expanding consumer culture that included public entertainment.[21]

Daniel Martínez observed that such intraethnic/intercultural courtship came at a high price, remarking that often, women who dated or married Mexican nationals "were ostracized by the community as well as by their families." Women with children who had been abandoned by *braceros* received particularly harsh treatment at the hands of local residents. In need of a job to support their families, some of these women sought employment as prostitutes in bars designated for Mexican nationals. Bar owners took advantage of their situation, for as one proprietor explained, "Since they have become outcasts in the community for associating with *braceros,* this is the only type of work they can find." The bar owner tried to justify his actions, explaining that "the *braceros* would look for [women] anyway so why not provide them with the companions in a place where they could not get into trouble with the locals and at the same time be protected from being 'rolled' (robbed and beaten while under the influence of alcohol)?" The proprietor saw his business as a service to "the nicer girls from the community" since *braceros* would not be as inclined to seek them out for dates when they had plenty of opportunities to meet "outcasts" in the bar. The prevalence of prostitution within these drinking establishments, however, influenced the attitudes of many locals who questioned the morality of any Mexican American women seen publicly with a Mexican national.[22]

In spite of attempts to keep locals and Mexican nationals separate, conflicts often came to a head in the vice-ridden bar districts located in areas adjacent to *bracero* camps and Mexican American *colonias*. In Cucamonga's Northtown, for example, business from young, local men, some Mexican American women, and Mexican nationals supported six bars that provided a lively nightlife on the weekends.[23] Captain Mayer of the San Bernardino County Sheriff's Department and Cucamonga constable Oscar Raven reported a consistent escalation of crime and violence in the area since World War II, attributing most of the problems to unemployment, prostitution, and juvenile delinquency. Neither official, however, felt inclined to remedy the situation, since both believed "there is very little that can be done until the residents themselves try to do something about it." Quite often, law enforcement authorities were slow to respond to conflicts due to their distance from these outlying areas and a pervasive attitude of apathy and neglect. Cucamonga's Judge Hutton reflected the true feelings of many local officials when he explained, "[I] personally do not think that the residents of Northtown know the meaning of the word morals; otherwise they would try to clean up their own mess." Managers and doctors in charge of *bracero* camps occasionally exhibited similar prejudices and were equally disinclined to intervene during moments of social conflict. For example, Doctor Baro, a physician serving a camp in Irwindale, allegedly told Daniel Martínez that he believed very little could be done to solve the problems associated with Mexican nationals since "all the braceros have an I.Q. of a one year old."[24]

Intraethnic tension between Mexican Americans and Mexican nationals reached a boiling point on April 19, 1952, when four Mexican American youths murdered Ricardo Mancilla Gómez, a *bracero* employed in the Cucamonga area. The tragic death of the twenty-two-year-old Gómez typified a season of growing violence in which one other Mexican national, Magdaleno Cornejo, had been killed and several others beaten. Reported as an "assassination" in the Pomona Valley newspaper *El Espectador,* the "cold blooded" killing disturbed Ignacio "Nacho" López, a local defender of Mexican American civil rights and co-owner of the Spanish-language weekly. Lamenting that Gómez's death had come "at the hands of brothers of the same race," López editorialized that if such murders continued, "El México de Afuera" (México of the Exterior) will exterminate the "México de Adentro" (México of the Interior). He blamed the mistreatment of *braceros* (whom he called "ambassadors in overalls") on the moral deprivation of young Mexican American *valientes* (bullies) corrupted by ignorance, vice, and the spiritual decay of a country living in the shadow of the atomic bomb attacks on Hiroshima and Nagasaki, Japan. According to López, a government capable of killing millions with a single bomb shared some of the responsibility for creating "a morbid psychosis in society at large."[25]

Reports that Gómez's underage assailants—Manuel Fierro, Frank Mendoza, Felix Montoya, and Sabiel Mayo—had been smoking marijuana and drinking at the Cucamonga cantina "La Cita" re-ignited moral panic over juvenile delinquency among minority youth.

Sharing the concerns of a generation of educated Mexican Americans who came of age just prior to World War II, López worried that many young Mexican men had forsaken education for a lifestyle of "hoodlumism." During the 1940s, López became an outspoken critic of zoot-suiters whom he regarded as "pachuco miscreants" that inspired prejudicial attitudes among Anglos toward all Mexican Americans.[26] Yet, unlike the Los Angeles County Sheriff's Department who attributed the problem of Mexican American juvenile delinquency to the "inherent vicious[ness]" of all Mexicans, López believed that the roots of "El Pachuquismo" were "deeply entrenched in the economic and social discrimination practices inflicted on minorities by the dominant groups of our nation." Consequently, although Mexican American critics like López blamed youth for the violence against *braceros,* they identified the larger societal problems of racism and warfare rather than the biological proclivities of the Mexican race as the origin of such delinquency.[27]

In response to the murder, Mexican consuls Salvador Duhart of Los Angeles and Roberto Urrea of San Bernardino immediately withdrew 178 Mexican contract workers from Cucamonga and announced the suspension of the *bracero* programs throughout the Pomona Valley. Acknowledging that the murder was not an isolated incident but rather part of a larger trend, Duhart expressed outrage at the "repeated abuses against our braceros that have been the motive [for the suspension]." Deliveries of workers, they concluded, would not resume until all possible measures had been taken to correct the problem of violence against Mexican nationals.[28] In all, Mexico recalled over 500 contract workers from the Southern California Farmers Association, the primary distributor of *braceros* in the Pomona Valley. Many *braceros* expressed their support of the consulate's decision in a letter signed by 123 coworkers of Ricardo Gómez asking for the immediate termination of their contracts.[29]

The Mexican government's actions precipitated a community-wide conversation held at the local elementary school that revealed many of the social and economic tensions created by the *bracero* program. Not surprisingly, local ranchers expressed their disappointment over the loss of Mexican contract laborers and promised to exercise their political influence to bring about the reinstatement of the program for the Pomona Valley. Mexican Americans were less unified in their response to Mexico's actions since defining "the community interest" had become a complicated matter in the ten years leading up to the crisis. The Southern California Farmers Association encouraged the marginalization of Mexican nationals by placing work camps on the outskirts of towns near Mexican American *colonias.* Some Mexican American merchants and business owners took advantage of this arrangement by setting up shops and establishing bars that catered mainly to the Mexican contract workers. Although *bracero* patronage benefited a few middle-class Mexican *comerciantes,* the working-class majority of Mexican Americans opposed the program on the grounds that the presence of Mexican nationals created unfair competition in the workplace and inspired violence and vice in their community.[30]

Siding with the majority, López became the mouthpiece for aggrieved Cucamonga residents. Affixing blame to contracting agents, government officials, and local bar owners for the crisis, López also reported that the meeting produced a "plan of action" that prescribed a tentative solution to the intraethnic violence. A majority of the 150 participants expressed a desire for camp managers and law enforcement officials to enforce the separation of young Mexican American men and *braceros* upon the return of Mexican nationals. In spite of strong objections to the program, López conceded its eventual reinstatement given the significant political influence of ranchers. Instead, López saved his harshest criticism for profit-driven bar owners who, he explained, "have let loose a plague on the good citizens of Cucamonga." Alarmed by escalating violence in the bar districts of Northtown, López and other meeting participants called for a unified community movement to clean up Cucamonga by making it more difficult for irresponsible proprietors to acquire liquor licenses. López argued that only pressure from concerned citizens could alter the ethics of bar owners whom he called "ostriches hiding their heads in the corrupt sand."[31]

By early August 1952, growers successfully petitioned for the return of the *braceros* to the Pomona Valley. Between April and August, López and local leaders joined together to produce a list of seven recommendations that encompassed the complete concerns of Northtown residents. In his weekly column "Marginal," López offered the following suggestions to returning Mexican nationals: they should dedicate themselves completely to their work; they should avoid, as much as possible, bar fights; they should respect the private property and dignity of locals; they should avoid personal friction that could lead to tragedy; they should establish cordial relations with local families and all their members; they should always demand employment conditions and salaries equal to that of domestic workers; and they should avoid displacing local workers in their jobs. Following up on his initial concerns of juvenile delinquency, López also issued a separate warning to parents and young people about the spread of alcoholism among youth in Cucamonga.

The list went beyond the blame game previously played by López and local leaders to confront the larger social and economic problems associated with the *bracero* program. In particular the last two suggestions addressed the issue of job competition and the program's negative impact on wages and job security for local Mexican Americans. López, despite his middle-class background, shared the concerns of working-class Mexican Americans. He supported the AFL and CIO's opposition to the bilateral agreement and questioned why Mexico, with its rich agricultural lands, could not develop a program to sustain rural life in the Mexican countryside. Anticipating observations made by current scholars on the subject, López further argued that the *bracero* program prompted "illegal immigration" by creating an "obsession" among all Mexicans to "cross the Rio Bravo" for work.[32] In another editorial he likened the conflict of the "Mexican brothers" (*braceros* and Mexican Americans) to the biblical story of Cain and Abel. Coming down squarely on the side of local laborers, López pointedly argued, "field workers of this country must have primacy over those other elements—even in the sad case when these elements are of our same race and language."[33]

Aimed at Mexican nationals, López's recommendations sought to curb *bracero* behavior while marking the domain of Mexican Americans, particularly the social spaces occupied by men. The language of López's editorials positioned Mexican nationals as eternal outsiders whose place in society could be accepted only after their acquiescence to rights and privileges that belong first and foremost to Mexican Americans. Moreover, requests for *braceros* to respect the dignity, personal property, and families of locals allude to the *braceros'* marginality. Given that most physical assaults had been perpetrated against, not by *braceros,* and that theft did not constitute a major source of tension between the two groups, such vague references left much room for interpretation. For example, one could speculate that the coded message communicated to Mexican nationals by López meant that Mexican American men assumed ownership and privileges over "their" women just as they assumed access to "their" jobs. Furthermore, his recommendation that *braceros* "dedicate themselves completely to their work" conveyed the hope that Mexican nationals would remain singularly focused on their jobs and not seek diversions with local women in *colonia* bars and pool halls, and at public dances.

Ultimately, community efforts to revise the *bracero* program and clean up vice districts garnered only symbolic reforms from local law enforcement officials and ranchers. In the wake of the Gómez tragedy, Cucamonga sheriff Charles Jones promised to reduce disorder in Northtown, while the contracting agency, the Agricultural Association of Southern California, assigned a new camp director, Ray Orton, to oversee improvements and foster better public relations with the community. Orton addressed Mexican American concerns that *braceros* would be used to replace local workers by stating, "in the first place it is prohibited by the terms of the signed agreement, and in the second, this was not the intention of local ranchers." Nevertheless, many Cucamonga residents interviewed by Daniel Martínez in 1957 continued to cite wage differences between Mexican nationals and local workers and blamed the *bracero* program for the loss of jobs and a steady decline in pay.[34] Moreover, the problems of violence continued to simmer in bars and pool halls throughout the region. In 1957, for example, a group of Mexican American men stripped and robbed *bracero* Pedro Carrillo in Pomona after offering him a ride back to his camp located in Montclair. Three years later, another bar fight in Cucamonga between three Mexican American men and a Mexican national resulted in the murder of *bracero* José Gómez Trejo.[35] Although these occasional robberies, beatings, and killings of *braceros* hardly constituted a pattern, such incidents are indicative of simmering resentments and tensions as the program entered its third decade of operation.

The citrus growers' postwar system of employment received a fatal blow on December 31, 1964, when civil rights advocates and labor organizations turned public opinion strongly against the *bracero* program and forced Congress to formally end Mexican contract labor in the United States. By that time, however, growers had discovered a new source of labor impervious to fluctuations in international relations: undocumented Mexican labor. As López had observed in 1952, the *bracero* program contributed to the expansion of immigration flows from Mexico during the postwar period. Between 1940 and 1943, the U.S. Immigration and Naturalization Service (INS) reported apprehending an annual average of 7,023 undocumented migrants; but that number rose rapidly to 29,176 in 1944. Three years later, apprehensions reached nearly 200,000, prompting INS officials to declare a war on immigration from Mexico in the form of "Operation Wetback."[36] In spite of aggressive policing at the border and neighborhood sweeps in

Mexican American neighborhoods, undocumented immigrants continued to come to the United States enticed by agribusiness employers. According to labor activist and immigration scholar Ernesto Galarza, growers regarded *indocumentados* not only as an alternative source of labor to *braceros* but also as more skilled workers than their fellow Mexican nationals. Galarza explained:

> Braceros found the Wetbacks as anxious to please as they were willing to endure. From among them the employer selected the more able workers for tasks requiring skill, such as irrigating and truck driving. They became differentiated from the common run of illegals, serving in specialized operations and becoming *stable, regular* employees. The employer would make unusual efforts to keep them and to arrange for their return if by chance they were picked up by the Border Patrol. (emphasis added)[37]

Referred to as "specials" by employers, these undocumented laborers rose above the status of *bracero* or "stoop laborer" to become essential members of the agricultural labor force. Daniel Martínez noted this same trend in the Pomona Valley when he discovered that "many farmers preferred 'wetbacks' to locals *or* braceros mainly because the wetbacks worked twice as hard for half the pay."[38]

Indocumentados presented agricultural employers with several advantages over *braceros*. Unlike Mexican contract workers whose limited work certifications required them to be replaced at regular intervals, undocumented workers could remain in their positions as long as employers wished them to stay. The longer job tenure allowed *indocumentados* to acquire skills that elevated them above the average farmworker and made them indispensable to many ranchers. Indeed, such advantages inspired many *braceros* simply to "skip" their contracts and become undocumented workers.[39]

Equally important, the ideology and practice of citizenship pursued by labor and civil rights group inadvertently laid the foundations for the post-*bracero* labor system. Civil rights leaders like Ignacio López and labor organizations like the AFL and CIO forged a unified front against the Mexican contract system by calling for rights and privileges for citizens of the United States. Although demands for citizenship rights helped end the *bracero* program, they also drew the line of membership around a national community that accentuated the differences between members and nonmembers. This line of inclusion/exclusion cut at right angles against potential class and ethnic solidarity, and ultimately helped increase the vulnerability of those at the bottom of the community: initially *braceros,* and eventually undocumented workers. Uneven economic development between Mexico and the United States and the lack of entitlements for noncitizen workers under the welfare state denied *indocumentados* a "safety net" and forced many to seek low-paid agricultural jobs typically reserved for *braceros* and resident Mexican workers. Furthermore, in spite of achieving skills that garnered pay raises for citizen workers, the political vulnerability of undocumented laborers (for example, fear of deportation) prevented them from either petitioning for state regulation or pursuing collective bargaining with their employers. Presented with few alternatives, undocumented workers toiled silently, remaining active in the U.S. workforce at high levels of productivity in order to survive.[40]

Notes

1. Manuel García y Griego, "The Importation of Mexican Contract Laborers to the United States, 1942–1964." In *Between Two Worlds: Mexican Immigrants in the United States,* edited by David Gutierrez (Wilmington, Del.: Jaguar/SR Books, 1996), 45–85; Ernesto Galarza, *Merchants of Labor: The Mexican Bracero Story* (Charlotte, N.C.: McNally and Loftin, 1964).

2. Report of the President's Commission of Migratory Labor, *Migratory Labor in American Agriculture* (Washington, D.C.: U.S. Government Printing Office, 1951), 226; and Wayne D. Rasmussen, *A History of the Emergency Farm Labor Program, 1943–1947,* U.S. Department of Agriculture, Bureau of Agriculture Economics (Washington, D.C.: Government Printing Office, 1951), 200–204, as cited in Daniel Martínez Jr., "The Impact of the Bracero Program on a Southern California Mexican-American Community: A Field Study of Cucamonga, California" (M.A. thesis, The Claremont Graduate School, 1958), 17.

3. Daniel Martínez, "The Impact of the Bracero Program," 24.

4. Paul Garland Williamson, "Labor in the California Citrus Industry" (M.A. thesis, University of California, Berkeley, 1946), 51–52; "Mexican National Program to Continue," The Sunkist Courier Department, *California Citrograph* (February 1946): 114.

5. Daniel Martínez, "The Impact of the Bracero Program," 34–35, 49.

6. Interview with Donato and Alfonsa Bustos, interview by Margo McBane, December 23, 1994; Daniel Martínez, "The Impact of the Bracero Program," 35. Many men like Donato Bustos lost this money when they "skipped" their contracts.

7. Daniel Martínez, "The Impact of the Bracero Program," 36–37.

8. Ibid., 44.

9. Bustos interview; Interview with Julia Salazar, interview by Ginger Elliot, February 17, 1997, at Claremont Heritage Foundation, Claremont, Calif.; Interview with Frank Hernández, interview by Margo McBane, December 18, 1994, La Verne Mutual Orange Distributors Citrus Packinghouse Oral History Project, City Hall, La Verne, Calif.

10. Bustos interview.

11. Most *bracero* strikes were over work camp conditions, especially the poor quality of food, not wages. See Mario T. García, *Mexican Americans: Leadership, Ideology, and Identity, 1930–1960* (New Haven: Yale University Press, 1989), 95, and Bustos interview. For evidence of wage differentials between Mexican Americans and *braceros* in California agricultural labor, see Daniel Martínez, "The Impact of the Bracero Program," 49; and Robert J. Thomas, *Citizenship, Gender, and Work: Social Organization of Industrial Agriculture* (Berkeley: University of California Press, 1985), 62–73.

12. Bustos interview.

13. Daniel Martínez, "The Impact of the Bracero Program," 55, 67.

14. Ibid., 55.

15. Salazar interview.

16. Although *braceros* had camps, they were permitted to live outside these prescribed areas if they could find a host or provide for themselves. Bustos interview.

17. Interview with Candelario Mendoza, interview by author, May 6, 1994; February 17, 1995; March 13, 1996; April 22, 1998, transcript at Special Collections, Pomona Public Library. This interview was conducted on April 22, 1998.

18. Salazar interview.

19. Mendoza interview. Salazar also acknowledged that some of her coworkers and barrio neighbors dated and married *braceros.*

20. Bustos interview.

21. Douglas Monroy, "An Essay on Understanding the Work Experiences of Mexicans in Southern California, 1900–1939." *Aztlán* 12 (Spring 1981): 70; Vicki Ruiz, *From Out of the Shadows: Mexican Women in Twentieth-Century America* (New York: Oxford University Press, 1998), 63. See also Mary

E. Odem, "Teenage Girls, Sexuality, and Working-Class Parents in Early Twentieth-Century California." In *Generations of Youth: Youth Cultures and History in Twentieth-Century America,* edited by Joe Austin and Michael Nevin Willard (New York: New York University Press, 1998).

22. Daniel Martínez, "The Impact of the Bracero Program," 56–57. Discussing the problem of prostitution with one bar owner in the Cucamonga's Northtown, Martínez reported: "The proprietor was asked what type of woman has been hired at his bar and at the other bars. He said that some of them are women who were left behind by *braceros* who promised to marry them. Because most of them have children to support, they have to find some type of employment. Since they have become outcasts in the community for associating with *braceros,* this is the only type of work they can find."

23. Mendoza interview, April 22, 1998.

24. Daniel Martínez, "The Impact of the Bracero Program," 60–61, 70.

25. *El Espectador* (Pomona Valley), June 22, 1952.

26. Ignacio López, "Grist for the Mills of the Axis," *El Espectador,* June 11, 1943, reprinted in Ignacio López's FBI file, No. 100–200298, part 1.

27. Ibid. For an example of another Mexican American critic of juvenile delinquency, see Manual Ruiz Jr. Papers. The career of Manual Ruiz Jr. is discussed in Eduardo Obregón Pagán, "Sleepy Lagoon: The Politics of Youth and Race in Wartime Los Angeles, 1940–1945" (Ph.D. diss., Princeton Universtiy, 1996).

28. *El Espectador,* June 22, 1952, 1.

29. *El Espectador,* May 2, 1952, 1.

30. *El Espectador,* May 9, 1952, 1, 2, 7; Daniel Martínez, "The Impact of the Bracero Program," 73. Martínez reported, "The 200 residents of Northtown interviewed, with the exception of the businessmen, all believe that their problems have been aggravated by the presence of the Braceros." He concluded, "They feel very strongly against the Bracero Programs and if a solution is not found soon, additional complications will result."

31. *El Espectador,* May 9, 1952, 7. López said of local growers: "All these men, will use their political prestige and force for the general benefit of the entire community."

32. *El Espectador,* June 22, 1952. For recent interpretations of the connections between the *bracero* program and undocumented immigration, see García y Griego, "The Importation of Mexican Contract Laborers," 73–75; and David Gutiérrez, *Walls and Mirrors: Mexican Americans, Mexican Immigrants, and the Politics of Ethnicity* (Berkeley: University of California Press, 1995), 142. Although López only mentioned the AFL, the CIO also opposed the *bracero* program. See testimony of Elizabeth Sasuly, U.S. Congress, Senate Committee on Agriculture and Forestry, *Hearings on Farm-Labor Supply Program,* 80th Cong., 1st sess., 1947.

33. *El Espectador,* October 6, 1950.

34. *El Espectador,* June 22, 1952; Daniel Martínez, "The Impact of the Bracero Program," 44.

35. *El Espectador,* March 29, 1957; *El Espectador,* April 1, 1960.

36. Gutiérrez, *Walls and Mirrors,* 142.

37. Galarza, *Merchants of Labor,* 30, 59. See also Thomas, *Citizenship, Gender, and Work,* 68.

38. Daniel Martínez, "The Impact of the Bracero Program," 39.

39. Thomas, *Citizenship, Gender, and Work,* 67.

40. Ibid., 71, 75, 206.

17

Across Generations

Polish Americans and Polish Immigrants

MARY PATRICE ERDMANS

April 5, 1988

Dear Mr. Mazewski,

Whatever the merits—or confusion and unnecessary recriminations—in the recent radio discussion series of refugees' complaints, I believe that the problem merits consideration. Polonia has adopted a "hands-off" attitude towards the refugees leaving the matter to the Immigration Committee [PAIRC], which I don't think is handling the problem satisfactorily, appearing to regard the refugees as a troublesome burden. . . . The question thus is: does Polonia continue its disinterested attitude, or consider extending to them a helping hand? I am well aware of the justified complaints against many newcomers. But surely, raw anger voiced by older immigrants, that the newcomers are communist agents, and if they don't like it here they should return to socialist Poland is inadmissible. Such people oversimplify the problem. It hurt me to listen to mutual accusations, vociferous and angry, voiced by both the newcomers and older immigrants, as if they were adversaries, and not all of them Poles. . . .

Kazimierz Lukomski, a World War II émigré and vice-president of the Polish American Congress (PAC) wrote the above letter to Aloysius Mazewski, president of both the PAC and the Polish National Alliance (PNA). In a memo dated April 9, 1988, Mazewski wrote back, "I concur that the refugees need our help. To whom will they turn if not to us? We must forget their attitude, the experiences of ingratitude, the demands they make as if we were obliged to help them, etc. But not all are like that— so with the hope that they will change—we must continue to help them."

This exchange provides a glimpse into one of the main conflicts in Polonia (the Polish American community) during the 1980s. Polonia included several hundred thousand new immigrants, a significant and vocal group of post-WWII émigrés, and millions of second- and third-generation Polish Americans. The new Polish immigrants [had] emigrated from communist Poland for both economic and political reasons. Many new immigrants, discouraged by Poland's failing economy came to America seeking economic gain; others, especially those involved in the opposition movement known as Solidarity, were escaping political repression. All came because they thought America offered them a better chance to do something with their lives. The economic and political immigrants were similar in age, occupations, and education, but they differed in terms of their legal status in the United States and their premigration involvement with the opposition in Poland. Those with permanent resident status and ties to the opposition were more likely to be involved in collective action than temporary migrants and those without a history of activism.

The presence of a new migrant cohort within Polonia was most evident in the 1980s, when refugees and an increased number of *wakacjusze* (literally "vacationers," which refers to temporary immigrants who often work illegally in the United States) accompanied the steady inflow of immigrants. Most notably recognized were the politically active Solidarity refugees and the large population of *wakacjusze,* each visible in the community but for different reasons—the latter because they resisted assimilation and the former because of their involvement in collective action for Poland. New immigrants usually settled in cities with large Polish populations (e.g., Chicago, New York, Detroit), and these century-old Polonian communities were structured around and through ethnic organizations.

New immigrants wanted ethnic organizations to lend them a helping hand; ethnics interpreted this outstretched hand as dependency, a negative vestige of their communist upbringing. Both new immigrants' demands and Polish Americans' feelings of obligation were premised on the understanding that they were "all Poles," for "to whom would they turn if not to us." Yet this perceived affinity did not translate into strong and concrete attachments to each other. Their interactions were often better characterized as "mutual accusation" rather than helpful cooperation.

Polish Americans and Polish immigrants may have shared an historical identity but they did not share a contemporary identity. Polish Americans were ethnics not immigrants, and their identity was rooted in twentieth-century capitalist America. Polish American ethnics were established members of American society while Polish immigrants were newcomers. Moreover, Polish immigrants had been socialized in twentieth-century communist Poland. These different social identities (as ethnics and immigrants) and experiences (in capitalist America and communist Poland) created different lenses through which they perceived and interpreted the behavior of each other. In sum, they had different cultures. Culture is not a static identity, but it is socially constructed, shaped by place and time. Because they came from different cultures they interpreted behavior differently.

All groups—Americans, Polish Americans, World War II émigrés, and new Polish immigrants—used communism as a discourse for interpreting behavior. Ruth Frankenberg defines discourses as "historically constituted bodies of ideas providing conceptual frameworks for individuals." Frameworks are schemata for interpreting behavior. Erving Goffman stated that a primary framework "allows its users to locate, perceive, identify, and label a seemingly infinite number of concrete occurrences defined in its terms." The framework provides background information and helps to answer the question: What's going on here? Cross-cultural conflict can be understood as an issue of frame discordance that produces varying interpretations of behavior.[1] In Chicago Polonia, the new immigrants and Polish Americans were socialized in different social contexts, with different symbolic meaning systems (especially as they related to communism).

When discussing the behavior of the new immigrants, every Polish American and World War II émigré I interviewed mentioned communism at least once, and some of them used the discourse of communism to explain numerous aspects of new immigrant behavior, such as work habits, attitudes toward government assistance, and unwillingness to join established Polish American organizations. In comparison, only a few new immigrants used the discourse of communism to explain new immigrant behavior; those that did were more likely to have arrived in the early 1960s as young adults and, as a result, had twenty-five to thirty years of socialization in American culture. New immigrants who arrived post-1980 seldom used the discourse of communism, and when they did, they used it to describe Polish American organizations (which they saw as resembling communist organizations).

Irene Claremont de Castillejo, a Jungian analyst, has argued that communism was America's national shadow. In Jungian analysis, we project upon a shadow all those qualities that we do not desire, but that most likely reside within ourselves.[2] America's abhorrence of communism was based on more than simply military fear; communism was positioned as antithetical to the basic American value of freedom. In other words, Americans cast communism as the Other. The Other, constructed in opposition to the Self, is invested with all the negative traits that the Self denies. The Other illuminates the Self in a value-oriented way so that the Self is of higher value than the Other. Casting communism as the Other, then, helped define democracy and capitalism: Democracy was freedom, communism was slavery; democracy was participatory decentralized government, communism was hierarchical centralized government; capitalism rewarded ambition, hard work and self-reliance, communism created disincentives to work and state-dependency.[3]

In American Polonia, this hatred of communism and communists, intensified by the presence of the communist regime in Warsaw, had been nourished for decades. What, then, were Polish Americans and World War II émigrés to make of these new immigrants who had been born in communist hospitals, educated in communist schools, and employed by communist bosses? Polonia was somewhat suspicious of these immigrants. A Polish American working for Catholic Charities, an agency that helps resettle refugees, said she had difficulty finding sponsors. "I called one woman, a Polish American, and asked if she would help resettle this new Polish immigrant and she refused because, she said, 'He's probably a communist.'"

Because communism was seen as antithetical to capitalist democracy, resettlement agencies assumed Polish immigrants would have a hard time adjusting to life in the "land of the free." One document from World Relief, a U.S. organization that helps resettle refugees, noted the following about Polish immigrants:

> The Polish people are very independent-minded . . . [they] like to decide their own lives and work for their own goals. However, 30 years of communist rule have not gone by without making an impression on the present generation of Poles. Even though most of the Polish refugees dislike their political system, they are a prod-

uct of it and do not question many of its components. In fact, they are used to, and expect that many decisions are made for them, and that they will be taken care of by the state. When the state's control is removed upon coming to the United States, they may be unprepared to take full charge of all aspects of their lives in a free society. Polish people are not used to picking from a variety of choices. In Poland, you don't even need to make a decision of what to have for supper. . . . The most difficult adjustment the Polish refugee has to make is adjusting to the freedom in American society, which means the freedom of choice, including the freedom to make profit, but also the freedom to be poor.[4]

This pamphlet reflected the attitudes of people who had not lived in communist Poland. They expected immigrants to have a basic problem understanding "freedom" (for example, they won't even know how to decide what to have for dinner!). Although emigration represented a rejection of communism, they believed the refugees had nonetheless internalized its practices. Refugees were unwitting victims of communism.

Polish Americans and World War II émigrés did not blame the immigrants for being influenced by the communist system—they blamed the communist system. Yet, with heads nodding in measured sympathy, they often stated that the immigrants themselves were unaware of how extremely "indoctrinated" they were. The World War II émigrés repeatedly described communism as an inescapable dogma that contaminated the psyches of its citizens. One World War II émigré compared communism to smog, "You can't help breathing it, and those who breath it are polluted." Another World War II émigré said: "Forty years ago the system was introduced, so the generation that comes over here is already a result of the communist indoctrination. . . . [W]e have to understand that it will take time before they shake everything what we think the system has imposed on their minds." These émigrés frequently used the term "indoctrination" and "brainwashed" to explain this socialization process. One World War II émigré said:

> They [the new immigrants] are not communists, they are against communists, which is a surprise to some degree because they were brainwashed from childhood—in schools, media, newspaper, radio, everything—they were brainwashed. . . . They were born there and educated there and worked there, from childhood until they left they were under constant influence. So I am surprised they are so anticommunist in spite of all this. . . . But at the same time they picked up a certain way of life, [hushed tones] way of thinking even, way of writing.

These quotes illustrate the sympathetic yet suspicious perceptions of Polonians toward the new immigrants. They constructed a reality whereby even though the immigrants engaged in anticommunist activities, even though some of them were imprisoned because of their antistate activities, and even though they chose to flee the communist system, still, these people carried the taint of communism with them to America. They believed the immigrants were politically against the communist state but socially and psychologically influenced by the communist system.

A few new immigrants also spoke of the ubiquitous nature of communism. One new immigrant who arrived in the late 1970s said:

> We were raised in communist system with quite different mentality, with quite different problems, work, everything. Because there's no doubt, I don't think that anybody could somehow avoid the influence of communist propaganda. There's no way, because they control your life from the very beginning. You were born in a government hospital, then you go to government pre-school, then you go to government elementary school, then government high school, then government university, and each step of the life is controlled by the government. The media is controlled by the government. Teachers have to follow very strict instructions from the government. Art is controlled by the government. So, there is very strong influence of the government philosophy on their individual lives. There is no way, you can't resist.

This man, however, when giving examples of how the system influenced him, spoke more about false information rather than about some deep psychological alteration that would incapacitate him in a democratic capitalist system. His "shock" when he left Poland was about the "lies" he had been told; he never spoke about not being able to adjust to life in a democratic society. He said:

> I know Polish literature, for example, very well. And I didn't realize when I escaped from Poland I went to Sweden, and I somehow met a guy who gots piles of books, published in the West, and most of them written by the writers in exile. You know, I was surprised, it was for me such an unbelievable shock, I realized that literature abroad is equally good and in some cases even better than that in Poland. And I considered myself as an educated man. And there was many and more shocks like that. For example, my wife went to Sweden and suddenly she was so surprised that the education in Sweden is free, even government provides papers, pencils for students. She was convinced, and she's not stupid, believe me, she was convinced that in capitalist country everybody has to pay for education.

This man did not convey the notion that communism seeped into his unconscious, but that he had been told stories that he later learned were false. Learning about the lies confirmed the negative feelings he already had toward the communist government in Poland.

Only three other new immigrants mentioned the indoctrination of the communist system, and they all had been in the United Stated for twenty to thirty years. They did not speak of this indoctrination as something that was causing them problems personally, but as something they saw in other immigrants—especially the newest immigrants. They used the language of "them" rather than "us" and talked about "those new immigrants" as a way of separating themselves from this indoctrination. One immigrant who arrived in the 1960s stated: "These Polish people there's a lot of misunderstanding. They don't understand. Because in Poland the government is manipulate people. . . . The party has complete control over radio, TV, and press. And so when these people come in here they don't understand." The only immigrant (1968 arrival) who referred to his own indoctrination also pointed out that he had changed. "You have to remember that every one of us, I am supposed to say myself, because I am quite a bit here, I change, for sure I am not the same person who came here. We have to realize that we are like a child of that system, too, I mean the communist system. They brainwash us that far that it's not like that [snaps fingers] to get rid of it."

The quotes chosen represent only a sample of the types of the statements I heard from Polish Americans and World War II émigrés. In contrast, they represent all of the discussion on this topic from new immigrants (and I interviewed and talked with more new immigrants than with members from either of the other two cohorts). The new immigrants simply did not trace their resettlement problems to the communist system. Immigrants related their problems to their newcomer status. As recent arrivals, they needed to learn a new language, find a job and a place to live, and learn how to maneuver through a new set of institutions. They did not say they had problems with too much freedom or that they were uncertain about what to have for dinner; they had problems learning English and finding good jobs.

Another perception was that communism destroyed the Poles' work ethic and fostered an attitude of dependency on the state. An America director of the Polish Welfare Association (PWA), which employed Polish immigrants and also helped new immigrants find employment, was extremely critical of the work habits of new immigrants.

> You're dealing with people that lived under socialism, where people don't work hard . . . the old Polish work ethic is not there. This is something I see on my staff, there's not a lot of initiative. . . . Their expectations of the American work force are completely unrealistic. We have a lot of people being sent on jobs quitting the first day—it's too hard, they go to people and ask for more money the first week, right away, it's crazy, it really is.[5]

This director also thought that communism made people manipulative:

> I think that growing up in Poland under communism you get to be very manipulative. You learn how to manipulate the best you can. And if it means in Poland you bribe an official for a better house, you do. You learn how to manipulate the system in America. You work illegally, there are people who over-extend their visa, you are here illegally, or even if you are here on a six-month visa and when you don't have work authorization, again you're manipulating the system, you're doing something illegally.

These statements were contradictory. At one moment, Polish immigrants did not want to work because communism destroyed their work ethic; in the next moment, the immigrants were sneaking around trying to get jobs. This second behavior was also attributed to communism. In the hands of people socialized in capitalist democratic America, communism was a conceptual tool used to invent explanations for a variety of behaviors. It became the catch-all term for explaining conflict and the scapegoat for undesirable behavior.

A few of the earlier arrivals in the new cohort expressed kindred viewpoints about the destruction of the work ethic. One man who arrived as a teen in the early 1960s stated: "In the first place there is the work ethic, which is basically missing, especially from the so-called intellectual elite." But other new immigrants, even ones who arrived in the 1960s, offered a more elaborate analysis of immigrant work habits. One new immigrant (1962 arrival) explained, "They have to work hard here. If in Poland they work hard there are no results, you don't see. Over here you can see results if you want. In Poland you don't, because all your efforts are destroyed by the Party, by the system." She noted that Poles were eager to work in a system that rewarded hard work, implying that people acted differently in America than in Poland. In effect, she was saying that behavior could be explained by systemic rather than psychological factors.

Immigrants who left Poland in their late teens and early twenties had less experience than someone who had actually worked in a communist system for several years. Immigrants who had more experience working in Poland were also very critical of the communist system, but they were not critical of Polish workers. One new immigrant vehemently countered this criticism of poor work ethics. He said:

> The people say, "Oh, you no like work over there because you nothing do." But this not true. The Polish people, I know, because I been in shipyards, in Szczecin, the people work very hard, very hard. . . . Like coal miners, he make big money in Poland, *ale* [but] he work seven days straight, Saturday and Sunday even, and very, very hard. . . . And why the Polish people come to America, because he been good worker. I no say everyone, but I am sure 80 percent of people who work in the United States and the factories, the owners been very happy for the work. He say the Polish worker he work very hard and very correct, he have no problem with these people. Why, because he learn in Poland. Because he work very hard for nothing in Poland. If he come here to America and he see the dollar and how much he make at the end of the week, how much he make for the month in Poland, he make here a lot more, so after that he very, very good worker. You no find better worker than Polish worker.

This statement represents the attitude most new immigrants had—that they preferred working in America because there was a positive relation between the number of hours worked and the size of the paycheck. Work habits were more related to the system within which one worked than the character of the worker.

In addition to the perception of poor work habits, members of established Polonia also believed that the immigrants had been socialized to depend more on the government. This was expressed by Americans, Polish Americans, and World War II émigrés, but no new immigrants (not even the early arrivals) expressed this belief. The perception was based on the understanding that communist governments provided their citizens with health care services, education, and jobs and therefore the immigrants arrived in the United States expecting the American government to do the same. The director of the Office of Refugee Resettlement in Chicago, an American, stated:

> Their homeland experiences precondition their expectations. The fact that Poles have immigrated from a communist country affects their behavior when they arrive here. This is true of Poles, Rumanians, Soviets, Czechs, Bulgarians and all those from communist countries. . . . They do have a certain inherent response to government programs, they feel that the government has a responsibility to them.

One Polish American said, "When they come here they have this Socialist mentality. They come here with their hands out." Another said, "They want everything done for free." A Polish American who worked for the PAC stated: "They have been indoctrinated in Poland for thirty years. The state gives you a job, the state gives you medical insurance, the state gives you free education. Then when they come to America they are lost." Another Polish American woman expressed the same idea:

> The Eastern Europeans have problems adjusting to the system in America. They come from a system where the state takes care of their education and all their medical problems. The state supports much more of the system there than it does here. They have problems because of that. . . . They can't understand that the state doesn't take care of their medical problems; see the health care is subsidized in Poland. Another example is the theater people who come over here. See, the state also subsidizes the theater and the arts in Poland. If one is an actress or an artist then the state pays them a salary to do that. They are shocked when they find out that if they want to do theater work here they also have to work, that it's not government subsidized like it is in Poland.

Polish Americans and World War II émigrés framed their understanding within an American cultural system that venerates hard work and scorns state dependency, a system wherein capitalism was sacred and communism profane.

In addition to using American frames of discourse, Polish Americans also interpreted the immigrants' behavior from an ethnic framework. Polish Americans used their own constructed identity of Polishness (thrift, discipline, and hard work) and their parents' and grandparents' stories of immigrant struggles to explain why they were against state support for new immigrants. In ethnic folklore passed down through the generations, Polish Americans told how their parents, or grandparents, or the generic "early Polish immigrants" started at the bottom and nobody helped them, they had to make it on their own without expecting a handout (reminiscent of the "I walked ten miles to school in the snow uphill, without shoes" cant). An older second-generation Polish American said in reference to the new immigration: "It's the new thing. It isn't only the Polish. They just hold their hand out." And then, in reference to her parent's generation, she said: "None of them felt that this country owed them anything. They knew they had to work. They expected to work. You know, no work, no eat." The Polish Americans believed the new immigrants should "pull themselves up by their own bootstraps" as their ancestors did. One World War II émigré compared the behavior of new immigrants to older Polish Americans who had lived through the Depression and did not have enough Social Security in their later years.

> Then came those food stamps and we tried to convince them [older Polish Americans], but they don't want to go. They said, "I am not beggar." It was hard to convince them that this is nothing wrong, you deserve it, you should go and get them. Well, with this people coming now, it is just the reverse. They are looking what they can get for nothing, you see. I know many cases, for example, that they could get a job for four dollars an hour; well they don't want it. They figure out, I am on welfare. I get more than if I am working. And the old-timer it was awfully hard to convince them even to get unemployment compensation because they say, "I am not beggar."

The equation here is that to receive state support implies that one is a beggar, and the suggestion is that new immigrants would rather go on public aid than get a job.

The World War II émigrés also had their own immigrant experiences to draw upon. Having arrived in the 1950s before the Great Society era, many pointed to their own hardships as immigrants and took pride in the fact that members of their generation resisted state support. One World War II émigré said: "When they were young, most of my friends, when we first came here, had at least one and a half jobs. In other words, one regular job and then at least a couple of evenings in some sort of money-making situation." Another World War II émigré made the following comparisons between his cohort and the new immigrants:

> This forty years or thirty years of the communist rule, going to communist school, they had to change little the psychology of the people. And their psychology was changed. For example, I give you the example of the difference. Let's say when our immigration was coming here to the United States we didn't expect somebody's going to welcome us with the red flowers, the red carpet at the airport or at the train station or on the boat in the seaport or anything like this. We just came, we just realized that we are coming here to make a living . . . that we practically have to start from the beginning. And we didn't look for someone to help us financially or give us money for start or things like this. Nothing like this happened. This people [new immigrants], in many cases, they think that somebody should await them with couple of few thousand dollars so they have a start, and they sort of holding the grief against us that we not doing this.

In contrast to the perception that new immigrants expected a handout, I found just the opposite to be true. Polish immigrants had low rates of welfare usage, underutilized state resources, often worked more than forty hours a week, and in fact were critical of Americans who did "go on welfare." A group of Polish immigrants who were students in an English language course I taught at the Polish University Abroad (*Polski Uniwersytet na Obczyźnie*) (PUNO) in Chicago, had the following conversation about American life. One student said:

> People [in America] are poor because they no want to work. . . . [P]eople from Poland taking this $3.75. That's normal pay for us. And they have family here. . . . Even with this money you can live, maybe not normal life, you have to be careful how you spending money. But if you using it right you not poor. I am not thinking I am poor and I making this $3.75. And there's enough to even save some.

This student (and others expressed similar attitudes) perceived the benefits of the American system to be that they were given an opportunity to work, not that they were given a handout. They defined "poorness" as a fault of the individual in this "land of opportunity" and did not expect the state to give them a job or a house (though they did think of education and health care as a citizen right). In 1988, Lorrain Majka, who worked in refugee services for the Jewish Federation of Metropolitan Chicago, said:

> The Poles are different because they hang onto jobs, they don't want to go on state welfare. They think there is some crime or shame. It is very difficult, for example with the PWA [the Polish Welfare Association], they can't fill their quotas. A certain percentage of their clients have to be on public aid, and they just can't find that many Poles on public aid to help out. So they had to request less money for next

year because they can't find enough people on public aid. They have a lot of clients, but most of them get a job and then hang on to their job.

Polish refugees in Chicago accessed fewer state resources than other refugee groups. One study of non-Southeast Asian refugees found that Polish refugees used assistance at half the rate as other refugee groups; in 1985 only 18 percent of Polish refugees in Cook County who had been there three years or less were receiving public assistance, while 38 percent of all refugees in the county were receiving assistance. They also reported that Polish refugees found jobs quickly and "underutilized" the employment services. In another study of refugees in Chicago by Catholic Charities, Anne Templeton found that 84 percent of the Polish refugees were employed within the first six months of arrival, compared to only 68 percent of the Assyrian refugees (who were coming from a noncommunist country). Moreover, of the ten refugee groups included in the study, Poles received the least amount of cash assistance averaging only $81 per capita compared to a rate of $659 for the Vietnamese. Templeton argued that this finding was "not unexpected" because the Polish refugees "found employment more quickly than any other nationality group."[6]

Taken together, these studies show that Polish refugees do not appear to be state-dependency slackers looking for a hand out and unwilling to take a job. It is important to remember that these studies were of refugees, newcomers who were eligible for the most state assistance. Other immigrants were not eligible for state resources until they had permanent residency status, and then they were only eligible for state and federal funds appropriated for all U.S. residents (such as Aid to Families with Dependent Children and food stamps). Temporary visitors with valid or invalid visas are by definition not permanent residents and thus not eligible for any assistance. If assistance usage rates were low for Polish refugees, we can assume that illegal immigrants and legal immigrants were even less "dependent" on the state.

In addition to these reports of low welfare usage, my ethnographic data indicate that new immigrants were more likely to be workhorses than freeloaders. Owners of construction and maid companies told me they considered Polish immigrants to be among the best laborers. Many immigrants worked two jobs and sixty hour weeks. No one I interviewed was receiving state assistance. Some refugees, however, did report that when they first arrived they stayed out of the labor market for a few months (seven- to eighteen-month range) to improve their language skills, recertify degrees, or seek additional training. This initial preference to accept state assistance rather than take a low-paying job may explain why Polish Americans had the perception that newcomers were looking for a handout. Polish refugees reported that "Polish American service providers accuse them of being lazy if they want to go to school and learn English."[7] Still, state support was a luxury that only a small percentage of the new cohort could afford. Less than 10 percent of the newcomers were refugees; the other 90 percent of the newcomers were not eligible for these state assistance programs.

So why did the established Polonian community perceive the new immigrants as coming here "with their hands out" and wanting "everything for free?" First, as mentioned above, they interpreted the behavior of immigrants from communist Poland through a frame that assumed they would be state dependent. Second, while new immigrants did not rely much on the state, they did in fact expect Polonia to help them. At a community forum in February 1989, immigrants directed hostile questions at the speaker (an employee of one of the Polish American fraternals) concerning the lack of help given to immigrants. One man said, "The [fraternal] doesn't help us; they look pretty but they don't do anything. They have meetings and *Wigilia* [the Christmas Eve supper] but they don't help us." Another man bluntly asked the speaker, "Why don't you give us jobs?" One immigrant blamed the Polish American community for the large number of professional, well-educated Polish refugees who were forced into menial labor positions in Chicago. He expected the Polish American organizations to help new immigrants improve their occupational status in America. On a Polish-language radio talk show in Chicago in March 1988, two new refugees called to complain about the lack of support they were receiving from Polish American organizations. One said, "If you find a job or an apartment it's usually through friends, or a friend of a friend," that is, not through one of the ethnic organizations.[8] Ewa Betka, executive director of the PAC Illinois Division, said that immigrants often called asking for help. She explained:

> They arrive in Chicago [and] they start calling the Polish organizations. And they find out that I don't have an apartment to give them. I don't have a job to give them because I don't know of any today. The most I can do today is to make sure they get a basket of food. I can have the city put them up in one of these overnight shelters. And then the resentments start. "What, you're a Polish organization, what are you here for? You're supposed to be helping me." . . . They come in and they expect the Polish organization to be ready and waiting to give them a job, housing, clothing and school.

While the new immigrants often complained about lack of support, the two studies of Polish refugees in Chicago in the 1980s found that Polish refugees had more community and sponsorship support than other refugee communities, and the lower welfare usage among Polish refugees was partially attributed to this strong sponsorship and community support. Nonetheless, this second study also noted, in several places, that the Polish refugees expressed strong dissatisfaction with and alienation from the established Polish American community.[9]

The new immigrants expected help from Polish Americans and criticized the organizations for not helping. The Polish Americans defended themselves by redefining the conflict as a negative consequence of communism. In many cases, it was during a conversation about conflicts in Polonia that Polish Americans and World War II émigrés brought up the topic of welfare dependency. The real problem, they said, was not that they were not helping the newcomers, but that communism had made the new immigrants expect too much.

Leaders of Polish American organizations were particularly galled by the fact that the new immigrants would ask them for help but were unwilling to join their organizations. Helen Zielinska, president of the Polish Women's Alliance, related the following story of a family involving wife abuse, visa problems, and financial need.

> I had a man call up yesterday and say, "I came from Poland, can you help me." And he had a problem and talked for half an hour and I said, "Sir, I can not give you any more

time." I said, "because what you want I can not help. . . . You have a problem and I don't want to mix into it." . . . See those are the problems. Everyday I get calls from people to help. Yet they won't belong to a fraternal, yet they'll call us for help. . . . I said to the man "I can not help you." And he said, "But I come from Poland." And I said, "Well, if you had money to come here from Poland, you could have used that money and get help."

The frustration Polish Americans felt toward immigrants asking for help but unwilling to help in return is expressed in the following comment:

> For the past twenty years or more the new immigrants that have come to America have shown themselves to be above our Polonia. They are not interested in joining organizations, fraternals, churches, or even help groups that work for the assistance to Poland or new immigrants coming to America. The Polish American organizations are criticizing us for catering to people who want our help but will rarely help the organization offering assistance.[10]

Not joining organizations was problematic because Polish American organizations needed new members. Many Polonian organizations formed in the first half of the twentieth century had a declining and aging membership in the 1980s. Fraternal organizations like the PNA peaked in terms of membership and lodges in the post–World War II era and total membership declined from 336,159 in 1960 to 294,761 in 1980. Membership for all but one of the top five Polish American fraternals (the Polish Falcons was the exception) declined from 1970 to 1980.[11] Moreover, the organizations' remaining members were aging, which is fiscally problematic for fraternal organizations whose assets are built on life insurance policies. An aging membership is also dangerous for any volunteer organization. Without new and young members the organization faces the threat of dying with its members. One director of the Polish-American Women's Coalition said, "The problem is that it really needs some new blood. Most of the women are old and we were supposed to make an effort to recruit young women but we haven't been too successful." Helen Zielinska, the president of the Polish Women's Alliance, said, "We are looking for a lot of young members to take our place. . . . To run a fraternal you have to have members, you have to have an increase in members, especially young members. . . . I mean up to about 38 to 45, you know, that's young people, compared to us older people." Francis Rutkowski, who in 1986 served briefly as the president of the Polish Roman Catholic Union, said, "A lot of the members are old, they are dying . . . all fraternals are faced with the problem of fluctuating membership." Anthony Piwowarczyk, a vice-president of the PNA, stated that "in the PAC, there is a need of new blood. Absolutely." He also explained that the PNA is top-heavy, and as an insurance company it needs to bring in young members: "That's why we run the youth jamboree . . . this is the purpose, to get them involved in activities so that they go out and get in the organization. We have to propagate."

The organizations were unable to attract enough new members from the second-, third-, and fourth-generation ethnics. They hoped to enroll large numbers of new immigrants arriving in the 1970s and 1980s. Yet, no significant number of new immigrants joined the organizations in the 1980s. An administrative assistant for the PAC said, "No, they are not coming to the PNA. Even though there is a big campaign to get them, they are not joining. Even the Solidarity people, the intelligent, educated ones, they are sticking to themselves. It's the same thing with the artistic community. They gather in one place, and they include only this one group of people." For the most part, the new immigrants did not join the established Polish American organizations. Among those I interviewed in Chicago, the only organization the new immigrants joined was the Polish National Alliance (PNA) by forming new fraternal lodges, and a few were active in the Illinois division of the PAC. No one in my sample of home health care workers joined Polish American organizations, and less than 20 percent of my sample of the members of Forum and less than 10 percent of my sample of ESL students at PUNO belonged to any Polish American organization. And even though immigrants attended Polish churches, they were not as inclined to officially join the parish.[12]

To explain this nonjoiner behavior, the Polish Americans and World War II émigrés turned to their favorite whipping boy—communism. They believed that communism had destroyed the "natural instinct for groupness." PAC members, especially World War II émigrés, explained the new immigrants' behavior as a rebellion against their earlier experience of being forced to join organizations in the communist system. One PAC director stated: "Any organization in Poland had to be regime sponsored. They grew up antiorganizational, and they still carry it to some extent." Another World War II émigré stated: "They stay away from others. They have this suspicion of organizations. They just want to be dispersed. Free. Not organized." The following quotes by World War II émigrés active in the PAC make evident this opinion.

> These people were brought up in slavery and they have a different attitude. They will have some chips on their shoulders, maybe even some Sovietization. They don't know it, but there's terrific propaganda which comes from Moscow in the schools—false history, false literature, false information. And then they come over here hating these organizations because they were forced to join them in Poland.

Another said:

> Our generation [World War II émigrés] could be described as very prone to organize itself. When you have the next generation, which comes now from Poland, they stay from organizing themselves, they stay away, because they were pushed by the communist government to organize. They attended these forced meetings so much that they hate even the word organization.

The leaders of these established ethnic organizations did not reflect on aspects about their organizations that may have made new immigrants unwilling to join. They started with the assumption that their organizations were good and necessary and if new immigrants were not joining there was something wrong with the new immigrants. The explanation was that the experiences in a communist society destroyed associational behavior.

A handful of new immigrants used this same explanation. Both of the following quotes are from immigrants who arrived in the United States in the late 1970s. Notice again that when discussing new immigrants they do not use the inclusive "we" pronoun but the otherized "they" pronoun. "The problem with the new immigrants is that they were raised in communist Poland. See, it is the natural desire of people to identify with some other group of people, to belong, feel they belong to a group. This desire was crushed by the communists. After forty years of communism they have destroyed this natural instinct for groupness." The other said, "These people who have arrived here from Poland, who have been forced for years to join the Party, to join this or to join that, they come here and they want to remain anonymous. They don't want to join organizations. Because they've been forced to do this, for years, and I think this is part of the problem."

It was true that Poles were "forced" to join organizations in communist Poland, and the organizations were created and controlled by the communist state. (KOR, formed in 1976, was one of the first autonomous and open organizations in communist Poland.) In interviews with Poles in Poland in 1987, many talked about this manipulation and forced participation. One Pole succinctly described such a situation:

> People were automatically signed into organizations like the ZMP [Youth Organization], it was mechanical. Most of us didn't know we were assigned, we didn't sign up. Our directors, principals in the *liceum* [high school] informed us one day, "Oh you are members of ZMP." One had to be really brave to stand up and say, "Director, I don't want to be member of this organization. Cross me out."

Nonetheless, this is the same country that gave birth to Solidarity, a union that at one point almost a third of the population joined voluntarily. The comments from the new immigrants above represent the ideas of those who left Poland before Solidarity. Only one post-1980 immigrant noted her reluctance to join organizations.

> Yes, I am a member of KIK [the Club of Catholic Intellectuals in Chicago.] It is the only organization I am really a member. It is my decision not to belong to any organization here. It was also my program in Poland since Stalinist period when I dropped Youth organization. I say, "Enough" any organizations, but, of course, later, I was a co-operator of KOR, I was co-founder of Solidarity in my factory and so on. But it wasn't, I *must* do it.

The interesting thing is that these three immigrants—and they were the only ones from the new cohort who made statements about communism spoiling their desire to join organizations—were, in fact, all members of organizations. This last women was also a member of KOR and a co-founder of the Solidarity union in her region. In America, however, they were members of small, informal new immigrant organizations rather then the larger, more formal Polish American organizations.

While established Polonia blamed communism for the new immigrants' nonjoining behavior, the new immigrants blamed the established ethnic organizations. Some newcomers stated that the reason they were reluctant to join established Polonian organizations was that they were too formal, autocratic, and centralized. When discussing their reasons for not joining, new immigrants used phrases from and analogies to the communist system to disparage the organizations. One immigrant said, "This organization [the PAC] is run like an oligarchy and we are very familiar with this system, we lived for a long time in totalitarian rule so we know how they are running things." Another immigrant said in reference to the PAC, "There is no opposition, there is only autocratic rule." Because of the older age of the average PAC members, another new immigrant likened them to the Central Committee of the Communist Party. When the twenty-year PAC president died in 1988, a new refugee compared the situation to the death of Stalin: "In communism, you have a specific dominant authoritarian leader like in [the PAC], where at the top you have only one leader. When this leader dies there is a gap, like when Stalin died." One refugee who worked for WPNA, the radio station owned by the PNA, said in reference to a directive telling announcers not to broadcast news about a demonstration in February 1989, "I obeyed the . . . official party line." Another new immigrant said, "New immigrants are pissed off because Moskal [the PAC president] took his guys, his *aparatczy* from his office to go with him" when he went to Poland. Another immigrant called one PAC board member "the main political member of the politburo." At a public meeting with a representative from the PNA, who was speaking to a room of mostly new immigrants, one immigrant who had come in the late 1970s said, in reference to the fact that Polish American organizations did not help the new immigrants, that the ethnic fraternals did not really do anything and therefore "looked like the communist system in Poland." At that statement, roughly half of the audience of one hundred clapped. In one article published in a Polonian magazine, a new immigrant wrote, "The pressure of social conformity here is no less effective than censorship in the PRL."[13]

Many immigrants criticized the way that leaders were chosen for the PAC. The national PAC had a nominating committee that suggested a slate of candidates. The standard procedure was that the slate was either accepted or rejected at the National Council of Directors meetings. In reference to the PAC elections, one new immigrant said that because the voting was done by raising hands and not by secret ballot it was "like the communists do in Poland." The appointment of people to positions in the PAC was called "negative selection," which one immigrant described as "an expression from Poland, the Party selects for the president of a company or dean of a university the people who will follow the rules which are stated for them." One new immigrant, referring to the elections said, "I don't think there is much difference in the actions in Poland and the actions here." Another said, "I don't see in PAC enough democracy. I think there is no democracy, their, uh, elections is not democratic because there are some people nominated by previous president, they are not chosen from the people."[14] These quotes are not meant to imply that the new immigrants thought that the PAC was a communist organization but only to show how their experiences in the communist system influenced the way that the new immigrants thought (or at least talked) about Polish American organizations. The new immigrants superimposed the image of the rigid authoritarian structure of the communist regime onto the centralized bureaucracy of organizations like the PNA and the PAC. New immigrants did not appreciate these structural characteristics, and preferred not to join these formalized, centralized, and bureaucratic organizations.

Another reason new immigrants did not join was because they saw no benefit to joining. The immigrants wanted and needed organizations that would help them satisfy newcomer needs. The established organizations, however, were ethnic organizations set up to service ethnic needs. Ethnic needs included maintaining a cultural attachment to an ancestral homeland, fighting for state resources distributed on the basis of ethnic identification, working to maintain and increase their share of decision-making positions (that is, as elected and appointed public officials and top managerial and executive positions in the private sector), and fighting to minimize ethnic prejudice and discrimination.

The sorts of ethnic goods the organizations provided are reflected in their activities and goals: They sponsored Polish American Heritage Month activities; they published pamphlets on Pulaski and Kosciuszko, both heroes of the American Revolution; they organized parades and festivals, cultural tours to Poland, and fund-raisers for the renovation of the Statue of Liberty. Ethnic projects the PAC was involved in during the 1980s included: an examination of the unfair and prejudicial portrayal of ethnic groups in the media; a nationwide library project entitled "Not For Polish-Americans Only" (1983–84); support for parochial schools in America and the Polish seminary at Orchard Lake; and funding for ethnic studies programs. The purpose of the Copernicus Center, as stated in their public relations pamphlet, was: "Our generation will construct the Center as an expression of the pride we have in them and our heritage." Activities at the Copernicus Center included Polish language classes, polka classes, an art fair, and the Taste of Polonia summer festival. President Mazewski describing the PNA stated, "We are more fraternal than anything. We just got two new dance groups, from two lodges. We spend a lot of money, over a million dollars on fraternalism, on dance groups and choral groups, and youth and sports clubs. This is all fraternalism." A pamphlet, describing the Polish Women's Alliance (April 1986), stated that "this fraternal has worked to preserve Polish customs and traditions and Polish culture." Toward this end the "Alliance sponsors Polish Language, literature, folklore, history and craft classes as well as Polish song and folk-dance lessons, festivals, commemorative programs and quadrennial youth conferences." The pamphlet of the Polish Roman Catholic Union fraternal states that it "promotes Catholic action, fosters Polish language, and maintains Polish traditions, promoted various sports activities, provides various activities such as folk dancing, singing, hobby classes, youth festivals, and language classes, [and] works to enhance the image and prestige of Americans of Polish descent." Organizations serving ethnic needs concentrate on the needs of an ethnic group in a pluralist nation: cultural maintenance, ethnic discrimination, political representation, and securing state resources for such things as museums and public festivals.

The new immigrants, however, were not yet ethnics. While their children may have needed Polish language classes or to learn about their Polish heritage, the new immigrants did not. Immigrant needs were attached to their newcomer status. They needed help resettling in a new culture and society; in this case, Poles had to learn what it meant to be American and how to live in the United States. Organizations serving immigrant needs would do things such as teach English, help newcomers fill out immigration and residency documents, and disseminate information regarding practical concerns (city transit schedules or instructions about utility company policies, for example). Teresa Golebiewska, at the time a graduate student in geography and a new immigrant herself, studied the residential choices of new immigrants. She noted the problems immigrants had deciding where to live.

In Poland they assign you a place to live, you don't choose it. Therefore there are not things like good and bad neighborhoods, at least not in the extreme sense that we know of it. Someone is just lucky to get an apartment, they don't care where it is. Because people don't have a choice, they are not judged by what their building looks like, or what neighborhood it is in, instead they are judged by what it looks like inside, something they have control over. When they come to America they have to learn what "good neighborhood" means, they have to learn how to choose a good neighborhood, but first they have to learn that there is a thing such as good and bad neighborhoods, and then how to know what is the good one.

While all Americans have to find a place to live, Americans do not have to learn that there are differences between good and bad neighborhoods, and established residents in a city already know where these good and bad neighborhoods are. Another institution immigrants needed to negotiate was the education system. Hubert Romanowki, the director of the Polish University Abroad, said that he set up information seminars for new immigrants because, "the biggest problem for the new Poles is a lack of information about how to use the educational system." Immigrants did not know how to recertify foreign degrees or prepare for college entrance exams. Moreover, similar to the problems with residential choice, immigrants did not realize the importance of the different prestige levels of universities, that not all college degrees were equivalent. Finding a good neighborhood and knowing that a degree from Northwestern University was worth more than one from a community college were not things Polish Americans had to learn. Newcomers to a society have to learn new routines and new values (even if they decide not to adopt them), and they have to establish new networks.

Immigrant needs were concrete and immediate, involving the routines of day to day life. Ethnic needs were cultural and less exigent. The two identities—ethnic and immigrant—are not mutually exclusive. The newcomer status that structures immigrant choices fades over time and the ethnic identity matures. In between new immigrants and the established Polish American ethnics were the World War II émigrés, who, by the late 1980s, represented a group of immigrants who were no longer newcomers. They expended more effort than did the immigrants at maintaining a cultural identity, but were also more directly tied to the homeland than were the ethnics.

The PAC addressed immigrant issues on a national level but not on a local level. The PAC lobbied to increase the number of slots for Polish refugees and change immigration laws to make them more favorable to Polish immigrants. The PAC Washington D.C. Office Report, covering the period November 1988 through May 1989, outlined the main activities of the lobbying arm of the PAC, which included efforts on behalf of the Polish refugees to bring them to the United States and support of other immigration legislation (Immigration Reform and Control Act [IRCA], Bills S.358 and S.448) directed at altering the immigration quota preference system. In 1988, the PAC helped pass legislation that allowed Polish immigrants with Extended Voluntary Departure status to be granted temporary, and then permanent, residency in the United States. This national level action, however, did not directly address the immediate needs that immigrants faced upon arrival in this country. The only immigrant-oriented activity that the PAC Illinois Division undertook in the late 1980s was to provide ESL classes to the immigrants who received residency status through the IRCA. The PAC received government funds for these classes, so it was a profit-generating service. The PNA provided a few other immigrant services; for example, it organized a Polish Information Center in the late 1970s to assist members of Polonia. At one conference in 1988, held for delegates from various foreign countries interested in immigration affairs, the director of this PNA program described the goal of the center: "The principle of our program is not to give out food but to give information." The information provided, however, was directed toward the elderly members of the community (information on pensions, health insurance, Medicare, federal supplements, social security income). They did provide some services for new immigrants—mostly information about how to contact local, state, and federal agencies and programs, and help filling out forms. Still, the PNA was not an employment agency and it did not help immigrants find housing.[15] In general, organizations like the PAC and the fraternal organizations were not set up to help new immigrants.[16] In President Mazewski's response to Lukomski's plea to help the new immigrants (quoted at the beginning of the chapter), he did not mention anything the PNA or PAC could do to help them, but simply stated there needed to be an assessment of organizations providing immigrant services and a plan drawn up to procure increased funds for these needs. But the ethnic organizations themselves could not help the newcomers. Even if they wanted to, they were not set up for that function. As one director of the PAC said, "None of us are in a position or have the power to hire these people."

Several Polish immigrant service organizations existed in Chicago, such as the Polish Welfare Association and the Polish American Immigration and Relief Committee, but these were not membership-based organizations.[17] The conflict in the community centered around the fact that new immigrants were not joining ethnic organizations and large ethnic organizations, such as the PAC and the fraternals, were not helping new immigrants. This conflict is well summarized in the following quote from a woman who emigrated as a child in the late 1940s and was a secretary to the president of the PNA.

> We are all Poles but very different. There are the ones that came a long time ago, and the ones that came in the 1950s, and then now. People that I meet at work now are recent arrivals. These new arrivals think that Polonia owes them everything. When it doesn't give them everything then they are very disappointed and discouraged. They expect a lot from these organizations. But these are private institutions, not like in Poland where they are owned by the state. I have had contact with these new arrivals at the PNA, they just want a job and they want the organization to do something for them, all the time making demands and saying they want, they want. It's not like the post–World War II Poles. When they came they had their tails between their legs and they were meek and humble and they were willing to take any work at all. With these recent arrivals, if the organizations don't do what they want then it's very difficult to get them to join the PNA. What do they need insurance for, they aren't used to buying insurance. In Poland the state pays for everything—life and medical insurance. Its hard to convince them that they should buy this insurance. For most people the main interest is to make money to live here or go back to Poland. That's why they have two or three jobs. See the problem is that they were raised in a communist country so they have been brainwashed. They have a communist mentality, they don't understand how things work over here. And there is a

lot of problems because they don't want to join these organizations but they only want the organizations to help them.

Requests for assistance were interpreted as artifacts of communist socialization rather than as immigrant needs. Immigrants, she believed, asked for help because they came from communist Poland not because they were newcomers in America.

Although immigrants did not join ethnic organizations, they did form their own. In Chicago, new immigrants helped rebuild the Polish University Abroad (PUNO), and they created a chapter of the Club of Catholic Intelligentsia (KIK, *Klub Inteligencji Katolickiej*), modeled after a similar organization in Poland. They also formed numerous political organizations. In addition, the immigrants organized several new PNA lodges (and in this way did in fact "join" the fraternals, but they did not do so in large numbers). President Mazewski identified seven new fraternal lodges formed by new immigrants by 1988. Other new immigrant organizations included the Polish American Economic Forum, Polish Art's Club, Joseph Conrad Yacht Club, and *Klub Samotnych* (Singles Club).

The creation of new organizations was not as troublesome as their failure to join established organizations. The World War II émigrés themselves had created their own organizations,[18] so it was difficult for them to criticize the newcomers for the same behavior. Jan Nowak, a prominent World War II émigré, argued that new immigrants had different attachments to Poland and thought in different "categories" than did Polish Americans; they needed to form their own associations so as to ward off threats of dispersion and inactivity.

> People who share the same experiences and memories easily find common ground and become exclusive, often without realizing it. The younger generation which was raised in Poland, finding itself in a foreign land, instinctively is drawn toward groups of their countrymen, but soon see that they are only marginally tolerated. They often do not understand the old structures and symbols, to which the past soldiers emigration [World War II cohort] is so attached. . . . Criticizing the old emigration and Polonia is also useless. Let's take people as they are. Let's not expect an American (second- or third-generation of Polish decent) who still feels some attachment with Poland to think in the same categories as a young, newly arrived Pole. Let's not expect from him, for example, the same degree of loyalty towards democratic movements in Poland, as we expect from ourselves.[19]

Polish American leaders also agreed that new immigrants needed their own organizations. Explaining the formation of new fraternal lodges, PNA President Aloysius Mazewski said:

> See, it's better for them to have their own lodges because they understand each other. You see if it's an old lodge, you see, then there's some animosity, you know. And they have set ways of doing it. And even these newcomers have a different language. See the Polish language of the old is different, they have their particular style that has to be catered to.

The new immigrants strongly advocated their right and desire to form their own autonomous organizations. The new immigrants wanted to distinguish themselves from the already existent ethnic group. One founding member of Pomost, a new organization, wrote that this organization's goal was "to unite the politically active members of our generation and enable them to express their own judgments and to act outside the constraints of the current émigré routine. . . . Each new generation of emigrants must emphasize its own distinctive features."[20] The two groups—Polish American ethnics and Polish immigrants—needed different organization because they saw themselves as different. These differences originated in their different group biographies, which produced different symbolic meaning systems.

Within the community, this difference between the new immigrants and Polish Americans ethnics was at times described as a class difference. There was some consensus between the groups that class differences were important, but there was no consensus as to which group had the higher status. Both the immigrants and the Polish Americans believed they were of higher class. The educated immigrants compared themselves to, as one man said, "the sausage-selling grandchildren of the early peasants"; the suburban-dwelling Polish Americans compared themselves to "ghetto-dwelling hordes" of *wakacjusze* living and drinking in *Jackowo* "wearing funky nail polish" and living "like animals in a barn."[21] The fact is, there was more variation within cohorts than between cohorts. Both groups were economically, educationally, and occupationally diverse. As a migrant cohort, the new cohort was better educated and more cosmopolitan than the earlier "peasant" cohort. On average, however, the new immigrants did not have higher paying jobs or more wealth than Polish Americans. They were newcomers. Yet class is also related to education. New immigrants were often highly educated—more than half of them had some postsecondary education. Polish Americans had rates of educational attainment similar to those of other ethnics of European descent in America—roughly a third of the population attended some postsecondary school.[22] In America, however, education is generally linked to class through occupation. More schooling leads to better jobs with either higher wages or more prestige and most often both. This relation between education and occupation was more direct for native-born Americans than immigrants. New immigrants seldom worked in the occupations they were trained for or at the level they had before they emigrated. Emigration represented a decline in occupational status for most immigrants. Comparing the two groups in terms of income and occupation, Polish Americans fared better than immigrants; comparing the two groups in terms of education, the immigrants surpassed the ethnics. In a strict analysis that defines class only in economic terms, immigrants fell behind ethnics. However, immigrants had fewer resources because of their newcomer status, not because they had less education or fewer occupational skills.

Class also has a cultural component. Polish immigrants often remarked that they had a greater appreciation for "high culture," meaning art, operas, symphonies, and literature, and defined Polish Americans as having ties to a "folk culture" Polishness. Yet, the new immigrants' appreciation for high culture was not primarily related to their class position, but to their experiences in communist Poland. Polish Americans had less exposure to high culture because they lived in an American capitalist economy with a market-driven mass media culture, and had a greater affinity for Polish folk culture because they were descendants of a mostly peasant cohort. High culture is the domain of the middle and upper classes in America, where tickets to symphonies and operas are expensive.

In contrast, the communist government in Poland provided inexpensive and accessible admissions to concert halls and theaters.[23] Moreover, Poland's state-controlled television had only two channels, which, while showing some sports, slapstick comedies, and Hollywood serials (*Dallas* did make it to Poland), for the most part offered educational shows, documentaries, and musical entertainment. The offerings on Polish television resembled America's Public Broadcasting System. Americans would also be exposed to more "high culture" if the only television channel was PBS. Polish Americans' lack of appreciation for high culture is related to their predominantly working-class position in capitalist America.

The ethnic culture that working-class Polish Americans celebrated was the folk culture of their ancestors who came from rural Poland. Obidinski writes that Polonian customs are "residues of Polish American immigrant community activity derived from native peasant folkways." Helen Stankiewicz Zand describes some of the folk traditions that have survived in American Polonia. "We see that the dances, the 'polka' as a ballroom dance and the 'krakowiak' as an exhibition dance, have a great vitality and are likely to last for a long time. The 'krakowiak' costume, somewhat stylized but very close to the original, has almost become a conventional symbol of the Polish people."[24] The dances and costumes are descendant from a rural peasant culture and persist, especially the polka dance, primarily in the culture of working-class Polish American communities.

Not all Polish Americans are working class. Charles Keil argues that class divisions within ethnic Polonia are reflected in the types of culture they celebrate. He argues that most Polonian scholars and Polonian leaders prefer to emphasize high-culture Polishness, which connects descendants not to peasant roots but to aristocratic roots. Middle-class Polish Americans imaginatively romanticize themselves as "heirs of Polish kings and knights with ancient codes of chivalry and honor to uphold." Keil writes that middle-class Polonia "hates the polka with a passion" and shuns the corner bars, bowling alleys, and Knights of Columbus halls of the Polish American working class.[25] Within Polonia, these middle-class values and culture are reinforced by the smaller elite intellectual strata and the World War II émigré cohort.[26] This culture prefers to listen to Chopin rather that 'Lil Wally's Polka Band, they spend their time at the Polish Cultural Garden Club rather than the fraternal sports clubs, and with the Halina Singing Society rather than at the *Dom Polski.*

Whether it is a working-class tie to the peasantry or a middle-class tie to the aristocracy, Polish American culture nonetheless originates in nineteenth-century Poland. The cultural identity of the new immigrants is also rooted in their ancestors (no culture is ahistorical; they read Adam Mickiewicz and dance the Polonaise), but their cultural identity was transformed in twentieth-century Poland, so it has a contemporary as well as historical base in Poland. In contrast, the meaning of Polishness for Polish Americans was not modernized in Poland. At the Polonaise festival in July 1986, sponsored by the PAC Illinois Division, the brochure describing the Miss Polonaise contest stated, "Polish women kept the Old World Traits alive. They kneaded the *pierogi* and rolled the *gołąbki.*" Over the century, however, the "Old World" changed. The women in the new immigration were defined not by their kneading and rolling, but by their behavior in contemporary Poland. Polish women were accountants and doctors, they managed household when their activist husbands were sent to prison, and they themselves were union organizers. Moreover, Polonian culture rooted in peasant traditions was not familiar to new immigrants who came from urban areas in Poland; this folk history was not their history, so the symbols of this culture held little meaning for them.

The cultural and social landscape of Poland changed over the last fifty to one hundred years, and with it the symbols associated with Polishness. One new immigrant couple living in Michigan talked about these cultural differences between new immigrants and Polish Americans that became evident when they joined a Polish American organization. They started by saying they "cannot communicate with" Polish Americans. The husband said:

> Many [Polish Americans] do not speak correct Polish. And not only that, even people who came here thirty years ago, we are different. We have different values, we come from a different Poland. Poland now is all industry. There are no more farmlands. We all live in the city. My whole life I am living in the city.

And the wife said:

> And we cannot even talk to them. They are different. For example, we come here and everyone is having polka parties. In Poland no one polkas, oh maybe some folk groups, or for special ethnic days, but we dance the same dances as the Western world do now. And when we are together, I remember this one time we went to some thing at the Polish Heritage Foundation, and there were like two different cultures. The old Poles all sat on on one side of the room and we sat on the other side. . . . And at the Polish Heritage Foundation they do not even speak Polish!

Another immigrant complained because the PAC chose to finance the publication of a nineteenth-century novel rather than something by a more well-known contemporary Polish writer.

> It's really stupid, because it's something like the novel about in this country, if we can compare, the Wild West, with all the shooting and riding horses. It was great, OK, but when I was fourteen. And they consider this a great novel. Oh. I don't know. It's a little bit different situation, because in some point in Polish history it was the important book. But not right now. We have world-wide recognized writers. Why don't they print these things? Because they don't know.

Polish culture for new immigrants included contemporary symbols and figures. Polish culture for ethnics was rooted in the past.

Culture is not a static identity; it changes and evolves within a sociohistoric context. For Polish Americans this was an American context, and for new immigrants it was a Polish context. The best illustration of this is in language. Speaking a common language is often one indicator of shared identity. In Polonia, however, the Polish language was not a shared symbol system but a source of internal group borders. Many Polish Americans did not speak Polish, and when they did, it was often grammatically incorrect, full of outmoded expressions, with a heavy American accent or representative of regional dialects. One immigrant said, "You know we are a different group from these older Poles. . . . Many Poles do not even speak Polish, and some that do speak Polish, speak it very bad." Another newcomer said, "The old Poles are different; they are like chop suey. Not really Polish; not really America. When I hear them speak, I say, 'What's that? I never heard that before.'" One new immigrant referring to several directors of the PNA said: "It's really beautiful, their Polish, it has all these old phrases, but it's not the Polish spoken today. Some have these old accents that make it hard for you to understand them." And another immigrant said:

> Some of these old Poles, [laughs] they are really funny, their Polish. It is not American, it is not Polish. Some I can not even understand. Those that came from the turn of the century from these poorer regions, mostly Galicia, they are speaking a different Polish than we do. And then they are here and it changes. It is really funny to listen to them. Some of them are so colorful. There was this one man, he knew some Polish and this man from Poland, some famous guy, came and he wanted to impress him so he wanted to use his Polish and he told the man to sit down in Polish and said, "*siedź na dupie*" which means "sit on your ass." And this man doesn't even know what he is saying, but that he thinks he is politely saying to this man to sit down, because maybe this is how he hears his father say it.

Communication between new immigrants and Polish Americans was difficult even when they were both speaking Polish. As one Polish American stated, "There is still a language problem, even when I am speaking Polish with them." Languages are grounded in social contexts. The Polish of Polish Americans was an "old" Polish (grounded in nineteenth-century rural Poland), but it was also, in a sense, a "new" Polish because it was a language transformed in American. Languages are not dead as long as they continue to be used. The Polish used by Polish Americans was a hybrid, a new language: not Polish, not American but like "chop suey."[27]

The Polish language had changed over the generations in twentieth-century Polonia, but the new immigrants' use of language was also altered within the context of communist Poland. One of the ways this manifest itself was in the writing styles of the new immigrants. One World War II émigré, a former editor of the Polonia newspaper *Dziennik Związkowy,* had hired new immigrants as staff writers. He connected the writing styles of the new immigrants to the state-controlled media in Poland. "They were born and they were raised and they know the Soviet style of journalism. . . . For example, they love to have interview, because in Soviets you have interview in the paper splashed all over, interview with Natasia Aleksandrownia who was the top tractor operator in some factory so she is a good hero, so interview in all the paper." He also believed that censorship in communist Poland shaped their writing skills so that they learned to write extremely long articles, "to figure out the space to talk and not to say anything."

The different writing styles became an issue in the Polish American Economic Forum (Forum), an organization established in 1989 composed of Polish Americans and new Polish immigrants. Several Forum documents, promotional letters, and information bulletins originally written in Polish had to be both translated into English and, as one Polish American said, "Americanized," which meant "changing the mood" of the articles. To put it into an American language meant to put it into a language that sells. For example, the Polish version of Forum's main promotional letter was six long paragraphs (five to six sentences per paragraph) and described in excruciating detail the inaugural meeting, the upcoming convention, Forum's offices, and membership fees. It was a very dry and boring document. The American version was only half as long, had ten short paragraphs (one or two sentences per paragraph), only briefly mentioned the inaugural meeting, convention, and membership fees, and focused mainly on the "extraordinary transition" occurring in Poland and the "inevitable opportunity" for profits. The American version was marked with punchy propaganda and included spicy adjectives and phrases about the "great change" and "urgent need" in Poland because the "alien system was being dismantled."

Language was also a source of divisiveness in the community when groups were forced to choose between Polish and English. Forum members debated which language to use (Polish or English) and, though the debate had certain practical tones, it also had symbolic meaning. Forum members spent half of one business meeting arguing over "the official language of Forum." A Polish American member identified this debate over language as "a philosophical question: Is Forum a Polish organization or an American organization?" In Forum's formative stages, the Polish American chairman (who spoke Polish) stated that English would be the official organizational language, although 98 percent of the members were not native English speakers and most were not proficient in English. In addition, most of the people in Poland with whom Forum negotiated did not speak English. In the beginning, despite the chairman's pronouncements, most of the literature leaving the office was in Polish only. The discussion of the official language surfaced again at the first board of directors' meeting. Although the majority of board members (78 percent) were native Polish speakers, the Polish American chairman decided that Forum was "an American organization. We should have English as the official language." He decreed that all board meetings were to be conducted in English. The result was that conversation was in English when the chairman was in the room, but in Polish when he was not present. Though the Polish Americans wanted to "Americanize" Forum, the nature of the membership base demanded that business be conducted in Polish. In the end, most business was conducted in Polish; however, the office staff meetings, literature, and the conventions were bilingual.

Language did not bring the two groups together. For Polish Americans, their Polish was tied to their immigrant ancestors and had transformed in American society; the new immigrants' language had evolved in twentieth-century communist Poland. In some instances, language became a site of struggle between the immigrants and ethnics as they vied for the power to define the situation as either American (English) or Polish. In the community, the Polish, Polish American, and English languages represented three different symbol systems, and these differences became in-house borders, or ways of defining "us" and "them."

Other symbols of Polishness were also not easily shared. One arena that illustrated symbolic differences was the May 3d Polish Constitution Day parade. This is "The" Polish parade in the City of Chicago. During the parade in 1988, over one hundred floats and groups marched down LaSalle Street, including Americans, Polish Americans, World War II émigrés, and new Polish immigrants. The first set of symbols displayed expressed Poland's contemporary struggles. In the "Solidarity group" (there was only one) most of the marchers (all new immigrants) wore T-shirts with the slogan "Alive *Solidarność*," and some had a number below this slogan that was the wearer's former prison number. The banners in this group reflected the contemporary political situation in Poland (for example, "*Solidarność*," "Free Elections in Poland, Jaruzelski Out," "Free Political Prisoners," a swastika and the Soviet emblem with an equal sign between them, "Support Polish Strikes"). The group chanted political slogans (among them, "Solidarity—Yes, Communism—No," "Free Elections in Poland," "Stop Red Peril," "Lech Walesa," "*Solidarność*," "Jaruzelski Out"). This was the only group whose symbolic representation was based solely on contemporary Poland. Other groups displayed banners with symbols of Poland's opposition, however, these symbols of Poland's contemporary struggles were intertwined with ethnic or American symbols. For example, groups representing Polish American fraternal lodges and Polish Saturday schools also carried *Solidarność* placards, and the Illinois Right to Life group carried Polish flags and *Solidarność* placards. They used the symbols of Solidarity to complement and legitimate their own Polonian and American symbols.

A second set of symbols represented traditional Polish culture, much of which has found its way into Polish American (Polonian) culture. For example, people in the Krakus Ham float wore folk costumes, as did people marching to represent ethnic fraternal lodges. Others drew on Poland's political history of democracy, such as politician (and non-Pole) Tom Hynes, whose group carried a picture of him with the words, "We Salute the Polish Constitution." The constitution was written in 1791, just before the second partition of Poland and is a national Polish symbol of democracy and independence. The folk costumes and constitution are representations of Polish national history; these are symbols that have been incorporated into Polonian culture yet also remain meaningful in contemporary Poland.

A third set of symbols represented Polonian culture. For example, one group sang Bobby Vinton's song, "*Moja droga, ja ci kocham.*" Bobby Vinton is a popular singer in American Polonia with very little name recognition in Poland. Another Polonian association carried a banner that read, "Pride in our Country's Heritage." Pride and heritage reflect ethnic concerns in America. Other Polonian symbols of pride included T-shirts and pins with such pro-Polish heritage logos as: "Proud to Be Polish," "Half Polish Is Better Than None," "Genuine Polish Parts, Happiness Is Being Polish," and "Polish Power." These are not slogans one finds on T-shirts in Poland (except, perhaps, in shops catering to Polish American tourists). The fraternals, who sponsored the parade and whose lodges represented numerous groups in the parade, are themselves Polonian symbols. Fraternalism is an ethnic American institution rooted in late nineteenth- and early twentieth-century immigrant culture. The bands playing polkas also symbolized Polonian, not Polish, culture. In America the polka is almost synonymous with Polish Americans (perhaps to Polonian scholars and leaders it is synonymous with working-class Polish American culture, but to the rest of America it represents Polish American culture in general). The polka is actually a Czech dance that has become incorporated into Polish American culture. It is not a meaningful symbol of Polish national culture in Poland.

During the parade, new immigrants identified with the historical (the constitution) and contemporary Polish symbols but not the Polonian symbols. They wore buttons supporting *Solidarność* rather than ones that said, "Kiss Me I'm Polish." The new immigrants watching the parade joked when the "polka floats" passed, telling each other to go and join the music; "That's your group," they ribbed to each other and then laughed. Another said sarcastically, "Yes, yes, I loooove that music." These symbols of ethnic Polonia did not resonate with the new immigrant.[28]

In one exchange, a Polish immigrant who was a radio talk show host had to defend, or at least justify, to a confused Polish American woman why his radio program did not play polka. The Polish American woman suggested, "You should spice it up a bit with some polkas. . . . What do you talk about anyway?" This was in the spring of 1988 and the immigrant mentioned the strikes in Poland and the activities of Solidarity. The ethnic responded, "I still say go for the polkas, they would add some life." For the ethnic, the polka was a symbol of Polish radio. For the immigrant, contemporary issues in Poland—social, political, literary, and economic—defined the context of new Polish media.

While immigrants have concrete ties to a contemporary homeland, ethnic ties are mediated through their ancestors. As a result, the two groups do not always share the same culture or even the same language. Social benefits such as friendship or entertainment that are derived from participation in organizations operate in those arenas where there is a like-mindedness among members. New immigrants did not experience a like-mindedness with Polish American ethnics, and therefore were unlikely to join an organization for its social benefits. Moreover, one primary goal of ethnic organizations was to promote cultural maintenance. Even if the immigrants decided they wanted to work on maintaining their culture, they did not necessarily agree with the Polish Americans on the symbolic basis of Polishness. These symbolic differences interfered with the practical problems of working together in the same organizations, and partly explain why new immigrants formed their own organizations.

Was Forum a Polish or an American organization? Symbols identify and maintain borders between groups. Much the same way that Pierre Bourdieu discusses borders between class groups, borders between social groups[29]—in this case ethnics and immigrants—are also symbolically produced. Symbols are used by members of a group to define who they are as well as who they are not. Each group in Polonia fought to preserve its definition of Self; and ownership of the community depended in part on each group's power to symbolically define the public arena. The new immigrants would find themselves outside the community if Polonia were defined as speaking English and celebrating folk culture; the Polish Americans would find themselves shoved aside in a polka-hating, Polish-speaking community.

Contentious conflicts in the community were over the new immigrants' unwillingness to join ethnic organizations and with the ethnic organizations' inability to satisfy new immigrant needs. The established Polonians used a discourse of communism to explain what they considered undesirable behavior. Socialized in a capitalistic-democratic society, they believed that pervasive, subtle, and cunning communism brainwashed its victims and made them unable to understand concepts like freedom and democracy, that the supply-market principles of the communist system destroyed the work ethic of its citizens, and finally, that communism fostered an attitude of dependency. While members of the new migrant cohort seldom became dependent on state resources, they did expect the ethnic community to help them. The ethnic community, however, was structured to satisfy ethnic needs, not newcomer, immigrant needs. As a result, the new immigrants saw no immediate reason to join the ethnic organizations. Moreover, the immigrants did not feel a solidarity of likeness with Polish Americans. The two groups had different experiences, they had different social identities (ethnic and immigrant) that occasioned different needs, and they had different understandings of Polishness. Immigrants had direct experience with communism, while Polish Americans experienced communism filtered through an American lens. Immigrants experienced being newcomers to a society; ethnics experienced being established members of a society. Polishness for ethnics (its language and symbols) reflected nineteenth-century Poland; immigrants had a more up-to-date version. The immigrants and ethnics shared an historical identity but not a contemporary one.

Notes

1. Snow and Benford's application of frame analysis to social movement participation is useful here. They argue that frames need to resonate in order to mobilize people to participate in collective action. Cross-cultural variations lead to different experiences, which explain, for example, why different frames were used to mobilize members of the peace movement in Europe and the United States. David Snow and Robert Benford, "Ideology, Frame Resonance, and Participant Mobilization." In *International Social Movement Research* (Greenwich, Conn.: JAI Press, 1988) 1:197–217. Ruth Frankenberg, *White Women, Race Matters: The Social Construction of Whiteness* (Minneapolis: University of Minnesota Press, 1993), 265; Erving Goffman, *Frame Analysis* (New York: Harper & Row, 1974), 21.

2. Writing in the 1970s, Claremont de Castillejo stated: "Today we spend a lot of energy rabidly hating the Russians or the Chinese for their disregard of individual life and individual liberty. . . . We see the tyrannies in Russia and China and hate them with our souls, but because we have not noticed that we are no longer free ourselves, we vent our hatred on the Chinese or Russians, instead of on the tyranny. Irene Claremont de Castijello, *Knowing Woman: A Feminine Psychology* (New York: Harper and Row, 1972), 31.

3. This argument does not suggest that there was no valid intellectual, military, or moral objections to communism, but it does maintain that America's anxiety was at times akin to a national phobia, which does imply that at times the threat was exaggerated and irrational. See Richard Crockatt, *The Fifty Years War: The United States and the Soviet Union in World Politics, 1941–1991* (New York: Routledge, 1995), for an analysis of the real military threats during the 1950s. Edward Said, *Orientalism* (New York: Vintage Books, 1978); bell hooks, *Black Looks: Race and Representation* (Boston: South End Press, 1992); Frankenberg, *White Women, Race Matters*.

4. Gertraude Roth Li, "The Polish People: The Challenge of Sponsorship." *World Relief, Ethnic Profile* (New York: Refugee Services Division, 1982), 5–7.

5. It is important to note that only legal immigrants could use the Polish Welfare Association (PWA) to find employment. This means that those people seeking work were looking for permanent employment, for careers rather than short-term jobs. Also, many members of the new cohort had been educated professionals in Poland, and they wanted the PWA to help them find similar occupations in the United States. The PWA did not have strong networks into the professional communities. In fact, the late 1980s the PWA advised Polish immigrants with professional credentials to go to Jewish Vocational Services.

5. Donald Cichon, Elzbieta Gozdziak, and Jane Grover, *The Economic and Social Development of Non-Southeast Asian Refugees,* vol. 2, *Chicago Poles* (Washington, D.C.: U.S. Department of Health and Human Services, Office of Refugee Resettlement, GPO, 1986), 14, 26, 48, 59.

6. Ann Templeton, "The Chicago Project: A Demonstration Refugee Resettlement Program Aimed at Self-Sufficiency" (Chicago: Catholic Charities of Chicago, 1984), 27, 37.

7. Cichon et al., *Economic and Social Development,* 18.

8. The study of non-Southeast Asian refugees found that 75 percent of employed Polish refugees found jobs through informal referrals, another 21 percent through newspapers or professional journals, and only one person found a job through an organization. Cichon et al., *Economic and Social Development,* 59.

9. In Mostwin's survey of 552 Polish immigrants who arrived between 1974 and 1984, the respondents listed their three most important needs in order as work, learning English, and finding a place to live. Danuta Mostwin, *Emigranci polscy w USA* (Polish immigrants in the USA) (Lublin, Poland: Catholic University of Lubin Press, 1991), 78. They were also very critical of "*stara Polonia*" (old Polonia) precisely because they did not help them meet these needs. One man wrote, "It's not worth writing about old Polonia; they would rather take than help" (80). Templeton, "The Chicago Project," 22, 34–35; Cichon et al., *Economic and Social Development,* 15, 18–19, 32

10. This statement came to me from Michael Blichasz, national chairman for the Polish American Heritage Month committee, sponsored by the PAC, who sent me information about the October 1988 activities in a letter dated February 2, 1989. He compiled a summary of the positive and negative comments he received about Heritage Month. These comments are not his own, but reflect a synthesis of the opinions of various members of Polonia.

11. Donald E. Pienkos, *PNA: A Centennial History of the Polish National Alliance of the United States of America* (Boulder, Colo.: East European Monographs, 1984), 323, 329.

12. Cichon et al., *Economic and Social Development;* Mostwin, *Emigranci polscy w USA;* interviews with Polish priests.

13. Maciej Wierzynski, "Dno" (Bottom). *Kurier,* July 4, p. 11.

14. At the national meetings in November 1988, the PAC had to choose a new president to replace the twenty-year president Aloysius Mazewski, who had died. A motion to vote by secret ballot for the president and to elect the president from a number of candidates, rather than accept or reject the entire slate of candidates, reflects the fact that this was a new procedure.

> Council member: Mr. Lukomski and delegates, with the death of our late president, it brings us to a very important turning point in the Polish American Congress. Right now, I think the Polish press and radio, the Polonia, are looking at us, to see how we will elect our next president. Will it be in the democratic form? Will it be in the suggestive form as it was in the past? . . . We're talking all the time about democratic opposition in Poland, we want free elections—at least the highest ranking person should be elected by this body.

Even within the PAC, the framework of democracy and communism was used to promote or sanction behavior.

15. The churches provided more immigrant services than did the ethnic organizations. For example, in 1987–88, when illegal immigrants could apply for residency through the Immigration Reform and Control Act (IRCA), the largest Polish church in Chicago, St. Hyacinth (*Kościół św. Jacka*) in *Jackowo,* held community meetings after its masses and brought in city officials and representatives from agencies to provide information and help the immigrants through the legalization process. It also had nightly ESL classes and programs that assisted immigrants who wanted to become naturalized citizens. The focus of this study was not, however, on churches, and so I cannot argue that this institution was more effective than the ethnic organization in serving immigrant needs. Several immigrants complained as bitterly about the Polish American churches as they did about the ethnic organizations, but for different reasons. Mostwin discusses new immigrant relations within old Polonian parishes more completely. She argues that the churches did not successfully meet the needs of new immigrants because the role of the priest was based on traditional models and suggests that the Polish American parish needed a new type of priest that was more sensitive to the psychological and social needs of new immigrants. Mostwin, *Emigranci polscy w USA.*

16. It should be mentioned that none of the ethnic organizations were financially well-off. Yet,

I do not think that a tight budget necessarily explains the conflict. The organizations chose to direct their funds (however meager they were) toward ethnic functions. They funded ethnic and choral groups rather than employment service programs. I am also not arguing that they *should* have provided for immigrant needs but only pointing out that new immigrants made demands on the organizations because they were "Polish," ignoring or not understanding the fact that they were ethnic organizations, not immigrant organizations. Perhaps, however, if they had been resource-rich organizations they could have provided for both ethnic and immigrant needs.

17. The Polish Welfare Association provided for specific immigrant needs including counseling services for newcomers, food and clothing banks, employment services, translation services, English language classes, and assistance negotiating American institutions, primarily government programs and the legal system. In the six-month period between July 1985 and January 1986, this agency served 631 Polish newcomers, 41 percent of whom were refugees. (Cichon et al., *Economic and Social Development*, 31). Unlike the early fraternal organizations that were strictly in-house operations, this agency was funded mostly by state and federal programs. It occasionally received modest donations from the larger Polish American fraternals but this made up only a small percentage of its annual income. In 1989, almost two-thirds of its funds came from the state and federal governments, and only 4.7 percent came from the Polish American fraternals. (*Annual Report of the Polish Welfare Association,* Chicago, Ill., 1989, 15).

The Polish American Immigration and Relief Committee, Inc. (PAIRC) was founded after World War II to help resettle Polish refugees. It helps only refugees, not all immigrants. In the 1980s, the PAIRC was one of the official resettlement agencies in the United States and it received its funding primarily from federal funds appropriated through the Office of Refugee Resettlement. During the 1980s it resettled an average of five hundred Polish refugees a year. PAIRC's "paramount aim" was to help "newcomers become self-sufficient and productive members of their new homeland and not a drain on its economy." The PAIRC was not dedicated to helping refugees find employment in fields similar to the ones they had in Poland, but instead to getting them jobs as quickly as possible. Polish refugees who were resettled by PAIRC complained that this agency was more concerned about getting them any job than getting them a good job. To restate what Lukomski said in his letter to Mazewski, quoted at the beginning of this chapter, the PAIRC was not "handling the problem satisfactorily, appearing to regard the refugees as a troublesome burden." *Refugee Resettlement Program,* Report to Congress (Office of Refugee Resettlement, U.S. Department of Health and Human Services, Washington, D.C., 1983), 63.

18. Stanislaus Blejwas, "Old and New Polonias: Tension Within an Ethnic Community." *Polish American Studies* 38, 22 (1981): 55–83.

19. Jan Nowak, "Pomost." *Pomost Quarterly* 5 (Winter 1980): 3–4.

20. Wlademar Wlodarczyk, "Pomost After One Year." *Pomost Quarterly* 6 (Spring 1980): 40.

21. Like most Americans, they used class as synonymous with social status or prestige. I would like to thank Peggy Malecki for providing me with the tapes of three interviews she conducted with Polish Americans in the fall of 1986. This last quote came from one of her interviews.

22. Stanley Lieberson and Mary Waters, *From Many Strands: Ethnic and Racial Groups in Contemporary America* (New York: Russell Sage Foundation, 1988), 107–8.

23. Jeffrey Goldfarb, *On Cultural Freedom: An Exploration of Public Life in Poland and America* (Chicago: University of Chicago Press, 1982).

24. Eugene Obidinski, and Helen Stankiewicz Zand, *Polish Folkways in America: Community and Family* (New York: University Press of America, 1987), 118, 138.

25. Charles Keil, "Class and Ethnicity in Polish-America." *Journal of Ethnic Studies* 7 (2): 38–39, 43.

26. Obidinski and Zand, *Polish Folkways in America*; Felix Gross, "Notes on the Ethnic Revolution and the Polish Immigration in the U.S.A." *The Polish Review* 21 (3): 150–72.

27. Helen Stankiewicz Zand offers a wonderful discussion of how the Polish language changed in America (Obidinski and Zand, *Polish Folkways in America*, 40–49). She emphasizes that the Polish American tongue is distinct from the Polish spoken in contemporary Poland. Derived from mostly peasant origins, Polish American Polish reflects regional dialects and includes numerous

American words (spoken with Polish inflections) referring to objects and concepts that did not exist in Poland around the turn of the century. Moreover, when a Polish American speaks Polish the pronunciation is softened—"It sounds muffled as though it were spoken through flannel" as vowels and consonants "lose their sharp contours" (43).

28. I cannot make any well-supported claims about the extent to which customs maintained in Polish American families are maintained in new immigrant families. I have observed some key traditions of Polish American culture that are also practiced by new immigrants; for example, *Wigilia* (the Christmas Eve supper), *Święconka* (the blessing of the Easter baskets), and *Kolędy* (Christmas caroling). These are national traditions, not specifically peasant traditions. There are other traditions that I have not observed but I cannot state authoritatively that immigrants do or do not practice them (for example, Dyngus Day, the bridal dance, visiting relatives' graves on All Saints Day). Many of these traditions are family traditions or private matters, and my data collection focused on organizations. While I participated in family gatherings with new immigrants, the data are too weak to make any strong claims. I am not arguing that there was no common culture between new immigrants and Polish Americans, only that some symbols of Polonian culture (such as the polka) were not meaningful to new immigrants. For a wonderful discussion of Polish folkways in America, see Obidinski and Zand, *Polish Folkways in America*.

29. Pierre Bourdieu, "Social Space and Symbolic Power." *Sociological Theory* 7 (1): 14–25.

18

"Ser De Aquí"

Beyond the Cuban Exile Model

NANCY RAQUEL MIRABAL

I have no memory to recall what happened, I have no home to keep the memories.

—Emilio Bejel, 1995

¿Qué quiere decir "ser de aquí"?

—Dolores Prida, 1991

Memory and Home

There are two themes, however nuanced, which have surrounded, defined, and at times, haunted Cuban-United States historiography; memory and home. For the 1959 exile community and those born to it, they remain inseparable. The multiple meanings attached to each are invaluable starting points for unraveling what it means to be Cuban in the United States during a period of exile and separation. For the US Cuban writer and poet Achy Obejas, being Cuban in the United States has meant realizing and accepting that her parents' anti-Communist politics as well as their decision to leave Cuba marked her early on as an exile. Because of her parents' politics and their decision to leave Cuba for the United States as refugees, Obejas can only imagine what would have happened "if we'd stayed, and there had been no revolution?"

The question posed by Obejas is both deceptively simple and very powerful. With it she reveals how nostalgia operates in her own personal reinvention, in her own attempts to travel back and reconfigure time, politics, and space, during a period of global and political transition. While Obejas' wondering is not a new intervention in the exile dialogue, what makes it important is that at the same time that she allows memory to shape her identity as a Cuban exile, she is also cognizant of its potential dangers. "I try to imagine who I would have been if Fidel had never come into Havana sitting triumphantly on top of the tank, but I can't. I can only think of variations of who I am, not who I might have been."[1] As Obejas decides *not* to speculate on what could have happened had her family stayed in Cuba, and Castro had not come into power, she challenges the traditional narrative of the post-1959 Cuban exile, a narrative that has been consumed by images of dreaming, possibility, memory, and returning home. By reworking her own definitions of exile and revolution without falling into a litany of "what ifs," Obejas initiates a discussion on what it means to be *from here* in ways that reassert self, by both echoing and disrupting previous narratives concerning the exile experience in the US.

The images associated with exile arise, as Flavio Risech has written, from the fact that Cubans "only cross the border in one direction." Despite the expectation that many would soon return, "the crossing proved over time to be irrevocable and necessitated a reconceptualization of the meaning of leaving Cuba for the US."[2] In addition to re-evaluating what it means to leave Cuba, there also needs to be a rethinking of what it means to *stay* in the United Stated, to define, as the poet Dolores Prida has written, to be "*de aquí*" (from here). Deciphering as well as defining what it means to be from here, however, is not easy. The collective memory of the Cuban exile experience is deeply influenced by a language rooted in the longing for returns as well as the imagining of those returns. So lasting are these emotions that for many born in the United States to Cuban exiles, Cuba and being Cuban has evolved into a memory that is handed down and imparted through pictures, recollections, and a nostalgia that so often belongs to others.

Nostalgia serves multiple functions. It keeps whole that which is fractured and in pain. It creates identity and purpose; it reminds and it renews. It is both fixed and fluid enough to hold memory and experience. Yet, what is particular to one wave of exiles about this shared, if not at times, imagined nostalgia when, as Maria de los Angeles Torres has written, each new wave "has brought an updated vision of the island?"[3] How do these distinct "updated" visions reconfigure how we remember the island? To what extent have successive waves of exiles, especially those who arrived in the 1980s and 1990s, been defined and marked by a 1959 revolutionary nostalgia?

A defining element in the creation and reinforcement of nostalgia is that it can move past the individual recollection of events and memory to the community where, as Román de la Campa has observed, it breeds "a strong sense of Cuban [exile] nationalism."[4] At the same time, a politicized nostalgia of the other, of the one that has left and abandoned the revolution, can also create a distinct revolutionary nationalism based in Cuba. And yet, these competing nostalgic nationalisms are incompatible with the current political, social, economic, and cultural world systems defined primarily by globalization and transnationalism. Moreover, because this nostalgia is so heavily dependent and centered on geography—that is, the continual re-imagining of leaving and returning to the island—it further complicates how we reconcile community, memory, experience, and time.

This paper examines how such connections and disruptions have affected how we write the history of Cubans in the United States. Without lessening the role of the Cuban Revolution of 1959, this paper looks at the limitations of a framework that continues to be influenced by nostalgia, multiple nationalisms, rupture, longing, and separation. It situates and problematizes historiography by recognizing the process involved in the production of knowledge and the "infinite series of historical meanings"[5] implicit in that production—meanings that are indicative of politics, place, and the uses of space.

In so doing, this essay re-frames historiography in terms of possibility and change. It calls for a more expansive framework, one that links the history of the pre-1959 Cuban diaspora with that of the post-1959 diaspora. The contention is that such linkages allow for a rethinking of geographic movement across time, as well as the cultivation of the spaces necessary for examining the historical impact and relationship among varied migrations that have yet to fit well under the rubric of the exile model. Although consistently understudied, race and gender were pivotal to the formation of early Cuban exile and migrant communities. Early exile and migrant annexationist, separatist, and independence movements used negotiated meanings attached to "blackness," "whiteness," and "in-betweenness," to define and build nation.[6] In the same vein, the all-male leadership of the exile and migrant nationalist movement developed a masculinist rhetoric of independence and nation that placed women on the margins of the nation-building project, regardless of their activism in the exile and migrant nationalist movements of the 19th century.[7] Added to this theoretical questioning is an effort to further our understanding of the parameters and workings of historical thinking and writing by exploring the theoretical relocation of physical geographies, which is the recognition of the importance of "place" in historical re-inventions. It argues that in addition to Florida (i.e., Key West and Tampa), the Cuban migrants who lived and worked in cities like New York, New Orleans, and Washington DC also had a hand in redefining and re-creating a larger Cuban diasporic identity.

Between Currents: Politics, Location, and History Making

> . . . knowing Cuba may well depend on how strongly one is willing to imagine it.
> —Román de la Campa, 2000

> Now that I am here I don't know where to start.
> —Sonia Rivera-Valdés, 1998

What it means to be Cuban in a period of separation and change has been no less than an obsession for writers, thinkers, and scholars living on both ends of the currents. The artist and critic Coco Fusco attributes this to the fact "that we are always fighting with the people we love the most." For Fusco this intensity results from the "tremendous repression and forced separation that affects all people who are ethnically Cuban, wherever they reside."[8] Being Cuban, regardless of distance and geography, has informed much of the politics of the Cuban diaspora. Cuban exile politics has ranged from the virulently anti-Castro organization, *Cuban American National Foundation* (CANF) to the dialogue-centered *Cambio Cubano*. For close to 20 years, CANF supported candidates who shared its hard-lined views, raised millions of dollars to fuel its anti-Castro campaigns, and was involved in drafting legislation like the Helms–Burton Act of 1996 which consolidated the then 34–year-old embargo against Cuba. In 1997, CANF's leader Jorge Más Canosa died. Más Canosa's death signaled a break in the widespread acceptance of CANF's entrenched and inflexible political agenda. In its place, a more moderate style of exile politics emerged, aimed at ending past hostilities and opening a dialogue among Cubans on the island and in exile.

This is not to say, however, that Cuban exiles had not previously resisted the entrenched anti-Castro politics so closely associated with CANF. By advocating for dialogue and connection, members of the Antonio Maceo Brigades of the late 1970s initiated an alternative exile political agenda and identity.[9] By 1993 organizations such as the Cuban Committee for Democracy resisted CANF's political agenda by not only supporting a dialogue—un díalogo—among all Cubans, but also a reassessment of the "success" of the embargo, and an intercambio or exchange between Cuban and Cuban-American artists, writers, musicians, and politicians. These organizations resisted the politics of CANF and, in so doing, marked a shift in the political consciousness of many Cubans in the United States. The September 1995 edition of *NACLA: Report on the Americas* recognized this shift when it noted that much of "the purported right-wing hegemony of exile politics—the great Myth of the Miami Monolith—does not hold up under scrutiny." The report went on to argue that in terms of general ideological leanings, "about 45% of Cuban-Americans classify themselves as moderate or liberal."[10] At the same time, the political and economic system in Cuba has been changing. During the last 20 years, Cuba has weathered severe economic difficulties (i.e., the special period), and reinvented itself in a manner that combines ever-evolving definitions of capitalism with its own brand of Cuban socialism. This has resulted in an economy that integrates both dollars and pesos in an inequitable fashion, leading to economic and social divisions among those Cubans who have access to dollars and those who do not. Moreover, the Cuban government's interest in globalization has encouraged foreign investments in Cuba, a dramatic rise in tourism, and a new openness towards past adversaries.

The political, economic, and social changes in Cuba and among Cubans in the US have had a far-reaching impact on historical thinking and the field. Scholars, writers, artists, and researchers interested in Cuban-American studies are questioning theoretical frameworks that disproportionately focus on the experiences of Cubans who migrated after 1959 and before 1965. Not only does this framework characterize this period of migration as indicative of all Cuban migration experiences, but it also produces a set of exile and identity definitions that are difficult to penetrate and reconstitute. In her introduction to *Bridges to Cuba/Puentes a Cuba*, the anthropologist Ruth Behar comments on the inflexibility of a post-revolutionary Cuban identity when discussing the relationship between the polarizing and repercussive effects of a framework "born to the Cold War."

> Cuba, since the revolution, has been imagined as either a utopia or a backward police state. . . . Within this conflicting web of representations born to the Cold War, there is little room for a more nuanced and complex vision of how Cubans on the island and in the diaspora give meaning to their lives, their identity, and their culture in the aftermath of a battle that has split the nation at the root.[11]

Considering that Fidel Castro is celebrating over 40 years of power, that US migration policy has changed with the signing of Operation Distant Shore in 1994,[12] and that second generation Cuban migrants are re-evaluating the politics of their parents, it is more important than ever to draw not only "another map of Cuba," but also another map of the Cuban exile and migrant experience.

A necessary strategy in the re-mapping is to question why the bulk of the research has focused on examining the history of Cubans who migrated after the Communist Revolution. The problem with approaching the field with the assumption that the story begins in 1959 is that it promotes what the historian Gerald E. Poyo has argued to be an "inaccurate vision of the experience of Cubans in the United States." The heavy emphasis on 1959 has contributed to a scholarship that defines the Cuban migrant experience as beginning with the Cuban Revolution and "being essentially conservative, white, and middle class." For Poyo, the solution lies in the reconstruction of frameworks that involve pre-1959 communities, are geographically and theoretically located in the United States, and are "linked conceptually to the contemporary experience."[13]

A major paradigm that a reconfigured exile model would challenge is the over-riding interest in the "Cuban success story." Rooted in a post-1959 paradigm, the Cuban success model was designed to explain why Cubans were more "successful" than other migrants from Latin America. Scholars pointed to various variables to cast the Cuban exile as "unique," including the importance of social origins, the time of migration, the development of ethnic enclaves, and the existence of government programs like the Cuban Refugee Program of 1961 and the Cuban Adjustment Act of 1966.[14] One who warned against the proliferation of studies examining and measuring the success of Cuban migrants was the late Cuban writer and scholar Lourdes Casal. According to Casal, by focusing on "success," Cubans were not getting a clear picture of their true situation. In her opinion, "it desensitized them and others to the hidden costs of success, and it isolated them from other American minorities."[15] Casal's warning proved prophetic. The circumstances surrounding the Mariel Boatlift dramatically altered how the Cuban migration would be characterized. Scholars went from asking why Cubans were so successful to why Mariel Cubans failed to be *as* successful.

The Mariel Boatlift was unlike any other exile migration. Out of the 124,776 Cubans estimated to have arrived between April and October of 1980, a large percentage were males, Afro-Cuban, working-class, and part of a revolutionary society that was relatively unknown to the Cubans who left in the early to mid-1960s. Unlike previous waves of migration, most had little or no experience under any other regime outside of Castro. This meant that Mariel Cubans were more likely than past migrants to support elements of the regime including universal access to education and health care, while challenging the poor economy, the persecution of homosexuals, and the lack of consumer products.

The media attention and coverage given to the Mariel Boatlift was also very different. Whereas past migrations were viewed with a mixture of empathy and awe, this migration was seen as problematic. The media placed an inordinate amount of attention on those migrants who had been released from Cuban jails, even though they made up less than 5% of the overall migration.[16] Added to this, Mariel Cubans arrived during a period when migrants from El Salvador, Nicaragua, the Dominican Republic, Haiti, and Mexico were also entering the country in large numbers, prompting the Florida legislature to demand assistance from the federal government. The negative media coverage along with the massive migration of non-white migrants inspired a statewide immigration backlash. Despite their exile status, recent Cuban arrivals were treated much the same as other Latin American migrants. In the same year as the Mariel Boatlift, voters in Florida rejected the Bilingual–Bicultural Ordinance, making it unlawful to employ county funds to promote the use of "any language other than English . . . or any culture other than that of the United States."[17]. The campaign to reinforce English as the official language was a strong indicator that South Florida residents were becoming wary of this wave of exiles.

The growing anti-immigrant sentiment, the caution of older Cuban exiles, as well as the unflattering media coverage inspired a rethinking of Cuban migration policy. By the time the Cuban *balseros* (rafters) arrived in the early 1990s, the Clinton Administration had reversed a three decades old policy. In August 1994, President Clinton announced that Cubans picked up by the US Coast Guard would no longer be brought to the United States. Known as Operation Distant Shore, this policy reduced Cuban migration by making it more difficult than ever for Cubans to reach the US. Without much fanfare and very little media coverage, Cuban exiles were now forced to accept that they were no longer "special" or entitled to the same privileges enjoyed by past migrants. Much like the Mariel Boatlift, the Clinton Administration's decision to circumvent Cuban immigration policy led to a rethinking of past historical and theoretical models. Not only was the "success" model questioned, but also those that promoted the "unique" character of Cuban migration and settlement. The shift was nowhere more visible than when Cubans were turned away and resettled in Guantánamo Base.[18]

In addition to challenging past frameworks, the last two waves emphasized what has been missing and understudied in the field of Cuban–United States Studies: race. The racial character of both the Mariel Boatlift and the *balseros* (rafters) no doubt contributed to the changes in migration policy as well as to the unease among many in the "white," older, and more established Cuban community in Miami. When race is examined it is defined solely in terms of blackness. It would appear that the only people in the Cuban exile community who have "race" are those who are Afro-Cuban or racially mixed. The theoretical gaze needs to be redirected so that we can look at how "whiteness," or better the perception of "whiteness," has also been used to facilitate and sustain a privileged exile.[19]

Often an "unspoken" in the process of Cuban exile identity formation, race is often subsumed under the theoretical rubric of "culture," both fostering and reinforcing the belief that all Cubans in the United States share the same experiences, regardless of race. At the core of such invisibility is the use of a theoretical language that emphasizes a shared sense of loss and displacement over any discussion of difference. Because this language assumes that all post-1959 exiles are fundamentally defined by loss, there is little room for an analysis of racial, political, sexual, class, and gender distinctions among Cubans. Yet, as the different waves of migration clearly point out, Cubans in the United States are not all the same. The question that remains is, how do we write about the history of the Cuban exile and migrant community in a fashion that reflects distinction and variation? Or better, how can we not do so?

Diasporic Inventions: Race, Geography, and Historical Linkages

> The Struggle against a single History for the cross-fertilization of histories means repossessing both a true sense of one's time and identity: proposing in an unprecedented way a revaluation of power.
> —Edouard Glissant, 1989

In January 1880, José Martí arrived in New York City. After a trip to Venezuela in 1881, he returned the next year and eventually settled in New York City where he lived, wrote, and worked on behalf of the nationalist movement until his death in 1895. Over the last decade, scholars have re-evaluated Martí's life and experiences in New York, and re-positioned him within a larger Latino diasporic framework. Re-locating Martí as a theoretical architect of Latin American anti-imperialist thinking in the United States has allowed scholars to identify a distinctly Latin American, Caribbean, and migrant intellectual historical tradition in the United States.[20] In particular, scholars Edna Acosta-Belén and Carlos Santiago and José David Saldívar revisit one of José Martí's most famous essays, *Nuestra América* (Our America), written during the time he lived in New York City.[21]

The authors use Martí's *Nuestra América* to reassess the parameters of what constitutes "America" as well as to contest United States conceptions of geography, border delineation, and meaning. Saldívar employs Martí's discomfort with the "restrictions inherent in the privileged term America" to examine the implications and consequences of ignoring the existence of a mutual America. Saldívar looks to the Americas as a hemisphere to both "perceive what the literatures of the Americas have in common," and to reconstruct a "pan-American literary history."[22] In this instance, Martí and the notion of *Nuestra América* are tools for both cultivating "wholeness," and providing testimony and documentation. For Acosta-Belén and Santiago, the historical meanings of a *Nuestra América* are critical to theorizing a historical language that decolonizes "the cultural mythologies and received knowledge about ourselves as perpetuated within the dominant Western tradition." In addition, they also look to *Nuestra América* to understand the current "intricate and complex web of international (im)migration and labor flows that are causing multiple population displacement from the peripheral to the advanced capitalist nations."[23] For the authors, the conception of a *Nuestra América* is not confined to late 19th century or even to Martí. In both cases, *Nuestra América* is used and seen as a multi-directional map that allows a rethinking of larger frameworks that emphasize, among other things, hemispheric connection, historical writing, global movement, and displacement.

An important element in *Nuestra América* is Martí's ability to connect United States imperialism with race and racism. Martí openly disagreed with and publicly challenged the racial beliefs common to the late 19th century. As he wrote in *Nuestra América*, "Anyone who promotes and disseminates opposition or hatred among races is committing a sin against humanity."[24] For Acosta-Belén and Santiago, Martí's anti-racist writings serve as a "significant point of departure in the cultural analysis of the Americas," one which, according to the authors, acknowledges the "unprecedented mixing of races and cultural syncretism that took place in the Americas."[25] While Martí's writings can and do serve as a springboard for articulating a Latino theoretical language, they cannot be divorced from the historical context in which they were written.

Although Martí spent close to 15 years in the United States, he remained focused on the revolutionary wars in Cuba and the impact those wars had on the development of an independent Cuban nation and a separate Cuban identity. Martí's drive to publicly question United States imperialism took hold during the late 19th century when he helped form *El Partido Revolucionario Cubano* (PRC) in New York City. Founded in 1891, the PRC along with its official newspaper *Patria* was one of Martí's most effective tools for unifying the exile nationalist movement and solidifying its anti-imperialist position. The United States' growing interest in the island inspired Martí not only to write about the dangers of US imperialism and Eurocentrism, but also to articulate an oppositional vision of a racially mixed, American-rooted, Cuban identity that both defied and rejected the United States and Spain. It was during this period that Martí published some of his best-known and influential essays on race, including the oft cited *Mi raza*.

It is difficult, however, to discuss Martí's thoughts on race without taking into consideration his participation in the exile Cuban nationalist project. Members of the exile nationalist movement were acutely aware of the racial politics in Cuba and of the anti-racist language developed and used by rebels in Cuba. Proponents of the exile nationalist movement associated racism, slavery, racial disenfranchisement, and exclusion with Spanish colonial authority. By the same token, they connected anti-racism, inclusion, and the repudiation of racial categories with Cuban independence. As one of the intellectuals who scripted and used an anti-racist, exile nationalist language, Martí, as he wrote in *Nuestra América,* both condemned and attempted to erase the existence of racism by claiming that there "is no racial hatred, because there are no races."[26]

Martí's insistence that there was no such thing as race, and therefore no racism, can be read in multiple ways. In addition to speaking to events in Cuba and to racial conditions in the United States from a Latin American perspective, Martí's writings and actions also reveal the intricate connections between race and nation building. This connection, as the historian Ada Ferrer has argued, was complicated and open to different interpretation. By refusing to accept the existence of races as well as casting racism as an "infraction against the nation as a whole," Cuban rebels were able to "defeat the Spanish claims about the impossibility of Cuban nationhood." In other words, anti-racism and the rhetoric of racelessness—a rhetoric that Martí helped to script—became essential to the creation of a "raceless nationality." Yet, as Ferrer has demonstrated, this rhetoric gave black insurgents and citizens a powerful language with which to speak about race and racism "within the rebel polity—a language with which to show that the transcendence was yet to occur."[27] It is within this context, rife with tension, complexity, and possibility, that Martí is best understood.

While scholars of Latina/o Studies are relocating Martí as theoretical architect and re-situating the Americas as marker for multipositionality, scholars of Cuban–United States studies have yet to fully theorize Martí.[28] In many respects, José Martí's writings and experiences in the United States serve as necessary interventions in Cuban–United States historical thinking. First, Martí operates as a symbolic reminder that the Cuban diaspora cannot be confined to the late 20th century or to a specific exile community. As early as 1823, with the exile of both Father Felix Varela and the poet José Maria Heredia, Cuban exiles have looked to the United States to create and sustain political communities. Second, as Martí's writings testify, the early Cuban migrant community consisted not only of political exiles, but also of economic migrants who left the economic instability of Cuba to work in the United States. These migrants established and participated in powerful labor unions in the US and, during the early 20th century, were central to the development of Cuban cultural and political clubs in the United States. Third, it sets the terrain for examining the historical influence and impact of race and gender on the formation of early Cuban communities in the United States.[29] Lastly, Martí represents an intellectual tradition of US-based Latin American thought and exile political activism that challenges assumed silences and invisibility.

While Martí no doubt plays an important role in the theoretical reconstitution of Cuban–United States historiography, it is perhaps the period after Martí's death in 1895 and the United States intervention in Cuba in 1898 that best reveals the historical workings of the Cuban diaspora. The end of the war along with the dissolution of the PRC, and the exile war campaigns, left a vacuum in the political lives of Cuban migrants. Furthermore, the incorporation of the Platt Amendment of 1901 into the Cuban constitution—which allowed, among other things, the United States to intervene in Cuba any time it deemed necessary—convinced Cubans to acknowledge that the previously envisioned and imagined Cuban nation was now compromised and altered to fit a different political and economic reality. This reality transformed labor unions into sites where Cubans could reify their own sense of "Cuban-ness" in the face of growing United States power in Cuba.

This shift in migrant consciousness was most visible in the organization of the labor union *La Sociedad de Torcedores y sus Cercanías* also known as *La Resistencia* in 1899 by Cubans in Tampa.[30] Although Cuban migrants had had a long history of forming labor unions and going on strike, the organization of *La Resistencia,* with its public connection to labor unions in Cuba, signaled that Cubans in the US were unwilling to cut themselves off from the island. Besides being a powerful union, *La Resistencia* set the groundwork for a new reconfiguration of a post-war Cuban migrant identity in the United States. No longer focused on Cuban independence as a source of unity, Cubans now looked to labor unions, issues, and post-war politics to redefine themselves as both Cuban migrants and workers.

The period after the war also demanded a rethinking of race among Cubans and recognition of what the historian Aline Helg has called the "myth of racial equality" in Cuba.[31] The widespread belief among Afro-Cubans that they would have a stake in the building of a Cuban nation after gaining independence was betrayed. In 1902, with Tomás Estrada Palma as the acting president of Cuba, the government decided that no specific anti-discriminatory policy was necessary. Silences were not the prescribed antidote to a larger public language on race that in the past had resonated deeply with Afro-Cubans and supporters of the nationalist movement. This policy of silence traveled to the migrant community where Cubans found themselves renegotiating racial conditions, segregations, and disenfranchisement without the nationalist movement's language of racelessness. This resulted in a policy of separation that was both complex and unpredictable. Cultural and political clubs that had previously been integrated were now segregated, while cigar factories and labor unions remained, for the most part, integrated. Outside of the workplace, however, white Cubans established and frequented separate cultural clubs, mutual aid societies, and functions.[32]

For Afro-Cubans who moved north, the process of community formation was driven more by the ever-changing configuration of community than by a single economic factor. Unlike Tampa and Key West, New York was not as economically dependent on the cigar industry. This made it possible for Afro-Cuban migrants to find work in other businesses when the cigar industry began to falter in the 1930s. One of the industries that hired a large number of Afro-Cuban men and women was the garment industry. By the 1920s, a steady stream of Afro-Cuban migrants moved to New York to work in either the garment or textile industries. The workings of race among Cubans as well as the work environment manifested themselves differently in New York City. As Ybor City and Tampa were located in the South, Afro-Cuban migrants had little choice but to negotiate Florida's Black Codes and segregation laws. While the immigrant community of Ybor City did afford some mobility and access, their movements outside of the immigrant community were controlled and subject to many of the same restrictions as African-Americans.

In New York City, however, there were no formal policies of segregation that determined racial identity. This, however, does not mean that separations did not take place. Afro-Cuban migrants lived in black neighborhoods, frequented racially segregated clubs and, in general, followed the racial policies of the period. Yet, there was some level of fluidity that allowed some Afro-Cuban migrants like Lydia "Tata" Caraballosa, to live among "the Latin community in the Upper East Side."[33] This fluidity was seen by many in the African-American community as well as the growing West Indian community as being able to pass, or even in some instance as being "white."

In her insightful work on the Caribbean migration to New York, the historian Irma Watkins-Owens details how migrant status as well as speaking a foreign language was perceived by the West Indian and African-American community as a distinct advantage. Newspapers like the *Negro World* ran editorials expounding the merits of speaking Spanish as a way of gaining more employment and housing opportunities. As Watkins-Owens has shown, the relationship between housing and language was also evident in an article written by the Jamaican immigrant W. A. Domingo. Published in 1925, Domingo wrote that "black immigrants find it impossible to segregate themselves into colonies; too dark of complexion to pose as Cubans or some other Negroid but alien tongued foreigners, they are inevitably swallowed up in black Harlem."[34]

Separations, however, were not limited solely to the outside of the Cuban community. As Melba Alvarado's life story reveals, there were also separations among Cubans themselves. An Afro-Cuban migrant who arrived in New York during the 1930s, Alvarado was part of the larger migration of Cubans that left Cuba as a result of Gerardo Machado's presidency. Alvarado and her family settled in East Harlem in a community made up of Puerto Ricans and Cubans, where Spanish was spoken, Cuban products could be found, and where her family could belong to clubs and mutual aid societies like *El Club Julio*

Antonio Mello. While Alvarado viewed herself as "bien Cubana y siempre con los hispanos" (very Cuban and always with Hispanics) she continually negotiated her "blackness" in the United States. Being black determined what type of Cuban club she would become involved in, organize, and eventually lead, the people she would interact and work with, and, inevitably, the community she would help to form. Race delineated, distinguished, and, although few would openly admit it, at times divided the Cuban community in New York City during this period. As Alvarado herself put it,

> Cuando eran de color, eran de color, no importaba de que raza era. Entonces los cubanos negros se mezclaban con los negros Americanos. No podian estar con los blancos. Siempre ha habido su diferencia entre los negros y blancos.[35]

The separations, as Alvarado remembered, were not limited to clubs or formal functions; nor were they obvious or dictated by institutional policies. The separations were part of everyday interactions, and often gradual. One such experience was the celebration of the Caridad del Cobre, the patron saint of Cuba. According to Alvarado, this ritual had always been celebrated in a Catholic church on 114th street in New York City. Organized by "una señora de color," the service and ensuing celebration attracted all Cubans from New York City to come to "la Milagrosa." However, when the principal organizer of the event returned to Cuba in the mid-1950s, and more Cubans began to migrate, the once integrated celebration became now organized on the basis of race.

> En esa época pues entonces empezaron los cubanos a venir emigrado y empezó la propaganda que la verdadera Caridad estaba en la 156 en la iglesia de esperanza. Y empezaron los blancos a hacer las misas en la 156 en la iglesia de la esperanza y entonces los negros acá en la 114 y séptima avenida. Y se dividió. Los padres se pusieron muy disgustados porque ya se dividió y ya dejaron de ser las misas que eran.[36]

Alvarado's choice of works in this passage is very telling. She reveals the multiple workings of race among Cubans, a process that, while it includes the negotiation of "blackness," the privileging of "whiteness," and the changing meanings of Cuban-ness in the United States, cannot be solely understood in terms of binary United States racial definitions or ethnic affiliations. In fact, what Alvarado is responding to is the transmission and re-imagination of cultural experiences, as well as the disruption of that tradition. It is the disruption of the re-created diasporic tradition, the exclusion of Afro-Cubans from a distinctly Cuban cultural and religious event, that most articulates racial and cultural meaning. For Afro-Cuban migrants accustomed to negotiating separations as well as inclusions, such experiences forced a rethinking of what constituted community. This rethinking led to a re-working of mutual and shared communities that were deeply influenced and shaped by overlapping diasporas, and the distinct narratives that informed those diasporas.

The re-working of African diasporic communities in New York is evident in the records of the Afro-Cuban, New York–based club, *El Club Cubano Inter-Americano.* As past President of the club, Alvarado recounted how by the mid-1950s a significant number of the members were Puerto Ricans, Dominicans, and African-Americans. The intention was to establish a fluid space where membership of non-Cubans would not be restricted nor discouraged. It was important to the club members that the space be one for all Latino/as of African descent. Interestingly enough, it was also very important that politics *not* be part of the club's by-laws or agenda. The club's by-laws prohibited political events, functions, and endorsements. The decision by the members of *El Club Cubano Inter-Americano* not to mix politics, culture, and race lends an ironic twist to the history of Cuban diasporic communities. This time, migrant conceptions of nation, imagined shared politics, and transferred Cuban customs would not be enough to sustain community.

Intrigued by the various conceptions by which race has been historically defined, African-American scholars as well as writers including James Weldon Johnson and Langston Hughes have taken note of how Afro-Cuban migrants defined race in terms that resisted full integration into a larger African American identity. Similar to other black migrants, Afro-Cubans employed a different language to speak of their experiences and reality in the United States. This, as Earl Lewis has argued, is a strong reminder "of the diversity of black life," which, in turn, demands that we refine the "practice of writing African peoples into a history of overlapping diasporas."[37] Lewis' argument acknowledges that diasporic identities are continually changing in response to historical, social, cultural, and economic conditions and that different populations are in constant dialogue. For Tiffany Patterson and Robin D. G. Kelley, the move to complicate African diasporic research is intended to both challenge "the presumption that black people world-wide share a common culture," as well as to begin a collaborative dialogue that allows us to think, research, and write differently about the African diaspora. Moreover, their contention that the African diaspora exists within the "context of global race and gender hierarchies which are formulated and reconstituted across national boundaries and along several lines," provides the necessary opening for incorporating and using the African diaspora in larger Latino theoretical and intellectual projects.[38]

Conclusion

The over-emphasis on the 1959 exile model has resulted in a fragmented Cuban–United States historiography; one that has not weathered recent political and economic developments well. Extending the historiography to include pre-1959 Cuban migrant communities as well as employing diasporic studies, transnational migration theory, coloniality, geographical re-imaginings, and globalization complicates how we think, research, and write about Cubans in the United States. In addition, it allows an investigation of historical links, collaborations, alliances, conflict, and diaspora. It is also in these spaces that scholars of Cuban–United States historiography can initiate a larger discussion concerning the incorporation and integration of multiple histories over time.

One approach for complicating the analysis is to rethink the shifting theoretical parameters of the term America as a way to reconfigure transgeographical definitions of borders, movement, and place. Furthermore, by re-situating as well as problematizing Martí as theoretical architect, it is possible to identify and examine the historical uses of politics, rhetoric, and print media to get at a language of national consciousness, a language that continues to reverberate among Cuban exiles and migrants. The growing interest in African diasporic studies in the United States demonstrates an ever-growing awareness and interest in global historical connections that moves past the limits of the nation states. The value of such work for Cuban–United States history is that it unravels discussions of race, ethnicity, gender, identity, language, and diaspora from any naturalized or entrenched definitions that hinders the relocation of theoretical applications. The changes taking place in Cuba and among the Cuban exile and migrant community demand that historiographies and the way history is *made and written* also change. As Gonzalo Santos reminds us, "We will not remain the same. Either we remake ourselves or we will be remade by others."[39]

Notes

I thank Karina Cespedes for her careful reading, criticisms, and enthusiasm for this project. My gratitude to Norma Alárcon, Maylei Blackwell, DJ Cyphon, Suzanne Oboler, Mattie Richardson, José David Saldívar, Fernando Solorro and the anonymous reviewers for *Latino Studies* for their invaluable suggestions. This paper is dedicated to Melba Alvarado, whose words continue to inspire and to "Mayo" Mirabal, Nieves García, and Lydia "Tata" Caraballosa, for their stories and spirit.

1. Achy Obejas, *We Came All the Way from Cuba So You Could Dress Like This?* (San Francisco: Cleis Press, 1994), 124–25.

2. Flavio Risech, "Political and Cultural Cross-Dressing: Negotiating a Second Generation Cuban-American Identity," in *Bridges to Cuba, Puentes a Cuba: Cuban and Cuban-American Artists, Writers, and Scholars Explore Identity, Nationality and Homeland,* ed. Ruth Behar. (Ann Arbor: University of Michigan Press, 1995), 58.

3. María de los Angeles Torres, *In the Land of Mirrors: Cuban Exile Politics in the United States* (Ann Arbor: University of Michigan Press, 1999), 39.

4. Román de la Campa, *Cuba on My Mind: Journeys to a Severed Nation* (New York: Verso, 2000), 19.

5. Michel de Certeau, *The Writing of History* (New York: Columbia University Press, 1988), 34.

6. Gerald E. Poyo, *With All and for the Good of All: The Emergence of Popular Nationalism in the Cuban Communities in the United States, 1848–1898* (Durham: Duke University Press, 1989); Winston James, *Holding Aloft the Banner of Ethiopia: Caribbean Radicalism in Early Twentieth-Century America* (London: Verso Books, 1998); Nancy Raquel Mirabal, "'No Country But the One We Must Fight For': The Emergence of an Antillean Nation and Community in New York City, 1860–1901," in *Mambo Montage: The Latinization of New York,* ed. Augustin Laó-Montes and Arlene Davila (New York: Columbia University Press, 2001); Nancy Raquel Mirabal, "Telling Silences and Making Community: Afro-Cubans and African-Americans in Ybor City and Tampa, 1899–1915," in *Between Race and Empire,* ed. Brock and Castañeda Fuertes (Philadelphia: Temple University Press, 1998); Susan Greenbaum, *More than Black: Afro-Cubans in Tampa* (Gainesville: University Press of Florida, 2002).

7. Nancy Hewitt, *Southern Discomfort: Women's Activism in Tampa, Florida* (Urbana: University of Illinois Press, 2001).

8. Coco Fusco, *English Is Broken Here: Notes on Cultural Fusion in the Americas* (New York: New Press, 1995), 3.

9. According to María de los Angeles Torres, The Antonio Maceo Brigade was made up of members of the Areíto group who were granted entry into Cuba in 1977. A goal of the group was to meet with Cuban officials and the Cuban public to challenge the prevailing notion that everyone who left Cuba was "an enemy of the revolution." After returning to the US the members of the Brigade chose to open it up to other Cubans as long as they met a criteria that included opposition to the

economic blockade against Cuba, and support of normalized relations. For more information, see Torres' well-researched study. Torres, *In the Land of Mirrors,* 93.

10. *NACLA* (September/October 1995): 40. The question of Cuban exile politics is far too extensive to be explored in this article which is primarily interested in examining *how* exile politics informs and influences Cuban exile/migrant historiography and historical thinking. I also recognize that Cuban exile politics as well as Cuban politics are much more varied and wide ranging than the organizations/groups cited and used in this article.

11. Behar, *Bridges to Cuba,* 2.

12. In 1994, the Clinton Administration authored Operation Distant Shore. Before Operation Distant Shore, Cubans fleeing Cuba only needed to reach international waters to be rescued and brought to the US. After, Cubans had to reach the US (dry land) to be considered eligible for refugee status and benefits. In addition, this policy instructed the US Coast Guard to return Cubans who had not reached dry land back to Cuba. For an analysis of how this policy was received by the Cuban community in Miami, see editions of the *Miami Herald,* August 14–20, 1994.

13. Gerald E. Poyo, "Commentary: Cubans in the United States: Interpreting the Historical Literature," in *Cuban Studies Since the Revolution,* ed. Damián Fernández (Gainesville: University Press of Florida Press, 1992), 85.

14. In 1960, the Cuban Refugee Committee requested assistance from President Eisenhower. In response, Eisenhower released $1 million from the contingency funds of the Mutual Security Act to help with the resettlement programs. A few months later, the Eisenhower Administration formed a Cuban Refugee Emergency Center in downtown Miami to oversee the resettlement efforts. These actions prompted major changes in Cuban migration policy. First, it officially recognized Cubans as refugees and Cuba as a communist state. Second, it condoned the creation of a generous migration package. The Kennedy Administration followed suit the following year when it established the Cuban Refugee Program (CRP). The CRP provided Cuban exiles with monthly relief checks, health services, job training, adult education opportunities and surplus food distribution. In 1966, Congress further extended privileges to Cuban exiles when it passed the Cuban Adjustment Act of 1966, which allowed Cubans who lived in the United States for at least two years to apply for permanent residency. For information on the particulars of the Cuban Refugee Program and the Cuban Adjustment Act see Maria Cristina García, *Havana USA: Cuban Exiles and Cuban Americans in South Florida, 1959–1994* (Berkeley: University of California Press, 1996); Torres, *In the Land of Mirrors*; and Sylvia Pedraza, *Political and Economic Migrants in America: Cubans and Mexicans* (Austin: University of Texas Press, 1985).

15. Quoted in Pedraza, *Political and Economic Migrants,* 235.

16. García, *Havana USA,* 6. According to García, "While the felons comprised less than 4 percent of the total number of immigrants, they commanded a disproportionate amount of media attention."

17. García, *Havana USA,* 74.

18. According to *Miami Herald,* August 18–20, 1994, Cuban exiles had mixed feelings when it came to the resettlement of Cubans in Guantánamo Base. On the one hand, hard-lined Cubans believed that by preventing Fidel Castro from employing a safety-valve procedure, that is, allowing the departure of Cubans who were dissatisfied with the political system, the Communist system would eventually end. On the other hand, the media images of Cubans living in tents waiting to go back to a country intent on punishing them was also disheartening.

19. Cuban exiles and immigrants were rarely considered to be on the same footing as "white" United States citizens. Because they were Cuban and therefore, ethnic, their whiteness was conditional. Nonetheless, this conditional whiteness along with their exile status and the generous government programs of the early 1960s afforded Cuban exiles much more mobility and opportunities than other Latin American migrants in the US.

20. José David Saldívar, *The Dialectics of Our America: Genealogy, Cultural Critique, and Literary History* (Durham: Duke University Press, 1991); Edna Acosta-Belén and Santiago Acosta-Belén, "Merging Borders: The Remapping of America," in *The Latino Studies Reader: Culture, Economy*

and Society, ed. Antonia Darder and Rodolfo D. Torres, 29–42 (Oxford, UK and Malden, Mass.: Blackwell Publishers, 1998); Kirsten Gruesz, *Ambassadors of Culture: The Transamerican Origins of Latino Writing* (Princeton, N.J.: Princeton University Press, 2002); Julio Ramos, *Divergent Modernities: Culture and Politics in Nineteenth-Century Latin America* (Durham: Duke University Press, 2001).

21. *Nuestra América* first appeared in *La Revista Illustrada de Nueva York* on January 1, 1891, and on January 30, 1891, in *El Partido Liberal de Mexico.*

22. Saldívar, *The Dialectics of Our America,* 296.

23. Acosta-Belén and Acosta-Belén, "Merging Borders," in *The Latino Studies Reader,* ed. Darder and Torres, 31.

24. José Martí, *Selected Writings,* ed. and trans. Esther Allen (New York: Penguin Books, 2002), 296.

25. Acosta-Belén and Acosta-Belén, "Merging Borders," in *The Latino Studies Reader,* ed. Darder and Torres, 5–6.

26. Martí, *Selected Writings.*

27. Ada Ferrer, *Insurgent Cuba: Race, Nation, and Revolution, 1868–1898* (Chapel Hill: University of North Carolina Press, 1999), 9.

28. This, however, is not the case in literary studies. See works by Roberto González Echevarría, Arcadio Díaz Quiñones, Kirsten Gruesz, *Ambassadors of Culture*; Agnes Lugo-Ortiz, *Identidades Imaginada: Biografia y Nacionalidad en el Horizonte de la Guerra (Cuba 1860–1898)* (Rio Piedras: Editorial de la Universidad de Puerto, 1999); Julio Ramos; José David Saldívar; Jean Franco, and Ivan Schulman, among others.

29. Although Martí publicly supported the work of female patriots, including Inoncenia Martinez, Emilia Casanova de Villaverde, Carolina Rodriguez, and Paulina Pedroso, he did not see them as equal partners in the war effort. Martí rarely, if ever, publicly discussed or wrote about the merits of gender equality or the role of women in the building of a new Cuban republic. Women were not allowed formal membership in the PRC, nor to hold any key positions in the nationalist movement. Instead, they were expected to organize and participate in less powerful auxiliary organizations. See Hewitt, *Southern Discomfort,* and "Paulina Pedroso and Las Patriotas of Tampa," Ann L. Henderson and Gary Mormino, eds. (1991).

30. Durward Long, "La Resistencia: Tampa's Immigrant Labor Union," *Labor History* 6 (1965); Louis A. Jr. Pérez, "Cubans in Tampa: From Exiles to Immigrants, 1885–1901," *Florida Historical Quarterly* 56 (1978); Gary R. Mormino, "Tampa and the New Urban South: The Weight Strike of 1899," *Florida Historical Quarterly* 60 (1980).

31. Aline Helg, *Our Rightful Share: The Afro-Cuban Struggle for Equality, 1886–1912* (Chapel Hill: University of North Carolina, 1995), 16.

32. James, *Holding Aloft the Banner;* Mirabal, "Telling Silences," in *Between Race and Empire,* ed. Brock and Fuertes; Greenbaum, *More than Black.*

33. Interview with Lydia Caraballosa, conducted by Nancy Raquel Mirabal. November 26, 2001.

34. Irma Watkins-Owens, *Blood Relations: Caribbean Immigrants and the Harlem Community, 1900–1930* (Bloomington: Indiana University Press, 1996), 4.

35. Interview with Melba Alvarado by Nancy Raquel Mirabal, August, 1995, July 2002, South Bronx, New York. Translated, this passage reads, "When they were of color, they were of color, it didn't matter what race you were. This being the case, black Cubans interacted with black Americans. They couldn't be with the whites. There have always been their differences between the whites and blacks [Cubans]".

36. Alvarado, 1995. Translated this passage reads, "At that time, well, as Cuban immigrants began to arrive, so did the propaganda that the real Caridad was on 156 [street] in the Church of Hope. The whites [Cubans] began to have mass on 156 [street] at the Church of Hope and as a result, the blacks [Cubans] began to have mass here on 114 [street] and Seventh avenue. And it split. The priests were very upset because it had split and the masses were no longer the same." For a history

of Cuban women migrants, see Mirabal, "No Country But the One We Must Fight For," in *Mambo Montage,* ed. Laó-Montes and Davila Mirabal.

37. Earl Lewis, "To Turn as on a Pivot: Writing African-Americans into a History of Overlapping Diasporas," *American Historical Review* 100(3) (1995): 786.

38. Tiffany Patterson and Robin D. G. Kelly. "Unfinished Migrations: Reflections on the African Diaspora and the Making of the Modern World," *African Studies Review* 43(1) (2000): 45.

39. Gonzalo Santos, "Somos RUNA-FRIBES? The Future of Latino Ethnicity in the Americas." National Association of Chicano Studies Annual Conference Proceedings, 1992. Quoted in Antonia Darder, "The Politics of Biculturalism: Culture and Difference in the Formation of *Warriors for Gringostroika* and *The New Mestizas,*" in *The Latino Studies Reader,* ed. Darder and Torres, 129–43.

19

Between Culture and Politics

The Emma Lazarus Federation of Jewish Women's Clubs, 1944–89

JOYCE ANTLER

On November 22, 1909, over 2,000 New York women's garment workers, many of them already out on strike, crowded into Cooper Union to vote on an industry-wide action. In the ensuing hours of debate, speakers repeatedly urged caution in deciding whether to take the dramatic step of calling a general strike. Although the audience was more than half female, the only woman speaker was Mary Dreier, president of the New York Women's Trade Union League.

Then a worker called from the floor to be heard; despite complaints, she was permitted to speak. The woman was Clara Lemlich, a twenty-three-year-old who looked so slight that she was described in the next day's press as a teenage "girl." Yet Lemlich, a worker from the Leiserson shop, had been arrested seventeen times and was then recovering from a beating she had received two days earlier. In Yiddish, Lemlich proclaimed: "I am a working girl, one of those who are on strike against intolerable conditions. I am tired of listening to speakers who talk in general terms. What we are here for is to decide whether we shall or shall not strike. I offer a resolution that a general strike be declared—now."[1] As the delegates roared their approval, Benjamin Feigenbaum, the chairman of the meeting, sprang to Lemlich's side and thrust her right arm into the air.[2] "Will you take the old Hebrew oath?" he asked. According to a newspaper account of the strike, "Two and a half thousand right arms shot up. Two and a half thousand voices repeated the Yiddish words: 'May my right [hand] wither from [my] arm if I betray the cause I now pledge.'"[3] By the next evening over 20,000 workers had walked out; the strike thereafter became known as the Uprising of the 20,000. When the strike ended fourteen weeks later, 354 shirtwaist shop owners had signed union agreements. Although not all the workers' demands were met, the agreements generally raised wages, limited weekly work hours, and capped the amount of night work employers could demand.

The strike also dispelled the myth that women wage earners could not be organized and, by promoting unionization of the garment industry, helped shape the course of labor organizing in the twentieth century.

For her role in these events, Clara Lemlich has been allotted a place in the annals of labor history and in the history of women workers.[4] What has been ignored, however, is the emblematic quality of her actions in the strike as a female *Jewish* activist, an identity that she would claim all her life and that was particularly represented in the organization she helped to found in the 1940s: the Emma Lazarus Federation of Jewish Women's Clubs (ELF). For forty-five years the ELF stood at the forefront of Jewish women's cultural and political activism, staking out progressive stands on a variety of issues, including the fight against anti-Semitism and racial discrimination, and the promotion of women's rights. In their unflinching efforts to reconcile the female, radical, and Jewish components of their identity, Clara Lemlich Shavelson and the Emma Lazarus Federation illustrate the multiple, layered, and shifting amalgam of gender and ethnicity revealed on that momentous occasion in 1909 when Lemlich rose at Cooper Union. Lemlich had stood as a woman, a "girl" striker, speaking from the experience, and abuse, of women's work; as a radical labor movement activist, eager to create working-class unity and push the movement forward; and as a Jew, addressing in Yiddish an assembly of Jews who took a Jewish oath to affirm commitment to the radical cause of women. The search to join these three elements would occupy her and many colleagues throughout their lives; together they would create a new kind of American cultural Jewishness, embodied in the Emma Lazarus Federation, which fostered Jewish, feminist, and radical causes.

Although historians have recognized the importance of ethnic ties to the formation of Jewish women's working-class consciousness in the years prior to 1920, they have ignored the continuing cultural and political activities of these women, especially the primary importance to these activities of Jewish content.[5] The paradigm of assimilation has reigned supreme, with scholarly attention focused on the colorful immigrant period and the seeming denial of ethnic consciousness as Jews moved into the mainstream.[6] But the meaning of Clara Shavelson's life, and that of many of her allies, is that she managed to create a bridge that enabled her and others both to maintain their Jewish identity and to use it in a way that built (and built upon) their social and political commitments. In a world in which to be both radical and Jewish meant to be attacked in different ways and to be divided by ideological fissures (that between religion and communism, for example, or between nationalism and working-class unity), this was no small accomplishment. Even more unusual is the fact that it was built upon a foundation of knowledge in women's history during a period when the subject held little interest even for formally trained academicians. Creating new heroines out of women's experience and promulgating these figures to primarily working-class audiences, the ELF developed an agenda for collective action that linked women's rights and human rights to historical models. In this cultural work the "Emmas" fashioned a Jewish womanhood sensitive not only to issues of class but also to anti-Semitism and racism. Their post-Holocaust political identity sprang, then, both from a newly invigorated gender consciousness and an increasingly salient sense of themselves as Jewish Americans who were proud possessors of a unique cultural heritage.

Examining the federation's multiple interests—including women's history, Jewish culture, civil rights, peace, Israel, the women's movement, and working-class, consumer, and immigrant issues—this chapter will suggest that the federation illuminates a model of what I call "linked" identity, combining elements of gender, culture, politics, race, and ethnicity in a flexible, yet unusually engaged, fashion. The federation's simultaneous commitment to creating consciousness and to activism—another example of its "betweenness"—will also be explored.

From Trade Unionism to Jewish Culture:
Clara Lemlich Shavelson and the Emergence of the
Emma Lazarus Federation of Jewish Women's Clubs

Clara Lemlich Shavelson was born in 1886 in the town of Gorodok in the Ukraine, the daughter of an orthodox Jewish scholar and grocery storekeeper. The Lemlichs left their home in 1903, fleeing the Kishinev pogrom. After a few months in England, the family arrived in the United States: two weeks later, Clara found a job in the garment shops. In 1906 she became one of the founding members of Waistmakers Local 25, affiliated with the fledgling International Ladies' Garment Workers Union (ILGWU), then largely an organization of male cloak makers. Clara took part in a succession of bitter strikes: in 1907 at Welsen and Goldstein, in 1908 at the Gotham plant, and in 1909 and the Leiserson shop, where she was beaten up while walking the picket line. She was a seasoned strike veteran when the waist makers gathered at Cooper Union in November 1909.

After the waist makers' strike, Clara served as a delegate to union conventions, a member of the executive boards of Local 25 and of the Women's Trade Union League, an outspoken socialist, and a tireless organizer of women workers. As a working-class proponent of woman suffrage, she spoke frequently on the importance of the vote and its relationship to the labor movement.

In 1913 Lemlich married Joseph Shavelson, a printer and union activist. The couple had three children, a son and two daughters. Struggling to make ends meet on Joseph's $17-a-week salary, they shared a home with his sister and her family on DeKalb Avenue in Brownsville, Brooklyn, then a Jewish immigrant community with an activist tradition; Clara Shavelson returned to work in a tie shop on the ground floor of her own sister's building when her oldest child was two. She also resumed her organizing activities, becoming a familiar figure on neighborhood street corners. Shavelson's goal was to mobilize housewives around consumer and housing issues that affected the quality of working-class life. In 1917 she participated in a series of citywide riots and a boycott against the high price of Kosher meat. In 1919 she helped organize tenants in a tent strike against high housing costs; that same year, she became a charter member of the U.S. Communist Party. In 1926 she helped found the United Council of Working-Class Women, a consumer-based group organized to supplement the party's industrial organizing.

In the early 1930s the Shavelsons moved to the working-class community of Brighton Beach, where Clara established the area's first Unemployment Council and organized hunger marches, rent and food strikes, and kitchens for the jobless. She also participated in a neighborhood tenant council named after the Jewish essayist and poet, Emma Lazarus. In 1935 the United Council of Working-Class Women became the Progressive Women's Council. Though the council never intended to become exclusively Jewish, most members were Jewish immigrants; like Shavelson, many had been involved in the garment union before marriage. During the Great Depression, the council organized housewives to bring down food and housing costs; a 1935 meat boycott organized by Shavelson and Rose Nelson (Raynes) brought Shavelson to Washington to confront Secretary of Agriculture Henry Wallace and spread to dozens of cities.[7]

In the early 1930s Shavelson ran unsuccessfully for the State Assembly as a member of the Communist Party; she was the only female candidate. It was one of the rare times, her daughter recalled, that her mother purchased a new dress.[8] In 1944, with her husband's health in decline, Shavelson returned to the garment industry as a hand finisher in a cloak shop on Thirty-eighth Street in New York, joining Local 9. She remained there for almost a decade.

Shavelson was an activist in the fight against fascism as well. In 1934 she attended the first International Women's Congress against War and Fascism in Paris, traveling afterward to the Soviet Union. After her return, she lectured on the Soviet Union to the Progressive Women's Council, which she served as educational director, giving courses on fascism, war, and peace. She became a familiar figure on Brighton Beach street corners, rallying workers against Hitlerism.

At the time of World War II, the Progressive Women's Council, of which Shavelson was then president, merged with the women's clubs of the Jewish People's Fraternal Order (JPFO) of the International Workers Order (IWO), a fraternal benefit insurance company formed after a split in the Workmen's Circle (the Arbeiter Ring) between the centrist "*Forward* socialists" and the left-wing "progressive" radicals friendly to the Soviet Union; nearly 8,000 of the latter left the Workmen's Circle in 1930 to form the IWO as a "proletarian" fraternal organization.[9] After 1936, aided by the encouragement of the Communist Party, now in its popular front phase, the IWO launched a massive recruitment effort among immigrant workers. The party's support of ethnic awareness and pride, coupled with its active campaign against domestic anti-Semitism, made it attractive to Jews; by 1939 they constituted between 40 to 50 percent of party membership.[10]

Although not a political or labor organization, the IWO assisted the CIO's organizing drives and campaigned for unemployment insurance and for aid to Spain. With its health and insurance benefits and its sponsorship of ethnic language schools, summer camps, theater, dance, and other cultural programs, it became the fastest growing fraternal order in the country. By the end of World War II, the IWO counted almost 200,000 members in thirteen nationality societies, white and black; the JPFO, with 50,000 members, was the largest. In addition to its wide variety of benefit programs, many members were attracted by the IWO's multinational, multiracial character and its cutting-edge positions in racial relations and antidiscrimination matters. Even though the majority of rank-and-file members did not belong to the Communist Party (in contrast to major IWO leaders, who did), IWO politics generally mirrored those of the Communist Party.[11]

Clara Shavelson became New York City secretary of the IWO's Women's Division;

during the war she organized its knitting circles, first aid clubs, aluminum-collecting campaigns, and bond rallies. In March 1944 the IWO-JPFO gave birth to an Emma Lazarus Division: that year, the IWO published *Emma Lazarus: Selections from Her Poetry and Prose,* edited by Morris U. Schappes, the first collection of Lazarus's work in fifty years.[12] Schappes highlighted Lazarus's dual consciousness as a Jew and an American, a focus that the division adopted. Although earlier women's organizations, including the Brooklyn tenants' group established by Clara Shavelson, had been named after Lazarus, they did not focus on Lazarus's intellectual contributions as an American Jew, as the new division set out to do. Advertising itself as the "home of progressive Jewish women," the division attracted a membership of left-wing, largely Yiddish-speaking women, many of the immigrant generation.[13] Over the next five decades, though she was also an antiwar activist, campaigning against the proliferation of nuclear weapons and for improved international relations, Clara Lemlich Shavelson devoted much of her energy to the "Emmas."

In its broad strokes, Shavelson's biography does not differ greatly from those of other women who were instrumental in organizing and leading the Emma Lazarus Division and the ELF. June Croll Gordon, a founder and longtime executive director of the group, was born in Odessa in 1901; after immigrating to the United States at the age of three, she began working in New York City's needle trades. Gordon became a prominent trade unionist, leading strikes in the textile and millinery unions. By 1935 she was secretary of the Anti-Nazi Federation, helping to arouse public opinion against the Nazis' territorial ambitions. Rose Raynes, who became ELF's executive director after Gordon's death, came to the United States from Russia when she was ten. Soon employed in garment and millinery shops, Raynes became active in the textile and millinery unions. Like Lemlich, Raynes and Gordon were Communist Party members and officers of the United Council of Working-Class Women and the Progressive Women's Council. All three became targets of McCarthyism. An unsuccessful attempt was made to deport Gordon; Shavelson had her passport revoked. All were called before the House Un-American Activities Committee and harassed by the Federal Bureau of Investigation (FBI).[14]

The Emma Lazarus Division of the JPFO was established by these three women and others with similar backgrounds to combat anti-Semitism and racism, provide relief to wartime victims, and nurture positive Jewish identification through a broad program of Jewish education and women's rights. Founders believed that because of the Holocaust, thousands of women had become "newly aware of themselves as Jewish women," but they urgently needed "history, self-knowledge as Jews, and cultural products" that could sustain the fight against fascism. "Since the attack by Hitler against the Jewish people," Rose Raynes recalled, "we felt that [anti-Semitism] was not only an issue for Europe but for the U.S. as well. We felt that a progressive Jewish woman's organization was the order of the day."[15] Beginning in 1945, the division offered fellowships for works of fiction and history on Jewish themes; it was the first of its many efforts to heighten Jewish identity as a weapon against bigotry. It also supported a home for French war orphans and a day nursery in Israel and championed a broad range of women's issues: full employment for men and women; equal pay for equal work; maternity, unemployment, old age, health, and housing benefits; day nurseries and after-school care; and the inclusion of greater numbers of women in government.

From Division to Federation:
Promoting Jewish Women's History

In 1951 the division became the Emma Lazarus Federation of Jewish Women's Clubs, an independent organization. Although links to the progressive Left remained, the shift from division to federation marked an important transformation in the group's focus. The change in status was influenced by attacks against the Communist Party and the IWO. In 1951 the New York State attorney general initiated proceedings against the IWO as a subversive institution formed and directed under Communist Party auspices. Although the IWO denied that it used members' funds to support the Communist Party, New York State, aided by J. Edgar Hoover and the FBI, successfully prosecuted the order and forced it to liquidate in 1954. A much-reduced JPFO, without the financial advantages of a fraternal benefit society, reorganized as the Jewish Cultural Clubs and Societies, retaining several thousand members interested in cultural programs in Yiddish and English.[16] While Communist Party leaders played a part in reorganizing IWO constituencies, the Emma Lazarus Division had been moving toward a more independent, woman-centered stance in the 1940s in any case; cold war necessities further advanced its autonomy.

During the politically charged fifties, the ELF did not relinquish its radical commitments, although some leaders broke with the Communist Party. As an organization, the ELF vigorously protested against McCarthyism. The trial of Julius and Ethel Rosenberg, which frequently focused on their left-wing Jewish associations, especially alarmed federation leaders, who believed in the Rosenberg's innocence.[17] Although she never met Ethel Rosenberg, Clara Lemlich Shavelson spent two years working on her defense committee, recognizing in the accused woman's labor activism and ethnic associations a replica of her own background. As individuals and in some cases, as chapters, many ELF members rallied to the Rosenbergs' (especially Ethel's) support. After their deaths, the Rosenberg sons were adopted by Ann Meeropol, who was herself a member of the ELF, and her husband.[18]

Throughout the 1950s the federation emphasized the progressive voice of labor as the hallmark of democracy and called for coexistence with the Soviet Union. While Nikita Khrushchev's startling 1956 revelations about Stalinist terrors, and later information about the country's virulent anti-Semitism, left ELF members "shocked" and "grieved," publicly its leaders continued to hope that the USSR would return to its earlier encouragement of ethnic minorities. On at least one occasion, a branch delegate protested that the executive board did not condemn anti-Semitism within the Soviet Union as vigorously as it opposed domestic bigotry; the group remained split for many years between those who wanted to break all ties with the USSR and those who continued to support communism.[19]

Yet the division's unity around cultural work outweighed political differences. By the time the group called its first constitutional convention in 1951 to inaugurate the federation, the Emmas had decided that in the wake of Nazism's terrors, nothing was more important than integrating Jewish heritage into contemporary life. The terrors of McCarthyism, which stigmatized many Jewish radicals as "un-American" Communists, also contributed to the Emmas' desire to claim their own Jewish identity by promoting a progressive, secular Jewish heritage. "Our purpose was to add to the fabric of American culture and democracy by advancing all that is most humane and forward looking in Jewish culture," remarked ELF president Leah Nelson at its third convention in 1959.[20] If Jews were to survive as a people and contribute to world problems in morally responsible ways, they could not be isolated from the social mainstream.

The federation's emphasis on creating a "culturally enlightened American Jewry" coincided with the increasing acceptance of cultural pluralism in post-war life. Even as Jews moved ever more forcefully into the American mainstream, many seemed eager not to obliterate but to identify with their heritage. A so-called Jewish revival, indicated by the construction of synagogues and Jewish social centers, the enrollment of a new generation of youth in Jewish educational programs, and the proclamations of Jewish book, music, and history "months" revealed the desire of many Jews to connect to Jewish roots as well as the increasing acceptability of such expressions of "Americanized" ethnicity.[21]

Yet the ELF believed that this Jewish revival lacked depth and vision. Arguing that knowledge of Jewish tradition should extend beyond holidays and artifacts to an understanding of vital Jewish contributions to American history and democracy, the federation sought to promulgate the neglected history of American Jewish women—their contributions to American arts and letters, to abolition and the trade union movements, and to immigration policy—in order to create a framework for positive identification with Jewish culture and for understanding and acting on present problems. This did not mean assimilation, the Emmas believed, but its opposite: a reaffirmation of the long history of Jewish participation in American democracy *as Jews* and a recommitment to Jews' moral values and humanistic culture. Both the focus on women and the linkage of women's history to activism distinguished this goal from that of the Jewish Cultural Clubs and Societies, the reorganized JPFO group, whose emphasis lay in encouraging Yiddish culture while also supporting progressive Jewish culture in English (for example, aid to *Jewish Currents* magazine).[22]

In promulgating a secular progressive Judaism without relying on the special qualities of *yiddishkeit,* the Emmas resolved a paradox that had long troubled the immigrant Jewish Left. Jewish fraternal organizations had offered cultural programs, sports leagues, and medical services to members in an attempt to serve the interests of an increasingly assimilated Jewish immigrant population and their descendants; Yiddish newspapers began inserting English pages for similar reasons. But the Emmas were unusual in emphasizing a Jewish intellectual tradition that was both militantly secular and progressively American as the best appeal to the post-Yiddish-speaking generation.

In the early 1950s the ELF commissioned biographies of two Jewish women whose achievements they believed symbolized different, though compatible, directions in progressive American Jewish history. The first subject, writer Emma Lazarus (1849–87), the group's major inspiration, had concentrated on Jewish themes within a broad universalistic setting. The other, Ernestine Rose (1810–92), social reformer, abolitionist, and suf-fragist, had focused her energies on many important problems of the day, not especially Jewish ones. Although they had been radicals in their own time, both women's protests were clearly within the American democratic tradition; thus the Emmas selected models who helped ensure their own legitimacy as political and cultural dissenters.

Lazarus was, of course, the writer whose poem, "The New Colossus," engraved on a plaque on the Statue of Liberty in May 1903, has helped welcome generations of immi-grants to the United States. In the 1950s, however (and, it can be argued, even today), neither Lazarus's Jewish or woman's consciousness had been widely recognized. The standard belief was that Lazarus had become concerned with her Jewishness belatedly, only after the Russian pogroms of the 1880s; her contributions to the cause of women were even less commonly understood.

ELF members believed that Lazarus was an inspiration both for Jewish culture and women's rights. Though not associated with the women's rights movement, Lazarus had helped remove the "veils and screens" of women's life, with which the "woman-souled poet," as she called herself, had to grope. In the biography of Lazarus that the federation commissioned Eve Merriam to write (to celebrate the anniversary of the Jews' tercen-tennial in America in 1954), the author comments that "the figure representing work is a woman to Emma Lazarus, not the conventional symbol of a man."[23]

The federation also portrayed Lazarus as a woman who had spoken out forcefully and consistently against anti-Semitism and assimilation, and as a Jew who was concerned not only with what she called a narrow, "tribal" Judaism but also with oppressed peoples the world over. "Until we are all free, we are none of us free," was the Lazarus line most often quoted by the ELF to demonstrate the poet's concern for all humanity.[24]

Lazarus had originally used the line to refer to solidarity with the Jewish people. "When the life and property of a Jew in the uttermost provinces of the Caucasus are attacked," she wrote, "the dignity of a Jew in free America is humiliated. . . . Until we are all free, we are none of us free." Her universalism appeared in a line that stated that Jews should not "become too 'tribal' and narrow and Judaic rather than humane and cosmopolitan." Instead they must concern themselves with the misfortunes of "our unhappy brethren."[25] To the ELF, this "universal scope" coupled with Lazarus's sup-port for Jewish culture and women's freedom made her an admirable symbol of secular, humanistic values.

Ironically, the federation ignored one element in Lazarus's background that, as a left-wing organization, it might have been expected to highlight: her Jewish-based socialism. Lazarus argued, for example, that the root of the "modern theory of socialism" lay in the "Mosaic Code," which established the "principle of the rights of labor" and denied the "right of private property in land . . . we find the fathers of modern socialism to be three Jews—Ferdinand Lassalle, Karl Marx, and Johann Jacoby."[26] The federation also ignored another major Lazarus theme—her support for a Jewish homeland in Palestine. While the ELF endorsed both formulations, it found Lazarus's leadership in the campaign to promote Jewish culture, aid new immigrants, and fight anti-Semitism both more com-pelling and more characteristic.

For almost fifty years federation members never tired of presenting Lazarus's ideas to whichever group would listen. Every year the Emmas celebrated her birthday with a trip to Liberty Island; they succeeded in having the mayors of New York and Miami declare an Emma Lazarus Day, and later they arranged a commemorative stamp. The true meaning of Lazarus for the federation, however, lay less in these occasions than in the model of action, authority, and leadership that she claimed as a woman, a Jew, and an American. Basing their program on her work, the Emmas hoped to give "leadership to women in Jewish communities in our own time in the same spirit as Emma Lazarus did in hers."[27]

In 1954 the ELF published a biography of Ernestine Rose that it had commissioned Yuri Suhl to write. To the Emmas, Rose represented a model of activism even more than Lazarus, who spoke with her pen. They cited the fact that Susan B. Anthony had named Rose, along with Mary Wollstonecraft and Frances Wright, as the most important leader of the women's movement, praising her activism on behalf of women's property rights and suffrage.

Unlike Lazarus's, Rose's work did not have a Jewish orientation, yet the federation claimed her as the first Jewish woman reformer in the United States. Born in the ghetto of Piotrkow, in Russian Poland, Rose, the daughter of a rabbi, refused to accept the traditional destiny of young Jewish women. While still a teenager, she took her father to court, protesting his determination to marry her against her will and suing to obtain possession of the dowry her mother had left her. Rose won the lawsuit but returned most of the property to her father. Then, at age seventeen, she left the country, eventually settling in the United States.

Although Rose abandoned the formal practice of religion, she took a "fighting stand" against anti-Semitism, publicly disavowing its presence in her own circle of freethinkers. According to the Emmas, her work on behalf of abolition and women's rights and against anti-Semitism demonstrated the "interrelationships between Jew and non-Jew, Negro and white, men and women." Like Lazarus, she was seen to combine Jewish patriotism with a broader humanism. "Emancipation from every kind of bondage is my principle," they recalled her words. "I go for the recognition of human rights, without distinction of sect, party, sex or color." As she wrote to President Abraham Lincoln during the Civil War, "So long as one slave breathes in this Republic, we drag the chain with him."[28]

The Emmas considered Rose a model for her work in the peace movement; an activist for the Universal Peace Society, founded in Rhode Island, she was a delegate to several international peace congresses. To Rose, women had a special stake in peace crusades: "War is a terrible enemy of man," she observed, "a terrible school. . . . I trust that if every woman touched the sword it would be to sheath it in its scabbard forever."[29] The ELF often quoted these words to legitimate its own work for peace.

Though none received the attention given to Lazarus and Rose, the federation remembered other American Jewish women in its cultural work, spreading biographical reminiscences of Rebecca Gratz, Lillian Wald, Sophie Loeb, Penina Moise, and others. In the early 1950s it commissioned a history of Jewish women in the United States to be published in Yiddish and English but canceled the volume when the draft failed to meet its standards. The ELF debated publishing such a work into the late 1970s.

The federation documented the experience of Jewish women outside the United

States as well. In commemorating the anniversary of the uprising of the Warsaw Ghetto, it paid tribute to those who had taken part in the resistance and who had fought for freedom in partisan groups, women like Niuta Teitelboim, Dora Goldkorn, Zofia Yamalka, Rosa Robota, Mala Zimmetbaum, Regina Fuden, Zivia Lubetkin, Hana Senish, Vitka Kempner, and Frumke and Hentche Platnitksy. To federation members, the courageous stand of the "Mothers" of the Warsaw Ghetto merged with the traditions of women trailblazers in the United States — "Ernestine Rose, Sojourner Truth, Susan B. Anthony, Emma Lazarus, and the women from the shops and mills like Esther Greenleaf, a shoe worker, and the later immigrants like those of the Triangle Shirt and Waist shop who fought against sweatshop conditions."[30] Moreover, the ELF cited women's heroism in the fight for Israeli independence.

The federation also issued study outlines on themes in general Jewish and Yiddish history and culture, writing on such subjects as bigotry in school textbooks, the Jewish contribution to American law and letters, and Yiddish prose and poetry. In praising the work of Sholom Aleichem and I. L. Peretz, the Emmas singled out these writers' forward-looking, empathic treatment of women in the shtetls of Eastern Europe.

Toward An Inclusive Women's History: Dissidents, Working Women, White Women Reformers, and Black Women

Interested in the broader history of American women, the federation developed curricula on such subjects as the contributions of dissident women from Anne Hutchinson to Ethel Rosenberg and the role of America's working women in the Lowell mills and garment sweatshops. In 1954 it commissioned artist Philip Reisman to do a mural of the 1909 mass meeting at Cooper Union, depicting Clara Lemlich at the center; the five-foot-by-seven-foot painting was donated to the International Ladies' Garment Workers Union in 1982.

The link between women's rights and abolitionist movements was of vital interest. In the 1950s and 1960s the ELF prepared study guides on Sojourner Truth, Ida B. Wells, and Harriet Tubman and paid tribute to the leadership of Sarah Douglass, Mary Bibb, Grace Mapps, and Francis Ellen Harper. The federation also called attention to the contemporary achievements of Rosa Parks, Autherine Lucy, and other black women involved in the civil rights struggle.

Its most important contribution in this area was the pamphlet, "Women in the Life and Time of Abraham Lincoln," a reprint of the proceedings of a conference held by the National Women's Loyal League. Formed at a mass rally called by women's rights leaders (including Ernestine Rose) on May 14, 1863, at Cooper Union in New York City, the league assembled over one thousand northern white women abolitionists who pledged to rally women in their states to obtain one million signatures on a petition to endorse the Thirteenth Amendment. Though the league disbanded after the legislation passed, the Emmas believed that it had activated white women and advanced the women's rights movement. They hoped that its work for abolition would challenge contemporary white women (particularly Jewish women) to work for civil rights.

The ELF pamphlet about the Loyal League contained an introduction by Daisy Bates, leader of the desegregation struggle at Little Rock High School. Bates was also the principal speaker at a celebration held at Cooper Union by the federation's New York club in December 1963 to commemorate the one-hundredth anniversary of the national league's founding. Thirteen hundred people joined the Emmas on that occasion to celebrate the unity of white and black women in the common struggle for civil rights.

"Thinking . . . Expressed in Action": The Federation's Campaigns For Human Rights

For federation members, there was nothing pedantic or merely academic in its cultural work. The ELF believed that women's and Jewish history could inspire contemporary thought and policy by providing models of commitment and activism. "Thinking is expressed in action; culture is . . . promoted by projects," remarked Leah Nelson at the ELF's 1959 convention. Executive Director June Gordon used to say that the federation served the Jewish community as a true "university for women"; later she preferred to point to the ELF's work as a "Veker" and a "Wegweiser"—a pathfinder and awakener—involving members of other Jewish women's groups, as well as the community at large, in vital actions.[31]

The federation's practical work covered a wide spectrum. Its five-point program, adopted in 1951, established lasting goals. In addition to the promotion of Jewish culture (the "number one project"), these included the elimination of anti-Semitism and racism, the campaign for women's rights, support for the state of Israel, and world peace and consumer's issues.[32]

With the legacy of Emma Lazarus, Ernestine Rose, and the National Women's Loyal League pointing the way, the federation dedicated much of its efforts over four decades to work on behalf of civil rights. The "Negro question is ours," as one club member put it in 1955.[33] The Emmas acknowledged that while anti-Semitism and racism sprang from common roots and that American Jews and minorities shared the same dangerous enemy—the ultra-Right—oppression in the black community was not only significantly greater than that of Jews but also could be fueled by Jews' own racism. Consciousness of the impact of racial difference on women's roles and opportunities led the federation to focus on the needs of black women and racial minorities long before the white women's movement turned to these issues in the 1970s.

Its most important leaders, including Clara Shavelson, June Gordon, and Rose Raynes, had been members of the Communist Party at a time when interest in black culture and the promotion of civil rights was actively encouraged; June Gordon herself had married an African American artist, Eugene Gordon. For these reasons, and because of their guiding belief that discrimination in the form of anti-Semitism and that based on racism were deeply linked, the Emmas took on the challenge of promoting racial justice by engaging Jewish women in a joint campaign with blacks. "America's white women have been in semi-hibernation ever since the abolitionist movement," an Emma wrote in the first edition of the group's bulletin, *The Lamp,* in 1952.[34] Through concrete actions, it was time to wake them.

Shortly after its founding, the federation joined in a common statement of principle with the Sojourners for Truth and Justice, a black women's civil rights group. The Emmas made a regular financial contribution to the Sojourners, and the groups met at an annual luncheon.[35] The Los Angeles Emma Lazarus club established a similar relationship with the Southern Region of the California State Association of Colored Women's Clubs, jointly sponsoring an Interracial Mothers' Day event and other programs; in Miami, Emmas joined with black women in an Interracial Mothers' Association that worked on civil rights projects. In 1953 several Emmas traveled to Georgia as part of a delegation of black and white women to plead with the governor against the imprisonment of a black woman for the murder of a white man who had attacked her. (Two decades later they would defend black professor Angela Davis against what they considered unjust imprisonment.) By 1956 the Emmas were sending truckloads of food and clothing to Mississippi and joining boycotts and sit-ins. By the 1960s they were working with civil rights groups throughout the country, supporting the Freedom Rides and Freedom Summer, participating in civil rights marches in Washington, D.C., and organizing local demonstrations, rallies, and picket lines.

The Emmas fought segregation in housing and schools in their own communities, lobbying legislators, presenting petitions, and holding forums. They observed Negro History Week with readings, lectures, and joint programs with black organizations, often highlighting the contributions of black and Jewish women to the building of the country.[36] At annual Mother's Day celebrations, they typically honored a black women active in civil rights. Black women's associations in some regions honored the Emma Lazarus clubs at their own meetings and made contributions to the Emma Lazarus nursery in Israel.

The Emmas believed, however, that more was needed than occasional meetings with African American groups and ceremonial events; they called for "constant contact" and intensive, rather than token, support of black rights. To this end they established ongoing affiliations not only with the Sojourners but also with the NAACP, the National Association of Colored Women, and other groups, and they urged immediate and varied measures to end discrimination and increase opportunities in all arenas. But they warned against a "humanitarian" approach—whites "helping" blacks—rather than a "joint struggle." Jewish women's special task, modeled by the National Women's Loyal League, was to engage white women and Jews in the civil rights movement.[37]

The federation urged its own members to support equality for blacks by eliminating white supremacist attitudes they might unwittingly hold. In a 1951 position paper on "Racism, Enemy of the Jewish People," the ELF established two principles; first, that blacks suffered greater oppression in the United States than any other people, including Jews, whatever their experience with anti-Semitism; and second, that the main fight against discrimination was the responsibility of whites. While Jews were especially affected by discrimination, since anti-Semitism and racism derived from common white supremacist roots, the ELF argued that "every Jewish worker who wants to fight for peace and against fascism is hurting that struggle when he doesn't root out . . . every bit of racism in himself."[38]

The Emmas gave examples of how "Jewish nationalism and chauvinism" could feed the idea that Jews were superior to non-Jews—for example, the use of the terms *goyim* and *shikseh*. Such superior attitudes applied with double intensity to blacks: Jews who knew the derogatory meaning of anti-Semitic terms were cautioned against the use of *schvartse* and other stereotypical expressions about blacks. The Emmas voiced special concern for Negro women, who suffered "triple oppression, as women, as women-workers, and as Negroes": discriminated against in industry, they were forced to take menial jobs as houseworkers only to suffer from exploitation by white housewives.

The Emmas considered the campaign to secure passage of the United Nations (U.N.) Genocide Convention their most important political crusade. In 1963 the ELF initiated a petition campaign for the United States to ratify the Genocide Convention, which had been adopted by the U.N. General Assembly in 1948 and subsequently signed by seventy-five nations. ELF presented the first 4,000 signatures on the petitions to U.N. ambassador Adlai Stevenson in December 1963. Two years later, when the twentieth session of the General Assembly signed a new treaty to eliminate all forms of racism, it issued a new petition calling upon the United States to ratify both treaties. In 1966 the federation delivered 7,000 signatures to Ambassador Arthur Goldberg; in 1969 it sent a delegation (including three black women) to present 60,000 signatures to senator William Fulbright of the Senate Foreign Relations Committee. The Senate finally ratified the Genocide Convention on February 19, 1986.[39]

The Emmas never abandoned their faith in the potential of culture, and especially history itself, as an agent of change in the battle for human rights. In 1964 a member of the Emma Lazarus Boston club told the ELF national convention of an incident that confirmed this belief:

> At a panel discussion on the relationship of the Jew to the Negro in Roxbury, where there is considerable racial strife, the Jew did not fare so well. One Negro speaker bluntly said that he considered the Jews and the landlord and storekeeper as one who exploits him. The Jew on the panel, a representative of one of our big organizations, didn't elevate the level of the discussion. He started out, "No matter what," facing the Negro, "you still should be grateful that you live in America. You are still better off then if you lived in Russia."
>
> In the general discussion that followed Elizabeth Stern [president of the Boston Emma Lazarus club] took the floor and directed the attention of the audience to our Panel on the wall of that room and said in effect: "Let me show you a different relationship between Negro and Jew during our Civil War period," and she pointed to Ernestine Rose, Sojourner Truth and all the other characters depicted on the panel. One by one the audience came up to look at the Panel. It was closely scrutinized, discussed, admired by all. Our organization was commended for bringing to light this historical data and for the fashion in which it was presented, and the whole tone of the meeting was changed.[40]

Nor did the federation abandon its conviction that by working for social equality for blacks, its members were expressing their identity as good Jews and good Americans, as Emma Lazarus herself had proclaimed when she highlighted the harmony between America's multiple nationalities and its civic culture. For the Emmas, the civil rights crusade in which they played an early, vigorous, and continuous role was a perfect example of democratic pluralism at its best. Here, for example, is June Gordon's account of the Emmas demonstrating with thousands of black and white women during the historic March on Washington on August 18, 1963:

> At one point in the line of March, as we approached a spot where Lincoln Rockwell's brown-shirted bullies were on the lookout for an opportunity to jeer and make trouble, two young Episcopalian Ministers sprinted up in front of us and declared: "Ladies, pictures are being taken. We want our Bishop to see us leading the Emma Lazarus Contingent." At the same time a fellow Negro marcher chose to walk with us. He moved up front and said to one of our banner bearers: "You must be tired, let me carry it for a while." And so our contingent was headed by Episcopalians; one end of the banner—*on the side where the Nazi hoodlums were lined up*—was carried by a Negro marcher. Looking for Leah Nelson [the ELF president] to call her attention to the gloriously symbolic sight of unity we represented, we spotted her marching behind a banner of a *Catholic* organization. This truly was America.[41]

Because the Emmas believed that anti-Semitism and racism were inherently linked, they recognized that in working for civil rights, they were "not doing something for the black people, but . . . doing something for ourselves."[42] When in the late 1960s relations between blacks and Jews grew strained, the ELF affirmed the historic relationship between the two groups and insisted that differences on specific issues, which they felt had been inflamed by extremists on both sides, not be allowed to tamper with the groups' common interests. In contrast to many Jewish organizations, the Emmas supported affirmative action, community control of schools, and decentralization. Yet occasionally, when they found evidences of black anti-Semitism, they spoke out in protest: in 1967, for example, they called upon the Student Nonviolent Coordinating Committee (SNCC) to revise its "shocking and disturbing" position on Jewish organizations.[43]

From its inception, the federation was vigilant about anti-Semitism. It tracked, and opposed, the resurgence of Nazism through letters, telegrams, resolutions, pickets, and mass meetings; targets for its attacks included neo-Nazi movements in Germany, England, France, Italy, Argentina, and dozens of cities in the United States. The federation also protested the ominous spread of anti-Semitism among the general populations; too often, it noted, Jews were discriminated against at public resorts, at schools and colleges, and in the workplace. Quoting Emma Lazarus's protest against anti-Semitism that the word *Jew* was used constantly "even among so-called refined Christians" as a term of opprobrium and was increasingly employed as a verb "to denote the meanest tricks," the Emmas called for actions to protest pernicious stereotyping as well as discriminatory quota systems.[44] But they persistently argued that groups most guilty of anti-Semitic bigotry—at various times, the Ku Klux Klan, the American Nazi Party, the Liberty Lobby, or the Moral Majority—also posed the greatest danger to the rights of minorities.[45]

The blind spot in the federation's campaign against anti-Semitism remained the Soviet Union. The absence of a committed campaign against Soviet anti-Semitism was a consequence of the continuing political attachment of a significant number of federation members to the Communist Party; others within the leadership had broken with the party, or had become critical of its actions, because of revelations about Stalinist terror and Soviet anti-Semitism. The last president of the ELF, Rose Raynes, for example, was anti-Stalinist, whereas her second-in-command, Gertrude Decker, remained loyal to the USSR. This split prevented the executive board from taking a vigorous stand against Soviet brutality and harassment of Jews.[46]

The federation was involved in other issues outlined in its five-point program. From its inception, the ELF supported the cause of peace. At the Emmas' first annual Mothers' Day luncheon in 1951, members read poems of peace commemorating the struggles of women written by Gerda Lerner. Yet ELF leaders made clear to members that the role of the federation, as a cultural group, was to support existing peace organizations rather than create its own initiatives. ELF clubs cooperated with the Committee for a Sane Nuclear Policy (SANE), the Women's International League for Peace and Freedom (WILPF), and the Committee for World Development and World Disarmament. Within these groups the Emmas endeavored to help make policy as well as support petition drives and fund collections. As in the civil rights arena, they sought to become liaisons to Jewish women's organizations so as to bring these groups into the peace movement.[47]

While ELF shared a common agenda with SANE and other peace organizations, it criticized the minimal involvement of workers and their families in these groups. Here, too, the Emmas claimed a special role: "With our participating in the communities, we reach women from wage-earning families. Through work in the shops and raising this greatly important question in the union, where many of our sisters and their husbands belong, we can help strengthen and expand the peace organizations."[48] From their early interest in the elimination of nuclear weapons to their activities to end the Vietnam War, the Emmas remained involved in questions of war and peace, militarism, and foreign policy.[49]

As a Jewish women's organization, the federation was greatly concerned with the fate of Israel. The ELF was the first Jewish group to establish a daycare center in the new state (for the Jewish and Arab children of working mothers). The Emma Lazarus Nursery in Jaffa, later moved to Tel Aviv, was administered by the women's division of the Agudath Tarbuth L'Am (the Association for Peoples Culture), which worked mainly with families of immigrants and workers. The federation was the sole support of the nursery, which it considered its "pet project," until 1988, when the facility was forced to close because of the lack of funds. Many members journeyed to Israel specifically to visit the nursery; others knit sweaters for its children. The ELF also raised considerable sums of money for Israel at the time of the 1967 and Yom Kippur wars, and it regularly supported the Red Mogon Dovid.

In addition to holding forums and publishing study guides on Israel, the ELF attempted to focus the attention of peace groups on the need for a constructive stand on U.S. foreign policy in regard to Israel and peace in the Middle East. The federation distinguished its identification with Israel, however, from that of many other Jewish organizations. Its own positions were based on "kinship with the Israeli people and not on Israel as the core of Jewish life," as it understood was the case with other groups; the most vital service the ELF thought it could render to Israel was to heighten cultural identification among American Jews.

Concern for Israel, in any event, reflected the Emmas' class analysis of the Middle Eastern politics of oil, which it believed threatened the security of Israel and its Arab neighbors. The Emmas questioned whether the success of Arab national liberation movements might not benefit Israel in the long run and worried about the second-class treatment of Arabs within Israel. After the Six-Day War, the federation questioned whether Israel needed all the territory it had won but demanded that Arab neighbors accept Israel's right to exist without qualification.[50]

In November 1975 the federation adopted a resolution condemning the U.N. resolution equating "Zionism with racism" as "vicious anti-Semitism . . . directed against all Jews." But controversy erupted with ELF vice president Gertrude Decker declared in a public speech that she was "for the existence of Israel as a progressive State, not a Zionist state in the service of imperialism" and could not support the Israeli government's "discriminatory and *racist* policies." Board members condemned her remarks, and members of one local chapter circulated a petition opposing them.[51]

Promoting the rights and culture of immigrants and supporting consumer interests were also of deep concern. In the 1950s the federation engaged in a vigorous campaign for a statute of limitation against the deportation of foreign-born Americans; it was the only Jewish group to become a founder of the Museum of Immigration on Liberty Island. The ELF spoke out consistently against the high cost of living and for senior citizens' rights and entitlements; many local groups gave substantial support to the farm workers' union.

Women's issues, finally, were always central to federation interests. The ELF worked continuously to bring women's history to a wide public so that the lessons of the past might help shape the present. In 1956 it inaugurated a year of celebration for the thirty-fifth anniversary of woman suffrage, focusing on women's history. (Twenty years later, Congresswoman Bella Abzug addressed another large ELF-sponsored meeting honoring the achievement of suffrage.) After the advent of the new feminist movement in the 1960s, ELF members worked with women's rights organizations on myriad issues (including the Equal Rights Amendment); its International Women's Day celebration was an annual highlight.

The federation identified a host of economic and social problems that affected the lives of women, particularly working women. Far in advance of the times, its 1955 discussion guide, for example, focused on the lack of equal pay for equal work, "double" wage discrimination faced by black women, occupational segregation, unequal job security and promotional opportunities, lack of representation in trade union and management, and problems of working mothers (day nurseries and after-school care). Issues of educational access and the representation of women in politics, government, and the professions were also highlighted. Here, too, the ELF believed that it could play an important role by representing the needs of working women and implementing programs developed by union members. In addition, the federation hoped to bring a greater consciousness of black women's work, educational, and political situations to women's groups and other organizations to which it was affiliated. It supported these varied goals not only by raising its own members' consciousness through the production of study guides, dramatic presentations, lectures, exhibits, and other cultural programs but also through a continuing series of demonstrations, marches, picket lines, petition campaigns, celebrations and convocations, and other actions.

"Jewish Culture Does Not Limit One":
The ELF and Problems of Outreach

Spanning the country, with chapters in New York (Brooklyn, the Bronx, Rochester), New Jersey (Newark, Jersey City, Lakewood, Toms River), California (Los Angeles, San Francisco), and Boston, Chicago, Philadelphia, Detroit, and Miami, the Emma Lazarus Federation maintained its educational and political activities for close to forty years. Yet almost from the outset, questions of expanding its outreach had been raised. At their peak, some of the largest chapters in New York, Chicago, and Los Angeles had more than a dozen branches, with several hundred members each; other groups were much smaller. Though the organization kept no membership records, the best estimate is that the federation attracted approximately 4,000 to 5,000 members in one hundred clubs during the 1950s; membership remained fairly stable in the 1960s but fell in later years.

Though no match for Hadassah, with its hundreds of thousands of middle-class members, the ELF boasted an unusually active, committed membership. Like Clara Lemlich Shavelson, June Croll Gordon, and Rose Raynes, most of the original federation members were working-class women who had been associated with the IWO or other progressive labor-oriented groups. Many had worked in industry and had participated in the trade union movement; others had been radicalized as housewives and consumers. Most longtime members were Yiddish speaking; even when the balance began to shift with increasing numbers of members speaking only English, leaders advocated the bilingual approach: "The sisters [should] use the language which lends itself with greater ease to [their] verbal or written expression. Never, under any circumstances, should one be preferred over the other."[52] *The Lamp,* the monthly newsletter of the federation, appeared in both languages; meetings were usually conducted in English.

Leaders wondered, however, whether the ELF's relatively narrow membership base was sufficient to support the broad scope of its five-point program. Over the years they urged chapters to reach out to a wider circle of Jewish women. "We must be among women and unite on issues of concern to all women," the Newark club president declared.[53] From the beginning, the federation program appealed to a broader constituency than was reflected in its membership: regular presentations to Hadassah, B'nai Brith, synagogue sisterhoods, and similar groups enlarged the ELF's audiences by many thousands. Brooklyn and Los Angeles chapters were proud of their relationships with Jewish women's assemblies; several clubs enrolled non-Jewish, nonwhite members as well.

Although some ELF members did not want to lose their identity by doing "leg work for other organizations" or adjust their message to suit organizational partners, they realized that because new members were needed to keep the federation growing, so were new methods. "Know parliamentary procedures," advised the Philadelphia delegate to the 1955 ELF convention: "Learn to compromise our old methods without compromising our principles. Find new language—i.e., forward-looking people instead of the word 'progressive.' Use language that is acceptable to others . . . so they will come to listen to us. . . . Emphasize the issues that unite and bring with warmth and friendship our message to others."[54]

While some in the Jewish community dismissed the Emmas as "embittered women" with "heavy Yiddish accents," a number of prominent leaders were pleased to be publicly associated with them.[55] In 1947, when the Emma Lazarus Division was an IWO affiliate, Louise Waterman Wise, wife of eminent reform rabbi Stephen Wise and herself president of the Women's Division of the American Jewish Congress, took the podium to introduce a public session ("An Evening of Jewish Culture") at the division's First Constitutional Convention, held at Hunter College.[56] Illinois state legislator Esther Saperstein, impressed with the ELF-sponsored biography of Ernestine Rose by Yuri Suhl, joined the Chicago chapter in the 1950s and memorialized Rose's name in the legislature. New York congresswomen Bella Abzug and Elizabeth Holtzman also honored Rose and Lazarus and participated in federation events.[57]

The question of whether the ideas of the federation were too progressive to attract the support of more mainstream Jewish women—or whether subtle changes in language and procedure might win new members—frequently surfaced. At the 1965 ELF convention, June Gordon denied that the Emmas could not comfortably speak to a broad audience. "Many, all too many members think we are so far in advance of all other Jewish women in our progressive outlook that it is useless to approach them as prospective members and cultivate their interest in joining the club. This attitude is a disservice."[58] Though some members felt that other women's groups were too "reactionary," Gordon insisted that the federation offered a place for women of varied opinions.

Although new members joined Emma Lazarus clubs primarily for their educational programs, opportunities for sociability and friendship were important. "Even more precious than learning," recalled one Chicago member, was "a warm sisterly relation in the club, sisters we can share our joys and sorrows with—in short you feel a part of a great big noisy family." But most important was the connection to Jewish heritage this member (and many others) made as an Emma. She recalled her initiation to the Emmas at her first club meeting, where she had listened to a program about Chanukah and Emma Lazarus:

> I suddenly became aware that I was part of the struggles and triumphs of the Jewish people. How was it that I could not see it before? Perhaps because I wanted to forget I was a Jew, and thereby avoid facing the grim facts of my people not being accepted as equals even in our country. . . . I have always been interested in culture generally, and I thought at the time that pursuing Jewish culture only, is too narrow and limited. . . . My interest was aroused, and I joined the club at the following meeting. Since then, having participated in cultural as well as other projects, it became clear to me that Jewish culture does not limit one, but on the contrary, broadens one's horizon. I became conscious of a feeling of pride in my origin, particularly after reading the works of Emma Lazarus.[59]

Attracting young women who had been uprooted from their Jewish heritage was a continuing source of pride for the ELF.

While certain sections were able to attract new members, including young mothers, the graying of the membership became a major problem. Even though attendance at meetings was high, the ability of aging members to take on demanding campaigns diminished. Still, many ELF women remained vigorous well into their seventies and eighties. Here, too, Clara Shavelson led the way: as she aged along with the federation, Shavelson regularly attended its meetings and participated in its activities. In her seventies, she collected 1,500 signatures for the federation's Genocide Convention; the ELF gratefully acknowledged her contributions. Shavelson admitted that although she had been proud of the youthful Clara Lemlich, she thought that Clara Shavelson, a lifetime activist, had accomplished much more. When asked by a student interviewer to talk about the famous 1909 strike, she responded, at age eighty, that "I[n] so far as I am concerned, I am still at it."[60]

After 1968 Shavelson resided at the Hebrew Home for the Aged in Los Angeles, where she participated in political discussions and forums. She died in 1982 at the age of ninety-six. Like Shavelson, many federation members moved to suburban neighborhoods or retirement communities, at a distance from former comrades and Emma clubs. The federation tried to meet the problem by encouraging the formation of chapters in new communities; although Los Angeles was successful in starting suburban clubs, other regions could not adapt as readily to changing residence patterns.

The transformation of women's work, and the women's movement itself, also affected the federation's longevity. By midcentury, most Jewish working women did not share a trade union background with the original Emmas, though they might encounter gender discrimination at work and home. While many Jewish women were drawn to the women's movement, it was not as Jewishly identified women that they joined new feminist ranks. Sexism, although a major ELF concern, was not an exclusive one; women liberationists no doubt found it difficult to identify with the pantheon of federation causes. And while there was an incipient Jewish women's movement in the 1970s, it did not share the Emmas' secularism but rather focused on issues of religious patriarchy.

Despite their lack of progeny, federation members were not discouraged. Indeed, they were delighted that ideas they had promoted for a quarter of a century were attracting the attention of young feminists. "We did our small part," Rose Raynes commented; now it was time for others to take the lead.[61]

By the end of the 1980s ELF leaders like Clara Shavelson and June Gordon had passed on, and elderly members could not be replaced. Though some individual clubs in Chicago, Los Angeles, and the Bronx remained, the Emma Lazarus Federation of Jewish Women's Clubs disbanded in 1989.

The Federation and "Betweenness": "A Part of the Whole Multi-National Culture of American Life"

For nearly four decades, the federation played a distinct role in Jewish women's organizational life. It was, according to its leaders, the "only Jewish women's organization that encourages mass action, the movement of people," a "progressive organization . . . which meets the needs of those women who are on the move."[62] It had also, over this period, taken its message regarding the significance of Jewish women's history, culture, and ideals to a broad audience of women in more traditional Jewish organizations. At the same time, the Emmas joined successfully with black women and other minorities to work for an end to racism. Though not a peace group, the federation dedicated its energies to programs and education for peace.

All of its varied projects sprang, the Emmas believed, from a dedicated core of Jewish identity. As distinct from Hadassah or synagogue sisterhoods, whose identity focused on Israel or the religious aspects of Judaism, the ELF proudly asserted itself as a secular Jewish group centered in the culture of America and its Jewish population. Much as their ancestors turned to Judaic religious emblems, the Emmas selected a heroine compatible with their own multi-faceted identities as secular Jews, women, and Americans. Their primary identification with Emma Lazarus arose from her secularism, which the Emmas associated with a universalist humanism that they argued reflected the essence of Jewish values.

While the Emmas were a Jewish organization, their proud ethnicity did not hamper, but, in fact, promoted, their identification as women, as workers, and as Americans. As proclaimed in the ELF's first constitution in January 1951, the enhancement of Jewish culture was proposed "as a part of the whole multinational culture of American life." To be Jewish and American was not a contradiction but an interrelationship; as Lazarus's life had implied, "to be a good Jew was to be a better American."[63] Furthermore, gender was as fundamental to the group's identity as were ethnicity and nationality: as we have seen, women's issues and history were woven into all activities of the federation over the course of nearly forty years. Class consciousness was also deeply ingrained within the federation: like Shavelson, Gordon, and Raynes, most leaders and members came from trade union backgrounds or had married men who were active in workers' movements. Working-class consciousness distinguished the federation from middle-class Jewish women's organizations and helped shape its theory and practice.

The history of the Emma Lazarus Federation also raises provocative questions about racial identity and sensitivities. From the creation of the Emma Lazarus Division in 1944 to the demise of the federation forty-five years later, members consistently spoke to the necessity of eliminating white racism as well as anti-Semitism. In a series of continuing projects, they directed their efforts practically as well as rhetorically to the support of civil rights, particularly to the task of awakening white women (especially Jewish women) to the cause and allying themselves with black women to improve their situation.

In view of the ways in which the Emma Lazarus Federation amalgamated rather than separated the traditional markers of group identity—class, gender, nationality, ethnicity, and race—the experience of this group sheds light not only on Jewish women's activism in the twentieth century, but also on broader theoretical questions of feminism.[64] As feminists examine the various ways in which race, class, gender, and ethnicity interact and compete for the allegiance of individuals, organizations, and communities, the history of the Emma Lazarus Federation cautions us about the pitfalls of naming "discrete, coherent and absolutely separate" measures of identity.[65] For the Emmas, there was no dichotomy between class and gender, race and ethnicity. In one respect, the group itself represented a "racialized ethnicity," a people with a common ethnic past who came to regard itself as a "race" because of the traumatic experience of the Holocaust, recognizing connections with other victims of genocide and racism.[66]

Like Clara Shavelson, most members of the ELF had begun their organizational lives as trade union members. Yet while Shavelson in 1909 had spoken her famous words as a worker, the delegates to the Cooper Union meeting offered a Jewish prayer before voting on her strike resolution. Jewish solidarity supported workers' consciousness on that occasion, as it did for all the years in which Shavelson, Gordon, Raynes, and their friends took part in the Jewish People's Fraternal Order of the IWO. These women's participation in the United Council of Working-Class Women, the Progressive Women's Council, and the Women's Division of the IWO illustrates their early recognition of the importance of gender as well as class and ethnic consciousness.

Not, however, until the Holocaust had accomplished its unspeakable horrors did the Jewish component of their identity become most salient. Remembering the women victims who "sang lullabies to console their children while facing the open graves before them," Clara Shavelson and her progressive friends made themselves over into "Emmas," dedicating themselves to promote Jewish culture—albeit a woman-centered "people's" culture—as a "shield" against fascism and genocide. "We dare not forget or forgive . . . the crimes of Nazism," they repeatedly exclaimed.

The coming to consciousness of the Emmas as "racialized" Jews in a way that fully incorporated their identities as women, trade unionists, and Americans illuminates the importance of the Holocaust in shaping Jewish women's experience. Yet it was the microcosmic context of these women's lives over a long period of time—their roles and relationships as comrades in the sweatshops and unions, as housewives in their neighborhoods, on bread and meat picket lines, and as associates in the JPFO and Progressive Women's clubs—that provided the fulcrum for their gender-specific response to the Holocaust.

At its twentieth anniversary convention in 1971, the Emma Lazarus Federation reconsidered its organizational roots. "Why are we calling ourselves a Jewish women's organization?" one delegate asked. "Since we are progressive with our ideology and program to benefit all people, why the separation? Why emphasize our Jewishness?" "Why a woman's organization?" Rose Raynes repeated. "Why the Hadassah, the Pioneer Women, the Council of Jewish Women, the Women's Division of the American Jewish Congress, the Women Strike for Peace, the National Council of Negro Women, the Emma Lazarus Federation?"

In response, the ELF president reaffirmed the importance both of "unity as Jews, unity in variety" and the "special approach" needed to solve women's problems because of pervasive attitudes of "male superiority": "We are a part of American life generally, and of the Jewish community in particular," she reaffirmed, as well as a member of the "family" of women's organizations.[67] In pursuing this aim, the ELF created linkages with groups that complemented its purposes yet did not hesitate to criticize allies when they fell short of the mark—peace and women's groups for failure to represent working-class interests; minority organizations for anti-Semitism; "progressive" male Jewish clubs for ignoring the contributions of Jewish women.

Another "unity" in the federation's approach was its elimination of standard dualities between thought and action, history and policy. A cultural organization, the federation was deeply involved in politics: knowledge isolated from activity had little meaning. The Emmas repeatedly pointed out that culture was a "weapon" in the hard battle against bigotry and complacency. History, put forward on the first line of advance, would shape the present and the future.

Ironically, these dualities were bridged almost effortlessly not by feminist theorists but by the working-class women of the federation—both housewives and paid laborers—women who through their self-styled cultural work made themselves into intellectual activists. Here, too, Clara Shavelson had been a prototype. Growing up in the Ukraine, Clara read late at night after her housework and sewing were done, hiding her books to prevent her father's wrath. In New York, following a full day's work in the garment factory, she studied at the free night school, dreaming of becoming a doctor; when she had time, the public library was a favorite haunt. After Clara married and was busy with children, job, and community organizing, she still made time for several newspapers a day and a book "for dessert."[68]

Such hunger for learning was common to the Emmas, even though they belittled their skills and acknowledged the difficulty of being truly informed on the many issues that concerned them. "Sisters, believe me, it is not an easy task to do research, sit up nights and write outlines," confessed Miriam Silver, of the Bronx Coops, ELF's last cultural director. "I am not a professional writer, but I am willing and happy to do my job as long as I know that the material is being utilized."[69]

As demonstrated by these bridgings between theory and practice, Jewishness and universalism, and class, gender, ethnicity, race, and nationality more broadly, the women of the Emma Lazarus Federation cannot easily be ascribed with a fixed identity that framed them as a group apart—coherent, unitary, singular, and unchanging. Identity for the Emmas was neither linear nor static, but rather multiple, loose, fluid, and "linked." As anthropologist James Clifford suggests, when identity is conceived "not as a boundary to be maintained but as a nexus of relations and transactions actively engaging a subject," ethnicity becomes "more complex, less . . . teleological."[70]

Although the group consciousness of the Emmas grew and changed in interaction with historical events, the ability to unite conflicting values, bringing together disparate axes of experience in a new synthesis, remained constant. In many ways, the Emmas resembled the *mestiza* consciousness described by Gloria Anzaldua as a "consciousness of the borderland" that arises from constantly "crossing over" and thereby "uniting all that is separate . . . breaking down the unitary aspect of each new paradigm." Like the mestiza, the Emmas' struggle to live "between ways," between different cultures, developed into a "tolerance for contradictions [and] ambiguity" and the ability to transcend painfully limiting dualities.[71]

The quality of "betweenness" has long been ascribed to Jewish identity as well. Georg Simmel described the Jew as the perpetual "stranger" who combines "nearness and distance" in "reciprocal tension"; more recently, Daniel and Jonathan Boyarin have spoken of Jewishness as a "diasporic" identity, a living apart from and among others, "disrupt[ing] the very categories of identity because it is not national, not genealogical, not religious, but all of these in dialectical tension with one another."[72] The same kind of "disaggregated" identity—one that is partial and fluid rather than whole and linear—may apply to gender; the writers suggest the parallel notion of a "disaporized gender identity" that combines difference and sameness, specialness and universalism, in contradictory, yet positive and empowering, ways.

The Emma Lazarus Federation of Jewish Women's Clubs demonstrates the simultaneity—rather than the dispersion—of the components of American Jewish female identity in ways that exemplify these creative tensions. As women, as Jews, as proud members of the working class, as radical activists, and as Americans sensitive to the horrors of race prejudice, they fought anti-Semitism and pursued their mission of social injustice in ways that drew on the many strengths, as well as the weaknesses, of their shared background and experiences. Their lack of sustained attention to Soviet anti-Semitism was ironic, given how often they quoted Lazarus's line, "Until we are all free, none of us is free"—a reference to the plight of Russian Jews—and unfortunate.

The Emmas' response to domestic anti-Semitism after the Holocaust and their commitment to antiracist work was, however, continuing and vigorous; both efforts underscore the varied ways in which they joined cultural and political means to reaffirm Jewish identity even as the pull of assimilation grew ever more powerful. During a period when few others evidenced interest in women's historical consciousness, moreover, the Emmas supported innovative research in many areas of women's history, focusing on subjects that were Jewish and black, working-class and intellectual, American and international; they linked the production of this knowledge to active involvement in a variety of human rights campaigns. The contributions of the federation in these arenas helped transform our knowledge of Jewish culture and politics, and of women's lives, in postwar America.

Rather than accepting the generational trope that posits the denial of ethnic consciousness after the first generation as normative, women's historians would do well to probe the various patterns, exemplified by the Emma Lazarus Federation, by which ethnic, gender, class, racial, and national identities were linked in innovative and flexible ways across the generations. Crossing unsettled boundaries between these markers, the Emma Lazarus Federation struck out for new frontiers that, we, their feminist heirs, are still traversing.

Notes

I would like to thank the editors of *U.S. History of Women's History* for their insightful comments. Special thanks are also due Kathy Spray, archivist at the American Jewish Archives in Cincinnati, and members of the Brandeis University Faculty Seminar and Graduate Seminar in Jewish women's history and theory. Paul Buhle, Morris U. Schappes, and Rose Raynes provided a helpful context about the organization and the Jewish immigrant left.

1. Louis Levine, *The Women's Garment Workers* (New York: B. W. Huebsch, 1923), 154.

2. According to Morris U. Schappes, Feigenbaum used his knowledge of the Bible and Jewish tradition to promote socialist ideas. Among other works, he translated August Bebel's *Women and Socialism* and *Yiddishkeit and Sozialismus* (Jewishness and Socialism) into Yiddish. See Schappes, "Clara Lemlich Shavelson," *Jewish Currents* 36 (November 1982): 11.

3. Clara Lemlich Shavelson, "Remembering the Waistmakers General Strike, 1909," *Jewish Currents* 36 (November 1982): 11; also recounted in Paula Scheier, "Clara Lemlich Shavelson: Heroine of

the Garment Strike of 1909," *Morgen Freiheit,* September 17, 1982. See also Scheier, "Clara Lemlich Shavelson: Fifty Years in Labor's Front Line," *Jewish Life* (November 1954): 7–11; Arthur Zipser, "A Labor Heroine," *Daily Worker,* 13 August 1982; Miriam Silver, "Clara Shavelson—Heroine of Labor," and tape of Memorial Meeting for Shavelson, 24 October 1982, both in the Papers of the Emma Lazarus Federation of Jewish Women's Clubs, American Jewish Archives, Cincinnati (hereafter cited as ELF Papers). Shavelson's biography is drawn from these sources and from one of the few scholarly histories to treat Shavelson's mature activities, Annalise Orleck, "Common Sense and a Little Fire: Working-Class Women's Activism in the Twentieth-Century United States" (Ph.D. diss., New York University, 1990).

4. On the strike, see Meredith Tax, *The Rising of the Women: Feminist Solidarity and Class Conflict, 1880–1917* (New York: Monthly Review Press, 1980), 205–40, and Ann Schofield, "The Uprising of the 20,000: The Making of a Labor Legend," in *A Needle, a Bobbin, a Strike: Women Needleworkers in America,* Joan M. Jensen and Sue Davidson, eds. (Philadelphia: Temple University Press, 1984), 167–82. On Jewish women radicals, see Alice Kessler-Harris, "Organizing the Unorganizable: Three Jewish Women and Their Union," *Labor History* 17 (winter 1976): 5–23. Also of interest are Ruth A. Frager, *Sweatshop Strife: Class, Ethnicity, and Gender in the Jewish Labour Movement of Toronto, 1900–1939* (Toronto: University of Toronto Press, 1992), and Naomi Shepherd, *A Price below Rubies: Jewish Women as Rebels and Radicals* (Cambridge: Harvard University Press, 1993), which, with a few exceptions, concentrates on European women. On radical women generally, see Mari Jo Buhle, *Women and American Socialism, 1870–1920* (Urbana: University of Illinois Press, 1981), and Robert Schaffer, "Women and the Communist Party, USA, 1930–1940," *Socialist Review* 9 (May-June 1979): 73–118.

5. Among major studies in American Jewish women's history, see the pioneering volume by Charlotte Baum, Paula Hyman, and Sonya Michel, *The Jewish Women in America* (New York: New American Library, 1975); Jacob Rader Marcus, *The American Jewish Woman, 1654–1980* (New York: KTAV Publishing House, 1981); June Sochen, *Consecrate Every Day: The Public Lives of Jewish American Women, 1880–1980* (Albany: State University of New York Press, 1981); Sydney Stahl Weinberg, *The World of Our Mothers: The Lives of Jewish Immigrant Women* (Chapel Hill: University of North Carolina Press, 1988); Susan A. Glenn, *Daughters of the Shtetl: Life and Labor in the Immigrant Generation* (Ithaca, N.Y.: Cornell University Press, 1990); Linda Kuzmack, *Woman's Cause: The Jewish Woman's Movement in England and the United States, 1881–1933* (Columbus: Ohio State University Press, 1990); and Faith Rogow, *Gone to Another Meeting: The National Council of Jewish Women* (Tuscaloosa: University of Alabama Press, 1993).

6. See Arthur Hertzberg, *The Jews in America: Four Centuries of an Uneasy Encounter: A History* (New York: Simon and Schuster, 1989), and Edward S. Shapiro, *A Time for Healing: American Jewry since World War II* (Baltimore: Johns Hopkins University Press, 1992). Deborah Dash Moore's study of the children of immigrants, *At Home in America: Second-Generation New York Jews* (New York: Columbia University Press, 1981), offers a different argument. On the question of immigrant generations, see Peter Kivisto and Dag Blanck, eds., *American Immigrants and Their Generations: Studies and Commentaries on the Hansen Thesis after Fifty Years* (Urbana: University of Illinois Press, 1990).

7. On an earlier protest by Jewish housewives, see Paula Hyman, "Immigrant Women and Consumer Protest: The New York Kosher Meat Boycott of 1902," *American Jewish History* 70 (September 1980): 91–105. For an account of the housewives' movement in the Great Depression, see Annalise Orleck, "'We Are That Mythical Thing Called the Public': Militant Housewives during the Great Depression," *Feminist Studies* 19 (spring 1993): 147–72. See also Mark Naison, *Communists in Harlem during the Great Depression* (New York: Grove Press, 1983), 149–50, for an account of the 1935 meat boycott led by Shavelson and Rose Nelson [Raynes].

8. Tape of Memorial Meeting for Clara Lemlich Shavelson, October 1982, ELF Papers.

9. See, e.g., "Class Struggle in Fraternal Organization," *Daily Worker,* 18 July 1930, IWO Papers, Tamiment Library, New York University (hereafter cited as IWO Papers).

10. Mark Naison, "Remaking America: Communists and Liberals in the Popular Front," in Michael E. Brown, Randy Martin, Frank Rosengarten, and George Snedeker, eds., *New Studies in*

the Politics and Culture of U.S. Communism, (New York: Monthly Review Press, 1993), 58–59; Arthur Leibman, *Jews and the Left* (New York: John Wiley and Sons, 1978), 59, 350–51.

11. "Straight from the Shoulder Fraternalism," JPFO Bulletin, IWO Papers. On the IWO, see Arthur J. Sabin, *Red Scare in Court: New York versus the International Workers Order* (Philadelphia: University of Pennsylvania Press, 1993), 10–23; Rose Raynes, Gertrude Decker, Morris U. Schappes, and Annette Rosenthal, interviews by author, February-March 1993. On Jews and American Communism, see Paul Buhle, "Jews and American Communism: The Cultural Question," *Radical History Review* 23 (spring 1980): 9–33; Leibman, *Jews and the Left;* and David Leviatin, *Followers of the Trail: Jewish Working-Class Radicals in America* (New Haven: Yale University Press, 1969).

12. Morris U. Schappes, ed., *Emma Lazarus: Selections from Her Poetry and Prose* (New York: Cooperative Book League, Jewish-American Section, IWO, 1944); the ELF sponsored new editions of the volume in 1978 and 1982. Schappes also wrote an introduction and notes to *An Epistle to the Hebrews by Emma Lazarus,* centennial ed. (New York: Jewish Historical Society of New York, 1987), and he edited, with an introduction, *The Letters of Emma Lazarus, 1868–1885* (New York: New York Public Library, 1949).

13. Founding documents, ELF Papers.

14. Ibid.; Rose Raynes, interview by author, February 1993.

15. Rose Raynes, interview by Paul Buhle, 21 March 1979, Oral History Interviews of the Left, Tamiment Library, New York University.

16. In his book about the case, law professor Arthur J. Sabin describes the prosecution as without parallel in American law and concludes that the IWO had been destroyed for political reasons. See Sabin, *Red Scare in Court.* For further information see IWO Papers, including "Report of the Officers," IWO, 3–4 February 1951.

17. See, e.g., Leah Nelson, "They Shall Not Die," *The Lamp* 1, 3 (November-December 1952): 4–5.

18. Robert Meeropol, interview by author, May 1993.

19. "Resume of a Discussion by the Executive Committee of the Emma Lazarus Federation on the Destruction of Jewish Culture and Unjust Execution of Jewish Cultural and Civic Leadership," 10 July 1956, ELF Papers; Rose Raynes and Gertrude Decker, interviews by author. See also the discussion of the ELF and the Soviet Jewish question in *Israel Horizons and Labour Israel* 21 (January-February 1974): 2, 28–30.

20. *Proceedings of the Third Convention,* 6–8 February 1959, ELF Papers.

21. On postwar Jewry, see Moore, *At Home in America*; Shapiro, *A Time for Healing*; and Marshall Sklare and J. Greenblum, *Jewish Identity on the Suburban Frontier* (New York: Basic Books, 1967).

22. The Jewish Cultural Clubs and Societies, like the Yiddisher Kultur Farband, supported such institutions as the *Morgen Freiheit* newspaper, *Yiddishe Kultur* magazine, and Camp Kinderland and worked to publish Yiddish books.

23. Cited in ELF Papers; see Eve Merriam, *Woman with a Torch* (New York: Citadel Press, 1957).

24. Study outline on Emma Lazarus, ELF Papers.

25. Schappes, *Epistle to the Hebrews,* 30.

26. Lazarus, "The Jewish Problem," reprinted in Schappes, *Emma Lazarus: Selections from Her Poetry and Prose,* 78.

27. ELF constitution and by-laws, 20–21 January 1951, ELF Papers.

28. Cited in Ernestine Rose study guide, ELF Papers, from Yuri Suhl, *Ernestine L. Rose and the Battle for Human Rights* (New York: Reynal, 1959).

29. Study guide on Ernestine Rose, ELF Papers.

30. Discussion outline, "Women, Heroines of the Warsaw Ghetto," 1951, ELF Papers.

31. Report of June Gordon, Executive Director of the Third National Convention, *Proceedings of the Third Convention.*

32. See, e.g., Miriam Silver, Cultural Report, 4 December 1976, ELF Papers.

33. Report of Ida Sper to the Second National Convention, 23 October 1955, ELF Papers.

34. *The Lamp* 1, 1 (May 1952): 6.

35. Ibid., 6–7.

36. In 1959, for example, under the auspices of the Brooklyn Emma Lazarus clubs, hundreds of blacks and Jews attended a brotherhood meeting at the Eastern Parkway Jewish Center cosponsored by local affiliates of the American Jewish Congress, the NAACP, and the Brownsville Neighborhood Health Council. A new Brooklyn Emma Lazarus club, made up of young mothers, rejected the lecture/meeting format and organized a brotherhood puppet show about changing neighborhoods attended by 1,400 black and white children.

37. See, e.g., address of Leah Nudell, Vice President of the ELF and President of the Los Angeles club, to the Seventh National Convention, 14–16 November 1975, ELF Papers.

38. Speakers Guide, "Racism, Enemy of the Jewish People," ELF Papers.

39. To the Emmas, genocide not only was "actually killing" but also was caused by poverty, starvation, malnutrition, and the social ills that "killed people's spirit." See Miriam Silver, "Helping to Shape a Brighter Future for Our New Generation," 1969, and remarks of Rose Raynes, 9 April 1989, ELF Papers.

40. Report of Eva Mamber, Boston ELF, to the Fifth National Convention, 1964, ELF Papers.

41. Report of the Fifth National Convention, ibid.

42. Rose Raynes, keynote address, Seventh National Convention, 14–16 November 1975, ELF Papers.

43. Press release, 18 August 1967, ELF Papers.

44. *The Lamp* 1, 6 (May-June 1960): 6.

45. In 1959, for example, the ELF sponsored a mass meeting in Union Square that attracted 8,000 Americans who protested a swastika outbreak in West Germany and the United States. At the same time the Brooklyn chapter called a mass meeting with twelve other organizations at which Jackie Robinson spoke. Thus was the fight against anti-Semitism joined, they said, "with the Negro people's struggle for equality." Mollie Ilson, "As I See It," *The Lamp* 6, 12, ELF Papers.

46. Rose Raynes, Gertrude Decker, and Morris U. Schappes, interviews by author.

47. At the urging of the Emma Lazarus Committee in Los Angeles (which included fifteen member clubs), WILPF called a conference of Jewish women's organizations. ELF Papers.

48. Quotations from the Third National Convention, *Proceedings of the Third Convention.*

49. Local branches also supported regional issues: the Los Angeles group, for example, started a cooperative nursery school for Mexican American, Filipino, and Jewish children.

50. When some members of the Jewish community criticized the ELF for a member's anti-Israel statement, leadership disassociated the federation from the member, noting that its firm support for Israel had long been a matter of public record. See letters from Rose Raynes and Morris U. Schappes discussing the incident in *Israel Horizons and Labour Israel* 21 (January-February 1974): 2, 28–30.

51. Undated typescript, ELF Papers.

52. Leah Nelson, President's Report, *Proceedings of the Third Convention.*

53. Shirley Bolton, Newark, N.J., Second National Convention, October 1955, ELF Papers.

54. Helen Lewis, Second National Convention, ibid.

55. See letter of Rose Raynes in *Israel Horizons and Labour Israel* 21 (January-February 1974): 30.

56. IWO press release, 13 November 1947, IWO Papers. See also photos of Louise W. Wise and June Croll Gordon embracing on the stage of Assembly Hall, Hunter College, ELF Papers.

57. Abzug spoke on 25 October 1970, at the ELF's fiftieth anniversary celebration of woman suffrage; on 14 December 1974, she spoke at its celebration of Emma Lazarus's 125th birthday. Holtzman, described as a "twentieth century disciple of Ernestine Rose," was the guest of honor at a 25 March 1974, celebration of Rose.

58. June Gordon, Fifth National Convention, 1964, ELF Papers.

59. Ida Good, "Why I Joined the E.L. Club," *The Lamp* 4, 8 (October 1958): 4.

60. Scheier, "Clara Lemlich Shavelson: Fifty Years in Labor's Front Line," 11; Schappes, "Clara Lemlich Shavelson," 11.

61. Rose Raynes, interview by Buhle.

62. Leah Nelson, address at the Fourth National Convention, 3–5 November 1961, ELF Papers.

63. ELF constitution and by-laws, 20–21 January 1951, ELF Papers.

64. For example, on the problem of class/gender paradigms in women's history, see Nancy A. Hewitt, "Beyond the Search for Sisterhood: American Women's History in the 1980s," reprinted in Ellen Carol DuBois and Vicki L. Ruiz, eds., *Unequal Sisters: A Multicultural Reader in U.S. Women's History,* 2d ed. (New York: Routledge, 1990), 1–14.

65. Biddy Martin and Chandra Talpade Mahanty, "Feminist Politics: What's Home Got to Do with It?" in Teresa de Lauretis, ed., *Feminist Studies: Critical Studies* (Bloomington: Indiana University Press, 1986), 192.

66. The term used by Nancy Fraser in "Rethinking the Public Sphere: A Contribution to the Critique of Actually Existing Democracy," in Craig Calhoun, ed., *Habermas and the Public Sphere* (Cambridge: MIT Press, 1992), 118.

67. Address (unsigned) of Leah Nelson to the Sixth National Convention, 1971, ELF Papers.

68. Scheier, "Clara Lemlich Shavelson: Fifty Years in Labor's Front Line," 8.

69. Miriam Silver, "Report on Culture: Anti-Semitism and Resurgence of Nazism," ca. 1978, ELF Papers.

70. James Clifford, *The Predicament of Culture: Twentieth-Century Ethnography* (Cambridge: Harvard University Press, 1988), 341–42, 344.

71. Gloria Anzaldúa, "La conciencia de la mestiza: Towards a New Consciousness," in *Borderland/La Frontera: The New Mestiza* (San Francisco: Spinsters/Aunt Lute Books, 1987), 79. On feminist consciousness and "otherness," see esp. Martin and Mahanty, "Feminist Politics"; Teresa de Lauretis, "Eccentric Subjects: Feminist Theory and Historical Consciousness," *Feminist Studies* 16 (spring 1990): 115–50; Trinh T. Minh-Ha, *Woman Native Other: Writing Postcoloniality and Feminism* (Bloomington: Indiana University Press, 1989); and Shane Phelan, "(Be)Coming Out: Lesbian Identity and Politics," *Signs* 18 (1993): 765–90. Also useful are Barbara Smith, ed., *Home Girls: A Black Feminist Anthology* (New York: Kitchen Table/Women of Color Press, 1983), and Elly Bulkin, Minnie Bruce Pratt, and Barbara Smith, eds., *Yours in Struggle: Three Feminist Perspectives on Anti-Semitism and Racism* (Brooklyn, N.Y.: Long Haul Press, 1984).

72. Kurt H. Wolff, ed., *The Sociology of Georg Simmel* (New York: Free Press, 1950), 408; Daniel Boyarin and Jonathan Boyarin, "Diaspora: Generation and the Ground of Jewish Identity," *Critical Inquiry* 19 (summer 1993): 721.

20

"We Don't Sleep Around Like White Girls Do"

Family, Culture, and Gender in Filipina American Lives

YEN LE ESPIRITU

I want my daughters to be Filipino especially on sex. I always emphasize to them that they should not participate in sex if they are not married. We are also Catholic. We are raised so that we don't engage in going out with men while we are not married. And I don't like it to happen to my daughters as if they have no values. I don't like them to grow up that way, like the American girls.

—Filipina immigrant mother

I found that a lot of the Asian American friends of mine, we don't date like white girls date. We don't sleep around like white girls do. Everyone is really mellow at dating because your parents were constraining and restrictive.

—Second-generation Filipina daughter

Focusing on the relationship between Filipino immigrant parents and their daughters, this article argues that gender is a key to immigrant identity and a vehicle for racialized immigrants to assert cultural superiority over the dominant group. In immigrant communities, culture takes on a special significance: not only does it form a lifeline to the home country and a basis for group identity in a new country, it is also a base from which immigrants stake their political and sociocultural claims on their new country.[1] For Filipino immigrants, who come from a homeland that was once a U.S. colony, cultural reconstruction has been especially critical in the assertion of their presence in the United States—a way to counter the cultural Americanization of the Philippines, to resist the assimilative and alienating demands of U.S. society, and to reaffirm to themselves their self-worth in the face of colonial, racial, class, and gendered subordination. Before World War II, Filipinos were barred from becoming U.S. citizens, owning property, and marrying whites. They also encountered discriminatory housing policies, unfair labor practices, violent physical encounters, and racist as well as anti-immigrant discourse.[2] While blatant legal discrimination against Filipino Americans is largely a matter of the past, Filipinos continue to encounter many barriers that prevent full participation in the economic, social, and political institutions of the United States.[3] Moreover, the economic mobility and cultural assimilation that enables white ethnics to become "unhyphenated whites" is seldom extended to Filipino Americans.[4] Like other Asians, the Filipino is "always seen as an immigrant, as the 'foreigner-within,' even when born in the United States."[5] Finally, although Filipinos have been in the United States since the middle of the 1700s and Americans have been in the Philippines since at least the late 1800s, U.S. Filipinos—as racialized nationals, immigrants, and citizens—are "still practically an invisible and silent minority."[6] Drawing from my research on Filipino American families in San Diego, California, I explore in this article the ways racialized immigrants claim through gender the power denied them by racism.

My epigraphs, quotations of a Filipina immigrant mother and a second-generation Filipina daughter, suggest that the virtuous Filipina daughter is partially constructed on the conceptualization of white women as sexually immoral. This juxtaposition underscores the fact that femininity is a relational category, one that is co-constructed with other racial and cultural categories. These narratives also reveal that women's sexuality and their enforced "morality" are fundamental to the structuring of social inequalities. Historically, the sexuality of racialized women has been systematically demonized and disparaged by dominant or oppressor groups to justify and bolster nationalist movements, colonialism, and/or racism. But as these narratives indicate, racialized groups also criticize the morality of white women as a strategy of resistance—a means of asserting a morally superior public face to the dominant society.

By exploring how Filipino immigrants characterize white families and white women, I hope to contribute to a neglected area of research: how the "margins" imagine and construct the "mainstream" in order to assert superiority over it. But this strategy is not without costs. The elevation of Filipina chastity (particularly that of young women) has the effect of reinforcing masculinist and patriarchal power in the name of a greater ideal of national/ethnic self-respect. Because the control of women is one of the principal means of asserting moral superiority, young women in immigrant families face numerous restrictions on their autonomy, mobility, and personal decision making. Although this article addresses the experiences and attitudes of both parents and children, here I am more concerned with understanding the actions of immigrant parents with the reactions of their second-generation daughters.

Studying Filipinos in San Diego

San Diego, California has long been a favored area of settlement for Filipinos and is today the third-largest U.S. destination for Filipino immigrants.[7] As the site of the largest U.S. naval base and the Navy's primary West Coast training facility, San Diego has been a primary area of settlement for Filipino navy personnel and their families since the early 1900s. As in other Filipino communities along the Pacific Coast, the

San Diego community grew dramatically in the twenty-five years following passage of the 1965 Immigration Act. New immigration contributed greatly to the tripling of San Diego County's Filipino American population from 1970 to 1980 and its doubling from 1980 to 1990. In 1990, nearly 96,000 Filipinos resided in the country. Although they made up only 4 percent of the country's general population, they constituted close to 50 percent of the Asian American population.[8] Many post-1965 Filipino immigrants have come to San Diego as professionals — most conspicuously as health care workers. A 1992 analysis of the socioeconomic characteristics of recent Filipino immigrants in San Diego indicated that they were predominantly middle-class, college-educated, and English-speaking professionals who were more likely to own than rent their homes.[9] At the same time, about two-thirds of the Filipinos surveyed indicated that they had experienced racial and ethnic discrimination.[10]

The information on which this article is based comes mostly from in-depth interviews that I conducted with almost one hundred Filipinos in San Diego.[11] Using the "snowball" sampling technique, I started by interviewing Filipino Americans whom I knew and then asking them to refer me to others who might be willing to be interviewed. In other words, I chose participants not randomly but rather through a network of Filipino American contacts whom the first group of respondents trusted. To capture the diversity within the Filipino American community, I sought and selected respondents of different backgrounds and with diverse viewpoints. The sample is about equally divided between first-generation immigrants (those who came to the United States as adults) and Filipinas/os who were born and/or raised in the United States. It is more difficult to pinpoint the class status of the people I interviewed. To be sure, they included poor working-class immigrants who barely eked out a living, as well as educated professionals who thrived in middle- and upper-class suburban neighborhoods. However, the class status of most was much more ambiguous. I met Filipinos/as who toiled as assembly workers but who, through the pooling of income and finances, owned homes in middle-class communities. I also discovered that class status was transnational, determined as much by one's economic position in the Philippines as by that in the United States. For example, I encountered individuals who struggled economically in the United States but owned sizable properties in the Philippines. And I interviewed immigrants who continued to view themselves as "upper class" even while living in dire conditions in the United States. These examples suggest that the upper/middle/working-class typology, while useful, does not capture the complexity of immigrant lives. Reflecting the prominence of the U.S. Navy in San Diego, more than half of my respondents were affiliated with or had relatives affiliated with the U.S. Navy.

My tape-recorded interviews, conducted in English, ranged from three to ten hours each and took place in offices, coffee shops, and homes. My questions were open-ended and covered three general areas: family and immigration history, ethnic identity and practices, and community development among San Diego's Filipinos. The interviewing process varied widely: some respondents needed to be prompted with specific questions, while others spoke at great length on their own. Some chose to cover the span of their lives; others focused on specific events that were particularly important to them. The initial impetus for this article on the relationship between immigrant parents and their daughters came from my observation that the dynamics of gender emerged more clearly in the interviews with women than in those with men. Because gender has been a marked category for women, the mothers and daughters I interviewed rarely told their life stories without reference to the dynamics of gender.[12] Even without prompting, young Filipinas almost always recounted stories of restrictive gender roles and gender expectations, particularly of parental control over their whereabouts and sexuality.

I believe that my own personal and social characteristics influenced the actual process of data collection, the quality of the materials that I gathered, and my analysis of them. As a Vietnam-born woman who immigrated to the United States at the age of twelve, I came to the research project not as an "objective" outsider but as a fellow Asian immigrant who shared some of the life experiences of my respondents. During the fieldwork process, I did not remain detached but actively shared with my informants my own experiences of being an Asian immigrant woman: of being perceived as an outsider in U.S. society, of speaking English as a second language, of being a woman of color in a racialized patriarchal society, and of negotiating intergenerational tensions within my own family. I do not claim that these shared struggles grant me "insider status" into the Filipino American community; the differences in our histories, cultures, languages, and, at times, class backgrounds, remain important. But I do claim that these shared experiences enable me to bring to the work a comparative perspective that is implicit, intuitive, and informed by my own identities and positionalities—and with it a commitment to approach these subjects with both sensitivity and rigor. In a cogent call for scholars of color to expand on the premise of studying "our own" by studying other "others," Ruby Tapia argues that such implicitly comparative projects are important because they permit us to "highlight the different and *differentiating* functional forces of racialization."[13] It is with this deep interest in discovering—and forging—commonalities out of our specific and disparate experiences that I began this study on Filipino Americans in San Diego.

"American" and Whiteness: "To Me, American Means White"

In U.S. racial discourse and practices, unless otherwise specified, "Americans" means "whites."[14] In the case of Asian Americans, U.S. exclusion acts, naturalization laws, and national culture have simultaneously marked Asians as the inassimilable aliens and whites as the quintessential Americans.[15] Excluded from the collective memory of who constitutes a "real" American, Asians in the United States, even as citizens, remain "foreigners-within"—"non-Americans." In a study of third- and later-generation Chinese and Japanese Americans, Mia Tuan concludes that, despite being longtime Americans, Asians—as racialized ethnics—are often assumed to be foreign unless proven otherwise. In the case of Filipinos who emigrated from a former U.S. colony, their formation as racialized minorities does not begin in the United States but rather in a "homeland" already affected by U.S. economic, social, and cultural influences.[16]

Cognizant of this racialized history, my Filipino respondents seldom identify themselves as American. As will be evident in the discussion below, they equate "American" with "white" and often use these two terms interchangeably. For example, a Filipina who is married to a white American refers to her husband as "American" but to her African American and Filipino American brothers-in-law as "black" and "Filipino," respectively. Others speak about "American ways," "American culture," or "American lifestyle" when they really mean *white* American ways, culture, and lifestyle. A Filipino man who has lived in the United States for thirty years explains why he still does not identify himself as American: "I don't see myself just as an American because I cannot hide the fact that my skin is brown. To me, American means white." A second-generation Filipina recounted the following story when asked whether she defined herself as American:

> I went to an all-white school. I knew I was different. I wasn't American. See, you are not taught that you're American because you are not white. When I was in the tenth grade, our English teacher asked us what our nationality was, and she goes how many of you are Mexican, how many of you are Filipino, and how many of you are Samoan and things like that. And when she asked how many of you are American, just the white people raised their hands.

Other Asian Americans also conflate *American* and *white*. In an ethnographic study of Asian American high school students, Stacey Lee reports that Korean immigrant parents often instructed their children to socialize only with Koreans and "Americans." When asked to define the term *American,* the Korean students responded in unison with "White! Korean parents like white."[17] Tuan found the same practice among later-generation Chinese and Japanese Americans: the majority use the term *American* to refer to whites.[18]

Constructing the Dominant Group: The Moral Flaws of White Americans

Given the centrality of moral themes in popular discussions on racial differences, Michele Lamont has suggested that morality is a crucial site to study the cultural mechanisms of reproduction of racial inequality.[19] While much has been written on how whites have represented the (im)morality of people of color,[20] there has been less critical attention to how people of color have represented whites.[21] Shifting attention from the otherness of the subordinate group (as dictated by the "mainstream") to the otherness of the dominant group (as constructed by the "margins"), this section focuses on the alternative frames of meaning that racially subordinate groups mobilize to (re)define their status in relation to the dominant group. I argue that female morality—defined as women's dedication to their families and sexual restraint—is one of the few sites where economically and politically dominated groups can construct the dominant group as other and themselves as superior. Because womanhood is idealized as the repository of tradition, the norms that regulate women's behaviors become a means of determining and defining group status and boundaries. As a consequence, the burdens and complexities of cultural representation fall most heavily on immigrant women and their daughters. Below, I show that Filipino immigrants claim moral distinctiveness for their community by re-presenting

"Americans" as morally flawed, themselves as family-oriented model minorities, and their wives and daughters as paragons of morality.

Family-oriented Model Minorities: "White Women Will Leave You"

In his work on Italian immigrant parents and children in the 1930s, Robert Anthony Orsi reports that parents invented a virtuous Italy (based on memories of their childhood) that they then used to castigate the morality of the United States and their U.S.-born or -raised children.[22] In a similar way, many of my respondents constructed their "ethnic" culture as principled and "American" culture as deviant. Most often, this morality narrative revolves around family life and family relations. When asked what set Filipinos apart from other Americans, my respondents—of all ages and class backgrounds—repeatedly contrasted close-knit Filipino families to what they perceived to be the more impersonal quality of U.S. family relations.[23] In the following narratives, "Americans" are characterized as lacking in strong family ties and collective identity, less willing to do the work of family and cultural maintenance, and less willing to abide by patriarchal norms in husband/wife relations:

> American society lacks caring. The American way of life is more individual rather than collective. The American way is to say I want to have my own way. (Filipina immigrant, fifty-four years old)
> Our [Filipino] culture is different. We are more close-knit. We tend to help one another. Americans, ya know, they are all right, but they don't help each other that much. As a matter of fact, if the parents are old, they take them to a convalescent home and let them rot there. We would never do that in our culture. We would nurse them; we would help them until the very end. (Filipino immigrant, sixty years old)

> Our [Filipino] culture is very communal. You know that your family will always be there, that you don't have to work when you turn eighteen, you don't have to pay rent when you are eighteen, which is the American way of thinking. You also know that if things don't work out in the outside world, you can always come home and mommy and daddy will always take you and your children in. (Second-generation Filipina, thirty-three years old)

> Asian parents take care of their children. Americans have a different attitude. They leave their children to their own resources. They get baby sitters to take care of their children or leave them in day care. That's why when they get old, their children don't even care about them. (Filipina immigrant, forty-six years old)

Implicit in negative depictions of U.S. families as uncaring, selfish, and distant is the allegation that white women are not as dedicated to their families as Filipina women are to theirs. Several Filipino men who married white women recalled being warned by their parents and relatives that "white women will leave you." As one man related, "My mother said to me, 'Well, you know, don't marry a white person because they would take everything that you own and leave you.'" For some Filipino men, perceived differences in attitudes about women's roles between Filipina and non-Filipina women influenced their marital choice. A Filipino American navy man explained why he went back to the Philippines to look for a wife:

> My goal was to marry a Filipina. I requested to be stationed in the Philippines to get married to a Filipina. I'd seen the women here and basically they are spoiled. They have a tendency of not going along together with their husband. They behave differently. They chase the male, instead of the male, the normal way of the traditional way is for the male to go after the female. They have sex without marrying. They want to do their own things. So my idea was to go back home and marry somebody who has never been here. I tell my son the same thing: if he does what I did and finds himself a good lady there, he will be in good hands.

Another man who had dated mostly white women in high school recounted that when it came time for him to marry, he "looked for the kind of women" he met while stationed in the Philippines: "I hate to sound chauvinistic about marriages, but Filipinas have a way of making you feel like you are a king. They also have that tenderness, that elegance. And we share the same values about family, education, religion, and raising children."

The claims of family closeness are not unique to Filipino immigrants. For example, when asked what makes their group distinctive, Italian Americans, Vietnamese Americans, South Asian Americans, and African Americans all point proudly to the close-knit character of their family life.[24] Although it is difficult to know whether these claims are actual perceptions or favored self-legitimating answers, it is nevertheless important to note the gender implications of these claims. That is, while both men and women identify the family system as a tremendous source of cultural pride, it is women—through their unpaid housework and kin work—who shoulder the primary responsibility for maintaining family closeness. As the organizers of family rituals, transmitters of homeland folklores, and socializers of young children, women have been crucial for the maintenance of family ties and cultural traditions. In a study of kinship, class, and gender among California Italian Americans, di Leonardo argues that women's kin work, "the work of knitting households together into 'close, extended families,'" maintains the family networks that give ethnicity meaning.[25]

Because the moral status of the community rests on women's labor, women, as wives and daughters, are expected to dedicate themselves to the family. Writing on the constructed image of ethnic family and gender, di Leonardo argues that "a large part of stressing ethnic identity amounts to burdening women with increased responsibilities for preparing special foods, planning rituals, and enforcing 'ethnic' socialization of children."[26] A twenty-three-year-old Filipina spoke about the reproductive work that her mother performed and expected her to learn:

> In my family, I was the only girl, so my mom expected a lot from me. She wanted me to help her to take care of the household. I felt like there was a lot of pressure on me. It's very important to my mom to have the house in order: to wash the dishes, to keep the kitchen in order, vacuuming, and dusting and things like that. She wants me to be a perfect housewife. It's difficult. I have been married now for about four months and my mother asks me every now and then what have I cooked for my husband. My mom is also very strict about families getting together on holidays,

and I would always help her to organize that. Each holiday, I would try to decorate the house for her, to make it more special.

The burden of unpaid reproductive and kin work is particularly stressful for women who work outside the home. In the following narrative, a Filipina wife and mother described the pulls of family and work that she experienced when she went back to school to pursue a doctoral degree in nursing:

> The Filipinos, we are very collective, very connected. Going through the doctoral program, sometimes I think it is better just to forget about my relatives and just concentrate on school. All that connectedness, it steals parts of myself because all of my energies are devoted to my family. And that is the reason why I think Americans are successful. The majority of the American people they can do what they want. They don't feel guilty because they only have a few people to relate to. For us Filipinos, its like roots under the tree, you have all these connections. The Americans are more like the trunk. I am still trying to go up to the trunk of the tree but it is too hard. I want to be more independent, more like the Americans. I want to be good to my family but what about me? And all the things that I am doing. It's hard. It's always a struggle.

It is important to note that this Filipina interprets her exclusion and added responsibilities as only racial when they are also gendered. For example, when she says, "the American people they can do what they want," she ignores the differences in the lives of white men and white women—the fact that most white women experience similar competing pulls of family, education, and work.

Racialized Sexuality and (Im)morality: "In America, . . . Sex Is Nothing"

Sexuality, as a core aspect of social identity, is fundamental to the structuring of gender inequality.[27]. Sexuality is also a salient marker of otherness and has figured prominently in racist and imperialist ideologies.[28] Historically, the sexuality of subordinate groups—particularly that of racialized women—has been systematically stereotyped by the dominant groups.[29] At stake in these stereotypes is the construction of women of color as morally lacking in the areas of sexual restraint and traditional morality. Asian women—both in Asia and in the United States—have been racialized as sexually immoral, and the "Orient" (and its women) has long served as a site of European male-power fantasies, replete with lurid images of sexual license, gynecological aberrations, and general perversion.[30] In colonial Asia in the nineteenth and early twentieth centuries, for example, female sexuality was a site for colonial rulers to assert their moral superiority and thus their supposed natural and legitimate right to rule. The colonial rhetoric of moral superiority was based on the construction of colonized Asian women as subjects of sexual desire and fulfillment and European colonial women as the paragons of virtue and the bearers of a redefined colonial morality.[31] The discourse of morality has also been used to mark the "unassimilability" of Asians in the United States. At the turn of the twentieth century, the public perception of Chinese women as disease-ridden, drug-addicted prostitutes served to underline the depravity of "Orientals" and played a decisive role in the eventual passage of exclusion laws against all Asians.[32] The stereotypical view that all Asian women were prostitutes, first formed in the 1850s, persisted. Contemporary American popular culture continues to endow Asian women with an excess of "womanhood," sexualizing them but also impugning their sexuality.[33]

Filipinas—both in the Philippines and in the United States—have been marked as desirable but dangerous "prostitutes" and/or submissive "mail-order brides."[34] These stereotypes emerged out of the colonial process, especially the extensive U.S. military presence in the Philippines. Until the early 1990s, the Philippines, at times unwillingly, housed some of the United States's largest overseas airforce and naval bases.[35] Many Filipino nationalists have charged that "the prostitution problem" in the Philippines stemmed from U.S. and Philppine government policies that promoted a sex industry— brothels, bars, and massage parlors—for servicemen stationed or on leave in the Philippines. During the Vietnam War, the Philippines was known as the "rest and recreation" center of Asia, hosting approximately ten thousand U.S. servicemen daily.[36] In this context, *all* Filipinas were racialized as sexual commodities, usable and expendable. A U.S.-born Filipina recounted the sexual harassment she faced while visiting Subic Bay Naval Station in Olongapo City:

> One day, I went to the base dispensary. . . . I was dressed nicely, and as I walked by the fire station, I heard catcalls and snide remarks being made by some of the firemen. . . . I was fuming inside. The next thing I heard was, "How much do you charge?" I kept on walking. "Hey, are you deaf or something? How much do you charge? You have a good body." That was an incident that I will never forget.[37]

The sexualized racialization of Filipina women is also captured in Marianne Vilanueva's short story "Opportunity."[38] As the protagonist, a "mail-order bride" from the Philippines, enters a hotel lobby to meet her American fiancé, the bellboys snicker and whisper *puta* (whore): a reminder that U.S. economic and cultural colonization in the Philippines always forms a backdrop to any relations between Filipinos and Americans.[39]

Cognizant of the pervasive hypersexualization of Filipina women, my respondents, especially women who grew up near military bases, were quick to denounce prostitution, to condemn sex laborers, and to declare (unasked) that they themselves did not frequent "that part of town." As one Filipina immigrant said,

> Growing up [in the Philippines], I could never date an American because my dad's concept of a friendship with an American is with a G.I. The only reason why my dad wouldn't let us date an American is that people will think that the only way you met was because of the base. I have never seen the inside of any bases because we were just forbidden to go there.

Many of my respondents also distanced themselves culturally from the Filipinas who serviced U.S. soldiers by branding them "more Americanized" and "more Westernized." In other words, these women were sexually promiscuous because they had assumed the sexual mores of white women. This characterization allows my respondents to symbolically disown the Filipina "bad girl" and, in so doing, to uphold the narrative of Filipina sexual virtuosity and white female sexual promiscuity. In the following narrative, a mother who came to the United States in her thirties contrasted the controlled sexuality of women in the Philippines with the perceived promiscuity of white women in the United States:

> In the Philippines, we always have chaperons when we go out. When we go to dances, we have our uncle, our grandfather, and auntie all behind us to make sure that we behave in the dance hall. Nobody goes necking outside. You don't even let a man put his hand on your shoulders. When you were brought up in a conservative country, it is hard to come here and see that it is all freedom of speech and freedom of action. Sex was never mentioned in our generation. I was thirty already when I learned about sex. But to the young generation in America, sex is nothing.

Similarly, another immigrant woman criticized the way young American women are raised: "Americans are so liberated. They allow their children, their girls, to go out even when they are still so young." In contrast, she stated that, in "the Filipino way, it is very important, the value of the woman, that she is a virgin when she gets married."

The ideal "Filipina," then, is partially constructed on the community's conceptualization of white women. She is everything that they are not: she is sexually modest and dedicated to her family; they are sexually promiscuous and uncaring. Within the context of the dominant culture's pervasive hypersexualization of Filipinas, the construction of the "ideal" Filipina—as family-oriented and chaste—can be read as an effort to reclaim the morality of the community. This effort erases the Filipina "bad girl," ignores competing sexual practices in the Filipino communities, and uncritically embraces the myth of "Oriental femininity." Cast as the embodiment of perfect womanhood and exotic femininity, Filipinas (and other Asian women) in recent years have been idealized in U.S. popular culture as more truly "feminine" (i.e., devoted, dependent, domestic) and therefore more desirable than their more modern, emancipated sisters.[40] Capitalizing on this image of the "superfemme," mail-order bride agencies market Filipina women as "'exotic, subservient wife imports' for sale and as alternatives for men sick of independent 'liberal' Western women."[41]

Embodying the moral integrity of the idealized ethnic community, immigrant women, particularly young daughters, are expected to comply with male-defined criteria of what constitute "ideal" feminine virtues. While the sexual behavior of adult women is confined to a monogamous, heterosexual context, that of young women is denied completely.[42] In the next section, I detail the ways Filipino immigrant parents, under the rubric of "cultural preservation," police their daughters' behaviors in order to safeguard their sexual innocence and virginity. These attempts at policing generate hierarchies and tensions within immigrant families—between parents and children and between brothers and sisters.

The Construction(s) of the "Ideal" Filipina: "Boys Are Boys and Girls Are Different"

As the designated "keepers of the culture,"[43] immigrant women and their behavior come under intensive scrutiny both from men and women of their own groups and from U.S.-born Americans.[44] In a study of the Italian Harlem community from 1880 to 1950, Orsi reports that "all the community's fears for the reputation and integrity of the domus came to focus on the behavior of young women."[45] Because women's moral and sexual loyalties were deemed central to the maintenance of group status, changes in female behavior, especially that of growing daughters, were interpreted as signs of moral decay and ethnic suicide and were carefully monitored and sanctioned.[46]

Although details vary, young women of various groups and across space and time—for example, second-generation Chinese women in San Francisco in the 1920s, U.S.-born Italian women in East Harlem in the 1930s, young Mexican women in the Southwest during the interwar years, and daughters of Caribbean and Asian Indian immigrants on the East Coast in the 1990s[47]—have identified strict parental control on their activities and movements as the primary source of intergenerational conflict. Recent studies of immigrant families also identify gender as a significant determinant of parent-child conflict, with daughters more likely than sons to be involved in such conflicts and instances of parental derogation.[48]

Although immigrant families have always been preoccupied with passing on their native culture, language, and traditions to both male and female children, it is daughters who have the primary burden of protecting and preserving the family. Because sons do not have to conform to the image of an "ideal" ethnic subject as daughters do, they often receive special day-to-day privileges denied to daughters.[49] This is not to say that immigrant parents do not place undue expectations on their sons; rather, these expectations do not pivot around the sons' sexuality or dating choices.[50] In contrast, parental control over the movement and action of daughters begins the moment they are perceived as young adults and sexually vulnerable. It regularly consists of monitoring their whereabouts and forbidding dating.[51] For example, the immigrant parents I interviewed seldom allowed their daughters to date, to stay out late, to spend the night at a friend's house, or to take an out-of-town trip.

Many of the second-generation women I spoke to complained bitterly about these parental restrictions. They particularly resented what they saw as gender inequity in their families: the fact that their parents placed far more restrictions on their activities and movements than on their brothers'. Some decried the fact that even their younger brothers had more freedom than they did. "It was really hard growing up because my parents would let my younger brothers do what they wanted but I didn't get to do what I wanted even though I was the oldest. I had a curfew and my brothers didn't. I had to ask if I could go places and they didn't. My parents never even asked my brothers when they were coming home." As indicated in the following excerpt, many Filipino males are cognizant of this double standard in their families:

> My sister would always say to me, "It's not fair, just because you are a guy, you can go wherever you want." I think my parents do treat me and my sister differently. Like in high school, may be 10:30 at night, which is pretty late on a school night, and I say I have to go pick up some notes at my friend's house, my parents wouldn't say anything. But if my sister were to do that, there would be no way. Even now when my sister is in college already, if she wants to leave at midnight to go to a friend's house, they would tell her that she shouldn't do it.

When questioned about this double standard, parents generally responded by explaining that "girls are different":

> I have that Filipino mentality that boys are boys and girls are different. Girls are supposed to be protected, to be clean. In the early years, my daughters have to have chaperones and curfews. And they know that they have to be virgins until they get married. The girls always say that is not fair. What is the difference between their brothers and them? And my answer always is, "In the Philippines, you know, we don't do that. The girls stay home. The boys go out." It was the way that I was raised. I still want to have part of that culture instilled in my children. And I want them to have that to pass on to their children.

Even among self-described Western-educated and "tolerant" parents, many continue to ascribe to "the Filipino way" when it comes to raising daughters. As one college-educated father explains,

> Because of my Western education, I don't raise my children the way my parents raised me. I tended to be a little more tolerant. But at times, especially in certain issues like dating, I find myself more towards the Filipino way in the sense that I have only one daughter so I tended to be a little bit stricter. So the double standard kind of operates: its alright for the boys to explore the field but I tended to be overly protective of my daughter. My wife feels the same way because the boys will not lose anything, but the daughter will lose something, her virginity, and it can be also a question of losing face, that kind of thing.

Although many parents discourage or forbid dating for daughters, they still fully expect these young women to fulfill their traditional roles as women: to marry and have children. A young Filipina recounted the mixed messages she received from her parents:

> This is the way it is supposed to work: Okay, you go to school. You go to college. You graduate. You find a job. *Then* you find your husband, and you have children. That's the whole time line. *But* my question is, if you are not allowed to date, how are you supposed to find your husband? They say "no" to the whole dating scene because that is secondary to your education, secondary to your family. They do push marriage, but at a later date. So basically my parents are telling me that I should get married and I should have children but that I should not date.

In a study of second-generation Filipino Americans in northern California, Diane Wolf reports the same pattern of parental pressures: Parents expect daughters to remain virgins until marriage, to have a career, *and* to combine their work lives with marriage and children.[52]

The restrictions on girls' movement sometimes spill over to the realm of academics. Dasgupta and DasGupta recount that in the Indian American community, while young men were expected to attend faraway competitive colleges, many of their female peers were encouraged by their parents to go to the local colleges so that they could live at or close to home.[53] Similarly, Wolf reports that some Filipino parents pursued contradictory tactics with their children, particularly their daughters, by pushing them to achieve academic excellence in high school but then "pulling the emergency brake" when they contemplated college by expecting them to stay at home, even if it meant going to a less competitive college, or not going at all.[54] In the following account, a young Filipina relates that her parents' desire to "protect" her surpassed their concerns for her academic preparation:

> My brother [was] given a lot more opportunity educationally. He was given the opportunity to go to Miller High School that has a renowned college preparatory program but [for] which you have to be bussed out of our area.[55] I've come from a college prep program in junior high and I was asked to apply for the program at Miller. But my parents said "No, absolutely not." This was even during the time, too, when Southside [the neighborhood high school] had one of the lowest test scores in the state of California. So it was like, "You know, mom, I'll get a better chance at Miller." "No, no, you're going to Southside. There is no ifs, ands, or buts. Miller is too far. What if something happens to you?" But two years later, when my brother got ready to go on to high school, he was allowed to go to Miller. My sister and I were like, "Obviously, whose education do you value more? If you're telling us that education is important, why do we see a double standard?"

The above narratives suggest that the process of parenting is gendered in that immigrant parents tend to restrict the autonomy, mobility, and personal decision making of their daughters more than that of their sons. I argue that these parental restrictions are attempts to construct a model of Filipina womanhood that is chaste, modest, nurturing, and family-oriented. Women are seen as responsible for holding the cultural line, maintaining racial boundaries, and marking cultural difference. This is not to say that parent-daughter conflicts exist in all Filipino immigrant families. Certainly, Filipino parents do not respond in a uniform way to the challenges of being racial-ethnic minorities, and I met parents who have had to change some of their ideas and practices in response to their inability to control their children's movements and choices:

> I have three girls and one boy. I used to think that I wouldn't allow my daughters to go dating and things like that, but there is no way I could do that. I can't stop it. It's the way of life here in America. Sometimes you kind of question yourself, if you are doing what is right. It is hard to accept but you got to accept it. That's the way they are here. (Professional Filipino immigrant father)

> My children are born and raised here, so they do pretty much what they want. They think they know everything. I can only do so much as a parent. . . . When I try to teach my kids things, they tell me that I sound like an old record. They even talk back to me sometimes. . . . The first time my daughter brought her boyfriend to the house, she was eighteen years old. I almost passed away, knocked out. Lord, tell me what to do? (Working-class Filipino immigrant mother)

These narratives call attention to the shifts in the generational power caused by the migration process and to the possible gap between what parents say they want for their children and their ability to control the young. However, the interview data do suggest that intergenerational conflicts are socially recognized occurrences in Filipino communities. Even when respondents themselves had not experienced intergenerational tensions, they could always recall a cousin, a girlfriend, or a friend's daughter who had.

Sanctions and Reactions:
"That Is Not What a Decent Filipino Girl Should Do"

I do not wish to suggest that immigrant communities are the only ones in which parents regulate their daughters' mobility and sexuality. Feminist scholars have long documented the construction, containment, and exploitation of women's sexuality in various societies.[56] We also know that the cultural anxiety over unbounded female sexuality is most apparent with regard to adolescent girls.[57] The difference is in the ways immigrant and nonimmigrant families sanction girls' sexuality. To control sexually assertive girls nonimmigrant parents rely on the gender-based good girl/bad girl dichotomy in which "good girls" are passive, threatened sexual objects while "bad girls" are active, desiring sexual agents.[58] As Dasgupta and DasGupta write, "the two most pervasive images of women across cultures are the goddess and whore, the good and bad women."[59] This good girl/bad girl cultural story conflates femininity with sexuality, increases women's vulnerability to sexual coercion, and justifies women's containment in the domestic sphere.

Immigrant families, though, have an additional strategy: they can discipline their daughters as racial/national subjects as well as gendered ones. That is, as self-appointed guardians of "authentic" cultural memory, immigrant parents can attempt to regulate their daughters' independent choices by linking them to cultural ignorance or betrayal. As both parents and children recounted, young women who disobeyed parental strictures were often branded "non-ethnic," "untraditional," "radical," "selfish," and "not caring about the family." Female sexual choices were also linked to moral degeneracy, defined in relation to a narrative of a hegemonic white norm. Parents were quick to warn their daughters about "bad" Filipinas who had become pregnant outside marriage.[60] As in the case of "bar girls" in the Philippines, Filipina Americans who veered from acceptable behaviors were deemed "Americanized"—as women who have adopted the sexual mores and practices of white women. As one Filipino immigrant father described "Americanized" Filipinas: "They are spoiled because they have seen the American way. They go out at night. Late at night. They go out on dates. Smoking. They have sex without marrying."

From the perspective of the second-generation daughters, these charges are stinging. The young women I interviewed were visibly pained—with many breaking down and crying—when they recounted their parents' charges. This deep pain, stemming in part from their desire to be validated as Filipina, existed even among the more "rebellious" daughters. One twenty-four-year-old daughter explained:

> My mom is very traditional. She wants to follow the Filipino customs, just really adhere to them, like what is proper for a girl, what she can and can't do, and what other people are going to think of her if she doesn't follow that way. When I pushed these restrictions, when I rebelled and stayed out later than allowed, my mom would always say, "That is not what a decent Filipino girl should do. You should come home at a decent hour. What are people going to think of you?" And that would get me really upset, you know, because I think that my character is very much the way it should be for a Filipina. I wear my hair long, I wear decent makeup. I dress properly, conservative. I am family oriented. It hurts me that she doesn't see that I am

> decent, that I am proper and that I am not going to bring shame to the family or anything like that.

This narrative suggests that even when parents are unable to control the behaviors of their children, their (dis)approval remains powerful in shaping the emotional lives of their daughters.[61] Although better-off parents can and do exert greater controls over their children's behaviors than do poorer parents,[62] I would argue that all immigrant parents—regardless of class background—possess this emotional hold on their children. Therein lies the source of their power: As immigrant parents, they have the authority to determine if their daughters are "authentic" members of their racial-ethnic community. Largely unacquainted with the "home" country, U.S.-born children depend on their parents' tutelage to craft and affirm their ethnic self and thus are particularly vulnerable to charges of cultural ignorance and/or betrayal.[63]

Despite these emotional pains, many young Filipinas I interviewed contest and negotiate parental restrictions in their daily lives. Faced with parental restrictions on their mobility, young Filipinas struggle to gain some control over their own social lives, particularly over dating. In many cases, daughters simply misinform their parents of their whereabouts or date without their parents' knowledge. They also rebel by vowing to create more egalitarian relationships with their own husbands and children. A thirty-year-old Filipina who is married to a white American explained why she chose to marry outside her culture:

> In high school, I dated mostly Mexican and Filipino. It never occurred to me to date a white or black guy. I was not attracted to them. But as I kept growing up and my father and I were having all these conflicts, I knew that if I married a Mexican or a Filipino, [he] would be exactly like my father. And so I tried to date anyone that would not remind me of my dad. A lot of my Filipina friends that I grew up with had similar experiences. So I knew that it wasn't only me. I was determined to marry a white person because he would treat me as an individual.[64]

Another Filipina who was labeled "radical" by her parents indicated that she would be more open-minded in raising her own children: "I see myself as very traditional in upbringing but I don't see myself as constricting on my children one day and I wouldn't put the gender roles on them. I wouldn't lock them into any particular way of behaving." It is important to note that even as these Filipinas desired new gender norms and practices for their own families, the majority hoped that their children would remain connected to Filipino culture.

My respondents also reported more serious reactions to parental restrictions, recalling incidents of someone they knew who had run away, joined a gang, or attempted suicide. A Filipina high-school counselor relates that most of the Filipinas she worked with "are really scared because a lot of them know friends that are pregnant and they all pretty much know girls who have attempted suicide." A 1995 random survey of San Diego public high schools conducted by the Federal Centers for Disease Control and Prevention (CDC) found that, in comparison with other ethnic groups, female Filipino students had the highest rates of seriously considering suicide (45.6 percent) as well as the highest rates of actually attempting suicide (23 percent) in the year preceding the survey. In comparison, 33.4 percent of Latinas, 26.2 percent of white women, and 25.3 percent of black women surveyed said they had suicidal thoughts.[65]

Conclusion

Mainstream American society defines white middle-class culture as the norm and whiteness as the unmarked marker of others' difference.[66] In this article, I have shown that many Filipino immigrants use the largely gendered discourse of morality as one strategy to decenter whiteness and to locate themselves above the dominant group, demonizing it in the process. Like other immigrant groups, Filipinos praise the United States as a land of significant economic opportunity but simultaneously denounce it as a country inhabited by corrupted and individualistic people of questionable morals. In particular, they criticize American family life, American individualism, and American women.[67] Enforced by distorting powers of memory and nostalgia, this rhetoric of moral superiority often leads to patriarchal calls for a cultural "authenticity" that locates family honor and national integrity in the group's female members. Because the policing of women's bodies is one of the main means of asserting moral superiority, young women face numerous restrictions on their autonomy, mobility, and personal decision making. This practice of cultural (re)construction reveals how deeply the conduct of private life can be tied to larger social structures.

The construction of white Americans as the "other" and American culture as deviant serves a dual purpose: It allows immigrant communities both to reinforce patriarchy through the sanctioning of women's (mis)behavior and to present an unblemished, if not morally superior, public face to the dominant society. Strong in family values, heterosexual morality, and a hierarchical family structure, this public face erases the Filipina "bad girl" and ignores competing (im)moral practices in the Filipino communities. Through the oppression of Filipina women and the denunciation of white women's morality, the immigrant community attempts to exert its moral superiority over the dominant Western culture and to reaffirm to itself its self-worth in the face of economic, social, political, and legal subordination. In other words, the immigrant community uses restrictions on women's lives as one form of resistance to racism. This form of cultural resistance, however, severely restricts the lives of women, particularly those of the second generation, and it casts the family as a potential site of intense conflict and oppressive demands in immigrant lives.

Notes

I gratefully acknowledge the many useful suggestions and comments of George Lipsitz, Vince Rafael, Lisa Lowe, Joane Nagel, Diane Wolf, Karen Pyke, and two anonymous reviewers for *Signs*. I also would like to thank all those Filipinos/as who participated in this study for their time, help, and insights into immigrant lives.

1. Marita Eastmond, "Reconstructing Life: Chilean Refugee Women and the Dilemmas of Exile," in *Migrant Women: Crossing Boundaries and Changing Identities,* ed. Gina Buijs (Oxford: Berg, 1993), 40.

2. Fred Cordova, *Filipinos: Forgotten Asian Americans, a Pictorial Essay, 1763–1963* (Dubuque, Iowa: Kendall/Hunt, 1983); Miriam Sharma, "Labor Migration and Class Formation among the Filipi-

nos in Hawaii, 1906–46," in *Labor Immigration under Capitalism: Asian Workers in the United States before World War II,* ed. Lucie Cheng and Edna Bonacich (Berkeley: University of California Press, 1984), 579–611; Craig Scharlin and Lilia V. Villanueva, *Philip Vera Cruz: A Personal History of Filipino Immigrants and the Farmworkers Movement* (Los Angeles: University of California, Los Angeles Labor Center, Institute of Labor Relations, and Asian American Studies Center, 1992); Moon-Kie Jung, "No Whites: No Asians: Race, Marxism and Hawaii's Pre-emergent Working Class." *Social Science History* 23:3 (1999): 357–93.

3. Tania Fortunata M. Azores-Gunter, "Educational Attainment and Upward Mobility: Prospects for Filipino Americans." *Amerasia Journal* 13:1 (1999): 39–52; Amado Cabezas, Larry H. Shinagawa, and Gary Kawaguchi, "New Inquiries into the Socioeconomic Status of Filipino Americans in California." *Amerasia Journal* 13:1 (1980): 1–21; Jonathan Okamura and Amefil Agbayani, "*Pamantasan:* Filipino American Higher Education," in *Filipino Americans: Transformation and Identity,* ed. Maria P. Root (Thousand Oaks, Calif.: Sage, 1997), 183–97.

4. Yen Le Espiritu, "The Intersection of Race, Ethnicity, and Class: The Multiple Identities of Second Generation Filipinos." *Identities* 1:2–3 (1994): 249–73.

5. Lisa Lowe, *Immigrant Acts: On Asian American Cultural Politics* (Durham, N.C.: Duke University Press, 1996), 5.

6. E. San Juan, Jr., "Mapping the Boundaries: The Filipino Writer in the U.S." *Journal of Ethnic Studies* 19:1 (1991): 117.

7. Filipino settlement in San Diego dates back to 1903, when a group of young Filipino *pensionados* enrolled at the State Normal School (now San Diego State University). Ruben Rumbaut, "Passages to America: Perspectives on the New Immigration," in *America at Century's End*, ed. Alan Wolfe (Berkeley University of California Press, 1991), 220.

8. Yen Le Espiritu, *Filipino American Lives* (Philadelphia: Temple University Press, 1995)

9. Rumbaut, "The Crucible Within: Ethnic Identity, Self-Esteem, and Segmented Assimilation among Children of Immigrants." *International Migration Review* 28:4 (1994): 748–94.

10. Yen Le Espiritu and Diane L. Wolf, "The Paradox of Assimilation: Children of Filipino Immigrants in San Diego," in *Ethnicities: Children of Immigrants in America,* ed. Ruben Rumbaut and Alejandro Portes (Berkeley: University of California Press; New York: Russell Sage Foundation, forthcoming).

11. My understanding of Filipino American lives is also based on the many conversations I have had with my Filipino American students at the University of California, San Diego, and with Filipino American friends in the San Diego area and elsewhere.

12. Personal Narratives Group, "Origins," in *Interpreting Women's Lives: Feminist Theory and Personal Narratives,* ed. Personal Narratives Group (Bloomington: Indiana University Press, 1989), 4–5.

13. Ruby Tapia, "Studying Other 'Others.'" Paper presented at the Association of Pacific Americans in Higher Education, San Diego, Calif. May 24, 1997, 2.

14. George Lipsitz, *The Possessive Investment in Whiteness: How White People Profit from Identity Politics* (Philadelphia: Temple University Press, 1998), 1.

15. Lowe, *Immigrant Acts.*

16. Ibid., 8; Mia Tuan, *Forever Foreigners or Honorary Whites? The Asian Ethnic Experience Today* (New Brunswick, N.J.: Rutgers University Press, 1998).

17. Stacey J. Lee, *Unraveling the "Model Minority" Stereotype: Listening to Asian American Youth* (New York: Teachers College Press, 1996), 24.

18. Mia Tuan, *Forever Foreigners or Honorary Whites?*

19. Michele Lamont, "Colliding Moralities between Black and White Workers," in *From Sociology to Cultural Studies: New Perspectives,* ed. Elisabeth Long (New York: Blackwell, 1997), 263–85.

20. Patricia Hill Collins, *Black Feminist Thought: Knowledge, Consciousness, and the Politics of Empowerment* (New York: Routledge, 1991); Gina Marchetti, *Romance and the "Yellow Peril": Race, Sex, and Discursive Strategies in Hollywood Fiction* (Berkeley: University of California Press, 1993); Darrell Y. Hamamoto, *Monitored Peril: Asian Americans and the Politics of Representation* (Minneapolis: University of Minnesota Press, 1994).

21. A few studies have documented the ways racialized communities have represented white Americans. For example, in his anthropological work on Chicano joking, José Limón, "History, Chicano Joking, and the Varieties of Higher Education: Tradition and Performance as Critical Symbolic Action," *Journal of the Folklore Institute* reports that young Mexican Americans elevate themselves over whites through the telling of "Stupid-American" jokes in which an Anglo American is consistently duped by a Mexican character. In her interviews with African American working-class men, Michele Lamont, "Colliding Moralities," finds that these men tend to perceive Euro Americans as immoral, sneaky, and not to be trusted. Although these studies provide an interesting and compelling window into racialized communities' views of white Americans, they do not analyze how the rhetoric of moral superiority often depends on gender categories.

22. Robert Anthony Orsi, *The Madonna of 115th Street: Faith and Community in Italian Harlem, 1880–1950* (New Haven, Conn.: Yale University Press, 1985).

23. Indeed, people around the world often believe that Americans have no real family ties. For example, on a visit to my family in Vietnam, my cousin asked me earnestly if it was true that American children put their elderly parents in nursing homes instead of caring for them at home. She was horrified at this practice and proclaimed that, because they care for their elders, Vietnamese families are morally superior to American families.

24. Micaela di Leonardo, *The Varieties of Ethnic Experience: Kinship, Class, and Gender among California Italian-Americans* (Ithaca, N.Y.: Cornell University Press, 1984); Nazli Kibria, *Family Tightrope: The Changing Lives of Vietnamese Immigrant Community* (Princeton, N.J.: Princeton University Press, 1993); M. Gail Hickey, "'Go to College, Get a Job, and Don't Leave the House without Your Brother': Oral Histories with Immigrant Women and Their Daughters." *Oral History Review* 23:2 (1996): 63–92; Michele Lamont, "Colliding Moralities."

25. di Leonardo, *Varieties of Ethnic Experience,* 229.

26. Ibid., 222

27. Kate Millett, *Sexual Politics* (Garden City, N.Y.: Doubleday, 1970).

28. Sander L. Gilman, *Difference and Pathology: Stereotypes of Sexuality, Race, and Madness* (Ithaca, N.Y.: Cornell University Press, 1985); Ann Laura Stoler, "Carnal Knowledge and Imperial Power: Gender, Race, and Morality in Colonial Asia," in *Gender at the Crossroads of Knowledge: Feminist Anthropology in the Postmodern Era,* ed. Micaela di Leonardo (Berkeley: University of California Press, 1991), 51–104.

29. Writing on the objectification of black women, Patricia Hill Collins, *Black Feminist Thought,* argues that popular representations of black families—mammy, welfare queen, and Jezebel—all pivot around their sexuality, either desexualizing or hypersexualizing them. Along the same line, Native American women have been portrayed as sexually excessive (Rayna Green, "The Pocahontas Perplex: The Image of India Women in American Culture." *Massachusetts Review* 16:4 [1975]: 698–714), Chicana women as "exotic and erotic" (Alfredo Mirande, "The Chicano Family: A Reanalysis of Conflicting Views," in *Rethinking Marriage, Child Rearing, and Family Organization,* ed. Arlene S. Skolnick and Jerome H. Skolnick [Berkeley: University of California Press, 1980], 479–93), and Puerto Rican and Cuban women as "tropical bombshells, . . . sexy, sexed and interested" (Carmen Tafolla, *To Split a Human: Mitos, Machos y la Mujer Chicana* [San Antonio, Tex.: Mexican American Cultural Center, 1985], 39).

30. Gilman, *Difference and Pathology,* 89.

31. Stoler, "Carnal Knowledge and Imperial Power," in *Gender at the Crossroads,* ed. di Leonardo.

32. Sucheta Mazumdar, "General Introduction: A Woman-Centered Perspective on Asian American History," in *Making Waves: An Anthology by and about Asian American Women,* ed. Asian Women United of California (Boston: Beacon, 1989), 3–4.

33. Yen Le Espiritu, *Asian American Women and Men: Labor, Laws, and Love* (Thousand Oaks, Calif.: Sage, 1997), 93.

34. Rona Tamiko Halualani, "The Intersecting Hegemonic Discourses of an Asian Mail-Order Bride Catalog: Pilipina 'Oriental Butterfly' Dolls for Sale," *Women's Studies in Communication* 18:1

(1995): 45–64; Timothy Egan, "Mail-Order Marriage, Immigrant Dreams and Death," *New York Times,* May 26, 1996, 12.

35. Espiritu, *Filipino American Lives,* 14.

36. Sheila Coronel and Ninotchka Rosca, "For the Boys: Filipinas Expose Years of Sexual Slavery by the U.S. and Japan," *Ms.,* November/December 1993, 10–15.; Jennifer Warren, "Suit Asks Navy to Aid Children Left in Philippines," *Los Angeles Times,* March 5, 1993, A3.

37. Quoted in Espiritu, *Filipino American Lives,* 77.

38. M. Villanueva, *Ginseng and Other Tales from Manila* (Corvallis, Oreg.: Calyx, 1991).

39. Sau-ling Wong, *Reading Asian American Literature: From Necessity to Extravagance* (Princeton, N.J.: Princeton University Press, 1993), 53.

40. Espiritu, *Asian American Women and Men,* 113

41. Halualani, "The Intersecting Hegemonic Discourses," 49; see also Raquel Z. Ordonez, "Mail-Order Brides: An Emerging Community," in *Filipino Americans: Transformation and Identity,* ed. Maria P. Root (Thousand Oaks, Calif.: Sage, 1997), 122.

42. Shamita Das Dasgupta and Sayantani DasGupta, "Public Face, Private Space: Asian Indian Women and Sexuality," in *"Bad Girls/Good Girls": Women, Sex, and Power in the Nineties,* ed. Nan Bauer Maglin and Donna Perry (New Brunswick, N.J.: Rutgers University Press, 1996), 229–31.

43. Janet Mancini Billson, *Keepers of the Culture: The Power of Tradition in Women's Lives* (New York: Lexington, 1995).

44. Donna Gabaccia, *From the Other Side: Women, Gender, and Immigrant Life in the U.S., 1820–1990* (Bloomington: Indiana University Press, 1994), xi.

45. Orsi, *Madonna of 115th Street,* 135.

46. Gabaccia, *From the Other Side,* 113.

47. Judy Yung, *Unbound Feet: A Social History of Chinese Women in San Francisco* (Berkeley: University of California Press, 1995); Orsi, *Madonna of 115th Street;* Vicki L. Ruiz, "The Flapper and the Chaperone: Historical Memory among Mexican-American Women," in *Seeking Common Ground: Multidisciplinary Studies,* ed. Donna Gabaccia (Westport, Conn.: Greenwood, 1992); Dasgupta and DasGupta, "Public Face, Private Space"; Mary C. Walters, "The Intersection of Gender, Race, and Ethnicity in Identity Development of Caribbean American Teens," in *Urban Girls: Resisting Stereotypes, Creating Identities,* ed. Bonnie J. Ross Leadbeater and Niobe Way (New York: New York University Press, 1996), 65–81.

48. Ruben Rumbaut and Kenji Ima, *The Adaptation of Southeast Asian Refugee Youth: A Comparative Study* (Washington, D.C.: U.S. Office of Refugee Resettlement, 1988); T. M. Woldemikael, *Becoming Black American: Haitians and American Institutions in Evanston, Illinois* (New York: AMS Press, 1989); Maria Eugenia Matute-Bianchi, "Situational Ethnicity and Patterns of School Performance among Immigrant and Nonimmigrant Mexican-Descent Students," in *Minority Status and Schooling: A Comparative Study of Immigrant and Involuntary Minorities,* ed. Margaret A. Gibson and John U. Ogbu (New York: Garland, 1991), 205–47; Margaret A. Gibson, "Additive Acculturation as a Strategy for School Improvement," in *California's Immigrant Children: Theory, Research, and Implications for Educational Policy,* ed. Ruben Rumbaut and Wayne A. Cornelius (La Jolla: Center for U.S.-Mexican Studies, University Of California, San Diego, 1995), 77–105.

49. Yvonne Y. Haddad and Jane I. Smith, "Islamic Values among American Muslims," in *Family and Gender among American Muslims: Issues Facing Middle Eastern Immigrants and Their Descendants,* ed. Barbara C. Aswad and Barbara Bilge (Philadelphia: Temple University Press, 1996), 19–40; Waters, "Intersection of Gender, Race, and Ethnicity," 75–76.

50. The relationship between immigrant parents and their sons deserves an article of its own. According to Gabaccia, *From the Other Side,* 79, "Immigrant parents fought with sons, too, but over different issues: parents' complaints about rebellious sons focused more on criminal activity than on male sexuality or independent courtship." Moreover, because of their mobility, young men have more means to escape—at least temporarily—the pressures of the family than young women. In his study of Italian American families, Orsi reports that young men rebelled by sleeping in cars or joining the army, but young women did not have such opportunities. *Madonna of 115th Street,* 143.

51. Diane L. Wolf, "Family Secrets: Transnational Struggles among Children of Filipino Immigrants." *Sociological Perspectives* 40:3 (1997): 457–82.

52. Ibid.

53. Dasgupta and DasGupta, "Public Face, Private Space," 230.

54. Wolf, "Family Secrets," 467.

55. The names of the two high schools in this excerpt are fictitious.

56. Nan Bauer Maglin and Donna Perry, "Introduction," in *"Bad Girls/Good Girls": Women, Sex, and Power in the Nineties,* ed. Nan Bauer Maglin and Donna Perry, (New Brunswick, N.J.: Rutgers University Press, 1996), xiii–xxvi.

57. Deborah L. Tolman and Tracy E. Higgins, "How Being a Good Girl Can Be Bad for Girls," in *"Bad Girls/Good Girls": Women, Sex, and Power in the Nineties,* ed. Nan Bauer Maglin and Donna Perry (New Brunswick, N.J.: Rutgers University Press, 1996), 206.

58. Ibid., 205–25.

59. Dasgupta and DasGupta, "Public Face, Private Space," 236.

60. According to a 1992 health assessment report of Filipinos in San Francisco, Filipino teens have the highest pregnancy rates among all Asian groups and, in 1991, the highest rate of increase in the number of births as compared with all other racial or ethnic groups. Antonio T. Tiongson, Jr., "Throwing the Baby Out with the Bath Water," in *Filipino Americans: Transformation and Identity,* ed. Maria P. Root (Thousand Oaks, Calif.: Sage, 1997), 257.

61. See Wolf, "Family Secrets."

62. Diane L. Wolf, *Factory Daughters: Gender, Household Dynamics, and Rural Industrialization in Java* (Berkeley: University of California Press, 1992); Nazli Kibria, *Family Tightrope: The Changing Lives of Vietnamese Immigrant Community* (Princeton, N.J.: Princeton University Press, 1993).

63. Espiritu, "The Intersection of Race, Ethnicity, and Class."

64. The few available studies on Filipino American intermarriage indicate a high rate relative to other Asian groups. In 1980, Filipino men in California recorded the highest intermarriage rate among all Asian groups, and Filipina women had the second-highest rate, after Japanese American women. Pauline Agbayani-Siewert and Linda Revilla, "Filipino Americans," in *Asian Americans: Contemporary Trends and Issues,* ed. Pyong Gap Min (Thousand Oaks, Calif.: Sage), 156.

65. Angela Lau, "Filipino Girls Think Suicide at Number One Rate," *San Diego Union-Tribune,* February 11, 1995, A-1.

66. Ruth Frankenberg, *White Women, Race Matters: The Social Construction of Whiteness* (Minneapolis: University of Minnesota Press, 1993), 113.

67. Gabaccia, *From the Other Side.*

21

Born Again in East L.A.

The Congregation as Border Space

LUÍS LEÓN

> Currently, Los Angeles International Airport welcomes more immigrants than any other port of entry in American history. Public mythology, however, still reveres Ellis Island and the Statue of Liberty and looks toward Europe. Historical writing on immigration in the United States surely suffers from this severe regional imbalance; most studies still focus on the Northeast and selected cities of the Old Northwest. The fact that the American Southwest has been the locus of one of the most profound and complex interactions between variant cultures in American history is repeatedly overlooked.
>
> —George J. Sánchez, *Becoming Mexican American* (1993)

> Los Angeles is a veritable Jerusalem. Just the place for a mighty work of God to begin.
>
> —Frank Bartleman, *Azusa Street* (August 1, 1906)

> East Los Angeles was our Jerusalem and the birthplace for Victory Outreach. Spiritually speaking, California is our Judea and the United States is our Samaria. The "uttermost parts" is the rest of the world.
>
> —The Victory Outreach Mission Statement

Over the past ten years, the movement of Latino Catholics to forms of evangelical/pentecostal or "born-again" religion has captured the attention of scholars and journalists who are interested in the configuration and active reconfiguration of religion in the Americas.[1] Over the past thirty years, the once impenetrable walls of Catholicism in Central and South America have been shaken by waves of evangelical conversion, and now "nearly ten percent or more of the Latin American population identifies itself as *evangelico,* with the percentage substantially higher in Brazil, Chile, and most of Central America."[2] Scholarly interest in Latin American "born-again" conversion has been buttressed by the debate on the "failure" of the Catholic church to serve the needs of the Latino masses and more particularly the actual impact of liberation theology. That the Latin American Catholic church has functioned historically, in effect, as a bulwark

504

of the landed elites by mystifying class inequities is now axiomatic.[3] In spite of promising and well-intentioned post–Vatican II discursive and practical attempts at reforms in Latin American Catholicism engineered by the bishops and made manifest as liberation theology, some argue that theologies of liberation in Latin America have been "better at filling faculties, bookshelves, and graves than churches."[4]

At the moment, academic research on Latino pentecostalism is disproportionately focused on Latin America. In its assessments of motivations for evangelical conversion, this literature falls into two broad interpretive categories, which I have named *Marxist social determinism* and *rational-choice humanism.* Both are commonly applied to explain Chicano/United States Latino[5] evangelical conversion as well.[6] Hence, they are worth pursuing here.

What I call rational-choice humanism is an intellectual position that implies that the Latino religious "consumer" is endowed with all the necessary information and the requisite freedom and privilege to choose, based on *reason,* one religion over another and make that religion best fit his or her particular needs—in short, empowerment.[7] This position rarely takes into account the often limited and degrading choices available to working-class Latinos.

On the other hand, the Marxists proclaim that evangelical religion provides a mechanism for social disengagement by channeling people's repressed energies, anxieties, and general social dissatisfaction into a spiritual obsession and attendant eschatological hope that preclude critical political thought and revolutionary practice.[8] In the words of one pentecostal historian, the pentecostal movement teaches us "something about the way in which movements of the 'disinherited' that arise out of protest against the social order are transformed into religious forces that serve to perpetuate that order."[9] While some have separated the positions, I see as closely related David Martin's argument that Latin America has been religiously, socially, and politically latent, and that it is therefore only now experiencing its Protestant Reformation.[10] Evangelicalism, in this narrative of modernity, creates docile and complacent workers who are focused on the afterlife.

Although not unproblematic, Martin's theory is helpful for identifying the social space opened by pentecostalism where power, group loyalties, identity, and resistance can be reimagined and expressed. This space has been widened to include Latina feminist concerns. Some have recently argued that pentecostalism provides Latin American women with a sacred mallet for pounding the cultural beast of a peculiarly Latin American machismo into submission.[11] In this view, clever women choose pentecostalism as a mechanism of empowerment to restrain their husband's "machista" habits. In other words, the rational-choice humanism model posits a free—indeed *transcendent* subject— who, in spite of social limitations, can choose at will, whereas the Marxist social determinism model posits the opposite: a submissive pawn who is duped into submission by the elites for political and economic exploitation.

Neither of these binary paradigms explains fully the complex phenomenon of Mexican American or Chicano pentecostalism. Nonetheless, both are illuminating. Certainly there are escapist elements in pentecostalism, just as there are modes of empowerment. No human agent, however, is free from social context, and Chicanos face many social, political, symbolic, and economic forces that limit not only their choices but also their

ability to choose. Hence, I attempt in this essay to determine the conditions of possibility under which the choice for Alcance Victoria, a group of about two dozen Spanish-
language churches that are part of the mainly English-language evangelical church movement known as Victory Outreach, headquartered east of Los Angeles in La Puente, is
made possible. My thesis is that Alcance Victoria at once enables the reproduction of
both modes of empowerment and modes of docility or domination. In what follows, I
attempt to illuminate ethnographically how these modes are enabled in one particular
context: the Alcance Victoria congregation in the Boyle Heights district of East Los
Angeles.[12]

Given its institutional affiliation, the story of Alcance Victoria is a story within a
story, a tale of an elaborate religious organization located strategically within a larger,
highly articulated network of religious and social organizations. In the local congregation, Alcance Victorians negotiate and rework their identities in the context of often
overwhelming social conditions by spinning understandings of time and place, together
with self and society, into webs of religious-meaning systems. What follows attempts to
unravel the Alcance Victoria web to tell the stories of the individual lives that together
constitute what I call the "congregational narrative."

Victory Outreach/Alcance Victoria Ministries:
Possess the Land

Victory Outreach was founded by Sonny Arguinzoni in Boyle Heights in 1967 as a ministry to Chicano gangs. From its humble beginnings in the Pico Aliso public housing
projects during the late 1960s, Victory Outreach has become a vast and highly organized
movement spanning the globe and touching and improving the lives of many. Recounted
in a number of autobiographical books and on video- and audiotapes, Arguinzoni's story
(or "testimony," in pentecostal vernacular) has become a foundational myth for the Victory Outreach cosmos.[13] Arguinzoni's testimonial narrative functions as a template for
believers concerning matters of doctrine — as well as gender relations and expectations
of women. (It is required reading at many of the Victory Outreach women's retreats.)

A Puerto Rican (or better, "Newyorican"), Arguinzoni began using heroin as a youth
in Brooklyn. His parents were both active pentecostals and prayed for their son's "salvation." During the late 1950s, after he had spent time in jail and after an increasing
heroin addiction further alienated him from his parents, Arguinzoni became "saved"
one afternoon through the intervention of evangelist Nicky Cruz, a notorious ex–gang
leader. Arguinzoni's interest in pentecostalism was aroused by the dapper appearance
of a former heroin-addicted associate of his who had been "born again." Arguinzoni followed his former associate to the para-church organization Teen Challenge, founded by
David Wilkerson, author of *The Cross and the Switchblade*. There Arguinzoni encountered
Cruz, the former president of the infamous Puerto Rican "Mau Mau" gang who earned
fame in the Bronx for waging war on the police. Arguinzoni met his match in Cruz, who
physically prevented him from leaving the Teen Challenge Center until he was able to
kick drugs. In his personal narrative, Arguinzoni describes how he beat his addiction

and enrolled in La Puente Bible College located east of Los Angeles. While there, he met Julie Rivera, a Chicana from East Los Angeles.

Julie Rivera came from a Catholic home. Her entire family had converted to pentecostalism, however, after they came to believe that her brother had been revived from the dead after a drug overdose. The family attributed the brother's second chance at life to the prayerful intercession of Julie's aunt, a pentecostal. Julie and Sonny were married shortly after graduation in the early 1960s.

The Arguinzonis' first home was a rented unit in the Pico Aliso housing projects in Boyle Heights. There Sonny began preaching to the drug addicts, gang members, and ex-convicts who populated the tenements; he often sheltered them in his own tiny apartment for rehabilitation. Eventually he rented a church located within the city blocks that comprise the giant housing complex. Even after the church was rented, he and Julie sheltered a number of needy Chicanos in their home, helping them to kick the drug habit. It was in this way that the idea for Victory Outreach, a drug rehabilitation and rescue ministry, was born.

After its beginning in the 1960s, Victory Outreach moved to a number of rented locations to hold church services, including a discotheque that had to be sanitized early every Sunday morning. In the late 1980s, Victory Outreach acquired fourteen acres in a former school property in La Puente for $1.7 million. This property now houses the "mother church" (pastored by Arguinzoni), the Victory Outreach School of Ministry, and a bookstore. Each Sunday morning at 8:30 and 10:30, services are held at the mother church sanctuary, which seats one thousand people. Currently Victory Outreach is in the process of building a larger temple on that site that will seat between three and four thousand.

Today Victory Outreach is a sophisticated organization with over two hundred churches and twice that number of drug rehabilitation homes throughout the world. Not all congregations look alike; each assumes an identity that largely depends on its own geography and class. Most churches are made up of working-class members. The expressed goal of Victory Outreach, together with Alcance Victoria, is to have one thousand churches by the year 2000. In addition to the La Puente headquarters, Victory Outreach also rents two thousand feet of office space in West Covina, California, where the business offices of Arguinzoni and his staff are housed. Victory Outreach sponsors a number of programs designed especially for women, United Women in Ministry, and a television ministry that broadcasts infrequently on the Trinity Broadcasting Network.

One of the organization's most successful programs is a youth ministry called God's Anointed Now Generation (GANG). GANG creates a Christian image that mimics a Los Angeles Chicano youth gang aesthetic, encoding it within a Christian vernacular. Victory Outreach has its own rap groups that sample rhythms and riffs of popular songs but inscribe Christian lyrics over them. Many members of GANG continue to sport the hairstyles, makeup, and baggy clothes of Los Angeles youth culture, but they espouse Christian teachings.

When a convert feels a "burden" to open a church in a particular place, he is "launched out," or given one year of support from the organization for that ministry. The first church was "launched out" eastward from Boyle Heights to Pico Rivera, California. It is expected that such a church will become self-supporting within a year, although some exceptions are made and cutoff dates extended. Hence, the impressive growth of Victory Outreach can be explained largely by the individual initiative of its male members. Women are not able to become pastors or to head churches themselves, but they can become evangelists and work as leaders among other women.

As the Spanish-language branch of Victory Outreach, Alcance Victoria now has over twenty-five churches in Mexico, Spain, and the United States. Alcance Victoria began in 1983, in an abandoned synagogue on Bridge Street in Boyle Heights. This first congregation was taken over by Eliodoro Contreras, known as "Pastor Lolo," in 1989, after the original pastor became ill. Pastor Lolo had been "born again" in Victory Outreach ministries, and he felt a "burden" for Mexico. Although he spoke very little Spanish, armed with his Bible and $500, Lolo, along with his wife, Catty, and their infant son, made the pilgrimage to the sacred heart of Mexico: Mexico City. From that vantage point they planned to win Mexico for Jesus. Upon returning to the States several years later, Lolo assumed the leadership of the Spanish congregation, which had moved from the synagogue on Bridge Street to a storefront on McDonald Street. Soon the group grew too large, and in 1992 Lolo moved them into a former painters' union hall on Soto Street in the heart of Boyle Heights, which they rented monthly. In 1994, Pastor Lolo resigned his post after the stress of the job took its toll on his marriage and family life. The congregation was given over to one of Pastor Lolo's "generals," Jesus Figueroa, who goes by the nickname "Chuy." At the time Chuy was twenty-two-years-old, which made him the youngest pastor in the Victory Outreach organization.

Pentecostalism in the Borderlands

In 1994, Alcance Victoria Este de Los Angeles (East Los Angeles) moved from the painters' union hall to a defunct movie theater in Boyle Heights, where they still meet today. Although they rent the edifice, they have made substantial permanent changes to it and intend to buy it eventually; in the words of the pastor, they are "trusting God" for its purchase. The building's facade is dominated by a marquee, which in times past announced films starring Cantinflas and other Mexican legends. It now sports a hand-painted cloth sign announcing Alcance Victoria's presence and the order of their services, and welcoming all passersby. On the exterior wall that Alcance Victoria shares with another building an advertisement reads, "You can change your eye color." When passing, I never fail to reflect on the appropriateness of this statement as a welcoming sign for Alcance Victoria, whose message is of personal transformation and the omnipotence of God: "You too can be changed—spiritually, morally, *physically*."

Inside, the building is big but spare, with high ceilings and a plain decor. A banner behind the pulpit proclaims: "Alcance Victoria E.L.A. Posseer La Tierra" (Possess the Land). Eight flags of various nations, fresh flowers, a Plexiglas podium, and red carpeting complete the furnishings of the platform. At the very top center of the ceiling hang two flags, one Mexican, the other American. The auditorium is brightly lighted.

Men make up over half of this Alcance Victoria congregation, which is generally young. About 75 percent of the membership is under the age of fifty, and most are in their twenties, thirties, and forties. The average Sunday morning and evening attendance is three hundred, of which, according to the pastor's estimates, about one-half are recently arrived Mexican immigrants, and the other half Mexican Americans or Mexicans living permanently in the United States.

While East Los Angeles (not unlike its inhabitants) is officially "unincorporated" into the city, it is nonetheless Los Angeles, and this ambiguous fact is evident in the built environment, from the growing downtown skyline that, when not obscured by smog, is visible from most areas in this part of town. This section of Los Angeles is densely built for a western city; the buildings are two and three stories high with no side yards. The blocks are long, and the streets teem with humanity. During my typical one-block walk from where I park my car to the church on the corner of the block, I pass one Mexican grocery store, one general grocery store owned by immigrants from India, a large basketball gymnasium that is usually open (operated by the Hollenbeck Division of the Los Angeles Police Department, located opposite the Alcance Victoria edifice), and a pet store with its cages of birds and rabbits lining the broad sidewalk, making their presence known with their exotic sounds and odors.

During the dry, hot summer months, while making the trek from my car to the church (usually an adventure in itself), I have encountered young Chicanas and Chicanos loitering in front of the general grocery store drinking beer out of bottles wrapped in brown paper bags; Alcance Victoria members are usually in their midst, ministering to them passionately. Their evangelistic narratives resonate with the *consejo* in Mexican culture—proverbial words of wisdom gained from life experience imparted to the youth by elders. The youth outside the liquor store, suffering from the shortsightedness that plagues most young generations, endure this exchange with the Alcance Victoria members respectfully: they try to restrain giggles with smiles, and they nod quietly and patiently, all the while appearing generally appreciative of the elders' concern. This is the reaction of most gang members to whom Alcance Victorians preach on their weekly pilgrimages into the depths of the gang-infested neighborhoods of East Los Angeles—patient, respectful, even grateful.

That Boyle Heights is ridden with gangs might come as a surprise to the uninformed visitor. Indeed, there is a feeling of community here, of being among family; the maxim that "we are all in this together" seems to define the sentiments of the collectivity. Strangers initiate Spanish conversations in stores, in restaurants, and on the streets. Just a few blocks away from the church, where Cesar Chavez Avenue meets Soto Street, any warm summer night will find hundreds of people passing the time together. Under the mesmerizing Los Angeles moon, they eat together and barter with the vendors whose pottery and leather wares cover colorful blankets on the sidewalks in neat rows; on sizzling and steaming carts, Mexican pastries and tacos are prepared to be sold fresh. I often stop there before making the ninety-minute drive back to my home in pristine Santa Barbara. If this scene were taking place outside a massive park instead of in parking lots, it could easily be mistaken for Mexico City or Guadalajara. East Los Angeles's public culture is largely organized around food, and its effervescence is reflected in Alcance Victoria.[14]

In the center of the Alcance Victoria church vestibule stands a small island where food is prepared and served by the women members. Eating takes place at each service, and without question commensalism is the ritual practice definitive of Chicano culture. On one level, the relegation of women to food preparation and service is easily understood to be an extension and actualization of cultural norms that contribute to the marginalization of women. On the other hand, women too are agents in the production of religion, and their control of food provides them an arena of power. (The full exploration of this topic goes beyond the scope of this study.)

The gendered division of religious and cultural labor is further evident in the assignment of worship leaders. Ushers who stand at the entranceways and distribute worship programs are more often men, although women do sometimes serve as ushers. Sunday morning and evening services are led by a man who holds a title in the church hierarchy. The songs are projected onto a screen with an overhead projector. The music is provided by a band made up entirely of men. Electric keyboards, guitar, and bass play to the rhythm of acoustic drums. Perhaps the main attraction at the pulpit are three teenage and young adult female singers, who often wear slinky dresses or other colorful outfits and stand stage left of the male song leader. These women alternate song-leading responsibilities with other women, but one is always the pastor's wife. It is impossible to overlook the allure of the women's chorus for the typically single male audience member. This is indeed part of the appeal for the men: the likelihood of finding the idealized "virgin" woman to marry. It seems that in spite of the pentecostal iconoclastic rejection of the Virgin of Guadalupe, the realm of women's possibilities she symbolizes and circumscribes still dominates the Chicano imagination.[15]

The order of the Sunday morning and evening services is roughly the same. An opening prayer is followed by lively singing and even some dancing, interspersed with more prayers. Here, instead of the rock and roll and soulful beats borrowed from black churches and inscribed with the Spanish lyrics once characteristic of Latino pentecostal churches, the most popular songs in this congregation are taken from the Psalms of David, sung in minor keys with Hebrew lyrics. During the faster numbers, young children rush to the front of the church and jump around, forming a mosh pit of sorts, while several men spill into the aisles and begin twirling on one leg and lifting their arms above their heads.

After the congregation sings and prays for fifteen or twenty minutes, the pastor makes a dramatic entrance, walking stoically yet briskly from the rear of the church with two or more of his church officials, all sporting dark suits, ties, and short hair shaven on the sides. They assume the places reserved for them in the first row of the sanctuary and do not stop to greet anyone. In this way, they symbolically command the respect and authority of an intensely committed religious group; everyone knows who is in charge here. Several announcements are then made, and the offering prayed for and collected. A brief round of special songs follows, during which individuals who are prepared beforehand are asked to mount the pulpit and sing a solo. Others from the audience are asked to deliver special *testimonios,* or "testimonies." Finally, the pastor assumes the pulpit about one hour to ninety minutes after the service begins. He leads the congregation in choruses of rousing songs while swaying a tight fist up and down to form a U-shape. Next, he allows the congregation to be seated and announces a passage from the Bible that will serve as the text of his sermon. While waiting for the congregation to locate the Scripture and follow along, he asks how many love Jesus or some other rhetorical question. As he reads the text, the congregation is perfectly silent.

Pastor Chuy's sermons are animated and compelling. He begins by reading a passage from the Bible, and then illustrates (most often indirectly) how it is relevant to the congregation's life. His preaching has a folksy quality about it, and his topics vary. However, he always emphasizes personal responsibility and the transformative power of God. He typically exhorts congregation members to maintain their faith, to work hard for Jesus, to continue coming to church, and to love and help one another, for Jesus' return is near. His sermons average between forty-five minutes to an hour. On Father's Day of 1995, he preached about how to be a good and responsible father, and urged fathers to spend time with their children. He related a deeply moving story about his own father, who had abandoned his family when Chuy was very young. Pastor Chuy told the congregation about the time he contacted his father, whom he barely knew, to invite him to his high school graduation. His father declined. Pastor Chuy responded by telling him that all he wanted was for his father to be his friend. The point of the message was forgiveness. Pastor Chuy was admonishing his congregants to behave in kind and to forgive their fathers.

On Mother's Day of 1996, two women preached. This surprised me, for I had not seen women preach to the congregation previously. The first woman, probably in her fifties, had been in the United States most of her life. She gave a *consejo* about the power of a mother's love and the witness of a Christian mother to her children. She analogized a mother's love to God's claiming that just as mothers love their children in spite of their flaws, so too God does love his children in spite of their mistakes. She spoke for about twenty minutes before leaving the pulpit to the next speaker.

The woman following her was in her late twenties; she had arrived in the United States from Mexico within the last five years. Her message was very stern. She opened by asking, "What kind of influence are you on your husband?" She cited Jezebel as an example of a negative influence, because Jezebel was always speaking her mind and giving her kingly husband advice. This woman claimed that a woman's divinely stipulated role was to be a supportive helpmate, enabling her husband to work for God. The main task of women was to be a "positive" influence. However, she argued, women should not try to influence their husband's decisions. She assured the crowd that to "live the Bible" is "not nice: to live the Bible you have got to suffer." She ended her sermon by confessing that she realized that her message was going to anger some parishioners, but that it was the message that God had given her, and she had to please God, not the parishioners. She spoke for approximately thirty minutes.

Slow, emotional singing and an alter call follow the preaching; this is the climactic moment of collective effervescence. Most parishioners make their way up to the alter, resulting in heated crowding and sensual body contact. The music, the contact, the emotion, the groans, the passion—all intensify the sensuality of the moment. Indeed, men make much physical, emotional, and spiritual contact with other men during the periods of intense prayer. Worshipers embrace one another, hold hands, place their arms around one another, kneel down together, and hold each other tightly while cathartically weeping and praying together. During this time congregants speak in tongues and experience mystical trances as their bodies are repossessed anew by the Holy Ghost. This period of charismatic worship lasts up to a half-hour and is followed by more slow, emotional singing before the service ends. The whole service is about two hours long.

Pentecostal Mariachis and Other Cultural Oxymorons

Generally, congregational singing at Alcance Victoria Este de Los Angeles is regularly accompanied by two or three trumpeters, which gives the rhythms and choruses a distinctly Mexican sound. The trumpet players are brothers, and together with their father and mother they form a mariachi band called "Mariachi Genesis." During special services they are summoned to the pulpit—either all together, the father and mother together, or the father or mother alone. On very special occasions, the brothers and father will be accompanied by musicians playing an acoustic bass and acoustic guitars, with all band members wearing the tight-fitting red and black slacks, coats with gold trim, and big sombreros that define mariachi style. All the songs in their extensive repertoire are done in the classic mariachi fashion, but their lyrics express evangelical theology. At times, the band performs traditional Mexican songs that have no explicit religious message but convey instead a strong spiritual yearning for Mexico, a melancholy acquired during the long and difficult years spent in exile. One of Mariachi Genesis's most popular songs mixes secular and Christian themes. Entitled "Mexico para Cristo" (Mexico for Christ), the song's chorus goes as follows (the translation is my own): "I love my Mexico, I love the Lord, I love my people/race [*raza*] with all of my heart; I'm not ashamed of the Gospel, because it is power and salvation."

The first time I heard Mariachi Genesis perform a secular Mexican song without Christian references during a worship service I was stunned. I was at the same time overwhelmed by the wildly enthusiastic reaction of the crowd. The performance of a secular song might be disallowed in a pentecostal church with more severe fundamentalist underpinnings, for such a song belies the "holiness" interpretation of the biblical mandate calling for strict separation from the secular world.[16]

It was this willingness to address the needs of the people by appealing to cultural narratives that provided my first major piece in the complex puzzle of Alcance Victoria's success. Alcance Victoria is a pragmatic group, relying on contextual truth—within scriptural parameters. As mystics, they interpret truth in trance.[17] This pragmatic philosophy and praxis unfold to the pulse of everyday life in the heart of East Los Angeles, and is revealed in the creation and utilization of religious symbols and discourses that emerge to satisfy physical need, spiritual desire, and lust of memory. Mariachi Genesis is but one product of this cultural strategy that throws mysticism in the mix with pragmatism and arranges it around Mexican symbolism to produce a new cultural matrix that can sustain what at one time may have been a cultural oxymoron: pentecostal mariachis. When asked how a church that preaches a new life in Christ can support songs during worship services that are not explicitly Christian, Pastor Chuy explained that the churches must become "culturally relevant."

Often on Wednesday evenings members of the church meet in smaller groups called "cell units." These *grupos familiares,* or "family-style groups," assemble for prayer and reflection on the Bible. Church members invite friends and family to join them, so the group is intended to grow; once it reaches fifteen, however, it is divided into another group, with all members attending church.[18]

The congregation sponsors four drug rehabilitation homes. One of them is located directly across the street from the church, and the others are in surrounding areas. Three of the shelters house men, and one is for women. On average, the "rehabs" are home to fifteen people each, although turnover rates are high, and most of the members do not stay in the homes for the nine-month duration of the program. One home director, Kiko, who looks much older than his eighteen years, recounts to me his daily tasks dealing with gang members: "I get in their face and tell them who we are and what we are about. They respect us." Recently, he nearly evicted someone for speaking badly about him. Kiko, a tough young warrior, was reduced to tears by vicious gossip.

Alcance Victoria in East Los Angeles has experienced marked growth in the two years that Pastor Chuy has been at the helm. Chuy was attending Alcance Victoria as a member before Pastor Lolo brought him into the ministry full-time. Pastor Lolo made Chuy an attractive offer to work as his assistant for $6 an hour. At the time, however, Chuy was working for a Los Angeles high school earning $12 an hour, and the school was paying for Chuy to pursue a bachelor's degree in business administration at California State University, Los Angeles. Hence, Chuy told Pastor Lolo that he would "pray about it." His conversion experience precipitated the decision for full-time ministry, or what he calls his "Road to Damascus" experience.

> When my brother first started coming here to this church, I though it was good for him because it changed him. Then he started preaching to me. But I wasn't in any trouble, everything was going fine for me. I didn't need church. But deep inside of me something was missing. I was getting good grades, but in my heart I was wondering what was the purpose of this life. Why are we here? I use to lie awake at night meditating about this. It was the Lord speaking to me. So I accepted Jesus into my life. I began to feel a burden for the full-time ministry. I didn't want to. I thought God had blessed me with my job and school, and I knew that God was not an Indian-giver. But shortly after that, I was witnessing to a sister and her husband at her home, and, when I left, the sister gave me the pentecostal [hand]shake—she slipped a bill into my hand while shaking it. Usually this is about $10 or $20. But, later, driving in my car, I took out the bill, thinking it might be enough to get some tacos or a hamburger, and it was actually four-$20 bills all folded up! I began to cry in my car. I cried and knew at that point that God would take care of me in ministry. It was the Holy Spirit who spoke to me (May 22, 1995, Boyle Heights).

When Chuy was tapped for the Alcance Victoria pastorship in 1995, he was newly married and planning on "launching" a Victory Outreach church in Brazil. He claims, however, that God had other plans for him.

Pastor Chuy's "Road to Damascus" experience has proven to be a harbinger of the blessings he was destined to receive in ministry. In 1995 a member of the church arranged for him to buy a new condo in the Monterey Park hills. At the Father's Day morning service in 1995, much to Pastor Chuy's surprise, the congregation ceremoniously handed him a check for an amount they had collected among themselves that he was instructed to use as a down payment on a new car. Later that day, at the El Sereno drug rehabilitation home, an enthusiastic Pastor Chuy was busily walking around giving orders, supervising the making of the *carne asada* (roasted meat), greeting people, choosing the tapes that were being played on the huge boom box, and counseling members. There were to be baptisms in the aboveground pool that sits on the property. He stopped briefly to chat with me. "We baptize before we eat," Pastor Chuy explained, "or else everyone will leave before the baptisms" (May 22, 1995, Boyle Heights). Pastor Chuy is a *guerito,* or a "light-skinned Latino." He stands about five feet, ten inches, tall and wears a thick mustache. For this occasion he was wearing long athletic shorts, basketball shoes, and an oversized T-shirt with a picture of the Tasmanian devil that read "Houston Rockets." (He had recently returned from Houston, where he supervised the opening of a church.)

"I'm the youngest pastor here in Victory Outreach," Pastor Chuy told me. Hence, his biggest challenge, he feels, is to get the older men to respect him. For that reason, he tries to look older. In the two years that Pastor Chuy has led Alcance Victoria, he has met that challenge and has risen to deal with an even greater dilemma: with the variety of interests and problems represented in this congregation, how can it be managed cohesively? A turn now to the stories of Alcance Victoria parishioners, what I call the "congregational narrative," will address this question.

Constituents of the Church

One Victory Outreach preacher has called the movement's adherents the "Lazarus Generation," meant as an allegory for those who have been raised, metaphorically, from the dead, like Lazarus in the Christian Scriptures. In this context, the "dead" refers to the gang members, drug addicts, prostitutes, and the like who were "dead in sin" in Victory Outreach language. While the Lazarus element is certainly present in the Alcance Victoria congregation, they are not the only constituency. Indeed, Alcance Victoria welcomes newly arrived Mexican immigrants and their young families in addition to widows and widowers, divorcees, and young single men and women, some of whom are college and high school students. Many of the young congregants have never been on drugs and have other motivations for joining this rescue ministry. I identified several life situations of individuals in the Alcance Victoria collective. Below, I weave their stories together into the congregational narrative.

The former drug addicts, gang members, and prostitutes are in many respects the cornerstone of the congregation, for they are the foot soldiers that march and fight most loyally in the Victory Outreach army. Collectively the Lazarus Generation has done more to shape the congregational narrative than any other group, for they are the ushers, deacons, musicians, rehabilitation home leaders, and church administrators. More than any other, this group stressed the notion of "the change." Twenty-seven-year-old Manny Martinez, a former gang member who works as an usher in the church, spoke for them:

> The change, the change is the most important thing. I was a drug addict before [I came here]. I went to jail and everything, but now God has changed my life. Twenty-five years ago Pastor Sonny [Arguinzoni] got the burden, and that's why he opened the first church. So when people come here they can see with their own eyes, people can see the results. People are always happy here! It's knowing God. It's knowing who he really is. I know God is love, peace, happiness; God is like air—you don't see it, but you feel it. (April 30, 1995, Boyle Heights)

"The change" enables former gang members to take control of their lives, and to imagine and live in a coherent world.

As Martinez notes, there is a sensual, corporeal quality to Alcance Victoria worship. It is experienced as electric charges and ecstatic trancelike states that assure the believer that God is real and that believers have tapped the power of God—directly. Martinez also notes the centrality of Arguinzoni to the Victory Outreach cosmogony. Arguinzoni enjoys a virtual apotheosis in the minds of the Victory Outreach believers. He is the living embodiment of the power of God, the capacity for the quick change, the election, and material success. Arguinzoni lives in a large house in a fashionable Los Angeles suburb, drives a new BMW, and travels extensively. In his rise from gang member and drug addict on the streets of Brooklyn to successful religious entrepreneur, Sonny Arguinzoni is a living, breathing, preaching symbol of the American success story—from rags to riches.

The Victory Outreach empire was built by preaching that other men can do the same: become born again, marry a "nice girl," pastor a church, and become part of what the Victory Outreach collective refers to informally as the "corporation." Here, the rhythms and cycles of life are marked by renewal and progress: spiritual, symbolic, and material. All involved in the leadership of Victory Outreach will vehemently insist that the motivation to pastor a church is entirely spiritual. Nonetheless, they will in the same breath concede that many of the men come to church looking for a wife and that Alcance Victoria encourages the men to realize their individual calling as pastors and to open their own churches. This is the path taken by hundreds of men in Victory Outreach/Alcance Victoria. Certainly Manny is following this path. Less than a year before our interview he married a young woman he had met in the church; he had been active in the church leadership and was planning eventually to pastor his own church. Meanwhile he was, like the majority of the Chicanos in the congregation, working seasonally in construction.

Kiko, the former director of the men's transition home, is actively working in the Alcance Victoria offices, running errands for Pastor Chuy. He explains that he does not receive a regular salary for this work but that the pastor "blesses" him often. This means that the pastor will spontaneously hand Kiko some cash. The pastor of each church controls the financial resources. While becoming a pastor is the most common goal, it is not the sole upward path open to Alcance Victoria's men. Kiko plays keyboards in the church, and would like eventually to earn a living as an Alcance Victoria evangelist and marry an Alcance Victoria woman. In the mythology of the Victory Outreach movement, all these things were shown to be possible through the example of Arguinzoni, which is particularly meaningful for the men of the Lazarus Generation who have few other role models.

Women too are part of the Lazarus Generation. One such woman has been in the United States for four years and a member of the Alcance Victoria for three of those years; she is now forty-two-years-old and a director of an Alcance Victoria women's home. I call her Magdalena. Her "change," as in the case of others who appear at the doorstep of Victory Outreach, took place at a dramatically low point in her life. "I was going crazy," she recounts. "I was looking for answers, but only Jesus is the answer" (July 9, 1996, Boyle Heights, interview conducted in Spanish). The answer to Magdalena's existential crisis came first in the form of witchcraft (*echiseria*) and lesbianism, which she now attributes to her witchcraft practices—all while she was a confirmed Catholic living in Mexico City. Her change occurred while she was confined to a bed in a mental hospital. It was Magdalena's sister who preached the evangelical Gospel to her, as refracted through the Alcance Victoria prism. She freely employs military metaphors in explaining that only God can help her to "fight that battle" with temptation, against the enemy. In her maneuvers on the battle lines, she leads six other women who live in the home. One is a former gang member, a twenty-two-year-old Chicana who has a baby with her in the home. Four others are Mexican immigrants who have nowhere else to go. A pregnant woman from Guatemala also lives there with her baby; she came to the States to earn money to support her husband back home.

Magdalena claims that the mission of the home is to restore women's "dignity" and to teach them to be "blessings in their homes and with their children." Some women have had their children taken away from them by the county, Magdalena explains. Therefore, the home helps to rehabilitate them and to have their children returned to them. In these efforts, the women are hired out to help support the basic needs of the home.

I asked Victory Outreach members what they imagine themselves doing in five or ten years. Magdalena wants to return to Mexico City to work with the children of the streets: "This country [the United States] is blessed; this God will bless us [Mexicans too], not with money but with faith in God." Like the Mexican and Chicano myth of "La Llorona" (a myth of infanticide), Magdalena says she knows Mexican mothers who have killed their children because they cannot feed them. She believes that her work in the Alcance Victoria women's home is "preparation" for the work she feels called to do in Mexico City.

When this same question about life ten years hence was posed to the Lazarus men, most seemed puzzled and had to mediate solemnly before responding. One twenty-nine-year-old Chicano spoke to me in Spanish; he had been in the home for eight weeks and just wanted to stay there for three months without "messing up." If he could make it for that long, he was almost certain that he could go the full nine months. Ultimately, he said, he would like to be married with a family and "have a regular life." I asked him if he would like to work in the ministry, and like all the others in the Lazarus category, he said he definitely would. At the moment, however, his energies were focused on overcoming a five-balloon-a-day heroin habit. He could not think much further than tomorrow or the next week.

Beyond the Lazarus Generation:
The First Second Generation

Another group of Alcance Victorians is distinct from the Lazarus Generation, for they have clear goals and time lines for achieving them. Most of these people I name the "First Second Generation" (FSG): they are the first group of Chicanos to be second-generation pentecostals, unlike many of the Lazarus Generation. All of them have pentecostal parents—they did not convert from Catholicism, as did the rest of the church—but their lives have followed two distinct patterns. Some in the FSG were involved in drugs and gang warfare; others were not. Of those who were not, many are pursuing an education and have ambitious career goals. Those formerly involved in gangs and drugs have career ambitions directly related to the church. A number of these folks are simply trying to make it in the intensity of turn-of-the-century Los Angeles while waiting to start their own Alcance Victoria church. Both types of FSG individuals seem keenly aware of the elasticity of social boundaries.

An example of a member of the group who is just getting by is an eighteen-year-old woman named Catalina. Both her mother and father were "saved" in the English-speaking Victory Outreach ministries, and Catalina was reared in the rehab homes that her parents directed. Catalina married a Victory Outreach minister, Brother Saul, who directed a home where they lived for nearly two years after their marriage. Like many in the FSG, although she was raised in the church, she marks the exact age of her conversion: "I was thirteen," Catalina reflects, "when I felt the Lord pulling at my heartstrings. I was partying and rebellious; I would run away and come back. I didn't want to surrender [to God]" (June 29, 1996, Boyle Heights). She remembers the critical moment when she hit bottom: "I got into a fistfight with my mom. My stepdad had fallen—he was using heroin again. But he's saved [again] now. After that, we just felt led to the Spanish ministry." Nearly every FSG member I interviewed had a story of religious devotional lapse that ended with a return and a stronger commitment to the church.

I asked Catalina about her views on women and men in the church. She said that she believes that if you don't count the fifty or so men who live in the homes, there are more women in the church than men. Most women who come are *solteras,* or free or single women who "come and refuge themselves in the Lord. A lot [of women] come here because they are lonely; some get married. My mom came with one kid, me, and had another one here after she was married again." The church has no official teaching on divorce and remarriage. Catalina believes that women and men share responsibility in working with people and spreading the Gospel. According to her, men take responsibility in ministry, and women help them; this conviction was echoed in the vast majority of my interviews with the Alcance Victoria women.

This is also the teaching expressed by the co-founder of Victory Outreach, Julie Arguinzoni. In "Preparing Women for the Vision 2000," a sermon she delivered and recorded on June 25, 1996, at a Victory Outreach women's retreat, Julie Arguinzoni told the women what they must do and what they could expect from ministry. She recounted that women approach her all the time and tell her that they "want ministry."

In response, she tells them that they don't really know what they want, because to be a woman in ministry, "you must suffer." (When Julie referred to "women in ministry," she meant women married to a pastor.) She explains that while in ministry will mean dressing "real pretty" and "sitting in the front of the church," women must also be prepared to do "whatever it takes" to help the ministry grow. But, overall, they must "love the Lord."

While waiting for "ministry," Catalina has been looking for a job that will pay her enough money to support herself and her husband, thus enabling him to devote himself to full-time work in the local church ministry and eventually become the pastor of an Alcance Victoria church, perhaps in Mexico. She related a story about a job in West Los Angeles, where she worked as a secretary in a copy shop until she quit because the manager was "verbally abusing" her. Apparently, he was calling her "stupid" and telling her that she was "good for nothing." In spite of this, she hastens to add that she is "smart" and "skilled," and has had many good jobs in the past; she nearly finished high school but ultimately "didn't make it." She expressed the desire for her children to "finish school."

I asked Catalina about her political views. She believed that abortion in all cases is murder, for even if a woman is raped, "sometimes God permits things for a purpose." She voiced support for affirmative action, claiming that "everyone deserves a chance." When asked about California's anti-immigration measures, her answer resounded with ambivalence. She hesitated for a long time before replying. She said that to be in the United States without "papers" (legal immigration documents or status) was "lying," but that it was "not really a sin." Still, living here without documents "will trouble you for a long time, because you are not right with the law." Ultimately, Catalina concluded, it was a matter of personal responsibility and moral choice—a matter of conscience. Her attitude was the same regarding individuals and families who receive welfare or other types of government assistance. She thought that what really mattered were the intentions and actions of the individual or family: "Some people are trying to better their lives by being here without papers or getting welfare, and that is a good thing. Other people are just messing up."

Catalina's thoughtful opinions were echoed in the narratives of other FSG members I interviewed, most of whom expressed ambivalence on issues of political commitment. However, there seemed to be uniform opposition to the anti-immigration and anti-affirmative action ballot initiatives.

Lulu, a thirty-year-old homemaker, volunteers several hours each week in the business office of Alcance Victoria. Born in Mexico, she came to the United States as a young girl and dropped out of school when she was fourteen to help at home with her family. Although her parents were pentecostal, she marks her own conversion to pentecostalism at age fifteen. While Sister Lulu was not involved in gangs, she explains that she was "looking for love," and found it in Jesus and the "love of God" located in the Alcance Victoria congregation. She shared with me a little about her experiences growing up in East Los Angeles and her very informed views on the California ballot initiatives concerning immigration:

> All my friends were either killed or overdosed on drugs. If it wasn't for Jesus I wouldn't be here right now! Fourteen of my friends from school have died! But

my family was different: we were the only pentecostals on our block, and we are the only ones left. The most important thing he [God] has done for me is the change, that love he gave to me. If I didn't have love I couldn't be going out to another person, a stranger, and telling them about God. The laws they want to pass against immigration are totally unfair. If a baby is born in the U.S., then that baby is an American, a citizen. That's the way it's always been. It shouldn't matter if the parents are Mexicans—that's racist! (April 30, 1994)

These views were echoed by Lupe, a twenty-one-year-old woman who moved to the United States from Mexico at age thirteen and joined Alcance Victoria soon thereafter. Her parents were pentecostal. Following high school graduation, she attended East Los Angeles City College and worked in a children's store for a year before marrying. I asked her what she believed was the most attractive or important element of Alcance Victoria. She said, "Love!" "What does love mean?" I asked. She replied:

Well, the love we share here is a very special kind of love. Anyone can love their family, but we show people, strangers, we love them the way they are! No matter if they are drug addicts, prostitutes, whatever—we accept them just like that. Sometimes we take them into our own homes. Now, that is the kind of love that attracted me to this church. (April 11, 1994, Boyle Heights, interview conducted in Spanish)

In response to my queries regarding the immigration laws, she was adamant: "I think that the new law they are proposing is wrong—that your baby born here won't be a citizen! I thought that this was supposed to be America! America is different from any other country—that's why we came here!" When asked about abortion, she paused thoughtfully to formulate her response: "Abortion is wrong because you are killing a baby, right? But you don't have the right to take another person's rights away."

Lupe delineated the Alcance Victoria teaching on women's and men's roles in church, claiming that "women can preach only amongst themselves to other women if there is a special reunion or something. Women can also be missionaries and evangelists. Women have come here to our church to preach to everyone. Women cannot become pastors, but all the pastors have wives."

Another FSG man, Noé, had similar responses. At the time of our interview, he was twenty-one years old. He was born in Guadalajara, Mexico, and has been in the United States since age five. He plays the trumpet in the church with his brothers and is part of Mariachi Genesis. He has never been involved in gangs or drugs. He graduated from high school, attended East Los Angeles City College for one semester, and worked delivering phone books around East Los Angeles until he was injured on the job in a car accident. At the time of our interview, he was settling this claim and looking for a job. His narrative typifies many of the FSG in its political outlook as well as in its focus on a faith crisis that was resolved in an epiphany resulting in a renewed and deeper commitment to the church:

I never really experienced the streets. But at one point a few years ago I just got real cold in the Lord. I was addicted to sports. That's all I wanted to do—watch sports on TV, play basketball, and read about sports. If you would ask me anything about sports I would know. I put that first before God. Sports is not a sin, but it shouldn't be your number one priority. For a Christian the number-one priority is God. I realize that now. (June 18, 1995, East Lost Angeles)

Noé has strong feelings about the Catholic church and the problems in East LA. He carefully distinguishes the Catholic religion from experiential religion and commitment, explaining that Alcance Victoria is not "religion"; instead it is "a relationship with God—this must be the most important thing in your life. The Catholics are a religion. They don't have the Holy Spirit, they have the Virgin [of Guadalupe] and saints—but no God. This [lack] is the biggest problem in East Los Angeles today: gangs, drugs, taggers [spray-paint graffiti artists], and violence." When I asked about justice or injustice for the undocumented, he observed, "One of the things people don't see, economically, is that people don't have the income to live in Boyle Heights; they live in poverty. Lots of people come here, but they don't have what it takes to make it here, so they live in poverty—lots of people living in poverty." Hence, Noé suggests that economic success is intimately related to justice in immigration.

I asked him what Alcance Victoria could do to work for economic justice and empowerment. His response was representative of the Victory Outreach philosophy on these issues: "There is not really a place for the church to confront poverty, except for in rehab homes," he explained. "We get blessed with God at church; the favor of God is there. You can't point out in our church a need. We offer something solid to help out the community; whatever we can do, we do it." Ministry, as Sonny Arguinzoni teaches, must always come before spending energies on social justice "causes:"

> It is not our job to propose legislation resolving immigration conflicts. The bigger and more visible a ministry becomes, the more people are going to come with their agendas. They will want you to get involved with this movement or that cause. It is not uncommon for people to want for us to join a worthwhile project, and then want us to promote it. Unless we are clear as to the vision of our church, the temptation may draw us off track. The enemy has a way of diverting us, getting us involved in so many things that we are unable to accomplish anything. James Chapter 1:8 tells us that the life of a man with divided loyalty will reveal instability in every turn. You simply ask, "What will this program do to help fulfill our vision?"[19]

In spite of Arguinzoni's official teaching, defined by a singular and uniform vision and purpose, Alcance Victorians do formulate individual opinions and support various causes. Individuals become masterfully adept at weaving social and political discourses into their own understandings of the Gospel and of the Alcance Victoria message. They arrive at a particular vision of the world that responds to their own crises and issues, yet this peculiar stance is based on their communion with a community of biblical interpretation.

Alcance Victoria has been nicknamed the "Junkie Church" because the majority of its constituents since the beginning had once been drug addicts. However, as Victory Outreach continues to grow in numbers and in fame, the church has simultaneously increased its respectability. Hence, it has found appeal among sections of Chicano youth previously untapped.

I interviewed a group of eight second-generation Americans, four women and four men, ranging in age from fifteen to twenty (June 5, 1996, Boyle Heights). Each interviewee had parents involved in born-again religion, and all had attended church regularly since they were children. Seven of the eight had "rebelled" briefly, experimenting with the "things of this world," before returning to the church with a deeper commitment. All participants were serious about their education, whether they were in high school, heading to college, or in a local state or community college. All in this group were single, and none had children. One sixteen-year-old woman had a straight-A record in her college prep courses, and because of this she had assumed the identity bestowed by her peers as someone heading for Harvard. "I'm going to apply there," she tells me when I ask if she is indeed Harvard bound. "We'll see what happens." Most in the group were introduced to the church through their parents, or they were invited by a family member or friend close to their own age. Interestingly, many of their parents had ceased regular church attendance themselves.

The men dominated the conversation, but the women expressed nonverbally their dissatisfaction with the men's manipulation of the interview. Three of the men took the opportunity to relate long, detailed narratives about their lives, while the women were very aware of the project as a group effort and kept their responses short. One twenty-year-old man, Cyrus, took the lead of the group. Cyrus is currently president of the student body at his California State University campus. He is emotionally torn between pursuing a career in public service or in ministry. At the time of our interview he was working in the offices of his local state assemblyman, who is also Mexican American.

I asked why they attended Alcance Victoria in particular; their answers varied, but all turned on matters of personal choice. Two of the women explained that they had been attending another Protestant church, but that it did not have the active youth programs they found in Alcance Victoria. The meaningful participation of the youth in the life of the congregation was the attraction for these women. Another woman had been attending an all-white Protestant church in Burbank where she did not feel entirely at home. At Alcance Victoria the music combined with the general enthusiasm put her at ease, reminding her of the church she had attended with her parents as a child, whereas in the Anglo church she felt isolated by the cold conservatism. Most members in this group were connected to each other through bonds of kinship, or in the case of the men, by "homeboy" bonds. They invited one another to church. One of the men, Ramón, spoke of the inspiration he finds in church:

> The thing that keeps me motivated in coming to church is that whenever I'm feeling down, or whenever I need help with whatever part of my life, with anything at school or here at church, my social life or my family, the thing that keeps me motivated is that I can bend my knees and just look up to heaven and ask God for that extra help and that extra push that I need in my life, and that just keeps me motivated and keeps me going on. So I think God for that.

Another twenty-year-old man, Eddie, echoed Ramón's testimony, claiming that the key to understanding God and having a rewarding life is obedience to church doctrine. He contended that God must be the priority in one's life, and all other goals will follow. His aphorism was greeted with cheerful agreement: "If you just listen to his word and everything, make God first, everything will go all right."

The youngest woman, Flora, fifteen years old, said that she liked Alcance Victoria because all her cousins attended, and there were many teenagers in the congregation. Gabby, age sixteen, claimed that she too came to Alcance Victoria because her cousins were there, and because she found what she "needed" in Alcance Victoria. Like the others, she then broke into a rehearsed testimony: "That emptiness. I don't have it anymore. I don't need anything because here I found what I needed. I know that God will supply the things that I need. Because he is there for us, to do for us."

I asked them to compare themselves to their parents. The women said that they differ from their mothers because their mothers are "traditional" homemakers. The men said that they differ from their fathers because their fathers work in factories. All agreed that the critical difference is that they now have the opportunity to get an education and "to have a better life" that their parents were denied, as Cyrus and others explained. They recognized that their parents' lives were much harder than their own. When asked what they imagine themselves to be doing in ten years, none identified the ministry as an option. All said they wanted to finish their education. One wanted to become a sociologist, another a doctor, another a teacher, another a child psychologist, and another a police officer. All claimed that they "of course" wanted to be doing "big things for God" and to have families.

All members of this group identified themselves as Chicano or Chicana, with clear and forceful conviction. However, they were conflicted about political issues. All hesitated to express favor for either the Democratic or Republican parties, but claimed instead to vote on particular issues and identified themselves as nonpartisan. Cyrus confessed that he was a registered Democrat, although some of his "moral values are with Republicans." All supported affirmative-action programs and felt that anti-immigration laws were racist and ungodly. They claimed that the laws were "unjust" because they discriminated against Mexicans. Cyrus expressed the views of the group when he attempted to navigate through the complexity of social and political issues: "I'm antiwar but the Republicans are prowar; I'm anti-abortion but the Democrats are pro-abortion." All members of this group were against abortion and all, led by Cyrus, claimed that the Bible provides the definitive template for gender relations—women are to be subordinate to men in the home and in ministry. The women led the response in affirming equal political rights for women, but all agreed that men should be the leaders in church; for that, they claimed with certainty, is what the Bible teaches.

Lapsed Catholics

Finally, I identified a group I describe simply as "lapsed Catholics." Many of the members of the church had not maintained strong ties to Catholicism before conversion and started attending Alcance Victoria because they were actively pursued. The people in this category were not battling drug problems or involved with gangs. They were simply widows and widowers, mostly older, or families with children who had immigrated recently. They tend to be drawn by the dynamic social life Alcance Victoria offers, and many take a while to learn a distrust for Catholicism. In their view, Pentecostalism and Catholicism are both Christianity. Señora Carmela, a fifty-one-year-old unemployed widow, has been a member of Alcance Victoria since coming to the United States from Mexico seven years ago. She serves as an usher, showing people to their seats, collecting the offerings, and preventing people from entering the sanctuary during prayer. She explained her "testimony" as follows: "I've never had any real vices. I maintain myself there in my house—I live close by here. Between my house and my church, that's all I do. And occasionally I go to the store, but that's all, really. I came to Alcance Victoria because they invited me" (May 16, 1994, Boyle Heights, interview conducted in Spanish). Another woman, Modesta, in her thirties, an immigrant from Mexico and mother of four, summarized the feelings of most of the parents by voicing a troubled concern for her children: "There are so many gangs around here. And Alcance Victoria is really doing something to help stop the violence" (June 6, 1996, Boyle Heights, interview conducted in Spanish).

Most of the "lapsed Catholics" came to Alcance Victoria because they enjoyed the company of others, the feeling of belonging, the music, the message of security and control over life—at least symbolically. In the congregation they find emotional security, friendship, and intimacy. For immigrants and Mexican Americans who lack social skills, the congregation functions as a mechanism of cultural brokerage. Symbolically and physically secluded from so many other centers in Los Angeles, they find in Alcance Victoria vibrant fellowship where they remake self, community, and the nation.

In an utterly pragmatic and pithy statement, Pastor Chuy powerfully explained the reason for the success of their church: "Alcance Victoria is successful because we are meeting the needs of the people!"

Recasting the American Dream through Religious Performance

"Meeting the needs of the people" is no easy task, especially given the diversity of interests and multiple foci of the members. Pragmatism is the pivot on which each judgment turns. This pragmatic turn is most evident in the teaching regarding immigration. Many in the congregation are undocumented workers. The condition of being in the United States without legal sanction is, in effect, living a lie. Pastor Chuy overlooks this fact, and will pray for the successful illegal border crossings of his congregants and their families when asked. He explains that this issue is a matter of personal conscience.

Central to this pragmatic course of meeting needs is endowing each participant with a sense of individual election, calling, and an "inner-worldly asceticism." At the same time each believer is imparted with a sense for the importance of and membership in the collective representation, where success does not exist outside of the collective ability to imagine and represent it, to legitimate and authorize it. Thus, understanding the religious drive of Alcance Victoria pentecostalism requires a mapping of the paradoxical space constituted at the intersection between the imperatives of the collective representation and the demand for individual achievement: between Mexico and the United States—especially between the collective drama and tragedy of Mexican Catholicism and the American Protestant myth of prosperity and success, with its individual orientation and enshrinement of personal responsibility. The borderland provides the cultural stage on which these dynamics are effectively performed.

Victory Outreach is known throughout California for its elaborate stage plays that dramatize the Chicano gang lifestyle and ultimately end with the protagonist's conversion to born-again Christianity through the efforts of Victory Outreach evangelism. These plays are in English, normally portraying a Mexican American experience as opposed to an immigrant's narrative. They are performed at churches, schools, and other meeting halls. Recently, however, the Spanish churches have produced their own play, *Sueño Americano* (American Dream), which represents an immigrant experience. Written and produced by an Alcance Victoria congregation, the play, at once social critique and soteriology, is a native, organic dramatization of the Alcance Victoria congregational narrative. It tells the story of one Mexican Catholic family—a mother, father, and three small children—who immigrate (illegally) to Los Angeles. Their "American dream" is for the children to have a better life in the United States.

The theme song, originally in English, is called "Just a Dream," and its chorus expresses in lyrical melody the message of the play: "Just a dream, just a dream, all our hopes and all our schemes." That is, the social aspirations of Mexican immigrants into the United States are "just a dream," nothing else. Before the family leaves Mexico, a close friend, a *compadre,* pleads for them not to go to Los Angeles, for there, he claims, they will find only "perdition." While being ejected from their home for preaching the evangelical Gospel, the *compadre* exhorts the father to remember in time of trouble that Christ loves him and that Christ is the answer to all his problems. The rest of the story is predictable. In Los Angeles the father becomes an alcoholic, and the children end up in gangs. Ultimately, the family converts to pentecostalism through the efforts of an evangelizer who tells them that even though all their dreams were lost on the streets, Jesus Christ can give them new dreams. The evangelizer tells the audience that they may have come to the United States with dreams that have not come true, yet Jesus Christ can make all of their dreams come true: Christ can give them hope and change them.

The play may hold the key to unlocking the mystery of one aspect of Latino born-again conversion. In the play, evangelical salvation is presented as a panacea, an antidote to social ills. Through evangelical conversion, one can be changed and then rechannel frustrated energies in constructive directions. In his journalistic writing on Victory Outreach, Richard Rodriguez has emphasized the importance of this sudden and dramatic change. "To immigrants who came to the American city expecting new beginnings, and who found instead the city corrupt," he writes, "the evangelical missionary offers the possibility of refreshment, of cleansing. To the children of immigrants, trapped by inherited failures, the evangelical offers the assurance of power over life. The promise of the quick change."[20] This notion of change was stressed by the majority of people interviewed for this study. Key to the experience of pentecostalism, metanoia is the initiatory event that registers membership in a powerful community of God.

Alcance Victoria is continually being reinvented, situationally, in response to particular contexts; this is possible because of the group's approach to Scripture. While based in a literalist reading of the Bible, pentecostal theology is malleable enough so that doctrine can be pragmatically molded to fit the needs of very different constituencies. Thus pentecostalism, in effect, has something for just about everyone. So what does it offer to Alcance Victorians? How do these people change?

Pentecostalism has been described as the *Vision of the Disinherited*.[21] Alcance Victorians are disinherited in particular ways. As immigrants, as people with great ambition who moved thousands of miles and jumped many hurdles in the hopes of improving their lives, many found instead the corruption, racism, structural inequality, and xenophobia that plagues much of contemporary Los Angeles.

But what about the individuals who are part of the FSG and the "lapsed Catholics" who are not suffering in the same way as the Lazarus Generation? Perhaps the key to understanding the attraction of pentecostalism to all of these groups is in understanding their belief and practice. Catholics who convert to pentecostalism are not asked to discard Christian theology outright. Rather, they are expected to refuse *mediation* of the sacraments from priests; to discard, in a sense, the priesthood, or "religious specialists." Rejection of sacramental mediation allows pentecostalists to become agents in their salvation and more. To eschew the religious specialists enables the group to authorize by consensus the terms and symbols of the religious life. These are decided upon collectively; Scriptures are interpreted through mystical experiences with the congregation working together as a cohesive unit. Like true Protestants, however, each religious agent must be authorized individually, and success and election are proven through the "bearing [of] religious fruit," and, implicitly, through economic achievement.

To "bear fruit," men become active in the ministry. In contrast to Catholicism, Alcance Victoria allows married men without education to have active and rewarding careers in ministry. In the congregation men discover their entrepreneurial potential.[22] Through ministerial work in the congregation, they can improve their lot in life and live comfortably. The congregation expects their ministers to live well, because ministers symbolize the aspirations of the group. A man can come to church, marry the woman he has dreamed about, become active in ministry, and move up through the Alcance Victoria/Victory Outreach chain of command. Like Sonny Arguinzoni himself, many of his staff drive BMWs—symbols of prosperity. Thus, included in the gospel of rescue and salvation are narratives of prosperity and well-being. For immigrants with broken dreams, these promises are made to willing listeners.

For the FSG, the message of prosperity is one of possibility. Undergirded by the Alcance Victoria message of power, those in the FSG are enabled to achieve the things in life they have come to desire, so that going to Harvard or holding public office is possible, following from the simple premise that "all things are possible with God." This message for many of the FSG is also one of prevention and maintenance. As Eddie indicated, "If you just listen to his word and everything, make God first, everything will go all right." These bright, ambitious young women and men have much at stake, and they do not want to lose it. They look to God not as an antidote for failed social dreams, and to the congregation not as a way to redirect failed ambitions, but to both as vehicles for fulfilling their dreams—things that remain unimaginable to many of their Chicano peers.

The Alcance Victorians whom I refer to as "lapsed Catholics" come with their own needs and hopes of salvation. The Catholic church, for whatever reason, was simply not able to hold their attention and loyalty, and Alcance Victoria does. This may in part be so because Alcance Victoria is in a sense a total institution that captivates the interests and desires of its membership, keeping them busy and making them feel part of a global movement. This American Protestant voluntarism is nothing new; it has defined American religion since the beginning of the republic. However, Alcance Victoria also offers dignity to each believer. Through Alcance Victoria, those without much economic success, the disinherited, become instated in the American myth: their lives matter; they are special, chosen, given a divine commission direct from God himself. By stressing individual election and achievement, the discursive and ritual community of Alcance Victoria confers self-worth, ultimate meaning, purpose, and a way to make sense of a harsh world.

Additionally, Alcance Victoria does not ask believers to eschew their ethnic heritage. Rather, it spins its message in such a way that it becomes blended with the thinly veiled Protestant symbolism that permeates the American consciousness and ethos. In this sense, Alcance Victoria is a border phenomenon, one that combines Mexican, American, and Christian evangelical archetypes and mythologies into a fresh identity, one that can support such seeming contradictions as pentecostal mariachis.

All of these observations suggest, then, that by taking control of the religious field, by becoming the religious specialists themselves, Alcance Victorians have tapped a new mechanism of empowerment. (The control that the hierarchy within Alcance Victoria exerts over the laity remains to be studied.) I am willing to conclude that insofar as Alcance Victorians are able to achieve the things they desire, through religious discourse and practice — performance — Alcance Victoria is an empowering phenomenon. However, the choices of many of these folks have been so deeply determined by their social conditions that the ability to imagine choices is itself limited. That is, years of oppression have limited not only choices but the ability to choose. Alcance Victoria enables people to work happily and productively within their social limitations, but its members for the most part are not unlimited bourgeois subjects endowed with privilege and the ability to make rational choices. Rather, most are people who pick and choose from within their social limitations; and the choices available to them are often exploitative and degrading. The exception would be those in the FSG who can imagine beyond common boundaries.

This research does not suggest, however, that Alcance Victoria members have been duped into becoming passive citizens and thus more productive workers. Undoubtedly, pentecostalism helps them to deal with overwhelming circumstances immediately, sensually, and experientially. There is also no question that Alcance Victoria quiets potential uprisings and social protest. Still, if there is resistance and protest in Alcance Victoria, they lie in the cultivation of ecstasy and in the critique of American society. These aspects of Alcance Victoria, along with others, warrant further exploration.

The roles of women, gender dynamics, and the construction of masculinity in Victory Outreach/Alcance Victoria are areas of research that need to be pursued further. My access to the intricacies of the Alcance Victoria women's world was limited by my male gender; I was not privy to intimate conversation and was unable to spend much time alone with the women. This limitation notwithstanding, my sense from this research is that in Alcance Victoria women attain status as authorized religious/social agents by means of a personal and intensely symbolic relationship to God. Some women use this authority to challenge social and cultural arrangements that confer status and privilege to men, claiming status and privilege for themselves in ways that are often subtle and concealed from public view. Others reiterate narratives of women's submission to God and men. In either case, women here are afforded the space to create their own symbolic worlds, and to live in them in ways authorized by someone even more authoritative than their husbands, fathers, brothers, and ministers: God. What is done with this newly discovered authority varies from case to case.

Still more, the relationship between the local congregation and the Victory Outreach headquarters in La Puente is a topic that deserves further research. Sonny Arguinzoni operates a program called "United We Can," which asks members to donate $1 a day to support Victory Outreach global ministries. In spite of the wide support that Arguinzoni enjoys, only a handful of Alcance Victorians pay membership dues—it is nowhere near the 20 percent of the congregation that the headquarters in La Puente would like, and probably under 5 percent. A study of Sonny Arguinzoni himself would make an interesting report. It will also be interesting to watch the emergence of a new class of religious specialists. What type of congregational control will operate as the hierarchy becomes even more elaborate, powerful, and distinct from the laity? A chart of the lives of individual believers, determining how many remain in the congregation and how many fall back into their old ways or move into another religion, would also be valuable. Recidivism is a problem that characterizes "revolving-door" pentecostalism and is yet to be mapped.

By way of conclusion, I want to repeat that in Alcance Victoria there is hegemony as well as liberation: it is not a question of domination *or* empowerment but rather *modes* of domination *and modes* of empowerment. These two binaries should be seen as markers, as ends of a continuum on which the Alcance Victorians fluctuate. Overall, Alcance Victoria provides a fresh and expansive locus from which to invent an evolving Chicano cultural form. It is the continual reinvention of Mexican American identity by drawing from a number of symbolic reserves that defines the borderlands thesis. Vicki L. Ruiz has described this process of creation as "cultural coalescence":

> There is not a single hermetic Mexican or Mexican-American culture, but rather permeable cultures rooted in generation, gender, region, class, and personal experience. Immigrants and their children pick, borrow, retain, and create distinctive cultural forms. People navigate across cultural boundaries as well as make conscious decisions in the production of culture.[23]

The discourse of Alcance Victoria functions most cogently in the arena of the production and reproduction of consciousness; that is, in the active construction of social expectations and the socialization of desire. "But, bear in mind," cautions Ruiz, "people of color have not had unlimited choice. Racism, sexism, imperialism, persecution, and social, political, and economic segmentation have constrained aspirations, expectations, and decision making."[24]

For some, the discourse of divine election and rebirth functioning within a community of believers places within reach possibilities that were at one time unimaginable. For others, biblical narratives contract worlds and expectations—including gender roles—and thus limit social intercourse and achievement: symbolic and social boundaries can be narrowed in Alcance Victoria. There is diversity among believers and thus in the congregational narrative.

In this study I have sought to demonstrate the great variety that exists among pentecostal believers. Perhaps the need to respect difference among pentecostals was impressed upon my consciousness because of my own experience growing up in my father's small Spanish pentecostal church in East Oakland, a very traditional church comprised mostly of families who had not been in trouble with drugs or the law. The spectrum of Latino pentecostal churches ranges from traditional and stoic to the emotional rescue ministry of Victory Outreach. For this reason, it was important for me and for the New Ethnic and Immigrant Congregations Project to attach human faces to an otherwise faceless academic discourse on Latino pentecostalism.

Alcance Victoria is a *place* filled with extraordinary people, most of whom have been dealt a bad hand in life but remain happy and optimistic in spite of it. Pentecostal practice equips them with the discursive, ritual, and other symbolic tools to negotiate deftly the precarious social terrain of postmodern Los Angeles. When I entered their lives four years ago, I did so with a bit of fear and trembling, for it was a return, in a sense, to my own cultural memory. To my great fortune, they welcomed me with open arms. Very few of them understood exactly what I was doing there, but still they trusted me and cooperated fully. They made me a part of their family. Without doubt, I learned as much from them as I did about them, and in this, I am enriched.

Notes

1. Allan Figueroa Deck, "The Challenge of Evangelical/Pentecostal Christianity to Hispanic Catholicism, in *Hispanic Catholic Culture in the U.S.,* edited by Jay Dolan and Allan Figueroa Deck (Notre Dame, Ind.: University of Notre Dame Press, 1994), 409–39; Luis León, "Somos un Cuerpo en Cristo: Notes on Power and the Body in an East Los Angeles Chicano/Mexicano Pentecostal Community," *Latino Studies Journal* 5 (September 1994): 60–86; David Stoll, *Is Latin America Turning Protestant? The Politics of Evangelical Growth* (Berkeley: University of California Press, 1990); David Stoll and Virginia Garrard-Burnett, eds., *Rethinking Protestantism in Latin America* (Philadelphia: Temple University Press, 1993); Robert Suro, "Switch by Hispanic Catholics Changes Face of U.S. Religion," *New York Times,* May 14, 1989, pp. 1, 22.

2. Stoll and Garrard-Burnett, eds., *Rethinking Protestantism,* 2.

3. Stoll, *Is Latin America Turning Protestant?*

4. Ibid., 310.

5. I use the term "Chicano" descriptively and interchangeably with "Mexican American" to refer to people of Mexican descent living permanently in the United States, whether born in the United States or in Mexico. Most of those in this study either refer to themselves as Chicano, or do not object to being referred to as such. While I recognize the problems inherent in this descriptive definition, I find these problems the least objectionable among the array of problems other descriptive terms of Mexican Americans engender. I use the term "Latino" to designate people of Latin American heritage, including but not limited to Mexican Americans.

6. Deck, "Challenge of Evangelical/Pentecostal Christianity," in *Hispanic Catholic Culture,* edited by Dolan and Deck.

7. Gaston Espinosa, *"Borderland Religion: The Origins of Latino Pentecostalism"* (Ph.D. dissertation,

Department of History, University of California, Santa Barbara, forthcoming); Stoll and Garrard-Burnett, *Rethinking Protestantism.*

8. Robert Mapes Anderson, *Vision of the Disinherited* (New York: Oxford University Press, 1979); Lalive D'Epinay, *Haven of the Masses* (London: Lutterworth Press, 1969).

9. Anderson, *Vision of the Disinherited,* 8.

10. David Martin, *Tongues of Fire: The Explosion of Protestantism in Latin America* (Oxford: Basil Blackwell, 1990).

11. Elizabeth E. Brusco, *The Reformation of Machismo: Evangelical Conversion and Gender in Colombia* (Austin: University of Texas Press, 1995); Bernice Martin, "New Mutations of the Protestant Ethic Among Latin American Pentecostals," *Religion* 25 (1995): 101–17.

12. The population of Boyle Heights is estimated at 89,000. Unless otherwise noted, interviews were conducted in English. Where the note "interview conducted in Spanish" appears, the translation from English to Spanish is my own.

13. Sonny Arguinzoni and Julie Arguinzoni, *Treasures Out of Darkness* (Green Forest, Ark.: New Leaf Press, 1991); Sonny Arguinzoni, *Internalizing the Vision* (La Puente, Calif.: Victory Outreach Publications, 1995).

14. León, "Somos un Cuerpo en Cristo," 79.

15. For a discussion of female religious symbols and the ways they have circumscribed Mexican and Chicana female roles, see Normal Alarcon, "Traddutora, Traditora: A Paradigmatic Figure of Chicana Feminism," *Cultural Critique* 13 (Fall 1989): 57–87.

16. Many fundamentalists and pentecostals base this teaching on the Christian Scriptures, especially the passage found in 2 Corinthians 6:17. Donald W. Dayton, *The Theological Roots of Pentecostalism* (Metuchen, N.J.: Scarecrow, 1987).

17. Harvey Cox, *Fire from Heaven: The Rise of Pentecostal Spirituality and the Reshaping of American Religion in the Twenty-First Century* (Boston: Addison, 1995).

18. This is a strategy Victory Outreach borrowed from Dr. David Yonggi Cho, whose 800,000-member Korean pentecostal congregation is said to be the largest in the world. Cox, *Fire from Heaven.*

19. Arguinzoni, *Internalizing the Vision,* 140.

20. Richard Rodriguez, "Evangelicos: Changes of Habit, Changes of Heart: The Crusade for the Soul of the Mission," *Image Magazine,* October 26, 1986.

21. Anderson, *Vision of the Disinherited.*

22. R. Stephen Warner, "Work in Progress Toward a New Paradigm for the Sociological Study of Religion in the United States," *American Journal of Sociology* 98 (March 1993): 1044–93.

23. L. Vicki Ruiz, "'It's the People Who Drive the Book': A View from the West," *American Quarterly* 45 (June 1993): 246.

24. Ibid.

22

From Ellis Island to JFK

Transnational Ties

NANCY FONER

The conception of citizenship itself is rapidly changing and we may have
to recognize a sort of world or international citizenship as more logical
than the present peripatetic kind, which makes a man an American while
here, and an Italian while in Italy. International conferences are not so rare
nowadays. Health, the apprehension or exclusion of criminals, financial
standards, postage, telegraphs and shipping are today to a great extent,
regulated by international action. . . . The old barriers are everywhere
breaking down. We may even bring ourselves to the point of recognizing
foreign "colonies" in our midst, on our own soil, as entitled to partake in the
parliamentary life of their mother country.

—Gino Speranza

S ound familiar? This reflection on the globalizing world and the possibility of electoral representation for Italians abroad describes issues that immigration scholars are debating and discussing today. The words were written, however, in 1906
by the secretary of the Society of the Protection of Italian Immigrants.[1] They are a powerful reminder that processes that scholars now call transnational have a long history.
Contemporary immigrant New Yorkers are not the first newcomers to live transnational
lives. Although immigrants' transnational connections and communities today reflect
many new dynamics, there are also significant continuities with the past.

The term transnationalism, as developed in the work of Linda Basch and her colleagues, refers to processes by which immigrants "forge and sustain multi-stranded social
relations that link together their societies of origin and settlement. . . . An essential element . . . is the multiplicity of involvements that transmigrants sustain in both home and
host societies." It's not just a question of political ties that span borders of the kind that
Gino Speranza had in mind. In a transnational perspective, contemporary immigrants
are seen as maintaining familial, economic, cultural, and political ties across international borders, in effect making the home and host society a single arena of social action.[2]

Migrants may be living in New York, but, at the same time, they maintain strong involvements in their societies of origin, which, tellingly, they continue to call home.

In much of what is written on the subject, transnationalism is treated as if it were a new invention; a common assumption is that earlier European immigration cannot be described in transnational terms that apply today. Perhaps, as Nina Glick Schiller notes, the excitement over the "first flurry of discovery of the transnational aspects of contemporary migration" led to a "tendency to declare . . . transnational migration . . . a completely new phenomenon."[3] A few years earlier, she and her colleagues argued that transnationalism was a new type of migrant experience—that a new conceptualization, indeed a new term, transmigrant, was needed to understand the immigrants of today.[4] Recently, Alejandro Portes has argued that present-day transnational communities— dense networks across political borders created by immigrants in their quest for economic advancement and social recognition—possess a distinctive character that justifies coining a new concept to refer to them.[5]

Of course, there have been hints in the literature that modern-day transnationalism is not altogether new—suggestions, for example, that it differs in "range and depth" or "density and significance" from patterns in earlier eras.[6] A recent essay by Glick Schiller marks an important step forward by beginning to systematically compare current transnational migration to the United States with past patterns.[7] Following this lead, Luis Guarnizo analyzes differences in the meanings, implications, and effects of transnational political practices among contemporary and turn-of-the-century immigrants.[8] Historians, too, have been jumping on the transnationalism bandwagon, pointing out that they've been writing about transnational practices and processes all along—they just haven't used the term.[9]

In this chapter I take a closer look at what's really new about transnationalism through an analysis of New York's immigrants in two eras. What emerges is that many transnational patterns often said to be new have been around for a long time—and some of the sources of transnationalism seen as unique today also operated in the past. At the same time, there is no denying that much is distinctive about transnationalism today, not only because earlier patterns have been intensified or become more common but also because new processes and dynamics are involved.

Continuities between Past and Present

Like contemporary immigrants, Russian Jews and Italians in turn-of-the-century New York established and sustained familial, economic, political, and cultural links to their home societies at the same time as they developed ties and connections in their new land. They did so for many of the same reasons that have been advanced to explain transnationalism today. There were relatives left behind and ties of sentiment to home communities and countries. Many immigrants came to America with the notion that they would eventually return. If, as one anthropologist notes, labor-exporting nations now acknowledge that "members of their diaspora communities are resources that should not and need not be lost to the home country," this was also true of the Italian government in the past.[10] Moreover, lack of economic security and full acceptance in America also plagued the earlier immigrants and may have fostered their continued involvement in and allegiance to their home societies. Of the two groups, Italians best fit the ideal transmigrant described in the contemporary literature; many led the kind of dual lives said to characterize transmigrants today.

Russian Jews and Italian immigrants in New York's past, like their modern-day counterparts, continued to be engaged with those they left behind. What social scientists now call "transnational households," with members scattered across borders, were not uncommon a century ago. Most Italian men—from 1870 to 1910 nearly 80 percent of Italian immigrants to the United States were men—left behind wives, children, and parents; Jewish men, too, were often pioneers who later sent money to pay for the passage of other family members. Those who came to New York sent letters to relatives and friends in the Old World—and significant amounts of money. Jake, the young Jewish immigrant in Abraham Cahan's story *Yekl,* was following a common pattern when he regularly sent money to his wife in Russia. Whenever he got a letter from his wife, Jake would hold onto his reply "until he had spare United States money enough to convert to ten rubles, and then he would betake himself to the draft office and have the amount, together with the well-crumpled epistle, forwarded to Poveodye." The New York Post Office sent 12.3 million individual money orders to foreign lands in 1900–1906, half the dollar amount going to Italy, Hungary, and Slavic countries.[11] Gino Speranza claimed that "it was quite probably that 'Little Italy' in New York contributes more to the tax roll of Italy than some of the poorer provinces in Sicily or Calabria."[12]

There were organized kinds of aid, too. Between 1914 and 1924, New York's Jewish *landsmanshaftn,* or home town associations, sent millions of dollars to their war-ravaged home communities. The societies' traditional activities—concerts, balls, banquets, regular meetings, and Sabbath services—all became occasions for raising money. Special mass meetings were held as well. In one week in December 1914 more than twenty rallies took place in New York, raising between seventy-five and fifteen hundred dollars each for the war victims of various towns. After the war, many Jewish immigrant associations sent delegates who actually delivered the money. A writer in one Yiddish daily wrote: "The 'delegate' has become, so to speak, an institution in the Jewish community. There is not a single *landsmanshaft* here in America . . . which has not sent, is not sending, or will not send a delegate with money and letters to the *landslayt* on the other side of the ocean."[13]

Putting away money in New York to buy land or houses in the home country is another long-term habit among immigrants who intend to return. In the last great wave, Italian immigrants were most likely to invest in projects back home. "He who crosses the ocean can buy a house," was a popular refrain celebrating one goal of emigration.[14] An inspector for the port of New York quizzed fifteen entering Italians who had previously been to the United States. "When I asked them what they did with the money they carried over, I think about two-thirds told me that had bought a little place in Italy, a little house and a plot of ground; that they had paid a certain sum; that there was a mortgage on it; that they were returning to this country for the purpose of making enough money to pay that mortgage off." It was not unusual for Italians in New York to send funds home with instructions about land purchases. An Italian told of his five years of back-breaking construction work in New York. Each day, he recalled, "I dreamed of the land I would one day buy with my savings. Land anywhere else has no value to me."[15]

Many did more than just dream of going back—they actually returned. Nationwide, return migration rates are actually lower now than they were in the past. In the first two decades of the century, for every one hundred immigrants entering the United States, thirty-six left; between 1971 and 1990, the number had fallen to twenty-three.[16] Return migration, as Glick Schiller observes, should be viewed as part of a broader pattern of transnational connection. Those who have come to America with the notion of going back truly have their "feet in two societies." Organizing a return, Glick Schiller argues, necessitates the maintenance of home ties and entails a continuing commitment to the norms, values, and aspirations of the home society.[17]

Russian Jews in turn-of-the-century New York were unusual for their time in the degree to which they were permanent settlers. Having fled political repression and virulent anti-Semitism, the vast majority came to the New World to stay. Even so there was more return migration than is generally assumed. Between 1880 and 1900, perhaps as many as 15 to 20 percent who came to the United States returned to Europe.[18]

Many Russian Jewish migrants planned to return only temporarily in order to visit their home towns, although "not a few turned out to be one-way visits." Some had aged relatives whom they longed to see; others sought brides, young Jewish women being in short supply in America; still others went home merely to show off, to demonstrate that they had somehow made good; and in a few cases immigrants returned home to study. Some Russian Jews went back, savings in hand, to found businesses. Sarna tells us that a few "enterprising immigrants employed their knowledge of English and Russian to engage in commerce. In 1903, according to Alexander Hume Ford, there was 'a Russian American Hebrew in each of the large Manchurian cities securing in Russia the cream of the contracts for American material used in Manchuria.'" Russian statistics indicate that 12,313 more U.S. citizens entered Russian territory from 1881 to 1914 than left. According to American government investigators, "Plenty of Jews living in Russia held United States passports, the most famous being Cantor Pinchas Minkowsky of Odessa, formerly of New York."[19]

After 1900, however, events in Russia led immigrants in New York to abandon the notion of return. With revolutionary upheaval and the increasing intensity of pogroms, the rate of return migration among Russian Jews fell off to about 5 percent.[20] In the post-1900 period there were also few repeat crossers. Of the Jews who entered the United Stated between 1899 and 1910, only 2 percent had been in the country before, the lowest rate of any immigrant group in the United States in this period.[21]

Many more Italians arrived with the expectation of returning home. They were the quintessential transnational New Yorkers of their time, as much commuters as many contemporary immigrants. Many were "birds of passage" who went back to their villages seasonally or after a few years in America. Italians called the United States "the workshop"; many arrived in March, April, and May and returned in October, November, and December, when layoffs were most numerous.[22] For many Italian men, navigating freely between their villages and America became a way of life.[23] They flitted "back and forth," writes Mark Wyman, "always trying to get enough for that additional plot, to pay off previous purchases, or to remove the load of debt from their backs." By the end of the nineteenth century, steamships were bigger, faster, and safer than before; tickets for the sixteen- or seventeen-day passage in steerage from Naples to New York cost fifteen dollars in 1880 and twenty-five in 1907 and could be paid for in installments.[24] Prefiguring terms used today, one early twentieth-century observer of Italian migration wrote of how improved methods of transportation were leading to the "annihilation of time and space."[25] Overall, between the 1880s and World War I, of every ten Italians who left for the United States, five returned. Many of these returnees—*ritornati,* as the Italians called them—remigrated to the United States. According to reports of the United States Immigration Commission, about 15 percent of Italian immigrants between 1899 and 1910 had been in the United States before.[26]

If economic insecurity, both at home and abroad, now leads many migrants to hedge their bets by participating in two economies, it was also a factor motivating Italians to travel back and forth across the Atlantic. The work Italian men found in New York's docks and construction sites was physically strenuous and often dangerous: the pay was low and the hours long; and the seasonal nature of the building trades meant that laborers had many weeks without any work. During economic downturns, work was scarcer, and, not surprisingly, Italian rates of return went up during the financial depression of 1894 and the panic years of 1904 and 1907.[27] Many Jews in the late nineteenth century, according to Jonathan Sarna, returned to Russia because they could not find decent work in America—owing to "the boom-bust cycle, the miserable working conditions, the loneliness, the insecurity."[28] Fannie Shapiro remembers crying when her father returned from a three-month stay in America, since she had wanted to join him. (She later emigrated on her own in 1906.) In Russia, she explained, her father "put people to work . . . [because] he was the boss," but in New York "they put him in a coal cellar."[29]

Lack of acceptance in America then, as now, probably contributed to a desire to return. Certainly, it fostered a continued identification with the home country, or, in the case of Jews, a sense of belonging to a large, diaspora population. Because most current immigrants are people of color, it is argued that modern-day racism is an important underpinning of transnationalism; nonwhite immigrants, denied full acceptance in America, maintain and build ties to their communities of origin to have a place they can call home.[30] Unfortunately, rejection of immigrants on the grounds of race has a long history, and, in the days before "white ethnics," Jews and Italians were thought to be racially distinct from—and inferior to—people with origins in northern and western Europe.

Whether because they felt marginalized and insecure in America or maintained ethnic allegiances for other reasons, Italians and Jews then, like many immigrants today, avidly followed news of and remained actively involved in home-country politics. As Matthew Jacobson puts it in his study of the "diasporic imagination" of Irish, Polish, and Jewish immigrants, the homelands did not lose their centrality in "migrants' ideological geographies." Life in the diaspora, he writes, remained in many ways oriented to the politics of the old center. Although the immigrant press was a force for Americanization, equally striking, says Jacobson, "is the tenacity with which many of these journals positioned their readers within the envisaged 'nation' and its worldwide diaspora. . . . In its front-page devotion to Old World news, in its focus upon the ethnic enclave as the locus of U.S. news, in its regular features on the groups' history and literature, in its ethnocentric frame on American affairs, the immigrant journal located the reader in an ideological universe whose very center was Poland, Ireland, or Zion."[31] Continued connections to the homeland influenced immigrants' political orientations and involvements in other ways. According to Michael Topp, the ideas, activities, and strategies of Italian American radicals in the years just before and just after World War I were shaped, at least in part, by communications with unionists and other activists in Italy, their reactions to events in Italy, and their physical movement back and forth between countries.[32]

New York immigrants have also long been tapped by home-country politicians and political parties as a source of financial support. Today, Caribbean politicians regularly come to New York to campaign and raise money; earlier in the century, Irish nationalist politicians made similar pilgrimages to the city. Irish immigrants, who arrived in large numbers in the mid-1800s, were deeply involved in the Irish nationalist cause in the early decades of the twentieth century. In 1918, the Friends of Irish Freedom sponsored a rally in Madison Square Garden attended by fifteen thousand people, and street orators for Irish freedom spoke "every night of the week" in Irish neighborhoods around the city. In 1920, Eamon de Valera traveled to New York seeking support for Sinn Fein and an independent Irish Republic, raising $10 million for his cause.[33]

Moreover, home governments were involved with their citizens abroad. The enormous exodus to America and return wave brought a reaction from the Italian government, which, like many states that send immigrants today, was concerned about the treatment of its dispersed populations—and also saw them as a global resource.[34] The Italian government gave subsidies to a number of organizations in America that offered social services to Italian immigrants and set up an emigration office on Ellis Island to provide the newly arrived with information on employment opportunities in the United States. The current of remigration, an Italian senator said in 1910, "represents an economic force of the first order for us. It will be an enormous benefit for us if we can increase this flow of force in and out of our country." In 1901, the Italian government passed a law empowering the Banco di Napoli to open branches or deputize intermediaries overseas to receive emigrant savings that could be used for Italian development. Beyond wanting to ensure the flow of remittances and savings homeward, Italy tried to retain the loyalty of emigrants overseas as part of its own nation-building project. A 1913 law addressed the citizenship issue: returnees who had taken foreign citizenship could regain Italian citizenship simply by living two years in Italy; their children were considered Italian citizens even if born elsewhere.[35] Although it never came to pass, there was even discussion of allowing the colonies abroad to have political representation in Italy.

What's New

Clearly, transnationalism was alive and well a hundred years ago. But if there are continuities with the past, there is also much that is new. Technological changes have made it possible for immigrants to maintain more frequent and closer contact with their home societies and, in a real sense, have changed the very nature of transnational connections. Today's global economy encourages international business operations; the large number of professional and prosperous immigrants in contemporary America are well positioned to operate in a transnational field. Dual nationality provisions by home governments have, in conjunction with other changes in the political context, added new dimensions to transnational political involvements. Moreover, greater tolerance for ethnic pluralism and multiculturalism in late twentieth-century America, and changed perspectives of immigration scholars themselves, have put transnational connections in a new, more positive light.

Transformations in the technologies of transportation and communication have increased the density, multiplicity, and importance of transnational interconnections and made it possible for the first time for immigrants to operate more or less simultaneously in a variety of places.[36] A century ago, the trip back to Italy took about two weeks, and more than a month elapsed between sending a letter home and receiving a reply. Today, immigrants can hop on a plane or make a phone call to check out how things are going at home.[37] As Patricia Pessar observes with regard to New York Dominicans: "It merely requires a walk to the corner newsstand, a flick of the radio or television dial to a Spanish-language station, or the placement of an overseas call" to learn about news in the Dominican Republic.[38]

In the jet age, inexpensive air fares mean that immigrants, especially from nearby places in the Caribbean and Central America, can fly home for emergencies, like funerals, or celebrations, like weddings; go back to visit their friends and relatives; and sometimes move back and forth, in the manner of commuters, between New York and their home community. Round-trip fares to the Dominican Republic in 1998 ran as low as $330. Among the immigrant workers I studied several years ago in a New York nursing home, some routinely spent their annual vacation in their home community in the Caribbean; others visited every few years.[39] A study of New York's Asian Indians notes that despite the distance and cost, they usually take their families back to visit India every year or two.[40] Inexpensive air travel means that relatives from home also often come to New York to visit. In the warmer months, Lessinger reports, when relatives from India make return visits to the United States, "a family's young men are often assigned to what is laughingly called 'airport duty,' going repeatedly to greet the flights of arriving grandparents, aunts and uncles, cousins and family friends."[41] Thanks to modern communications and air travel, a group of Mexicans in New York involved in raising money to improve their home community's water supply was able to conduct meetings with the *municipio* via conference call and to fly back to the community for the weekend to confer with contractors and authorities when they learned the new tubing had been delivered.[42]

Now that telephones reach into the far corners of most sending societies, immigrants can hear about news and people from home right away and participate immediately in family discussions on major decisions. Rates have become cheap—in 1998 a three-minute call to the Dominican Republic cost as little as $1.71, and to India $3.66; phone parlors, ubiquitous in New York, and prepaid phone calls are even cheaper.[43] Cristina Szanton Blanc describes how a Filipino couple in New York maintained a key role in child-rearing decisions although several of their children remained in Manila. On the phone, they could give advice and orders and respond to day-to-day problems. When their only daughter in Manila had an unfortunate romance, they dispatched a friend visiting the Philippines to investigate the situation. Adela, the mother of the family, had herself been back to the Philippines three times in six years.[44] Asian Indian New Yorkers typically phone relatives in India weekly or biweekly, and Johanna Lessinger reports that one rich young woman called her mother in Delhi every day.[45] Most Brazilians whom Maxine Margolis interviewed in New York City ran up phone bills of between $85 and $150 a month, and a few admitted that they typically spent $200 a month or more. She offers an illustration of how readily Brazilians call home: "When I was in a home furnishing store in Manhattan and asked the Brazilian owner, a long time resident of New York City, how to say 'wine rack' in Portuguese, he was disturbed when he could not recall the phrase. As quickly as one might consult a dictionary, he dialed Brazil to ask a friend."[46]

Faxes and videotapes also allow immigrants to keep in close touch with those they left behind. Some Brazilians in New York, Margolis tells us, regularly record or videotape sixty- to ninety-minute messages for family and friends back home. Like other immigrant New Yorkers, they can participate vicariously, through videotape, in important family events.[47] Johanna Lessinger recounts how Indians in Queens gather to watch full-length videos of weddings of widely scattered relatives, able to admire the dress and jewelry of the bride and calculate the value of pictured wedding gifts.[48] The better-off and better-educated may use e-mail as well. Said an Irish journalist in New York: "My grandfather, who came here in the late 1800s . . . he was an immigrant. . . . We don't have the finality of the old days. I can send E-mail. I can phone. I can be in Bantry in twelve hours."[49] Immigrant cable-television channels, moreover, allow an immediate, and up-close view, of homeland news for many groups; Koreans in Queens can watch the news from Seoul on the twenty-four-hour Korean channel, while Russian émigrés can turn to WMNB-TV for live performances from a Moscow concert hall.[50]

Modern forms of transportation and communications, in combination with new international forms of economic activity in the new global marketplace, have meant that more immigrants today are involved in economic endeavors that span national borders. Certainly, it is much easier today than a hundred years ago for immigrants to manage businesses thousands of miles away, given, among other things, modern telecommunications, information technologies, and instantaneous money transfers. Alejandro Portes and Luis Guarnizo describe how Dominican entrepreneurs in New York reap rewards by using their time in New York to build a base of property, bank accounts, and business contacts and then travel back and forth to take advantage of economic opportunities in both countries.[51] A few years after a Dominican man Patricia Pessar knew bought a garment factory in New York, he expanded his operations by purchasing (with his father and brother) a garment factory in the Dominican Republic's export processing zone. He and his wife and children continue to live in New York, where he has become a U.S. citizen, though he has also built a large house in the Dominican Republic.[52]

Many Asian Indian New Yorkers, encouraged by the Indian government's attempt to capture immigrant capital for development, invest in profit-making ventures in India, including buying urban real estate and constructing factories, for-profit hospitals, and medical centers. Often, relatives in India provide on-the-spot help in managing the business there. After receiving a graduate degree in engineering in the United States, Dr.

S. Vadivelu founded a factory in New Jersey that makes electrolytic capacitors. He later opened two factories in his home state of Andhra Pradesh, where he manufactures ceramic capacitors for sale to Indian electronics manufacturers. His father and brothers manage both plants on a daily basis; Dr. Vadivelu travels back and forth several times a year to check on the factories.[53]

The Indian example points to something else that's new about transnationalism today. Compared to the past, a much higher proportion of newcomers today come with advanced education, professional skills, and sometimes substantial amounts of financial capital that facilitate transnational connections—and allow some immigrants to participate, in the manner of modern-day cosmopolitans, in high-level institutions and enterprises here and in their home society. The affluence of Indian New Yorkers, Lessinger argues, makes them one of the most consistently transnational immigrants in behavior and outlook. Indeed, *within* the Asian Indian community, it is the wealthiest and most successful professionals and business people who maintain the closest links with India and for whom "extensive transnationalism is a way of life." They are the ones who invest in India, make numerous phone calls, and fly home frequently, where they mix business with pleasure; such individuals have "a certain influence and standing wherever they go."[54] The Chinese "astronauts" who shuttle back and forth by air between Taiwan or Hong Kong and America are typically well-educated and well-off professionals, executives, and entrepreneurs who move easily in financial, scientific, and business worlds around the globe.[55] Pyong Gap Min describes international commuter marriages involving high-level Korean professionals and business executives who have returned to Korea for better jobs while their wives and children remain in New York for educational opportunities. The couples talk on the phone several times a week; the husbands fly to New York two to five times a year while the wives visit Korea once or twice a year.[56]

When it comes to transnational political involvements, here, too, technological advances play a role. The newest New Yorkers can hop on a plane to vote in national elections in their home countries, as thousands did in a recent Dominican presidential election. (With new Dominican electoral reforms, due to go into effect in 2002, such trips will be unnecessary, since it will be possible to vote in Dominican elections from polling places in New York.) Politicians from home, in turn, can make quick trips to New York to campaign and raise funds. Candidates for U.S. electoral positions have been known to return to their country of origin for the same reason. Guillermo Linares, for example, during his 1991 campaign for New York's City Council, briefly visited the Dominican Republic, where rallies held in support of his candidacy generated campaign funds and afforded opportunities for photos that were featured in New York newspapers.[57]

Apart from technological advances, there are other new aspects to transnational political practices today. Russian Jews brought with them a notion of belonging to a broader Jewish diaspora community, but they had no interest in being part of the oppressive Russian state they left behind. Italians, coming from a country in the midst of nation-state consolidation, did not arrive with a modern "national identity." Except for a tiny group of political exiles, migrants did not care much about building an Italian state that "would welcome them back, protect them from the need to migrate further, or represent the character and glories of the Italian people."[58] Among other groups in the past, such as the Irish, migration became part of their continuing struggle for national liberation. What's different today is that immigrants are arriving from sovereign countries, with established nationalist ideologies and institutions, and are a potential basis of support for government projects, policies, and leaders in the homeland. As a new way of building support among migrants abroad, former president Jean-Bertrand Aristide of Haiti popularized the notion of overseas Haitians as the Tenth Department in a country that is divided into nine administrative departments and set up a Ministry of Haitians Living Abroad within the Haitian cabinet.[59]

Moreover, today when the United States plays such a dominant role in the global political system and development strategies depend heavily on U.S. political and economic support, a number of sending states view their migrant populations as potential lobbies. It has been argued that one reason some nations are encouraging their nationals to become United States citizens is their desire to nurture a group of advocates to serve the home country's interests in the American political arena.[60]

Of enormous importance are the dual-nationality provisions that now cover a growing number of New York's immigrants. Early in the century, a new citizen forfeited U.S. citizenship by voting in foreign elections or holding political office in another country. Today, the United States tolerates (though does not formally recognize or encourage) dual nationality—and many countries sending immigrants here have been rushing to allow it. As of December 1996, seven of the ten largest immigrant groups in New York City had the right to be dual nationals.[61] Legislation passed in Mexico in 1998 allows Mexicans, one of the fastest-growing immigrant groups in the city, to hold Mexican nationality as well as U.S. citizenship although, as of this writing, dual nationals cannot vote in Mexican national elections or hold high office there.[62]

The details of dual-nationality policies vary from country to country. In Trinidad and Tobago, for example, dual nationals can vote only if they have lived there for a year prior to the elections, whereas Colombian nationals can vote at the Colombian Consulate or polling site in Queens and run for office in their homeland even after they become U.S. citizens. In 1994 the Dominican Republic recognized the right to dual nationality; three years later, as part of an electoral reform package, the government adopted a proposal to give naturalized American citizens of Dominican descent the right to vote in Dominican elections and run for office while living in New York. When implemented, the reforms will make the Dominican community in New York the second largest concentration of voters in any Dominican election, exceeded only by Santo Domingo.[63] Currently, there are proposals in the Dominican Congress to create seats to represent Dominican emigrants.

A powerful economic incentive is involved in the recognition of dual nationality by various sending countries. In the Dominican Republic, for example, immigrant remittances rank as the most important source of foreign exchange, and there, as elsewhere, the government wants to ensure the flow of money and business investment homeward.[64] The record-breaking naturalization rates in the United States, in large part a response to recent U.S. legislation depriving noncitizens of various public social benefits, may have increased concern about losing the allegiance—and dollars—of emigrants.[65] On his first visit to New York City as president of the Dominican Republic, Lionel Fernandez Reyna (who grew up in New York City, where he attended elementary and high school on the

Upper West Side) publicly urged Dominicans to feel free to pursue dual citizenship. "If you, young mother, or you, elderly gentlemen, or you, young student, feel the need to adopt the nationality of the United States in order to confront the vicissitudes of that society stemming from the end of the welfare era, do not feel tormented by this," he said in a speech televised on New York's Channel 41. "Do it with a peaceful conscience, for you will continue being Dominicans, and we will welcome you as such when you set foot on the soil of our republic."[66] Political calculations come into play, too. The extension of dual nationality or citizenship provisions may be a way of trying to secure the role of overseas nationals as "advocates of *la patria's* interests in the United States, the new global hegemon."[67] And though the migrant community's economic clout is an important reason why, as in the Dominican case, migrant lobbying efforts for dual citizenship were successful, political developments and conflicts in the home country are also involved.[68]

Although some scholars and public figures worry about the trend toward dual nationality—it makes citizenship akin to bigamy, says journalist Georgie Anne Geyer, in *Americans No More: The Death of American Citizenship*—by and large transnational connections are viewed in a more favorable light today than they were in the past.[69] Early in the century, return migration inflamed popular opinion. "Immigrants were expected to stay once they arrived," writes historian Walter Nugent. "To leave again implied that the migrant came only for money; was too crass to appreciate America as a noble experiment in democracy; and spurned American good will and helping hands."[70] Another historian notes: "After 1907, there was tremendous hostility . . . toward temporary or return migrants. . . . The inference frequently drawn was that [they] considered the United States good enough to plunder but not to adopt. The result was a high degree of antipathy."[71] Indeed, Randolph Bourne's classic essay, "Transnational America," published in 1916, responded to rising anti-immigrant sentiment, arguing that the nation should "accept . . . free and mobile passage of the immigrant between America and his native land. . . . To stigmatize the alien who works in America for a few years and returns to his own land, only perhaps to seek American fortune again, is to think in narrow nationalistic terms."[72]

At the time, a common concern was that the new arrivals were not making serious efforts to become citizens and real Americans. Public schools, settlement houses, and progressive reformers put pressure on immigrants to abandon their old-fashioned customs and languages. A popular guide on becoming American advised immigrant Jews to "forget your past, your customs, and your ideals." The Americanization movement's "melting pot" pageants, inspired by Israel Zangwill's play, depicted strangely attired foreigners stepping into a huge pot and emerging as immaculate, well-dressed, accent-free "American-looking" Americans.[73] Expressions of ethnicity were suffocated in New York City's schools, where, in the words of Superintendent Maxwell, the goal was "to train the immigrant child . . . to become a good American citizen."[74] Much of the scholarship concerning the earlier immigration emphasized the way immigrants were assimilating and becoming American; ties to the home society were often interpreted as "evidence for, or against, Americanization" and, in many accounts, were seen as impeding the assimilation process.[75]

Today, when there's an official commitment to cultural pluralism and cultural diversity, transnational ties are more visible and acceptable—and sometimes even celebrated in public settings. Anti-immigrant sentiment is still with us, and immigrant loyalties are still often questioned, but rates of return are not, as in the past, a key part of immigration debates. In an era of significant international money flow and huge U.S. corporate operations abroad, there is also less concern that immigrants are looting America by sending remittances home. Indeed, as Luis Guarnizo observes, U.S. corporations unintentionally reinforce and encourage transnationalism by developing marketing incentives to promote migrants' monetary transfers, long-distance communications, and frequent visits to their countries of origin.[76] Increasingly today, the message is that there is nothing un-American about expressing one's ethnicity. In New York, officials and social service agencies actively promote festivals and events to foster ethnic pride and glorify the city's multiethnic character. Practically every ethnic group has its own festival or parade, the largest being the West Indian American Day parade on Brooklyn's Eastern Parkway, which attracts between one and two million people every Labor Day. Exhibits in local museums and libraries highlight the cultural background of different immigrant groups; special school events feature the foods, music, and costumes of various homelands; and school curricula include material on diverse ethnic heritages. In the quest for votes, established New York politicians of all stripes recognize the value of visits to immigrant homelands. As part of her mayoral campaign, for example, Democratic candidate Ruth Messinger traveled to the Dominican Republic and Haiti for four days of official meetings, news conferences, and honorary dinners, which led to coverage in newspapers and radio and television stations reaching Dominicans and Haitians in New York.[77] This kind of campaigning across borders, Luis Guarnizo argues, lends legitimacy, status, and a sense of empowerment to groups like Dominicans, who maintain intense transnational relations.[78]

Scholars are now more interested in transnational ties and see them in a more positive light than in the past. In emerging transnational perspectives, the maintenance of multiple identities and loyalties is viewed as a normal feature of immigrant life; ties to the home society complement—rather than detract from—commitments in this country. At the same time, as immgrants buy property, build houses, start businesses, make marriages, and influence political developments in their home societies, they are also shown to be deeply involved in building lives in New York, where they buy homes, work on block associations and community boards, join unions, run school boards, and set up businesses.[79] Generally, the literature stresses the way transnational relationships and connections benefit immigrants, enhancing the possibility of survival in places full of uncertainty. In an era when globalization is a major subject of scholarly study, it is perhaps not surprising that immigrants are seen as actors who operate in a transnational framework or that commentators in the media are following suit. "Today," writes journalist Roger Rosenblatt, "when every major business enterprise is international, when money is international, when instant international experiences are pictured on T.V., more people think of themselves as world citizens. Why should not immigrants do likewise?"[80]

Obviously, there is much that is new about transnationalism. Modern technology, the new global economy and culture, and new laws and political arrangements have all combined to produce transnational connections that differ in fundamental ways from those maintained by immigrants a century ago. Once ignored or reviled, transnational ties are now a favorite topic at conferences and are sometimes even celebrated in today's multicultural age. Yet the novelty of contemporary conditions should not be exaggerated. Immigrants who move from one country to another seldom cut off ties and allegiances to those left behind, and turn-of-the-century immigrant New Yorkers were no exception. It may have been harder to maintain contacts across the ocean than it is today, but many immigrants in the last great wave maintained extensive, and intensive, transnational ties and operated in what social scientists now call a transnational social field.

A comparison of transnationalism then and now raises some additional issues. If many academic observers who studied earlier immigrants were guilty of overlooking transnational ties in the quest to document assimilation, there is now a risk of overemphasizing the centrality of transnationalism and minimizing the extent to which contemporary immigrants "become American" and undergo changes in behavior and outlook in response to circumstances in this country. Indeed, as David Hollinger notes, today's immigrants "are more prepared for a measure of assimilation by the worldwide influence of American popular culture; most are more culturally attuned to the United States before they arrive here than were their counterparts a century ago."[81] Moreover, as a recent study of Mexican and Central American migrants points out, transnationalism tends to put too much stress on ephemeral migration circuits and understates the permanency of migrant settlement.[82] Although many, perhaps most, immigrants come with the idea of improving their lot and returning home, as they extend their stay and as more family members join them, they become increasingly involved with life and people in this country. Ties to the homeland seldom disappear, but they often become fewer and thinner over time.

Perhaps because studies using a transnational approach are in their infancy, we still know little about how pervasive and extensive various transnational ties actually are for different groups. The new immigration, like the old, to quote Hollinger again, is very mixed. "It displays a variety of degrees of engagement with the United States and with prior homelands, and it yields some strong assimilationist impulses alongside vivid expressions of diasporic consciousness."[83] In the past, Italians were more transnational in behavior and outlook than Russian Jews. This was mainly because Jews came to stay, whereas large numbers of Italians were labor migrants, who aimed to—and often did—go back home after a spell of work in New York.

Today, as well, some groups are likely to maintain more intense, regular, and dense transnational connections than others, but we don't know which ones—or why. It is much more than a question of having significant numbers who go back and forth in low-level jobs like the Italian sojourners of old. Peggy Levitt suggests several factors that help explain why the groups she is studying in Boston differ in type, intensity, and durability of transnational ties. She lists geography, including the home country's distance from the United States and the extent of residential clustering here; institutional completeness or the degree to which the group creates institutions enabling migrants to satisfy most of their needs within their own ethnic community, particularly transnational institutions such as churches that extend across borders; and the role of the state, both the home government's role in reinforcing and encouraging migrants' ties with people back home and the American government's history of political and economic involvement in the homeland. She also mentions socioeconomic factors, including high levels of social parity between migrants and those in the home community that make it easier for members to stay attached to one another and to sanction those who do not.[84] Additional factors are also likely to be important: the nature of social organization and cultural patterns in the home community that may encourage the maintenance of transnational connections as well as the particularities of homeland political movements, leaders, and organizations that may lead them to actively recruit support abroad.

There is also variation *within* groups in the frequency, depth, and range of transnational ties. Just as well-off Asian Indian immigrants have more resources to maintain transnational connections than their poorer counterparts, so, too, this may be true in other immigrant groups. Legal status is likely to affect the types and extent of transnational connections maintained; undocumented immigrants cannot easily go back and forth, to give one obvious example. Whether migrants came on their own or with their families also must be considered. There are also bound to be differences in the nature and impact of transnational ties between men and women and between the old, young, and middle-aged. And as I've noted, transnational conditions may well lose force with the length of stay in America, as suggested by research showing that remittances tend to taper off over time.

Finally, there are the consequences of transnational connections for migrants' lives here. If scholars of turn-of-the-century immigration once tended to blame home-country ties for a host of problems, from poor English skills to lack of interest in naturalizing, today's transnational perspectives often have a celebratory tone. Transnational ties are seen as helping migrants cope with discrimination and prejudice in this country and providing access to a wide range of resources, including business and investment opportunities, political and organizational leadership positions, and assistance with child care. In an insecure world, they allow migrants to keep their options open. As Glick Schiller and her colleagues write: "By stretching, reconfiguring, and activating . . . networks across national boundaries, families are able to maximize the utilization of labor and resources and survive within situations of economic uncertainty and subordination."[85] Even involvement in home country-based organizations is often said to strengthen migrants' ability to mobilize a base support for political issues and elections in New York.[86]

But it is important to bear in mind that modern-day transnationalism has costs as well. Financial obligations to relatives left behind may be a drain on resources needed for projects in New York.[87] The family separation involved in transnationalism often brings great personal strain. Transnational mothers worry about the children left behind in the home country—about the care they're receiving, whether they'll get in trouble in adolescence, and whether they will transfer their allegiance and affection to the "other mother."[88] In the realm of politics, involvement in political and organizational affairs of the home country may draw energies and interests away from political engagement and activism on behalf of the immigrant community here; this is what one study suggests happens among Latin American men in Queens. Having experienced a loss of occupational status in New York, many of the men want to return to Latin America, and, as a result, they tend to form, participate in, and lead ethnic organizations that focus on the country of origin. These ethnic organizations raise money for charitable concerns in the home country, not the United States. It's unlikely, Jones-Correa predicts, such ethnic institutions will, in the short run, be an instrument for redirecting immigrants' focus to political and social issues in the United States.[89]

That scholars are debating the contradictory pressures of transnational ties is a sign of their importance for today's immigrants—and perhaps for their children as well. What is clear is that for the first generation, transnational practices are very much part of the modern scene. It is also clear, to return to the comparison, that they are not just a late twentieth-century phenomenon. Transnationalism has been with us for a long time, although in its modern guise it appears to be more far-reaching and more intense—and may also turn out to be more durable and long-lasting.

Notes

1. Gino Speranza, "Political Representation of Italo-American Colonies in the Italian Parliament," in Francisco Cordasco and Eugene Bucchioni (eds.), *The Italians: Social Backgrounds of an American Group* (Clifton, N.J.: Augustus M. Kelley, 1974 [1906]), 310.

2. Linda Basch, Nina Glick Schiller, and Cristina Szanton Blanc, *Nations Unbound: Transnational Projects, Postcolonial Predicaments, and Deterritorialized Nation-States* (Langhorne, Penn.: Gordon and Breach, 1994), 7.

3. Nina Glick Schiller, "Who Are Those Guys? A Transnational Reading of the U.S. Immigrant Experience." Paper presented at a conference of the Social Science Research Council, Becoming American/America Becoming, Sanibel Island, Fla., 1996, 4.

4. Nina Glick Schiller, Linda Basch, and Cristina Blanc-Szanton, "Transnationalism: A New Analytic Framework for Understanding Migration," in Nina Glick Schiller, Linda Basch, and Cristina Blanc-Szanton (eds.), *Towards a Transnational Perspective on Migration* (New York: New York Academy of Sciences, 1992), 1; Basch et al. *Nations Unbound*, 7; see also Constance Sutton, "Transnational Identities and Cultures: Caribbean Immigrants in the United States," in Michael D'Innocenzo and Josef Sirefman (eds.), *Immigration and Ethnicity* (Westport, Conn.: Greenwood, 1992).

5. Alejandro Portes, "Immigration Theory for a New Century: Some Problems and Opportunities," *International Migration Review* 31 (1997): 799–825.

6. Barry Goldberg, "Historical Reflections on Transnationalism, Race, and the American Immigrant Saga," in Schiller, *Towards a Transnational Perspective on Migration*, 205; Delmos Jones, "Which Migrant? Permanent or Temporary?" in Ibid., 219.

7. Schiller, "Who Are Those Guys?" For a revised version of this paper, see Nina Glick Schiller, "Transmigrants and Nation-States: Something Old and Something New in the U.S. Immigrant Experiences," in Charles Hirschman, Philip Kasinitz, and Josh DeWind (eds.), *The Handbook of International Migration* (New York: Russell Sage Foundation, 1999).

8. Luis Guarnizo, "On the Political Participation of Transnational Migrants: Old Practices and New Trends." Paper presented at a Social Science Research Council workshop, Immigrants, Civic Culture, and Modes of Political Incorporation: A Contemporary and Historical Comparison, Santa Fe, N. Mex., 1997; Luis Guarnizo, "The Rise of Transnational Migration," *Political Power and Social Theory* 12 (1998): 45–94; see also Robert Smith, "Transnational Migration, Assimilation, and Political Community," in Margaret Crahan and Alberto Vourvoulias Bush (eds.), *The City and the World: New York's Global Future* (New York: Council on Foreign Relations, 1997); Robert Smith, "Reflections on Migration, the State and the Construction, Durability and Newness of Transnational Life," *Soziale Welt* 12 (1998): 197–217.

9. For example, Michael Miller Topp, "The Transnationalism of the Italian American Left: The

Lawrence Strike of 1912 and the Italian Chamber of Commerce of New York City," *Journal of American Ethnic History* 17 (1997): 39–63.

10. Patricia Pessar, *A Visa for a Dream* (Boston: Allyn and Bacon, 1995), 76.

11. Abraham Cahan, *Yekl and Other Stories of Yiddish New York* (New York: Dover, 1970 [1896]), 27; Mark Wyman, *Round-Trip America: The Immigrants Return to Europe, 1880–1930* (Ithaca: Cornell University Press, 1993), 61.

12. Speranza, "Political Representation of Italo-American Colonies," in Cordasco and Bucchioni (eds.), *The Italians*, 309. According to the Italian Bureau of Emigration, in 1903 23 million lire arrived in Italy from abroad (about $7.75 million), 18 million of which came from the United States. Except for 1906 and 1907, the remittances from overseas increased every year, passing 150 million lire in 1916 and reaching one billion lire in 1920. Dino Cinel, *From Italy to San Francisco: The Immigrant Experience* (Stanford: Stanford University Press, 1982), 75.

13. Daniel Soyer, *Jewish Immigrant Associations and American Identity in New York, 1880–1939* (Cambridge: Harvard University Press, 1997), 172, 177.

14. Cinel, *From Italy to San Francisco*, 71.

15. Wyman, *Round-Trip America*, 130–31.

16. Michael Jones-Correa, *Between Two Nations: The Political Predicament of Latinos in New York* (Ithaca: Cornell University Press, 1998b), 96.

17. Schiller, "Who Are Those Guys?"

18. Jonathan Sarna, "The Myth of No Return: Jewish Return Migration to Eastern Europe, 1881–1914," *American Jewish History* 71 (1981): 256–68.

19. Ibid., 264.

20. Wyman, *Round-Trip America*.

21. Samuel Joseph, *Jewish Immigration to the United States: From 1881–1910* (New York: AMS Press, 1967), 139.

22. Wyman, *Round-Trip America*, 79.

23. Michael La Sorte, *La Merica: Images of Italian Greenhorn Experience* (Philadelphia: Temple University Press, 1985), 218.

24. Wyman, *Round-Trip America*, 23–24, 131.

25. Speranza, "Political Representation of Italo-American Colonies," in Cordasco and Bucchioni (eds.), *The Italians*.

26. On Italian "birds of passage" and return migration, see Thomas Archdeacon, *Becoming American* (New York: Free Press, 1983); Cinel, *From Italy to San Francisco*; Dino Cinel, "The Seasonal Emigration of Italians in the Nineteenth Century: From Internal to International Migration," *Journal of Ethnic Studies* 10 (1982): 43–68; Robert Foerster, *The Italian Emigration of Our Times* (Harvard: Harvard University Press, 1919); Silvano Tomasi, *Piety and Power* (New York: Center for Migration Studies, 1975); and Wyman, *Round-Trip America*. For a general discussion of return migration to Europe, see also Ewa Morawska, "Return Migrations: Theoretical and Research Agenda," in Rudolph Vecoli and Suzanne Sinke (eds.), *A Century of European Migrations, 1830–1930* (Urbana: University of Illinois Press, 1991).

27. Wyman, *Round-Trip America*, 79.

28. Sarna, " Myth of No Return", 266.

29. Sydelle Kramer and Jenny Masur (eds.), *Jewish Grandmothers* (Boston: Beacon Press, 1976), 2.

30. Schiller, "Who Are Those Guys?"

31. Matthew Jacobson, *Special Sorrows* (Cambridge: Harvard University Press, 1995), 2, 62.

32. Topp, "The Transnationalism of the Italian American Left."

33. Joe Doyle, "Striking for Ireland on the New York Docks," in Ronald Bayor and Thomas Meagher (eds.), *The New York Irish* (Baltimore: Johns Hopkins University Press, 1996); Chris McNickle, "When New York Was Irish, and After," in Ibid.

34. For an interesting comparison of the involvement of the Italian and Mexican states in their emigrant populations, see Robert Smith, "Reflections on Migration."

35. Wyman, *Round-Trip America*, 93–94, 199.

36. Nina Glick Schiller, Linda Basch, and Cristina Blanc-Szanton, "From Immigrant to Transmigrant: Theorizing Transnational Migration," *Anthropological Quarterly* 68 (1995): 48–63; Roger Rouse, "Thinking Through Transnationalism: Notes on the Cultural Politics of Class Relations in a Contemporary United States," *Public Culture* 7 (1995): 353–402.

37. See Portes, "Immigration Theory for a New Century."

38. Pessar, *A Visa for a Dream*, 69.

39. Nancy Foner, *The Caregiving Dilemma: Work in an American Nursing Home* (Berkeley: University of California Press, 1994).

40. Johanna Lessinger, "Investing or Going Home? A Transnational Strategy among Indian Immigrants in the United States," in Schiller, et al., *Towards a Transnational Perspective on Migration.*

41. Johanna Lessinger, *From the Ganges to the Hudson* (Boston: Allyn and Bacon, 1995), 42.

42. Robert Smith, "Transnational Localities: Community, Technology and the Politics of Membership within the Context of Mexico and US Migration," in Michael Peter Smith and Luis Guarnizo (eds.), *Transnationalism from Below* (New Brunswick: Transaction, 1998).

43. It was not possible to make a transatlantic phone call until 1927, and then it was prohibitively expensive—two hundred dollars in present-day currency for a three-minute call to London. These days, phone parlors and card businesses buy telephone minutes in bulk from long-distance carriers and sell them at sharply discounted rates (see Deborah Sontag and Celia Dugger, "The New Immigrant Tide: A Shuttle Between Worlds," *New York Times,* July 19, 1998.)

44. Basch et al. *Nations Unbound*, 237.

45. Lessinger, "Investing or Going Home?" in Glick Schiller et al. (eds.), *Towards a Transnational Perspective,* 61; On Koreans' phone contact with family members back home, see Pyong Gap Min, *Changes and Conflicts: Korean Immigrant Families in New York* (Boston: Allyn and Bacon, 1998).

46. Maxine Margolis, *An Invisible Minority: Brazilians in New York City* (Boston: Allyn and Bacon, 1998), 115.

47. Maxine Margolis, "Transnationalism and Popular Culture: The Case of Brazilian Immigrants in the United States," *Journal of Popular Culture* 29 (1995): 29–41.

48. Lessinger, *From the Ganges to the Hudson*, 41.

49. Joan Mathieu, *Zulu: An Irish Journey* (New York: Farrar, Straus and Giroux, 1998), 140.

50. Sontag and Dugger, "The New Immigrant Tide."

51. Portes, "Immigration Theory for a New Century."

52. Pessar, *A Visa for a Dream*, 77.

53. Lessinger, *From the Ganges to the Hudson*, 91; see also Lessinger, "Investing or Going Home?" in Glick Schiller et al. (eds.), *Towards a Transnational Perspective.*

54. Lessinger, *From the Ganges to the Hudson*, 89.

55. See Bernard Wong, *Ethnicity and Entrepreneurship: The New Chinese Immigrants in the San Francisco Bay Area* (Boston: Allyn and Bacon, 1998).

56. Min, *Changes and Conflicts*, 113–18.

57. Pessar, *A Visa for a Dream*, 75.

58. Donna Gabaccia, "Italians and Their Diasporas: Cosmopolitans, Exiles and Workers of the World." Paper presented at the conference States and Diasporas, Casa Italiana, Columbia University, 1998.

59. Aristide's successor, René Préval, distanced himself from Aristide on many points, including the use of the term "Tenth Department," although he retained the Ministry of Haitians Living Abroad. Nina Glick Schiller and Georges Fouron, "Transnational Lives and National Identities: The Identity Politics of Haitian Immigrants," in Smith and Guarnizo (eds.), *Transnationalism from Below,* 148–49.

60. Louis DeSipio, "Building a New Foreign Policy among Friends: National Efforts to Construct Long-Term Relationships with Latin American Emigres in the United States." Paper presented at the conference States and Diasporas, Casa Italiana, Columbia University, 1998; Guarnizo, "The Rise of Transnational Migration"; Smith, "Reflections on Migration."

61. Somini Sengupta, "Immigrants in New York Pressing for Drive for Dual Nationality." *New York Times,* December 30, 1996.

62. James Smith, "Mexico's Dual Nationality Opens Doors," *Los Angeles Times,* March 20, 1998.

63. Deborah Sontag and Larry Rohter, "Dominicans May Allow Voting Abroad," *New York Times,* November 15, 1997.

64. Guarnizo, "On the Political Participation of Transnational Migrants."

65. For a fascinating analysis of the contents and conditions influencing immigrants' views and decisions about naturalization, based on a case study of an extended family of Dominican immigrants in the late 1990s, see Greta Gilbertson and Audrey Singer, "Naturalization under Changing Conditions of Membership: Dominican Immigrants in New York City," in Nancy Foner, Rubén Rumbaut, and Steven Gold (eds.), *Immigration Research for a New Century* (New York: Russell Sage Foundation, 2000). Nationwide, in 1997 alone, 1.4 million applications for naturalization were filed with the Immigration and Naturalization Service, a threefold increase over those filed in 1994.

66. Larry Rohter, "U.S. Benefits Go: Allure to Dominicans Doesn't," *New York Times,* October 12, 1996.

67. Guarnizo, "The Rise of Transnational Migration", 79.

68. On the politics of dual nationality legislation in the Colombian and Dominican cases, see Arturo Sanchez, "Transnational Political Agency and Identity Formation among Colombian Immigrants" and Pamela Graham, "Political Incorporation and Re-Incorporation: Simultaneity in the Dominican Migrant Experience." Papers presented at the conference Transnational Communities and the Political Economy of New York City in the 1990s, New School for Social Research, New York, 1997; and Guarnizo, "On the Political Participation of Transnational Migrants." Also see Jones-Correa, *Between Two Nations*, 60–68, on lobbying efforts for dual citizenship among Colombians, Ecuadorians, and Dominicans in New York.

69. Georgie Anne Geyer, *Americans No More: The Death of American Citizenship* (New York: Atlantic Monthly Press, 1996).

70. Walter Nugent, *Crossings: The Great Transatlantic Migrations, 1870–1914* (Bloomington: Indiana University Press, 1992), 159.

71. Shumsky, quoted in Nugent *Crossings*, 159; see Neil Shumsky, "Let No Man Stop to Plunder: American Hostility to Return Migration, 1880–1924," *Journal of American Ethnic History* 11 (1992): 56–75.

72. Quoted in Goldberg, "Historical Reflections on Transnationalism," in Glick Schiller et al. (eds.), *Towards a Transnational Perspective*, 212.

73. Benjamin Schwartz, "The Diversity Myth: America's Leading Export," *Atlantic Monthly,* May 1995, 57–67.

74. Stephan Brumberg, *Going to America, Going to School: The Jewish Immigrant Public School Encounter in Turn-of-the-Century New York City* (New York: Praeger, 1986), 71.

75. Schiller, "Who Are Those Guys?"

76. Guarnizo, "On the Political Participation of Transnational Migrants."

77. Adam Nagourney, "Long Roads to City Hall Get Longer," *New York Times,* December 4, 1996.

78. Guarnizo, "On the Political Participation of Transnational Migrants."

79. Basch et al. *Nations Unbound.*

80. Roger Rosenblatt, "Sunset, Sunrise," *New Republic,* December 27, 1993, 20–23.

81. David Hollinger, *Postethnic America* (New York: Basic, 1995), 154.

82. Pierrette Hondagneu-Sotelo and Ernestine Avila, *Gendered Transitions* (Berkeley: University of California Press, 1997).

83. Hollinger *Postethnic America*, 153.

84. Peggy Levitt, "Forms of Transnational Community and Their Impact on the Second Generation: Preliminary Findings." Paper presented at the conference Transnationalism and the Second Generation, Harvard University, 1998; Peggy Levitt, "Migrants Participate across Borders: Towards an Understanding of Forms and Consequences," in Foner et al., (eds.), *Immigration Research for a New Century*.

85. Glick Schiller et al., "From Immigrant to Transmigrant," 54.

86. Linda Basch, "The Vincentians and Grenadians: The Role of Voluntary Associations in Immigrant Adaptation to New York City," in Nancy Foster (ed.), *New Immigrants in New York* (New York: Columbia University Press, 1987).

87. See Sarah Mahler, *American Dreaming: Immigrant Life on the Margins* (Princeton: Princeton University Press, 1995).

88. Hondagneu-Sotelo and Avila, *Gendered Transitions*.

89. Michael Jones-Correa, "Different Paths: Gender, Immigration and Political Participation," *International Migration Review* 32 (1998): 326–49. According to Jones-Correa, it is Latin American women activists who are able to combine loyalty to the home country with an engagement in American politics. Having gained independence and power in New York with their income, they have a greater desire than men to stay in this country. They also have more experience dealing with public institutions through their children. The result is that migrant women activists are more likely than men to involve themselves in New York City politics and the problems of the immigrant community there.

Credits

Chapter 1 is originally from *The Minds of the West: Ethnocultural Evolution in the Rural Middle West, 1830–1917* by Jon Gjerde. Copyright (c) 1997 by the University of North Carolina Press. Used by permission of the publisher.

Chapter 2 is originally from Martha A. Hodes, "The Mercurial Nature and Abiding Power of Race: A Transnational Family Story." *American Historical Review* 108, 1 (February 2003).

Chapter 3 is orginally from *Contented among Strangers: Rural German-Speaking Women and Their Families in the Nineteenth-Century Midwest.* Copyright (c) 1996 by the Board of Trustees of the University of Illinois. Used with permission of the University of Illinois Press.

Chapter 4 is originally from Shirley J. Yee, "Gender Ideology and Black Women as Community Builders in Ontario, Canada, 1850–1870," *Canadian Historical Review* 75, 1 (March 1994). Reprinted by permission of University of Toronto Press Incorporated.

Chapter 5 is originally from *Across the Great Divide* edited by Matthew Basso, Dee Garceau, and Laura McCall (c) 2001. Reproduced by permission of Routledge/Taylor & Francis Books, Inc.

Chapter 6 is originally from Erika Lee, "Enforcing the Borders: Chinese Exclusion along the U.S. Borders with Canada and Mexico, 1882–1924," *Journal of American History* 89, 1 (2002). Copyright (c) 2002 Organization of American Historians. Reprinted with permission.

Chapter 7 is originally from Donna R. Gabaccia, "When the Migrants are Men: Italy's Women and Transnationalism," in *Women, Gender and Labour Migration: Historical and Global Perspectives,* edited by Pamela Sharpe. Reprinted by permission of Routledge.

Chapter 8 is originally from John Mason Hart, "Boomers, Sooners, and Settlers: Americanos in Mexico," in Hart's *Empire and Revolution: The Americans in Mexico since the Civil War.* Copyright (c) 2002 The Regents of the University of California. Reprinted with permission

Chapter 9 is originally from Akram Fouad Khater, "Back to the Mountain: Emigration, Gender and the Middle Class in Lebannon," in Khater's *Inventing Home: Emigration, Gender and the Middle Class in Lebanon, 1870–1920.* Copyright (c) 2001 The Regents of the University of California. Reprinted with permission.

Chapter 10 is originally from Gunther Peck, "Reinventing Free Labor: Immigrant Padrones

Contributors

DONNA GABACCIA is the Vecoli Professor of Immigration History at the University of Minnesota. She has written extensively on immigrant life in the United States, on Italian migration around the world, and on global and transnational perspectives on human mobility. Recent books include *Immigration and American Diversity* (Blackwell, 2003); *Italy's Many Diasporas* (University College of London Press, 2000) and *We Are What We Eat: Ethnic Food and the Making of Americans* (Harvard University Press, 1998).

VICKI L. RUIZ is a Professor of History and Chicano/Latino Studies at the University of California, Irvine. Her many publications include *From Out of the Shadows: Mexican Women in 20th Century America* (Oxford University Press, 1998) and *Cannery Women, Cannery Lives* (University of New Mexico Press, 1987). Most recently, she and Virginia Sánchez Korrol edited *Latina Legacies* (Oxford University Press, 2005) and *Latinas in the United States: An Historical Encyclopedia* (Indiana University Press, 2005). She is President of the Organization of American Historians.

THOMAS G. ANDREWS is an Assistant Professor of History at California State University, Northridge. He has published articles on Native American and environmental history, and is the author of *Power, Toil, and Trouble: The Nature of Industrial Struggle in Colorado's Bloody Coalfields from the 1870s through the Ludlow Massacre of 1914* (in preparation).

JOYCE ANTLER is the Samuel Lane Professor of American Jewish History and Culture at Brandeis University. She has authored or edited eight books, including *The Journey Home: How Jewish Women Shaped Modern America* (Schocken Books, 1998), *Talking Back: Images of Jewish Women in American Popular Culture* (University Press of New England, 1997), and *American and I: Short Stories by American Jewish Women Writers* (Beacon Press, 1990).

MARY PATRICE ERDMANS is an Associate Professor of Sociology at Central Connecticut State University. She is the author of *The Grasinski Girls: The Choices They Had and the Choices They Made* (Ohio University Press, 2004), and *Opposite Poles: Immigrants and Ethnics in Polish Chicago, 1976–1990* (Penn State University Press, 1998).

YEN LE ESPIRITU is a Professor of Ethnic Studies at the University of California, San Diego. She is the author of *Home Bound: Filipino American Lives across Cultures, Communities, and Countries* (University of California Press, 2003), *Asian American Women and Men: Labor, Laws, and Love* (Sage, 1997), and *Asian American Panethnicity: Bridging Institutions and Identities* (Temple University Press, 1992).

NEIL FOLEY is an Associate Professor of History and Associate Dean at the University of Texas at Austin. He is the author of *White Scourge: Mexicans, Blacks, and Poor Whites in Texas Cotton Culture* (University of California Press, 1997). He is also the coauthor, with John Chávez, of *Teaching Mexican American History* (American Historical Association, 2002), and editor of *Reflexiones: New Directions in Mexican American Studies* (University of Texas Press, 1998).

NANCY FONER is a Distinguished Professor of Sociology at Hunter College, City University of New York. She is the author of eleven books, including *American Arrivals: Anthropology Engages the New Immigration* (School of American Research Press, 2003), *New Immigrants in New York* (Columbia University Press, 2001), *Islands in the City: West Indian Migration to New York* (University of California Press, 2001), and *From Ellis Island to JFK: New York's Two Great Waves of Immigration* (Yale University Press, 2000). She is also an elected member of the Executive Board of the Immigration and Ethnic History Society.

MATTHEW GARCÍA is an Associate Professor of American Civilization at Brown University. He is the author of *A World of Its Own: Intercultural Relations in the Citrus Belt of Southern California, 1900–1970* (University of North Carolina Press, 2001), and has written numerous articles on dance hall culture in post-World War II Southern California.

JON GJERDE is a Professor of History at the University of California, Berkeley. He is the author of *The Minds of the West: Ethnocultural Evolution in the Rural Middle West, 1830–1917* (University of North Carolina Press, 1997), and *From Peasants to Farmers: The Migration from Balestrand, Norway to the Upper Middle West* (Cambridge University Press, 1985), and edited *Major Problems in American Immigration and Ethnic History* (Houghton Mifflin, 1998).

EVELYN NAKANO GLENN is a Professor of Women's Studies and Ethnic Studies at the University of California, Berkeley. She is the author of *Unequal Freedom: How Race and Gender Shaped American Citizenship and Labor* (Harvard University Press, 2002), *Mothering: Ideology, Experience and Agency* (Routledge, 1994), and *Issei, Nisei, War Bride: Three Generations of Japanese American Women in Domestic Service* (Temple University Press, 1986).

JOHN MASON HART is a Professor of History at the University of Houston. He is the author of *Empire and Revolution: The Americans in Mexico since the Civil War* (University of California Press, 2002), *Revolutionary Mexico: The Coming and Process of the Mexican Revolution* (University of California Press, 1988), and *Anarchism and the Mexican Working Class, 1860–1931* (University of Texas Press, 1978). He also edited *Border Crossings: Mexican and Mexican-American Workers* (Scholarly Resources, 1998).

MARTHA HODES is an Associate Professor of History at New York University. She is the author of *White Women, Black Men: Illicit Sex in the Nineteenth-Century South* (Yale University Press, 1997), which won the Allan Nevins Prize of the Society of American Historians, and edited *Sex, Love, Race: Crossing Boundaries in North American History* (New York University Press, 1999).

AKRAM FOUAD KHATER is an Associate Professor of History at North Carolina State University. He is the author of *Inventing Home: Emigration, Gender and the Making of a Lebanese Middle Class, 1861–1921* (University of California Press, 2001), and editor of *Sources in the History of the Middle East* (Houghton Mifflin, 2003).

ERIKA LEE is an Associate Professor of History at the University of Minnesota. She is the author of *At America's Gates: Chinese Immigration and American Exclusion, 1882–1943* (University of North Carolina Press, 2003).

LUÍS LEÓN is a Visiting Assistant Professor of Ethnic Studies and Religious Studies at the University of California, Berkeley. He is the author of *La Llorona's Children: Religion, Life, and Death in the U.S.-Mexican Borderlands* (University of California Press, 2004), and coeditor, with Gary Laderman, of *Religion and American Cultures: An Encyclopedia of Traditions, Diversity, and Popular Expressions* (ABC-Clio, 2003).

KAREN J. LEONG is an Assistant Professor of Women's Studies at Arizona State University. She is the author of *The China Mystique: Mayling Soong Chiang, Pearl S. Buck, and Anna May Wong in the American Imagination* (University of California Press, 2005).

NANCY RAQUEL MIRABAL is an Associate Professor of Raza Studies at San Francisco State University. She has published several articles on the history of Cuban and Puerto Rican Afro-diasporic migrations and is coeditor of *Techno-Futuros: Critical Intervention in Latina/o Studies* (forthcoming). She is also the director of a community oral history project on the impact of gentrification on the Latina/o community in the Mission District of San Francico.

GUNTHER PECK is an Associate Professor of Public Policy Studies and History at Duke University. He is the author of *Reinventing Free Labor: Padrones and Immigrant Workers in the North American West* (Cambridge University Press, 2000).

LINDA SCHELBITZKI PICKLE is Professor of German at Western Kentucky University. She is the author of *Contented among Strangers: Rural German-Speaking Women and their Families in the Nineteenth Century American Midwest* (University of Illinois Press, 1996), and of a number of other studies on nineteenth-century German-speaking immigrants.

JUDY TZU-CHUN WU is an Associate Professor of History at Ohio State University. She is the author of *Doctor Mom Chung of the Fair-Haired Bastards: The Life of a Wartime Celebrity* (University of California Press, 2005).

SHIRLEY J. YEE is an Associate Professor of Women Studies at the University of Washington. She is the author of *Black Women Abolitionists: A Study in Activism, 1828–60* (University of Tennessee Press, 1992), which was nominated for the Pulitzer Prize in History.

Index

STATUE OF LIBERTY–ELLIS ISLAND CENTENNIAL SERIES

The Immigrant World of Ybor City: Italians and Their Latin Neighbors in Tampa, 1885–1985
  Gary R. Mormino and George E. Pozzetta
The Butte Irish: Class and Ethnicity in an American Mining Town, 1875–1925 *David M. Emmons*
The Making of an American Pluralism: Buffalo, New York, 1825–60 *David A. Gerber*
Germans in the New World: Essays in the History of Immigration *Frederick C. Luebke*
A Century of European Migrations, 1830–1930 *Edited by Rudolph J. Vecoli and Suzanne M. Sinke*
The Persistence of Ethnicity: Dutch Calvinist Pioneers in Amsterdam, Montana *Rob Kroes*
Family, Church, and Market: A Mennonite Community in the Old and the New Worlds, 1850–1930
  Royden K. Loewen
Between Race and Ethnicity: Cape Verdean American Immigrants, 1860–1965 *Marilyn Halter*
Les Icariens: The Utopian Dream in Europe and America *Robert P. Sutton*
Labor and Community: Mexican Citrus Worker Villages in a Southern California County, 1900–1950
  Gilbert G. González
Contented among Strangers: Rural German-Speaking Women and Their Families in the Nineteenth-
  Century Midwest *Linda Schelbitzki Pickle*
Dutch Farmer in the Missouri Valley: The Life and Letters of Ulbe Eringa, 1866–1950
  Brian W. Beltman
Good-bye, Piccadilly: British War Brides in America *Jenel Virden*
For Faith and Fortune: The Education of Catholic Immigrants in Detroit, 1805–1925
  JoEllen McNergney Vinyard
Britain to America: Mid-Nineteenth-Century Immigrants to the United States *William E. Van Vugt*
Immigrant Minds, American Identities: Making the United States Home, 1870–1930
  Orm Øverland
Italian Workers of the World: Labor Migration and the Formation of Multiethnic States *Edited by
  Donna R. Gabaccia and Fraser M. Ottanelli*
Dutch Immigrant Women in the United States, 1880–1920 *Suzanne M. Sinke*
Beyond Cannery Row: Sicilian Women, Immigration, and Community in Monterey, California,
  1915–99 *Carol Lynn McKibben*
Merchants, Midwives, and Laboring Women: Italian Migrants in Urban America *Diane C. Vecchio*
American Dreaming, Global Realities: Rethinking U.S. Immigration History *Edited by
  Donna R. Gabaccia and Vicki L. Ruiz*

The University of Illinois Press is a founding member of the
Association of American University Presses.

Composed in 10/13 Hoefler Text with Triplex display
by Celia Shapland for the University of Illinois Press
Designed by Copenhaver Cumpston
Manufactured by Sheridan Books, Inc.

UNIVERSITY OF ILLINOIS PRESS
1325 South Oak Street   Champaign, IL 61820-6903
www.press.uillinois.edu